Governance by Emulation

Social media giants like Meta and transnational regulators such as the European Union are transforming private governance by creatively emulating public law frameworks. Drawing on exclusive interviews and in-depth analysis of Meta's Oversight Board and the EU's Digital Services Act, this book explores how these approaches blend European and American perspectives, bridging distinct legal traditions to address the challenges of platform governance. Analysis of content moderation practices and their implications uncovers a critical pattern in the evolution of governance for industries that will define the future, from digital platforms to emerging technologies. Combining public and private law in innovative ways, the book sheds light on bold governance experiments that will shape the digital world – for better or worse. This title is also available as Open Access on Cambridge Core.

Moritz A. Schramm is a research scholar and adjunct professor at New York University School of Law. He holds a PhD in law from Humboldt-University of Berlin and completed a postdoctoral fellowship at NYU. He has received multiple international awards for his work.

Cambridge Studies in European Law and Policy

The focus of this series is European law broadly understood. It aims to publish original monographs in all fields of European law, from work focusing on the institutions of the EU and the Council of Europe to books examining substantive fields of European law as well as examining the relationship between European law and domestic, regional and international legal orders. The series publishes works adopting a wide variety of methods: comparative, doctrinal, theoretical and interdisciplinary approaches to European law are equally welcome, as are works looking at the historical and political facets of the development of European law and policy. The main criterion is excellence, i.e. the publication of innovative work, which will help to shape the legal, political and scholarly debate on the future of European law.

Books in the Series

Governance by Emulation: The Oversight Board, the Digital Services Act, and the Struggle for Platform Accountability
Moritz A. Schramm

Sustainability and EU Migration Law: Tracing the History of a Contemporary Concept
Alezini Loxa

Reimagining Prosperity: Toward a New Imaginary of Law and Political Economy in the EU
Marija Bartl

Open Strategic Autonomy in EU Trade Policy: Assessing the Turn to Stronger Enforcement and More Robust Interest Representation
Wolfgang Weiß and Cornelia Furculiță

Trilogues: The Democratic Secret of European Legislation
Giacomo Rugge

The European Union, Emerging Global Business and Human Rights
Aleydis Nissen

The European Central Bank and the European Macroeconomic Constitution
Klaus Tuori

The Procedural and Organisational Law of the European Court of Justice: An Incomplete Transformation
Christoph Krenn

The New Economic Governance of the Eurozone: A Rule of Law Analysis
Paul Dermine

Digital Constitutionalism in Europe: Reframing Rights and Powers in the Algorithmic Society
Giovanni De Gregorio

Can the European Court of Human Rights Shape European Public Order?
Kanstantsin Dzehtsiarou

The Constitutional Boundaries of European Fiscal Federalism
Brady Gordon

Private Selves: Legal Personhood in European Privacy Protection
Susanna Lindroos-Hovinheimo

Fissures in EU Citizenship: The Deconstruction and Reconstruction of the Legal Evolution of EU Citizenship
Martin Steinfeld

The Boundaries of the EU Internal Market: Participation without Membership
Marja-Liisa Öberg

The Currency of Solidarity: Constitutional Transformation during the Euro Crisis
Vestert Borger

Empire of Law: Nazi Germany, Exile Scholars and the Battle for the Future of Europe
Kaius Tuori

In the Court We Trust: Cooperation, Coordination and Collaboration between the ECJ and Supreme Administrative Courts
Rob van Gestel and Jurgen de Poorter

Beyond Minimum Harmonisation: Gold-Plating and Green-Plating of European Environmental Law
Lorenzo Squintani

The Court of Justice of the European Union as an Institutional Actor: Judicial Lawmaking and its Limits
Thomas Horsley

The Politics of Justice in European Private Law: Social Justice, Access Justice, Societal Justice
Hans-W Micklitz

The Transformation of EU Treaty Making: The Rise of Parliaments, Referendums and Courts Since 1950
Dermot Hodson and Imelda Maher

Redefining European Economic Integration
Dariusz Adamski

Human Rights in the Council of Europe and the European Union: Achievements, Trends and Challenges
Steven Greer, Janneke Gerards and Rosie Slowe

Core Socio-Economic Rights and the European Court of Human Rights
Ingrid Leijten

Green Trade and Fair Trade in and with the EU: Process-based Measures within the EU Legal Order
Laurens Ankersmit

New Labour Laws in Old Member States: Trade Union Responses to European Enlargement
Rebecca Zahn

The Governance of EU Fundamental Rights
Mark Dawson

The International Responsibility of the European Union: From Competence to Normative Control
Andrés Delgado Casteleiro

Frontex and Non-Refoulement: The International Responsibility of the EU
Roberta Mungianu

Gendering European Working Time Regimes: The Working Time Directive and the Case of Poland
Ania Zbyszewska

EU Renewable Electricity Law and Policy: From National Targets to a Common Market
Tim Maxian Rusche

European Constitutionalism
Kaarlo Tuori

Brokering Europe: Euro-Lawyers and the Making of a Transnational Polity
Antoine Vauchez

Services Liberalization in the EU and the WTO: Concepts, Standards and Regulatory Approaches
Marcus Klamert

Referendums and the European Union: A Comparative Enquiry
Fernando Mendez, Mario Mendez and Vasiliki Triga

The Allocation of Regulatory Competence in the EU Emissions Trading Scheme
Josephine van Zeben

The Eurozone Crisis: A Constitutional Analysis
Kaarlo Tuori and Klaus Tuori

International Trade Disputes and EU Liability
Anne Thies

The Limits of Legal Reasoning and the European Court of Justice
Gerard Conway

New Governance and the Transformation of European Law: Coordinating EU Social Law and Policy
Mark Dawson

The Lisbon Treaty: A Legal and Political Analysis
Jean-Claude Piris

The European Union's Fight Against Corruption: The Evolving Policy Towards Member States and Candidate Countries
Patrycja Szarek-Mason

The Ethos of Europe: Values, Law and Justice in the EU
Andrew Williams

State and Market in European Union Law: The Public and Private Spheres of the Internal Market before the EU Courts
Wolf Sauter and Harm Schepel

The European Civil Code: The Way Forward
Hugh Collins

Ethical Dimensions of the Foreign Policy of the European Union: A Legal Appraisal
Urfan Khaliq

Implementing EU Pollution Control: Law and Integration
Bettina Lange

European Broadcasting Law and Policy
Jackie Harrison and Lorna Woods

The Transformation of Citizenship in the European Union: Electoral Rights and the Restructuring of Political Space
Jo Shaw

The Constitution for Europe: A Legal Analysis
Jean-Claude Piris

The European Convention on Human Rights: Achievements, Problems and Prospects
Steven Greer

Social Rights and Market Freedom in the European Constitution: A Labour Law Perspective
Stefano Giubboni

EU Enlargement and the Constitutions of Central and Eastern Europe
Anneli Albi

Governance by Emulation

The Oversight Board, the Digital Services Act, and the Struggle for Platform Accountability

Moritz A. Schramm
New York University

CAMBRIDGE
UNIVERSITY PRESS

CAMBRIDGE
UNIVERSITY PRESS

Shaftesbury Road, Cambridge CB2 8EA, United Kingdom

One Liberty Plaza, 20th Floor, New York, NY 10006, USA

477 Williamstown Road, Port Melbourne, VIC 3207, Australia

314–321, 3rd Floor, Plot 3, Splendor Forum, Jasola District Centre, New Delhi – 110025, India

Cambridge University Press is part of Cambridge University Press & Assessment, a department of the University of Cambridge.

We share the University's mission to contribute to society through the pursuit of education, learning and research at the highest international levels of excellence.

www.cambridge.org
Information on this title: www.cambridge.org/9781009639781

DOI: 10.1017/9781009639750

When citing this work, please include a reference to the DOI 10.1017/9781009639750

First published 2026

Cover image: Francis Bacon, Detail of *Portrait of George Dyer in a Mirror*, 1968

Photo: Hugo Maertens

A catalogue record for this publication is available from the British Library

A Cataloging-in-Publication data record for this book is available from the Library of Congress

ISBN 978-1-009-63978-1 Hardback
ISBN 978-1-009-63977-4 Paperback

The publication was funded by the Open Access Publication Fund of Humboldt-Universität zu Berlin.

Revised version of the dissertation submitted in fulfillment of the requirements for the *Doctor iuris* awarded by Humboldt-Universität zu Berlin, Faculty of Law (2023), original dissertation title: Emulated Guardians: On the Practice, Politics, and Performativity of the DSA and the Oversight Board.

HUMBOLDT-UNIVERSITÄT ZU BERLIN

The research was funded by the Deutsche Forschungsgemeinschaft (DFG – German Research Foundation) – [397044234] via the Graduate School, Dynamic Integration.

Deutsche Forschungsgemeinschaft
German Research Foundation

To my parents, and my sister.

Nostalgia is a luxury.

Zadie Smith (Swing Time)

Dann bin ich da gehockt, natürlich gerne konzentriert, im fensterlosen Raum, draußen wusste man den Sommer toben, wie sich das gehört, und man selber saß hoch oben in der Universität, versammelt, inmitten all der anderen, die auch mit ihren Hirnen werkten, selber in die Arbeit rein gebückt, absichtlich, froh und still, als würde ich, nicht Neon an der hohen Decke, den ganzen Raum beleuchten.

Rainald Goetz (Kontrolliert)

Contents

Figures

Series Editors' Preface

The focus of Moritz Schramm's examination of core aspects of digital governance in the "online age," which we are delighted to welcome to the *Cambridge Studies in European Law and Policy*, is the issue of "content moderation." This might seem a somewhat abstruse starting point for the investigation. In fact, for many people, content moderation is at the core of digital governance as it affects their online lives. Schramm defines content moderation as "the umbrella term for social media companies' governance of online communication." It is the process of reviewing (and policing) user-generated content placed on, as noted, social media websites. The control of user-generated content – that is, *speech* – is important because it clearly links to normative principles we hold dear, around freedom, human dignity and respect, and equality.

These values are important, as Schramm's analysis makes clear, in ways that cut across the traditional divides of public law and private law. Thus, Schramm's approach supplements the existing approaches focused on constitutionalism, liability, and private governance by invoking the regulatory power of "administrative law," which is one of the paradigm elements of the legitimate control of the exercise of (public) power. So, while Schramm cleaves to the mechanisms of public law, he sets aside constitutionally inspired approaches as being too loose knit and indeed too contested to be of use in offering a framework of recourse for digital "consumers."

Examining two core cases of the Meta Oversight Board and the out-of-court dispute settlement bodies foreseen in the European Union's Digital Services Act, Schramm notes that these entities "emulate" adjudicatory mechanisms which have evolved in the context of the growth of administrative law at the national level. The examination of emulation – a practice long seen by legal comparativists – is the analytical heart of the book.

It is important for Schramm's argument that we acknowledge that administrative law can work in contexts which escape the state. It does not matter who infringes private rights. The capaciousness of administrative law can also stretch to the governance of private rights and infringements by private actors, notably the large corporates who, in the context of the emergence of increasingly disruptive digital technologies, exercise almost unheard of levels of power over the ordinary lives of citizens.

But the issue is even bigger than this. For Schramm, we are seeing the likely first signs of a major transformation of law, suited for the global, digital age. Schramm provides in the text some brief comments about the aftermath of the US Presidential Election in November 2024, which fall, as he notes, into the box marked "for future investigation and research." However, the complex relationships between corporate power and public power which we have seen emerging in those weeks and months will need to be mapped and tracked as we go forward. Disruptive technologies, especially digital technologies, will remain at the core of the enquiry. As ever with the most important topics, there will be further work to be done in the future, but it will be able to build upon this pioneering and original study of how law can frame and control mechanisms of content moderation.

Jo Shaw
Mark Dawson
Laurence Gormley

Preface

This book, like the world it describes, is transitional. It explores what I believe to be a groundbreaking shift in how the normativity of public law ideals – such as individual rights, formalized accountability, and self-governance – unfolds in an era where the state, the traditional locus of organized authority for several hundred years, gradually recedes. Rather than focusing on the starting point or ultimate destination of this transition, the book delves into the process itself. It conceptualizes, problematizes, and evaluates *emulation* as a fundamental pattern of governance beyond the state, especially in private and regulatory contexts. Emulation describes how organizational actors, such as the European Union or Meta, build new policies and formal structures by imitating older institutionalized policies from other contexts. In our context, these older institutionalized policies are those commonly known from administrative, constitutional, and civil rights law. In short, when in need for good governance, many turn to public law for inspiration. Remarkably, this inspiration transcends political divides. Throughout the 2010s and early 2020s, debates centered largely on "liberal" public law elements – rights, adjudication, and due process. These demands form the core focus of this book. Yet, rather recently – and at an exponential pace during the final months of this manuscript's production – a crescendo of countervailing voices has grown so powerful that it ultimately swept the White House with the second Trump administration. In a stunning shift, it also appears to have partially reshaped corporate policy among major social media companies, especially Meta. How lasting and entrenched these changes are remains to be seen (and how entrenched prior liberal configurations indeed ever were is one of the continuing questions of this book). Further, a closer look reveals that even Silicon Valley's apparent political realignment with Trump's "Make America Great Again" (MAGA)-conservatism remains framed in (potentially twisted understandings of) public law terms. Calls for majoritarianism, free speech absolutism, and the curbing of alleged viewpoint discrimination follow a superficially different but structurally similar logic to the liberal arguments that dominated the previous decade. Both sides evoke public law concepts, sometimes twisted and self-serving but nonetheless thoroughly rooted in a common frame of reference. That frame of reference is public law. In effect, we are witnessing a revival of classic public law debates – on individual freedom, the counter-majoritarian difficulty, minority protections, the rule of law – now transposed onto the private governance of social media platforms, and potentially other emerging centers of power such as artificial intelligence. In short, public law ideals – from rights to majoritarianism, from courts to self-governance – continue to exert immense cultural and normative influence, even as traditional legal institutions struggle to enforce them. Consequently, regulators and corporations, driven partly by self-interest and partly by the proven utility of public law as a counterbalance to concentrated power, have begun to adopt and internalize these ideals within managerial frameworks. Remarkably, they do so not exclusively, perhaps not even predominantly, because of traditional regulation, but through discourse, appropriation, repackaging, and so forth. Unsurprisingly, that internalization of public law ideas by private and regulatory actors is feeble and imperfect. But the following 300 pages or so make the case that such an internalization of public law mechanisms in contractual, corporate, and regulatory settings may be ambivalent, yet an important avenue to further explore to tame power structures beyond the state.

The empirical heart of the book lies in its case studies on content moderation and the novel, yet fragile adjudicators tasked with overseeing it. These are, namely, Meta's Oversight Board and the European Union's out-of-court dispute settlement bodies established under Article 21 of the Digital Services Act. These adjudicators emulate key aspects of public law, particularly the adjudication of individual rights vis-à-vis bureaucratic power structures. While these cases are compelling in their own right, I believe they also exemplify a larger trend. As governance increasingly shifts to powerful, vertically integrated, infrastructure-controlling corporations, demands for accountability are bound to follow. Why not, for better or worse, model these new accountability structures after those that have worked – imperfectly but effectively – within the state? Whether this emulation succeeds is, of course, a matter of how its conditions and ends are defined. In that sense, this book is just one chapter in a much longer story about liberalism's struggles, promises, and pitfalls in an increasingly digital, complex, and interconnected world. A world that now teeters between tech-feudalism, the resurgence of brute-force territorialism, and the uncertainty of planetary futures yet to unfold.

The book's transitional nature also reflects its creation. It began as a PhD project at Humboldt-University of Berlin in October 2019, sustained through the dark winters of the pandemic, punctuated by travel, fellowships, and conferences once the world reopened, and reached its first culmination in 2023 with its defense.

The dissertation was awarded several prizes. These were, in chronological order, the Best Doctoral Thesis Award by the European Law Faculties Association (Edinburgh, 2024), the Konrad-Redeker-Prize for the best dissertation in administrative law and constitutional law, awarded by the Faculty of Law of Humboldt-University of Berlin and endowed by the Konrad Redeker Foundation (Berlin, 2024), and the Best Thesis Prize by the European Public Law Organization (Athens, 2024). Also, the thesis was shortlisted for the Best Thesis Award by the Institute for World Business Law of the International Chamber of Commerce (Paris, 2023).

What you hold in your hands (or read on your screen) is the evolved product of that dissertation, shaped by the new perspectives and opportunities afforded to me since summer 2023 at New York University. The book transitions, much like its subject, between European and American perspectives. Ironically, it belongs fully to neither. In Europe, my project is often perceived as oddly American, while in the United States, my occasional skepticism toward profit-driven corporations acting in the public interest betrays my European roots. Yet, as the issues discussed here transcend Europe, the United States, or any specific jurisdiction, this interplay of perspectives is, I hope, among the book's strengths.

This book engages with material up until November 2024, with events beyond that – particularly those surrounding the 2024 US elections – falling largely outside its scope. As the Oversight Board and the Digital Services Act continue their bold, ambivalent, and complex experiments, the mid 2020s mark the beginning of a new, more uncertain chapter. I try to provide a comprehensive account of how we got here. For one book, that should, hopefully, be enough.

Apart from the two public foundations mentioned in the acknowledgments and the support of New York University School of Law through Guarini Global Law & Tech, I never accepted – nor was offered – any funding by other actors. I affirm that, to the best of my knowledge, no conflicts of interest exist in relation to the research, writing, or publication of this book.

A final word on the book's cover. To spare myself the indignity of overly earnest (and likely cringeworthy) forays into art history, I limit myself to three simple observations. First, the cover features Francis Bacon's 1968 painting *Portrait of George Dyer in a Mirror*. Second, I selected Bacon as an artist specifically for his nuanced engagement with emulation. Third, though many of Bacon's pieces explicitly reference other artworks, this one does not. Yet, as the distorted reflection in the mirror reveals, it grapples with themes of perception, guise, and societal power in ways that resonate deeply with the book's subject.

Moritz A. Schramm

Acknowledgments

Working on this project came with the privilege of spending time at fascinating places – especially Berlin, Florence, and New York – as well as meeting an extraordinary group of individuals. Their generosity, insights, and friendship have profoundly enriched the years that went into this book. I extend my deepest gratitude to each of them, as well as to the many others I cannot name individually here.

First and foremost, my immense gratitude goes to Professor Matthias Ruffert for his unwavering support, the freedom he granted me throughout this adventure, and the intellectual guardrails he provided, which proved invaluable in refining what was, at times, a somewhat wayward undertaking. Equally, I want to deeply thank Professor Christoph Möllers, whose early belief in this project and argumentative creativity was both humbling and motivating. Writing my PhD within a structured program – a rarity in German academia – was a true sanctuary. Among my colleagues at Humboldt's graduate school Dynamic Integration, I am especially grateful to Paul Friedl, Friederike Grischek, Lukas Huthmann, Charlotte Langenfeld, Carolin Lerch and Jakob Gašperin Wischhoff. I owe special thanks to Meret Plucis for her sharp mind, incisive criticism, and for patiently discussing many of the themes explored in this book.

In Florence, I am particularly indebted to Professor Deirdre Curtin for her incisive feedback and encouragement, as well as to the entire Digital Public Sphere Working Group, especially Francisco de Abreu Duarte, Valerie Albus, Francesca Palmiotto, Sarah Tas, and Anna Morandini.

Now in New York, this book – and my life – has entered a new chapter. I owe immense gratitude to Professors Benedict Kingsbury and Joseph H. H. Weiler for inviting me over and generously continuing to support my endeavors. A special thanks also goes to Professor Thomas Streinz, who, despite now being in Florence, remains one of the most generous mentors I encountered at NYU.

Further, I wish to extend my enduring gratitude to those whose invaluable support, offered in various capacities and at different stages – sometimes unknowingly – proved instrumental and motivational, including Michael Beauvais, Maxim Bönnemann, David Boss, Anja Bossow, Josh Cowls, Philipp Dann, Philipp Darius, Sebastian Darius, Joyce De Coninck, Claudia Golden, Giovanni De Gregorio, Niklas Eder, Martin Eifert, Veronika Fikfak, Angelina Fisher, Daniel Holznagel, Martin Husovec, Patricia Jeronimo, Thomas Kadri, Kate Klonick, Andrew Krochalk, Aysel Küçüksu, Scott Martingell, María Paula Mondragón, Päivi Neuvonen, Enrico Peuker, Oreste Pollicino, Robert Post, Katherine Rizkalla, Sofia Ranchordás, Ximene Rego, Dominiquo Santistevan, Kerstin Schuster, Rüdiger Schwarz, the late Heike Schweitzer, Nathalie Smuha, Max Steinbeis, Bent Stohlmann, Katherine Strandburg, Yirong Sun, Nicolas Suzor, Yane Svetiev, Rodrigo Vallejo, Nils Weinberg, Claire Whitman, Thomas Wischmeyer, Raphaële Xenidis, and Friedrich Zillessen.

A particularly warm thank you goes to all interviewees, who took the time in their often very busy jobs to talk to me for this book. I was deeply humbled by the richness of their perspectives and dedication to their work. Although academic custom demands to engage critically with the empirical material, I believe the eventual result of these many hours of conversations paints a fair picture of the opportunities and challenges of governance by emulation.

I am deeply grateful to Professors Mark Dawson, Laurence Gormley, and Jo Shaw for including this book in the esteemed Cambridge Studies in European Law and Policy. My heartfelt thanks also go to Matt Gallaway, Sharon McCann, Gemma Smith, Sri Hari Kumar Sugumaran, and Helen Kitto of Cambridge University Press for their invaluable guidance in bringing this project to fruition. Additionally, I am profoundly appreciative of Humboldt University's Open Access Fund, whose generous support has significantly contributed to making this book accessible to a wider audience.

This book was made possible through the generous support of the German Research Foundation (Deutsche Forschungsgemeinschaft) via the graduate school Dynamic Integration at Humboldt-University of Berlin, as well as the German Academic Exchange Service (Deutscher Akademischer Austauschdienst). I am deeply thankful for their contributions, which provided the foundation for this research. In its final stages, the work benefitted immensely from the gracious support of Guarini Global Law & Tech at New York University School of Law, for which I am equally grateful.

I am wholeheartedly grateful to the European Public Law Organization, the European Law Faculties Association, the Faculty of Law at Humboldt-University, the Konrad-Redeker-Foundation, and the Institute of World Business Law at the International Chamber of Commerce (ICC) for their generous recognition of my thesis – whether through awarding prizes or, in the case of the ICC, shortlisting it for consideration.

Lastly, I owe a particular debt of gratitude to my family, especially my sister, whose support and occasional prod made all of this possible.

To you, dear reader: My apologies for the lengthy preliminaries. As this is my first endeavor of this kind, I trust you will indulge me. With that, I hope these six chapters offer something to provoke thought, complexify, persuade, or at the very least, entertain.

Table of Cases and Decisions by the Oversight Board

Domestic Courts

Abweichende Meinung der Richterin Lübbe-Wolff zum Beschluss des Zweiten Senats vom 14 Januar 2014 [2014] Federal Constitutional Court (Bundesverfassungsgericht) 2 BvR 2728/13, BVerfGE 134, 366

COPPAR v Rizzo District Court 357 F. Supp. 1289 (E.D. Pa. 1973), add'd sub nom

Federal Trade Commission v Facebook Inc, United States District Court, District of Columbia, Case No 1:20-cv-03590 (Complaint for injunctive and other equitable relief)

Goode v Rizzo, 506 F.2d 542 (3rd Cir. 1974), rev'd, 96 S. Ct. 598 (1976)

Hassrede [2021] Federal Court of Justice (Bundesgerichtshof) III ZR 179/20 and III ZR 192/20

Klimabeschluss [2021] Federal Constitutional Court (Bundesverfassungsgericht) 1 BvR 2656/18, BVerfGE 157, 30

Moody v Netchoice [2024] United States Supreme Court 603 US ____ (2024)

Oury Jalloh [2014] Federal Court of Justice (Bundesgerichtshof) 4 StR 473/13

Rizzo v Goode United States Supreme Court 96 S. Ct. 598 (1976)

Stadionverbot [2018] Federal Constitutional Court (Bundesverfassungsgericht) 1 BvR 3080/09, BVerfGE 148, 267–290

European Court of Justice

Associação Sindical dos Juízes Portugueses v Tribunal de Contas [2018] European Court of Justice (Grand Chamber) C-64/16, ECLI:EU:C:2018:117

Defrenne v Belgian State [1971] European Court of Justice C-80/70, ECLI:EU: C:1971:55

Defrenne v SABENA [1976] European Court of Justice C-43/75, ECLI:EU:C:1976:56
Egenberger [2018] European Court of Justice C-414/16, ECLI:EU:C:2018:257
GC and Others (De-referencing of sensitive data) [2019] European Court of Justice C-136/17, ECLI:EU:C:2019:773
Glawischnig-Piesczek [2019] European Court of Justice C-18/18, ECLI:EU:C:2019:821
Independence of the Polish Supreme Court [2019] European Court of Justice (Grand Chamber) C-619/18, ECLI:EU:C:2019:531
Nold [1960] European Court of Justice Joined cases 36, 37, 38–59, 40–59, ECLI:EU:C:1960:36
NS [2011] European Court of Justice (Grand Chamber) C-411/10, ECLI:EU:C:2011:865
Stauder [1969] European Court of Justice C 26–69, ECLI:EU:C:1969:57
Stork [1959] European Court of Justice C 1/58, ECLI:EU:C:1959:4
Technische Universität München [1991] European Court of Justice C-269/90, ECLI:EU:C:1991:438

International Courts

Basu v Germany, European Court of Human Rights [215/19], 18 January 2023

Oversight Board

Alleged Crimes in Raya Kobo [2021] Oversight Board 2021–014-FB-UA
Armenians in Azerbaijan [2021] Oversight Board 2020–003-FB-UA
Asking for Adderall® [2022] Oversight Board 2921–015-FB-UA
Ayahuasca brew [2021] Oversight Board 2021–013-IG-UA
Breast Cancer symptoms and nudity [2021] Oversight Board 2020–004-IG-UA
Cambodian Prime Minister [2023] Oversight Board 2023–003-FB-MR
Claimed COVID cure [2021] Oversight Board 2020–006-FB-FBR
Colombia Protests [2021] Oversight Board 2021–010-FB-UA
Colombian police cartoon [2022] Oversight Board 2022–004-FB-UA
COVID lockdowns in Brazil [2021] Oversight Board 2021–008-FB-FBR
Depiction of Zwarte Piet [2021] Oversight Board 2021–002-FB-UA
Former President Trump's suspension [2021] Oversight Board 2021–001-FB-FBR
Knin Cartoon [2022] Oversight Board 2022–001-FB-UA
Myanmar post about Muslims [2021] Oversight Board 2020–002-FB-UA

Nazi Quote [2021] Oversight Board 2020–005-FB-UA
Öcalan's Isolation [2021] Oversight Board 2021–006-IG-UA
Pro-Navalny Protests in Russia [2021] Oversight Board 2021–004-FB-UA
Protest in India against France [2021] Oversight Board 2020–007-FB-FBR
Punjabi Concern over the RSS in India [2021] Oversight Board 2021–003-FB-UA
Shared Al Jazeera Post [2021] Oversight Board 2021–009-FB-UA
South Africa slurs [2021] Oversight Board 2021–011-FB-UA
Two Buttons Meme [2021] Oversight Board 2021–005-FB-UA
UK drill music [2022] Oversight Board 2022–007-IG-MR
United States posts discussing abortion [2023] Oversight Board 2023–01-IG-UA, 2023–012-FB-UA, 2023–013-FB-UA
Wampum Belt [2021] Oversight Board 2021–012-FB-UA

Table of Legislation

Directive 2000/31/EC of the European Parliament and of the Council of 8 June 2000 on certain legal aspects of information society services, in particular electronic commerce, in the Internal Market ('eCommerce Directive')

Directive 2013/11 [OJ L 178, 17.7.2000, pp. 1–16] /EU of the European Parliament and of the Council of 21 May 2013 on alternative dispute resolution for consumer disputes and amending Regulation (EC) No 2006/2004 and Directive 2009/22/EC (Directive on consumer ADR) [OJ L 165, 18.6.2013, pp 1–12]

Directive (EU) 2019/790 of the European Parliament and of the Council of 17 April 2019 on copyright and related rights in the Digital Single Market and amending Directives 96/9/EC and 2001/29/EC (Digital Single Market Directive) (OJ L 130, 17.5.2019, pp. 92–125)

Gesetz zur Verbesserung der Rechtsdurchsetzung in sozialen Netzwerken (Netzwerkdurchsetzungsgesetz – NetzDG) (BGBl I S 3352, last amended through BGBl 2024 I Nr 149)

Regulation (EU) 2019/1150 of the European Parliament and of the Council of 20 June 2019 on promoting fairness and transparency for business users of online intermediation services (OJ L 186, 1172019, pp. 57–79)

Regulation (EU) 2021/784 of the European Parliament and of the Council of 29 April 2021 on addressing the dissemination of terrorist content online (OJ L 172, 17.5.2021, pp. 79–109)

Regulation (EU) 2022/2065 of the European Parliament and of the Council of 19 October 2022 on a Single Market for Digital Services and amending Directive 2000/31/EC (Digital Services Act)

UK Online Safety Bill [HL Bill 87-EN]

Abbreviations

ADR – Alternative Dispute Resolution
CAS – Court of Arbitration for Sport
CFR – Charter of Fundamental Rights and Freedoms of the European Union
DMA – Regulation (EU) 2022/1925 (Digital Markets Act)
DSA – Regulation (EU) 2022/2065 (Digital Services Act)
ECJ – European Court of Justice
ECHR – European Charter of Human Rights
ECtHR – European Court of Human Rights
EU – European Union
GAL – Global Administrative Law
ICANN – International Corporation for Assigned Names and Numbers
ICCPR – International Covenant on Civil and Political Rights
ICTR – International Criminal Tribunal for Rwanda
LLC – Limited Liability Company
ODS – Out-of-Court Dispute Settlement Body in the sense of Article 21 DSA
TEU – Treaty on European Union
TFEU – Treaty on the Functioning of the European Union
UN – United Nations
UNGP – United Nations Guiding Principles for Business and Human Rights
WTO – World Trade Organization

1 Introduction

1.1 Setting the Scene

How to control private power beyond the state? How to guard individual rights in an ever more globalized and digitized world, where traditional markers of authority, like state-centered sovereignty, territory, and black-letter law seem to gradually fade? How to discipline bourgeoning private power structures that seem to be dominating ever more aspects of our lives? What role for public authority, particularly the European Union (EU) – a vanguard of transnationalism since the 1960s – in that transformation? Does its regulatory power indeed reverberate into the transnational, globalized space of the informational economy? What exactly are the Union's normative mechanisms to assert European rights and values, apart from contextual factors like leveraging its formidable market size? Or, in general, what tools remain for state actors to enforce their policies vis-à-vis vastly powerful digital corporations?

So far, a common approach to these issues has been to reuse tried and tested vocabularies, mechanisms, and ideas known for controlling public power, especially those from public law. Those public law ideas are then reused for private governance. Rights, adjudication, due process, majoritarianism, and accountability to name a few. That reusing regularly necessitates creating *new* versions of these older role models, especially existing institutions. The institutions already in place, for example courts, are often considered to be ill-equipped to counter the scale and velocity of ascendent private power structures, especially globally active, vertically integrated digital corporations like Meta, Google, OpenAI, ByteDance, or Tencent. Hence, academics, politicians, and activists often demand new accountability mechanisms to answer these new challenges. This demand for "new" institutions, especially in private and regulatory governance, however, regularly turns to old ideas for inspiration and, quite inevitably, remains discursively embedded in the dominant cultural, legal, and epistemological paradigms of the time. Therefore, when the topic is controlling large power structures, many such old ideas and discursive frameworks stem from public law. By public law, I mean mostly constitutional, civil rights, and, especially, administrative law. To confront the massively concentrated, infrastructural, and globe-spanning power of some private actors - social media companies, in our case - many turn to the emulation of classic public law mechanisms to keep profit-driven power in check.

This book examines what I take to be a fundamental transformation in the way the normativity of public law ideals – individual rights, formalized accountability, and self-governance – unfolds in an era in which the state, long the central locus of organized authority, is gradually receding. Rather than fixating on beginning or endpoints, the analysis centers on the transition itself – foregrounding the process of emergence. It conceptualizes and critically assesses *Governance by Emulation* as a key mode of ordering beyond the state, particularly in private and regulatory domains.

Emulation captures the dynamic by which organizational actors – such as the European Union or Meta – construct new policies and institutional frameworks by imitating pre-existing, institutionalized models from other contexts. In this case, those models stem from the familiar repertoire of administrative, constitutional, and civil rights law. In short: when searching for credible governance, many now look to public law for inspiration. However, the nascent institutions emerging from this mode of governance carry a complex legacy. Untangling this legacy provides the book's red thread

In the following chapters, we will study two particularly prominent examples of this common approach. First, the out-of-court dispute settlement bodies, or short ODSs, as foreseen in the EU's Digital Services Act as a mix of classic alternative dispute settlement and administrative-style civil rights protector. Second, the social media company Meta's Oversight Board, hailed as "something like a Supreme Court for Facebook" by Mark Zuckerberg.[1] Albeit vastly different in detail, both exemplify the same idea: emulating the adjudication of individual rights vis-à-vis a large and often quite bureaucratic power structure. In our example here, that

[1] Ezra Klein, 'Mark Zuckerberg on Facebook's Hardest Year, and What Comes Next' *Vox.com* (2 April 2018) <https://perma.cc/5W3N-Y37S>.

power structure are social media companies, more precisely their content moderation machinery. To put it simply, this book studies how the EU and Meta, quite remarkably, both came up with a novel kind of adjudicator to control content moderation and protect the rights of billions of users – or at least appear to do so.

Those novel adjudicators epitomize the thinking of a whole generation of lawyers. The choice to introduce rights-based adjudication into private and regulatory governance of digital power structures reflects liberal convictions and presumptions about the role of rights in democratic discourse and the power of adjudicators to advance social justice. On a more abstract level, the underlying pattern – novel power structure, public demand for accountability, emulation of public law role model like courts, rights, and so forth – seems so self-evident, so obvious, that we will most likely see it again in future reforms in other sectors.

Building on that, we shall call the concrete form of emulation we study here, that of individualized accountability structures, *Emulated Guardians*. Guardians in reference to their – purported – accountability function and one of public law's aporiae: Who guards the guardians? The term emulation then highlights their distinctive emulative nature. These guardians seek to reproduce but also to adjust and, potentially, appropriate the symbolism of preexisting role models. I use the term emulation without connotation. In principle, emulating is neither good nor bad. We will see in the case studies, once these Emulated Guardians begin to practice, they develop a life of their own, aspects of which are positive, others more negative.

Emulative arguments and ideas are pervasive in debates about regulation and self-regulation of corporate power structures. We perceive social media platforms as increasingly dangerous and unaccountable threats to individual freedom, social order, and democracy itself. Again, social media platforms are a placeholder here. We could engage in strikingly similar discussions on topics such as artificial intelligence, privacy, data governance, and (digital) infrastructure, alongside other unfolding economic developments. Looking beyond these already tangible realities, consider the largely unregulated domains of extraterrestrial resource extraction, commerce, and – should it ever come to fruition – space colonization.

Simultaneously, we consider public law and its institutions to be perhaps the best way to contain powerful organizations that might threaten liberty, society, and potentially even democratic governance. Why? Because, in the past, public law delivered. We, or rather the ancestors of some of us, overcame absolutism, fascism, and various other ghastly modes of governance. Public law did play an important part in this. Courts then assumed a prominent role in that process, especially since the late 1950s. Therefore, why not paving new avenues for individuals to litigate their rights vis-à-vis private power structures that are widely likened to authoritarian or feudal regimes?

Because it is not so easy. This book identifies and problematizes the deeply ambivalent consequences of emulation as a technique of ordering, be it through norms, organizations, or else. The pathways explored here are based on ideas from a range of disciplines, insights from textual analysis, conclusions from empirical findings this present work has produced, among these – perhaps most illuminating – evidence from expert interviews with people working inside and outside the EU and the Oversight Board, as well as activists, and prior Meta employees. As a result, this book offers fresh perspectives on these practical, normative, and institutional aspects of the discourse and (self-)regulatory practice regarding content moderation and, by extension, private governance in general. Crucially, the book empirically traces how emulative techniques and arguments structure decision-making and institutional design in public regulators as well as private companies. And, the book is, to the best of my knowledge, the first monograph on the Oversight Board and one of the very first on the Digital Services Act. By comparing the Digital Services Act's ODSs and the Oversight Board, one originating from the EU's regulatory agenda, the other from Meta's self-governance, the book shows the varied shades of normativity that canonical public law ideas may take in transnational constellations. The lessons we may draw from this are relevant way beyond content moderation. Holding globalized private power structures accountable is a truly global concern. Today, one of that concern's most pressing manifestations is content moderation. More will follow.

Emulating public law ideas – and more broadly, using public law as an ideational framework to analyze private power structures in the twenty-first century, particularly digital corporations – transcends political divisions. This book primarily examines the emulation of rights, adjudication, and administrative justice. These are, at their core, "liberal" concepts (in the political theory meaning of the term), especially in an American context. They take center stage here because they dominated the debate on social media governance throughout the 2010s and early 2020s. Yet these ideas have never gone unchallenged. Over time, conservative and more libertarian voices have mounted multifaceted critiques, targeting the speech governance exercised by online platforms in the USA, the regulatory ambitions of the EU, and, more fundamentally, the very choice of values, principles, and institutions operationalized vis-à-vis digital corporations. However, much of this criticism operates within a public law framework as well. Conservative critics also invoke nondiscrimination but shift the focus to who, exactly, is being discriminated against. While early advocates of applying public law concepts to digital corporations warned against the marginalization of minorities or women, others have now flipped the script, often in alarmist terms, to decry the alleged suppression of "conservative" viewpoints or even "masculinity." These critiques are frequently paired with calls for free speech absolutism and greater majoritarian control over platform governance. Hence, despite their diverging trajectories and rhetorical styles, much of this conservative backlash – particularly its post-pandemic surge – mirrors the public law-inspired argumentative structure of the "liberal" debates from the 2010s and early 2020s. Conservative critics of earlier, more liberal approaches to platform governance now champion a different set of public law concepts. The counterthesis is not that platforms should be governed by rights and adjudication, but rather by majoritarianism and unrestricted speech – both foundational public law principles in their own right. In short, each approach borrows from public law, adapting its principles in ways that are novel, occasionally self-serving, and slightly askew – yet still anchored in a shared frame of reference. This dynamic reveals two key points. First, public law remains the epistemological and discursive framework through which many grapple with new, immensely powerful private institutions like social media companies, and likely others in the future. Second, because of this, the core positions in these debates closely resemble those of classic public law controversies: countermajoritarian difficulty, rights-based approaches, and the legitimacy of institutional constraints.

This book focuses primarily on the first phase of these debates from the 2010s to the early 2020s, a period that might be called the liberal (in the Obama-era understanding of the term) phase of platform governance. That time was shaped by the rise of (or at least discussions about) rights, adjudication, and proceduralism. The book traces how these "liberal" concepts emerged in legislation and managerial practice while also exposing their fault lines, compromises, and contradictions. Crucially, where pertinent, the book also considers whether these approaches should be championed at all or whether more fundamental, structural changes might offer a better path. This question is particularly relevant given the backlash now reaching the highest echelons of policymaking in Washington and Brussels, as well as boardrooms in California – and, increasingly, Texas. Many of today's critiques respond, at least in part, to the very ambivalences this book uncovers. However, the second wave of public law concepts now reshaping private and regulatory governance – majoritarianism, viewpoint discrimination, and other facets of the conservative backlash – have to be discussed in future research.

The book has an interdisciplinary and comparative approach to connect its findings with related phenomena and perspectives. The book draws from law, sociology, and political science and focuses on two of the three biggest digital economies, Europe and the USA. I dearly hope the book's findings may be of interest to people working on these issues in law schools, social science departments, bureaucracies, and parliaments, from Brussels to London and Washington, DC, to Addis Abeba, Beijing, Brasília, and Delhi.

One such finding is that building on key elements of what worked in the past to solve contemporary problems inevitably requires careful adaptation. That is especially so because seemingly potent institutions like courts only work if embedded in and enabled by contextual factors. Those contextual factors – the rule of law, widespread commitment to judicial authority, legitimate rules and norms – are, however, seldom reproduced as easily as the institutional shell itself. Simply put, advancing justice and controlling power requires much more than adjudicators and normative material. It requires deeply rooted structural changes in governance, culture, economics, and sociological makeup of the power structure one intends to tame.

Therefore, when it comes to our distinct public–private situation, emulation sometimes carries a whiff of, let us say, moral ambiguity. Clearly, reproducing best practice makes sense. Yet, referencing publicly legitimate role models in private governance – but not their enabling contextual factors – nonetheless goes down so well in general discourse. If there is a flamboyant adjudicator, who cares for the nitty-gritty of practical implementation? In other words, emulation often comes with oratorical grandiosity. However, at times, borrowing public legitimacy by appropriating ceremony and symbolism may not be sufficiently corroborated by contextual factors that enable effectively adjudicating rights in private, profit-oriented contexts.

If that would be it, however, this would be a rather one-sided book. This book does not propose abandoning to emulate well-working older ideas in new contexts. This would be naïve. Learning from what we know makes sense. One cannot reinvent the wheel every single time. Also, not everything that claims to be novel indeed is, hence using what worked well in the past, often, is just fine. And to be fair, even actual courts are far from the powerful change-makers many lawyers would like them to be. So, criticizing novel adjudicators for being not sufficiently effective may be, somewhat, trite. Of course they are not. It took actual courts hundreds of years to incrementally assert their authority – and it remains a constant struggle to maintain that authority.

Therefore, the book also offers a scenario – neutrally, but in my mind not impossible – in which emulated adjudicators potentially do become relevant guardians in the global arena. They do so not because of their formal mandate but because of their public perception and public support. Organizational authority is deeply performative. If you act as if you have authority and people believe you, you kind of have it. From a normative perspective this may be troubling at times. But it seems to be a sociological fact. Borrowing public legitimacy through narration, symbolism, and overall perception potentially *empowers* new guardians that reproduce existing structures, in our case courts. The two guardians I will study here – Emulated Guardians as I call them – are potentially powerful not because they are courts (they are not) but because they *appear like* courts. Their organizational setup and normative practice is, too, deeply performative. They seek to control vastly powerful organizations, even though their formal mandate is rather limited. Yet, as they – and this goes especially for the Oversight Board – manage to portray themselves as adjudicators, they tap into the public legitimacy linked to the almost universally acclaimed notion of adjudicating individual rights vis-à-vis a dominant power structure. Surely, now is too early to tell but the performative possibilities that come with emulation may herald a fundamental shift in the governance of private power. Evidently, classic modes of public regulation became – at least partly – ineffective in a globalized and digitized world economy. Yet, demand that power ought to be controlled did not waver. Public discourse still demands accountability for organizations that appear threatening our individual rights. If public regulation cannot do it alone, new actors seem indeed necessary. From a pragmatic perspective, therefore, the actual fight is that for Emulated Guardians' character and potency, rather than their overall desirability. Emulated Guardians exist and, due to the mechanisms of politics, the information economy and public relations, more will follow.

Building on this sociological rather than traditionally legal perspective, the book eventually argues that the crucial resource of power for Emulated Guardians is *not* (only) the law but public perception. Effectuating independent, norm-based, *ex post* control vis-à-vis a dominant new power structure inevitably requires public pressure.

Even for Europe, which hails itself for "constitutionalizing" the digital economy, this book shows how many substantive regulatory demands like proportionality and fundamental rights protection will likely remain empty promises if the European public fails to vigorously push for their stringent application in private governance.

In abstract terms, and quite remarkably so, this whole setup reminds of the genesis of judicial review of administrative action itself, which also responded to public demand rather than external regulation. Whenever big changes occur, normativity eventually originates from the people – not from institutions. In the eighteenth century, there was no EU to protect individuals from monarchs. It was the people who did that. The people took to the streets to topple monarchs and fund republics. The people carved out individual liberties from overreaching normative regimes superimposed on them by absolutism and the Church. The people fought for civil rights from abolitionism to suffrage, and various other forms of equality. Surely, some of those fights were supported by institutions like courts. Yet, at the end of the day, holding large, vastly powerful and recalcitrant organizations accountable is a job for all of society, not only lawyers, judges, and regulators. In fact, bereft of societal support, lawyers, judges, and regulators are utterly powerless. Law and regulation do not work in a vacuum. They are a social phenomenon. And if the social current fails to expedite regulatory demands, those demands will become empty ceremonies.

In that sense, highlighting the ambivalence of emulation seeks to challenge the prevailing mood of "depression" among law and technology scholars – a depression that often masquerades as optimism, as Julie Cohen observes.[2] In their quest for meaning and direction amidst a bleak landscape, many law and technology scholars frequently reinforce, rather than critically examine, self-serving corporate legitimacy claims and the inertia of regulatory complacency. Do not fall for all these performances, Cohen argues in reference to Ari Ezra Waldman.[3] As discussed in this introduction, I concur with that argument. However, precisely because performativity is such a potent tool – arguably the very foundation of organizational power – it can be directed toward diverse

[2] Julie Cohen, 'From Lex Informatica to the Control Revolution' (2021) 36 Berkeley Technology Law Journal 1017, 1038.

[3] Cohen (n 2) 1038 et seq (esp. 1041); for Waldman's work see esp. Ari Ezra Waldman, *Industry Unbound: The Inside Story of Privacy, Data, and Corporate Power* (Cambridge University Press 2021); Ari Ezra Waldman, 'Privacy Law's False Promise' (2020) 97 Washington University Law Review 773.

ends. Performativity, discourse, and the social construction of power require a frame of reference. Ironically, in the realm of private governance, an increasingly important frame of reference is public law or, in Cohen's words, "rule-of-law" language. This dynamic is profoundly influential and could be leveraged to counter the troubling tendencies that Cohen and Waldman so insightfully critique. Therefore, all is not lost. Here, I part ways with some of the more pessimistic voices, as I genuinely believe – and hope this book demonstrates – that there is a positive, even cautiously optimistic, narrative to be found in the performative interplay between public law ideals, innovative lawyering, and private governance; especially so in times of great unraveling and groundbreaking changes. Luckily, Cohen seems to agree, arguing that

> "rule of law" language is intended to supply a framework for talking about power, calling it to account, and constraining its systematic abuse. Designing governance institutions for the networked information era requires new thinking about how to translate those broadly framed rule-of-law commitments into mid-level principles capable of being operationalized within networked digital environments.[4]

Thus, in conclusion, the book proposes to think of many of Emulated Guardians and all the other empirical aspects covered here as potential harbingers of a new public law or, not to borrow legitimizing verbiage myself, new accountability norms. These new accountability norms emerge in spheres beyond public authority. They build through public, private, and hybrid forms (these labels are immaterial at the end of the day). Emulated Guardians are crucial interlocutors but only some out of many. Both the norms and the actors shaping this debate remain fiercely contested. The balance between rights-based institutionalism, unrestrained majoritarianism, administrative justice, and entrepreneurial freedom has yet to be struck. After roughly a decade of experimentation with

[4] Ibid 1047. I should note, however, that Cohen explicitly criticizes "those who conceived and designed" the Oversight Board for implementing a rule of law "in name only" (cf. ibid 1048). What matters, though, and what I hope Chapter 4 demonstrates, is that the performative engagement with public law concepts, the process of institutionalization, and the broader dynamics at play require a distinction between the efforts undertaken by the Oversight Board since it became operational and Meta as a company, both in its initial creation of the Board and in its subsequent interactions with it. How these dynamics will evolve after Meta CEO Mark Zuckerberg's sweeping policy changes in January 2025, many of which may not necessarily align with the Board's mission, remains to be seen. A similar uncertainty surrounds the implementation of the Digital Services Act, whose strictness remains in flux as the European Commission, at the time of writing, navigates an increasingly tense geopolitical and economic standoff with the USA after Donald Trump's return to the White House.

rights, the pendulum appears swinging in another direction since the mid-2020s. In short, these emerging new norms build also on emulations of other forms of control and participation, they are by no means inherently "liberal" but, if at all, in the process of being negotiated. These new accountability norms are effectuated, however, mostly through public pressure and infrastructural control rather than formal legal mandate. This reminds then of the historic emergence of public law itself, which, over a period of hundreds of years, became the mode of societies to control their states. Perhaps, we will see reminiscent processes of – ideally participatory – norm-creation, power-contestation, institution-building, and public participation also vis-à-vis digital corporations (or whatever succeeds them). In this light, today's struggles, breakthroughs, rituals, and backlashes unfold within a broader historical arc. Nothing is ever entirely lost, and few gains are ever permanent.

1.2 Protagonists

With this prelude complete, I now turn to presenting the book's two main protagonists: out-of-court dispute settlement bodies (ODSs) and the Oversight Board. Out-of-court dispute settlement bodies are new but ultimately rather weak private adjudicators, foreseen and licensed by the EU to essentially outsource ex-post accountability for content moderation in Europe. They are envisaged to decide millions of cases per year. Out-of-court dispute settlement bodies will be staffed with specialized lawyers and technology experts (although the exact qualifications are unclear) and decide appeals by European users whenever Facebook, X, TikTok, or other social media sites delete or even downrank their communication. However, after much horse-trading in the Council, one of the EU's main legislative bodies, ODSs decisional authority was gutted, and their decisions are not legally binding. Some hope that public pressure and financial incentives will lend some normative force to the decisions, nonetheless. The hope is that the sheer mass of these cases will improve content moderation in Europe. Another word on vocabulary. There are many ODSs under the DSA, I will speak of ODSs in general here. Whenever I mean a specific ODS, I will highlight that.

The Oversight Board, in contrast, was devised by the highest echelons of Meta, the world's largest social media company. It is also not a particularly strong adjudicator if one looks at its mandate. It consists of roughly twenty high profile members from all world regions, some former heads of government, journalists, law professors, and a Nobel

Peace Prize laureate. Those Board members are supported by a highly capable staff of full-time lawyers. So far, the Board has delivered "decisions" on salient issues like whether Meta could ban then US President Donald Trump from Facebook and Instagram or what type of speech shall be permissible in cases of ongoing violence and ethnic unrest. The Board strategically borrows public law symbolism and personnel, giving normative guidance to Meta on cases it deems representative of structural problems in its governance. This makes the Board a method to channel public critique and orchestrate public pressure vis-à-vis a company that so far appeared largely evasive of comprehensive regulation.

Before we proceed a few words on comparability. As we learned, ODSs are private but licensed by the EU, a public actor. They would not exist if not for Article 21 Digital Services Act, which envisages them as a vital, yet privatized, part of the accountability architecture for online platforms in Europe. The Oversight Board, in contrast, exists because Mark Zuckerberg, Meta's CEO and dominant shareholder, wants it to. Article 21 DSA emerged in a democratic process; the Oversight Board came about as a management decision. Out-of-court dispute settlement bodies shall, in theory, advance European laws vis-à-vis powerful companies. The Oversight Board in turn was repeatedly described primarily a deflection of Meta's responsibilities. Does it make sense to compare these two types of bodies?

The answer is yes! This book studies accountability forums of various origin as *complementary* (and increasingly intertwined) tools to control power. It is not only interesting but imperative to look at public and private approaches together, especially so if the public approach is here to largely privatize a task that can be understood as quintessentially public: individual rights adjudication. Meta's entirely private approach with the Oversight Board, in turn, takes inspiration from and performatively plays with public conceptions of judicial control over public power. Hence, precisely *because* the Oversight Board and ODSs are different in many respects it is fascinating to learn how both seek to emulate public law ideas to constrain platforms and, by extension, publicly legitimize platform power. It is their proclivity to emulation (and the desire for the public legitimacy ascribed to it) that is similar – not the emulation's execution or overall legitimacy from a public law or classic political theory perspective.

Further, things are more complex than schematic public–private distinctions suggest. We must distinguish between public law *ideas* (like individual rights adjudication) and public *actors* (like the EU). One key finding of the book is that public law ideas remain strong while public law actors face ever greater challenges to effectively execute their laws vis-à-vis digital corporations. In other words, individual rights adjudication and other public law ideas remain powerful templates to force upon recalcitrant private power structures like platforms. We can learn from what worked to control public power and apply it, mutatis mutandis, to the private power structures that threaten our liberty today. However, it appears, that classic regulation faces its limits when trying to force structurally foreign modes of governance onto profit-oriented actors. Rather, other sources of pressure – public opinion and economics – may be needed.

Equally, we must distinguish between the actors who create the new adjudicators and the new adjudicators themselves. The *creators* are the EU and Meta, the EU being a public actor and Meta being a private actor. The new adjudicators, however, do not fit as clearly on a purist public/private scale. While the Oversight Board is clearly entirely private in form, it hired mostly people with a human rights background. In turn, ODSs are private bodies but established pursuant to Article 21 of the Digital Services Act. They are licensed and supervised by the EU and would not exist if not for the EU. Yet they are not EU bodies in a formal sense. Simply put, ODSs are privatized and outsourced adjudicators on behalf of the EU. Shuffling a lot of responsibilities on private actors is characteristic for the EU's approach to platform regulation, and, hence, ODSs epitomize the EU's current regulatory thrust in the digital sphere.

Both bodies imperfectly mirror the idea of judicial control over administrative action in private governance. Both face the challenge to effectively transfer selected public-law mechanisms into private power structures. Despite differences in functionality and scope, both represent practical evidence for the increasing institutionalization of adjudication-focused public-law norms when it comes to content moderation. In principle, content moderation can be viewed as functionally administrative because it concerns the comprehensive regulation of public rights and infrastructures while also remaining predominantly informed by private law-inspired regulatory forms and, crucially, buttressed by informal, technologically devised, tools and mechanisms. This apparent institutionalization of public-law elements in private governance is a striking development because it incrementally combines North American and European conceptions into a completely new transnational, administrative space dominated by private powers. It is this space where Chapter 6 sketches elements of what could be understood as new accountability norms introduced above. The Oversight Board and the ODSs – which I characterize throughout this book as Emulated Guardians – are supposed to "bring" accountability to that space, protect individual rights, and improve platforms' internal governance structures.

But the more we focus on this picture, the more the details appear blurred. How far-reaching is the adaptation of public law-inspired mechanisms to private governance? Do glitches occur between the publicly announced and the internally practiced? What are the functional and normative requirements for adjudicating individual rights online – and is it enough to simply increase the number of potential adjudicators? Will those adjudicators' incomplete institutional design and feeble jurisprudential authority performatively affect our understanding of how "enforceable" individual rights are online? To take the example of privacy, we know how dangerous a continual chipping away of a once venerated institution can be. It has only taken a few years for many – perhaps most – people to accept that egregious breaches of privacy are simply the new normal in the information economy. Will the same thing happen when it comes to other individual rights?

Against this backdrop, this book questions whether Emulated Guardians are, for all their inbuilt flaws, the first significant evidence of the demise of individual rights protection online, or are they potentially the first step toward safeguarding individual rights online? In other words, is public law still the *leitmotif* to control power beyond public authority – even if not through legislation but more sociological, performative factors? Further, from an EU law perspective, the book offers a fresh, interdisciplinary perspective on the bloc's attempt to position itself as a global regulator and to – internally and externally – legitimize itself by protecting its citizens from overly powerful platforms. As we will see, the theoretical perspectives and empirical findings offered here paint a complex and nuanced picture of contemporary struggles to maintain legitimate governance and normative orders in today's increasingly mediated world. Many rules that have been put in place to harmonize the EU's internal market might end up cleaving normative orders along other fissures. In addition, many of the DSA's regulatory demands are vaguely worded and, as of now, woefully unspecific; as we will see, this invites a mere ceremonial emulation of public-law mechanisms and ineffective implementation within platforms. If the DSA's main purpose were to level power imbalances between people and platforms, we can see signs that the EU has unintentionally consolidated platform power because the DSA autonomizes rather than controls how platforms make the rules governing online communication. To end positively though, many of these flaws may be reconciled through subsequent practice, strict interpretation, and, crucially, a vigilant public.

1.3 Contributions

Albeit content moderation is a relatively novel phenomenon, private governance and the EU's attempts to shape global norms are not. Against the backdrop of seminal accounts on all these issues, this book seeks to make several contributions.

1.3.1 Emulation and Emulated Guardians

First, drawing from organization theory and the political science concept of policy diffusion, I identify *emulation* as a crucial mechanism for incorporating – or trying to incorporate – public norms into private power structures.[5] Emulation – in other contexts also called mimesis, imitation, or reproduction – refers to the reproduction of conventional role models in novel contexts.[6] The key driver behind emulation is the desire for the legitimacy attached to the role model as well as institutional uncertainty over an organization's future course of action. In principle, emulation is neither good nor bad. However, it often comes with two risks.

Successful emulation requires a contextualized understanding of the problem one intends to solve by it. Emulating governance mechanisms is much more complex than replicating the most visible level of formal structures and institutions. For example, functional – and thereby legitimate – adjudicators are typically embedded within a system of democratic rules and a general culture of accountability. Only the interplay of these factors

[5] See esp. John W Meyer and Brian Rowan, 'Institutionalized Organizations: Formal Structure as Myth and Ceremony' (1977) 83 American Journal of Sociology 340; Paul J DiMaggio and Walter W Powell, 'The Iron Cage Revisited: Institutional Isomorphism and Collective Rationality in Organizational Fields' (1983) 48 American Sociological Review 147; Eleanor Westney, *Imitation and Innovation The Transfer of Western Organizational Patterns to Meiji Japan* (Harvard University Press 1987); Paul DiMaggio and Walter W Powell (eds.), *The Neo-Institutionalism in Organizational Analysis* (University of Chicago Press 1991); Beth A Simmons, Frank Dobbin and Geoffrey Garrett, 'Introduction: The Diffusion of Liberalization' in Beth A Simmons, Frank Dobbin and Geoffrey Garrett (eds.), *The Global Diffusion of Markets and Democracy* (Cambridge University Press 2008); Charles R Shipan and Craig Volden, 'The Mechanisms of Policy Diffusion' (2008) 52 American Journal of Political Science 840; Mark Lawrence Schrad, *The Power of Bad Ideas: Networks, Institutions, and the Global Prohibition Wave* (Oxford University Press 2010).

[6] See at 2.1 and 2.4.

constructs and reinforces their authority vis-à-vis the power structures they have been constituted to control. On the other hand, if predominantly emulative bodies lack the wherewithal to do the work of control, emulation will often be an incomplete and imperfect phenomenon. Emulation necessitates learning and modification but, once it becomes clear that such emulative accountability structures often lack the equipment necessary to do their job, it may well be merely ceremonial. As anticipated above, I call such novel but emulated accountability structures *Emulated Guardians*. Given the significance of this phenomenon and the likely increase in demand for similar accountability structures – though perhaps not identical, but certainly analogous – this book deems such a new concept warranted. Whether this conceptual framing constitutes a contribution in itself is for the reader to judge. I would argue it does, as merely labeling these bodies "quasi-courts" or "pseudo-adjudicators" offers little insight into their true nature and fails to reflect their importance.

But why make such a fuss about emulation, especially if it is a standard mechanism of policymaking, institutional development, or for that matter our overall cognitive and behavioral learning? Indeed, we could even dismiss emulative practices as a self-evident and straightforward answer to a particular problem. Yet much legal reform and scholarly commentary repeatedly falls into a common epistemological trap. That trap is to think in dichotomies. Focusing on what I call emulation helps to avoid falling into that trap.

Often, a phenomenon is considered either old or new, legal or illegal, a court or an executive body. Either the Oversight Board or ODSs are perceived as constitutionalizing revolution, or as representing a cabal of corporate reactionism. But emulated institutions, at least in the realm of private power, are more than just shiny updates of old models. Neither should we view them as isolated from their epistemological and sociocultural contexts. In principle, stipulating distinguishable categories is a necessary condition for many arguments, comparisons, and our overall path toward better understanding. For example, this book distinguishes between public and private power, a distinction that, if we are not careful, can end up being decidedly simplistic and even too binary. Contrasting one thing with another can be a valuable way to highlight differences and divergence while also indicating similarities and convergence.[7] At the same time, we are aware that societal phenomena are rarely as clear-cut

[7] Which is why the one dichotomy this book employs extensively is that of "role model" and "emulation." Of course, said dichotomy can be equally deconstructed, see at 6.2.1.

as their sociological, philosophical, political, economic, or legal categorizations suggest.

Focusing on emulation therefore highlights, rather than evades the implications of the fluidity of practice – especially in a rapidly developing field such as digitization. Studying phenomena through the prism of emulation – or, as a literary theorist might say, mimesis – means to focus on what a structure or practice picks up from the past and from its context, how a phenomenon digests and newly assembles preexisting ingredients, and to describe the effects this newly fashioned phenomenon has on its context and its own role models.

The power of emulation is to *remind* us of traditional, revered concepts. Thus, squeezing such phenomena into dichotomous boxes will inevitably under- or overemphasize their potential – as well as their potential dangers. For example, if we compare the Oversight Board or ODSs to traditional courts, it will not take us long to realize that neither of these bodies is a (de facto) court, a human rights tribunal, or any other traditional label that other actors may be trying to stick on them. But does that fact make them irrelevant from a public law perspective? After all, the Oversight Board is an entirely private body and most ODSs will be private as well. Perhaps we should view these as just a particularly sophisticated form of customer service. However, such thinking might prove shortsighted. In a world where private power structures command increasing power over public rights, in this case freedom of speech, calls for accountability of such private power will only grow louder, and rightly so. Yet the resulting struggle for accountability in (privatized) global governance produces phenomena that are inspired by traditional models but hardly ever meet equivalent conditions and contexts in their new field of application. Thus, contrasting the "new" and the "old" risks missing out on the hidden and, as we will see, sometimes rather ostentatious links between then and now, between traditional role model and contemporary emulation. This work, therefore, predominantly focuses on identifying, describing, and contextualizing emulation as a phenomenon in legal practice.

Using the concept of emulation offers a new, critical perspective on many contemporary as well as, arguably, future phenomena in (private) global governance. More power structures will emerge, and more people will come up with ideas for revamping traditional, public-law ideas to control those new power structures. Therefore, instead of concentrating on the alleged "novelty," "unprecedentedness," or "innovation" of emergent phenomena, the approach developed here should, I hope, broaden our analytical perspective.

This approach might also make emulation a valuable contribution to administrative law-inspired perspectives on global governance as it unlocks the so far largely concealed door of corporations. Since an emulation-oriented perspective keeps an eye on ceremonial side effects and the risk of appropriation of symbolism through emulation, it also helps in identifying normatively undesirable developments. Focusing on emulation thus enables us weaving together a phenomenon's past and future, narration, and practice. In this way, focusing on emulation can help overcome such dichotomous thinking.

1.3.2 *Performativity*

Second, emulating traditional role models for new contexts could have far-reaching potential when it comes to institution-building. Embedded in narratives about freedom of expression, judicial review, and individual agency, Emulated Guardians dip deep into the sociocultural imaginary about protecting individual rights against the state. In other words, the book seeks to highlight the *performativity* of the phenomena it describes.[8] These emulative bodies may well eventually modify our traditional concepts and interpretations, especially regarding the enforceability of individual rights online and the accountability of platforms, which – somewhat presumptuously – appear to consider themselves "more like a government than a traditional company," in Mark Zuckerberg's words.[9] Some of those changes might be all to the good, but others perhaps will be worse. For now, the focus here on emulation seeks to mark out the potentially performative effects of Emulated Guardians for content moderation and, by extension, the place of public law and power in a globalized world in general.

1.3.3 *Ceremony*

Third, once we become aware of the performative effects of Emulated Guardians and the discourse that enables them, the dangers of purely *ceremonial* emulation become ever more apparent.[10] Ceremonial emulation presents itself as something (i.e., an effective protector of rights or

[8] See at 2.1.2 and for specific examples 3.8 and 4.6 and 5.3.

[9] The quote is by Meta CEO Mark Zuckerberg. See Henry Farrell, Margaret Levi and Tim O'Reilly, 'Mark Zuckerberg Runs a Nation-State, and He's the King' (*Vox.com*, 10 April 2018) <https://perma.cc/UVD9-MDNK>.

[10] The term "ceremonial" is borrowed from Meyer and Rowan (n 2) who speak of formal organizational structures as "myth and ceremony." See at 2.1 and 2.4 (esp. 2.4.1).

controller of power) it is not, or at least not to the extent it claims to be. However, by virtue of perceptions of it, ceremonial emulation potentially legitimizes phenomena in the public eye that are scarcely legitimate from a normative perspective. Therefore, as argued elsewhere already,[11] we should carefully weigh the discursive effects before bestowing symbolism-drenched and potentially legitimizing concepts and roles on these new players. Already at the level of terminology, bodies like the Oversight Board should neither be understood nor narrated using older and sometimes loaded terms like "(supreme) court." Their essential trait is the fact that they *remind* us of courts, the procedures of adjudication, and historical examples of the protection of individual rights. In other words, both bodies performatively play with juridical discourse and constitutional metaphors to performatively build up their legitimacy.[12] To reflect these characteristics, I propose calling bodies like the Oversight Board, or the EU's out-of-court dispute settlement bodies *Emulated Guardians*. Constructing such an overarching conceptual frame seems a justifiable way to surmount descriptively vague analogies to courts that might inadvertently help these emulative bodies in being mere legitimizers of the status quo.

1.3.4 *Authority and Experiments*

Fourth, I explore the practical ability of Emulated Guardians to performatively expand their *authority* and thereby advance accountability.[13] Based on internal accounts of EU lawmaking, the Oversight Board's practice, and the very first, fresh-off-the-shelf ODSs, the book identifies and highlights several inherent shortcomings, unresolved questions, and practical developments to sketch out a reformist roadmap. For example, Emulated Guardians try, with some success, to make up for weak mandates by

[11] See Josh Cowls, Philipp Darius, Dominiquo Santistevan and Moritz Schramm, 'Constitutional Metaphors: Facebook's "Supreme Court" and the Legitimation of Platform Governance' (2024) 26 New Media & Society 2448.

[12] See also Thomas Kadri, 'Juridical Discourse for Platforms' (2022) 136 Harvard Law Review (Forum) 163.

[13] Here, my argument builds on scholarship on the incremental construction of authority by international courts. Clearly, no Emulated Guardian bears similar authority to classic international or transnational courts but arguments regarding the iterative, context-dependent construction of authority appear comparable. See e.g. Eric Stein, 'Lawyers, Judges, and the Making of a Transnational Constitution' (1981) 75 American Journal of International Law 1; Karen J Alter, Laurence R Helfer and Mikael Rask Madsen, 'How Context Shapes the Authority of International Courts' in Karen J Alter, Laurence R Helfer and Mikael Rask Madsen (eds.), *International Court Authority* (Oxford University Press 2018).

well-reasoned decisions whose implementation they themselves assess very publicly – irrespective of the fact that the controlled organization is under no legal obligation to abide by the Guardian's feedback. In turn, analyzing these phenomena through the prism of emulation highlights their reflexive relationship to traditional concepts of individual rights protection, which they partly reproduce but never entirely match. Coming back to the example, Emulated Guardians reference traditional legal concepts, institutions, and styles extensively. They self-present and, arguably, self-perceive as juridifiers of otherwise unruly corporate superstructures. Emulated Guardians' common frame of reference then is, more often than not, public law. This resemblance without identity might have, at some point, repercussions on the original concept, because the emergence of Emulated Guardians should be interpreted as the next phase in the struggle over individual rights online (and beyond the state in general).

Moreover, since ODSs particularly rely on scaling effects, many are likely to lead the way in incorporating large language models into automated justice architectures. This could provide a valuable opportunity to *experiment* with such automated systems, especially since these bodies pose tolerable immediate risk – after all, their decisions are not legally binding. It remains to be seen whether this will be a step toward more – and more effective – protection of rights, or whether the path leads toward more ceremonial, and hence less effective, rights protection.

1.3.5 *Externality of EU Law*

Fifth, from an EU-law perspective, these developments are intriguing as they epitomize the risk that some EU laws may lack normative force at the margins of traditional law.[14] On the one hand, many hail the EU – and the EU certainly hails itself – as a global regulatory force muscling through European norms and values vis-à-vis other regulators and big business. The *Brussels Effect* was ubiquitously referenced during the legislative procedures leading to the Regulation (EU) 2022/2065 (Digital Services Act) (DSA) and Regulation (EU) 2022/1925 (Digital Markets Act) (DMA) package. And indeed, with the DSA and DMA the EU has presented perhaps the most ambitious regulation of platform power worldwide. However, the case studies presented below cast doubt on the true normative force these EU regulations will be able to exert. At the moment, the EU's regulatory approach to content moderation is to infuse principles like objectivity,

[14] See at 3.2.4 and 3.8.2.3 and 5.2.

proportionality, normative clarity, a duty to give reasons, individual rights adjudication into the private governance of platforms. But in its efforts to do this, the DSA is only formulating relatively broad procedural, functional, and normative goals for the platforms. The social media platforms retain "unfettered"[15] discretion on implementing this normative framework – pushing the door wide open for ceremonial formalities, structures, and procedures that will not settle the deeply embedded governance issues currently faced. Encountering the centripetal forces of private regulation and public pressure, the DSA's somewhat ceremonial attempt to advance individual rights adjudication therefore autonomizes private rulemaking power instead of confining it.[16] The DSA has triggered a path dependency that seemingly only has two, equally unsatisfactory, routes. If out-of-court dispute settlement bodies "work" in the way the DSA's stipulations would seem to be implying, the former may end up remedying only arbitrary rule enforcement while failing to address the deeper problem of unelected, private executives making the rules of free speech in Europe and beyond. If out-of-court dispute settlement bodies do not work, they nonetheless manifest the platforms' normative force. Out-of-court dispute settlement bodies' adjudication or inaction will be likely to autonomize rather than legally delineate the appropriate extent of private rulemaking and rule enforcement.

1.3.6 *Administrative Perspective on Private Governance*

Sixth, regarding content moderation, the book offers *administrative law* as a complementary perspective to the currently prevailing approaches of constitutionalism, liability, or private governance.[17] So far, much of the (legal) debate on content moderation has been approached through the

[15] Martin Eifert, Axel Metzger, Heike Schweitzer and Gerhard Wagner, 'Taming the Giants: The DMA/DSA Package' (2021) 58 Common Market Law Review 987, 1013.

[16] See at 3.2.4.3.

[17] Specifically Jack M Balkin, 'Free Speech Is a Triangle' (2018) 118 Columbia Law Review 2011 (regarding "private bureaucracies"); Kate Klonick, 'The New Governors: The People, Rules, and Processes Governing Online Speech' (2018) 131 Harvard Law Review 1598 (describes the internal bureaucracies of content moderation); Hannah Bloch-Wehba, 'Global Platform Governance: Private Power in the Shadow of the State' (2019) 72 SMU Law Review 27 (also makes the link to GAL); Evelyn Douek, 'Content Moderation as Systems Thinking' (2022) 136 Harvard Law Review 526 (mentions administrative law in passing); Giovanni De Gregorio, *Digital Constitutionalism in Europe: Reframing Rights and Powers in the Algorithmic Society* (Cambridge University Press 2022) (focuses on "digital constitutionalism" but briefly mentions the DSA's administrative dimension). See further from a private law perspective Rodrigo Vallejo Garretón, 'After Governance? The Idea of

lens of (digital) constitutionalism[18] or viewed through the private-law lens of liability.[19] Neither of these lenses focuses on internal practices as they are manifested in platforms. Constitutionalism is too loose-knit an approach to fully tease out the technical, but arguably crucial, details of the inner workings of content moderators. In turn, most liability-focused perspectives focus mainly on the external acts of platforms, whose effects might then elicit liability claims, but much less on the internal, structural reasons for such putatively liable acts. Last, some authors are staunch opponents of intensifying government regulation, often deploying variations of arguments that platforms are too big, too globalized, or too innovative to be effectively regulated. This latter approach is, I believe, ahistorical and misguided. Over the centuries we have seen time and again that public law itself is an innovative, flexible, and adaptable mechanism for furthering the control of overweening power. Of course, everything changes all the time, yet few developments are ever truly unprecedented. Platforms create, regulate, and police infrastructures vital to the exercise of public discourse. They regulate – in various ways – the way so many of us communicate online. In short, platforms

a Private Administrative Law' in Poul F Kjaer (ed.), *The Law of Political Economy* (Cambridge University Press 2020).

18 The epistemological basis can be found in Günther Teubner's work. For proponents of "digital" constitutionalism see e.g. Dennis Redeker, Lex Gill and Urs Gasser, 'Towards Digital Constitutionalism? Mapping Attempts to Craft an Internet Bill of Rights' (2018) 80 International Communication Gazette 302; De Gregorio (n 17); Nicolas P Suzor, 'Digital Constitutionalism: Using the Rule of Law to Evaluate the Legitimacy of Governance by Platforms' (2018) 4 Social Media + Society 1; Edoardo Celeste, 'Digital Constitutionalism: A New Systematic Theorisation' (2019) 33 International Review of Law, Computers & Technology 76; Oreste Pollicino, *Judicial Protection of Fundamental Rights on the Internet: A Road towards Digital Constitutionalism?* (Hart 2021); Edoardo Celeste, Amélie Heldt and Clara Iglesias Keller (eds.), *Constitutionalising Social Media* (Hart 2022); critical: Moritz Schramm, 'Where Is Olive? Or: Lessons from Democratic Theory for Legitimate Platform Governance' (*The Digital Constitutionalist*, 26 January 2022) <https://perma.cc/RL93-CGSY>; Róisín Á Costello, 'Faux Ami? Interrogating the Normative Coherence of "Digital Constitutionalism"' (2023) 12 Global Constitutionalism 326.

19 See especially but also not exhaustively Ronald J Mann and Seth R Belzley, 'The Promise of Internet Intermediary Liability' (2005) 47 William & Mary Law Review 239; Martin Husovec, *Injunctions against Intermediaries in the European Union* (Cambridge University Press 2018); Daphne Keller, 'The Right Tools: Europe's Intermediary Liability Laws and the EU 2016 General Data Protection Regulation' [2018] Berkeley Technology Law Journal 297; Klonick (n 17) 1603 et seq; Giancarlo Frosio and Martin Husovec, 'Accountability and Responsibility of Online Intermediaries' in Giancarlo Frosio (ed.), *Oxford Handbook of Online Intermediary Liability* (Oxford University Press 2020); Christophe Geiger, Giancarlo Frosio and Elena Izyumenko, 'Intermediary Liability and Fundamental Rights' in Giancarlo Frosio (ed.), *Oxford Handbook of Online Intermediary Liability* (Oxford University Press 2020).

unilaterally exercise power over individuals in traditional public-law areas, such as public discourse, artistic freedom, the right to do business, and the protection of free speech. Further, regulators increasingly co-opt platforms for policy agendas like the enforcement of criminal law online. Thus, content moderation can be seen, with several caveats of course, as quintessentially administrative. There is a narrative that private power, in our case content moderation, would be so groundbreaking and innovative that "conventional" thinking about guaranteed freedoms and their accompanying guardians would be missing the point. But this story risks chipping away at the basic assumption that domination ought to be normatively justified. Platforms exercise power in crucial public respects. Public law has an orchestra of instruments for controlling power. Within the field of public law, administrative law would offer a much-needed analytical variety to digital constitutionalists, and a much-needed normative program, which would complement still-relevant elements of private regulatory mechanisms like liability. The DSA now ignites another stage of what could be called the *administrification* of content moderation. The administrative-law perspective proposed here seeks to incorporate and further develop aspects of the Global Administrative Law project and beyond.

1.3.7 New Accountability Norms

Seven, we take a step back and use the empirically validated descriptions of the origins, practice, and potential of Emulated Guardians to reflect more generally on whether the emulation of the specific set of public-law mechanisms, most notably rights and process, which dominate discussions about content moderation (but also about global governance more widely) are indeed the most appropriate normative choice. Perhaps overemphasizing rights and adjudication risks underemphasizing other, more input-oriented, mechanisms like participation in rulemaking. At the end of the day, contemporary reforms of content moderation like the DSA appear incomplete in their focus on the ex-post legitimation of power in individualized relationships. Here, individualized procedures and review mechanisms might help in remedying individual violations. However, many reformers seem to underestimate the fact that most transgressions of platforms vis-à-vis individuals only reflect normative choices made earlier in the process, further up the ladder, and chiseled into platforms' business models. Reforms thus ought to be much more structural than a mere individualized, ex-post alleviating of symptoms.

Therefore, we must broaden the conversation. Especially, there is a much more fundamental discussion to be held on repurposing private law and its mechanisms, not only to incorporate more elements of publicness but, crucially, to reflect the infrastructural realities of technology and code.[20] However, in these discussions, public law concepts will remain essential. It may be that their efficacy no longer depends solely on traditional regulation, but also on discourse and social pressure. Yet, public law ideas – potentially repackaged and redefined – are such a potent and persuasive "method and mindset" that they will continue to play a significant role in governing private power beyond the state.[21] In many ways, this book intends to serve merely as a prologue to a much larger conversation.

1.4 Approach and Methodology

This is a socio-legal and a comparative book. It *describes* and *evaluates* Emulated Guardians. Both description and evaluation rely on a theoretical frame, and various methods.

1.4.1 Theoretical Approach

The theoretical frame combines three distinct but interrelated strands of literature. These are organization theory, more specifically neo-institutionalist sociology;[22] the related political science literature on policy diffusion;[23] and administrative law (in its broadest sense).[24] Academic

[20] Laura DeNardis and Francesca Musiani, 'Governance by Infrastructure' in Francesca Musiani and others (eds.), *The Turn to Infrastructure in Internet Governance* (Palgrave Macmillan 2016); Benedict Kingsbury, 'Infrastructure and InfraReg: On Rousing the International Law "Wizards of Is"' (2019) 8 Cambridge International Law Journal 171; Benedict Kingsbury and Nahuel Maisley, 'Infrastructures and Laws: Publics and Publicness' (2021) 17 Annual Review of Law and Social Science 353.

[21] Megan Donaldson and Benedict Kingsbury, 'Ersatz Normativity or Public Law in Global Governance: The Hard Case of International Prescriptions for National Infrastructure Regulation' (2013) 14 Chicago Journal of International Law 1, 48.

[22] The key texts are cited in n 5.

[23] See especially Westney (n 5); Beth A Simmons, Frank Dobbin and Geoffrey Garrett (eds.), *The Global Diffusion of Markets and Democracy* (Cambridge University Press 2008); Shipan and Volden (n 5).

[24] Benedict Kingsbury, Nico Krisch and Richard B Stewart, 'The Emergence of Global Administrative Law' (2005) 68 Law and Contemporary Problems 15; Benedict Kingsbury, 'Frontiers of Global Administrative Law in the 2020s' in Jason NE Varuhas and Shona Wilson Stark (eds.), *The Frontiers of Public Law* (Hart Publishing 2020); Orit Fischman-Afori, 'Taking Global Administrative Law One Step Ahead: Online Giants and the Digital Democratic Sphere' (2022) 20 International Journal of Constitutional Law 1006;

works relating to organization theory and policy diffusion have helped to explain why organizations, like the EU or Meta, establish certain formal structures and decide for or against specific policies. In contrast to "rationalist" explanations, which view organizational development or policy diffusion as constituting a "rational" means toward an equally "rational" (i.e. economic, efficiency-oriented) goal, neo-institutionalist and (large parts of) policy diffusion scholarship argue that organizational design, formal structures, and policy or management choices reflect the expectations and "myths" of their institutional environments.[25] In other words, many formal structures (like novel adjudicators) or policies (such as establishing a new adjudicator and using individual rights as an instrument to control formalized power structures) exist not because they work in a rationalist sense – but because they are socially, culturally, legally, and politically institutionalized and therefore expected. Once institutionalized, a formal structure or policy's efficacy is hardly questioned, and their "fit" for new contexts is considered natural, obvious, and appropriate.[26] Sociologists highlighted the role of such "imitation" in the early-twentieth century,[27] while the first theories of the role of imitation in organizational development emerged in the 1950s.[28] In the 1970s, tenets of neo-institutionalism began to uproot rationalist[29] (at least in the economic sense) conceptions of organizational development and the law's role in it.[30] However, scholars of

Moritz Schramm, 'Platform Administrative Law: A Research Agenda' (SSRN, 24 July 2024) <https://perma.cc/JH2A-8ZW2>.

25 See at 2.4. The "myth" references neo-institutionalism's founding article, Meyer and Rowan (n 5).

26 See for that argument in organization theory: ibid 343–353; for political science: Simmons, Dobbin and Garrett (n 5) 31–40.

27 See esp. Gabriel Tarde, *The Laws of Imitation* (Henry Holt 1903); for context: Barbara Czarniawska, 'Gabriel Tarde and Organization Theory' in Paul Adler (ed.), *The Oxford Handbook of Sociology and Organization Studies* (Oxford University Press 2009) 246 et seq.

28 See esp. Alchian's reflection on how "imperfect attempts to imitate others, unconsciously innovate by unwittingly acquiring some unexpected or unsought unique attributes." Armen A Alchian, 'Uncertainty, Evolution, and Economic Theory' (1950) 58 Journal of Political Economy 211, 218–219.

29 Rationalist in that sense refers predominantly to economically grounded rational choice and efficacy-oriented theories, cf. Meyer and Rowan (n 5) 341–342. In a broader sense, neo-institutionalism also is "rationalist", said rationality's goal, however, is not economic (or other substantive) efficacy but socio-cultural and political legitimacy of the organization. Within that rationality, emulating even economically disastrous or entirely dysfunctional policies may be "rational" for their legitimacy yields.

30 For a brief historical overview see Swaran Sandhu, 'Grundlagen und Kernbegriffe des Neo-Institutionalismus' in Swaran Sandhu, *Public Relations und Legitimität* (Verlag für Sozialwissenschaften 2012) 73–74; see in general Ronald L Jepperson, 'Institutions,

administrative law, EU law, and international law have so far not extensively interacted with them.[31]

Emulated Guardians' underlying idea is to control large-scale, formalized power structures – in particular, social media platforms – by subjecting them to individual rights review by an adjudicator. Social media platforms, partly because of regulatory embedding that the companies which owned them had often unilaterally undertaken, have evolved into huge rulemaking and rule-enforcing structures that can in fact be viewed as "private bureaucracies" (Balkin) and "systems of administration" (Douek).[32] This functionality mirrors administrative law. The third constitutive strand of literature, therefore, builds on the existing corpus of Global Administrative Law (GAL),[33] developed since the 2000s and which conceives of administrative law in a broad sense, as pertaining to the theories, doctrines, mechanisms, institutions, and principles regulating the exercise and control of administration-like power.

1.4.2 *Interviewing*

The genesis of Emulated Guardians is complex, and their practices – in the case of Meta's Oversight Board which, unlike the EU's out-of-court dispute settlement bodies, is already up and running for several years at the time of writing – fast-moving and relatively untransparent. To generate insights beyond already published texts and to more effectively interpret the primary and secondary sources at hand, I conducted qualitative, semi-structured interviews with experts over a period of three years. It is essential to emphasize that these interviews served as a complementary source rather than the primary or, in many respects, even a decisive one.

Institutional Effects, and Institutionalism' in Walter W Powell and Paul J DiMaggio (eds.), *The New Institutionalism in Organizational Analysis* (University of Chicago Press 1991).

[31] A rare (but critical) mention can be found in Laura Dickinson, 'Organizational Structure and Culture in an Era of Privatization: The Case of United States Military and Security Contractors' in Susan Rose-Ackerman, Blake Emerson and Peter L Lindseth (eds.), *Comparative Administrative Law* (2nd ed., Edward Elgar Publishing 2017) 566, 570.

[32] See at 2.3 and Balkin (n 17) 2021–2032; Bloch-Wehba (n 17) 31 et seq; Douek (n 17) 531; Schramm (n 24).

[33] GAL was founded and prominently advanced by Benedict Kingsbury, Richard Steward, and Sabino Cassese and many others. GAL sought to normatively reconceptualize phenomena of global governance through the lens of administrative law. For an introduction see Kingsbury, Krisch and Stewart (n 24); Sabino Cassese, 'Administrative Law without the State? The Challenge of Global Regulation' (2005) 37 International Law and Politics 663; Sabino Cassese, *Research Handbook on Global Administrative Law* (Edward Elgar 2016); Kingsbury (n 24).

Between September 2021 and November 2024, I carried out twenty-four qualitative interviews with twenty-one interviewees. Most interviews were conducted between September 2021 and November 2022, roughly a third then in 2024 to inquire for follow-ups prior to publication of this book (see Table 1.1). All interviewees were "experts" in that they had special knowledge of the research object due to their occupation.[34] They represent a diverse set of perspectives from the "inside" and "outside" of Emulated Guardians. Interviewees' expertise stems from their work in the European Commission, the European Parliament, the Oversight Board, prior or current employment or consultancy activities for Meta/Facebook, newly founded ODSs such as ADROIT, User Rights, and the Appeals Centre, academic work, and activism. Most interviewees had a legal background. They filled positions of varying seniority, with the bulk of perspectives coming from higher mid-level to high-level positions in the respective organizational setup. Most interviewees were embedded in their respective organizations' hierarchies but still seemed to have considerable leeway in interpreting their roles. Their positions were mostly specialized and professional rather than political or executive. Put simply, in one way or another, most interviewees prepare, influence, and facilitate their organization's acts but are not the ones publicly accountable for them. The focus on such higher mid-level interviewees was made for three reasons. First, large organizations like the EU or Meta rely on highly skilled staffers.[35] A great deal of internal wrestling, decision-making, and tacit policy decisions are made by expert staffers and framed in "legal" or "technical" terms.[36] Such staffers are regularly more entrenched in the details of specific policy proposals, aware of options that did not make it into the published texts, and speak more openly about substance than do PR-savvy executives. Second, analyzing how legal institutions' "ghostwriters" (in Tommaso Pavone's term) impact organizational practice is increasingly,

[34] For further information what constitutes an "expert" see Michael Meuser and Ulrike Nagel, 'The Expert Interview and Changes in Knowledge Production' in Alexander Bogner, Beate Littig and Wolfgang Menz (eds.), Interviewing Experts (Palgrave Macmillan UK 2009) 17 et seq. Note, however, that what constitutes expertise and who is considered an "expert" remains a construction by the researcher, cf. Emilia Korkea-aho and Päivi Leino-Sandberg, 'Interviewing Lawyers: A Critical Self-Reflection on Expert Interviews as a Method of EU Legal Research' (2019) European Journal of Legal Studies (Special Issue) 17, 31–32.

[35] Pointing to the importance of the EU's highly qualified staffers for the Union's regulatory capacity: Anu Bradford, *The Brussels Effect: How the European Union Rules the World* (Oxford University Press 2020) 31 et seq.

[36] Päivi Leino-Sandberg, *The Politics of Legal Expertise in EU Policy-Making* (Cambridge University Press 2021) 58 et seq.

Table 1.1 *Interviews*

Date Interview(s)	Interviewee	Institutional Background
21 September 2021	1	Trustee Oversight Board, consultant for Facebook during Oversight Board's creation (2018–2020)
1 October 2021	2	Academic, embedded observer at Facebook during Oversight Board's creation (2019–2020)
29 October 2021	3	Staffer, European Commission
29 October 2021, 8 July 2022	4	Staffer, European Commission
1 November 2021	5	Academic, consultant for Facebook during Oversight Board's creation (2018)
17 November 2021	6	Staffer 1, European Parliament
1 December 2021	7	Activist
5 January 2022 25 March 2022	8	Staffer, Oversight Board
13 April 2022	9	Staffer 1, Oversight Board
6 May 2022	10	Staffer 2, Oversight Board
27 May 2022	11	Staffer 3, Oversight Board
2 June 2022	12	Staffer 4, Oversight Board
23 November 2022	13	Staffer 5, Oversight Board
29 June 2022, 16 November 2022	14	Academic, Consultant to the European Commission
15 November 2022	15	Member, Oversight Board
25 November 2022	16	Staffer 2, European Parliament
25 October 2024	17	Co-Founder, User Rights
30 October 2024	18	Founder, ADROIT
30 October 2024	19	Staffer 1, ADROIT
30 October 2024	20	Staffer 2, ADROIT
1 November 2024	21	Director, Appeals Centre

and I believe rightly, recognized as a central theme in socio-legal scholarship relating to legal institutions.[37] Third, higher mid-level staffers are often more accessible than people further up the ladder.

[37] Hannah Birkenkötter, 'What the Secretariat Makes It: How International Civil Servants Shape Contemporary International Law' (2023) 20 International Organizations Law

Generally speaking, the accessibility of interviewees varied widely.[38] In particular, accommodating confidentiality concerns required lengthy and slow-moving negotiations, a fact that was itself informative regarding organizational habitus.[39] I retained full control over the research output and confidentiality concerns were met through consent forms and anonymization. Conducting interviews about the DSA faced the additional challenge that the legislative procedure's speed outpaced expectations, which affected the amount of time when (potential) interviewees from EU institutions were available.

To include a broad set of perspectives, I engaged in so-called snowball sampling.[40] Of course, the interviewees should not be thought of as a "representative" sample from a quantitative viewpoint.[41] Instead, the range of empirical insights gathered for this work depicts a plausible account of organizational practices. Diverging accounts of these practices are equally plausible.

Most interviews were conducted via videoconferencing. Except for two group interviews, all the interviews were one-to-one. Typically, interviews lasted roughly an hour. All interviewees gave informed consent to their statements being used in this research. As a principle, interviews were audio recorded and transcribed. Not every interviewee consented to being recorded. For these cases, I made handwritten and computer-typed notes as well as immediately produced "memory minutes." Unfortunately, this resulted in varying data quality. However, for these exploratory and

Review 426; Tommaso Pavone, *The Ghostwriters: Lawyers and the Politics behind the Judicial Construction of Europe* (Cambridge University Press 2022); Joost Pauwelyn and Krzysztof Pelc, 'Who Guards the "Guardians of the System"? The Role of the Secretariat in WTO Dispute Settlement' (2022) 116 American Journal of International Law 534; Tommaso Soave, *The Everyday Makers of International Law: From Great Halls to Back Rooms* (Cambridge University Press 2022); from a critical perspective Fuad Zarbiyev, 'On the Judge Centredness of the International Legal Self' (2021) 32 European Journal of International Law 1139; see already Yves Dezalay and Bryant G Garth, *Dealing with Virtue: International Commercial Arbitration and the Construction of a Transnational Legal Order* (University of Chicago Press 1998); Charles R Epp, *The Rights Revolution: Lawyers, Activists, and Supreme Courts in Comparative Perspective* (University of Chicago Press 1998); criticizing lacking perspectives is also at the heart of Kathryn M Stanchi, Linda L Berger and Bridget J Crawford (eds.), *Feminist Judgments: Rewritten Opinions of the United States Supreme Court* (Cambridge University Press 2016).

38 See in that regard generally Korkea-aho and Leino-Sandberg (n 34) 37–41.

39 See in general ibid 41–44.

40 Ibid 32.

41 In that regard see the practical observations in Anne Galletta, *Mastering the Semi-Structured Interview and Beyond: From Research Design to Analysis and Publication* (New York University Press 2013) 31; Korkea-aho and Leino-Sandberg (n 34) 32–33.

systematizing interviews, varying data quality can be a nuisance but not an insurmountable obstacle.[42] All generated textual data (transcripts, notes, memory minutes) were collated and analyzed using *MaxQDA* software. All data were saved with password-protection locally and on servers located in Germany, and all interviewees have been anonymized. Interviewing was ethically reviewed, approved, and supervised according to the procedures at Humboldt-University of Berlin.

Apart from the interviews listed in the table above, I enjoyed numerous, roughly thirty, "background talks" with activists, academics, EU member-state officials, judges, and other experts. These background talks were not connected to the interview script and did not generate equivalent data (like transcripts, notes, or memory minutes), and are therefore not included as interviews. Nevertheless, they provided valuable contextual material that I was then able to feed into my analysis.

1.4.3 *Word Count*

The Oversight Board case study contains a brief word count analysis.[43] The word count analysis quantitatively scrutinizes claims made by interviewees, scholarly commentators, and my own impressions – based on a close reading of all Board decisions issued until November 2024 – that the Board in its normative conceptions focuses mainly on Article 19 of the International Covenant on Civil and Political Rights (ICCPR) and not on the "rules" that Meta's lawyers and executives have themselves devised. In other words, although the charter and the bylaws envisaged the Oversight Board's review as based mainly on Meta's *internal* rules, the Board arguably turned to *external* rules to construct a more concise and legitimate normative framework for its adjudication.[44] To gauge whether the Board was working closely with human rights law on a more general level, I decided to compare how many words the Board allots to human rights analyses in its decisions in contrast to its analyses of other norm-oriented material.

Generating quantitative insights requires an irreducible baseline unit. The Board issues three types of decisions: standard, expedited, and summary. This word count analysis focuses on standard decisions, as they

[42] That is because the information retrieved from the data does not require, for example, linguistic analysis or extensive coding. Even though transcriptions are always better, notes and memory minutes can serve as a robust alternative.

[43] See at 4.5.

[44] See at 4.4.

offer the most in-depth normative analysis. All Oversight Board standard decisions (from now on "decisions") feature similar parts.[45] Each decision contains a part called "Oversight Board Analysis," which exclusively contains the Board's normative reasoning. Initially, that "Oversight Board Analysis" was split into three sections: one section contained the reasoning regarding Meta's "Community Standards"; another where the case is situated in relation to Meta's "values"; and one which deals with the particular case's possible relevance to the provisions of certain pieces of international human rights law, especially Article 19 ICCPR.[46] In mid-2023, a prior section on Meta's values was essentially gutted.

The subsection on human rights further subdivides into a three-pronged proportionality test; each prong is announced with a subheading. Counting the number of words that the Oversight Board allots to each of these sections provides such an irreducible baseline unit as it does not require an act of interpretation by the researcher. Each word is one unit, a so-called unigram, and the total number of units in a section – for example, the subsection on human rights – constitutes the word count of that unit. This minimizes the risk of biases entering the dataset. Therefore, assertions regarding word count can be *true*, whereas more far-reaching claims on the basis of a text's linguistic or syntactic characteristics rest on complex premises and require interpretation beyond the scope of this book.[47]

A disadvantage of word-counting as a method is that adjudicators, especially with increasing confidence and practice, may tend to express themselves more succinctly or reference an acquis without bothering to

45 See at 4.5.1.

46 See at ibid. In one case in November 2022, the Board added a subsection 8.4 on "identical content with parallel context" in the sense of Article 4 of the Charter, cf. *UK drill music* [2022] Oversight Board 2022-007-IG-MR.

47 I personally entertain reservations towards too confident – in the sense of absolute and exclusive – truth claims relating to social phenomena. For more elaborate reflections on the matters of "truth" and the "objectivity" of its representation see Max Weber, 'Die "Objektivität" sozialwissenschaftlicher und sozialpolitischer Erkenntnis' (1904) 19 Archiv für Sozialwissenschaft und Sozialpolitik 22, 31 et seq; Lisa Webley, 'Qualitative Approaches to Empirical Legal Research' in Peter Cane and Herbert M Kritzer (eds.), *The Oxford Handbook of Empirical Legal Research* (Oxford University Press 2010) 77–78; see in that sense also Foucault who argues that "one does not attach the constants of discourse to the ideal structures [i.e. 'truth'] of the concept, but one describes the conceptual network on the basis of intrinsic regularities of discourse"; Michel Foucault, *The Archaeology of Knowledge* (Pantheon Books 1972) 62; see for the opposite (slightly polemical) position Paul Boghossian, *Fear of Knowledge* (Oxford University Press 2006) esp. 25 et seq. More balanced, Ian Hacking, *The Social Construction of What?* (Harvard University Press) 63 et seq.

explain their normative reasoning all over again.[48] However, this aspect seems negligible for the Oversight Board as it enjoys discretion in case selection (subject to the prior approval of Meta executives, however, which goes to the heart of the Board's genuine substantive power).[49] It seems unlikely that the Board would select cases that fail to raise new normative issues. It does pick cases that cover issues the Board has addressed in the past but which it did not deem to have been sufficiently addressed by Meta – although in these cases the Board typically cites older decisions *and* presents its argumentation regarding the issue in question.

Based on the interviews, a close reading of the decisions, and existing theories about the value of argumentation and citation in adjudicative texts, I contend that, within its "analysis" section, the Board writes most about what it considers normatively important. Writing more increases word count. Hence, within the Board's normative reasoning (which is always confined to the "Oversight Board Analysis" part of a decision), each section's word count may serve as a proxy indicator for that section's importance.[50]

The Oversight Board publishes all outcomes of procedures (also when there is no decision) on its website. Until the time of this writing in mid-November 2024, the Board issued sixty-eight standard decisions.[51] All were downloaded as pdfs. As mentioned before, the Board normatively reasons only in the part entitled "Oversight Board Analysis." Evaluating the total word count of this part and the distribution between and within sections therefore tells us how many words the Oversight Board allots to which issues.[52] These quantitative insights in turn supplement the close reading and legal analysis of the Board's argumentation.

All words belonging to the main corpus, headings, and subheadings of each decision's "Oversight Board Analysis" were manually copied to a table in a Word document.[53] This table featured one column for each

48 Angelika Nußberger, 'Wer Zitiert Wen? Zur Funktion von Zitaten bei der Herausbildung Gemeineuropäischen Verfassungsrechts' (2006) 61 JuristenZeitung 763.

49 See at 4.3.

50 Note that a similar claim could not be equally made regarding the comparison of the word count of the argumentative part and the descriptive parts. In the latter, the Board merely describes existing material. That it does so at great length indicates, on the one hand, the complexity of the issues at stake, and on the other hand, the presumed aim of the Board to present its reasoning as flowing from the normative material and the facts of a case.

51 The very first decision was essentially empty as the user withdrew the appeal and the Board did not decide on the subject matter.

52 This premises that the Board's reasoning corresponds to the respective subsections' heading. A close reading of all decisions indicated that this was indeed the case.

53 That document is on file with the author.

decision and one row for each of the sections (community standards, values, human rights). In the table, the words were manually cleaned of copy/paste errors or hyphenations. Within the rows mirroring the decisions' human rights section, the sub-sections on legality, legitimate aim, and necessity and proportionality were highlighted in different colors. Any text within the human rights section that did not belong to one of these categories was left unhighlighted.

Using *Microsoft Word*'s "mark text" and "word count" functions, I counted each section in total as well as the highlighted paragraphs separately. This yielded numerical data relating to the number of words in each section regarding the applicable rules (values, community standards, human rights) and, within the human rights assessment, the highlighted paragraphs (regarding legality, aim, and necessity and proportionality).

Last, I entered this numerical data into an *Excel* table.[54] Using basic *Excel* functions (for instance, column average) and analysis tools (exponential regressions), I then analyzed the numerical data and turned the relevant findings into graphs.[55]

1.5 Situating the Research(er)

Following those methodological remarks, a short reflection on the research's (and the researcher's) epistemic background seems warranted. Research is a contingent practice, swayed by discourse, preexisting interests, opinions, experience, attitudinal stance, and temporality.[56] Generally, findings are contingent on research design, which in turn is contingent on prior epistemologies, interests, and material conditions.

Subjecting powerful organizations to individualized redress resonates with core tenets of contemporary political science, legal scholarship, and culture. Emulated Guardians reflect what their creators thought were effective, legitimate, and legitimizing mechanisms to control platform

[54] That table is on file with the author.

[55] See at 4.5, 4.6, and 5.3.

[56] For Bourdieu's perspective on epistemic reflexivity see: Pierre Bourdieu, 'The Practice of Reflexive Sociology (The Paris Workshop)' in Pierre Bourdieu and Loïc JD Wacquant (eds.), *An Invitation to Reflexive Sociology* (Polity Press 1992) 224–234; Loïc JD Wacquant, 'Towards a Social Praxeology: The Structure and Logic of Bourdieu's Sociology' in Pierre Bourdieu and Loïc JD Wacquant (eds.), *An Invitation to Reflexive Sociology* (Polity Press 1992) 36–46. See already the basis at Foucault (n 49) 3–21, 178 et seq.

power (or to be perceived as controllers of this power). But this is only one way of looking at the picture. Reflecting on the researcher's "subliminal categories of thought" unearths several underlying premises and preconceptions.[57]

As a German-educated (public) lawyer, I tend to have a mild suspicion of anything private that purports to be public. This neither implies a bias against private governance, nor does it reflect a statist agenda.[58] Martti Koskenniemi considers it "trite" to advocate for the state to "take back control" in transnational governance.[59] But if private power structures are increasingly exercising such governance, it appears intuitive to install guardians, insert control rods, and contain power. Perhaps the most significant risk in debates about content moderation, technology, and private governance in general is the entrenching of polarized positions between defeatism – "nobody can regulate the Internet" – and simplistic state-oriented approaches – "private governance is inherently problematic." As this book shows, private and regulatory *emulation* of public-law legislation manifests itself in an intricate dance of regulators, corporations, public opinion, academics, and activists. Emulated Guardians' functionality and normative legitimacy does not lend itself to black-and-white thinking.

Another (not so) "subliminal" aspect affecting the form of this book is fieldwork. I conducted numerous interviews with a range of experts from inside and outside the two Emulated Guardians (see Section 1.4.2). The interviews yielded indispensable insights into relatively untransparent institutions. Talking at length with people from various backgrounds challenged some predispositions that I owe to my (German) public-law background.

Therefore, the perspectives reflected in this book echo the diverse voices of the people I talked to. Only their diverse viewpoints enabled a multi-perspectival and balanced analysis. Talking to people crafting the

57 See also Moritz Schramm, 'Shrinks, Priests, and Academic Soul-Searching: Epistemic Reflexivity in Socio-Legal Research' (*Frontiers of Socio-Legal Studies*, 5 July 2023) <https://perma.cc/EV9F-ZZ72>.

58 Note, however, that Anu Bradford rightly pointed out that "Europeans are generally less trusting of markets and more comfortable with government intervention. The state enjoys greater public trust in the EU and can therefore assume a more prominent role in regulating markets" (n 35) 39.

59 Referring not exclusively to private power in transnational governance though, Martti Koskenniemi, 'Performing Legal Expertise: Reflections on the Construction of Transnational Authority' in Emilia Korkea-aho and Päivi Leino-Sandberg (eds.), *Law, Legal Expertise and EU Policy-Making* (Cambridge University Press 2022) 40.

Digital Services Act, working for the Oversight Board or trying to set up an out-of-court dispute settlement body allowed the "research object" to narrate its own version of the story. This is of course never a risk-free undertaking because empirical analysis reflexively influences normative analysis, preconceptions, and understanding.[60]

Meeting the people toiling hard and passionately on these pressing issues inevitably left its mark. Notwithstanding my above-mentioned initial suspicions and the skeptical viewpoint, I sometimes take in the book, this text is certainly not a defeatist critique of lawyers, policymakers, or managers. I was genuinely impressed by the strong commitment of many interviewees to shifting the governance of online discourse onto a better path – despite sometimes crippling institutional constraints.[61] The culmination of my research and thinking presented here therefore seeks to balance constructive, normatively driven skepticism with empirically informed restraint in light of the complexities of real-world practice. Certainly, engaging in empirical work made me more cautious – the easy answer is often a false friend. Evidently, the observations and arguments presented stake no claims to exclusivity or absolute truth.

Last, a word on AI. As a non-native speaker, my use of artificial intelligence tools has been limited to refining prose here and there. I did not rely on AI in any substantive way beyond improving the wording of text I had already written.

1.6 Terminology and Structure

Before we proceed, a few words on terminology. Throughout the book we will jump back and forth between law and social sciences (mainly sociology and political science), as well as between European and North American perspectives.[62] This calls for a large degree of terminological caution as not everything that looks or sounds similar denotes similar things in various disciplines or jurisdictions. Thus, before I outline the structure of the book, I briefly highlight what several key concepts are presumed to mean as I use them in each of the ensuing chapters.

[60] See in that sense Sarah MH Nouwen, '"As You Set out for Ithaka": Practical, Epistemological, Ethical, and Existential Questions about Socio-Legal Empirical Research in Conflict' (2014) 27 Leiden Journal of International Law 227.

[61] See for similar reflections about EU agents' commitment to the EU interest: Leino-Sandberg (n 36) 24.

[62] Lacking empirics about comparable phenomena outside the EU and the US are another, rather painful testament to my positionality and indicate a promising field of further research.

In this introduction we have met two dimensions of legitimacy: public and normative legitimacy. Public legitimacy is used here purely descriptively as societal acceptance of a certain power structure paired with the perception that said power structure has the right to act the way it does.[63] In contrast, normative legitimacy is a reflection of that power structure's conformity with certain preset norms irrespective of its public reception.[64] Through emulation, an actor may accrue both types of legitimacy.[65] However, if an emulation predominantly focuses on establishing publicly visible ceremonies without substantive practical effects, it may yield public legitimacy. This occurs because the ceremonial emulation appears legitimate, as it resembles a normatively legitimate model. Yet, it might also lack actual normative legitimacy, as the ceremonial emulation does not function as effectively as the genuinely normatively legitimate role model. Simply put, constructing something that vaguely reminds of a court, does not immediately make a powerful guardian of individual rights.

Further the book distinguishes between public and private power as well as public and private law. Clearly, ironclad distinctions between public and private law and power would paint an oversimplified picture.[66] Private law exists within a constitutional framework and is

[63] I build on Weber's classical account of "*Legitimität*," which I translate to legitimacy. I call that dimension of legitimacy "public" ("perceived" or "descriptive" would have been equally possible terminology) to highlight the element of massification as well as its discursive elements. See Max Weber, *Wirtschaft Und Gesellschaft* (1922) (Zweitausendeins 2005) Erster Halbband, Erster Teil, Drittes Kapitel, § 1 (p. 157); Enrico Peuker, *Bürokratie und Demokratie in Europa: Legitimität im europäischen Verwaltungsverbund* (Mohr Siebeck 2011) 97 et seq; Christoph Möllers, 'Legalität, Legitimität und Legitimation des Bundesverfassungsgerichts' in Matthias Jestaedt et al. (eds.), *Das entgrenzte Gericht* (Suhrkamp 2011) 297.

[64] I call this normative legitimacy as it abstractly links an actor's legitimacy to a preset normative system and not to public perception. Legitimation specifically denotes the process of accruing legitimacy. Peuker (n 65) 96–97; (speaking of legitimation) Möllers (n 65) 308 et seq; (also speaking of legitimation) Michael Zürn, *A Theory of Global Governance: Authority, Legitimacy, and Contestation* (Oxford University Press 2018) 62 et seq.

[65] Debates about the exact theoretical contours of legitimacy (and legitimation) fill whole libraries. See recently and not-so-recently e.g., Niklas Luhmann, *Legitimation durch Verfahren* (Suhrkamp 1983); David Beetham, *The Legitimation of Power* (Humanities Press International 1991); Linnet Taylor, 'Public Actors Without Public Values: Legitimacy, Domination and the Regulation of the Technology Sector' (2021) 34 Philosophy & Technology 897.

[66] In that sense, but from varying perspectives see especially: Morris Cohen, 'Property and Sovereignty' (1927) 13 Cornell Law Quarterly 8; Duncan Kennedy, 'The Stages of the Decline of the Public/Private Distinction' (1982) 130 University of Pennsylvania Law Review 1349; Alfred C Aman, 'The Globalizing State: A Future-Oriented Perspective on the

(increasingly) imbued with public-law principles like nondiscrimination. In turn, public law and power co-opt private actors for effective enforcement and reflect, at least in theory and confined by the outer bounds of a constitution, the demands of the "private" majority. Yet "public" and "private" are still useful signifiers that point to significant differences in an actor's mandate, culture, capacity, and values.[67] Public, in this conception, refers to organizations associated with state power on the national or international level – or like the EU, for example, which is neither a state nor a typical international organization. Accompanying this observation is the (often implicit) assumption that public actors work, by and large, in the public interest. Private power, in turn, is usually exercised by organizations like companies, which operate on a profit-oriented basis and whose main driver is, in principle, not the public interest but operational benefit.

One last concept that deserves anticipatory attention is institution. In sociological parlance, institutions are stable, repeated, and expected practices.[68] The term is open-ended and may refer to different phenomena like marriage, parliamentary democracy, or, as in our case, the adjudication of individual rights. In a narrower sense, which is more common in legal literature, the term "institution" refers to a formally constituted organization, like an Emulated Guardian, a specific court or the EU institutions cited in Articles 13 to 19 in the Treaty on European Union (TEU). These are then called "organizations" in sociological parlance.

The book progresses in three steps. The first step, consisting of Chapters 1 to 2, lays the theoretical and contextual framework. After this brief introduction, Chapter 2 theorizes how organizations emulate societal institutions to yield public legitimacy. The second step builds on the theoretical program and presents two empirical case studies of two Emulated Guardians. These are, in Chapter 3, the DSA's out-of-court dispute settlement bodies and, in Chapter 4, Meta's Oversight Board. Based on extensive textual analysis and complemented by numerous expert interviews, the case studies lay bare the origins and practice of

Public/Private Distinction, Federalism, and Democracy' (1998) 31 Vanderbilt Journal of Transnational Law 769.

[67] See e.g. Jody Freeman, 'The Private Role in Public Governance' (2000) 75 New York University Law Review 543, 551 et seq; Jack M Balkin, 'Populism and Progressivism as Constitutional Categories (Book Review)' (1995) 104 Yale Law Journal 1935, 1968–1969.

[68] See in general Meyer and Rowan (n 5); Jepperson (n 30); Sandhu (n 30) 76 et seq; Schrad (n 5) 13.

Emulated Guardians. The third and final step evaluates the empirical findings of both case studies from a public-law perspective. Chapter 5 assesses whether the two Emulated Guardians feature sufficient contextual backing to effectively control platform power and identifies positive, optimistic developments as well as more pessimistic, ceremonial elements. Eventually, both Emulated Guardians feature considerable ceremonial elements but might, in practice, become meaningful accountability forums. For several context-related reasons – especially its turn to international human rights law as external normative framework, its resources, its focus on structural governance issues instead of mass-litigation of individual rights, and its ability to attract public attention – the Oversight Board indeed seems to have taken promising first steps toward providing meaningful accountability. Finally, the last chapter critically reflects on the findings and argues that we witness the emergence of a new set of transnational norms, oscillating between the public and the private. The conclusion, therefore, is cautiously optimistic: while traditional public law actors and regulations alone may not be the answer, public law ideas remain highly relevant in incrementally establishing a form of public guardianship over corporate power structures beyond the state.

2 Theory and Context

Governance by emulation describes a mode of governance that relies on reproducing preexisting models of public governance – here long-standing ideas of administrative and constitutional law – in new, privately governed contexts. In our case, these privately governed contexts are the corporate-controlled content moderation machineries of social media platforms. The emulated public law role model here is individual rights adjudication, meaning the rights-based control and, ideally, long-term improvement of administrative governance structures through courts. Some of the most prominent examples of this approach – think of human and civil rights cases or the European Court of Justice's role in European integration – have become part of the shared politico-legal canon, especially in Europe and the United States. Throughout the last seven decades or so, courts assumed a very active and, despite ambivalent downstream effects, widely venerated role in operationalizing individual rights as mediators for structural change in large governance structures like administrative agencies, the police, or the workplace. Remarkably, governance by emulation appears to be a strategy that, yet for slightly different reasons, appeals as much to democratic actors like the European Union as it does to corporate actors like Meta.

This book investigates the construction of this new type of governance regime by focusing on two paradigmatic examples of such governance by emulation: the European Union's out-of-court dispute settlement bodies (ODSs) and Meta's Oversight Board. As anticipated in the introduction, I call them Emulated Guardians. That is because they seek to emulate aspects of individual rights adjudication and in reference to one of the aporia of public accountability: Who guards the guardians?

Both Emulated Guardians are designed to protect – or at least appear to be protecting – individual rights and to control massive and increasingly bureaucratic private power structures. Although these specific power structures – social media platforms – are relatively novel (with social media and its content moderation existing for only the better part of two decades at the time of writing), the underlying questions, ideas, and mechanisms shaping the power dynamics between platforms and their users are far from new. The demands to emulate individual rights adjudication draw from long-established traditions. These dynamics are not only legal but also deeply political, social, and cultural, grounded in the familiar rather than the innovative.

Therefore, the key observations made and questions raised in this book go well beyond the already important issue of content moderation and digital governance. Rather this book provides a way to think about developments that seem all but certain to play out in similar form in other future sectors whose global governance is dominated by centralized and vertically integrated private power structures like today's social media companies. The power dynamic we observe here – corporate control over infrastructure, rulemaking, and rule enforcement, combined with the absence of viable exit options for individuals – may be particularly stark and easy to grasp in the regulation of speech by platforms, but it is by no means confined to that area. Consider sectors such as artificial intelligence, satellite internet, commercial space travel, human "enhancement," carbon capture, biotechnology, and many others. Not all of these fields will thrive, but some certainly will. And all appear poised to be respectively dominated by a few, perhaps even just one, centralized entity – a private corporation, likely based in the United States or China, rather than a democratically governed institution operating within a rule of law framework. Private ordering is, of course, not inherently problematic. Do not mistake my concern as ideological refusal of the inevitable. Private ordering is important and especially the profit motive – derided by some and with indeed complicated downstream impacts as we will see in the case studies – is an important driver of innovation and efficiency. However, it is equally obvious that some things of public concern ought to be governed according to some higher order principles like representation and a sense of publicness. An informed look into the papers shows that the structures we currently conceptualize as private ordering (in the American wording) or private governance (the European way to put it) cannot achieve these public goals solely through innovation, efficacy, and managerial Icarianism.

Therefore, once the power of these corporations becomes apparent, public demand for accountability will inevitably follow. And when people call for accountability in response to a massive, organized power structure, borrowing concepts from public law – particularly administrative and constitutional law – seems a natural course of action. Rights, due process, independent review, participatory rulemaking. All these principles will resurface in the discussions ahead. This book identifies and critically engages with that mode of thinking – governance by emulation – and offers analytical tools to better understand and assess it.

It is important to emphasize that I do not argue that governance by emulation is inherently good or bad. It is, above all, a reality. Emulating public law ideals to manage private power structures holds significant potential – as we will explore throughout the coming chapters – but also presents serious risks, which we will encounter in equal measure.

To these ends, this chapter lays the contextual and theoretical groundwork for our investigation, zeroing in again on content moderation. In the following four sections, we address four key questions. First, who are the main actors in this story? Second, what exactly are these actors – our so-called Emulated Guardians – tasked with doing? Third, what is content moderation and why does it make sense to look at it through the prism of administrative law? And finally, since governance by emulation involves adapting public law models to private governance, how does this leap from the public to the private actually unfold?

Along the lines of these four questions, this chapter follows four lines of enquiry. First, I briefly introduce Emulated Guardians as the key concept of the book. Emulated Guardian is the overarching term used here for bodies like the EU's out-of-court dispute settlement bodies or the Oversight Board. The term "Emulated Guardians" points to both bodies' two key characteristics: First, they are presumed to act as guardians of individual rights, in the same way that courts or other adjudicators became guardians that protect individuals from overweening public power. Second, they are novel bodies whose structural features reflect or *emulate* ideas regarding judicial protection, individual rights, adjudication, and judicial review. This aspect is crucial. Emulated Guardians are important and potentially powerful because they *remind* us of courts and adjudication – not necessarily because they can already fully do the job. From a grander historical perspective, Emulated Guardians may be a first version of new accountability structures for power beyond public authority. Fascinatingly, traditions and revered imaginaries of courts and judicial power live on in those "novel" institutions. Here we also reflect on Emulated Guardians' performativity. Their performativity works bidirectionally. On the one hand, they may performatively self-legitimize by mere appearance while, on the other, they might incrementally modify conceptions of whether and to what extent individual rights are protectable and enforceable online and in so-called "post-state" governance.

Second, we look at what Emulated Guardians are supposed to do: adjudicate individual rights. *Individual rights adjudication* is a widely practiced and culturally venerated mechanism to control power. Here, we step far back from our notional "information age" and recapitulate the elements required to subject power structures to an adjudicatory review of individual rights. This analysis condenses legal-political practice from the last two centuries of liberal government.

Third, we look at the power structures Emulated Guardians shall control, that is, social media platforms. We will address how social media platforms design, regulate, and police digital infrastructures, particularly with regard to how regulatory co-option and self-interest has driven platforms to become private governance actors that devise increasingly sophisticated administrative and bureaucratic ways of working. Consequently, there have been growing demands to introduce control mechanisms into these private power structures whose lack of accountability has become increasingly concerning from the mid-2010s. Here, I draw on administrative law to explain how elements like hierarchy and heteronomy, deference and coherence, review, regulation and reform transform content moderation into an ever more administration-like enterprise.

Fourth, by this point, tensions were becoming apparent – between, on one side, fledgling guardian institutions and, on the other, extensive yet unaccountable power in private hands. To examine the fruits of that tension, descriptively (and later normatively), this chapter draws from research in organization theory and political science to explain why and how organizations *emulate* institutions like individual rights adjudication. In simple terms, to emulate means to imitate, reproduce (or even strive to improve upon) a role model. The primary drive to emulate is to appear more legitimate. As organizations seek legitimacy, emulation becomes an increasingly widespread mechanism of organizational development. Yet emulation's track record may be Janus-faced. Does it diffuse tried and tested practices or merely build ceremonial façades?

2.1 Emulated Guardians

This chapter looks at the contextual and theoretical framework of *Emulated Guardians*. Starting point for those observations are Emulated Guardians themselves. What are their characteristics? How do they reproduce adjudicative functionality and performatively play with judicial symbolism? I develop the term Emulated Guardians inductively from the theoretical framework and empirics presented in this book. In that sense, the term predominantly addresses a distinct phenomenon: the emulation of adjudication to control content moderation. However, as I argue more detailed in the introduction and in Chapter 6, the Oversight Board and Article 21 Digital Services Act (DSA) should be seen as placeholders for a more fundamental development in global governance. Since ever more power is exercised beyond public authority, designing "new" accountability structures will become more pertinent. I argue that many of these allegedly "new" accountability structures are anything but new and unprecedented. Instead, they *emulate* bits and pieces of preexisting role models to publicly legitimize and – ideally – control emergent power structures. Emulated Guardians that seek to adjudicate individual rights are one particularly salient example of that development and, therefore, the focus of this book. But I encourage the reader to keep this meta level in mind when reading through the coming chapters.

2.1.1 *Characteristics*

Emulated Guardian is the overarching term used here for bodies like ODSs or the Oversight Board. The term points to both bodies' two key characteristics. First, they are presumed to act as guardians of individual rights, in a similar way that courts or other adjudicators became guardians that protect individuals from overweening public power. I use the term *guardian* to reminisce the famous "who guards the guardians" issue in public law.[1] Second, they are novel bodies whose structural features reflect or *emulate* ideas regarding judicial protection, individual rights, adjudication, and judicial review.

Emulation describes how organizational actors, such as the EU or Meta, build new policies and formal structures by imitating older institutionalized policies from other contexts. Emulating existing institutions has two advantages: first, emulating something is easier than entirely reinventing the wheel.[2] Second, because institutionalized policies and formal structures are generally (that is, publicly) considered legitimate, emulating these to address novel problems maps the perception of legitimacy from

[1] Originally, that phrase predates the emergence of public law altogether. It originates from Roman poet *Iuvenal's* "Quis custodiet ipsos custodes?" For a modern adaptation see Martin M Shapiro, *Who Guards the Guardians? Judicial Control of Administration* (University of Georgia Press 1988).

[2] With the caveat, of course, that only very few ideas are truly new.

the old context onto the new institution.[3] Simply put, emulating adjudicatory control over public – and especially administrative – power promises a smooth path toward controlling social media platforms and enables those social media platforms to present themselves as (more) legitimate.

Viewed through a legal lens, emulation is an unwieldy category, because actors like ODSs or the Oversight Board do not fit traditional conceptual frames. By dint of their emulative natures, ODSs and the Oversight Board reflect diverse aspects of various adjudicatory role models without, however, becoming the "original" – either in concept or in practice. Recent conceptual takes on Emulated Guardians range from supreme court,[4] to sub-courts,[5] de facto courts,[6] to human rights tribunals,[7] to (as yet unspecified) transnational adjudicators.[8] But, in my view, superimposing traditional concepts onto novel phenomena might risk "foreclos[ing] rather than foreground[ing] debates" about the current reshuffle of power relations at play.[9] In turn, to borrow Martin Shapiro's words, "[i]f we turn to the work of those persons and institutions to which we normally award the titles judges and courts, we shall see that in reality they are simply at one end of a spectrum rather than constituting an absolutely distinct entity."[10]

[3] The idea of "mapping" traditional meaning onto a novel context originates from Lakoff's work on metaphors, George Lakoff and Mark Johnson, *Metaphors We Live By* (University of Chicago Press 1980).

Metaphorical mapping with the effect of legitimizing design choices and practices is a common practice in discourses about Emulated Guardians as a showed elsewhere: Josh Cowls, Philipp Darius, Dominiquo Santistevan and Moritz Schramm, 'Constitutional Metaphors: Facebook's "Supreme Court" and the Legitimation of Platform Governance' (2024) 26 New Media & Society 2448.

[4] Ezra Klein, 'Mark Zuckerberg on Facebook's Hardest Year, and What Comes Next' *Vox.com* (2 April 2018) <https://perma.cc/5W3N-Y37S>; Kate Klonick, 'Inside the Making of Facebook's Supreme Court' *New Yorker* (12 February 2021) <https://perma.cc/44Y7-S8VH>; Cowls, Darius, Santistevan and Schramm (n 3).

[5] European Parliament Committee on Legal Affairs and Tiemo Wölken (Rapporteur), 'DRAFT REPORT with Recommendations to the Commission on a Digital Services Act: Adapting Commercial and Civil Law Rules for Commercial Entities Operating Online (2020/2019(INL))' 21 et seq <https://perma.cc/VC3U-7Y97>.

[6] Daniel Holznagel, 'The Digital Services Act Wants You to "Sue" Facebook over Content Decisions in Private de Facto Courts' (*Verfassungsblog*, 24 June 2021) <https://perma.cc/6W8K-E3GM>.

[7] Laurence R Helfer and Molly K Land, 'The Facebook Oversight Board's Human Rights Future' (2023) 44 Cardozo Law Review 2223.

[8] Rishi Gulati, 'Meta's Oversight Board and Transnational Hybrid Adjudication: What Consequences for International Law' KFG Working Paper Series No. 53 March 2022.

[9] See, referring to the Supreme Court metaphor regarding the Oversight Board Cowls, Darius, Santistevan and Schramm (n 3) 17.

[10] Martin M Shapiro, *Courts, a Comparative and Political Analysis* (University of Chicago Press 1981) 8.

On the contrary, analogizing amorphous and ambiguous emulators like ODSs or the Oversight Board to existing – and often patently legitimizing – ideas like "supreme" or "quasi-courts," attaches public legitimacy and an assumed certainty to phenomena (yet) undeserving of these epithets.[11] Simultaneously, as outlined in the introduction, pressing Emulated Guardians in schematic templates of public or private oversimplifies reality. For example, ODSs are formally private bodies. Yet, they only exist because the EU envisaged them in the DSA and national administrators license them. The EU's "vision" for ODSs in turn, albeit formally emerging in legislative procedures, was shaped at least in parts by lobbying and backchanneling during legislation. Tucking phenomena into somewhat undercomplex conceptual boxes like "public" and the "private" is important to highlight indeed existing and important differences, yet the reality in those boxes seldom manifests as purely as dichotomous labels would suggest.

Therefore, I assume a deferential approach toward the criteria of adjudication just outlined. I investigate the diverse and at times convoluted practices in the case studies through the prism of individual rights adjudication as their paragon, point of reference, and model – but not as a strict deductive category.[12] The practices of the Oversight Board and the out-of-court dispute settlement bodies appear to be heavily inspired by individual rights adjudication. Yet this observation does not necessarily tick all the boxes.[13] For example, the out-of-court dispute settlement bodies cannot bindingly decide cases and Meta retained some influence over the Board's composition and docket, thereby undermining its independence.[14] Nonetheless, both bodies mirror many functional aspects of adjudicators and performatively play with their (limited) reproduction of adjudicative features like individual appeals, impartiality, norm-based decision-making, and juridical "habitus."[15]

[11] See for an empirical analysis and critical discussion of the prevalence of the Oversight Board as Supreme Court Metaphor in US News media discourse Cowls, Darius, Santistevan and Schramm (n 3). See also Thomas Kadri, 'Juridical Discourse for Platforms' (2022) 136 Harvard Law Review (Forum) 163.

[12] See in that regard also Bourdieu's reflection on the mistaken antinomy of "subjective" and "objective" accounts in social sciences, Pierre Bourdieu, *The Logic of Practice* (Stanford University Press 1992) 25–29.

[13] See at Chapter 5.

[14] See at 3.6, 3.7, and 4.3.3.

[15] Highlighting the discursive dominance of juridical concepts and imaginaries in debates about platform governance, Kadri (n 11) 169 et seq; see already Cowls, Darius, Santistevan and Schramm (n 3).

The key trait of Emulated Guardians is, therefore, not that they are indeed courts or human rights tribunals but that they *remind* us of adjudicators without being "classic" specimens of the species. Resemblance without identity, one could say. Thus, focusing on the aspect of *emulation* acknowledges Emulated Guardians' reflexive status as operating in a space between law and self-regulation, public expectation, self-serving interest, institutionalized and culturally dependent beliefs about controlling power structures, and the real practice of controlling power structures.

2.1.2 Performativity

If Emulated Guardians' characteristic is that they oscillate between positive law and self-regulation, public imagination and actual authority, ceremony and actual control, they are quintessentially performative. In other words, Emulated Guardians' practice, symbolism, and perception reflect changes in common and legal discourse and, reflexively, may change the very discourse itself. The idea is simple. Emulated Guardians can – and do[16] – bring with them a rich arsenal of symbols, practices, and argument-based resources that might channel some of the public legitimacy attached to classic adjudicatory institutions.[17] They appear – and are designed to appear[18] – as adjudicative institutions. However, compared to traditional individual rights adjudication, Emulated Guardians suffer from in-built design flaws. For example, the Oversight Board remains financially dependent on Meta, and neither ODSs nor the Oversight Board can issue binding decisions at scale.[19]

Yet if their practice is perceived as sufficiently adjudicative, they may be able to incrementally build their own public legitimacy and authority vis-à-vis the power structure they shall control. Through practice and narration, Emulated Guardians may dress themselves in the publicly legitimizing guise of adjudicatory appearance. Because adjudication is such a powerful and revered societal institution Emulated Guardians may construct their own authority, outgrow inbuilt design flaws, and yield larger cultural changes toward more meaningful accountability. That

[16] See at 3.7, 3.8, 4.5, 4.6, and Chapter 5.

[17] See already Cowls, Darius, Santistevan and Schramm (n 3) 1–8, 16–19; for an empirical analysis of the "Supreme Court metaphor's" prevalence in the US news discourse between 2018 and 2021 see: ibid 8–16. For a normative critique of platforms' overuse of juridical concepts see Kadri (n 11) 186 et seq.

[18] See at 3.2, 3.3, 4.2, and 4.3.

[19] See 3.6, 4.3.3, and 4.6.

would be public legitimation by emulation or, from a cynical point of view, self-legitimation by appropriation.

In turn, Emulated Guardians' practice, which is related to but not quite adjudication in a classic sense, might reflexively alter the shared understanding of how individual rights adjudication works in the digital sphere or, perhaps, in the whole realm of post-state governance. We can observe similar performative reconstructions of crucial social concepts in many aspects of life.

Take the example of privacy. Changing societal perspectives on privacy and its enforceability offer a cautionary tale in a closely related field.[20] Only two decades ago, much of the hyper-personalized data mining of Amazon, Google, and Meta would have arguably been viewed as an outrageous breach of individual privacy. In her comprehensive genealogy of what she calls "surveillance capitalism" in Silicon Valley during the 1990s and early 2000s, Shoshana Zuboff points out Google's pioneering role in privacy-eroding "datafication":

> Google would no longer mine behavioral data strictly to improve service for users but rather to read users' minds for the purposes of matching ads to their interests, as those interests are deduced from the collateral traces of online behavior. With Google's unique access to behavioral data, it would now be possible to know what a particular individual in a particular time and place was thinking, feeling, and doing. That this no longer seems astonishing to us, or perhaps even worthy of note, is evidence of the profound psychic numbing that has inured us to a bold and unprecedented shift in capitalist methods.[21]

Yet by virtue of practice and rhetoric[22] (especially through imaginaries of endless connectivity, possibility and, ironically, individual freedom) our

[20] The term "enforceability" underscores the importance of perspective in understanding whether individuals reinterpret the ideal of privacy – what is considered protected from outside view and what is not – or merely adjust their stance toward accepting breaches of that ideal, along with the extent to which they modify their behavior accordingly. This tension – between a persistently strong normative desire for privacy and the increasing acceptance of privacy violations – is often framed as the "privacy paradox." For an overview see Spyros Kokolakis, 'Privacy Attitudes and Privacy Behaviour: A Review of Current Research on the Privacy Paradox Phenomenon' (2017) 64 Computers & Security 122; Tobias Dienlin, Philipp K Masur and Sabine Trepte, 'A Longitudinal Analysis of the Privacy Paradox' (2023) 25 New Media & Society 1043.

[21] Shoshana Zuboff, *The Age of Surveillance Capitalism: The Fight for a Human Future at the New Frontier of Power* (PublicAffairs 2019) 78.

[22] The importance of rhetorical devices to discursively construct specific, and regularly industry-serving, imaginaries cannot be overstated. See e.g. Tarleton Gillespie, 'The Politics of "Platforms"' (2010) 12 New Media & Society 347; referring to the conceptual "blank area" of informational capitalism, which is then flooded with legitimizing

conceptions of privacy, or at least of privacy's enforceability, have fundamentally changed.[23] Quantitative empirical research found that "previous privacy violation experiences" had only "small effects on … subsequent online privacy concerns and no substantial effects on online information disclosure."[24] In other words, past experiences of eroding privacy do not raise a great deal of concern and most of the time do not elicit behavioral consequences, like withdrawing from social media platforms. Thus, the shared understanding of privacy changed.

Qualitative empirical findings corroborate these quantitative results. For example, after a privacy breach of eighty-seven million North American Facebook accounts by Cambridge Analytica in 2018, many users around the globe (especially younger ones) appear to have changed their perception of what Facebook could legitimately do with its – and by extension, their – data.[25] Instead of anger or discomfort, which could have changed their usage of social media, some people began to modify their perception of privacy. As Hagar Afriat et al. argue:

> At that critical moment, users reestablished in their minds Facebook's legitimacy and right to harvest data … In this view, it is the users' responsibility to manage

metaphors: Shoshana Zuboff, 'Big Other: Surveillance Capitalism and the Prospects of an Information Civilization' (2015) 30 Journal of Information Technology 75, 83; Maria Lindh and Jan Michael Nolin, 'GAFA Speaks: Metaphors in the Promotion of Cloud Technology' (2017) 73 Journal of Documentation 160; Zuboff (n 21) 74; Julia Slupska, 'War, Health and Ecosystem: Generative Metaphors in Cybersecurity Governance' (2021) 34 Philosophy & Technology 463; Cowls, Darius, Santistevan and Schramm (n 3); Kadri (n 11). See also the grim picture painted by Ari Ezra Waldman based on qualitative field work with data protection professionals: Ari Ezra Waldman, *Industry Unbound: The Inside Story of Privacy, Data, and Corporate Power* (Cambridge University Press 2021) 210 et seq.

23 Various studies provide ample empirical evidence for this phenomenon. For example, Mary Culnan and Pamela Armstrong found already in 1999, that individuals were willing to give away data more freely "when people were explicitly told that fairness procedures in the form of fair information practices are observed" – irrespective of whether that practices were really observed. That trend manifested over time. In a 2011 literature survey of 500 studies on privacy, France Bélanger and Robert Crossler found that "[t]he most intriguing finding in information privacy attitudes research is that, in the presence of privacy attitudes, greater concern for information privacy no longer influences willingness to disclose personal information." See for the first quote Mary J Culnan and Pamela K Armstrong, 'Information Privacy Concerns, Procedural Fairness, and Impersonal Trust: An Empirical Investigation' (1999) 10 Organization Science 112; for the second quote see France Bélanger and Robert E Crossler, 'Privacy in the Digital Age: A Review of Information Privacy Research in Information Systems' (2011) 35 MIS Quarterly 1017, 1021.

24 Philipp K Masur and Sabine Trepte, 'Transformative or Not? How Privacy Violation Experiences Influence Online Privacy Concerns and Online Information Disclosure' (2021) 47 Human Communication Research 49, 66–67.

25 For the relevance of the Cambridge Analytica scandal in the creation of the Oversight Board see at 5.2.

their privacy, as it is Facebook and other social media companies' right to profit from activities on their platforms. After all, as one participant remarked: "This is capitalism. It is not illegal."[26]

Such changes of overall perception induced by changing practice and language can be (broadly) described as performative.[27] The iterative repetition of concepts, practices, and symbols in different times and places *attaches* a general meaning to these concepts, practices, and symbols, but over time *alters* the general meaning of these concepts and the significance of practices and symbols pertaining to them.[28]

The formative effects of practice and language on reality, power, politics, and, therefore, law should not be misunderstood as a merely constructionist or postmodern quip.[29] History is full of examples, ranging

[26] The findings are based on fifty qualitative interviews conducted in Israel partly before and partly after the Cambridge Analytical scandal, Hagar Afriat, Shira Dvir-Gvirsman, Keren Tsuriel, and Lidor Ivan '"This Is Capitalism. It Is Not Illegal": Users' Attitudes toward Institutional Privacy Following the Cambridge Analytica Scandal' (2021) 37 The Information Society 115, 116.

[27] The concept of performativity goes back to John Austin's philosophy of language and has been adapted in various and sometimes conflicting ways in linguistics, the philosophy of language, sociology, cultural studies, and law. Austin's "performative utterances" highlighted that speech acts – depending on context, speaker, and utterance – may materially alter people's lives (or what Husserl called the "life world"). See e.g. the "christening Mr. Stalin" example in John L Austin, *How to Do Things with Words* (Oxford University Press 1962) 4 et seq; posing at 7 the famous question "can saying make it so?" For various adaptations of performativity throughout the disciplines see e.g., Julie Cohen's observations of performativity at work in platforms' terms of service, Julie Cohen, *Between Truth and Power: The Legal Constructions of Informational Capitalism* (Oxford University Press 2019) 45. For European law: Thomas Diez, 'Speaking "Europe": The Politics of Integration Discourse' (1999) 6 Journal of European Public Policy 598. In the United States see already the related work on rhetoric and narratives by Peter Brooks and Paul Gewirtz (eds.), *Law's Stories: Narrative and Rhetoric in the Law* (Yale University Press 1996); see also Ingo Venzke's application of linguistic philosophy to the interpretation of international law (and especially also regarding Austin and Brandom): Ingo Venzke, *How Interpretation Makes International Law* (Oxford University Press 2012) 54–57 (regarding performativity), 144 et seq (regarding the performative effects of international adjudication) esp. 167 et seq (on the influence of institutional changes).

[28] Variations of this idea can be found also in Foucauldian conceptions of "discourse," cf. Michel Foucault, *The Archaeology of Knowledge* (Pantheon Books 1972) 56 et seq; Michel Foucault, *The Order of Things: An Archaeology of the Human Sciences* (Vintage Books 1973) 17 et seq.

[29] Reinhart Koselleck, *Begriffsgeschichten* (Suhrkamp 2006) 32 et seq, 297 et seq; Venzke (n 27) 27–29, 58–64. Importantly, one would be mistaken to consider language-focused perspectives inherently "progressive" or "liberal." Venzke points to a quote by an (infamously) renowned twentieth century German scholar, who, in a letter to another eminent anti-Weimar intellectual, equated power with the ability to form concepts and meaning (see ibid at 59). Regarding the later unfolding interpretative changes in German law during the Third Reich, which can also be understood as performative, see seminally:

from the extreme to the mundane. A vivid example of the former were the "*propagandistes*" in post-Revolutionary France who sought to revamp the entire French language by fixating revolutionary spirit in everyday parlance to enable (but also to guardrail) citizens to speak (and think) only in revolutionary terms.[30] Many examples of performative change and incremental shifts in meaning are less flashy and abrupt than the one just mentioned. Arguably, those changes that really stick are not paternalistically declared, but gradually normalized.

2.2 Individual Rights Adjudication

That being said, we begin zooming in on the contextual details of Emulated Guardians. To repeat, Emulated Guardian is the overarching term used here for bodies that (partly) reproduce individual rights adjudication in private governance. The two studied examples are the out-of-court dispute settlement bodies and the Oversight Board. The former are a child of the European Union's DSA, the letter an offspring of the world's largest social media company, Meta, formerly known as Facebook. The following section deconstructs what exactly Emulated Guardians emulate here, that is, individual rights adjudication.[31] The key takeaway is that the very basic configurations that Emulated Guardians seek to reproduce mirror a century-old model of public governance, that is, in plain language, going to court to sue the police department whose officer battered you.

We will therefore dig into the theory and history of enforcing individual rights through an adjudicator vis-à-vis a dominant power structure, which is, historically, the state. Therefore, we leave contemporary

Bernd Rüthers, *Die unbegrenzte Auslegung: zum Wandel der Privatrechtsordnung im Nationalsozialismus* (8th ed, Mohr Siebeck 2017). Insightful in addressing how to navigate epistemes of questionable provenance in legal scholarship – a topic that warrants deeper reflection than I can offer: Gwinyai Machona, 'Das Provenienz-Problem der Rechtswissenschaften: Zum Umgang mit Antisemitismus, Rassismus und Sexismus im Juristischen Wissenskanon' (2022) 55 Kritische Justiz 437, 447, 452.

30 Reinhart Koselleck unearthed several quotes from the French revolutionary era that declared language the ultimate sovereign, e.g. "*les paroles nationales seront souverains de tous les souverains*" ("the national words will be sovereign of all sovereigns"), Koselleck (n 29) 297–302.

31 This book predominantly uses the term "individual rights adjudication" rather than "courts," as the latter excludes numerous adjudicative actors that are essential to the external, independent, and rights-based review of power structures but are not labelled as courts. Ultimately, the concept of a court is largely a projection shaped by a range of diverse institutional preconceptions.

phenomena like social media platforms or private governance altogether and take a step back, to look at the bigger picture.

The next few pages will be somewhat theory-heavy and abstract. But bear with me, it is important to deconstruct these underlying patterns to later identify structural flaws and missing contextual factors in the practice of Emulated Guardians.

2.2.1 *Individual Rights*

Individual rights adjudication refers to rights-based, adjudicative ex-post control over power structures. If, for example, a police officer exceeds their power against a protestor, the latter may initiate individual rights adjudication, claiming civil rights violation and the likes. Individual rights adjudication rests on two pillars. These are, on one side, power mediators in the hands of individuals, or what I call broadly individual rights.[32] In the police example given above, the relevant individual rights could be those to bodily integrity, free expression, and freedom of assembly. On the other side, individual rights adjudication relies on adjudication as a mechanism to effectuate these power mediators. The adjudicator would be, in all likelihood, some kind of court.

The normative basis of individual rights adjudication are individual rights. The term "individual rights" is a functional concept. Functionally, individual rights can be viewed as normative practices that enable individuals (or other rights holders) to make normative claims to limit the exercise of power on the part of a dominant power structure.[33] Individual rights can be human, constitutional, civil, or fundamental rights (depending on one's jurisdiction) and other more specialized or derivative rights. Individual rights can be substantive (e.g., the right to freedom of expression) or procedural (e.g., the right to judicial protection). Individual rights need not follow a specific terminology or form, nor must they share a specific normative or philosophical underpinning.[34] The key idea behind individual rights, which is the only relevant aspect at this point, is that

[32] I borrow the term "power mediator" from Christian Reus-Smit, *Individual Rights and the Making of the International System* (Cambridge University Press 2013) 196.

[33] For a historical functionalist conceptualization of individual rights as mechanism in the incremental construction of sovereignty see ibid 36 et seq.

[34] Of course, in Europe and North America individual rights share common historical and philosophical contexts. These contexts are, among other things, the emancipation of politics from the Church and the ascent of Westphalian sovereignty, Enlightenment, and the rise of individualism. Yet, the practice of individual rights widely diversified throughout space and time.

they provide the basis for normative claims formulated by individuals to structure their relationship with a powerful actor. In this sense, rights are solely a functional category. They are "usefully understood as power mediators, as normative [practices] that materially weak actors can invoke to alter the power relationship between themselves and materially preponderant actors or institutions (empires, sovereign states, etc.)."[35] That could entail, for example, claims that a powerful actor must not curtail personal liberties or take property without due process, cannot discriminate based on gender or race, or is prohibited from constraining intra-European trade for protectionist reasons.

Equalizing these power relations by exercising individual rights inevitably *individualizes* said relationships because it shifts the focus from underlying, structural factors to the exercise of power vis-à-vis individual rights holders. This aspect of individualization simultaneously constitutes individual rights' main advantage and impediment. On the one hand, individual rights grant far-reaching agency to individuals, allowing them to challenge the exercise of power and thereby to act as agents for the common good.[36] On the other hand, many rights violations occur arguably not as individual transgressions but reflect more deeply underlying issues relating to embedded structures, habits, procedures, and policies. Salvaging those structural issues requires proactive reforms that regularly go beyond vindication of individual legal guarantees.

2.2.2 *Enforcement and Adjudication*

Individual rights require an enforcement mechanism. Only if enforced, individual rights function as "power mediators." Various enforcement mechanisms exist. Every individual can verbalize a claim, directly or implicitly referencing that they believe a *right* corroborates their normative position. Sometimes, the power structure might respond to such voice and voluntarily subject itself to cogently formulated arguments.[37] However, that is not always the case. Therefore, many "guardians" of (public) power exist. We are familiar with various accountability mechanisms, procedures, and entities that hold to account large power structures, especially entities embodying public power. We may distinguish

[35] Reus-Smit (n 32) 38.

[36] Highlighting the "massification" of individual rights adjudication: Mauro Cappelletti, *The Judicial Process in Comparative Perspective* (Clarendon Press 1989) 268–274.

[37] Albert O Hirschman, Exit, *Voice, and Loyalty: Responses to Decline in Firms, Organizations, and States* (Harvard University Press 1970).

ex-ante influence exercised via participatory mechanisms[38] from continuous oversight and scrutiny by elected representatives,[39] auditors,[40] ombudspersons,[41] the public,[42] or the press. Further, many administrative organizations feature individually accessible, internal though not independent review mechanisms.

However, one of the oldest, most institutionalized and revered practices for enforcing individual rights vis-à-vis administrative power is *adjudication*. Adjudication is characterized here as independent, norm-based dispute settlement between an individual and a power structure. "Adjudicator" refers to the independent entity that resolves the dispute and thereby exerts control over the power structure.

Depending on time and context, adjudication is formalized and institutionalized in various shapes and with diverse labels. The most prominent term for adjudicators is the "court" label.[43] But there are other names as well. Adjudicators controlling administrative power might be called (administrative) tribunals,[44] administrative courts,[45]

[38] Articles 10, 11 TFEU.

[39] Highlighting the role of parliamentary accountability in English administrative law: Matthias Ruffert, *Law of Administrative Organization of the EU: A Comparative Approach* (Edward Elgar 2020) 140 et seq.

[40] Alex Brenninkmeijer, Laura Frederika Lalikova and Dylan Siry, 'Public Audit Accountability' in Peter Cane and others (eds,), *The Oxford Handbook of Comparative Administrative Law* (Oxford University Press 2020) 789.

[41] cf. Michał Krajewski, *Relative Authority of Judicial and Extra-Judicial Review: EU Courts, Boards of Appeal, Ombudsman* (Hart 2021) 139 et seq; Herwig Hofmann and Jacques Ziller (eds.), *Accountability in the EU: The Role of the European Ombudsman* (Edward Elgar 2017).

[42] Public pressure can influence governance in many ways. A widely used mechanism with, however, volatile efficacy is so-called "naming and shaming," see further Emilie M Hafner-Burton, 'Sticks and Stones: Naming and Shaming the Human Rights Enforcement Problem' (2008) 62 International Organization 289.

[43] For the institutionalization of courts in various political systems throughout history see: Shapiro, *Courts, a Comparative and Political Analysis* (n 10). For the ascent of courts as controllers of public power see Peter Cane, *Controlling Administrative Power: An Historical Comparison* (Cambridge University Press 2016) 325 et seq.

[44] Peter Cane, *Administrative Tribunals and Adjudication* (Hart 2010); Kieran Bradley, 'Tribunals and Adjudication' in Peter Cane, Herwig C Hofmann, Eric C Ip, Peter L Lindseth (eds.), *The Oxford Handbook of Comparative Administrative Law* (Oxford University Press 2020); Lewis Mayers, *The American Legal System: The Administration of Justice in the United States by Judicial, Administrative, Military, and Arbitral Tribunals* (Rothman 1981); James E Pfander, 'Article I Tribunals, Article III Courts, and the Judicial Power of the United States' (2004) 118 Harvard Law Review 643; Chantal Stebbings, *Legal Foundations of Tribunals in Nineteenth-Century England* (Cambridge University Press 2006).

[45] Christine Steinbeiß-Winkelmann, '§ 4 Formen Der Verwaltungsgerichtsbarkeit Auf Reichsebene' in Karl-Peter Sommermann and Bert Schaffarzik (eds.), *Handbuch der Geschichte der Verwaltungsgerichtsbarkeit in Deutschland und Europa* (Springer 2019).

commissions,[46] boards,[47] or committees.[48] Adjudication as a control mechanism of rule enforcement and rulemaking exists on the international level,[49] in the EU,[50] and within any rule of law system. Generally speaking, adjudication occupies a special place on the cusp of our sociocultural imaginary of taming the sovereign, advancing the rule of law, and making the putatively "liberal" political project a reality. Over time, adjudicators have also devised strategies for moving beyond individualized vindication of rights and aim at ameliorating those structural governance problems that give rise to individual rights violations in the first place.[51] Yet remedying structural governance flaws inductively by adjudicating individual rights remains complicated for several reasons – accessibility, adjudicative expertise when it comes

46 Hiroshi Okayama, *Judicializing the Administrative State: The Rise of the Independent Regulatory Commissions in the United States, 1883–1937* (Routledge 2021) 39 et seq.

47 With a comprehensive empirical analysis of the (dysfunctional) review exercised by the Board of Immigration Appeals in the US: David Hausman, 'The Failure of Immigration Appeals' (2016) 164 University of Pennsylvania Law Review 1177.

48 Questionable prominence achieved the Greek Asylum Appeal Committees, which decide appeals by asylum seekers against deportation based on the so-called "EU-Turkey Deal." See Mariana Gkliati, 'The EU-Turkey Deal and the Safe Third Country Concept before the Greek Asylum Appeals Committees' (2017) 3 movements 213.

49 See Benedict Kingsbury, Nico Krisch and Richard B Stewart, 'The Emergence of Global Administrative Law' (2005) 68 Law and Contemporary Problems 15, 39 et seq; Karen J Alter, *The New Terrain of International Law: Courts, Politics, Rights* (Princeton University Press 2014) 199 et seq; focusing mostly on internal adjudication: Armin von Bogdandy and Ingo Venzke, *In wessen Namen? Internationale Gerichte in Zeiten globalen Regierens* (Suhrkamp 2014) 107 et seq; but more general at 283.

50 In EU law, the normative anchor point is Article 47 CFR, see Volker Roeben, 'Judicial Protection as the Meta-Norm in the EU Judicial Architecture' (2020) 12 Hague Journal on the Rule of Law 29; and Anthony Arnull, 'The Principle of Effective Judicial Protection in EU Law: An Unruly Horse?' (2011) 36 European Law Review 51. In contrast, the emergence of adjudication beyond formal judicial institutions since the 1990s presents a so far unresolved conceptual challenge to EU law, cf. Jacopo Alberti, 'The Position of Boards of Appeal: Between Functional Continuity and Independence' in Merijn Chamon and Mariolina Eliantonio (eds.), *Boards of Appeal of EU Agencies* (Oxford University Press 2022) 245 et seq; Marco Lamandini and David Ramos Muñoz, 'Law and Practice of Financial Appeal Bodies (ESAs' Board of Appeal, SRB Appeal Panel): A View from the Inside' [2020] Common Market Law Review 119, 120; in contrast, see Krämer's convincing functional perspective: Hannes Krämer, *Rechtsschutz im EG-Eigenverwaltungsrecht zwischen Einheitlichkeit und sektorieller Ausdifferenzierung: eine Untersuchung unter besonderer Berücksichtigung des Gemeinschaftsmarkenrechts* (Duncker & Humblot 2007) 90–93.

51 Abram Chayes, 'The Role of the Judge in Public Law Litigation' (1976) 89 Harvard Law Review 1281; Judith Resnik, 'Managerial Judges' (1982) 96 Harvard Law Review 374; from a constitutional law perspective see: Martin Shapiro and Alec Stone Sweet, *On Law, Politics, and Judicialization* (Oxford University Press 2002); Alec Stone Sweet, 'Judicialization and the Construction of Governance' (1999) 42 Comparative Political Studies 147.

to administrative practices, and advisable adjudicative restraint due to the notion of tripartite government.

Demands for, and the affirming of, the practice of adjudicatory control of administrative power are not limited to traditional administrative contexts. In modified form, adjudication that seeks to protect individuals from dominant power structures exists in various governance frameworks. For example, the UN Guiding Principles on Business and Human Rights oblige private power structures to be subject to public judicial and administrative review mechanisms and encourage businesses to make use, if necessary, of independent review mechanisms. Referring to the entire range of administrative or administration-like[52] actors, Kingsbury, Stewart, and Krisch noted,

> administrative infringement of individual rights … generally requires … the possibility of review by an independent body. Under such an approach, it is presumed to be irrelevant who interferes with rights: whether it is a domestic regulator, or an international administrative body does not matter.[53]

In sum, practice and theory have yielded idealized and widely diffused concepts of adjudication that build on and structure adjudicators, which again are much more diverse than purported by idealized notions. Further, many scholars, practitioners, and discourses identify adjudicative control of power as something we aspire to and desire.

2.2.3 Disputes and Power Relations

The ignition spark of adjudication is a dispute or, in other words, the desire to control an adverse, potentially dominant power structure.[54] Regularly,

[52] Note that the term "administration" is here not understood in the US American way, where it is sometimes used synonymously with (federal) government.

[53] Kingsbury, Krisch and Stewart (n 49) 46.

[54] The functions of adjudication – resolving disputes and controlling power – are deeply interconnected. However, domestic conceptions of these functions vary significantly. In Germany, for instance, a "dispute" (*Rechtsstreit*) arises only when individuals bring a case to court, whereas interactions between individuals and administrative actors are typically not framed as disputes. Moreover, the adjudicative control of administrative power in Germany is often viewed primarily as serving individual interests, rooted in the concept of the "subjektives Recht" (*subjective right, i.e. a litigable individualized legal position*) rather than addressing broader societal concerns or power control.

In contrast, the United States embraces a broader understanding of "dispute" – and of adversarial proceedings more generally – encompassing many forms of administrative adjudication. Even first-order decision-making can appear as a "dispute," as in the trial-like proceedings of individual claims before an administrative law judge. At the same time, ex post adjudicative control of administrative power in the US is widely understood as serving the public interest and contributing to societal oversight.

the dispute concerns some form of prior exchange, act, or communication. Further, an individual's desire to "control" a potentially adverse, dominant power structure. If there is no such desire, then there is no dispute, and consequently no need for adjudication. The disputes discussed in this book arise as a result of power imbalances, namely between individuals and social media platforms' content moderation policies.[55] The disputes concern how social media platforms unilaterally regulate and police the communication of their users. As this chapter explains in greater detail in Section 2.3, people often have little possibility to exit the platforms due to network effects and generally have no say in the rules applied to them.[56]

2.2.4 *Impartiality and Independence*

To settle disagreements about the exercise of power that cannot be resolved directly between the individual and the power structure, the individual might turn to a third party.[57] That third party, the adjudicator, provides the forum for effectuating individual rights as "power mediators."[58] Or, in Alex Stone Sweet's more abstract formulation,

For context see Johannes Buchheim and Christoph Möllers, '§ 46 Gerichtliche Verwaltungskontrollen als Steuerungsinstrument' in Andreas Voßkuhle, Martin Eifert and Christoph Möllers (eds.), *Grundlagen des Verwaltungsrechts*, vol II (3rd ed., Beck 2022) paras 9–15, 38–44 (esp. 41, 42a); for the broad US American understanding of "disputes" see again Michael Asimov, 'Five Models of Administrative Adjudication' (2015) 63 The American Journal of Comparative Law 3, 4.

[55] For a useful introduction to the phenomena "platform" and "content moderation" see: Tarleton Gillespie, *Custodians of the Internet: Platforms, Content Moderation, and the Hidden Decisions That Shape Social Media* (Yale University Press 2019); Cohen (n 27) 98 et seq; Kate Klonick, 'The New Governors: The People, Rules, and Processes Governing Online Speech' (2018) 131 Harvard Law Review 1598; Evelyn Douek, 'Content Moderation as Systems Thinking' (2022) 136 Harvard Law Review 526, 539 et seq.

[56] Regarding the structure of digital (platform) markets and platforms' network effects see Stigler Center for the Study of the Economy and the State (University of Chicago), 'Stigler Committee on Digital Platforms Final Report' (2019) 7 et seq, 34–43 (esp. 38–39).
Individuals' lack of "voice" in platform rulemaking was criticized repeatedly, see e.g. Rebecca MacKinnon, *Consent of the Networked: The Worldwide Struggle for Internet Freedom* (Basic Books 2012) 12–14; Zuboff (n 22) 83; Nicolas P Suzor, 'Digital Constitutionalism: Using the Rule of Law to Evaluate the Legitimacy of Governance by Platforms' (2018) 4 Social Media + Society 1, 5–8; Moritz Schramm, 'Where Is Olive? Or: Lessons from Democratic Theory for Legitimate Platform Governance' (*The Digital Constitutionalist*, 26 January 2022) <https://perma.cc/RL93-CGSY>.

[57] For a theorization of triadic dispute resolution in general see Stone Sweet (n 51) 149, 153–155.

[58] For a private law-oriented theorization of courts dispute-resolvers in triadic situations see Shapiro, *Courts, a Comparative and Political Analysis* (n 10). See further Cappelletti (n 36) 217–222. For the conception of individual rights as "power mediators" see Reus-Smit (n 35).

a dyadic relationship between two parties transforms into a triad consisting of two parties and an adjudicator.[59]

To fulfill its umpire-like[60] role in the triad, an adjudicator must be *impartial* toward the parties and hence cannot be a "part" of either disputant. Typically, that separation between the impartial third party and the disputing parties is conceived of as *independence*.

The relationship between impartiality and independence is not entirely intuitive. Whereas we might use the two concepts interchangeably in common parlance, they denote different aspects of adjudication. Independence denotes a predominantly *organizational* and *external* criterion whereas impartiality refers to a mainly *functional* and *internal* one. For example, in its decisions on Polish judicial "reforms," the European Court of Justice (ECJ)'s judges interpreted impartiality as an adjudicator's fair-mindedness and objectivity.[61] Adjudicators are therefore impartial if their staff make decisions uninfluenced by considerations other than those based on the relevant norms. In this idealized view, (adjudicatory) impartiality is clearly a myth. Implicit norm-derived sentiments are so embedded in our thinking, language, and informational landscape that "truly" impartial decision-making seems impossible.[62] A pragmatic solution, therefore,

59 Stone Sweet (n 51) 149.

60 Simon Palmer and Michael Roberts conceptualize this third-party role as umpiring – in contrast to mediation (which does not result in decisions). In historical context, such umpires could be either private arbitrators, or public and religious courts. For the control of administrative power however, adjudication remained a largely public endeavor. See Michael JE Palmer and Simon Roberts, *Dispute Processes: ADR and Primary Forms of Decision-Making* (2nd ed., Cambridge University Press 2005) (building on Shapiro) 221–223, 264–266.

61 Commission v Poland (Indépendance de la Cour suprême), Judgment European Court of Justice C-619/18, ECLI:EU:C:2019:531 [73–74].

62 Impartial decision-making can be conceptualized as a specific rationality. However, as psychological and sociological research shows, humans have difficulties following through on such binary rationalities due to internal, often subconscious "biases," competing rationalities and other factors. See the work of Daniel Kahneman and Amos Tversky, summarized in Daniel Kahneman, *Thinking, Fast and Slow* (Farrar, Straus and Giroux 2011). See for a critical legal studies perspective discussing the 'indeterminacy' of judging Jules L Coleman and Brian Leiter, 'Determinacy, Objectivity, and Authority' (1993) 142 University of Pennsylvania Law Review 549, 559 et seq.

Implicit biases' relevance for (criminal) adjudication is empirically well documented, especially in racialized contexts. For example, Rachlinski et al. find that judges hold implicit biases that influence their judgment. However, "[j]udges can, at least in some instances, compensate for their implicit biases": Jeffrey J Rachlinski, Sheri Johnson, Andrew J Wistrich and Chris Guthrie 'Does Unconscious Racial Bias Affect Trial Judges?' (2009) 84 Notre Dame Law Review 1195, 1197; see further: Justin D Levinson, Mark W Bennett and Koichi Hioki, 'Judging Implicit Bias: A National Empirical Study of Judicial Stereotypes' (2017) 69 Florida Law Review 63, 70 et seq, 82 et seq, 110 et seq.

is to confine elements and influences that might unduly affect decision-making and at least maintain the impression of a decision's impartiality and safeguard its norm-based verifiability through normative reasoning, which ties adjudication to the existing normative backdrop.

In turn, *independence* can be seen as the adjudicating organization's autonomy from outside pressure or factual constraint.[63] In other words, independence is the organizational and somewhat objectifiable means toward the goal of impartial decision-making.[64] Contemporary discussions mainly revolve around these organizational aspects, summarized as judicial independence.[65] On the most fundamental level, independence demands that adjudicators be free from any external command, hierarchy, or intervention. As the ECJ formulates it:

> The concept of independence presupposes, in particular, that the body concerned exercises its judicial functions wholly autonomously, without being subject to any hierarchical constraint or subordinated to any other body and without taking orders or instructions from any source whatsoever, and that it is thus protected against external interventions or pressure liable to impair the independent judgment of its members and to influence their decisions.[66]

[63] Commission v Poland (Indépendance de la Cour suprême), Judgment (n 61) paras 77, 108; Associação Sindical dos Juízes Portugueses v Tribunal de Contas [2018] European Court of Justice (Grand Chamber) C-64/16, ECLI:EU:C:2018:117 [43–45].

[64] In that sense see also Vauchez' conceptualization of independence as a "technique that allows one to insulate decision-making from the pressure of partisan politics," Antoine Vauchez, 'The Genie of Independence and the European Bottle: How Independence Became Europe's Most Contentious Legal and Political Category' (2022) 20 International Journal of Constitutional Law 1, 4.

[65] That goes for the UN level, the Venice Commission, and the European Union. For example, since 1994, the United Nations entertain a Special Rapporteur on the Independence of Judges and Lawyers. See further the Basic Principles on the Independence of the Judiciary, adopted by the Seventh United Nations Congress on the Prevention of Crime and the Treatment of Offenders held at Milan from 26 August to 6 September 1985.

See further: European Commission for Democracy through Law (Venice Commission), 'Report on the Independence of the Judicial System Part I: The Independence of Judges' (2010) Study No. 494/2008; CDL-AD(2010)004.

In the EU, see recently Associação Sindical dos Juízes Portugueses v Tribunal de Contas (n 63) paras 43–52; Commission v Poland (Indépendance de la Cour suprême), Judgment (n 61) paras 71–97, 108–124. In that context, see e.g. Krista Kovács and Kim Lane Scheppele, 'The Fragility of an Independent Judiciary: Lessons from Hungary and Poland – and the European Union' (2018) 51 Journal of Communist and Post-Communist Studies 189; Laurent Pech and Kim Lane Scheppele, 'Illiberalism Within: Rule of Law Backsliding in the EU' (2017) 19 Cambridge Yearbook of European Legal Studies 3, 9 et seq.

[66] Associação Sindical dos Juízes Portugueses v Tribunal de Contas (n 63) para 44; Commission v Poland (Indépendance de la Cour suprême), Judgment (n 61) para 74.

Although its precise contours vary, independence requires a guarantee that there are independently derived, specified procedures for appointment and nomination, fixed tenure and remuneration of the adjudicating personnel, removal for cause only, a preset budget and, crucially, no encroachment on the power structures an adjudicator is tasked with controlling.[67]

Yet from a historical perspective, adjudication's foundational criterion is impartiality, not independence. Adjudication of private disputes (but to a degree also for disputes between individuals and the organized and powerful, yet private nobility)[68] predates independent judiciaries in the modern sense. Also, as various judicial institutions in the Catholic Church or imperial China indicate, courts as institutions are not limited to constitutional power structures in liberal democracies.[69] That being said, adjudicating individual rights against a given context's dominant power structure, instead of merely smoothing over social and commercial disputes, remains largely exclusive to the liberal project. Individual rights adjudication, in that sense, reflexively relates to the very emergence of modern public law itself.[70] Even though, as Mauro Cappelletti highlights, "nobody would deny that even at the time of the absolute state . . . there

[67] For an overview of the relevant legal standards in Europe see European Commission for Democracy through Law (Venice Commission) (n 65) 5–17. See further, highlighting the importance of remuneration, tenure and removal only for cause, absence of hierarchical command or other undue influence, and budget, Associação Sindical dos Juízes Portugueses v Tribunal de Contas (n 63) paras 43–52; Commission v Poland (Indépendance de la Cour suprême), Judgment (n 61) 71–97.

From an American perspective see Kaufman's historical contextualization of judicial independence in England and the United States, Irving R Kaufman, 'The Essence of Judicial Independence' (1980) 80 Columbia Law Review 671, 672 et seq, resp. 679 et seq.

[68] cf. Rita Sailer, *Untertanenprozesse vor dem Reichskammergericht: Rechtsschutz gegen die Obrigkeit in der zweiten Hälfte des 18. Jahrhunderts* (Hochschulschrift Universität Freiburg i. Br. 1999).

[69] Especially Mauro Cappelletti, referring to private-law disputes, highlighted that adjudication and judicial decision-making is not at all limited to "independent" judiciaries but can be found also in absolutist, unitarian regimes. There "[t]he ruler, in person or through his officers, was from time to time the legislator, the administrator, and the judge. He functioned as judge when he settled his subjects' disputes, condemning, absolving, and, in sum, adjudicating as an imperial organ super partes." Cappelletti (n 36) 218. See in that sense also Kaufman's historic contextualization of the American understanding of judicial independence that developed out of an English judiciary whose history "is largely that of an institution dependent upon and deferential to the King or Parliament," Kaufman (n 67) 672; see further regarding imperial China Shapiro, *Courts, a Comparative and Political Analysis* (n 10) 157 et seq.

[70] See Martin Loughlin's insightful genealogy how medieval "fundamental law" discursively morphed into modern "public law" (which should be understood more broadly than as mere positive-legal counterpart to private law): Martin Loughlin, *Foundations of Public Law* (Oxford University Press 2010).

were nevertheless judicial decisions,"[71] absolutist adjudication's liberty-impairing and erratic nature ended up necessitating and enabling an independent judiciary and individual rights adjudication.[72] Using individual rights as power mediators requires disentangling the accountability mechanism from the encroaching power structure. Metaphorically put, a leash is no use if nobody is holding it.

The degree and design of independence remain contingent on each adjudicator's organizational setup.[73] As Cappelletti says, "[T]here exist, of course, thousands of definitions of the terms 'court,' 'judge' and 'judicial,' and no one who has a comparativist's mind would insist on any of them as absolute."[74] The focus on an independent judiciary permeated through Europe and the United States after the American and French revolutions and the ensuing adoption of the principle of tripartite government.[75] As a means of controlling public power in general as well as the burgeoning forms of administrative power, judicial independence stabilized external accountability but also created frictions between idealized notions and practice. Debates are legion, from the much discussed "counter-majoritarian difficulty" to courts' legitimacy and practical ability to control the expanding administrative state's "independent" agencies and informal acts.[76] The control of administrative power by adjudicating individual rights is never detached from public power or, in the case of administrative

[71] Cappelletti (n 36) 218.

[72] cf. Montesquieu, *The Spirit of Laws* (1748) XI.6.

[73] Shapiro, *Courts: A Comparative and Political Analysis* (n 10).

[74] Cappelletti (n 36) 217.

[75] Practical foundations of judicial independence originate especially from England. The Magna Carta of 1215 exempted barons from the Crown's jurisdiction (Clause 21 Magna Carta 1215). Later, after repeated influence by the Crown over judges in the seventeenth century, the 1701 Act of Settlement guaranteed judges *quamdiu se bene gesserint*, i.e., tenure and removal only for cause. Based on these English experiences, Montesquieu theorized in his 1748 *l'esprit des lois* that "there is no liberty, if the judicial power be not separated from the legislative and executive," Montesquieu, *The Spirit of Laws* (1748) XI.6. Montesquieu's theorization then influenced the drafters of the American constitution, whose first three Articles sharply distinguish the federal government's three branches. Consequentially, Alexander Hamilton highlighted that "[t]he complete independence of the courts of justice is peculiarly essential" in the new constitutional system, Hamilton, 'Federalist No. 78' (28 May 1788).

[76] From the vast literature see, for example, regarding the counter-majoritarian difficulty: Alexander M Bickel, *The Least Dangerous Branch: The Supreme Court at the Bar of Politics* (2nd ed., Yale University Press 1986) 16–28; for the interplay of courts and agencies in the US: Martin Shapiro, 'APA: Past, Present, Future' (1986) 72 Virginia Law Review 447, 455; for the EU: Mariolina Eliantonio, 'Judicial Review in an Integrated Administration: The Case of "Composite Procedures"' (2015) 7 Review of European Administrative Law 65.

adjudicators, not even independent of administrative power structures.[77] In these contexts, adjudication was *itself* an exercise of public power.

To reconcile impartial and independent adjudication with the practical need to finance, staff, and (democratically) legitimize[78] adjudicators, public-law adjudicators developed various, graded stages of adjudicatory independence. Courts and the judiciary are not the sole torchbearers of the judicial function. Rather, many systems such as those of the European Union, the United States or England are familiar with sites of "administrative justice" revolving around adjudicators that are not courts.[79] These adjudicators often lack the same independence safeguards as those enjoyed by "classic" courts.[80] But such non-court adjudicators are, as a result of their respective legal and political systems' peculiarities, endowed with "sufficient" independence safeguards.[81] For example, members of EU Boards of Appeal also have fixed tenure, can only be removed for cause, are not entrenched in "their" agency's hierarchical apparatus, and are required to make decisions independently and impartially.[82] Particularly for adjudicators that

[77] See generally Christoph Möllers, *The Three Branches: A Comparative Model of Separation of Powers* (Oxford University Press 2013).

[78] cf. ibid 51 et seq.

[79] See the literature cited in n 44.

[80] See e.g., Moliterno's theorization of administrative law judges as impartial but not independent in a judicial sense. Note, however, that Moliterno refers to the American system only and consequentially employs the broad American understanding of adjudication as both the initial decision and appeals, James E Moliterno, 'The Administrative Judiciary's Independence Myth' (2006) 41 Wake Forest Law Review 1191, 1211 et seq.

[81] For the United States see William Baude, 'Adjudication Outside Article III' (2020) 133 Harvard Law Review 1511, 1515 et seq.

[82] Boards of Appeal are, in principle, equipped with robust institutional and normative safeguards to ensure their independence. This is why the four oldest Boards of Appeal were established as mandatory first-instance review bodies before annulment actions could be brought before the General Court. Article 58a (1) of the CJEU Statute explicitly refers to an "independent board of appeal." Nevertheless, scholarly evaluations of the independence of Boards of Appeal – particularly those beyond these four – often grapple with the tension between their safeguards and the ideal of "pure" judicial independence. See e.g., the diverging perspectives by, on the one hand, Chamon and Frommage and, on the other hand, Tovo on whether Boards of Appeal should be understood as "independent," Merijn Chamon and Diane Fromage, 'Between Added Value and Untapped Potential: The Boards of Appeal in the Field of EU Financial Regulation' in Merijn Chamon, Annalisa Volpato and Mariolina Eliantonio (eds.), *Boards of Appeal of EU Agencies: Towards Judicialization of Administrative Review?* (Oxford University Press 2022) 13; Carlo Tovo, 'The Boards of Appeal of Networked Services Agencies: Specialized Arbitrators of Transnational Regulatory Conflicts?' in ibid 36–40. Others argue that Boards of Appeals can be conceptualized as functional courts. From a German administrative law perspective, that argument indeed makes sense as in Germany, in contrast to the UK or the US, the judicial function in administrative matters is indeed largely restricted to administrative courts, cf. Krämer (n 50) 90–93.

provide accountability to administrative power structures, tensions between impartial decision-making, organizational independence, and structural entrenchment are a necessary side effect of the diffusion of judicial functions beyond the traditional judicial system.[83] Assessing an adjudicator's independence thus remains necessarily context-sensitive and flexible.

2.2.5 *Rules*

Once an individual who seeks to protect their rights has turned to an impartial and independent adjudicator, the adjudicator cannot decide at whim but only based on a particular normative framework.[84] This normative framework must meet several requirements. On the one hand, it should be *preset*. This means that rules should not be made ad hoc but should reflect the relationship between the individual and the power structure as it was when the alleged rights-infringement took place. The preset rules upon which the adjudicator bases its decisions can be of various origins; typically, they will be the law of a given state, public organization, or stipulations contained in international law. Further, it is crucial that the rules are – at least in part – *external* to the controlled entity. For example, adjudicators control whether administrative agencies comply with external provisions like the EU treaties, the US Constitution, the agency's founding regulation, or the relevant act of Congress. The adjudicator then applies the facts of the case, in terms of how the power structure exercised its power, to the normative material at hand – that is, the law regulating the agent's powers – and then decides whether the agent's acts conform with this normative material or not.

If the normative material violates higher-ranking rules, individual rights adjudication may also include reviewing the normative material itself. For example, if the adjudicator considers statutory provisions to conflict with constitutional requirements, depending on its authority, the adjudicator might declare the lower-level rules void or inapplicable. However, whereas reviewing rule enforcement is the bread and butter of individual rights adjudication, reviewing rulemaking is a more complex endeavor.

[83] See, for example, tensions about Administrative Law Judge's endangered decisional independence by reforms of their nomination process under the Trump administration, Jennifer Nou, 'Dismissing Decisional Independence Suits' (2019) 86 University of Chicago Law Review 1187.

[84] cf. Christoph Möllers, *Gewaltengliederung: Legitimation und Dogmatik im nationalen und internationalen Rechtsvergleich* (Mohr Siebeck 2005) 95 et seq.

2.2.6 *Outcomes*

When an individual goes to an adjudicator to enforce their rights and control power, adjudication may yield several outcomes. The stereotypical outcome of adjudication – especially if conceptualized mainly as a dispute – is a *decision*. A decision assesses the normative material and typically orders the losing party to commit or omit a certain act. For example, a court may decide that an agency's approval for specific medication did not follow the required procedural steps and violated the relevant normative material. The court would then annul said approval and perhaps order the agency to examine the approval again, following all the necessary procedural steps. Thus, the role of individual rights adjudication is typically to review and control decisions made by (administrative) actors – and not to make a new "administrative" decision.

In a historical context, an adjudicator's decision is typically legally *binding* for both parties, especially the public agent. In constitutional democracies, public power is conditioned by the rule of law. In fact, the ability to make legally binding decisions constitutes perhaps *the* crucial feature distinguishing adjudicators who really *control* public power, like courts, from other more marginal guardians that provide more circumscribed services like mediation, arbitration, expert review, or transparency.[85]

However, from a functional perspective, we should not overemphasize the importance of a decision's legally binding nature, because the efficacy of legally binding decisions is conditioned by the degree to which the controlled actor abides by the rule of law. Reversing this formulation, legally binding decisions are only effective in rule of law systems whereas less stable, novel, and still emerging normative systems require other mechanisms to safeguard a decision's real-world effectiveness.

Even within stable rule of law systems, adjudicators use a variety of instruments to control organizational behavior. Binding decisions are an important instrument, but by no means the only one. As argued above, disputes about individual rights often merely reflect more deeply rooted governance problems. Such problems could manifest as recurring patterns or institutionalized structures within an organization that inevitably and persistently produce individual rights violations. We can identify various examples whereby adjudicators addressed deeper organizational patterns that had led to various kinds of individual rights violations. Among the

[85] Shapiro, *Courts: A Comparative and Political Analysis* (n 10) 8 passim.

most notable are racial bias within police departments,[86] administrative inadequacies leading to "systemic deficiencies" in EU Member States' asylum systems,[87] or the lack of political will to take measures necessary for meeting carbon reduction targets.[88] In such cases, judges often act in ways that are "forward looking, fashioned ad hoc on flexible and broadly remedial lines, often having important consequences for many persons including absentees."[89] This is because correcting structurally flawed patterns within a powerful organization, especially administrative ones, is ultimately "not a dispute between private individuals about private rights, but a grievance about the operation of public policy."[90] Remedying structural patterns or, in Abram Chayes' words, to "operate public policy," adjudicators resort to flexible, more forward-looking remedial approaches. These can be more effective than singular, backward-looking, but binding decisions. In all the abovementioned cases – despite their variety – the adjudicator outlined future handrails for the controlled organization that would remedy the underlying governance issue. In *COPPAR v Rizzo*, an example I borrow from Chayes, a District Court required a police department to "submit ... a comprehensive program for dealing adequately with civilian complaints alleging police misconduct."[91] Such a program should, for example, safeguard "[a]ppropriate revision of police manuals and rules of procedure spelling out in some detail, in simple language, the 'dos and don'ts' of permissible conduct in dealing with civilians."[92] In *N.S.*, the ECJ described how a Member State could assess whether "systemic deficiencies" imbue the asylum procedures in another Member State, namely by resorting to "regular and unanimous reports of international non-governmental organizations bearing witness to the practical difficulties in the implementation

[86] COPPAR v Rizzo District Court, 357 F. Supp. 1289 (E.D. Pa. 1973), add'd sub nom. Goode v Rizzo, 506 F.2d 542 (3rd Cir. 1974), rev'd, 96 S. Ct. 598 (1976); see esp. the remarks in Chayes (n 51) 1305–1309; see further Rizzo v Goode, US Supreme Court 96 S. Ct. 598 (1976).

Adjudication's track record of tackling such structural problems is ambivalent. In the abovementioned case, the US Supreme Court overturned the District Court's decision with questionable factual assessments. Further, cases raising concerns of structural maltreatment of persons of color by police departments are by no means a US American particularity, cf. Oury Jalloh, Bundesgerichtshof 4 StR 473/13; Basu v Germany, European Court of Human Rights [215/19], 18 January 2023 paras 31–39.

[87] NS [2011] European Court of Justice (Grand Chamber) C-411/10, ECLI:EU:C:2011:865.

[88] Klimabeschluss, Federal Constitutional Court (Bundesverfassungsgericht) 1 BvR 2656/18.

[89] Chayes (n 51) 1302.

[90] Ibid.

[91] COPPAR v Rizzo (n 86) 1321.

[92] Ibid.

of the Common European Asylum System."[93] The Bundesverfassungsgericht (Germany's constitutional court) ordered the German legislator (!) to ramp up its carbon reduction plans "according to the guidelines [*Maßgaben*]" formulated by the Bundesverfassungsgericht.[94]

Taking a normative perspective on the separation of functions, adjudicatory review of the deeper flaws of power structures seems intuitively more contentious than superficial remedies of individual rights violations.[95] However, drawing the line between "effective" adjudication that tackles the root of governance problems on the one hand and misguided adjudicatory creep into the realm of policymaking on the other requires fine-tuned measuring instead of principled simplifying.[96] Adjudicatory efficacy depends on an adjudicator's authority within its legal system, the applicable normative framework, and other control tools at hand.[97] Hence, a clear-cut, generalizable normative solution as to what exactly constitutes effective judicial protection arguably does not – and cannot – exist.

For the purposes of this book, we can conclude that adjudicators use various tools to exercise control over large scale organizations, ranging from binary, binding decisions to open-ended, flexible recommendations, which are of course reinforced by most adjudicators' *ability* to issue binding decisions in cases of noncompliance. Therefore, to ensure that adjudicators' influence over structural reforms at large organizations can be properly wielded, binding decision-making powers serve as a sword of Damocles lending weight to non-binding normative sentences issued by the adjudicator.

2.2.7 *Appellate Review*

As we are jumping back and forth between Europe and the United States, another terminological note seems warranted. The term "adjudication" has different connotations in England (and most other countries that

93 NS (n 87) paras 90–91 (the ECJ formulates less directly but makes it clear nonetheless what sources Member States should consult to assess systemic deficiencies in other Member States).

94 Klimabeschluss (n 88) para 268.

95 See concretely Chayes (n 51) 1313–1316.

96 Famously: Abweichende Meinung der Richterin Lübbe-Wolff zum Beschluss des Zweiten Senats vom 14 Januar 2014 [2014] Bundesverfassungsgericht 2 BvR 2728/13, BVerfGE 134/366.

97 For the relevance of narratives in judgments see recently Freya Schramm, 'Judges as Narrators of the Climate Crisis? An Illustrative Analysis of the Decision of the German Constitutional Court from 24 March 2021' (2022) 7 European Papers 361.

follow common law) than in the United States.[98] In England,[99] adjudication refers to third party appellate review of administrative decisions.[100] In contrast, in US parlance, adjudication broadly refers to independent decision-making related to administrative decisions as well as to their appellate review by a third party.[101] This broader American concept of adjudication reflects the US's Administrative Procedure Act of 1946, which applies adjudicating as an umbrella term for various types of administrative decision-making.[102]

Here, our concern is with the ex-post control of platforms' administration-like rulemaking and, especially, rule enforcement. Thus, we use the narrower understanding of adjudication as appellate review as this is more common, especially in England and many of its former colonial areas (such as Canada or Australia).

2.3 Platforms as Administrators

Above, I introduced individual rights adjudication as a mechanism to control power. But how should we understand the power of social media companies, which are ultimately the power structures the here studied Emulated Guardians shall provide accountability for?

Historically, individual rights adjudication resolves disputes regarding the exercise of *public* power by a large power structure, for example, an administrative actor vis-à-vis an individual. In our context, the EU's

98 Prompting Jeffrey Lubbers to call the US Model "the outlier," Jeffrey S Lubbers, 'Administrative Adjudication: The United States Is the Outlier' in Marc Hertogh and others (eds.), *The Oxford Handbook of Administrative Justice* (Oxford University Press 2022) 45.

99 I refer to England and not the United Kingdom in general as there are (considerable) differences in the English, Welsh (between these two not so much), Scottish, and Northern Irish legal subsystems within the UK.

100 Cane (n 43) 325–326.

101 Arguably, the historical context of the broader US American understanding is that, in the US, many first-instance decisions are made by independent officers (so-called administrative law judges) who are not subject to hierarchical command. From a functional perspective, "judicializing" already the first-instance decision emphasizes the various ways in which organizations can reinterpret the separation of functions. See the comprehensive historical study by Jerry L Mashaw, *Creating the Administrative Constitution: The Lost One Hundred Years of American Administrative Law* (Yale University Press 2012) esp. 251 et seq. See further Okayama (n 46) 10 et seq; Lubbers (n 98) 49 et seq; Jeffrey S Lubbers, 'Federal Administrative Law Judges: A Focus on Our Invisible Judiciary' (1981) 33 Administrative Law Review 109, 110–112.

102 Adjudicating is here understood as the administrative process to formulate an order (in contrast to rulemaking), cf. 5 US Code Subchapter II §§ 551(7), 554–558.

out-of-court dispute settlement bodies and Meta's Oversight Board emulate individual rights adjudication to resolve disputes about how a *private* power structure exercises its rulemaking and rule enforcement power vis-à-vis individuals. These private power structures are social media platforms. Social media platforms make and enforce rules concerning individual and social communication and thereby affect, as mediating entities, how individuals exercise their public rights, especially freedom of expression. Vice versa, regulating how individuals exercise their freedom of expression reflexively affects how political communities engage in societal, political, economic, and cultural discourse. Thus, social media platforms' private exercise of power can be viewed as affecting the public rights of individuals and the public interest of democratic societies. These *private* power structures then become de facto administrators.

This section therefore further develops – along prior work – the analytical toolkit and normative effects of understanding social media platforms as administrators.[103] This is, I believe, particularly important given current debates in the United States and particularly in Europe, which champion a predominantly constitutional law perspective on platform power.[104] However, as I will outline below, administrative law – alongside the broader sociological and economic studies of bureaucracy and organization theory – provides sharper analytical tools and more effective prescriptive solutions.

2.3.1 *Constitutional or Administrative?*

It is by now a truism that some of these digital corporations – or whatever comes after them – became so pervasive, inescapable, and powerful that

[103] Moritz Schramm, 'Platform Administrative Law: A Research Agenda' (SSRN, 24 July 2024) <https://perma.cc/JH2A-8ZW2>; Moritz Schramm, 'Averting Zombie Mode: Learning from (the Critique of) Global Constitutionalism for Digital Constitutionalism' in Giovanni De Gregorio, Oreste Pollicino and Peggy Valcke (eds.), *Oxford Handbook on Digital Constitutionalism* (Oxford University Press 2025).

[104] See from the broad field of "Digital Constitutionalism" esp. Andrea Simoncini, *The Constitutional Dimension of the Internet – Some Research Paths, EUI Working Papers LAW 2016/15* (2016); Dennis Redeker, Lex Gill and Urs Gasser, 'Towards Digital Constitutionalism? Mapping Attempts to Craft an Internet Bill of Rights' (2018) 80 International Communication Gazette 302; Oreste Pollicino, *Judicial Protection of Fundamental Rights on the Internet: A Road towards Digital Constitutionalism?* (Hart 2021); Giovanni De Gregorio, *Digital Constitutionalism in Europe: Reframing Rights and Powers in the Algorithmic Society* (Cambridge University Press 2022); notably without engaging with any of the above Anu Bradford, 'Europe's Digital Constitution' (2023) 64 Virginia Journal of International Law 1. For complementary accounts see Schramm, 'Where Is Olive? Or: Lessons from Democratic Theory for Legitimate Platform Governance' (n 56); Róisín Á Costello, 'Faux

we must think about them in public law terms.[105] Public law imagery is so pervasive that it transcends political divides. Liberal voices call for expanded rights, adjudication, and procedural safeguards, while increasingly vocal "conservative" critics, especially since the 2024 US elections, demand greater majoritarianism, denounce alleged viewpoint discrimination, and rail against "woke" content moderation policies.

This book focuses on the first wave of public law arguments: rights, adjudication, and due process. Yet many of the critiques leveled against these frameworks are themselves rooted in public law reasoning. In a sense, we are witnessing a reenactment of familiar public law debates – countermajoritarianism, freedom of speech, and institutional design – now transposed onto the realm of private and regulatory governance.

However, in general and scholarly discourse, these public law terms are often framed as *constitutional* rather than *administrative*. That is especially the case for discourses about content moderation. In principle, that dominance of constitutionalist discourse about platforms is not surprising. Content moderation intuitively links to freedom of speech, which is often understood as a quintessentially constitutional issue.

However, this book takes a slightly different approach. I emphasize the administrative and bureaucratic elements of much of content moderation and, for the fact of the matter, private governance in general. This complements the descriptive insights and prescriptive ideas by digital constitutionalists.[106] The motivation to focus on the administrative instead of the constitutional dimension comes predominantly from an empirical, rather than a solely normative perspective. Of course, many norms of constitutional law like non-discrimination or a minimum of legal coherence as it is implicit in any rule of law-based system would improve platform governance. However, if one looks at how content moderation actually looks like, analogies to administration and bureaucracies appear much more obvious. Platforms design, regulate, and police

Ami? Interrogating the Normative Coherence of "Digital Constitutionalism"' (2023) 12 Global Constitutionalism 326; Angelo Jr Golia, 'Critique of Digital Constitutionalism: Deconstruction and Reconstruction from a Societal Perspective' (2023) 10 Global Constitutionalism 1; Petros Terzis, 'Against Digital Constitutionalism' [2024] European Law Open 1; Schramm, 'Averting Zombie Mode: Learning from (the Critique of) Global Constitutionalism for Digital Constitutionalism' (n 103).

105 This book is mostly about content moderation, but see e.g. regarding Google (and the lingering question of fundamental rights and the state action doctrine): David Gray, 'Is Google a State Agent?' (2024) 27 Stanford Technology Law Review 206.

106 Schramm, 'Averting Zombie Mode: Learning from (the Critique of) Global Constitutionalism for Digital Constitutionalism' (n 103).

infrastructures with eminent importance for public life. They enact a myriad of extremely detailed norms – much more detailed than "free expression" – and devise the most intricate specifics of their technological infrastructures. Platforms organize these practices globally, partly accommodating to specific normative needs of local jurisdictions, partly striving for global coherence to maintain their economies of scale. These elements entail choices and practices that could be described as hierarchy and deviation, deferral and review, coherence and flexibility. Seen in the abstract these normative and organizational dilemmas remind us of structural features of the administrative state. In that sense, content moderation – especially through its co-optation by regulators – becomes a globalized transnational yet privately dominated administrative space.

Crucially, I use the notion administration or administrative law broadly. It refers to the acquis of transnational administrative law as we know it from the European Union or global governance structures but also domestic administrative law. In that sense, I particularly draw inspiration from the body of theories devised in the 2000s as "Global Administrative Law" (GAL) initiated by Benedict Kingsbury, Richard Stewart, and Nico Krisch. Importantly, (global) administrative law is now also met with great interest by private lawyers. Especially the work of Rodrigo Vallejo on "Private Administrative Law" highlighted the administrative elements in private standardization mechanisms and administrative law's potential beyond the ubiquitous but epistemologically laden "governance" paradigm.[107] Others have rightly highlighted the relevance of standards, transnational private governance, and private ordering.[108]

Coming from that empirical starting point, focusing on the administrative and bureaucratic rather than the constitutional dimension of content moderation and private governance offers several advantages. To begin with, administrative law is more detailed than constitutional law. Freedom of speech in an individual case is a constitutional issue

[107] Rodrigo Vallejo Garretón, 'The Private Administrative Law of Technical Standardization' (2022) 40 Yearbook of European Law 172; Rodrigo Vallejo Garretón, 'After Governance?: The Idea of a Private Administrative Law' in Poul F Kjaer (ed.), *The Law of Political Economy* (Cambridge University Press 2020); see the critique of the concept of "governance" in the EU context Christoph Möllers, 'European Governance: Meaning and Value of a Concept' (2006) 43 Common Market Law Review 313.

[108] Avery Katz, 'Taking Private Ordering Seriously' (1996) 144 University of Pennsylvania Law Review 1745; Harm Schepel, *The Constitution of Private Governance: Product Standards in the Regulation of Integrating Markets* (Hart 2005); Olia Kanevskaia, 'Governance of ICT Standardization: Due Process in Technocratic Decision-Making' (2020) 45 North Carolina Journal of Law & Technology 549; Anna Beckers, Hans-Werner Micklitz, Rodrigo Vallejo and Pia Letto-Vanamo, *The Foundations of European Transnational Private Law* (Hart 2024).

about balancing one fundamental right against another. In contrast, governance of millions of speech acts becomes primarily an administrative issue as said balancing exercise hinges upon effective and faithful implementation down the line. Constitutional law's brushstrokes are often too broad for the phenomenally complex and thickly layered content moderation bureaucracies we have today. Surely, procedures ought to be fair and nondiscriminatory and align with all kinds of constitutionalist values. But what does that mean for the organizational and procedural structuring of contemporary moderation behemoths? Especially so if our political economy protects platforms' profitability in often very absolute terms. These companies direct tens of thousands of human moderators, lawyers, engineers and, to a still ill-understood extent, automatic decision-making. Administrative law offers answers to these questions.

In addition, administrative law comes with way fewer side effects than constitutional law. Applying constitutional law notions descriptively to private actors like Meta may be justified through the latter's humungous power. But doing so may remain a bad description as most to all big social media companies are anything but "constitutional" in a liberal sense.[109] Neither do they feature meaningful participatory – not to say democratic – elements, nor do social media platforms meaningfully self-restrict their power or value the "public interest" higher than their own interest in profit. To be clear, that is not at all meant pejoratively. It is just the very purpose of a company. However, adorning companies too quickly with the label of being "constitutionalized" may cloak them in a legitimacy they do not deserve. Administrative law on the other hand, although also developed in the context of public power, comes with way less legitimatory grandezza. Administrative law is often perceived as boring. That is, in this case, an asset. Saying that platforms *administrate* is descriptively accurate, as they deal with millions of customers and do so – intriguingly – increasingly more informed (if not necessarily guided) by a public law understanding of what good administration entails.

Emulating individual rights adjudication for content moderation is expected therefore to achieve a similar goal as historic individual rights adjudication achieved vis-à-vis administrative actors: protecting

[109] The underlying problem here is the extent to which it is meaningful to examine factually powerful structures of order through the inherently normative lens of the "constitutional," or more specifically, "constitutionalism." While these structures clearly wield significant power, the question remains whether (uncritically) applying constitutional frameworks – typically reserved for public, i.e. democratic, governance – offers a useful or accurate perspective on private or hybrid forms of authority.

individual rights, advancing accountability, and controlling otherwise largely unchecked power structures.

2.3.2 *Platforms*

To substantiate this plea for a more administrative-focused perspective on content moderation, platforms, and private governance in general, I proceed with a quick look at the phenomenon of the *platform*. Although predominantly economic, it gives rise to social and normative implications. The term "platform" is a metaphor relating to a specific way in which data is presented and economic transactions are conducted in the information economy.[110]

In the abstract, a platform can be conceived of as an intermediary, virtual "structure" that allows people to communicate publicly.[111] Remarkably, the very term "platform" epitomizes the inevitable performative spin of any discourse about or practice of emergent digital power structures. As Gillespie has argued, companies have been strategically advancing the term "platform" to promote ideals of egalitarian connectivity at least since this century's first decade.[112] By framing companies like Facebook or Amazon as "platforms" and not, for example, as "online wholesale outlets" or "data mines," the metaphor implies the very criteria by which those companies will be judged.[113]

We can distinguish platforms from other communication tools like messaging, email, or chatrooms by their degree of public availability, accessibility, and direction of communication. Although the details vary, the underlying idea of a platform is to facilitate contemporaneous communication among a group of people. Communicative acts on platforms are "public" in that they are multidirectional since communication on platforms is often directed to a specific or unspecified audience. In contrast, emails or chats tend to be bidirectional because communication often occurs along the lines of existing social relations and, crucially, cannot be accessed or detected by other program users.[114] The term

110 Information economy refers to the data-driven, largely dematerialized, and increasingly platform-dominated digital economic sector. For prominent theorizations and genealogies of the information economy see especially: Cohen (n 27) 15 et seq; and generally: Zuboff (n 21).

111 For a brief overview see Robert Gorwa, 'What Is Platform Governance?' (2019) 22 Information, Communication & Society 854, 856.

112 Gillespie, 'The Politics of "Platforms"' (n 22) 348 et seq.

113 Ibid 359–360.

114 Metaphorically distinguishing between "platforms" and "channels," Paul M Leonardi, Marleen Huysman and Charles Steinfield, 'Enterprise Social Media: Definition, History,

"platform" also entered black letter law, with the EU's DSA defining the platform as an online infrastructure that "stores and disseminates information to the public" at the request of users.[115]

On some platforms, like Amazon or Alibaba, interaction is mainly commercial and based on trading. This type of platform can be seen as a marketplace bringing together buyers and sellers.[116] On other platforms, such as X, formerly Twitter, communication is generally social, cultural, or political. Many platforms blend elements, for example Facebook, which is primarily a social network but also includes more transaction-oriented features on its site. Even gaming or pornography sites can be seen as platforms as many offer channels of communication or even monetary exchange.

Platforms that focus mainly on social, cultural, or political communication are called *social media* or social networks and are sometimes described as a "digital marketplace of ideas" or, in reference to Habermas, a "digital public sphere."[117] However, the events of the last decade emphasize the deeply ambivalent effects of social media.[118] On one side, social media platforms have helped to foment discourses and social movements that have upended or at least shaken normatively questionable power structures.[119] Yet social media has also enabled and intensified discourses and movements that many

and Prospects for the Study of Social Technologies in Organizations' (2013) 19 Journal of Computer-Mediated Communication 1, 2.

[115] cf. Article 2(1)(i) DSA.

[116] Cohen (n 27) 37.

[117] For a good summary of contemporary perspectives using that approach (based on Reckwitz and Habermas) see Philipp Staab and Thorsten Thiel, 'Social Media and the Digital Structural Transformation of the Public Sphere' (2022) 39 Theory, Culture & Society 129. See further Joshua Cohen and Archon Fung, 'Democracy and the Digital Public Sphere' in Lucy Bernholz, Hélène Landemore and Rob Reich (eds.), *Digital Technology and Democratic Theory* (University of Chicago Press 2021) 23 et seq. For the originals see Jürgen Habermas, *Strukturwandel der Öffentlichkeit: Untersuchungen zu einer Kategorie der bürgerlichen Gesellschaft* (Suhrkamp 1990). Recently, Habermas revisited some of his arguments in: Jürgen Habermas, 'Überlegungen und Hypothesen zu einem erneuten Strukturwandel der politischen Öffentlichkeit' in Martin Seeliger and Sebastian Sevignani (eds.), *Ein neuer Strukturwandel der Öffentlichkeit?* (Nomos 2021) 487 et seq.

[118] Habermas put it more dramatically: "[T]he lava of this simultaneously anti-authoritarian and egalitarian potential, which was still palpable in the early Californian entrepreneurial spirit, soon solidified in Silicon Valley into the libertarian grimace of world-dominating digital corporations." see Habermas, 'Überlegungen und Hypothesen zu einem erneuten Strukturwandel der politischen Öffentlichkeit' (n 117) 488 (translation by the author).

[119] Examples abound, from the Arab Spring to the #MeToo movement, Black Lives Matter, or Fridays for Future. All these developments would not have transpired the same way if not for their publicity on social media.

view as normatively problematic, such as misinformation and anti-vaccine sentiments during the Covid-19 pandemic, as well as a slurry of xenophobic, racist, misogynous, antisemitic, or otherwise hateful content. To a degree, social media's "democratization" of discourse has given airtime to unsavory viewpoints that were formerly hard to access by most people because editorially mediated news outlets tended not to feature these kinds of content. It seems almost ironic that many now point to Habermas when lamenting the demise of twentieth century mass media – television, newspapers, radio – as Habermas himself held those very outlets responsible for what he described as the demise of the public sphere when compared to direct, face-to-face debates in bourgeois European circles in nineteenth-century Vienna, Berlin, London, and Paris. But aristocrat-studded salons have their own problems. Whether nineteenth-century discussions in salons and at dinner tables – all male and with a lot of smoking, I suppose – were indeed preferable to what we have today may be ultimately a matter of taste. Either way, idealizing phenomena we did not experience ourselves – especially historic ones – often risks idealizing a narrative that reflects only a fraction of what in and of itself is a rather complicated and ambivalent phenomenon.

Last, we should not misinterpret the notion that social media is about social, cultural, or political communication. Communication on social media platforms is inherently commercial. Many social media companies rely on advertising, which is personalized and then placed on their sites and those of others. Social media companies "mine" the behavioral data of their users and exploit it for advertising, profiling, and other forms of monetization.[120] Against this backdrop, any communication, even someone's not explicitly communicative behavior or activity, is of commercial value to the company that owns and maintains the platform because it still yields information – data which can then be monetized – about that person.

2.3.3 *Design, Regulation, Enforcement*

These observations bring us to *content moderation*, the umbrella term for social media companies' governance of online communication.[121] Content

[120] However, note that companies increasingly work with "synthetic" data, i.e. data that is not mined from users but modeled by "artificial intelligence" to emulate mined data, cf. Cade Metz and others, 'How Tech Giants Cut Corners to Harvest Data for AI' *New York Times* (6 April 2024) <https://perma.cc/WW5D-EXXS>; Shirin Ghaffary, 'Microsoft, Google and Meta Bet on Fake Data to Build AI Models' *Bloomberg* (2 May 2024) <https://perma.cc/MX2F-NSLU>.

[121] For example, James Grimmelmann positively defines content moderation as "the governance mechanisms that structure participation in a community to facilitate cooperation and prevent abuse." Grimmelmann, 'The Virtues of Moderation' (2015) 17 Yale

moderation as well as the broader term "platform governance"[122] has been described in detail by others.[123] For our purposes, it suffices to carve out several key elements of current, and still evolving, conceptions of content moderation.

First, content moderation should be interpreted *broadly*. It refers to the design and construction of a type of digital infrastructure – the platform – and the devising of rules that govern the operations of that infrastructure as well as the enforcement of those rules. As argued above, content moderation comprises at least three elements: design, rulemaking, and rule enforcement. As Kate Klonick's influential piece in the Harvard Law Review argued, the governance by "new governors" of online speech "bear[s] remarkable resemblance to heuristics and structures familiar in

Journal of Law & Tech 42, 47. Kate Klonick uses "governance" and "content moderation" largely synonymously, arguing that "platforms have developed a detailed system rooted in the American legal system with regularly revised rules, trained human decision-making, and reliance on a system of external influence." See Klonick, 'The New Governors: The People, Rules, and Processes Governing Online Speech' (n 55) 1599, 1617 et seq, 1630 et seq, 1664. Evelyn Douek broadened that picture, highlighting that content moderation "is a vast system of administration that includes a far broader range of decisions and decisionmakers than the standard picture admits." Douek, 'Content Moderation as Systems Thinking' (n 55) 531; see also Elettra Bietti, 'A Genealogy of Digital Platform Regulation' (2023) 7 Georgetown Law and Technology Review 1; Robert Gorwa, *The Politics of Platform Governance: How Governments Shape Online Content Moderation* (Oxford University Press 2024).

122 The term platform governance is, or at least used to be more prevalent in political science literature. Broadly, one can distinguish between the governance of platforms by regulators and the governance of users by platforms. Historically, platform governance was often understood broadly, also including aspects like data management and platform design. Following the conceptual broadening of content moderation (esp. by Evelyn Douek, regarding its implications for future reforms at 6.2), the two concepts appear increasingly aligned. The only exception may be data and privacy, which often remains a somewhat siloed discussion. For the concept of platform governance see Gorwa (n 111); thinking content moderation and data together esp.: Cohen (n 27); De Gregorio (n 104) 216 et seq. For the discursive effects of separating discussions on content moderation and data see also 4.2.4.

123 See in general especially: Grimmelmann (n 121) 48 et seq; Klonick, 'The New Governors: The People, Rules, and Processes Governing Online Speech' (n 55); Gillespie, *Custodians of the Internet* (n 55); Jack M Balkin, 'Free Speech Is a Triangle' (2018) 118 Columbia Law Review 2011; Nicolas P Suzor, *Lawless: The Secret Rules That Govern Our Digital Lives* (Cambridge University Press 2019); Sarah T Roberts, *Behind the Screen: Content Moderation in the Shadows of Social Media* (Yale University Press 2019); Douek (n 55); see further regarding more specific aspects like automated decision-making and "design" aspects: Tarleton Gillespie, 'Content Moderation, AI, and the Question of Scale' (2020) 7 Big Data & Society; Jing Zeng and D Bondy Valdovinos Kaye, 'From Content Moderation to Visibility Moderation: A Case Study of Platform Governance on TikTok' (2022) 14 Policy & Internet 79.

legal decision-making."[124] These rules prohibit certain kinds of communication and are unilaterally devised by social media companies[125] as well as often bleeding into various other contexts. As we will encounter those rules repeatedly in the empirical parts of the book, we will not go into greater detail here.[126]

But content moderation is more than just rulemaking and rule enforcement.[127] Content moderation also refers to the *design* of a platform and its business model.[128] The type of content a platform's algorithm amplifies, the data on which a platform's algorithms base their operations, and the many other normative decisions and technological issues involved in creating and operating a platform all, one way or another, moderate the content that users access.[129]

Second, platform power in content moderation is largely *unilateral* and generally unaccountable. Although social media platforms operate within legal systems, their leeway in designing content moderation systems is broad. Sheltered by particular conceptions of liability developed in US and European legal frameworks, platforms are considered by their owners to be mere "intermediaries" that are not liable for the content of information posted by their users. Historically, platform owners' motivation to moderate is not predominantly for legal reasons, as they tend not to be liable for illegal content anyway, but rather on the basis of their own interest in maintaining a (relatively socially acceptable) discursive environment that keeps users on the platform and accommodates the advertisers and potential buyers of the products those ads promote. To keep communication "civil," platforms therefore began formulating ever more specific rules and intensified the initially human and then algorithmic enforcement of those rules. Simultaneously, platform owners and employees sometimes made conflicting choices, designing their offerings

[124] Klonick, 'The New Governors: The People, Rules, and Processes Governing Online Speech' (n 55) 1630.

[125] Ibid 1631 et seq; Gillespie, *Custodians of the Internet* (n 55) 45 et seq; Suzor (n 123) 10 et seq.

[126] See 3.3 and 4.3 as well as, highlighting the DSA's omission of regulating platform rulemaking 3.2.4.3.

[127] Douek (n 55).

[128] Highlighting the importance to reform social media companies' business model: Jack M Balkin, 'How to Regulate (and Not Regulate) Social Media' (2021) 1 Journal of Free Speech Law 71; Jack M Balkin, 'To Reform Social Media, Reform Informational Capitalism', in Lee C Bollinger and Geoffrey R Stone (eds.), *Social Media, Freedom of Speech, and the Future of Democracy* (Oxford University Press 2022) 233.

[129] In the US, the key texts are: Klonick, 'The New Governors: The People, Rules, and Processes Governing Online Speech' (n 55); Douek (n 55); Kate Klonick, 'Of Systems Thinking and Straw Men' (2023) 136 Harvard Law Review Forum 339.

in such a way as to amplify offensive content, which they discovered would intensify user engagement more than "positive" content.[130]

Third, as mentioned above, we should think of content moderation as an *exemplar*. Clearly, social media is a relatively novel phenomenon. Nonetheless, private rulemaking and private governance of communication, resources, and people is by no means new. Although the future picture of world politics, trade, and digitization is necessarily blurry, it seems plausible that globally active, vertically integrated corporations with unilateral governance capacities over important sectors, in one form or the other, come what may, will become an ever more prevalent trend. Perhaps even more plausible is that digitization will play a huge role in future governance and that the power of a few, oligopolistic private power structures will strongly shape these developments. In other words, social media platforms and content moderation are not the first, nor will they be the last, power structure in potential need new forms of adjudicative guardianship.

Assuming future policymakers, managers, lawyers, and other experts might again come up with the idea to emulate individual rights adjudication to control private power, this study seeks to keep this overarching context in mind. For that reason, I do not speak of content moderation all the time but also about, for example, *private governance* or private ordering.

2.3.4 Private Content Moderation

After outlining these definitional contours, we now move on to dissect the public and private aspects of social media platforms' content moderation. We begin with the private aspects.

Social media platforms like Meta or X are private organizations – in other words, they are almost all pivately owned and controlled.[131]

[130] Jeremy B Merril and Will Oremus, 'Five Points for Anger, One for a "Like": How Facebook's Formula Fostered Rage and Misinformation' *Washington Post* (26 October 2021) <https://perma.cc/7E55-RPZL>.

[131] The two US giants Meta and X are either listed at the New York Stock Exchange (Meta) or got de-listed in a change of private ownership (Twitter, now X). The only notable exception is TikTok, which has more than 220 million monthly active users in Europe, 150 million in the US and whose parent company ByteDance is partly owned by the Chinese government. The government of the People's Republic of China owns so-called "golden shares" of various internet companies. According to insiders, the government particularly focuses on companies "possessing large amounts of key data." However, momentarily, these golden shares apparently only concern ByteDance's business within the People's Republic but not the TikTok version that is available in the rest of the world. In

Generally speaking, one can portray the relationships between these private organizations and hundreds of millions of individuals as solely private. A corporation offers a service and consumers access and use it, paying mainly by making their private data available to the company.[132] In that sense, controlling the private bureaucracies of platforms is only "customer service" – a characterization used by an interviewee working for Meta's Oversight Board.[133] Correspondingly, we see many private-law elements in Emulated Guardians' formal structure. For example, corporate law imbues the Oversight Board's formal structure, set up by a noncharitable trust based in Wilmington, Delaware.[134] Similarly, one core ideational role model for the DSA's out-of-court dispute settlement bodies was alternative dispute resolution in consumer relations. As we will see in Chapter 3, the European Commission modeled its proposed adjudicators that were supposed to "tame the giants" in parts on oversight bodies that, for instance, enforce passenger rights in disputes with airlines or resolve contractual disputes between customers and car insurers.[135]

However, analyzing the power relation between social media platforms and individuals based only on their formal structure obfuscates the functional dynamics at play.[136] As Deirdre Curtin and Linda Senden argued, "[t]he distinction between private and public regulation is, in any event, blurred and unclear, with traditional public administration becoming ever more 'unbounded' as outside actors become involved to varying degrees."[137] So "private law is public law in the sense that private

the mid-2020s, the US sought to transfer ownership of TikTok's US operations to a group of US investors. At the time of writing the results of that process were not yet clear. See Reuters Staff, 'Fretting about Data Security, China's Government Expands Its Use of "Golden Shares"' (*Reuters*, 16 December 2021) <https://perma.cc/XT6C-LFHT>

132 Seminal: Zuboff (n 21).

133 Interview with Oversight Board Staffer 3 (6 May 2022); see in that respect also Catalina Goanta and Pietro Ortolani, 'Unpacking Content Moderation: The Rise of Social Media Platforms as Online Civil Courts' in Xandra Ellen Kramer and others (eds.), *Frontiers in Civil Justice: Privatisation, Monetisation and Digitisation* (Edward Elgar 2022).

134 See at 4.3.1.

135 See 3.2 and 3.3.

136 cf. Hannah Bloch-Wehba, 'Global Platform Governance: Private Power in the Shadow of the State' (2019) 72 SMU Law Review 27, 33 et seq.

137 Deirdre Curtin and Linda Senden, 'Public Accountability of Transnational Private Regulation: Chimera or Reality?' (2011) 38 Journal of Law and Society 163, 164. See already: Alfred C Aman, 'The Globalizing State: A Future-Oriented Perspective on the Public/Private Distinction, Federalism, and Democracy' (1998) 31 Vanderbilt Journal of

regulation is part and parcel of democratic self-rule by a collective."[138] In turn, privately organized actors, like platforms, are subject to public-law scrutiny as they exercise power as it affects people on issues related to public law, such as freedom of expression. Yet, in our context, an idealized picture of private rulemaking as "democratic self-rule by a collective" is euphemistic. The rules governing the relationship between social media platforms and users are formal contracts. But a meeting of minds when it comes to such contracts is pure fiction; their provisions are periodically amended and unilaterally dominated by social media companies. Some researchers have even begun questioning whether social media platforms' terms of service can even be interpreted as contracts at all.[139] Others highlighted that "the law" stabilizes platform power through accommodating the political economy in which informational capitalism operates. In other words, platforms do not need to break the law as the law itself became part of the power relationship between platform, public authority, and user.[140] It would then follow that neither rulemaking by platforms, nor public regulation thereof can be reasonably construed as pure democratic self-government.

2.3.5 *Communication and Fundamental Rights*

However, despite the private law elements just mentioned, understanding (social media) platforms through a public law lens is now widely accepted. Such a public-law perspective becomes especially relevant whenever a private protagonist *acts on* the public. Social media platforms touch upon two aspects of crucial public concern. These are, on the one hand, communication and, on the other, fundamental rights, especially freedom of expression.

The space social media platforms design for their users serves as a forum for public and private communication. The importance of communication as a formative source of the self and as a cornerstone of

Transnational Law 769, 816 et seq; Duncan Kennedy, 'The Stages of the Decline of the Public/Private Distinction' (1982) 130 University of Pennsylvania Law Review 1349, 1353.

138 Curtin and Senden (n 137) 164.

139 Przemyslaw Jacek Palka, 'Terms of Service Are Not Contracts: Beyond Contract Law in the Regulation of Online Platforms' in Stefan Grundmann (ed.), *European Contract Law in the Digital Age* (Intersentia 2018).

140 At the end of the day, both perspectives point to the same problem: the way platforms structure their relationship with their users veers far away from idealized, moral notions of egalitarian contracting and individual liberty. See e.g. Julie Cohen, 'Law of the Platform Economy' (2017) 51 University of California Davis Law Review 133, 154–155.

society and politics is well-known.[141] Society and politics are products of communication, which perhaps points to the core of the human condition.[142] People are "political animals" by virtue of their ability to communicate.[143] Hence, enabling and regulating communication – as social media platforms like Meta and X do – means enabling and regulating a key ingredient of the social and political order we inhabit. Later theorists of justice,[144] deliberative democracy,[145] or the linguistic "turn"[146] have emphasized the importance (and fragility) of communication. Therefore, the governance of people's communication on social media platforms will inevitably warrant public-law scrutiny. As Linnet Taylor put it,

> This creates the potential for power relations of domination, and demands that we decide what constitutes the legitimacy to act on the public. Business ethics and private law are not designed to answer these questions, which are primarily political. If people have lost the right to disengage with commercial technologies, we may need to hold the companies that offer them to the same standards to which we hold the public sector.[147]

Second, communication's value is not only a philosophical or sociological truism but has long been established in law. The fundamental right of freedom of expression protects online communication.[148] Further, many specific fundamental rights, ranging from freedom of religion, and

[141] The classic text on communication's societal importance is Habermas, *Strukturwandel der Öffentlichkeit* (n 117). If you read German, see the recent special issue in this matter: Martin Seeliger and Sebastian Sevignani (eds.), 'Ein Neuer Strukturwandel Der Öffentlichkeit?' [2021] Leviathan Sonderband 37.

[142] Hannah Arendt, *The Human Condition* (2nd ed. [1998], University of Chicago Press 1958) 22 et seq (esp. 25–26).

[143] Aristotle, *Politics*, III iv 2.

[144] John Rawls' *Theory of Justice* built on the deliberative elements of agreeing on what is "just" instead of deducing it from abstract, higher order principles. He argued that "[t]he intuitive idea of justice as fairness is to think … of an original agreement in a suitably defined initial situation. [Justice is whatever] rational persons concerned to advance their interests would accept in this position of equality to settle the basic terms of their association." See John Rawls, *A Theory of Justice* (Rev ed., Belknap 1999 [1971]) 102.

[145] See the two Habermas texts cited in n 117.

[146] From the perspective of the philosophy of language see Austin (n 27); Ludwig Wittgenstein, *Philosophical Investigations* (1st ed., Basil Blackwell 1953); John R Searle, *Speech Acts: An Essay in the Philosophy of Language* (Cambridge University Press 1969); Judith Butler, *Excitable Speech: A Politics of the Performative* (Routledge 1997).

[147] See in general: Linnet Taylor, 'Public Actors Without Public Values: Legitimacy, Domination and the Regulation of the Technology Sector' (2021) 34 Philosophy & Technology 897.

[148] Article 11 CFR.

association, to the freedom to conduct business as enshrined in the EU's Charter of Fundamental Rights, make up a panoply of applicable rights. Platforms have become indispensable forums for the exercising of such rights, especially freedom of expression but also freedom of religion and the freedom to conduct business.[149] As the EU's DSA states in its preamble, to "exercise their fundamental rights," EU citizens are dependent on "responsible and diligent behavior" by platforms.[150] Public and especially administrative law offers a toolkit for normatively evaluating the organizational behavior that enables and sometimes restricts fundamental rights. Albeit platforms are not directly bound by fundamental rights, their actions shape how others exercise theirs. Further, platforms' gatekeeping function may impose procedural duties on them, such as those outlined by Germany's constitutional court in its *Stadionverbot* decision.[151] In the United States, in contrast, the Supreme Court appears not at all poised to envelope social media platforms in a denser net of obligations of how to moderate the content of their users.[152]

2.3.6 *Regulatory Administrification*

However, as important as communication and fundamental rights are, they cover only the subject of platform power but not its functionality. Because platforms deal with "public goods" like public communication and fundamental rights at a massive scale, they are increasingly regulated to abide to public law norms. These norms regulate how platforms

[149] See in general De Gregorio (n 104) 157 et seq; regarding US doctrine Klonick, 'The New Governors: The People, Rules, and Processes Governing Online Speech' (n 55) 1609–1613; Regarding German doctrine Sophie Knebel, *Die Drittwirkung der Grundrechte und -freiheiten gegenüber Privaten: Regulierungsmöglichkeiten sozialer Netzwerke* (Nomos 2018); human rights perspective: Jonathan Andrew and Frédéric Bernard (eds.), *Human Rights Responsibilities in the Digital Age: States, Companies, and Individuals* (Hart 2021); Rikke Frank Jørgensen (ed.), *Human Rights in the Age of Platforms* (MIT Press 2019); human and fundamental rights responsibilities for non-state actors, of course, are nothing new: Andrew Clapham, *Human Rights Obligations of Non-State Actors* (Oxford University Press 2006); See further: Evangelia Psychogiopoulou and Federica Casarosa, 'Social Media before Domestic Courts in Europe: An Analysis of Free Speech Cases' (2020) 27 Maastricht Journal of European and Comparative Law 791; Redeker, Gill and Gasser (n 104); Edoardo Celeste, Amélie Heldt and Clara Iglesias Keller (eds.), *Constitutionalising Social Media* (Hart 2022).

[150] Recital 3 DSA.

[151] Stadionverbot [2018] Bundesverfassungsgericht 1 BvR 3080/09, BVerfGE 148, 267-290; Hassrede [2021] Federal Court of Justice (Bundesgerichtshof) III ZR 179/20 and III ZR 192/20.

[152] Moody v NetChoice LLC [2024] Supreme Court of the United States 22-277 and 22-555, 603 ____ (2024); cf. Gray (n 105).

shall deal with their users. The normative model for many such rules – fundamental rights, due process, proportionality, nondiscrimination, hearing rights, duties to give reasons, and so on – is public law, or more precisely administrative law. I call this the *administrification* of platform governance.

There are two key drivers behind platforms' increasing administrification.[153] These are, on the one hand, regulatory co-opting of platforms and, on the other, increasing public scrutiny and demands for heightened platform accountability.[154] Social media platforms represent what the GAL project has characterized as *hybrid intergovernmental-private administrations* (in the case of the endowment to a public mandate) or entirely *private administrators*.[155] Such private governance organizations, like companies, "have adopted certain procedures of accountability and review in order to enhance their effectiveness and legitimacy; these may have parallels in domestic administrative and private law that are so far underexplored."[156] Hence, studying platforms as "part of global administration [allows us] to trace similarities as well as differences in mechanisms of accountability developed for public and private bodies."[157] This section outlines how regulatory co-option, which will only intensify with the newly enshrined DSA, incentivizes platforms to adopt administration-like procedures, rules, and formal structures. So far, except for remarks by Balkin, Bloch-Wehba, and Douek, this perspective was not explored in the literature.[158]

In 2016, several social media platforms, including Facebook and Twitter, now X, agreed with the European Commission on a code of conduct when it came to countering illegal hate speech online.[159] The social media platforms agreed to "have in place clear and effective processes to review notifications regarding illegal hate speech" and committed "to review such requests against their rules and community

[153] De Gregorio *en passant* called the DSA an "administrativization" of content moderation. Yet his framework focuses strongly on constitutionalism and not on administrative law. See De Gregorio (n 104) 213.

[154] Consequentially, even in the US, calls are increasingly emerging to treat digital corporations – especially social media companies – as state agents. cf. Gray (n 105).

[155] Kingsbury, Krisch and Stewart (n 49) 22.

[156] Ibid 54.

[157] Ibid 23.

[158] However, neither Douek nor Balkin dig (much) deeper into administrative law's prescriptive potential for improving platform governance, cf. Douek (n 55) 584 et seq; Balkin, 'Free Speech Is a Triangle' (n 123) 2028 et seq; in later pieces, the administrative law aspect disappeared: Balkin, 'To Reform Social Media, Reform Informational Capitalism' (n 128).

[159] Platform Code of Conduct on countering illegal hate speech online in the EU 2016.

guidelines."[160] Since platforms operate at scale, their commitments toward EU authorities are likely to affect, and perhaps water down, their global standards. In this context, Anu Bradford argued in her eminent book that platforms' normative material (the so-called community standards) increasingly mirrors the normative acquis of EU law.[161] However, it remains unclear whether their terms of service really "reflect the European standard of hate speech" as Bradford argues, or merely echo the overall tone of EU law rather than reflecting the EU acquis in any meaningful way.[162] Bradford points out that we do not know how these commitments are put into practice; especially since platform rules consist of many sublayers and platform lawyers "ultimately use their own judgment on what constitutes illegal hate speech. The outcome is therefore less likely to be perfectly aligned with the Commission's regulatory approach."[163] Building on the preexisting *division du travail* between social media platforms and European regulators, the Commission proposed a major overhaul of parts of the governance of social media platforms in December 2020.[164]

2.3.7 *Especially, the Digital Services Act*

This overhaul, the DSA, reiterated that platforms would be relatively free to devise their own procedures, decision-making processes, and substantive rules if they orient their dealings toward criteria like "objectivity," "proportionality," and "due regard for fundamental rights."[165] The DSA imposed several administrative law-inspired duties on platforms, for example the duty to give reasons for decisions against their users (Article 17 DSA) and to "act in a diligent, objective and proportionate manner in applying and enforcing" their terms of service (Article 14(2)).[166] The DSA stipulates that platforms should act with

[160] Ibid 2.

[161] Anu Bradford, *The Brussels Effect: How the European Union Rules the World* (Oxford University Press 2020) 161 et seq.

[162] Ibid 158; for a critical account see Moritz Schramm, 'Curb Your Enthusiasm: Why the Digital Services Act Might Not Have a "Brussels Effect"' (2025) European Journal of Legal Studies (Special Issue) 61.

[163] Ibid 162.

[164] See 3.2.

[165] See in detail 3.2.

[166] That trend is not limited to the DSA. Earlier frontrunners were the German Netzwerkdurchsetzungsgesetz or Regulation (EU) 2021/784 of the European Parliament and of the Council of 29 April 2021 on addressing the dissemination of terrorist content online (OJ L 172, 1752021, pp. 79–109).

due regard to the rights and legitimate interests of all parties involved, including the fundamental rights of the recipients of the service, such as the freedom of expression, freedom, and pluralism of the media, and other fundamental rights and freedoms as enshrined in the Charter.

In other words, the DSA infuses public-law ideas and administrative-law procedures into the otherwise private governance of online platforms. In response to this intensifying regulatory framework, platforms ramped up procedures, formulated norms, trained people, and formalized structures that could be characterized as "private bureaucracies."[167] Social media platforms must deal with notices, state reasons, and take down content that might be illegal.[168] In some cases, platforms are in effect auxiliary agents of public power.[169] In consequence, legal scholarship is increasingly conceptualizing platforms, more specifically content moderation, as systems of administration or even as bureaucracies.[170]

As a result, Balkin concludes, we observe a "burgeoning dialectic of governing power and public-private cooperation. Private infrastructure companies develop greater governing capacities than ever."[171] Indeed, governmental pressure on platforms has grown in recent years. In sum, regulatory frameworks like the DSA oblige platforms to enforce regulatory interests relating to copyright, personal rights or criminal law, for instance, which in practice compels platforms to be *functional* administrators. In turn, analyzing platforms through the lens of administrative law appears imperative.

2.3.8 *Autochthonous Administrification*

The previous sections showed how regulatory co-option molds social media platforms into ever more administration-like entities. However, regulatory endowment is not the only driver behind platforms' burgeoning private bureaucracies. Platforms' emulation of administration-inspired rulemaking and rule enforcement reflects demands from users – and, perhaps more importantly, ad-buyers – for "clean"

167 Balkin, 'Free Speech Is a Triangle' (n 123) 2021.

168 C-18/18 (Glawischnig-Piesczek) [2019] European Court of Justice ECLI:EU:C:2019:821 33–47; Clara Rauchegger and Aleksandra Kuczerawy, 'Injunctions to Remove Illegal Online Content under the eCommerce Directive: Glawischnig-Piesczek' (2020) 57 Common Market Law Review 1495.

169 That is particularly relevant in cases like Glawischnig-Piesczek (n 168).

170 Douek (n 55) 530 et seq; Balkin, 'Free Speech Is a Triangle' (n 123) 2021 et seq. Also arguing for a more administrative law inspired perspective on platform governance Schramm, 'Where Is Olive? Or: Lessons from Democratic Theory for Legitimate Platform Governance' (n 56).

171 Balkin, 'Free Speech Is a Triangle' (n 123) 2020.

platforms.[172] Users and investors demand a platform that is not littered with hate speech, sexism, or xenophobia.

To achieve this, platforms established their own rulemaking and enforcement regimes to monitor and regulate the communications of their users.[173] Faced with growing demands to take down harmful or violent speech, platform companies morphed from mere technology companies to complex regulatory bureaucracies.[174] As Kate Klonick's extensive empirical work shows, "platforms have developed a system that has marked similarities to legal or governance systems. This includes the creation of a detailed list of rules, trained human decision-making to apply those rules, and reliance on a system of external influence to update and amend those rules."[175] In turn, the intricate work of nudging such complex bureaucracies toward normatively desirable behavior is familiar – and has been well documented for social media platforms, particularly in the area of privacy.[176]

This private rulemaking appears deficient from an administrative law perspective or, in fact, any normative position linked to a notion of self-governance and publicness. Although platforms' private rulemaking is comprehensive, it remains incoherent and imprecise.[177] Still, social media platforms devise their rules unilaterally. Rulemaking remains largely decoupled from the "meaningful consent" (to quote Suzor) by the users whose behavior the platforms govern.[178] Rulemaking on platforms has been described as autocratic[179] and authoritarian[180] but, due to its pervasiveness and normative properties, also as "quasi-legislative" or simply as

[172] cf. Klonick, 'The New Governors: The People, Rules, and Processes Governing Online Speech' (n 55) 1625 et seq; Gillespie, *Custodians of the Internet* (n 55) 74 et seq.

[173] Seminal: Klonick, 'The New Governors: The People, Rules, and Processes Governing Online Speech' (n 55); see also Gillespie, *Custodians of the Internet* (n 55) 5 et seq.

[174] Klonick, 'The New Governors: The People, Rules, and Processes Governing Online Speech' (n 55) 1630–1669; Balkin, 'Free Speech Is a Triangle' (n 123) 2028–2032; De Gregorio (n 104) 110–122.

[175] Klonick, 'The New Governors: The People, Rules, and Processes Governing Online Speech' (n 55) 1602.

[176] See especially the empirically grounded contribution by Ari Ezra Waldman on information companies' (i.e., Google, Facebook, etc.) handling of privacy. Waldman argues that motivated and high-minded privacy professionals nonetheless tacitly embrace anti-privacy discourse and policies as they are swallowed by the platforms' thrust towards exploiting rather than protecting privacy, Waldman (n 22) 7–8, 210 et seq.

[177] See especially at 4.4 and 5.2.

[178] cf. Suzor, *Digital Constitutionalism: Using the Rule of Law to Evaluate the Legitimacy of Governance by Platforms* (n 56) 5.

[179] Balkin, 'Free Speech Is a Triangle' (n 123) 2024.

[180] De Gregorio (n 104) 116; Evelyn Douek, 'Facebook's "Oversight Board:" Move Fast with Stable Infrastructure and Humility' (2019) 21 North Carolina Journal of Law & Technology 1, 10.

"law."[181] Although I am skeptical when it comes to equating platform rulemaking with blurry, legitimacy-seeking notions like "quasi-legislative,"[182] the fact remains that platforms have huge influence in the way they frame and present the norms their private owners deem appropriate.

Further, the administration/administrative law analogy does not stop at cases where platforms are co-opted by governments or when they make and enforce "rules." The analogy also pertains to the way digital infrastructures are designed by platforms. This "administrification" goes beyond formal rulemaking but includes, especially, infrastructure design and programming.[183] What do users see, and when? Do algorithms nudge people to attack and insult other users?[184] A good way to think about all these questions is inspecting them through the method and mindset ofadministrative law. Imagine, for example, a big highway. When the local transport authority plans such a highway, it must discuss plans with the public, make an environmental impact assessment, and may not build it right through a national park. Similar design principles are imaginable for social media platforms too.

Arguing for a more nuanced understanding of the many ways platforms influence user behavior and regulate speech, Evelyn Douek has highlighted that it would be wrong to understand content moderation as "just the aggregation of many (many!) binary decisions to take down or leave up individual pieces of content."[185] Instead, Douek argues, content moderation "is a vast *system of administration* that includes a far broader range of decisions and decision-makers than the standard picture admits."[186] This book further explores the descriptive and normative

[181] De Gregorio (n 104) 117; Luca Belli, Pedro Augusto Francisco and Nicolo Zingales, 'Law of the Land or Law of the Platform? Beware of the Privatisation of Regulation and Police' in Luca Belli and Nicolo Zingales (eds.), *Platform Regulations: How Platforms Are Regulated and How They Regulate Us [Official Outcome of the UN IGF Dynamic Coalition on Platform Responsibility]* (FGV Direito Rio 2017) 44 et seq; Orly Lobel, 'The Law of the Platform' (2016) 101 Minnesota Law Review 87, 142 et seq; adopted by David Kaye, 'Report of the Special Rapporteur on the Promotion and Protection of the Right to Freedom of Opinion and Expression' (United Nations Human Rights Council 2018) A/HRC/38/35.

[182] See in detail Cowls, Darius, Santistevan and Schramm (n 3).

[183] See further Douek (n 55).

[184] This is apparently what happened at Facebook, cf. Merril and Oremus (n 130).

[185] Douek, 'Content Moderation as Systems Thinking' (n 55) 530–531; the extent to which what Douek calls the "standard picture" was indeed prevalent is disputed, see esp. Kate Klonick, 'Of Systems Thinking and Straw Men' (2023) 136 Harvard Law Review Forum 339; see also already regarding platform governance in general Robert Gorwa, 'What Is Platform Governance?' (2019) 22 Information, Communication & Society 854.

[186] Douek, 'Content Moderation as Systems Thinking' (n 55) 530–531 (emphasis added).

implications of content moderations (and, by extension, private governance's) resemblance to administration. So far, the literature only mentioned the resemblance or used administration as a metaphor but did not really dig into the normative "downstream consequences."[187]

2.4 From Public to Private: Emulation

We have now examined the phenomenon of individual rights adjudication and have justified our administrative-law perspective on social media platforms' private governance. Individual rights adjudication is an institutionalized – meaning, widely used and expected – method for controlling public power. Platforms now wield huge power. And yet, as the previous section argued, platforms are *private* organizations – so why and crucially, how would they adopt quintessentially *public*-law ideas?

To also theorize this last part of the analytical framework I now zoom out from the public-law perspective adopted above and invite the reader to don their sociology and political science glasses once again. In previous remarks, I anticipated that organizations conform to societal institutions, like individual rights adjudication, to increase their legitimacy.[188] We can now unpack this process of organizational conformance and identify its most important but double-edged tool: *emulation*.

The argument goes as follows: organizations want to appear legitimate. Platforms are powerful organizations that engage in extensive administration-like practices. They create a space where private individuals can exercise their rights, make rules regulating how their users interact, and enforce the rules governing this space. However, we – meaning the public, regulators, and scholars – instinctively perceive uncontrolled power as illegitimate, especially if it can potentially erode individual and societal communication and fundamental rights. At the political level, therefore, attempts are being made to regulate this "digital public sphere" and make private power's private governance of crucial public rights like freedom of expression more accountable. In turn, social media platforms arguably try to avoid regulation or even a breaking-up of their business models by making the exercise of their power appear more efficiently (self-)controlled and thus more legitimate.[189] In their attempts to legitimize this exercise of power –

[187] Ibid 584 et seq.

[188] See above at 2.1.

[189] The Federal Trade Commission (FTC), the US consumer protection and antitrust watchdog, lodged several complaints with the goal of potentially breaking up Facebook,

or at least, in the case of platforms, to make it appear legitimate – both actors decided roughly at the same time to do something that could represent a paradigm shift in private governance: they began *emulating* individual rights adjudication.

2.4.1 *Defining Emulation*

To emulate is to "imitate" and to "strive to equal or to excel."[190] Emulation comes from the Latin noun *aemulus*, or "rival," and the related verb *aemulare*, "to rival" or "to strive after another earnestly."[191] In this book we will encounter both meanings of emulation, connoting imitation, mimicry, and copying on the one hand, and innovation, rivalry, and competition on the other. In the social sciences, emulation is a concept used mainly in organizational sociology,[192] political science,[193] and, increasingly, law.[194] Political scientists and organizational sociologists have studied such patterns in intermingled but slightly diverging contexts, which are combined here to situate emulation in both the political and the sociological contexts of Emulated Guardians.

2.4.2 *Types of Emulation*

Based on Simmons et al., we can distinguish three types of emulation.[195] These types differ in how actors choose what policy or formal structure they deem "appropriate" to emulate. All types are featured in this book. In

Instagram, and WhatsApp. See e.g. Federal Trade Commission Facebook Inc, Case No 1:20-cv-03590 (Complaint for injunctive and other equitable relief) (United States District Court, District of Colombia).

190 Merriam Webster, emulate – meaning 1a and 1b, <https://perma.cc/GA24-A2H2>.

191 Online Etymology Dictionary, 'emulation (n),' accessible via: <https://perma.cc/8QED-6GXE>.

192 In sociology, emulation is used synonymously to "imitation" and "mimesis." See e.g. Paul J DiMaggio and Walter W Powell, 'The Iron Cage Revisited: Institutional Isomorphism and Collective Rationality in Organizational Fields' (1983) 48 American Sociological Review 147, 151 et seq.

193 In political science the term emulation was introduced by Eleanor Westney and became a discursive fixture. See Eleanor Westney, *Imitation and Innovation: The Transfer of Western Organizational Patterns to Meiji Japan* (Harvard University Press 1987) 9 et seq; Charles R Shipan and Craig Volden, 'The Mechanisms of Policy Diffusion' (2008) 52 American Journal of Political Science 840, 840 et seq; Beth A Simmons, Frank Dobbin and Geoffrey Garrett, 'Introduction: The Diffusion of Liberalization' in Beth A Simmons, Frank Dobbin and Geoffrey Garrett (eds.), *The Global Diffusion of Markets and Democracy* (Cambridge University Press 2008) 31 et seq; Fabrizio Gilardi and Fabio Wasserfallen, 'The Politics of Policy Diffusion' (2019) 58 European Journal of Political Research 1245.

194 Describing India's "emulation" of the GDPR: Bradford (n 161) 48.

195 Simmons, Dobbin and Garrett (n 193) 31 et seq.

practice, the types are interrelated and often converge. We distinguish between the "follow the leader" model, expert theorization, and normalization.

The first type is the "follow the leader" approach, in which social acceptance and notions of the "appropriateness" of policy choices emanate from exemplars of leading actors.[196] Emulating leading actors' policies and institutions is common practice in legal policies, especially in comparative law and the EU's legislative procedures.[197]

The second type is the emulation of policy choices or institutional designs because expert groups theorize and provide actors with a rationale to implement them.[198] Such "expert theorization" develops in epistemic communities that theorize, define, and sometimes lobby for new policy solutions or institutional designs for existing governance problems.[199] Here, no particular real-world example has to exist, although what it is that experts theorize about tends to be informed by existing policies and governance practices.[200]

Expert theorization was a strong driver behind the DSA's out-of-court dispute settlement bodies and the Oversight Board.[201] Decisive design choices for both the EU DSA's out-of-court dispute settlement bodies as well as Meta's Oversight Board were lobbied for and developed by scholars. The roles of experts, professionals, and scholars in legal and organizational practice have been extensively studied in organizational sociology and socio-legal scholarship.[202] Experts' stances and professional backgrounds will tend to inform their advice to policymakers and

[196] See ibid 34. See further Frances Stokes Berry and William Berry, 'Innovation and Diffusion Models in Policy Research' in Christopher M Weible and Paul A Sabatier (eds.), *Theories of Policy Process* (Routledge 2018) 230.

[197] Bradford (n 161) 10. See further David Vogel, *The Politics of Precaution: Regulating Health, Safety, and Environmental Risks in Europe and the United States* (Princeton University Press 2012).

[198] Simmons, Dobbin and Garrett (n 193) 34.

[199] Ibid 34–35.

[200] Ibid 35–36.

[201] See 4.2.

[202] See e.g. Päivi Leino-Sandberg, *The Politics of Legal Expertise in EU Policy-Making* (Cambridge University Press 2021); Antoine Vauchez, 'The Force of a Weak Field: Law and Lawyers in the Government of the European Union (For a Renewed Research Agenda)' (2008) 2 International Political Sociology 128; Tommaso Pavone, *The Ghostwriters: Lawyers and the Politics behind the Judicial Construction of Europe* (Cambridge University Press 2022); Antoine Vauchez and Bruno de Witte (eds.), *Lawyering Europe: European Law as a Transnational Social Field* (Hart 2013); Eric Stein, 'Lawyers, Judges, and the Making of a Transnational Constitution' (1981) 75 American Journal of International Law 1; Antonin Cohen and Antoine Vauchez, 'The Social Construction of Law: The European Court of Justice and Its Legal Revolution Revisited' (2011) 7 Annual Review of Law and Social Science 417.

executives of private companies. Or, put more bluntly, as one interviewee who advised Facebook on creating the Oversight Board put it:

> They could have started totally different paths. They could've issued three-page decisions like the [French] court of cassation does. It could've done that. It didn't. … It didn't do because of sociological factors, because they put a bunch of US lawyers in charge. What the fuck happens when you put a bunch of US lawyers in charge? Well, they started doing things that they're familiar with.[203]

This type of expert-driven emulation builds on input from experts conveyed to lawmakers or private-sector executives tasked with devising solutions to a particular governance problem. Whereas expert theorization's "appropriateness" may be more contested than the "follow the leader" type of emulation (two lawyers, three opinions, as the saying goes), expert-advised emulation banks on the social status of experts and their expertise. Another factor at play is the sheer constraint of time and resources faced by legislators. In particular, ambitious and time-sensitive projects like the DSA often rely on the expertise of people who deal with specific issues far more comprehensively than the average legislator can within the limits of their day-to-day.

Third, the emulation of policy choices or organizational designs often happens when the relevant policy choice and organizational design is considered by experts in the field or by the general public as a standard, a necessary operating procedure, or a norm.[204] The generating of norms, or "normalization," often builds on previous exemplars, which are then emulated based on the follow the leader model by other actors and on previous or subsequent theorization by experts.[205] As Simmons et al. note: "Once a new policy reaches a certain threshold, policymakers take it for granted as necessary."[206] This is very visible here. Platforms accrue more and more power. Therefore, accountability appears "appropriate." The "appropriate" form of accountability then, again, appears to be individual rights adjudication – after all freedom of speech is the one constant tune in this overture.

203 Interview with Academic, Consultant to Facebook in 2018 (1 November 2021).

204 See Simmons, Dobbin and Garrett (n 193) 37–40. What Simmons et al. describe as third and fourth type are bundled as one general type in this book.

205 Ibid 38.

206 Ibid 39.

2.4.3 *Policy Diffusion*

The intellectual history of emulation builds on two strands of scholarship. On one side it builds on research into policy diffusion, which examines how certain policies diffuse around the globe or within federal structures. Eleanor Westney first introduced the concept of emulation to comparative politics in a 1987 study of Japan's construction of "Western"-style institutions during the Meiji Restoration in the nineteenth century.[207] To evade colonization, Japan established a Western-style administrative system, legal frameworks, newspapers, and educational institutions. Within several years, formerly insular Japan had overhauled many of its institutional (as well as organizational) structures. Beth Simmons et al. contrast emulation with coercion (involuntary policy choices), competition (policy choices according to market expectations, that is, a general thrust toward liberalization), and learning (policy choices made after lengthy soul-searching, adapted to specific purposes, often inspired by others).[208] Political scientists describe such processes as *policy diffusion*.[209] Empirical research suggests that emulation is among the most common mechanisms of policy diffusion.[210] Actors reproduce preexisting policy choices because they deem them "appropriate."[211] What an actor considers "appropriate" is influenced by what the actor believes internal adversaries, relevant stakeholders, and the general public consider legitimate. As Eleanor Westney noted, "a foreign organizational model may be used [for emulation] to legitimate changes desired by innovators but which require justification by the appeal to the outside model."[212] Translated to our

[207] Westney (n 193) 9 et seq.

[208] Simmons, Dobbin and Garrett (n 193) 9 et seq.

[209] For an introduction see Simmons, Dobbin and Garrett (n 193); Shipan and Volden (n 193); Berry and Berry (n 196); Susanne Lütz, 'Policy-Transfer und Policy-Diffusion' in Arthur Benz and others (eds.), *Handbuch Governance: Theoretische Grundlagen und empirische Anwendungsfelder* (VS Verlag für Sozialwissenschaften 2007); Gilardi and Wasserfallen (n 193). For a critical assessment of the literature see Erin R Graham, Charles R Shipan and Craig Volden, 'The Diffusion of Policy Diffusion Research in Political Science' (2013) 43 British Journal of Political Science 673.

[210] Simmons, Dobbin and Garrett, 'Conclusion' in Simmons, Dobbin and Garrett (n 193) 353–355; Christine Min Wotipka and Francisco O Ramirez, 'World Society and Human Rights: An Event History Analysis of the Convention on the Elimination of All Forms of Discrimination against Women' in Simmons, Dobbin and Garrett (n 193); Shipan and Volden (n 193) 842–843.

[211] See also Chang Kil Lee and David Strang, 'The International Diffusion of Public Sector Downsizing: Network Emulation and Theory-Driven Learning' in Simmons, Dobbin and Garrett (n 193) 148.

[212] Westney (n 193) 27.

context: if a policy maker, Meta executive, or external consultant wants to change how the company is run, they might reference convincing outside examples how things are done in other contexts, for example, through "something like a Supreme Court." Correspondingly, a key denominator for what *is* considered appropriate and legitimate by actors throughout the case studies are the values and dogmas of two sociopolitical trends in Western governance since the 1950s: *juridification* and *judicialization*. Juridification is "a process in which human conflicts are torn through formalization out of their living context and distorted by being subject to legal processes."[213] In simple terms, juridification implies that we now interpret more issues as *legal* than we used to. The ever-increasing regulatory acquis on the domestic, supranational, and international levels provides ample anecdotal evidence.[214] Judicialization, in turn, refers to the institutions that benefit most from juridification: courts[215] and other adjudicators.[216] The more we see power imbalances as legal issues and the more we "juridify" and break down a governance actor's legitimacy into atomized rights disputes, the more powerful courts become. Evidence for judicialization has been observed for various systems, polities, and policies, from the United States to the European Union and its Member States, as well as in the workings of international law.[217] Examples range from the establishing of adjudicatory control over the burgeoning administrative state from the late-nineteenth century to landmark cases like *Brown v. Board of Education* in the United States

[213] Gunther Teubner, 'Juridification Concepts, Aspects, Limits, Solutions' in Gunther Teubner (ed.), *Juridification of Social Spheres* (De Gruyter 1987) 6. The main other text is Gunther Teubner (ed.), *Global Law without a State* (Dartmouth 1997). See for related approaches e.g. John H Barton, 'Behind the Legal Explosion' (1975) 27 Stanford Law Review 567; Eric A Posner, *The Perils of Global Legalism* (University of Chicago Press 2009); Lars C Blichner and Anders Molander, 'Mapping Juridification' (2008) 14 European Law Journal 36.

[214] Blichner and Molander (n 213).

[215] See Stone Sweet (n 51); Shapiro and Stone Sweet (n 51); Alec Stone Sweet, *The Judicial Construction of Europe* (Oxford University Press 2004).

[216] See e.g. Okayama (n 46); Merijn Chamon, Annalisa Volpato and Mariolina Eliantonio (eds.), *Boards of Appeal of EU Agencies: Towards Judicialization of Administrative Review?* (Oxford University Press 2022); Lamandini and Muñoz (n 50).

[217] Alec Stone Sweet, 'Judicialization and the Construction of Governance' (1999) 42 Comparative Political Studies 147; Alec Stone Sweet, *The Judicial Construction of Europe* (Oxford University Press 2004); Martin Shapiro and Alec Stone Sweet, *On Law, Politics, and Judicialization* (Oxford University Press 2002). Recently, critical voices are becoming more prominent see Fuad Zarbiyev, 'On the Judge Centredness of the International Legal Self' (2021) 32 European Journal of International Law 1139.

to *van Gend & Loos* in Europe.[218] Hence, paired with the sociopolitical and cultural significance of courts in Western discourses and cultures, the appropriate policy to emulate, almost self-evidently, has been adjudicative control over power. Norms and traditions that help to construct ideals of appropriateness may well conflict in detail, often leading to hybrid or adapted emulations trying to balance competing objectives and rationales. Yet policy diffusion is not the only perspective – especially because it does not account in full for why and when emulations fall short or remain uncompleted. For that, in the next part we need to turn to organizational sociology.

2.4.4 *Organization Theory*

The sociological angle then highlights the role of public legitimacy and the lingering danger of mere sugarcoating or, as Meyer and Rowan put it, ceremonial reforms. Organizations strive to appear more legitimate by conforming often uniformly to public demands of how a good organization should look like. Organizational theorists describe this emulation of what is seen elsewhere and considered "a best practice" – that is, this trend toward conformity – as *institutional isomorphism*.[219] That strand of work, soon called "neo-institutionalist," emerged in the 1980s as a response to then-dominant "rational choice" theories in sociology (and economics).[220] Rational choice perspectives posited that "efficient"

[218] See this chapter at 2.2.

[219] The concept "isomorphism" originates from mathematics, denoting a resembling relationship between mathematic, typically algebraic, structures. It derives from the ancient Greek words ἴσος (translit: isos) for "equal," and μορφή (translit: morphe) for "shape" or "form."

For the pioneering but largely forgotten work of Gabriel Tarde see his *The Laws of Imitation* (Henry Holt 1903) 37 et seq. See further Barbara Czarniawska, 'Gabriel Tarde and Organization Theory' in Paul Adler (ed.), *The Oxford Handbook of Sociology and Organization Studies* (Oxford University Press 2009) 258–260.

[220] Pioneering authors are John Meyer and Brian Rowan and later Walter Powell and Paul DiMaggio who studied the emergence of recurring patterns among various organizations, mainly in the private sector. Neo-institutionalism builds on classic accounts by Durkheim and Weber and the (often forgotten) work of Gabriel Tarde on imitation as the driving force behind social resemblance. See DiMaggio and Powell (n 192); John W Meyer and Brian Rowan, 'Institutionalized Organizations: Formal Structure as Myth and Ceremony' (1977) 83 American Journal of Sociology 340. For an overview see Swaran Sandhu, 'Grundlagen und Kernbegriffe des Neo-Institutionalismus' in Swaran Sandhu, *Public Relations und Legitimität* (Verlag für Sozialwissenschaften 2012) 74 et seq; Paul DiMaggio and Walter W Powell (eds.), *The Neo-Institutionalism in Organizational Analysis* (University of Chicago Press 1991). For a good historical contextualization see R Jepperson, 'The Development and Application of Sociological Neoinstitutionalism

organizational patterns prevail, whereas inefficient patterns fade away. In contrast, neo-institutionalists argue that many organizational patterns and structures are not necessarily "rational" in terms of efficacy but reflect social and culturally constructed patterns, models, ideas, and a consensus regarding what constitutes a "good" and "legitimate" organization.[221] Since organizations compete for "political power and institutional legitimacy," they seek to appear as legitimate as possible.[222] One common and relatively easy way to do so is to emulate institutions and organizations that are widely accepted as legitimate. This is why corporate actors have established a panoply of guardianship-oriented institutions ranging from compliance departments to auditors, diversity reports or, as this book shows, self-styled adjudicators.

Notably, emulation often leads to *ceremonial* changes in the formal structure instead of deep-rooted changes in "policy or strategy."[223] Emulating ceremonies and formal structures is more easily observable by the public and is perhaps for this reason more effective from a self-regulatory perspective, even though more complex policy changes may be "less easily noticed."[224] Again, the reason is that a ceremonial add-on like a new adjudicator promises immediate societal legitimacy. In contrast, a lengthy overhaul of internal governance practices may go unnoticed by the public.[225] Hence, as Meyer and Rowan argued: "the formal structures of many organizations … dramatically reflect the myths of their institutional environments instead of the demands of their work activities."[226] In simple terms, the myth this book investigates is that ever more adjudicators bring more justice.

The "myths" of out-of-court dispute settlement bodies and the Oversight Board's institutional environment arise from the sociocultural significance of individual rights, judicial review, and widespread belief in an ever-increasing "judicialization" of politics and governance.[227] Empirical data compiled by sociologists for decades suggests that

(2002)' in John W Meyer and Ronald L Jepperson (eds.), *Institutional Theory: The Cultural Construction of Organizations, States, and Identities* (Cambridge University Press 2021) 67 et seq.

221 Seminal: Meyer and Rowan (n 220).

222 DiMaggio and Powell (n 192) 150.

223 Ibid 152.

224 Ibid.

225 Ibid 155.

226 Meyer and Rowan (n 220) 341.

227 See e.g. Stone Sweet (n 51); Shapiro and Stone Sweet (n 51); Stone Sweet (n 215); Stein (n 202); Pavone (n 202); Jack M Balkin, 'What Is Postmodern Constitutionalism?' (1992) 90 Michigan Law Review 1966. Largely critical, albeit from different perspectives: Hjalte Rasmussen, *On Law and Policy in the European Court of Justice: A Comparative Study in*

organizations use emulation to establish ceremonial, formal structures that are decoupled from the organizations' work requirements. Doing new things, building fresh formal structures, and (metaphorically) putting on a new ceremony may merely serve to project a legitimizing image onto essentially unchanged practices. From the start, organizational sociologists highlighted the risk of *decoupling* between emulated, ceremonial structures shown to the outside and organizations' internal practices which often did not conform to the narratives characterizing the organization's public image.[228] Meyer and Rowan argued: "To maintain ceremonial conformity, organizations that reflect institutional rules tend to buffer their formal structures from the uncertainties of technical activities by becoming loosely coupled, building gaps between their formal structures and actual work activities."[229] Such decoupling serves as a clear warning. If out-of-court dispute settlement bodies or the Oversight Board were merely ceremonial, formal structures decoupled from the activities they were supposed to control, then they could be considered a failure from a public law perspective.

2.4.5 Legal Transplants

Lastly, we should distinguish emulation, as presented in political science and sociological scholarship, from *legal transplants*, a notion from the field of comparative law. Legal transplants are normative regimes originating in a particular legal system that is then adopted by other legal systems.[230] These political science and sociological viewpoints have two advantages over a legal transplant perspective. First, legal transplants refer chiefly to legal norms and not to organizations. Even though more recent scholars studying legal transplants have taken a more context-oriented perspective, the key question is still how a specific set of norms fit into another

Judicial Policymaking (Nijhoff 1986); Gerald N Rosenberg, *The Hollow Hope Can Courts Bring About Social Change?* (University of Chicago Press 1991); Michael Blauberger and others, 'ECJ Judges Read the Morning Papers. Explaining the Turnaround of European Citizenship Jurisprudence' (2018) 25 Journal of European Public Policy 1422; Lani Guinier, 'From Racial Liberalism to Racial Literacy: Brown v. Board of Education and the Interest-Divergence Dilemma' (2004) 91 Journal of American History 92; Emma Kaufman, 'The New Legal Liberalism' (2019) 86 University of Chicago Law Review 187.

228 Meyer and Rowan (n 220) 341 et seq.

229 Ibid 341.

230 For a legal theory perspective on the latter see foundationally *Alan Watson, Legal Transplants: An Approach to Comparative Law* (2nd ed., University of Georgia Press 1993). As well as the useful introduction by William Ewald, 'Comparative Jurisprudence (II): The Logic of Legal Transplants' (1995) 43 The American Journal of Comparative Law 489.

legal system.[231] Here, however, we mainly see evidence of the emulation of a formal structure – for example, the Oversight Board and Article 21 DSA emulating adjudicators – but not necessarily the "transplanting" of legal norms. On the contrary. As we will see in the case studies, many legal norms that might be of great value are not "transplanted" to their new context in private governance. Perhaps the most crucial aspect is the adjudicators' authority. In any serious rule of law system, it is "axiomatic" (using Paul Craig's word) that adjudicators protect individual rights, in one way or another, by *bindingly* deciding disputes between individual and public power structures.[232] However, the authority of both the Emulated Guardians studied here to bindingly decide cases concerning the activities of social media platforms is severely limited. Hence, perhaps the most fundamental rule of individual rights adjudication has not been successfully transplanted into private governance. If this is the case, then out-of-court dispute settlement bodies and the Oversight Board are the opposite of legal transplants. They transplant an institution – the adjudicator – without transferring the underlying norms. Chapter 5 details how this incomplete emulation impedes both bodies' roles and activities as guardians.

2.4.6 *"Designing This Thing"*

Applied to the Emulated Guardians studied here, we may theorize that their creators – the EU and Meta – emulate existing practices, here: individual rights adjudication, to conform to societal expectations. In other words, organizations emulate other organizations, policies, or institutions because they wish to be perceived as legitimate and because existing policies, role models, and institutions demonstrably work. Bound by time and resource constraints, large organizations – private and public – cannot search for a comprehensive solution for each governance problem. Instead, they "borrow heavily from their neighbors and ideological peers."[233] As one interviewee said:

[231] See e.g. Pierre Legrand, 'The Return of the Repressed: Moving Comparative Legal Studies Beyond Pleasure' (2001) 75 Tulane Law Review 1033; Liesel Spencer, 'Comparative Legal Geography – Context and Place in "Legal Transplants"' in Tayanah O'Donnell, Daniel F Robinson and Josephine Gillespie (eds.), *Legal Geography: Perspectives and Methods* (Routledge 2020) 149 et seq.

[232] cf. Paul P Craig, *EU Administrative Law* (3rd ed., Oxford University Press 2018) 265.

[233] Graeme Boushey, *Policy Diffusion Dynamics in America* (Cambridge University Press 2010) 25; Simmons, Dobbin and Garrett (n 193) 32; DiMaggio and Powell (n 192).

[We looked at] an ideational structure ... like what understandings from the background could be learned ... to design this thing.[234]

Hence, when the EU regulates the internal digital market, or Meta presumably tries to escape regulation, this involves making a policy choice that would be widely understood as legitimate. In the very first memos sketching the outline of the Oversight Board, the Board's court-like structure was praised as its most important asset because this would make it, literally, "widely understood as legitimate."[235] In turn, the EU equally strove to infuse legitimate procedures into social media companies' private governance and thus initially sought to subject private power to "simplified legal procedures" that would "fit the nature of content moderation disputes."[236]

Creating adjudicatory oversight to protect the rights of individuals is something we might generally consider legitimate. After all, who would object to more individual rights protection? Politicians, managers, and consultants, for all kinds of justified practical reasons, cannot devise an "original" solution for every governance problem. Arguably, few genuinely "new" solutions exist anyway since all ideas build on previous notions and experiences. It is thus natural that decision-makers draw inspiration from the wealth of existing models; drawing inspiration and even reproducing and emulating is a common form of human and organizational learning. Therefore, in principle, emulation is neither "good" nor "bad."

However, adopting models that have been devised elsewhere requires careful fitting.[237] Even the most attractive-looking ready-to-wear garment will not fit if you pick the wrong size. In the next chapters we will assess whether ODSs and the Oversight Board indeed "fit" their new contexts.

2.4.7 *The Wrong Role Model?*

Further, from a more critical perspective and beyond questions surrounding the power relationships between individual and platform, the idea that more adjudication leads to more justice rests on shaky ground. If emulating judicial control over administrative power is to

234 Interview with Academic, Consultant to Facebook in 2018 (n 203).

235 Noah Feldman, 'Facebook Supreme Court: A Governance Solution (March 2018), Published in: Global Feedback and Input on the Facebook Oversight Board for Content Decisions Appendix, Appendix D' 104; See further Douek (n 180) 46 et seq.

236 European Parliament Committee on Legal Affairs and Tiemo Wölken (Rapporteur) (n 5) 22.

237 cf. Richard Harvey Brown, 'Bureaucracy as Practice: Towards a Political Phenomenology of Formal Organizations' (1978) 23 Administrative Science Quarterly 365, 375.

work, as argued above, it requires an actor in an agreed leadership position to follow or adapt theorization of a functioning model. The specific exemplars and theorizations contributing to Emulated Guardians share their epistemological basis in the rise of courts and rights-based approaches that have arisen since the 1950s in the United States and Europe.[238] However, these meta-narratives of "rights-based approaches" enabling individuals as controllers of powerful institutions have been criticized from historical, political, and sociological perspectives.[239] Famously, Gerald Rosenberg argued that courts are a "hollow hope," which often cannot bring about social change. Courts that tend to align, so the critique goes, with public opinion more often than not (as Friedman argues) often fail to implement structural changes. Even landmark cases like *Brown v. Board of Education* may be pyrrhic victories placating lawyers, activists, and policymakers with the self-aggrandizing idea of changing institutional practice with one normative verdict issued after judicial processes, or ceasing to control public power altogether because of institutional self-interest.

Therefore, the leading exemplars from the state context and their theories championing the power of courts and the normative traction of individual rights are perhaps compromised. In fact, over the short period of writing this book, the approval ratings of the US Supreme Court dipped from a ten-year high of 58 percent in July 2020 to a record low of only 39 percent approval in July 2025. And, to add more anecdotal evidence, whenever presenting the research on this book to a US American audience at least one person would question the wisdom of emulating what more and more people consider a flawed institution.[240] This does not mean that individual rights adjudication is

[238] For an overview see Charles R Epp, *The Rights Revolution: Lawyers, Activists, and Supreme Courts in Comparative Perspective* (University of Chicago Press 1998); Reza Banakar (ed.), *Rights in Context: Law and Justice in Late Modern Society* (Ashgate Pub Co 2010). Also, European integration and the "constitutionalization" of its treaties can be understood as a rights-based approach which made the individual an "auxiliary agent of the Community," see Robert Lecourt, *L'Europe des juges* (Bruylant 2008).

[239] Guinier (n 227). See further Rosenberg (n 227); Barry Friedman, *The Will of the People: How Public Opinion Has Influenced the Supreme Court and Shaped the Meaning of the Constitution* (Farrar, Straus and Giroux 2009); Kaufman (n 227). For the European context and the ECJ's backtracking of some of its citizenship jurisprudence see Blauberger and others (n 227).

[240] Skepticism toward prominent courts is, of course, a recurring phenomenon not necessarily limited to one particular political perspective.

not a hallmark of legitimate government and deserving of praise and repurposing in new governance contexts. Yet when emulating individual rights adjudication, such criticism provides valuable insights into the parameters, circumstances, and conditions essential for effective adjudicatory control of power.

This is not the place to discuss whether the above critiques are entirely accurate. Yet, the abovementioned criticism provokes the question of whether emulating individual rights adjudication to control platform power is the correct approach at all. Suppose traditionally constituted adjudicators are criticized for sometimes failing to protect individuals in the face of power imbalances vis-à-vis powerful administrative institutions. How can emulated adjudicators, often with markedly inferior authority and legitimacy, fare any better? Are there perhaps other, more innovative forms of controlling power equally able to protect individuals from the largest administrators of the twenty-first century? Evidence from the case studies presented here, especially those in the private realm, therefore require us to ask the question Martin Laughlin bitingly posed for public law in general: does it make sense to base "a political order on individual rights, and therefore paradoxically basing the legitimacy of society on a thoroughly asocial principle?"[241]

Chapter 6 engages deeper with these criticisms. But as the first wave of organizational and normative emulations in the form of the DSA and the Oversight Board consolidates itself, we can fairly say that thinking about rights permeates legislation, self-regulation, and academic approaches like "digital constitutionalism."[242] Ultimately, the fact that discourses around controlling platform power have homed in on relationships between individualized (and therefore relatively powerless) users and independent, autonomous, dominant platforms shows how individual rights can become merely an affirmatory feature in the operation of power instead of power's counterbalance.[243] In much the same vein, Douek recently called for a more systemic approach to content moderation, arguing that "the current regulatory focus on procedure in *individual cases* is a mistake."[244] Therefore, emulating individual rights adjudication must not appear as a "natural"

[241] Martin Loughlin, *The Idea of Public Law* (Oxford University Press 2004) 130.

[242] See e.g. Redeker, Gill and Gasser (n 104); De Gregorio (n 104) 273 et seq.

[243] cf. Nikolas Rose and Peter Miller, 'Political Power beyond the State: Problematics of Government' (1992) 43 British Journal of Sociology 173, 174.

[244] Douek (n 55) 532.

evolutionary step for the judicial process tailing the locus of power from the public domestic level to the supranational level and then to private actors. Instead, it may equally well reproduce those power dynamics and mechanisms that tend to stabilize existing power structures.

2.5 Conclusion

This chapter introduced Emulated Guardians as the book's key concept. Drawing from administrative law, political science, and organizational sociology it argued that ostensibly "new" governance solutions like the Oversight Board or the EU's out-of-court dispute settlement bodies are in fact reproductions of preexisting, culturally venerated role models. Such emulations are particularly attractive for the emulator as they often build on best practice in different contexts and, by extension, promise public legitimacy for the solution of the problem at hand. However, emulation is not easy. Many role models function only under specific contextual factors. These contextual factors – like an overall commitment to the rule of law, legitimate rulemaking, and extensive adjudicatory authority – are not necessarily given in new contexts. In such cases, emulation may demise to mere ceremony that cloaks organizations in the legitimizing appearance of accountability albeit the Emulated Guardians are rather powerless. However, crucially, the Emulated Guardians studied here reproduce individual rights adjudication, which is at the cusp of our contemporary sociocultural imaginary. That public imagination about courts, rights, and their power – potentially – lends power to Emulated Guardians vis-à-vis the power structures they control. After all, also courts incrementally expanded their authority vis-à-vis public power through bold moves and public support. The next two chapters, investigate to what extent out-of-court dispute settlement bodies and the Oversight Board can indeed deliver on that promise.

Thus, abstractly spoken, studying new phenomena through the prism of emulation is not limited to the Oversight Board, the DSA, content moderation or the internet. Quite the contrary. As emulations' underlying social mechanism – an easy way to attract public legitimacy – is so fundamental, we will likely see many more emulations of accountability mechanisms guarding (or pretending to guard) future power structures. Concretely, both the Oversight Board as well as out-of-court dispute settlement bodies are designed to be emulated.[245] Further, one may read the whole book as an allegory for future struggles of legal and adjudicatory authority in (privately dominated) transnational governance.

245 Meta's "Corporate Human Rights Policy" explicitly states: "We believe the Oversight Board breaks new ground for access to remedy in the social media industry, and hope it serves as a useful model for other companies and initiatives," at 03, accessible via: <https://perma.cc/EK3G-FC7E>. The EU designed the whole DSA to be a "global standard-setter," European Commission, Proposal for a Regulation of the European Parliament and of the Council on a Single Market for Digital Services (Digital Services Act) and amending Directive 2000/32/EC 2020 [COM(2020) 825 final] explanatory memorandum at 2.

3 Out-of-Court Dispute Settlement Bodies

3.1 Introduction

After the contextual *tour de force* in the previous chapter, we now focus on the first of our two protagonists, the European Union's out-of-court dispute settlement bodies (ODSs). This chapter explains the origin of these bodies, the legislative (and lobbying) fights that shaped them and scrutinizes their efficacy. As the book aims to offer generalizable insights as to how such regulatory projects are – and should (not) be – conducted, the chapter engages in some detail with *how* those bodies came about and whether they deliver on the Union's promise to make social media giants more accountable. Lastly, we will take a short look at the nascent implementation of the very first of these bodies, which became operational shortly before I finished this book. Although the final version of Article 21 Digital Services Act (DSA) – the legal foundation for ODSs – lacks several critical elements deemed essential by its proponents, early indications reveal a surprising, and perhaps hopeful, story of creativity and experimentation. However, that discussion is for later.[1] For now, it is essential – and, given the EU's broader regulatory drive to oversee diverse private governance regimes, from artificial intelligence to other sectors, highly insightful – to carefully examine the legal-political battles behind the EU's push to emulate individual rights adjudication for social media platforms in Europe. By *individual rights adjudication*, I mean the practice of constraining a large and powerful organization—historically the state, but now potentially digital corporations—through the independent adjudication of individual normative claims against that power structure.

[1] Impatient readers may leapfrog to 3.8.

So, how did the EU come up with the idea to emulate individual rights adjudication for social media platforms? It all begins with a tempting fresh narrative for the European Union, a uniquely integrated yet sometimes fragile norm-creating behemoth with occasional legitimacy anxieties. After more than a decade and an ongoing mélange of lagging reform, infighting over the Euro, populism, and Brexit, many EU officials picked up on the idea that the Union should again transform. This time, it was not the Court of Justice but the Union's regulatory machinery consisting of the legislating institutions and a host of agencies which, met with "benign neglect," grew to become a global regulatory powerhouse. By leveraging its own market size and contextual factors intrinsic to globalized markets, the EU, so the story goes, managed to position itself as a global norm-creator in matters ranging from food safety and privacy to freedom of expression.

Observations that the EU was expanding its global regulatory posture emerged concomitantly to much internal misfortune buffeting the Union since the failed 2006 constitutional reforms, and the financial and political crises that followed.[2] The phenomenon, which Anu Bradford coined the "Brussels Effect" in a 2012 article and popularized in a 2020 book, offered a fresh sense of purpose to a shaken and soul-searching Union.[3]

[2] The groundworks were laid by David Vogel's 2001 genealogy of the precautionary principle in food safety and environmental law, which risk-averse European regulators managed to (somewhat) globally establish as the US moved to a more laissez faire regulatory approach in the 1980s, David Vogel, 'The New Politics of Risk Regulation in Europe' [2001] Centre for Analysis of Risk and Regulation, London School of Economics and Political Science; David Vogel, *The Politics of Precaution: Regulating Health, Safety, and Environmental Risks in Europe and the United States* (Princeton University Press 2012). In a 2007 report, a Brussels think tank wrote "At the moment, the European Union and the United States are clearly the two 'regulators of the world,'" André Sapir, 'Fragmented Power: Europe and the Global Economy' (Bruegel 2007) 12. In 2009, Elliot Posner argued the dynamics in transatlantic regulation of financial services shifted "from cooperation skewed heavily toward the preferences of US officials and accepted grudgingly by European counterparts to a Euro-US regulatory condominium characterized by close interactions among decision makers and mutual accommodation," Elliot Posner, 'Making Rules for Global Finance: Transatlantic Regulatory Cooperation at the Turn of the Millennium' (2009) 63 International Organization 665, 666. In 2012, Anu Bradford coined the term *Brussels Effect* for what she described as "unprecedented and deeply underestimated global power that the European Union is exercising through its legal institutions and standards, and how it successfully exports that influence to the rest of the world," Anu Bradford, 'The Brussels Effect' (2012) 107 Northwestern University Law Review 1, 1. For more see Alasdair R Young, 'The European Union as a Global Regulator? Context and Comparison' (2015) 22 Journal of European Public Policy 1233, 1235; Joanne Scott, 'Extraterritoriality and Territorial Extension in EU Law' (2014) 63 American Journal of Comparative Law 87.

[3] Anu Bradford, *The Brussels Effect: How the European Union Rules the World* (Oxford University Press 2020); see also Scott (n 2).

According to Bradford, the Brussels Effect emerged incrementally, first as a side effect of internal market regulation, and then solidifying into a more external agenda.[4] Talk about the Brussels Effect seemed to have rejuvenated the political self-esteem of the EU as it generously offered yet another pillar of output legitimacy that seems to be widely embraced by EU politicians and officers. Once again, the good news came (largely) from the other side of the Atlantic,[5] and once again the protagonists were those EU institutions that were getting to grips with complex normative mechanisms and political strategies for advancing and safeguarding the Union's posture. Crucially, discussions about the Brussels Effect offered the EU a new arena to deliver results for its citizens and, thereby, bolster its output legitimacy. Interestingly, comparable developments can be seen in the United States, where weighing in on big tech appears to be one of the last bipartisan projects.[6]

Yet these debates about the Brussels Effect emerged against a backdrop of skepticism. Some scholars doubted the Union's ability to exert globe-spanning normative force, and criticism of the Brussels Effect grew louder as its assumptions, empirically derived assertions, and generalizations from specific cases came under increasing scrutiny.[7] Disregarding the skeptics, however, EU policymakers moved ahead and framed several signature initiatives at least partially in the language of the Brussels Effect.[8] A notable example of this is Regulation (EU) 2022/2065, commonly known as the DSA. Echoing Ursula von der Leyen's pitch in her State of the Union address in 2020 – the branding of that speech epitomizing political emulation

[4] cf. Bradford (n 3), 7 et seq, 25 et seq, Scott (n 2).

[5] As was already the case, famously, with Eric Stein, 'Lawyers, Judges, and the Making of a Transnational Constitution' (1981) 75 American Journal of International Law 1.

[6] See e.g. Lindsey Graham and Elizabeth Warren, 'When It Comes to Big Tech, Enough Is Enough (Guest Essay)' *New York Times* (27 July 2023).

[7] Alasdair R Young, 'The European Union as a Global Regulator? Context and Comparison' (2015) 22 Journal of European Public Policy 1233, 1236–1343; criticizing the "reductionist and monocausal" brushstrokes of the Brussels Effect: Abraham L Newman and Elliot Posner, 'Putting the EU in Its Place: Policy Strategies and the Global Regulatory Context' (2015) 22 Journal of European Public Policy 1316, 1321. Arguing that the EU is a global actor "past its peak" Charlotte Bretherton and John Vogler, 'A Global Actor Past Its Peak?' (2013) 27 International Relations 375, 386. See already much earlier assessments of the EU's lacking ability (or willingness) to "export" human rights norms via trade agreements Frank Hoffmeister, *Menschenrechts- und Demokratieklauseln in den vertraglichen Außenbeziehungen der Europäischen Gemeinschaft* (Springer 1998).

[8] See above n 6; For a general introduction to the DSA see esp. Martin Husovec, *Principles of the Digital Services Act* (Oxford University Press 2023).

on its own – the Commission "envisages the Digital Services Act as a standard-setter at global level."[9]

To set such a global standard and present itself to its citizens as potent protector of individual rights, most importantly of the rights to privacy and free expression, the EU embarked on an ambitious normative agenda. In essence, the DSA seeks to inject certain administrative-law principles – like nondiscrimination, proportionality, and a duty to give reasons for individual decisions – into platforms' private governance structures. I call this the "administrification" of content moderation (and platform governance in general).[10] This administrification provides the broader context in which Emulated Guardians operate. On the other hand, the DSA seeks to protect individuals by offering them individualized, independent, adjudication-inspired redress mechanisms, known as ODS. As their genesis and future practice shows, these ODSs are what this book calls Emulated Guardians.

Out-of-court dispute settlement bodies are private, certified, independent adjudicators that are set up to decide on disputes between individual users and online platforms regarding content moderation. Although ODSs were initially introduced as powerful alternatives to the judicial process, some lawmakers even labeled them "sub-courts", though their authority, as we shall see, was watered down in the legislative process.

The key observation is that ODSs innovatively merge public and private law control mechanisms, which might sharpen the regulatory tools needed to control platforms' private power. With public law I mean administrative and constitutional law.[11] Out-of-court dispute settlement bodies' accessibility, expertise, flexibility, and speed of response potentially make them serious actors in as yet the sole emerging panoply of guardian institutions for the digital public sphere. However, ODSs also have structural deficits that will likely impair their ability to exercise control over platforms' burgeoning private bureaucracies and algorithmic infrastructures. Among these structural deficits are their lack of binding decision-making powers, the timidity of their proposed cost incentives for platforms, and their narrow focus on rule enforcement for platforms rather than on platform design and rulemaking.

[9] European Commission, Proposal for a Regulation of the European Parliament and of the Council on a Single Market for Digital Services (Digital Services Act) and amending Directive 2000/32/EC 2020 [COM(2020) 825 final] explanatory memorandum at 2.

[10] See at 2.3 and generally Moritz Schramm, 'Platform Administrative Law: A Research Agenda' (SSRN, 24 July 2024) <https://perma.cc/JH2A-8ZW2>.

[11] This is the European understanding of the term public law, see 1.5 and 1.6.

Nonetheless, ODSs could still prove valuable in resolving disputes, potentially ending a significant portion of cases that might otherwise spiral into costly and uncertain litigation. While it remains unclear how the mediation of simpler cases will influence the underlying structures of platforms' private governance systems, the broader benefit of resolving disputes quickly – through a process reminiscent of mediation but without burdening the judicial system – should not be overlooked (even if "mediation" is not really what ODSs do as there seems to be little communication between the parties). Importantly, the early examples of practice emerging since the first ODSs became operational in the summer of 2024 suggest that we can expect a diverse range of approaches. These may incrementally lend normativity to formally nonbinding decisions. Crucially, ODSs also may become important experiments for integrating large language models into mass decision-making frameworks.

We progress as follows. We first examine the political context of the DSA and trace the European Commission's internal discussions and deliberations as well as the ensuing legislative steps it has taken. This will enable us to reveal how Article 21 of the DSA combines public and private law influences. With public law I mean administrative, constitutional, and civil rights law. In turn, the term private law in this book refers to the law governing the relationships between natural and legal persons, such as contracts or company law. Then, building on this contextualization, the chapter moves on to analyze ODSs' institutional structure, the rules they apply, and the decisions they make. The chapter discusses how effectively ODSs might eventually implement the limited accountability mechanisms at their disposal, especially as mediators, before finishing with some final remarks.

3.2 Origins

First, we look at the origins of ODSs, which would be ultimately passed in Article 21 of the DSA. This section unpacks how EU lawmakers drew from several adjudicatory role models to give individual users an instrument to control social media platforms' private governance. Initial visions for ODSs were bold and ostensibly mirrored the public-law mechanism of individual rights adjudication. However, some of ODSs' key features did not survive the legislative process. Most notably, the version of ODSs that was eventually passed lacks binding decision-making powers. Because of this, ODSs only imperfectly emulate individual rights adjudication.

The whole legislative procedure that went into the making of Article 21 of the DSA, and perhaps of the DSA as a whole, can be viewed as a constant wrestling – sometimes constructive, sometimes destructive – between two competing visions for individual rights-based control of social media platforms in Europe. On the one hand, prominent voices in the legislative process championed a public-law perspective, epitomized by early approaches adopted by the European Parliament as well as the bodies' resemblance to individual rights adjudication. Proponents of this public-law perspective lobbied for binding decision-making authority for bodies brought into being and empowered by Article 21 of the DSA. This section therefore uncovers how Commission, Parliament, and Council (often in meetings known as "trilogues"), closely monitored by industry groups, discussed whether ODSs should have the power to "bind" the platforms they control to their adjudication. Eventually, the Council prevented the enacting of binding decision-making powers for out-of-court dispute settlement bodies. On the other hand, Article 21 of the DSA emulates aspects of private law, especially based on expert theorization that the EU should establish "compensated alternative dispute resolution (ADR) bodies" to economically incentivize platforms to improve their governance. However, only parts of this private law-inspired vision made it into the final text.

3.2.1 *Why Now?*

The conceptual starting point for the EU's regulatory overhaul of social media platforms is a change in the mood music of discourses about online platforms in general and social media platforms in particular.[12] Whereas debates in the 1990s and 2000s were dominated by internet enthusiasm, a string of scandals (e.g., Cambridge Analytica, Russian election interference) and political events (e.g., Brexit, the 2016 US Presidential election,

[12] For a variety of critical perspectives representing that mood swing, which is sometimes called "techlash," see e.g. Julie Cohen, *Configuring the Networked Self* (Yale University Press 2012); Rebecca MacKinnon, *Consent of the Networked: The Worldwide Struggle for Internet Freedom* (Basic Books 2012); Julie Cohen, 'Law of the Platform Economy' (2017) 51 University of California Davis Law Review 133; Jaron Lanier, *Ten Arguments for Deleting Your Social Media Accounts Right Now* (Macmillan 2018); Kate Klonick, 'The New Governors: The People, Rules, and Processes Governing Online Speech' (2018) 131 Harvard Law Review 1598; Stigler Center, 'Stigler Committee on Digital Platforms Final Report' (2019); Nicolas P Suzor, *Lawless: The Secret Rules That Govern Our Digital Lives* (Cambridge University Press 2019); Shoshana Zuboff, *The Age of Surveillance Capitalism: The Fight for a Human Future at the New Frontier of Power* (PublicAffairs 2019); Robert Gorwa, *The Politics of Platform Governance: How Governments Shape Online Content Moderation* (Oxford University Press 2024).

the displacement of the Rohingya) soured the political mood in which platforms operated in the mid-2010s. We should note that social media's most devastating effects do not occur in – still – relatively stable and institutionalized political systems like those of the United States or EU Member States, but in more fragile polities.[13] For example, according to the United Nations, Facebook played a "significant" role in the context of human rights violations against the Rohingya people in Myanmar in the 2010s.[14]

Correspondingly, ongoing transformations in the information economy,[15] like ever increasing "datafication" and social media platforms' constitutive role for public discourse, were increasingly being seen as problematic in Europe and elsewhere.[16] In particular, social media platforms like Twitter, now X, and Facebook were portrayed as threats to fundamental rights, democracy, and societal discourse.[17]

But although criticisms of online platforms were being made across the globe, only a few regulatory institutions appeared powerful enough to take on social media platforms. Especially in the US, stricter platform regulation seemed politically impossible for a long time. Some EU Member States pressed ahead with national regulation, the German *Netzwerkdurchsetzungsgesetz* (*NetzDG*), or Network Enforcement Act, being one prominent example.[18] Diverging regulatory approaches within the

[13] Although several developments in the US and some European Member States since the mid-2010s might have eroded confidence into their democratic commitment, these issues seem to remain (so far) on a level that is not outright lethal to large groups of the population. In political situations of civil war, violent persecution, and lethal unrest, social media can have effects like a combustive agent; for a brief reflection on the aftermath of the US 2024 election on this issue see Moritz Schramm, Marie Müller-Elmau and Anja Bossow, 'His Time Has Come' (*Verfassungsblog*, 9 November 2024) <https://perma.cc/4ZF5-6BXS>. See at 5.2.4 for how the Oversight Board dealt with Meta's handling of one such situation.

[14] Recital 74 Human Rights Council, 'Report of the Independent International Fact-Finding Mission on Myanmar, A/HRC/39/64' (United Nations General Assembly 2018).

[15] See in more detail 2.3. For an in-depth genealogy see Zuboff (n 12); Julie Cohen, *Between Truth and Power: The Legal Constructions of Informational Capitalism* (Oxford University Press 2019); remarkably blunt also: Stigler Center (n 12).

[16] See for more context at 2.3, 3.2, and 4.2.

[17] Recitals 1, 3 Commission proposal (n 9).

[18] For an overview see Andrej Lang, 'Netzwerkdurchsetzungsgesetz und Meinungsfreiheit' (2018) 143 Archiv des öffentlichen Rechts 220; Martin Eifert and others, *Netzwerkdurchsetzungsgesetz in der Bewährung* (Nomos 2020); Marc Liesching and Chantal Funke, *Das NetzDG in der praktischen Anwendung: eine Teilevaluation des Netzwerkdurchsetzungsgesetzes* (Carl Grossmann Verlag 2021).

For the US discourse, in contrast, see e.g. Eric Goldman, 'Why Section 230 is Better than the First Amendment' (2019) 95 Notre Dame Law Review 33.

internal market pushed the Union's window of political opportunity wide open. Domestic regulatory attempts risked fragmenting the internal market while their capacity to rein in globally active corporations appeared doubtful to say the least.[19] In contrast, the idea took hold that EU institutions would be able to put in place a uniform regulatory framework to harmonize the "digital single market," protect individual citizens and at the same time seek ways of establishing a global standard.[20] In political messaging, the focus on protecting fundamental rights was particularly strong. The DSA was repeatedly portrayed as a "worldwide first" for "protecting users' fundamental rights online" and with an "asymmetrical" focus – in other words, one that aimed to address the power imbalance between individuals and online platforms.[21]

3.2.2 *The DSA as a Political Opportunity*

Against this backdrop, we can view the DSA not only as the worldwide, innovative way of regulating platform power it claims to be[22] (and indeed is) but also as a political opportunity for the EU. For the EU, regulating online platforms is legitimizing because even those skeptical of "Brussels" tended to agree that the idea of single states regulating the internet's inherently globalized and transnational powers was infeasible.[23] Throughout the

[19] cf. Explanatory Memorandum at 2, 7–13 and Recital 2 Commission proposal (n 19).

[20] Recital 4 of the Commission proposal (n 9) reads: "[T]o safeguard and improve the functioning of the internal market, a targeted set of uniform, effective and proportionate mandatory rules should be established at Union level. … The approximation of national regulatory measures at Union level concerning the requirements for providers of intermediary services is necessary in order to avoid and put an end to fragmentation of the internal market and to ensure legal certainty, thus reducing uncertainty for developers and fostering interoperability." See further Husovec (n 8) 371–442.

[21] The quotes are from Council of the European Union, 'DSA: Council Gives Final Approval to the Protection of Users' Rights Online (Press Release)' (2022) <https://perma.cc/F85X-4QKF>; very confident also: Alexandra Geese, 'Why the DSA Could Save Us from the Rise of Authoritarian Regimes' (*Verfassungsblog*, 8 November 2022) <https://perma.cc/E44F-CFU4>.

See also Ursula von der Leyen's comment when political agreement was reached on the final version of the DSA in April 2022: "Today's agreement on #DSA is historic. Our new rules will protect users online, ensure freedom of expression and opportunities for businesses. What is illegal offline will effectively be illegal online in the EU. A strong signal for people, business & countries worldwide." Ursula von der Leyen, Twitter, now X, 23 April 2022 12:21 am, see at: <https://perma.cc/H2YW-4PKC>.

[22] For example, the Council declared after political deliberations had ended that "[t]he DSA is considered a world first in the field of digital regulation: no other legislative act has this level of ambition as regards regulating platforms and online supervision while preserving the core principles of the internal market," Council of the European Union (n 21).

[23] See recently on the topic of global policy struggles between the US, Europe, and China: Anu Bradford, *Digital Empires: The Global Battle to Regulate Technology* (Oxford University

legislative procedure, EU and Member States agreed to increase the level of harmonization over and above the Commission's original stipulations. The official Commission proposal argued only that the legal framework for online platforms "across the internal market should be harmonized."[24] The version of the DSA that was eventually passed states that it "fully harmonizes the rules" and that "[a]ccordingly, Member States should not adopt or maintain additional national requirements relating to the matters falling within the scope of this Regulation, unless explicitly provided for in this Regulation."[25]

Hence, a mix of fear of the unknown, individual grievances, notions of fundamental rights, and an understanding of digital corporations as a diffused, globalized threat allowed the EU to present itself as the prime guarantor of individual freedom and public discourse. Just months before the Commission published the DSA proposal, von der Leyen proclaimed in her 2020 State of the Union speech that "[w]e want a set of rules that puts people at the centre."[26]

And the Commission rushed to deliver. In December 2020, during the grim winter months of the second Covid lockdown, Berlaymont issued two broad legislative initiatives. These were the "Digital Markets Act," which focuses on the antirust aspects of the information economy, and the DSA, which infuses public law-inspired procedural rules into the user–platform relationship, especially regarding content moderation.

While the DSA's predecessor, the eCommerce Directive of 2000,[27] established only very limited procedural obligations for "online intermediaries," discussions in Member States and at the EU level reflected a more skeptical stance toward social media platforms. For example, in its impact assessment to the DSA, the Commission argued that social media platforms like Facebook or Twitter, now X, "can sometimes be compared to

Press 2023); Angela Huyue Zhang, *High Wire: How China Regulates Big Tech and Governs Its Economy* (Oxford University Press 2024); Mathew S Erie and Thomas Streinz, 'The Beijing Effect: China's Digital Silk Road as Transnational Data Governance' (2021) 54 New York University Journal of International Law and Policy 1.

[24] Recital 2 Commission proposal (n 9).

[25] Recital 9 Regulation (EU) 2022/2065 of the European Parliament and of the Council of 19 October 2022 on a Single Market for Digital Services and amending Directive 2000/31/EC (Digital Services Act).

[26] Ursula von der Leyen, 'State of the Union Address by President von der Leyen at the European Parliament Plenary' (Brussel, 15 September 2020) <https://perma.cc/8KWR-K873>.

[27] See esp. Article 15 Directive 2000/31/EC of the European Parliament and of the Council of 8 June 2000 on certain legal aspects of information society services, in particular electronic commerce, in the Internal Market ("eCommerce Directive").

public spaces for expression and economic transactions" but lack accountability.[28] The Commission also criticized platforms' lack of "oversight" and identified "an absence of checks and balances [for the platforms]. . . . This leaves citizens' rights vulnerable."[29] As evidenced in documents from this time, the Commission lawmakers' initial motives for creating the DSA focused on two elements: improving platforms' overall procedures and advancing some form of individual rights adjudication. In the words of the Commission, the DSA was to bring "more fairness, transparency and accountability for digital services' content moderation processes, . . . ensure that fundamental rights are respected, and guarantee . . . independent recourse to judicial redress."[30]

Therefore, from the very beginning of the legislative process, the Commission – in line with many academics[31] – viewed private online platforms like Facebook or Twitter through a public-law lens. In other words, the problem the Commission wanted to solve with the DSA was, apart from the reference to a fragmenting internal market, the power imbalance between individuals and the online platforms. For example, the Commission proposal stated its aims for the DSA as "to guarantee different public policy objectives such as the safety and trust of the recipients of the service, . . . protect the relevant fundamental rights enshrined in the Charter, . . . ensure meaningful accountability of those providers and . . . empower recipients and other affected parties."[32]

[28] 'Commission Staff Working Document, Impact Assessment, Accompanying the Commission Proposal for the DSA, Part 1/2. SWD(2020) 348 Final' 27.

[29] Ibid 25.

[30] Explanatory Memorandum at 2 in Commission proposal (n 9).

[31] Ahead of her time in (exploring the role of automated decision-making as form of administration and recommending "due process" for automated systems): Danielle Keats Citron, 'Technological Due Process' (2008) 85 Washington University Law Review 1249, 1301 et seq; Danielle Keats Citron and Helen L Norton, 'Intermediaries and Hate Speech: Fostering Digital Citizenship for Our Information Age' (2011) 91 Boston University Law Review 1435. See for recent examples the hugely influential Stigler report, which states that "Digital platforms are uniquely powerful political actors: Google and Facebook may be the most powerful political agents of our time. They congregate five key characteristics that normally enable the capture of politicians and that hinder effective democratic oversight: [money, media, complexity, connectivity, and national dominance]." See further calling platforms our "New Governors," Klonick (n 7); labelling platforms as systems of administration, Evelyn Douek, 'Content Moderation as Systems Thinking' (2022) 136 Harvard Law Review 526; arguing that platforms usurped the role of speech regulator from nation states, Balkin (n 15).

[32] Recital 4 Commission proposal (n 9).

This focus on fundamental rights, empowered individuals, and 'meaningful accountability' paved the way for the EU to emulate individual rights adjudication to control platforms.

3.2.3 *From Dyad to Triad*

As part of a shift toward using administrative-law mechanisms to improve platform-based procedures, the Commission and the EU Parliament considered "meaningful accountability"[33] and "independent recourse to judicial redress"[34] as crucial for the envisaged administrification of platforms' private governance. Interviewees repeatedly stressed that the DSA seeks to strengthen the individual vis-à-vis online platforms and that some form of adjudicative procedure was deemed necessary to provide people with the possibility of fair legal redress.[35]

However, judicial redress is a complicated affair. Traditional judicial institutions like courts are intricate structures, requiring a sound legal framework, complex institutional design, highly qualified staff, and judicial authority (a feature most transnational adjudicators only assert claims to over time).[36] In its proposal, the Commission stated that individuals "should be able to easily and effectively contest certain decisions of online platforms that negatively affect them."[37] But how to establish such a review system?

The initial idea to safeguard "independent recourse to judicial redress" had already split into three distinct assumptions under umbrella terms

[33] Recital 34 ibid.

[34] Explanatory Memorandum at 2 ibid.

[35] Interview with European Parliament Staffer 1 (17 November 2021); Interview with European Commission Staffer 1 (8 July 2022); Interview with European Commission Staffer 1 (29 October 2021); Interview with European Parliament, Staffer 2 (25 November 2022).

[36] cf. Karen J Alter, Laurence R Helfer and Mikael Rask Madsen, 'How Context Shapes the Authority of International Courts' in Karen J Alter, Laurence R Helfer and Mikael Rask Madsen (eds.), *International Court Authority* (Oxford University Press 2018) 24 et seq.

[37] Recital 44 Commission proposal (n 9). The finally passed version of the respective recitals reads: "Recipients of the service should be able to easily and effectively contest certain decisions of providers of online platforms concerning the illegality of content or its incompatibility with the terms and conditions that negatively affect them. . . . In addition, provision should be made for the possibility of engaging, in good faith, in the out-of -court dispute settlement of such disputes, including those that could not be resolved in a satisfactory manner through the internal complaint-handling systems, by certified bodies that have the requisite independence, means and expertise to carry out their activities in a fair, swift and cost-effective manner," Recitals 58, 59 Regulation (EU) 2022/2065 of the European Parliament and of the Council of 19 October 2022 on a Single Market For Digital Services and amending Directive 2000/31/EC (Digital Services Act).

like "contesting decisions that negatively affect" individuals. These three are, first, traditional opportunities to seek judicial redress at the EU or Member State level. Second was the provision that individuals could contest decisions directly against the decision-maker. This second form of contesting decisions that negatively impact individuals can take place by means of internal, nonindependent procedures, as evidenced by myriad types of administrative appeal procedures in public contexts. Third, and this will be the main focus here, the EU was obliged to seek a compromise between the first two options as neither of these seemed feasible or sufficient.

3.2.3.1 Judicial Review

We begin with "classic" judicial review. Of course, Member States would have had courts and other adjudicators at their disposal. However, administrifying platforms at the Union level just to hand over a crucial procedural mechanism – governing the review procedures when it came to platforms – to heterogenous and differently paced national judiciaries would not have matched the DSA's overall thrust. The DSA seeks to harmonize, not to pluralize.[38] Further, some interviewees who had dealt with the legislative procedure at an early stage pointed to a widespread understanding among EU lawmakers that national judicial procedures were of varying quality and, perhaps even more important, too slow.[39] National judicial processes arguably cannot offer the accessibility and speed the Commission wanted. Of course, anyone who thinks their content has been wrongly removed by a social media platform may initiate civil litigation (and some people do). But many of these judgments, for example decisions by Germany's Bundesgerichtshof also do not offer much more than the DSA does in this regard.[40] Again, the chosen normative tools are those known from administrative law: nondiscrimination, a duty to give reasons, perhaps a right to be

[38] The DSA explicitly states: "Member States are increasingly introducing, or are considering introducing, national laws on the matters covered by this Regulation. … Those diverging national laws negatively affect the internal market. … Therefore, in order to safeguard and improve the functioning of the internal market, a targeted set of uniform, effective and proportionate mandatory rules should be established at Union level. This Regulation provides the conditions for innovative digital services to emerge and to scale up in the internal market." Recitals 2, 4.

[39] Interview with European Parliament Staffer 1 (n 35); Interview with Academic, Consultant to the European Commission (29 June 2022).

[40] cf. Hassrede [2021] Federal Court of Justice (Bundesgerichtshof) III ZR 179/20 and III ZR 192/20 [83–89].

heard, and perhaps proportionality.[41] Either way, litigating before national courts is time-consuming and expensive and thus unsuited to achieving what the Commission's lawmakers wanted.

Further, demanding that EU courts deal with the expected mass of content moderation-related litigation was also a nonstarter. The European Court of Justice (ECJ)'s docket has a huge backlog and adjudicatory protection against EU agencies has already been partially outsourced to so-called Boards of Appeal.[42]

3.2.3.2 Internal Review

The second option is contending decisions directly against the decision-maker. The right to go back to the administrative actor to demand a second look and voice criticism is a classic one in administrative law.[43] Thus, the Commission included it in the DSA, which offers individuals access to an "internal complaint-handling system." According to Article 20(4) of the DSA, social media platforms

> shall handle complaints submitted through their internal complaint-handling system in a timely, non-discriminatory, diligent and non-arbitrary manner. Where a complaint contains sufficient grounds for the provider of the online platform . . . that the information to which the complaint relates is not illegal and is not incompatible with its terms and conditions, . . . it shall reverse its decision . . . without undue delay.

This provision codifies many ideas swirling around and would warrant its own chapter, which is beyond the scope of this study.[44] The administrifying intent of this provision is clear. It subjects platforms to the principle of non-discrimination and procedural consistency because platforms

[41] Ibid.

[42] See Michał Krajewski, *Relative Authority of Judicial and Extra-Judicial Review: EU Courts, Boards of Appeal, Ombudsman* (Hart 2021); Merijn Chamon, Annalisa Volpato and Mariolina Eliantonio (eds.), *Boards of Appeal of EU Agencies: Towards Judicialization of Administrative Review?* (Oxford University Press 2022); Moritz Schramm, 'Michał Krajewski, Relative Authority of Judicial and Extra-Judicial Review: EU Courts, Boards of Appeal, Ombudsman (Book Review)' (2023) 16 Review of European Administrative Law 125; Moritz Schramm, 'EU Review Bodies beyond the Judiciary' in Melanie Fink (ed.), *Access to Justice and the EU's Remedies System* (Cambridge University Press 2025).

[43] Paul P Craig, *EU Administrative Law* (3rd ed., Oxford University Press 2018) 320 et seq.

[44] See briefly Martin Eifert, Axel Metzger, Heike Schweitzer and Gerhard Wagner, 'Taming the Giants: The DMA/DSA Package' (2021) 58 Common Market Law Review 987, 1009–1014.

are prohibited from acting arbitrarily. Although not new,[45] this positive codification might have huge practical effects as it requires platforms to develop a normative corpus to safeguard the consistency of rulings. Given the millions of decisions that content moderation platforms make all the time (and the myriad design choices and rulemaking choices coloring every aspect of user behavior) "nonarbitrariness" requires a system of general and hierarchically structured rules to guide "downstream," user-facing decisions. Perhaps, this provision will be identified as the nucleus of platform-oriented administrative law in the future. But that is not our concern for now.

However, internal complaint-handling systems have one irredeemable flaw. They are not independent. Instead, the "complaint handler" is internal and keeps the dispute within the dyadic relationship of individual user and platform. The main function of such dyadic, internal complaint-handling mechanisms is to enhance the quality of decisions and to give decision-makers a second chance to undo mistakes before they become expensive, time-consuming, and potentially embarrassing. Such a forum for exercising "voice" is critical for users and, in principle, the easiest and most efficient form of reconciling disputes prior to the option of expanding dispute resolution into a triad. However, the dyadic nature of internal complaint-handling has clear limitations. Most importantly, the decision-maker on behalf of the governance structure – in our case the platform – does not substantially change. Perhaps other bodies further up the ladder decide complaints but those will be part of the same organizational entity. The internal units deciding those complaints are still entrenched in the platforms' hierarchy, must report to superior executives, and are subject to corporate policies, chief of which is the pursuit of profit.

Article 20 of the DSA seeks to remedy this entrenchment by stipulating that internal complaints must be handled in a nondiscriminatory, diligent, and nonarbitrary fashion. But what these terms mean remains murky. We do not know the criteria for "diligence," nor does the DSA stipulate the legal yardsticks against which the platforms are "reasonably" supposed to measure their nonarbitrariness. Surely, platform

[45] Regarding nondiscrimination in EU law Defrenne v Belgian State [1971] European Court of Justice C-80/70; Defrenne v SABENA [1976] European Court of Justice C-43/75; establishing equal protection based procedural obligations for private actors Stadionverbot [2018] Bundesverfassungsgericht 1 BvR 3080/09, BVerfGE 148, 267–290 [45–56]; for a theoretical perspective see already Niklas Luhmann, *Legitimation durch Verfahren* (Suhrkamp 1983) 203–218.

decisions should be effective and not violate EU fundamental rights. But is cost efficiency, for example, a reasonable or an arbitrary consideration when handling internal appeals?

At this point, we may realize that one notion that would have provided a legal basis for better decision-making is missing: impartiality. In the previous chapter I showed that from a functional as well as a historical perspective, impartiality, and not (only) independence, is arguably the characterizing feature of good adjudication.[46] Traditional, public administrative actors are expected to act impartially in their relations with individuals.[47] For example, the ECJ expects the European Commission to "examine carefully and impartially all the relevant aspects of the individual case, the right of the person concerned to make his views known and to have an adequately reasoned decision."[48] Platforms' internal complaint-handling systems do not have to be impartial in that public-law sense. Article 20 of the DSA makes no reference to impartiality. It does reference nonarbitrariness though. However, the notion of "nonarbitrariness" can only be interpreted in the economic context in which platforms operate and to which the DSA should apply. Although the EU legislators are trying to an extent to administrify platforms, the latter will still be private, profit-oriented enterprises. Profit orientation, a preference for quick fixes,[49] and economies of scale saturate platforms' internal structures and the habits and attitudes of most social media platforms and employees.[50] For a profit-oriented company, handling internal complaints as cheaply as possible is not an "arbitrary" decision at all. In terms of platforms' legally protected freedom to do business, handling internal complaints cheaply – even if that lowers the quality of their services – might be a rational and even legally protected choice. Thus, platforms are expected to consider aspects like cost efficiency when internally handling appeals, if not by law, then in practice. We know from testimony by Frances Haugen, a former executive-turned whistleblower,

[46] See at 2.2.4.

[47] See in general Craig (n 43) 320–355.

[48] Technische Universität München [1991] European Court of Justice C-269/90, ECLI:EU:C:1991:438 [14].

[49] Facebook's year-long motto famously was "move fast and break things."

[50] For an overview see in general Adrian Daub, *What Tech Calls Thinking: An Inquiry into the Intellectual Bedrock of Silicon Valley* (Farrar, Straus and Giroux 2020); Jillian York, *Silicon Values: The Future of Free Speech under Surveillance Capitalism* (Verso 2021); Sarah T Roberts, *Behind the Screen: Content Moderation in the Shadows of Social Media* (Yale University Press 2019); specifically for Meta: Sheera Frenkel and Cecilia Kang, *An Ugly Truth: Inside Facebook's Battle for Domination* (Harper 2021); 'Statement of Frances Haugen' <https://perma.cc/3QN6-JMY4>.

that Meta executives (and arguably those of other platforms) regularly decide against improving administrative procedures if they consider these too costly to implement:

> During my time at Facebook, first working as the lead product manager for Civic Misinformation and later on Counter-Espionage, I saw that Facebook repeatedly encountered conflicts between its own profits and our safety. Facebook consistently resolved those conflicts in favor of its own profits. The result has been a system that amplifies division, extremism, and polarization – and undermining societies around the world.[51]

In general, the regulation also seeks to accommodate the business interests of platforms – a balancing act that seems to be constitutionally demanded by the provisions of Article 16 of the Charter of Fundamental Rights (CFR).[52] For example, the DSA should "provide ... the conditions for innovative digital services to emerge and to scale up in the internal market."[53] In practice, platforms already allow for internal appeals – with mixed results. To sum up, internal complaint-handling is a crucial brick in the edifice of administrative justice, hence its appearance in the DSA. Against this backdrop, the DSA's approach to granting considerable leeway to platforms regarding how to implement and interpret procedural and other normative targets like "nonarbitrary internal complaint-handling" appears a risky one. We will further reflect on this in the chapter dealing with outcomes.[54]

To conclude, the power imbalance between platforms and users remain unchanged in internal complaint-handling. Therefore, contending platform decisions solely in front of internal complaint-handlers offers only limited accountability. So, introducing internal complaint-handling systems for platforms may offer some – but arguably not enough – legitimacy to the EU's desire to be a regulator with teeth.

3.2.3.3 ODSs as Middle Ground

The shortcomings of the two previous options – real courts are complicated and having no adjudication at all risks underwhelming stakeholders – have given rise to a kind of institutional hermaphrodite. The

[51] 'Statement of Frances Haugen' (n 50) 2.

[52] Ruffert in Article 16 GRCh paras 1–3 Christian Calliess and Matthias Ruffert (eds.), *EUV/AEUV: Das Verfassungsrecht der Europäischen Union mit Europäischer Grundrechtecharta: Kommentar* (6th ed., Beck 2022).

[53] Recital 4 Commission proposal (n 9).

[54] See at Chapter 5.

Commission proposed establishing independent, adjudicatory bodies – the ODSs – which some commentators at the time have quite reasonably interpreted as "de facto courts."[55] Out-of-court dispute settlement bodies are independent bodies set up to decide on disputes between individuals and platforms. Out-of-court dispute settlement bodies are private, yet publicly mandated. They base their decisions either on platforms' terms of service or on the acquis of applicable EU and Member State law.[56] Platforms are legally obliged to participate in proceedings before ODSs. Initially, the bodies' decisions were designed to be binding, which would have made ODSs specialized adjudicators controlling content moderation. But as we will see later, the Council scrapped ODSs' adjudicative authority. In the eventually passed version of the legislation, their decisions are not binding (although, the EU seems to be pinning its hopes on other enforcement mechanisms).

Politically, ODSs offered – at least as a result of the authority initially invested in them – legitimacy benefits to the EU because they would have allowed the EU to pose as a guarantor of individual rights online. By establishing ODSs, the policymakers' goal was that EU citizens could "easily and effectively contest certain decisions of online platforms that negatively affect them."[57] This is indeed a global legislative novelty.[58] As argued in the previous chapter, individual rights adjudication is a revered sociocultural reference point and an institutionalized element of legitimate administrative power structures. Infusing such administrative-law principles into private power structures will naturally be accompanied by some sort of individual rights adjudication. Correspondingly, legal experts welcomed the Commission's initial proposal "for aiming to introduce a system of out-of-court dispute resolution that promises the expedient settlement of conflicts involving harmful user-generated content."[59]

[55] Daniel Holznagel, 'The Digital Services Act Wants You to "Sue" Facebook over Content Decisions in Private de Facto Courts' (*Verfassungsblog*, 24 June 2021) <https://perma.cc/6W8K-E3GM>.

[56] See Article 18 Commission proposal (n 9). See further Article 21 Regulation (EU) 2022/2065 (Digital Services Act).

[57] Recital 44 Commission proposal (n 9).

[58] Eifert, Metzger, Schweitzer and Wagner (n 44) 1024 et seq. See, however, developments in India, where the government recently established so-called 'Grievance Appellate Commissions' for users to file complaints against content moderation decisions. See Ministry of Electronics and Information Technology (India), 'Three Grievance Appellate Committees (GACs) Notified on the Recently Amended "IT Rules 2021" (Press Release)' (28 January 2023) <https://perma.cc/98M3-5DQG>.

[59] Eifert, Metzger, Schweitzer and Wagner (n 44) 1026. Eifert et al also critique ODSs. However, that criticism is limited to the fact that, in the Commission proposal, only users

Remarkably, ODSs are not the first adjudicatory institutions the EU has set up to address power imbalances in private governance. Particularly when it came to consumer protection, Directive 2013/11/EU established a system of equally nonbinding ADR bodies.[60] As we will discuss in Section 3.3.3, the Commission proposal for ODSs partly emulates the ADR Directive.[61] But one legal scholar, who had welcomed the Commission proposal for ODSs in 2020, criticized the ADR Directive. In a 2014 article, Gerhard Wagner argued "ADR is an inadequate means of law enforcement" and "European consumer law is by no means an area so simple as to render adjudication unimportant. ... [I]t is all the more surprising that the EU lawmakers put so much faith in alternative dispute resolution. How would a non-court entity be able to apply the law more easily than a court would?"[62]

However, that the Commission would draw from earlier experiences with ADR when devising the DSA can also be explained through contextual factors. Several of the Commission agents who drafted Articles 20 and 21 of the DSA had previously worked in the context of the consumer ADR Directive.[63] Other role models that might have influenced the Commission's thinking were arguably Article 17(9) subparagraph 2 sentence 2 Digital Single Market Directive, which mandated Member States to "ensure that out-of-court redress mechanisms are available for the settlement of disputes," Article 12 of the P2B Directive, which nudges online intermediaries toward participating in mediation procedures, and §3(c) of the German NetzDG, which also briefly established voluntary mediation services for (some) disputes between platforms and users in Germany.[64] Yet, none of these earlier

whose content was deleted could appeal to ODSs. ODSs personal "jurisdiction" broadened in the legislative procedure to also include people upon whose notice content was not removed.

60 Directive 2013/11/EU of the European Parliament and of the Council of 21 May 2013 on alternative dispute resolution for consumer disputes and amending Regulation (EC) No 2006/2004 and Directive 2009/22/EC (Directive on consumer ADR) [CELEX: 32013L0011].

61 Apart from evident structural borrowing – compare e.g., Articles 6–8 ibid with Article 18 Commission proposal (9) – several Commission agents highlighted this in interviews. Also Eifert et al. speak of "ADR entities" when discussing Article 18 Commission proposal, cf. Eifert, Metzger, Schweitzer and Wagner (n 44) 1010, 1012.

62 Gerhard Wagner, 'Private Law Enforcement Through ADR: Wonder Drug or Snake Oil?' (2014) 51 Common Market Law Review 165, 165, 178, declaring the Directive partly "disturbing" at 174, "highly problematic," and "troublesome" at 179.

63 Interview with European Commission Staffer 1 (n 35).

64 Directive (EU) 2019/790 of the European Parliament and of the Council of 17 April 2019 on copyright and related rights in the Digital Single Market and amending Directives 96/9/EC and 2001/29/EC (Digital Single Market Directive) (OJ L 130, 1752019, pp. 92–125);

provisions foresaw binding adjudication and mandatory participation by platforms. How the EU wove these private- and public-law perspectives together will be detailed below.[65] Before diving into the details of ODSs' origin, we should first look at the DSA's overall characteristics.

3.2.4 *Characteristics of the DSA*

One focus of debates on online platforms was (and is) to develop mechanisms to contest unwanted moderation.[66] So too, the DSA seeks to establish procedural mechanisms to the benefit of individual users and oversight bodies in the Member States. Further, the DSA establishes a new coordinating institution, the European Board for Digital Services. As Irene Roche Laguna, a high-level Commission employee, and Martin Husovec, an academic adviser to the Commission, put it, the DSA subjects platforms to "due diligence obligations" that "focus mainly on the process and design rather than the content itself."[67]

The consequence of such a procedure-focused approach is that private actors will become ever more powerful enforcers of law, and especially fundamental rights. Ironically, such an approach could have drawn criticism from traditionalists as well as legal scholars. Outsourcing fundamental rights protection – which inevitably affects interpretation, application, and, eventually, performative modification of these rights – to profit-oriented actors runs counter to traditional conceptions of who should do what for citizens. Similar reforms in some Member States, most notably the German NetzDG,[68] had met criticism only a few years previously.[69] Yet criticism of the DSA remained subdued, and most

Regulation (EU) 2019/1150 of the European Parliament and of the Council of 20 June 2019 on promoting fairness and transparency for business users of online intermediation services (OJ L 186, 1172019, pp. 57–79); Gesetz zur Verbesserung der Rechtsdurchsetzung in sozialen Netzwerken (Netzwerkdurchsetzungsgesetz – NetzDG) (BGBl I S 3352, last amended through BGBl 2024 I Nr 149).

65 See at 3.3.

66 See e.g., for the general debate about automated decision-making vis-à-vis individuals, demanding "meaningful notice" and "hearings" for automated administrative decisions Citron (n 31) 1305 et seq; picking up Citron's ideas for platforms Klonick (n 12) 1666 et seq; Tarleton Gillespie, *Custodians of the Internet: Platforms, Content Moderation, and the Hidden Decisions That Shape Social Media* (Yale University Press 2019) 44; Lang (n 18) 245–248.

67 Martin Husovec and Irene Roche Laguna, 'Digital Services Act: A Short Primer' (SSRN, 5 July 2022) 1 <https://perma.cc/JE3Q-55XA>.

68 The *NetzDG* was less comprehensive than the DSA. However, much like the DSA today, the *NetzDG* also required platforms to enforce public law in the online sphere.

69 I cannot repeat the entire debate here, but it seems fair to say that *NetzDG* was met – especially prior to its implementation – with widespread scholarly rejection. Criticism

commentators seemed pleased that anything was being done at all (while viewing the EU as better equipped to handle these issues than Member States).[70]

Apart from these platform-focused aspects the DSA substantially reformed the supervisory architecture for online platforms, especially the big ones. On the one hand, it reinterpreted the country of origin-principle, so that not all supervision would end up in Dublin. That concentration of enforcement power in a single Member State is widely considered one of the structural flaws of the EU's General Data Protection Regulation. On the other hand, the DSA concentrates supervision powers for very large online platforms – for example, Meta, X, TikTok – in the hands of the Commission.[71] The DSA became applicable on February 17, 2024.[72]

3.2.4.1 Procedure

Many of the procedures the DSA concentrates on are individualized in that they focus on the relationship between person and platform – and less on platforms' structural governance mechanisms that inform

ranged from principled arguments (law enforcement should not be privatized), to practical aspects (turnover deadlines were very, very short), to a seemingly overblown panic that *NetzDG* would lead to massive "overblocking." A few years into practice, it became apparent that *NetzDG* yielded negligible take-down rates compared with platforms' terms of service. Widespread criticism about "censorship" seemed reflective of US free speech absolutism, which operates in this context predominantly as argument against any form of regulation. For a balanced perspective and a good overview see: Andrej Lang, 'Netzwerkdurchsetzungsgesetz und Meinungsfreiheit' (2018) 143 Archiv des öffentlichen Rechts 220; Martin Eifert, 'Das Netzwerkdurchsetzungsgesetz und Plattformregulierung' in Martin Eifert and Tobias Gostomzyk (eds.), *Netzwerkrecht* (Nomos 2018) 9 et seq; critical e.g. Thorsten Feldmann, 'Zum Referentenentwurf eines NetzDG: eine kritische Betrachtung' (2017) 20 Kommunikation & Recht 295 et seq; Hubertus Gersdorf, 'Hate Speech in sozialen Netzwerken: Verfassungswidrigkeit des NetzDG-Entwurfs und grundrechtliche Einordnung der Anbieter sozialer Netzwerke' (2017) 20 MultiMedia und Recht 439, 446–447.

[70] See e.g. Miriam C Buiten, 'The Digital Services Act: From Intermediary Liability to Platform Regulation' (2021) JIPITEC 361, paras 86–92; Eifert, Metzger, Schweitzer and Wagner (n 44) 1024–1028; for a critical perspective see generally Daphne Keller, 'Internet Platforms: Observations on Speech, Danger, and Money, Hoover Institution's Aegis Paper Series No. 1807' (2018) 1–4, 16 et seq.

[71] Suzanne Vergnolle, 'Putting Collective Intelligence to the Enforcement of the Digital Services Act: Report on Possible Collaborations between the European Commission and Civil Society' Conservatoire National des Articles et Métiers (CNAM) Paper Series, 2023; Daniel Holznagel, 'Ireland Cannot Do It Alone' (*Verfassungsblog*, 27 April 2021) <https://perma.cc/36C6-LYJB>.

[72] Article 93(2) Regulation (EU) 2022/2065 (Digital Services Act).

individualized decisions.[73] Seen through the lens of rulemaking and rule enforcement, the DSA proceduralizes rule enforcement but not rulemaking. For example, platforms must establish internal complaint-handling mechanisms (Article 20) and are subject to the rulings of the relevant out-of-court dispute settlement bodies (Article 21). Here, the DSA seeks to empower individuals to use individual rights as power mediators vis-à-vis the platforms on two levels.

Beyond the individual level, the DSA introduced several, more general and structural, procedures to enhance the transparency of platforms. For example, extensive platforms "shall diligently identify, analyze and assess" whether they pose "systemic risks" for aspects such as "foreseeable negative effects on civic discourse and electoral process, and public security."[74] Further, platforms are subject to auditing (Article 37) and transparency obligations regarding their use of data (Articles 39, 40, and 42) and must establish a "compliance function" (Article 41). In contrast, the DSA offers very few specific, standard-related criteria in its definitions of what practices or normative judgments are allowed or prohibited. For example, Articles 34 and 35 leave standard-setting for matters like auditing (Article 34(1)(d)) to "voluntary industry standards" and equally "self"-devised codes of conduct.

3.2.4.2 Design

However, the DSA's reformist agenda arguably misses out on two crucial aspects: rulemaking and inner-platform decision-making prior to enforcement (in other words, the design of platforms). The previous chapter briefly sketched out how content moderation relies not only on the binary enforcement of company-made rules but also on the design, programming, and infrastructure employed by platforms vis-à-vis their users.[75] Initially, aspects of platform design or internal decision-making, although referenced,[76] were not a prominent feature in the Commission proposal.[77] Later, perhaps reflecting evolving academic views on content moderation, a newly introduced Article 25(1) of the DSA sketched a broad design framework for

[73] See e.g., Articles 16, 17, 20, 21, 22 ibid.

[74] Article 34(1)(c) ibid.

[75] See at 2.3.3 and 6.2.2.

[76] cf. Recitals 56–59 and Articles 22(7) and implicitly also Article 24 Commission proposal (n 9).

[77] Quite the contrary, the Commission proposal focused mainly on potential manipulation of platform services through outside influence like fake accounts and not on the manipulative aspects of platform services themselves. cf. Recital 57 (at the end) European Commission Proposal Digital Services Act (n 9).

platform–user relationships prior to questions of formal enforcement. This particular clause stipulated that social media platforms were to "design, organize or operate their online interfaces" in no way that "deceives or manipulates" or "materially distorts or impairs the ability" of individual users "to make free and informed decisions." According to Article 25(3) of the DSA, the Commission may publish further guidelines specifying design principles. For the moment, the legal status of those design "principles" remains vague. What counts as deception and impairment of "free" decision-making is still unclear. After all, building a doctrinally sound legal framework that protects the exercise of free will itself would be a Sisyphean task.[78] Nonetheless, the Commission could in theory fine platforms for violating these design principles.[79] A cynic might even say that any social media platform's design is anyway geared toward deceiving, manipulating, and impairing the exercise of free will on the part of its users.[80] Algorithms lure users into spending more time on-screen. Based on mined behavioral data the companies anticipate, encourage or even produce needs among their customers. Further, social media usage can lead to an increase in users experiencing a host of negative effects, ranging from multiplying cases of depression and anorexia to growing incidents of suicide.[81] From a rule of law perspective, such overly broad and in practice unrealizable design criteria perhaps should not be "enforceable" in the event of their absence by fining the companies up to 6 percent of their combined global annual turnover.[82]

[78] To compare, the German code against unfair business practices (*Gesetz gegen den unlauteren Wettbewerb*) defines in § 5(1–4) ten examples for the arguably much narrower act of making "deceptive commercial statements" (*irreführende geschäftliche Handlungen*).

[79] Article 73, 74 Regulation (EU) 2022/2065 (Digital Services Act).

[80] Niklas Eder, 'Beyond Automation: Machine Learning-Based Systems and Human Behavior in the Personalization Economy' (2021) 25 Stanford Technology Law Review 1, 19 et seq.

[81] In a literature-based study, Keles et al. find "evidence for a putative relationship between social media use and mental health problems in adolescents. . . . [D]epression was the most commonly measured outcome. . . . [T]he review found a general correlation between social media use and mental health problems. However, most authors noted that the observed relationship is too complex for straightforward statements." cf. Betul Keles, Niall McCrae and Annmarie Grealish, 'A Systematic Review: The Influence of Social Media on Depression, Anxiety and Psychological Distress in Adolescents' (2020) 25 International Journal of Adolescence and Youth 79, 88.

[82] That goes even for "negligent" infringements of presumably any DSA provision as neither provision specifies which provisions are "relevant," cf. Articles 73(1), 74(1)(a) Regulation (EU) 2022/2065 (Digital Services Act).

3.2.4.3 Rulemaking

The second crucial aspect the DSA does *not* regulate is rulemaking. Platform rulemaking – that is, platforms' unilateral generating of norms that delineate what kinds of communication they allow – is a key aspect of content moderation.[83] The Commission has pointed out: "platforms set the rules of the game, without effectively mitigating the risks and the societal and economic harm they cause."[84] And yet the DSA does not seek to weigh in on platform rulemaking. Specifically, it does not limit platforms' power to unilaterally make and on their own behalf change these "rules of the game."[85] Article 14(4) of the DSA obliges platforms to "act in a diligent, objective and proportionate manner *in applying* and *enforcing* the … [terms of service], with due regard to the rights and legitimate interests of all parties involved, including the applicable fundamental rights." Martin Eifert and others argue that this means the DSA grants platforms "unfettered discretion" to exercise private regulation of public discourse.[86]

The DSA's due diligence obligations only concern, as already mentioned, *individual* application and enforcement – not rulemaking. From a public-law perspective, binding these strands of individual enforcement decisions to individual rights seems to make intuitive sense. If decision-makers must pay "due regard" to fundamental rights when enforcing terms of service, the problem should disappear.[87]

In an ideal world, Article 14(4) of the DSA requires platforms to engage in a long-term balancing act, which should – the theory goes – prevent any infringements of individual rights. However, the reality is that balancing fundamental rights is complex, and content moderation decisions are

[83] See at 2.3.3.

[84] The Commission proposal argued that "[i]n the absence of effective regulation and enforcement, they [i.e. very large online platforms] can set the rules of the game," cf. recital 56 Commission proposal (n 9). This paragraph was modified in negotiations with the Council to "[e]ffective regulation and enforcement is necessary in order to effectively identify and mitigate the risks and the societal and economic harm that may arise," cf. Recital 56 Regulation (EU) 2022/2065 (Digital Services Act).

[85] Recital 56 Commission proposal (n 9).

[86] Eifert, Metzger, Schweitzer and Wagner (n 44) 1013.

[87] Yet even here the used language leaves room for interpretation as it does not simply oblige platforms to protect fundamental rights. As any first-year law student knows, any extra word, every tweak added to an otherwise solid obligation can be used to undercut an otherwise impressive-sounding legal guarantee. Therefore, what exactly "due" means in this context remains to be seen.

made within constraints of time and resources. To cite just two numbers: between January and March 2024, YouTube deleted almost 8 million videos and more than 1.4 billion comments worldwide.[88] Human moderators, usually low-paid and based in South-East Asia, normally have only a few seconds per enforcement decision.[89] This may also work similarly in the case of internally handled appeals, which might be dealt with by different teams that would, perhaps, tend to be working in slightly better material and institutional conditions. In short, the reality of content moderation appears irreconcilable with the ideal premised in Article 14(4) of the DSA.

Also, in its introductory "recitals," the DSA text does not explain *how* platforms are supposed to pay "due regard" to fundamental rights when restricting communication.[90] The idea of people being required to consciously balance conflicting fundamental rights positions for *every* moderation-related decision is an illusion. In turn, the DSA fails to define procedural obligations – except that terms of service must be published and summarized in the relevant languages – that would inform decision-making and rulemaking processes.

Given our emulation-oriented framework, this key provision will probably only lead to the lip-service of ceremonial compliance. On paper, establishing a kind of ceremonial commitment to "duly regard" fundamental rights in all these decisions will be easy. There will be briefings, commitments, training courses, and reports aiming to enhance moderators' "awareness" of fundamental rights. However, none of these extras will enable moderators to take more time over individual enforcement decisions, which ought to be the baseline requirement for any genuine attempts to balance the fundamental rights of different protagonists – including potentially several users and, we should not forget, the platform itself – against each other. To put it bluntly, Article 14 of the DSA may serve as a sedative for the widespread debate about whether social media platforms ought to be

[88] 'Google Transparency Report, YouTube-Community-Guidelines and Their Application (Q1 2024)' <https://perma.cc/67GV-R8HZ>.

[89] Insightful: Gillespie (n 66) 111-139 (esp. 120–124). See also, highlighting the often precarious working conditions for many outsourced human moderators Roberts (n 50) 173, 176–183; MacKenzie F Common, 'Fear the Reaper: How Content Moderation Rules Are Enforced on Social Media' (2020) 34 International Review of Law, Computers & Technology 126, 127 et seq.

[90] cf. Recitals 47, 48 Regulation (EU) 2022/2065 (Digital Services Act).

"bound" in any sense by fundamental rights.[91] But it most likely lacks precision and force to effectuate meaningful change.

What is truly astonishing is the following: The Commission not only seemingly knew but even openly acknowledged these limitations from the very beginning of our whole saga in winter 2020. Concretely, the Commission assumes that implementing Article 14(4) of the DSA will require so little effort from platforms that it will come at virtually no cost. This admission can be found buried in an impact assessment published in 2020 alongside the initial Commission proposal. As argued above, the effective implementation of Article 14(4) and other key provisions would necessitate substantial organizational, normative, and procedural overhauls within platforms. By definition, such overhauls would be costly, especially considering the high-minded balancing objectives embedded in Article 14(4). After all, driving significant governance reforms at platforms is the core purpose of the DSA. Yet, in that impact assessment released alongside the initial proposal, the Commission concedes that for most companies the costs for engaging in public-minded moderation practices would,

> *not represent an additional cost compared to current operations*, but require a process adaptation in the receipt and processing of notices and streamline costs stemming from fragmented obligations currently applicable.[92]

To reiterate, the Commission asserts that implementing key provisions of the DSA will be no more expensive than "current operations." But if that were true, why have platforms not already adopted the practices the DSA now mandates? If exemplary moderation costs the same as mediocre moderation, why has the state of content moderation in Europe become

[91] See recently for example: João Pedro Quintais, Naomi Appelman and Ronan Ó Fathaigh, 'Using Terms and Conditions to Apply Fundamental Rights to Content Moderation' (2023) 24 German Law Journal 881; Sophie Knebel, *Die Drittwirkung der Grundrechte und -freiheiten gegenüber Privaten: Regulierungsmöglichkeiten sozialer Netzwerke* (Nomos 2018) 174 et seq, 301–306; Andreas Kulick, *Horizontalwirkung im Vergleich* (Mohr Siebeck 2020) 351–355; Eifert (n 69) 28–30; descriptively: Konstantinos Stylianou, Nicolo Zingales and Stefania di Stefano, *Is Facebook Keeping up with International Standards on Freedom of Expression? A Time-Series Analysis 2005–2020* (2022).

[92] European Commission, 'Commission Staff Working Document, Impact Assessment, Accompanying the Commission Proposal for the DSA, Part 1/2. SWD(2020) 348 Final' (n 28) paras 197, table 4 at row 2 (emphasis added). Further, the EU's focus on "streamline cost" omits that according to Articles 2 and 20, platforms are also required to delete content that is illegal under Member State law. This necessitates at least partially diversified enforcement structures.

such a pressing issue that the European Union felt compelled to pass the DSA? Conversely, if the DSA's supposedly "groundbreaking" demands require so little change at the platforms, what do we need the DSA for? The best things in life are free, but good content moderation certainly is not.

Automated moderation, on the other hand, does not "consciously" weigh anything but builds on specific, preexisting, computed rules and probabilistic patterns generated from large data sets.[93] Although hailed as a solution to content moderation's problem of scale, automated decision-making seems not (yet) equipped to "understand" the apparent "meanings" of human communication, let alone engage in a balancing of fundamental rights.[94] Even though recent advances in large language models are indeed impressive, at the time of this writing, neither the quality of the applied normative material nor the employed algorithms seem to have yet salvaged the described problems. Anyone who studied administrative actors knows how difficult maintaining decisional quality can be even with human operators. If companies eventually manage to out-engineer this problem – and that might be possible, to an extent – maintaining intrinsically anthropomorphic ideals like "balancing" and

[93] For an analysis of the differences between legal systems and natural language processing, a key technology for automated content moderation, see: Paul Friedl, 'Dis/Similarities in the Design and Development of Legal and Algorithmic Normative Systems: The Case of Perspective API' (2023) 15 Law, Innovation and Technology 25.

[94] Tarleton Gillespie, 'Content Moderation, AI, and the Question of Scale' (2020) 7 Big Data & Society; Robert Gorwa, Reuben Binns and Christian Katzenbach, 'Algorithmic Content Moderation: Technical and Political Challenges in the Automation of Platform Governance' (2020) 7 Big Data & Society 1; Gary Marcus and Ernest Davis, *Rebooting AI* (Knopf 2019); Caroline Sinders, 'Toxicity and Tone Are Not the Same Thing: Analyzing the New Google API on Toxicity, PerspectiveAPI' (*Medium.com*, 24 February 2017) <https://perma.cc/MK66-NS9J>; foundational: Joseph Weizenbaum, *Computer Power and Human Reason: From Judgment to Calculation* (Freeman 1976). See further in general: Danielle Keats Citron, 'Technological Due Process' (2008) 85 Washington University Law Review 1249; Katherine J Strandburg, 'Rulemaking and Inscrutable Automated Decision Tools' (2019) 119 Columbia Law Review 1851.

However, note that since the launch of ChatGPT scholars grew much more confident that large language models might indeed improve moderation, cf. Mirko Franco, Ombretta Gaggi and Claudio E. Pallazzi, 'Analyzing the Use of Large Language Models for Content Moderation with ChatGPT Examples' 3rd International Workshop on Open Challenges in Online Social Networks (OASIS '23), September 04–08, 2023 <https://perma.cc/Z2LP-KHT9>; Fabrizio Gilardi, Meysam Alizadeh and Maël Kubli, 'ChatGPT Out-Performs Crowd-Workers for Text-Annotation Tasks' (27 March 2023), preprint arXiv:2303.15056; Deepak Kumar, Yousef AbuHashem, Zakir Durumeric, 'Watch Your Language: Investigating Content Moderation with Large Language Models' (17 January 2024) arXiv:2309.14517v2.

"proportionality" in a system that runs through code rather than humans will be ever more challenging.[95]

In sum, content moderation "decisions" are not so much individualized, case-by-case decisions but repeated applications of specific rules and other "upstream" normative decisions.[96] As recent research corroborates, the crucial normative questions of content moderation are *not* hidden in individual rule applications but entrenched in the vast landscape of specific rules, guidelines, design choices, and other normative material made by platforms.[97]

It appears questionable whether individual rights are the (only) appropriate tool to tackle this problem. If individual decisions are just reflections of previously generated rules and other normative choices embedded in a platform's hardware, directing appeals against individual enforcement decisions is pointless. Consequently, Evelyn Douek even speaks of "accountability theater" in that regard.[98]

3.3 The Legislative Process

After discussing some key aspects of the DSA for context, we now return to the key storyline of this case study: how the EU established ODSs as independent adjudicators to protect individual rights online but later scrapped their authority. To reiterate, ODSs had originally been devised as adjudicators that were to *bindingly* decide on disputes between platforms and users.[99] With ODSs, the EU initially intended to establish "a system of sub-courts" to control platforms' burgeoning administrative powers.[100] This idea mirrors that of individual rights

95 See especially Friedl (n 93).

96 Insightful: Tarleton Gillespie, *Custodians of the Internet: Platforms, Content Moderation, and the Hidden Decisions That Shape Social Media* (Yale University Press 2019) 47–66. Comprehensively, and with a broader understanding of the normative decisions influencing content moderation: Douek (n 31) 539 et seq. See also Olivier Sylvain, 'Platform Realism, Informational Inequality, and Section 230 Reform' (2021) 131 Yale Law Journal Forum 475, 494–500.

97 Also pointing to the relevance of computing and design choices by platforms: Douek (n 31) 530, 539 et seq; for a practical example see: Jing Zeng and Bondy Valdovinos Kaye, 'From Content Moderation to Visibility Moderation: A Case Study of Platform Governance on TikTok' (2022) 14 Policy & Internet 79.

98 Douek (n 31) 533.

99 Article 18 Commission proposal (n 9).

100 Explanatory Statement 22/23 European Parliament Committee on Legal Affairs and Tiemo Wölken (Rapporteur), 'DRAFT REPORT with Recommendations to the Commission on a Digital Services Act: Adapting Commercial and Civil Law Rules for Commercial Entities Operating Online (2020/2019(INL))' <https://perma.cc/VC3U-7Y97>.

adjudication.[101] Already prior to the DSA's drafting, we were seeing an increase in rights-based litigation against online platforms and search engines around issues like data protection, termination of service, and hate speech.[102] In Europe, confining platform power has been "increasingly framed in terms of fundamental rights" since the early 2010s.[103] As a consequence, EU policymakers defined platforms' handling of fundamental rights as one of the main problems they intended to resolve by means of the DSA.[104] In its impact assessment, the Commission argued that only "[v]ery few online platforms subject their enforcement policies to systematic independent oversight."[105] This was exacerbated, the Commission argued, by a prevailing "lack of redress and transparency of decisions unilaterally taken by the platforms."[106] Thus, the Commission sought to build an individualized, adjudicatory mechanism that would take the pressure off Member States' courts and allow more users to enforce their rights.[107] To level the power dynamics in that "standard picture," EU policymakers opted to give people the possibility of recourse to ODSs so that the users would have an online version of "their day in court."[108]

The main protagonists in this section are experts, the European Parliament, the European Commission, the Council, the Member States, and the tech industry. The Parliament, Commission, and Council are the three legislative bodies of the EU. The Commission proposes legislation, which is then discussed in the Parliament – the EU's only directly elected body – and then sent to the Council – the powerful conclave of the Member States.

101 See at 2.2.

102 See e.g. *GC and Others (De-referencing of sensitive data)* [2019] European Court of Justice C-136/17, ECLI:EU:C:2019:773; Anna Katharina Struth, *Hassrede und Freiheit der Meinungsäußerung* (Springer 2019).

103 Folkert Wilman, 'The EU's System of Knowledge-Based Liability for Hosting Service Providers in Respect of Illegal User Content: between the e-Commerce Directive and the Digital Services Act' (2021) 12 JIPITEC 317, para 24.

104 Recitals 3, 4 Commission proposal (n 9); Recitals 3, 4 Regulation (EU) 2022/2065 (Digital Services Act).

105 Ibid 19 (Recital 54).

106 Ibid.

107 Interview with European Commission Staffer 1 (n 35); Interview with European Commission Staffer 1 (n 35); Interview with European Parliament Staffer 1 (n 35).

108 cf. Douek (n 31) 538; as a sidenote: this "day in court"-framing was very prevalent in conversations with the people who later would found ODSs, especially at User Rights; cf. below at 3.8.

3.3.1 *Expert Theorizing*

However, based on this standard picture, one expert theorization proved particularly influential for this part of the DSA. As argued above, establishing some kind of hermaphroditic adjudicator – one that would not quite count as a court while passing the test as a more effective accountability forum than internal complaint-handling – promised "output legitimacy" for the EU.[109] ODSs are that hermaphrodite. The reasons for their insertion into the DSA and their specific characteristics, especially their asymmetric cost structure, were set out (at least in parts) in a paper produced by two experts who worked with the European Commission in informal consultations preceding the drafting of the Commission proposal.[110]

3.3.1.1 Informal Consultations

Expert theorization, often conveyed in informal consultations with policymakers, is a driving force behind *emulation*.[111] Emulation refers to a way by which preexisting role models are reproduced in policymaking and organizational design.[112] Policymakers are usually acting within time and resource constraints.[113] They therefore strive to include experts' insights and proposals in policymaking. As a result, experts will theorize based on preexisting assumptions and often advise policymakers to adopt policy choices or organizational designs that work in other contexts. In other words, experts will often advise their clients to emulate.

The role of expert advice is particularly salient for the European Commission. Tasked to formulate regulatory proposals in vastly complex fields, the Commission engages in extensive expert consultations before drafting a proposal.[114] Although the Commission also conducts open and public consultations, internal and relatively nontransparent

[109] See at 3.2.

[110] For the role of expert theorizing and consulting in emulation see 2.4.

[111] Ibid.

[112] See at 2.1 and 2.4.

[113] See at 2.4.3 and 2.4.4.

[114] See in general: Bart van Ballaert, 'The European Commission's Use of Consultation during Policy Formulation: The Effects of Policy Characteristics' (2017) 18 European Union Politics 406; see also the recent works by Emilia Korkea-aho, 'Legal Lobbying: The Evolving (But Hidden) Role of Lawyers and Law Firms in the EU Public Affairs Market' (2021) 22 German Law Journal 65; for reflections on why lobbying (understood broadly) so far largely escaped recognition of EU legal scholars Emilia Korkea-aho, 'No Longer Marginal? Finding a Place for Lobbyists and Lobbying in EU Law Research' (2022) 18 European Constitutional Law Review 682, 691 et seq.

"behind the scenes" discussions tend to precede public consultations. As empirical research has evidenced, internal, circumscribed, and "capacity-building" consultations with experts and other stakeholders outnumber public consultations, especially when it comes to high-profile policy proposals like the DSA.[115] Typically, Commission consultations may include "expert groups, as well as seminars, workshops, or conferences which are institutionalized to a minimum degree,"[116] with only a few of these accessible to the public. For the DSA, the Commission held public consultations between June and September 2020, just months before publishing the final proposal in December.[117] It received more than 2,800 pieces of feedback in these open consultations.[118] Arguably, none of these eleventh-hour consultations had any meaningful effect on the proposal. Big questions are usually cleared way before such a proposal enters the public stage.

In contrast, informal and internal discussions precede public consultations because the former lay the groundwork for the ideas and texts subsequently discussed in the latter.[119] This was also the case for the DSA. In supplementary material to its proposal, the Commission said it had "gathered expertise and views through targeted consultations and engagement activities, including a series of workshops, conferences, interviews with experts and judges, consultations of the Expert Group on e-commerce, as well as numerous bilateral meetings and analysis of ad hoc position and research papers from organizations, industry representatives, civil society and academia."[120]

Such informal discussions are typically only open to invited experts, often working in a particular policy field.[121] In practice, such early, informal influence is crucial and perhaps even decisive. As Päivi Leino-Sandberg notes, based on interviews with members of the Commission's Legal Service: "The real legal battles within the Commission take place prior to the adoption of a proposal."[122] Within the Commission, drafting a proposal relies on extensive "internal legal consultations [that] involve

[115] Finding based on analysis of 150 policy proposals adopted between 2010 and 2014. See van Ballaert (n 114) 419.
[116] Ibid 407.
[117] Explanatory Memorandum at 8 Commission proposal (n 9).
[118] Ibid.
[119] van Ballaert (n 114) 408–410.
[120] Explanatory Memorandum at 10 Commission proposal (n 9).
[121] van Ballaert (n 114) 409.
[122] Päivi Leino-Sandberg, *The Politics of Legal Expertise in EU Policy-Making* (Cambridge University Press 2021) 163.

exchanges between officials at the level of technical experts."[123] During these discussions, an intricate dance of expertise, personality, political agenda, the relevant Directorate General's ideas, and the Commission's Legal Service law-related (and sometimes political) observations coalesce into the details of the Commission proposal.[124]

3.3.1.2 'Compulsory and Compensated ADR'

For ODSs, we can trace the influence of expert theorizations even beyond the discourse-oriented influence described above. One specific expert theorization was apparently a strong influence on the inclusion of and particular design of ODSs in the Commission proposal. That expert theorization can be traced to Martin Husovec, a law professor. Professor Husovec amicably agreed to be interviewed for this book. In the mid-2010s, when the Commission was contemplating reform of its eCommerce Directive, Husovec pitched what he called "compulsory and compensated ADR" to Commission staff.[125] That was "well before" the DSA proposal was planned out in detail.[126] Husovec stressed that he "would not want to paint the picture" that he had come up with the initial idea for out-of-court dispute settlement bodies. And yet he was apparently the first expert to pitch to the Commission the notion of compulsory and compensated ADR bodies as potential controllers of platform power.[127] In the early 2010s, the number of lawmakers, academics, and lobbyists working on platform regulation was not that large.[128] For example, conference programs from the time show the relevant people from the Commission and academics sharing panels, indicating that some contacts dated back years.[129] At the same time, the Commission was (internally) looking at ADR as a potential role model for overhauling

[123] cf. ibid *passim*.
[124] cf. ibid 164–173.
[125] Interview with Academic, Consultant to the European Commission (n 39). The Commission disclosed "targeted consultations" with experts, industry representatives, and other stakeholders since 2012, 'Commission Staff Working Document, Impact Assessment, Accompanying the Commission Proposal for the DSA, Annex, Part 2/2, SWD (2020) 348 Final' 38.
[126] Ibid.
[127] Ibid.
[128] Back then, the commonly used term was mainly "intermediary liability."
[129] See in that regard also the foreword (written by Irene Roche Laguna) and the preface in Husovec (n 8) *Principles of the Digital Services Act* v–x. See further, for example the conference program of the "Internet Freedom Conference" hosted by the Council of Europe at the Hofburg in Vienna on 13 October 2017, accessible via <https://perma.cc/3L25-SFLV>.

the eCommerce Directive.[130] As Husovec had worked extensively on intermediary liability, he and a colleague designed an experimental study to empirically test the governance-improving effects of what would later become ODSs. In the final publication of this study (but also in the earlier published preprint version) Husovec and Lenka Fiala, his coauthor, wrote:

> The proposal for the upcoming Digital Services Act in the European Union, which will update the law in the area, *adopts* the mandated version *of our policy in* its *Article 18*. The provision establishes certification of non-state out-of-court bodies that can resolve content disputes and issue *binding* decisions. The content creators who win the disputes shall have their content reinstated and be reimbursed "for any fees and other reasonable expenses that the recipient has paid or is to pay in relation to the dispute settlement." Thus, the reimbursement is flexible enough to accommodate the self-sustaining fee structure of ADR bodies that will also act as an incentive for providers to avoid making mistakes. The provision thus illustrates how our model can be *translated into a policy*. Our paper provides *evidence* for its potential positive effects on the notice and take-down practice.[131]

Simply put, ODSs seem to be emulation in its purest form. The EU needed a publicly legitimate but also realistic solution for a crucial policy problem. With the help of advice from experts it used models drawn from other contexts – here, consumer protection and, in the case of Husovec and Fiala, copyright dispute resolution – and applied them to a new context. Eventually, the emulation translates into both a policy and a formal structure for enacting that policy.

To operationalize these theorizations, the Commission consulted with Husovec and other experts.[132] For example, buried in supplementary legislative materials, we find that Husovec organized a "small-scale workshop [for Commission agents] about the future of liability of digital platforms in Europe."[133] Apparently, this workshop focused on the drafting of Articles 17 and 18 of the Commission proposal, which dealt with internal complaint-handling mechanisms and, crucially, ODSs and would later become Articles 20 and 21 DSA. According to the Commission, "[t]he event's goal was to share the latest academic research with the EU officials and discuss potential solutions for the reform of the [eCommerce

[130] Interview with European Commission Staffer 1 (n 35); Interview with European Commission Staffer 1 (n 35).

[131] Martin Husovec and Lenka Fiala, 'Using Experimental Evidence to Improve Delegated Enforcement' (2022) 71 International Review of Law and Economics 106079, 11 (emphases added).

[132] See in general Impact Assessment DSA Part 2/2 (Annex) 43–47.

[133] Impact Assessment DSA Part 2/2 (Annex) (n 125) 43.

Directive], including *drafting suggestions* for the provisions related to intermediary liability and notice-and-action mechanisms."[134]

This is remarkable. We must assume that not only the broad idea but the very formulation of the text that would later become Article 21 was discussed with outside experts in these informal consultations. "Compulsory and compensated ADR," as proposed by Husovec and Fiala, should incentivize delegated enforcers like platforms to take a more nuanced approach to blocking content, especially with automated tools. It builds on the standard picture of content moderation as comprising a continual string of individual decisions.[135] Husovec argued that compulsory and compensated ADR would help align private companies' decision-making activities with fundamental rights.[136] Interestingly, the professor's background was not in public law but private law, with a focus on intermediary liability and law and economics.[137]

Compulsory and compensated ADR was proposed by Husovec and Fiala to work as follows. If a platform decides against a user, for example, by deleting content, that person can go to an ADR body to seek redress. Platforms are obliged to take part in ADR proceedings, that is to say, ADR becomes compulsory for platforms. If they lose, platforms must pay a fine, that is to say, the proceedings are compensated.[138] Thus, the key function of "compulsory and compensated" ADR proceedings is to inflict costs upon misgoverning online platforms. These costs would then incentivize platforms to improve their governance. In the words of Husovec and Fiala:

> in the event the ADR panel decides that content should be reinstated, the provider has to comply with it and fully compensate the creator's fee and pay additional fees to ADR. This should create an incentive for providers to further invest in the quality of their review in the long run.[139]

The authors argued that inflicting costs is such an essential measure that the adjudicatory body's design does not matter "as long as the financing structure remains the same."[140] In their model, individual rights adjudication merely serves as a procedural legitimizer of the *punitive* costs inflicted on the platform in each case. Adjudication determines whether

[134] Ibid (emphasis added).
[135] See at 2.3.8.
[136] Interview with Academic, Consultant to the European Commission (n 39).
[137] Ibid.
[138] Husovec and Fiala (n 131) 4 (there at footnote 15).
[139] Husovec and Fiala (n 131) 4 (emphasis added).
[140] Ibid at footnote 18.

platforms must “comply” and “pay additional fees.”[141] These additional fees were the crucial, punitive aspect of the model. If enough cases pile up, platforms would in theory be motivated to modify their rulemaking and rule enforcement, as they would presumably prefer to avoid repeatedly paying “additional fees” when the same or similar issues arose in future.[142] For profit-oriented actors, cost is an incentive to change their organizational behavior. This aspect is decisive. Coming from a law and economics background, the expert was skeptical as to whether profit-driven “private bureaucracies” would abide by public law-inspired normative targets. When asked about this, Husovec said, “I'm a very practical-minded person, and I just don't believe that you can have courts to resolve things. I don't think every company responds to that. They respond to incentives, mostly financial incentives.”[143] According at least to this expert's theorization, tying individual rights adjudication to costs for platforms would reconcile platforms' main motivator (profit) with public interests (individual rights-based appeals).

3.3.2 *The European Parliament*

Roughly at the time the Commission was putting the finishing touches to its proposal, the European Parliament began publicly formulating its demands for the DSA. In October 2020, the European Parliament recommended that the Commission include a stringent, public law-inspired version of individual rights adjudication to control platforms' private governance. The parliamentarians' proposal was much more closely aligned to traditional images of “domestic” courts and administrative power than the Commission's ADR-flavored recipe. The European Parliament's Special Rapporteur argued that “content hosting platforms have *de facto* become public spaces in the digital sphere ... [and] public spaces must be managed in a manner that respects fundamental rights.”[144] To control platforms, the European Parliament requested a “system of sub-courts” offering “extra-judicial review” to individuals in matters relating to the digital realm.[145] Notably, such “sub-courts” should be run by Member States and not by private companies. Wölken's proposal was that:

141 Ibid at 4.

142 Ibid.

143 Interview with Academic, Consultant to the European Commission (n 39).

144 European Parliament Committee on Legal Affairs and Tiemo Wölken (Rapporteur) (n 100) recital F.

145 See Article 13 and Explanatory Statement pp. 21 and 23 in ibid.

> Member States shall establish independent dispute settlement bodies for the purpose of providing quick and efficient extra-judicial recourse when decisions on content moderation are appealed against.[146]

Regardless of the stretched interpretation of Article 114 of the Treaty on the Functioning of the European Union (TFEU) that such a proposal would require, proposing a general redress mechanism for users was a signal for what was at stake. Wölken's model emulates traditional judicial control over administrative power because it mandates an adjudicator with specific jurisdiction over rule enforcement conducted by a powerful organization which is not an administrative agency or police department but a social media company. However, traditional judicial redress must be "effective and workable in practice" without "overburdening" Member States' judicial systems.[147] In his report, Wölken further explains:

> For this reason, the rapporteur suggests setting up independent dispute settlement bodies in the Member States, composed of legal experts tasked with settling disputes between content hosting platforms and users regarding content moderation decisions. Such a simplified legal procedure would be designed to fit to the nature of content moderation disputes, and at the same time ensure that national courts are not overburdened by such disputes. As these bodies would act as a sub-court system, they may not replace traditional courts and further redress before courts must remain possible in all cases.[148]

These adjudicators would be specialized, effective, and accessible. However, the idea immediately ran into conceptual quicksand because it remains unclear what the role of such "simplified legal procedures" and "sub-courts" would be in relation to each other and in relation to Member State courts.[149] Though the Parliament had called for "extra-judicial review" by "independent dispute-settlement" bodies,[150] it neither defined "extra-judicial review" nor outlined the procedural framework for ensuring this review could occur.[151] Even though the Parliament's notion of a "sub-court" soon lost ground to the Commission's more ADR-oriented language, perspectives regarding ODSs as court-resembling guardians that protect individual rights remained prevalent. Several amendments to the Commission

[146] Article 13(1) ibid.

[147] Explanatory Statement p. 22 in ibid.

[148] Ibid.

[149] Ibid.

[150] Ibid at Article 13.

[151] The term "extra-judicial" is imprecise and politically charged, see Schramm, 'Michał Krajewski' (n 42) 125, 130–131; European Parliament Committee on Legal Affairs and Tiemo Wölken (Rapporteur) (n 100) 22.

proposal tabled by parliamentarians later in the legislative process conceptualize out-of-court dispute settlement bodies as a third form of review akin to "administrative or judicial review" that would control the platforms' rule enforcement.[152] In a similar vein, a staffer from Wölken's team argued that Europe needs faster and accelerated adjudication, which only new mechanisms could deliver.[153] Such new mechanisms, like Articles 20 and 21 of the DSA, would, the staffer said, be "faster and more adequate" than "parochial judicial institutions." Wölken's proposal was, in all its relevant aspects, adopted by the Parliament in a resolution passed in October 2020, urging the European Commission to make a formal proposal for the DSA. However, by this time, the Commission had already drafted large parts of the DSA based on the more law- and economics-focused version of individual rights adjudication outlined above. Nonetheless, we can reasonably assume that the Parliament shared its views with the Commission even before October 2020 in the above-mentioned informal consultations and technical meetings that went into each legislative project. But whether it shared its views with the Council is less clear.

3.3.3 *The Commission Proposal*

On December 15, 2020, the Commission published its proposal for the DSA. And indeed, parts of Husovec and Fiala's idea and the Parliament's demands for individual rights adjudication made the cut. The proposal envisaged ODSs as powerful ADR bodies with binding decision-making authority. In Article 18(1), which would later become Art. 21, for example, the Commission proposal stipulated that platforms "shall be bound by the decision taken by the body."

However, the Commission proposal did not reflect several key details of various experts' theorizations. The Commission proposal envisioned a cost structure that was still asymmetric but lacked punitive "additional fees." To recapitulate, the expert theorization wanted platforms to "compensate the creator's fee *and pay additional fees* to the ADR."[154] According to Husovec and Fiala, this additional fee would potentially encourage

[152] See amendment 186 [at 15a(1)(a)] in the Legal Committee or amendment 1126, 1127 in the Internal Market and Consumer Protection Committees. See at European Parliament, Opinion of the Committee on Legal Affairs, 2020/0361(COD), of 11 October 2021, AD \1240050EN.docx; see also at European Parliament, Committee on the Internal Market and Consumer Protection, Amendments 1012-1301, 8 July 2021, 020/0361(COD), AM \1235640EN.docx.

[153] Interview with European Parliament Staffer 1 (n 35).

[154] Husovec and Fiala (n 131) 4 (emphasis added).

platforms to modify their business model. In contrast, the Commission proposal only requires platforms to "reimburse the recipient for any fees and other reasonable expenses that the recipient has paid," according to Article 18(3) of the Commission proposal. If plaintiffs lose their case, they are not obliged to reimburse the platform's legal expenses, again in line with Article 18(3),[155] and the bodies may charge "fees" which, however, must be "reasonable and shall in any event not exceed the costs" of the dispute settlement procedure, the same subsection stipulates.

This begs the question of whether the limited fees proposed by the Commission can have the same effects as the "additional fees" proposed by Husovec and Fiala. Likely, the answer is no. Only a fee that hurts has the potential to incentivize platforms to change their behavior. Correspondingly, Husovec and Fiala stated that "it is noteworthy that these [desired] effects are observed with a relatively high fee" and that "changing the fee might potentially lead to lower or higher success rates."[156] Further, in this same paper, the "compensation" paid by the platform to the appellant would be 60 percent higher than the appellants' costs for referring the complaint to the adjudicator.[157] By contrast, in the model proposed by the Commission, the fee's main function seems to be covering expenses. Therefore, in the Commission proposal, fees are not "relatively high," as the expert theorization had argued they ought to be.[158] In turn, Husovec and Fiala were skeptical that low fees – like those in the Commission proposal and the final version of the DSA – would work toward the goal of improving content moderation.[159]

On the other hand, the Commission proposal also reflects some of the Parliament's positions. Although the Commission uses different, and perhaps even vaguely formulated, wording (like "self-regulatory efforts" and "information asymmetry"), the Commission proposal focuses on leveling the power imbalance between platforms and users. The role of ODSs is then to mitigate this power imbalance. In Articles 17 and 18 of the Commission proposal (which would become Articles 20 and 21 in the final text), the Commission advances a comprehensive, administrative model of redress to protect users' individual rights. Articles 17 and 18 essentially copy the two-step model of *internal* administrative and *external* judicial

155 Regarding the asymmetric cost structure see already Holznagel, 'The Digital Services Act Wants You to "Sue" Facebook over Content Decisions in Private de Facto Courts' (n 55)

156 Husovec and Fiala (n 131) 11.

157 Ibid 10. See last two rows at "Table 1: Model Parametrization."

158 Ibid 10.

159 Ibid.

review of administrative action.[160] This means that individuals are allowed to complain to the platform, which must handle the complaint in "a timely, diligent and objective manner" manner, as Article 17(3) of the Commission proposal puts it.

Additionally, users can take their case to the external adjudicatory bodies, which then independently review how platforms enforce their rules. In the words of the Commission, users should be able to "contest" the decisions of online platforms in front of "certified bodies that have the requisite independence, means and expertise to carry out their activities in a fair, swift and cost-effective manner."[161] This proposed two-step model of external and internal review bodies broadly mirrors the pattern of individual rights-based adjudicative control over administrative power.[162] In interviews, Commission lawmakers involved in drafting Articles 17 and 18 of the proposal explained this shift as mixing an ADR logic with a more administrative-law logic. One interviewed Commission staffer said that, whereas traditional ADR is typically agnostic as to the specifics of the parties to a case and the contractual relations they might have, Article 18 of the Commission proposal shifts the traditional focus of such adjudicative mechanisms to a more administrative or more power-controlling role.[163] Another staffer of the Commission argued that the Commission's motivating idea for creating the DSA, and for devising Article 18 in particular, was to balance out the effects that decisions relating to platforms could have on users and society.[164] This interviewee also argued that ODSs should function as a kind of first-instance adjudicator similar to Member State courts.[165] In this conception, ODSs were designed to go through the expected stream of cases like a trawler, winnowing out the minor and unexceptional cases to leave only the big and important ones to pass through to Member State courts.

Based on the Commission proposal and the accompanying remarks, the significance the Commission and the Parliament envisaged for ODSs becomes clear. Out-of-court dispute settlement bodies were initially proposed as adjudicatory guardians controlling social media platforms' efforts at private governance. Out-of-court dispute settlement bodies were always envisaged to be subordinate to courts. Yet their

[160] For theory and context on individual rights adjudication see at 2.2.
[161] Recital 44 Commission proposal (n 9).
[162] See again at 2.2.
[163] Interview with Staffer 2, European Commission (29 October 2021).
[164] Interview with European Commission Staffer 1 (n 35).
[165] Ibid.

organizational design and procedural function initially represented clear emulations of individual rights adjudication. Making an analogy to the most obvious institutions of individual rights adjudication – courts – Daniel Holznagel wrote that the proposed out-of-court dispute settlement bodies would "add another layer of dispute settlement: self-regulatory bodies to which users can appeal after platform decisions, delivering (partly) binding decisions. Thus, Article 18 Commission proposal attempts to establish external private bodies that shall have all the essential characteristics of courts."[166] However, one of the key characteristics of adjudicators, the authority to issue binding decisions, was to meet fierce resistance in the European Council.

3.3.4 *The Trilogues*

The DSA's legislative procedure pressed forward. The Commission issued its proposal in mid-December 2020, with the final version being adopted in summer 2022, just eighteen months after the Commission had released its proposal. However, out-of-court dispute settlement bodies left the legislative procedures considerably slimmed down due to opposition by some Member States and, arguably, also because of opposition by the platform industry.

3.3.4.1 Resistance by Member States

In principle, Article 18 of the Commission proposal was said to have a "rather low profile" in interinstitutional negotiations,[167] the reason being that this article was viewed by some as "user-centric," which was accepted as politically expedient by the Commission, the Parliament, and the Council.[168] The Council represents the interests of Member States in the EU lawmaking process. Unlike federal bodies such as the US Senate, however, its members are not elected to their positions but are instead sent by their respective national governments. Although, in tripartite meetings of representatives of the EU's three main arms (known as "trilogues"), there was a clear rift between, on the one side, the Commission and the Parliament and, on the other side, the Council. All the parties

[166] Holznagel, 'The Digital Services Act Wants You to "Sue" Facebook over Content Decisions in Private de Facto Courts' (n 55); see in contrast, speaking only of 'expert review' regarding the final version of the DSA: Martin Husovec, 'Will the DSA Work?' (*Verfassungsblog*, 9 November 2022) <https://perma.cc/FV8G-UPHZ>.

[167] Interview with European Commission Staffer 2 (29 October 2021) 2.

[168] Ibid.

involved seemed to agree with the principle of introducing some kind of independent adjudicator.[169] Prior to or during negotiations between institutions, experts began to scrutinize and comment on the Commission proposal. Some produced critiques of the notion of an ODS,[170] while others welcomed the DSA's attempt to establish an independent, additional remedy.[171] However, with the inevitable talk among industry representatives, activists, and Member State officials, it became clear that various (more or less concerted) efforts were at work to undermine ODSs and especially their legal authority.[172] Powerful industry actors apparently adopted a stealth strategy that would not expose them to the public eye while they monitored developments and sought back-channels with stakeholders in and outside Member States and EU institutions.[173] In Council-level discussions, ODSs' jurisdiction broadened in scope. Further, their "jurisdiction" expanded to include appeals by users who were drawing attention to illegal or harmful content.[174] The Commission proposal, unlike the Council's deliberation, had not allowed for such appeals. It was criticized for "turning a blind eye to the victims" of defamation or other violations when appellants were unable for whatever reason to contest platforms' decisions.[175]

169 Interview with European Commission Staffer 1 (n 35); Interview with European Commission Staffer 1 (n 35); Interview with European Commission Staffer 2 (n 168); Interview with European Parliament, Staffer 2 (n 35).

170 Arguing that the EU should have harmonized litigation fees in the Member States instead: Caroline Cauffman and Catalina Goanta, 'A New Order: The Digital Services Act and Consumer Protection' (2021) 12 European Journal of Risk Regulation 758, 770; very critical Jörg Wimmers, 'The Out-of-Court Dispute Settlement Mechanism in the Digital Services Act' (2021) 12 JIPITEC 421, para 32 et seq; also very critical 'The Digital Services Act Wants You to "Sue" Facebook over Content Decisions in Private de Facto Courts' (n 55).

171 Eifert, Metzger, Schweitzer and Wagner (n 44) 1026.

172 For example, German children's rights activists voiced "grave concerns" about Articles 17 and 18 Commission proposal in an open letter to two cabinet members, see Netzwerk zur Umsetzung der UN-Kinderrechtskonvention, 'Kinderrechte und das Gesetz über digitale Dienste' (23 March 2022) <https://perma.cc/GZP3-WUUP>.

173 This builds on numerous background talks with government officials, civil society organizations, and employees of technology corporations. See further: Corporate Europe Observatory, 'Big Tech's Last Minute Attempt to Tame EU Tech Rules – Lobbying in Times of Trilogues' (2022) <https://perma.cc/U2G7-4ESJ>; Corporate Europe Observatory, 'How Corporate Lobbying Undermined the EU's Push to Ban Surveillance Ads' (2022) <https://perma.cc/GC3S-6DQJ>.

174 See Article 18(1) DSA-General Approach as well as in the final version Council of the European Union (ed.), 'General Approach: Proposal for a Regulation of the European Parliament and of the Council on a Single Market for Digital Services (Digital Services Act) and Amending Directive 2000/31/EC.'

175 Eifert, Metzger, Schweitzer and Wagner (n 44) 1010–1012.

Yet one major change regarding Article 18 of the Commission proposal did come about as a result of negotiations with the Council. Several Member States, especially some Nordic countries, resisted the Commission's plan that decisions made by ODSs should have the authority to *bind* platforms.[176] Commission staffers recalled that several Member States, especially in the north and around the Baltic, were raising even constitutional concerns if ODSs were to have the authority to issue legally binding decisions.[177] Thus, opposition to ODSs' ability to make binding decisions was "relatively straightforward" in the Council.[178] Hence, at the Council level, the phrase that online platforms "shall be bound by the decision taken by the body" was cut from Article 18(1) of the DSA proposal in the Council's "General Approach" of November 2021.[179] This was a big deal. What once were imagined as "sub-courts" lost the authority to issue binding decisions.

3.3.4.2 Industry Resistance

However, the Member States just mentioned were not the only actors critical of the Commission proposal regarding an ODS's authority to bindingly adjudicate. Industry groups representing online platforms lobbied against binding decision-making authority for out-of-court dispute settlement bodies. Some of these groups voiced criticism of the potentially binding force of Article 18 of the Commission proposal. For example, Digital Europe, the powerful alliance of large online platforms in Europe, argued in a position paper:

> It is, however, unclear why the DSA proposal opts for this [binding] system while giving up its key advantage over court procedures: the non-binding, open nature of proceedings. This would mean that rather than a dialogue between complainant and platform, the dispute settlement will turn into a legal process with the level of formality and resource intensity of normal court procedures, which begs the question of what the added value of such a system would be.[180]

Intriguingly, in conversations with Commission staffers, such examples of industry criticism – or even just conversations with industry representatives – were never mentioned. But even though Article 18

[176] Interview with European Commission Staffer 1 (n 35); Interview with European Commission Staffer 2 (n 168).

[177] Ibid.

[178] Interview with European Parliament, Staffer 2 (n 35).

[179] Staffer 2, European Commission, Email to Author (on file with the author) (27 July 2022).

[180] Digital Rights Europe, 'Digital Serves Act Position Paper' <https://perma.cc/FCP8-5HNW>.

of the Commission proposal was described as "low profile" in the trilogues, lawmakers were presumably aware of the broad industry consensus against potent ODSs. Between December 2019 and October 2020, the Commission held at least 158 informal consultations with industry groups and digital companies to discuss the DSA/DMA package.[181] Digital Europe, for instance, sent representatives to meet formally with the Commission on three occasions during that period.[182]

Alongside the Commission, industry lobbying regarding the DSA/DMA package focused especially on Council representatives.[183] While "informal consultations" between the Council and industry groups are relatively rare (or under-reported), industry groups are in constant exchange with Member State representatives, who then set out and negotiate the Council's positions. How the Member States' representatives formulate their positions and the extent to which industry groups approach them (in Brussels or in their respective capitals) is largely hidden from the public. In other words, lobbying of Member States' agents can sway discussions in the Council and thereby influence EU lawmaking. Yet Member States share little (or no) information regarding whether or how intensively they consult with industry groups or companies. Further, based on numerous background talks with industry representatives and civil society activists, I can assure that several large technology companies lobbied also on their own terms, that is apart from their backing for Digital Europe above, intensely against Article 18 of the DSA proposal coming into law. For example, a particularly interesting alliance formed between one large digital corporation and child rights activists, which gave the former cover not having to be the one criticizing ODSs in public.

Further, Digital Europe representatives were present in at least some of the eleven meetings disclosed between industry, Council, or Member State representatives at the Council level.[184] How effective the platforms' lobbying actually was remains a matter of speculation. However, it seems plausible to assume that there was, perhaps, some effective influencing at work.

[181] Lobby Control, 'DSA/DMA: Wie Big Tech neue Regeln für digitale Plattformen verhindern will' (2020) <https://perma.cc/V8TL-Q3B6>.
[182] Ibid.
[183] Ibid.
[184] Ibid.

3.3.5 *The Final Version*

In conclusion, an innovative idea – combining ADR and individual rights adjudication to control platforms' private bureaucracies – lost much of its possible grip in the EU's legislative process. It combined public- and private-law aspects and built on prior expert theorization shared in informal consultations. Yet, as regularly happens with expert theorizations, only bits and pieces survived the political process. The Commission proposal ended up emulating only parts of the expert theorization it had called for. Specifically, opposition by some Member State representatives and major figures from industry seems to have stymied efforts to vest ODSs with the authority to *bindingly* adjudicate. According to a Commission employee who participated in negotiations in the trilogues, binding decision-making power would have meant "the real deal" as it could have taken the burden off Member State courts.[185] Based on the final design of the ODSs, several staff members from the Commission and the European Council questioned whether nonbinding ODSs would offer added value.[186]

Further, the Commission proposal did not stipulate that platforms must pay high "additional fees" when losing proceedings. Without these punitive fees, the efficacy of ODSs' economic incentives remains untested. As discussed, early practice of ODSs essentially confirms this as some ODSs actively work together with platforms together to make proceedings cheaper.[187] The only extra platforms must cover when they lose are the user's "reasonable" expenses. It remains to be seen how high these fees will be, but they will not be very high. So, platforms must cover their own expenses anyways and the expenses of the user, which will be minuscule, when the ODS decides in favor of the user. Thereby, platforms do evade punitive fees, contrary to the original idea pitched to the Commission by the experts. This basically decouples the result of the ODS proceeding from the financial incentive. If the whole point was to link bad moderation to losing proceedings which then would be costly, the current model seems nonsensical. As of now, platforms are in fact incentivized to moderate *less* instead of *better* as fewer takedowns will arguably cause fewer cases, which is economically advantageous because

185 Interview with European Parliament, Staffer 2 (n 35).

186 Staffer 2, European Commission, Email to Author (on file with the author) (27 July 2022); European Parliament, Staffer 1, Email to the Author (on file with the author) (17 November 2021).

187 See at 3.8.1.1.

platforms must pay more or less the same anyways.[188] Arguably, the cost aspect was not as prominent in the initial Commission proposal because at that stage it was expected that ODSs would have been accorded *binding* decision-making powers.[189]

However, it is important to note that the nonbinding nature of the decisions – or should we say recommendations? – can be an advantage, especially so given the scale of the whole operation. ODSs are designed to be mass adjudicators or, perhaps more fittingly, mass recommenders of what platforms should do. That might very well solve, say, eight out of ten cases at the pre-litigation level. This would indeed be a huge advantage compared to the situation today where individuals either resort to often ill-functioning internal appeals or costly and slow court proceedings. Offering middle ground here might very well prove to be a crucial improvement in the majority of cases, especially those where the platform indeed did an obvious mistake, like misapplying its own rules (which regularly happens).

But there are two more potential side effects. On the one hand, it seems likely that ODSs will become a business themselves. ODSs make money through the fees they collect. They need litigants to initiate proceedings. Hence, it seems plausible that different ODSs will compete for being the most user-friendly ODS as this means more litigation and, thereby, more fees.[190] Albeit being a business is not necessarily problematic, it appears questionable whether the described incentive structure indeed advances online justice or only produces a somewhat useless litigation industry.

On the other hand, there is no mechanism to maintain procedural and substantive cohesion among the bodies. For the DSA, it does not seem to be a problem that one ODS may decide totally different to another. While variation has its virtues, especially in federal systems like the EU and regarding socially sensitive matters such as speech, the foreseeable lack of consistency opens the door for utter confusion and, eventually, even might erode the uniformity of EU law. While maintaining uniformity of EU law is usually an almost neurotic issue for Luxembourg and Brussels, the DSA shifts responsibility for predictable normative chaos in a crucial

188 See in that regard also Daniel Holznagel, 'Article 21' in Ralf Müller-Terpitz and Markus Köhler (eds.), *Digital Services Act Kommentar* (Beck 2024) paras 72–78.

189 Framing ODSs as mere "expert" review, therefore, does not reflect the Commission's and the Parliament's initial plan. Both institutions clearly wanted ODSs to act as functional adjudicators (just like the underlying expert theorization, which also premised "binding" adjudicators). See in contrast Husovec (n 167).

190 Holznagel, 'Article 21' (n 189) para 72 et seq.

arena – what can be said online in Europe? – to a group of imperfect adjudicators that have an institutional interest to align their "jurisprudence" not with what is "right" (whatever that may be) but what brings them the most customers while remaining at least somewhat legally plausible. Legal plausibility is, as we all know, a rather low bar.

The DSA was passed as Regulation (EU) 2022/2065 on 19 October 2022. Shortly after the final editorial modifications, the Official Journal published the final version of the DSA on October 27, 2022.[191] It entered into force in November 2022, and legally applies since February 17, 2024.[192]

3.4 Institution

Now, let us have a look at how the DSA envisages ODSs as institutions. The institutional hermaphrodite birthed from the legislative procedure is best seen as emulating various bits and pieces of existing role models from other contexts.[193] The institutional design of ODSs borrows, on the one hand, from private law and ADR bodies and, on the other, from adjudicatory control over administrative action. Tracing this in detail is, inevitably, a bit technical – but going through these details builds the groundwork to fully grasp and appreciate the experimentation we saw once ODSs became operational.

The ADR aspects are mostly represented by the bodies' private-law structure and, after a lot of bickering in the legislative process, their nonbinding decisions. However, ODSs borrow their underlying function from adjudicatory control over administrative action and not from ADR. Functionally, ODSs can be conceptualized – and were publicly presented as such – as independent guardians protecting individual rights and controlling platform power. ODSs' purpose is not to decide on contractual disputes between customers and businesses regarding financial claims – like normal ADRs. ODSs are designed to protect freedom of expression and control platforms' administrative governance structures.

3.4.1 *Individual Rights*

Platforms may issue various "decisions" against their users, as specified in Article 20 of the DSA. According to Article 20(1), platforms can "remove or disable access to or restrict visibility" of content posted by the user,

191 OJ L 277/1, 27.10.2022, pp. 1–102.
192 Article 93 Regulation (EU) 2022/2065 (Digital Services Act).
193 For the theoretical framework on emulation see 2.3.

terminate accounts, or stop a user from monetizing content. These stipulations are designed to obstruct users from communicating on a particular platform. In this way, every moderation-related provision can potentially constrain a user's right to freedom of expression.[194] Out-of-court dispute settlement bodies are there to resolve disputes between individual users and platforms in the contexts of their "decisions." In other words, dispute resolution based on rights claims by individual users is one of the main mechanisms the DSA can call upon to mediate the power of platforms. Therefore, ODSs concern individual rights in that their provisions are aspects of individual rights adjudication.[195]

3.4.2 *Certification and Cost Structure*

In principle, ODSs are private bodies requiring "certification" by EU Member States. According to Article 21(6)(1) of the DSA, Member States may also establish public ODSs or "support the activities of some or all out-of-court dispute settlement bodies that they have certified."[196]

National authorities, called Digital Services Coordinators, as set out in Article 21(3) and Articles 49 to 51 of the DSA, are responsible for certifying ODSs. Member States can certify ODSs for a maximum period of five years and must demonstrate that they meet criteria such as independence, impartiality, expertise, ease of accessibility, and "clear and fair rules of procedure."

The cost regime of ODSs is rather litigant-friendly. According to Article 21(5) of the DSA, "the dispute settlement shall be available free of charge or at a nominal fee." Further, as previously mentioned, ODSs feature an *asymmetric* cost regime.[197] This means that individual users need only cover their fees (which should be limited), but not the costs of the platform in cases where the ODS decides in favor of the platform. However, let us suppose that the ODS decides in favor of the individual. In this event, the platform "shall reimburse that [individual] ... for any other reasonable expenses that it has paid in relation to the dispute settlement," according to Article 21(5) of the DSA. This asymmetric cost structure makes ODSs attractive for individual users and might, in principle, elicit a slew of appeals against rulings relating to content moderation.

194 See at 2.4. See from the vast literature e.g. Balkin (n 31); Klonick (n 12) 1609–1613; Hassrede (n 40).

195 See 2.2.

196 Based on several conversations with EU lawmakers it seems that not many Member States intend to set up such bodies.

197 See at 3.3.1 and 3.3.3.

Upon certification, ODSs will have to present annual reports listing the number of cases they received and "identify best practices" regarding dispute resolution as well as "systemic or sectoral shortcomings," in the words of Article 21(4) of the DSA. If a certified body fails to meet the required criteria, the relevant Digital Services Coordinator can revoke the body's certification, pursuant to Article 21(7) of the DSA.

3.4.3 *Compulsory Jurisdiction*

Further, ODSs exercise what could be described as "compulsory jurisdiction" over platforms' private governance. To be clear, ODS's jurisdiction is not exclusive. Article 21(1) of the DSA states that individuals may resort to judicial proceedings "at any stage" and that individuals can "contest those decisions by the providers of online platforms before a court in accordance with the applicable law." However, whereas users can choose between internal complaint-handling (according to Article 20 of the DSA), ODSs (according to Article 21), or judicial proceedings in their respective jurisdiction, platforms are obliged to "engage, in good faith, with the selected, certified out-of-court dispute settlement body with a view to resolving the dispute," according to Article 21(2) of the DSA. According to Article 21(2) subparagraph 2 of the DSA, platforms may only refuse to engage "when the dispute concerning the same information and the same grounds of alleged illegality or incompatibility of the content has already been resolved." Therefore, an ODS's jurisdiction does not require the *consent* of online platforms; rather, it is mandatory for platforms. Platforms can only block proceedings where content *and* basis for illegality or incompatibility with terms of service have already been established. This means that only almost identical cases are excluded from the provisions. Linked to this point, a Commission lawmaker reiterated that mandatory participation by platforms in such procedures is important because Article 21 of the DSA was designed "for the weaker party, which are the users."[198] Platforms also cannot bring proceedings before ODSs.

3.4.4 *Specialization*

Moreover, ODSs are specialized bodies. This is typical for entities that exercise individual rights adjudication but are not "normal" courts. Such specialized adjudicators, like Article I tribunals in the United States or Boards of Appeal in the European Union, build their legitimacy based on

[198] Interview with European Commission Staffer 1 (n 35) 2.

expertise in the complex, technical fields they adjudicate.[199] One major selling point for ODSs was establishing them as especially capable and expertise-based adjudicators for the thorny and technical questions of online individual rights adjudication. To get certified, ODSs must show "the necessary expertise" regarding "illegal content, or in relation to the application and enforcement of terms and conditions," according to Article 21(3)(b) of the DSA. As discussed in Section 3.8 below, we already see that most ODSs certified since summer 2024 claim to have some form of specialization or unique approach. That could be, for example, a particular focus on gaming platforms, app stores, and influencers, a particular understanding of fundamental rights, or specific language skills.

Further, their "jurisdiction" is limited to "decisions" of platforms to remove, uphold, restrict visibility or monetization of content that is either "illegal" or "incompatible with the terms of service" of a given network (Article 21(1) in conjunction with Article 20(1) of the DSA). In simple terms, out-of-court dispute settlement bodies control the private enforcement by platforms (the "decision") of public rules ("illegal content") or private rules ("incompatible with the terms of service"). In both cases, platforms exercise power over individuals when interpreting public rules or make and enforce their own rules largely unilaterally.

3.4.5 *Impartiality and Independence*

Impartiality and independence are major themes running through Article 21 of the DSA. As argued in the previous chapter, adjudicators must be impartial and independent.[200] Independence refers to the adjudicating entity's organizational design, whereas impartiality refers to the fair-mindedness and objectivity of the person adjudicating.[201] An adjudicator must be externally autonomous – that is, not bound by hierarchical command structures or factual constraint – and "internally" (in other words, consciously) objective and fair-minded regarding the procedure's outcome and any rules applied.[202]

[199] cf. at 2.2.2.

[200] See at 2.2.4.

[201] For a US perspective see James E Moliterno, 'The Administrative Judiciary's Independence Myth' (2006) 41 Wake Forest Law Review 1191, 1199–1208.

[202] cf. the recent case law by the ECJ on Poland's judiciary, see Independence of the Polish Supreme Court [2019] European Court of Justice (Grand Chamber) C-619/18, ECLI:EU:C:2019:531 paras 71–77.

According to Article 21(3)(a) of the DSA, ODS bodies can only be certified if they are "impartial and independent, including financially, of providers of online platforms and of recipients of the service." This is the main difference from platforms' internal complaint-handling mechanisms, which are neither independent nor (at least based on the wording of this stipulation) impartial. In that regard, Article 21(3)(c) of the DSA points out that delineating the makeup of the body's membership cannot be "linked to the outcome of the procedure." Therefore, in principle, ODSs are designed as independent bodies.

3.4.6 *Distinguishing Other ADR Bodies*

Lastly, we should distinguish ODSs from the rich variety of other existing ADR bodies, especially consumer ADR.

On the one hand, Article 21 of the DSA directly borrows from existing ADR schemes. Such ADR schemes are a widely used tool, especially in business–consumer relations. In Directive 2013/11/EU (the ADR Directive), the Union established a framework for Member States to introduce or harmonize existing ADR schemes when it came to consumer protection. Correspondingly, one Commission employee interviewed recalled that ODSs follow the line of the ADR Directive.[203] The ADR Directive enabled consumers to "submit complaints against traders to entities offering independent, impartial, transparent, effective, fast and fair alternative dispute resolution procedures."[204] Just as in Article 21 of the DSA, the "outcome of … [proceedings according to the ADR Directive] is not binding."[205] However, in the context of the ADR Directive, Member States may introduce binding consumer ADRs if they deemed these fit for purpose. Currently, the EU lists more than 400 bodies operating in the various Member States under the umbrella term "(consumer) out-of-court dispute settlement bodies." These bodies range from the Austrian Agentur für Passagier- und Fahrgastrechte, which bindingly adjudicates contractual disputes between carriers and customers, to the Swedish Trafikskadenämnden, which *non*bindingly reviews the amount of compensation paid by car insurance companies to accident victims.[206] However, according to Article 21(9) of DSA, the ADR Directive is still

203 Interview with European Commission Staffer 1 (n 35) 1.

204 Article 1(1) Directive 2013/11/EU.

205 Article 12(1) Directive 2013/11/EU.

206 For the former see the two respective websites: <https://perma.cc/6DQQ-B7KX> and <https://perma.cc/H432-8CHZ>.

applicable in the context of disputes between consumers and online platforms. Therefore, consumer-facing ADR bodies, as implied by the terms of the ADR Directive and the DSA's ODSs, should be viewed as *complementary* rather than identical.

Crucially, the ADR Directive seeks to solve disputes about contractual obligations that regularly focus on *monetary* claims. In contrast, ODSs adjudicate claims that mostly concern public rights. They are designed to control platforms' private bureaucracies and protect, at least as mediators, the fundamental rights of individuals. This differs from consumer-oriented ADR. Whereas most other consumer-concerning ADRs focus on specifically defined (and often highly technical) contractual disputes, Article 21 of the DSA relates to disputes about the "illegality" or "incompatibility with terms of service" of acts of communication. Although disputes regarding platforms' enforcement of terms of service are formally contractual disputes, the decisive normative questions concern freedom of expression and the balancing of fundamental rights.[207] Accordingly, the substance of most individual disputes boils down to balancing fundamental rights.[208] Further, most disputes involve classic administrative-law issues like the level of discretion an agent (the platform) enjoys when enforcing or making rules and procedural aspects of platform decision-making (duty to give reasons, right to be heard, etc.).[209] This fundamentally differs from contractual claims about compensation or related matters resolved by consumer-oriented ADR mechanisms.

Correspondingly, the power relations and the individual rights potentially threatened by platforms' governance of online communication fundamentally differ from mundane contractual and economic issues known from consumer-related ADR. To put this in stark terms, disputes over passenger rights or insurance claims are politically less relevant than disputes about societal, cultural, economic, religious, and political communication. The "integrity of public discourse as a basic institution

[207] For a theoretical perspective see: Balkin (n 31); from a US perspective: Klonick (n 12); from the perspective of legal practice see: Hassrede (n 40) paras 61–89.

[208] See Struth (n 102) 37. For an American perspective see Jack Balkin, 'Free Speech Is a Triangle' (2018) 118 Columbia Law Review 2011, 2015 et seq.

[209] The German Bundesgerichtshof (highest federal court for civil and criminal matters) ordered Facebook to implement several administrative-law style procedural rules, e.g. to hear customers before blocking their accounts for terms of service violations. See Hassrede (n 40). Further, most cases at the Oversight Board include extensive administrative-law like reflections on matters like the clarity and "legality" of the company's rules as well as the proportionality of its enforcement. See e.g., Former President Trump's suspension [2021] Oversight Board 2021-001-FB-FBR.

of liberal democracy" warrants guardianship over platforms that goes beyond the well-trodden paths of consumer-facing ADR.[210] External factors resulting from a lack of control over platforms' rulemaking and rule enforcement are, by now, simply considered too complex to address.[211]

Therefore, if we assume that the private governance of online communication functionally resembles administration, we then have to conclude that controlling these private administrative actors is not simply a matter of dispute resolution via ADR but something that more *resembles* adjudicative control over administrative power. In other words, ODSs *emulate* individual rights adjudication to control the power of platforms. However, as we will see, ODS's presumed capabilities to follow through remain underdeveloped.

Interestingly, the first certified ODS, the Maltese ADROIT, positions itself as primarily focused on commercial, transactional disputes.[212] However, if one interprets Article 21 of the DSA beyond its conventional focus on content moderation and platform governance – as most public lawyers typically do – there are likely many other disputes, particularly those related to transactional matters, such as in-app purchases, that fall within its scope.

3.5 Rules

The rules upon which ODSs base their decisions fall into two categories. Platforms enforce public law rules, that is, applicable Member State and Union law, and private law rules, that is, terms of service.[213] Correspondingly, Article 21(1), in conjunction with Article 20(1) of the DSA, subjects both these decisions to ODS review. Remember, by public law I refer to law set by public authority, meaning a state or the European Union, that governs the relationship between individuals and that public authority. Public Law in that sense refers to administrative, constitutional, and civil rights law. By private law, I refer to law governing the relationship between private individuals and legal persons, such as contracts or company law.

[210] For the quote see Eifert, Metzger, Schweitzer and Wagner (n 44) 993.

[211] Ibid; for drastic examples, see Citron and Norton (n 31) 1447–1453.

[212] See at 3.8.1.1.

[213] cf. already at 2.3. See further regarding Facebook's "normative order" Dan Wielsch, 'Die Ordnungen Der Netzwerke: AGB – Code – Community Standards' in Martin Eifert and Tobias Gostomzyk (eds.), *Netzwerkrecht* (Nomos 2018) 61 et seq (esp. 63–71).

3.5.1 *Public Rules and Illegality*

As a starting point, ODSs adjudicate appeals against moderation that enforces public rules. In the DSA's phrasing, ODSs have jurisdiction over "decisions taken by the provider of the online platform on the ground that the information provided by the recipients is illegal content," according to Article 21(1) in conjunction with Article 20(1) of the DSA. Illegal content means "any information, which, … is not in compliance with Union law or the law of any Member State which is in compliance with Union law, irrespective of the precise subject matter or nature of that law" (Article 2(g) of the DSA). Such cases can include, for example, allegations of libel and defamation.

It is unclear how ODSs maintain coherence within Member States' legal systems as their jurisdiction is separate from the domestic judicial process. Whether the ECJ would assume some harmonizing role remains up in the sky. Preliminary reference proceedings based on Article 267 TFEU at least seem unrealistic for the moment, as it would be unclear whether ODSs are "courts or tribunals of a Member State" within the meaning of said provision.[214] Possibly, the various ODSs will develop diverging or even conflicting doctrines. In the long term, Digital Services Coordinators might intervene in cases of egregious fragmentation. However, an ODS's ability to autonomously interpret Member State and Union law that provides grounds for illegality is wide-ranging. Whereas the ECJ is quick to protect its autonomy when interpreting EU law, ODSs would, in theory, have the freedom to decide on potentially millions of free speech-related disputes between platforms and EU citizens without oversight from Luxembourg. Ironically, the nonbindingness of ODSs' decisions and the fact that they are not formal courts places them under the radar of many lawyers and, arguably, the ECJ. Yet, even as somewhat impaired adjudicators, ODSs seem set to come up with their very own interpretations of EU and Member State law once the DSA comes into legal effect. Because ODSs are mainly funded by case fees, many might be economically incentivized to adopt the most user-friendly reading of the rules they apply. The DSA aims to harmonize the digital internal market, which in the Commission's view was fragmented

[214] For several reasons, we must assume that ODSs would not fall under the ambit of Article 267 TFEU as it is currently interpreted. Whether ODSs are "courts" is far from clear and if they could be seen as "of a Member State" remains also uncertain. Further, the ECJ regularly demands the authority to bindingly decide the disputes that are brought to it – an authority ODSs lack.

along, rather than harmonized across, Member State borders.[215] However, because ODSs lack normative or procedural mechanisms to guarantee their independence or safeguard the coherence by which they interpret evidence and issue rulings, which could discourage Digital Services Coordinators from intervening in a case too quickly, ODSs might exponentially *pluralize* the normative orders governing EU citizens' online communication. Currently, the DSA offers no solution to this potentially great fragmenting of norms, which might have already begun as the first ODSs become operational in 2024. However, as it may tend to happen outside the classic judicial process that silent transformation might pass unnoticed by many lawyers.

3.5.2 *Private Rules and Incompatibility*

Arguably more important, ODSs have jurisdiction over cases concerning the enforcement of all platform-made rules.[216] In the DSA's wording, ODSs adjudicate appeals against platform decisions the appellant deems "incompatible with . . . [the platform's] terms and conditions," according to Article 21(1) in conjunction with Article 20(1) of the DSA. That means, in simple terms, that users can 'sue' platforms whenever they think moderation does not align with the rules the platform made itself. There is, as explained above, little to no outside influence what these rules are. Platforms make them – as the next chapter shows – ad hoc, in meetings, somewhere in California (or, increasingly, Texas), staffed with lawyers and engineers. Because most moderation enforces terms of service and not domestic laws, we can assume that most disputes in front of ODSs concern incompatibility with terms of service, not illegality.

That platforms enforce mostly their own (globally unified) rules rather than diverse domestic laws has a simple reason: it is much easier and cheaper for the platform. Also, there are actually not that many laws platforms must enforce anyways, as they are largely shielded from intermediary liability, which means that platforms are not legally responsible for the content users post on them.[217] In the DSA framework, platforms

[215] Recital 1 et seq Regulation (EU) 2022/2065 (Digital Services Act).

[216] The DSA only speaks of "terms and conditions." That is because the terms and conditions are the doctrinal anchor point here. They are formally included into the contract between platform and user. However, those terms and conditions are usually nothing more than normative sign posts, which reference thick layers of cascading norms, most notably the "community standards/guidelines."

[217] In the US, that is § 230 CDC; cf. Eric Goldman, 'Why Section 230 is Better than the First Amendment' (2019) 95 Notre Dame Law Review 33.

must not enforce actual laws unless they are obliged to do so by a specific "notice" from a user, according to Article 16 of the DSA.[218] On the contrary, the DSA reaffirms that platforms do not have a "general monitoring" obligation for identifying illegal content.[219] Yet if platforms are not obliged to look for illegal content, they will find none and therefore remove none. Moreover, as many user notices and appeals come from someone arguing against *removed* content, it seems plausible to assume that "illegal content" will constitute only a minority of cases decided by ODSs. When asked, a Commission lawmaker estimated the likely percentage of appeals concerning illegality at ODSs to be between 20 and 30 percent.[220] Further, a lot of content that is illegal also violates terms of service so it could be deleted for the violation of the latter.

In the wording of Articles 21 and 20 of the DSA, both categories are exclusionary, although much illegal content also violates terms of service. Vice versa, this is not necessarily the case. Terms of service usually cover a much broader set of content and are often much more detailed than the normative acquis of the EU or the Member States. For example, EU and Member State law work with relatively broad normative categories, which are then interpreted in individual cases. For example, libel laws outlaw personal insults but do not specify specific terms, formulations, or symbols that constitute a personal insult.

In contrast, terms of service and the cascading sub-layers of rules devised by platforms are designed to offer a much more fine-grained normative categorization of speech acts. The reasoning behind this is straightforward. There are simply too many decisions to be made. Thus, platforms try to formulate quite specific rules on which content they allow or prohibit. As human communication is so complex, the normative quality of these categorizations varies, which will pose perhaps insurmountable problems for adjudicative bodies.

The terms of service of online platforms and the cascading rules and guidelines are often convoluted, inconsistent, and opaque. Yet they will arguably be the main basis for the decisions of the ODSs.

[218] This goes only for the DSA itself. Platforms may be subject to more expansive monitoring obligations in other regulatory contexts, e.g. to counter the dissemination of terrorist content online or to effectively enforce anti-libel judgments, as in C-18/18 (Glawischnig-Piesczek) [2019] European Court of Justice ECLI:EU:C:2019:821.

[219] Recital 30 Regulation (EU) 2022/2065 (Digital Services Act).

[220] Interview with European Commission Staffer 1 (n 35).

3.6 Decisions

Out-of-court dispute settlement bodies "resolve" disputes between individual users and platforms, in the words of Article 21(1) of the DSA. The decisions are quick but nonbinding on the particular platform.

3.6.1 *Quickness*

ODSs have to make their "solution" available to the parties within "a reasonable period of time and no later than 90 calendar days after the receipt of the complaint."[221] This speed of response is perhaps one of the main advantages that ODSs would have over traditional courts.[222] In "highly complex cases," ODSs may double that timeframe at their own discretion, according to Article 21(4) subparagraph 3 of the DSA.

3.6.2 *Nonbindingness*

ODSs' decisions are not binding upon the platform. In contrast to the wording of the Commission proposal,[223] the European Council inserted a new section into Article 21(2) subparagraph 3 of the DSA stipulating that "the body shall not have the power to impose the binding settlement of the disputes on the parties."[224] Recital 59 clarifies that "the outcome of the out-of-court dispute settlement procedure is *not* binding."[225] This muddled wording (the term "settlement" in Article 21(2) subparagraph 3 is new; other parts only speak of "resolve" in Article 21(1), "outcome" in 21(3)I, or "decision" in Article 21(5)) and the final choice of verb ("*impose* the binding settlement") presumably owes much to rushed debates in trilogues. However, regardless of the inconsistent wording of Article 21 of the DSA, decisions by ODSs are not "binding" for the platform.

3.7 Implementation

Now that we know that ODSs' decisions are nonbinding on platforms, the issue of implementation becomes even more difficult. As argued in the previous chapter, adjudicators use various normative mechanisms to protect rights and control power. They mediate, issue nonbinding

221 Article 21(4) subpara 3 Regulation (EU) 2022/2065 (Digital Services Act).
222 See e.g. Eifert, Metzger, Schweitzer and Wagner (n 44) 1026.
223 cf. Article 18 Commission proposal (n 9).
224 cf. for the Council's general approach, Article 18(1b)(3) in Council of the European Union (n 173).
225 Recital 59 Regulation (EU) 2022/2065 (Digital Services Act) (emphasis added).

guidance, or give informal advice. However, the authority to successfully employ such flexible enforcement tools arguably depends on an adjudicator's ability to bindingly decide on a case if the need arises. Like Damocles' sword, a potentially coercive judgment dangles over the heads of the disputing parties, and especially the controlled administrative power structures. Often, large power structures might be motivated to comply with nonbinding solutions *because* they seek to avoid a costly, embarrassing, and publicly delegitimizing judgment. However, as such a judgment is not even on the table, ODSs might have a hard time convincing or incentivizing platforms to do one thing or the other.

Apart from these issues of structure, ODSs face other obstacles. To begin with and as already mentioned, the Commission proposal and its underlying expert theorization seem to have underemphasized a crucial factor in the design of ODSs: unilateral platform rulemaking.[226] Platforms' terms of service are expected to be the basis for most ODS adjudication. However, as creations of private companies, platforms unilaterally change these rules whenever they deem fit. Adjudication based on rules that the supposedly controlled organization may change at whim thus becomes ceremonial. Notably, this design flaw is independent of the adjudicator's authority to issue binding decisions. Starkly expressed, even if an ODS's decisions were legally "binding," platforms could simply change the underlying rules and ex post "legalize" their enforcement. Moreover, because ODS decisions are in any case nonbinding, the EU would likely lack an "accountability culture," which would be required to effectively enforce any nonbinding outcomes of Article 21 of the DSA. Both these observations point to an uncertain journey ahead for ODSs. However, perhaps, there might be an important place for mediation, if not so much as a means of improving social medias structural governance flaws but at least to cost-effectively settle a large portion of disputes that would otherwise have to be handled by courts.

3.7.1 *Adjudication Without External Rules?*

There is a structural problem relating to the DSA's emulation of individual rights adjudication for online platforms. Section 3.2 of this chapter highlighted that the DSA focused mainly on improving how platforms enforce rules against individuals. Guided by rights-related discourses and expert theorizations, the EU identified platform rule enforcement as a problem that manifests in a continuous string of individual rights

[226] See already at 3.2.4.3.

infringements. Thus, establishing novel adjudicators, the ODSs, should have solved that problem. However, adjudicating rule enforcement is insufficient if it relies only on rules made unilaterally by the rule-enforcing entity. In other words, adjudication requires *external* rules to enable it to control power.[227] Otherwise, adjudication merely tells us whether a power structure obeys its own rules irrespective of said rules' quality and legitimacy. As of now, the DSA largely restricts ODSs to controlling whether platforms comply with terms of service – in other words, whether platforms follow *their own* rules. Compared to early announcements of ODSs that termed them "sub-courts" that would control platform power in general, the final version of Article 21 of the DSA – in conjunction with Article 14 – delivers potentially ceremonial institutions with questionable substantive impact.[228]

In most cases, ODSs will adjudicate whether a platform acted in a way that was "incompatible with its terms and conditions" vis-à-vis individuals.[229] In cases like these, Article 21 of the DSA does not allow ODSs to review platforms' rulemaking and rule enforcement based on superordinate external rules (for example, EU or Member State law). Instead, Articles 21 and 14 of the DSA establish, stabilize, and autonomize platform-made terms of service as a prime normative benchmark for millions of cases on free expression in Europe. To repeat, platforms unilaterally devise terms and conditions. Platforms can modify, amend, change, or scrap their terms of service on a whim; and they routinely do.[230] For example, Facebook altered its hate speech "community standard" more than twenty times between 2018 and 2024.[231] And these are only the top layer norms. There are many thick layers of normative material cascading below it, becoming ever more specific, detailed, and, arguably, confusing. Thus, the DSA designed adjudicators that decide cases based on rules that remain entirely within the discretion of the organizations the DSA seeks to control: the platforms. From this

227 See at 2.2.5. Notably, the Oversight Board focused strongly on external rules, i.e. international human rights law, to prop up its position vis-à-vis the company, cf. at 4.4.2.

228 See for the distinction between ceremonial and substantive organizational changes, John W Meyer and Brian Rowan, 'Institutionalized Organizations: Formal Structure as Myth and Ceremony' (1977) 83 American Journal of Sociology 340, 348–353.

229 See Article 18(1) subpara 1 in conjunction with Article 17(1) second alternative Regulation (EU) 2022/2065 (Digital Services Act).

230 See e.g. Meta, Transparency Center, Policies, Hate Speech Community Standard, Change Log accessible via <https://perma.cc/2YRS-K46C>.

231 cf. Meta Transparency Center, Home, Policies, Hate Speech Standard, archived via: <https://perma.cc/2YRS-K46C>. See in that regard also the critical account of Mark Lemley, 'The Benefit of the Bargain' [2023] Wisconsin Law Review 237.

perspective, the lack of authority on the part of ODS to issue "binding" decisions, which led to a great deal of bickering in the European Parliament, is in fact a pseudo-problem.

As long as platforms can ex post modify rules as they see fit, even formally "binding" adjudication based on said rules would remain largely *ceremonial*. An Emulated Guardian built into such a control regime could not, in any event, assume lasting authority. On the contrary, as Section 3.7.4 explores in detail, "binding" adjudication might even be counterproductive because it might incentivize platforms to water down their rules or make their enforcement less stringent to avoid further appeals. While some free-speech absolutists might consider this a positive development that could do away with platform "censorship" altogether, a more considered (and in my view preferable) perspective acknowledges that cleansing digital realms of hate, misinformation, and other externalities is a vital task. From this viewpoint, however, watered-down rules or circumscribed enforcement are the opposite of what the DSA intended. Based on these observations we will toward the end of the book briefly discuss why future reforms should focus more on advancing meaningful participation in platform rulemaking.[232]

3.7.2 *Persuasion, Naming, and Shaming*

Because ODSs "lost" their authority to issue legally binding decisions on platforms, naming and shaming emerged as a second-order strategy for asserting their guardianship. Even though these decisions do not legally bind platforms, the latter might nonetheless implement recommendations the decisions have advanced. Such nonbinding normative sentences can be even more sustainable than binding decisions as they might foster a dialogue between the adjudicator and the overseen body.[233] Yet such adjudicatory oversight presupposes a certain level of adjudicatory authority – ideally acknowledged by both parties. Adjudicatory authority arguably correlates with an adjudicator's ability to resort to binding decisions.

In our case, platforms are obliged to engage in "good faith" with the procedures, as set out in Article 21(1) of the DSA, once they are apprised of the facts of a case. Further, repeated noncompliance might lead to public pressure to comply. Several experts from the Commission and the Council voiced hope that such a "naming and shaming" approach might pressure

[232] See Chapter 6.

[233] See at 2.2.2.

platforms into complying with nonbinding decisions.[234] In essence, naming and shaming relies on *publicizing* organizational misdemeanor. Either the public at large or specific groups (like shareholders) can then pressure an organization or company into changing its behavior as it runs counter to the interests of the relevant stakeholders of the wider community. Naming and shaming is a technique often used by various types of oversight bodies that either lack other enforcement capabilities or choose to resort to such informal sanctioning.[235] However, even though naming and shaming is a popular strategy – and sometimes perhaps the only one at hand – for many NGOs, watchdogs, or international organizations, its track record is complicated.[236] Institutional changes resulting from naming and shaming campaigns are often contradictory and do not necessarily lead to better institutional practices, especially in the context of human rights.[237]

Yet nonbinding ADR bodies can be very effective. For example, Finland has a system and tradition of nonbinding but largely effective ADR bodies in consumer relations.[238] In Finland, and to a degree in Scandinavia in general, compliance with nonbinding ADR rulings is socially expected and thereby "informally" yet effectively enforced.[239] But even though such informal enforcement regimes can work, they typically require a cultural and social underpinning to stabilize and enforce their normativity. Whether ODSs will mobilize sufficient cultural and social capital to pressure the private bureaucracies of Meta and X into a normatively more desirable direction seems doubtful. Chapter 5 analyzes how complicated and multifaceted these kinds of strategy are, even for the Oversight Board – an Emulated Guardian that relies on

[234] Interview with European Commission Staffer 1 (n 35) 1; Interview with European Commission Staffer 1 (n 35) 2; Interview with European Commission Staffer 2 (n 168) 2; Interview with European Parliament, Staffer 2 (n 35).

[235] See for an overview of German regulatory law Philipp Florian Irmscher, *Öffentlichkeit als Sanktion* (Mohr Siebeck 2019) 16–20. For an analysis of naming and shaming in the context of banking supervision see ibid 149 et seq.

[236] Skeptical: Emilie M Hafner-Burton, 'Sticks and Stones: Naming and Shaming the Human Rights Enforcement Problem' (2008) 62 International Organization 289.

[237] For a case study on naming and shaming as a regulatory measure to mitigate corporate human rights abuses Marcia Narine, 'From Kansas to the Congo: Why Naming and Shaming through the Dodd-Frank Act's Corporate Governance Disclosure Won't Solve a Human Rights Crisis' (2013) 25 Regent University Law Review 351, 391–396.

[238] See in general regarding nonbinding adjudication in Finland Kirsikka Linnanmäki, 'Mediation: A Change in Finnish Court Culture?' in Laura Ervo, Pia Letto-Vanamo and Anna Nylund (eds.), *Rethinking Nordic Courts* (Springer 2021) 235 et seq.

[239] See in general Laura Ervo, Pia Letto-Vanamo and Anna Nylund (eds.), *Rethinking Nordic Courts* (Springer 2021).

public pressure to discipline Meta. On a practical level, ODSs are not designed to orchestrate the large-scale media coverage and social-engagement campaigns required for effective naming and shaming. In contrast to the Oversight Board, the ODSs' role is to decide as many disputes as possible. Out-of-court dispute settlement bodies are not mandated to issue general normative sentences, offer advice, or recommend procedure-related policies to platforms.

3.7.3 *Reports*

Further, ODSs could in theory also publish general reports to discipline social media platforms. Based on Article 21(4) of the DSA, ODSs will report annually to their Digital Services Coordinators. The Digital Services Coordinators would then, at least every two years, publicly report on "systemic or sectoral shortcomings," which would perhaps include examples of misgovernance in the private sphere.[240] However, these reports focus mainly on "the functioning" of ODSs and not on the platforms.[241] Arguably, the "guardians" assessing "systemic" problems manifesting on platforms are the platforms themselves, which carry out mandatory risk assessments (see Article 26 of the DSA). According to Article 26(1) of the DSA, large online platforms "shall diligently identify, analyze and assess any systemic risks stemming from the design, including algorithmic systems, functioning, and use." In these risk assessments, major online platforms will assess how their "content moderation" and "terms of conditions and their enforcement" influence systemic risks. Since ODSs are specialized adjudicators for "terms and conditions and their enforcement," using ODSs' adjudicative expertise for aggregated reports of contested governance and enforcement practices represents a promising and pragmatic future policy option.

3.7.4 *Incentives*

To address ODSs' lack of binding decision-making powers and relatively limited duties to report, the final item in the control toolbox is (mostly economic) incentives. Such incentives are a broad category partly distinct from authoritative control and public legitimacy-oriented naming and shaming efforts. Economic incentives target companies' profit orientation. From the organization theory perspective assumed here, economic incentives have up- and down-sides. People and organizations do not

[240] Article 21(4) subpara 2 (c) Regulation (EU) 2022/2065 (Digital Services Act).
[241] Article 21(4) subpara 1 ibid.

always act in ways that economic theories of rational behavior presuppose. Instead, considerations of public legitimacy also play a role.[242] Economic incentives are also only one out of a range of instruments that can be applied. We also know that public legitimacy can be buttressed by an essentially ceremonial conformity to public expectations, for example by companies emulating allegedly rights-protecting policies. Thereby, actors can reconcile profit orientation (internal practice) with public legitimacy (external façade).

Regarding ODSs' scope for economic incentivizing, two aspects seem decisive. Article 21 DSA establishes an asymmetric cost structure. Participating in those proceedings costs platforms more than users. As platforms must participate, being dragged in front of these bodies will accrue costs on platforms. This cost then would – so the theory goes – motivate platforms to improve their enforcement.

We will now briefly discuss, first, how the finally passed version of Article 21 DSA pretty much flounders that idea and, second, whether the idea works – even from a theoretical angle – in the first place. Simply put, the first question is whether ODSs incentivize platforms to do *anything* and, second, if so, whether ODSs motivate platforms *to do the right thing*. While the answer to the first question may be affirmative, unfortunately, the answer to the second question seems to be negative.

3.7.4.1 ODS's Incentive Structure Is Insufficient

Let us begin with the first issue. Are the costs platforms must cover high enough to incentivize them to change anything in their moderation practices? The idea was to make ODSs *compulsory* for platforms and to make *losing* ADR proceedings *costly* for platforms. Article 21 of the DSA delivers on the first part of this idea. Also, when platforms lose these procedures, they must "bear all the fees charged by the body and shall reimburse the recipient . . . for any other reasonable expenses that they have paid," as Article 21(5) of the DSA sets out. Therefore, the "fees" and "any other reasonable expenses" charged by an ODS might incentivize platforms to improve their governance.

However, what the experts initially wanted – and claimed to have experimental evidence for its efficacy – are "relatively high fees" that would be "additional" to the costs of the parties.[243] In other words, not only participating in the proceedings but *losing* the proceedings was

[242] See at 2.4.4.
[243] Husovec and Roche Laguna (n 67) 27.

supposed to be costly. Essentially, these extra fees in case of losing the proceedings were supposed to function as "fines" and "penalties."[244] The expert theorization, as presumably pitched to the Commission, requires more than cost-covering "fees." However, in the passed version the bulk of the fees occur always, irrespectively of whether the platform loses or not. Such a model, already on a theoretical level, arguably fails to incentivize platforms not to lose proceedings but only to avoid proceedings altogether.[245] One particularly concerning prospect to avoid ODS proceedings would be to curb moderating in general. Less moderation, fewer proceedings.

Husovec, who participated in a workshop for the Commission on the drafting of what would later become Article 21 DSA and who had pitched "compulsory and compensated ADR" to the Commission therefore distanced himself from the Commission's restrictive wording that limited fees to "reasonable expenses."[246] In contrast, Husovec in an interview for this book stressed that the reasonable-expenses formulation in Article 21 of the DSA was "nothing" he "came up with."[247] Further, he argued that one can read Article 21 of the DSA's reasonable-fees phrase as in fact aligning with his proposal, because it refers to "this extra fine that comes on top of the nominal fee."[248] Nevertheless, one could also "read it as just the standard thing like you win the case, so there is some reasonable cost."[249] Thus, it seems doubtful whether the current model of mandatory fees will incentivize platforms to change anything in their content moderation.

3.7.4.2 Bereft of Rulemaking, Adjudication Cannot Deliver Accountability

That being said, one may question how viable some of the assumptions implicitly or explicitly made by the Commission and their consulting experts indeed are. It seems, from my perspective, questionable whether individualized incentive models like that proposed by Husovec and Fiala can – even on a theoretical level – incentivize platforms to *do the right*

244 "In line with what is typically observed on online platforms, we mimic penalties for providers such as fines and injunctions to stop service," Husovec and Fiala (n 131) 4 (there at footnote 16); ibid 10–11 (highlighting that the fees are "ADR penalties").
245 See in that sense also Holznagel, 'Article 21' (n 189) paras 76–78.
246 Interview with Academic, Consultant to the European Commission (n 39).
247 Ibid.
248 Ibid.
249 Ibid.

thing, that is to say, positively reform their content moderation machineries.

Husovec and Fiala claim to "provide ... empirical evidence for the potential positive effects of the proposed policy and identifies factors to consider when operationalizing it in practice."[250] However, the real-world validity of some of that alleged evidence appears doubtful. That is for one simple reason: platforms have (much) more choices than Husovec and Fiala suggest.[251] In their paper, they argue that platforms have basically two options when losing in front of an ODS: positively improving their content moderation or keeping it as it is, thereby risking more fines in the future. As platforms want to avoid fines, they would choose improving their content moderation, which then enables them to win future procedures. With such a narrowed bouquet of choices, the paper's encouraging results are hardly surprising.

If only they were realistic. In reality, platforms can resort to myriad other options to avoid losing more cases. They can, for example, blur their normative material so that it is unclear what is allowed and what is not. Where there is legal uncertainty, one is less likely to be held accountable. And indeed, platforms constantly modify their rules, not always adding to their clarity. In simple terms, costly adjudication based on individual cases but with virtually no influence on rulemaking, may incentivize platforms to ex post "legalize" what they are doing, blur the rules, scrap them, or simply curb moderating altogether to avoid cases.

Therefore, in conclusion, we see how adjudication on its own cannot solve these problems. Irrespective of whether a decision is binding or economically incentivizing – unless the DSA reins into the rulemaking and infrastructural set up of platforms, which it does not – most structural reform of content moderation remains entirely at the whim of platforms.

[250] Husovec and Fiala (n 131) 12.

[251] The experimental design built on a "finitely repeated sequential game of two players," conducted in 2018 and 2019 with 148 participants. In the experimental design, the rules determining the correctness/incorrectness of a take-down/keep decision – in this case relating to terms of service – are *stable*. These rules remain the same throughout the experiment. However, in reality, platforms regularly amend their terms of service and curb/ramp up their enforcement. Therefore, platforms have not one choice about improving enforcement (yes/no), as suggested by the experimental design, but many; I would argue at least three. They can either decide to modify their enforcement (yes/no) *or* their rules (yes/no), or they can decide to modify their enforcement *and* their rules (yes/yes). Both, the second and the third possible choice – in my understanding – seemed to be missing in the expert theorization, cf. Husovec and Fiala (n 131) 6–7, 12–16.

3.7.5 *Mediation*

The criticisms outlined above remain valid when the aim, as articulated by the DSA, is to curb platform power and enhance platform governance in Europe. However, there is a more optimistic perspective to consider if we shift our focus from large-scale governance reform to the amicable resolution of the many potential disputes between individuals and platforms. From this viewpoint, ODSs might simply serve as another forum for settling disputes – one that is certainly less costly than courts.

There may still be value in the mediatory role of ODSs, especially when they operate at scale. As this chapter has shown, establishing ODSs as robust adjudicators would have been exceedingly difficult, even if they had been given formally "binding" authority. However, their current lack of binding power can either be performatively circumvented – an approach seemingly preferred by actors like User Rights and the Oversight Board's Appeal Center, two of the first ODSs certified in summer 2024 – or leveraged through mediation processes. At the end of the day, ODSs have to combine both approaches; and we already see signs of this with User Rights and the Appeals Center. While mediation may not provide strong enforcement mechanisms, it offers a low-risk, cost-effective solution for resolving many disputes between individuals and platforms.

Although it remains unclear how such mediations would directly contribute to structural improvements, it is not beyond possibility. Platforms might, through repeated mediations, identify problematic patterns and use these insights to drive internal changes. Whether this approach will succeed is a question for future research, as it depends on the mediatory effectiveness of ODSs and the willingness of platforms to engage with these processes and proactively implement their outcomes.

That being said, the mediatory quality and trajectory of ODSs remains unclear. Neither of them seems to be specifically designed to facilitate communicative exchange between platform and user. They are designed to decide, not to set up a framework for two disputing parties to reach a mutual agreement. The human resources required for participating in tens or potentially hundred of thousands of proceedings also renders it unlikely that ODS will become mediators in the classic sense.

3.8 Fragments of Practice

Fast forward to late 2024, only weeks before final submission of the manuscript of this book. Shortly after the DSA entered into force, shrewd lawyers, consumer protection activists, academics, and entrepreneurs all over Europe had begun to explore how they could contribute to – and make a buck off – what seems indeed poised to grow into an ecosystem of different ODSs. After one and a half years of preparation, the first ODSs were certified in summer 2024 and became operational one after another through late summer and fall of that year. Although we are only at the very early stages of this implementation phase, the remaining pages of this chapter map the first fragments of practice relating to Article 21 DSA.

As always, reality turned out different than anticipated. Fascinatingly, the very lack of a coherent legislative vision seems to have unleashed creativity, experimentation, and what could end up being a healthy diversity of approaches. In some sense, the botched Article 21 DSA created a playground, a "sandbox" in regulatory legalese, for experiments with different approaches as to which model might work toward very diverse ends. Remarkably, ensuing practice shows elements of convergence, osmosis and, in the sociological framing of this book: emulation, between the two case studies. That is driven partly by personal overlaps. One of the first ODSs, User Rights, was cofounded by a former staff member of the Oversight Board. However, overlaps are also strategically driven by the Oversight Board itself, which founded its very own ODS, the Appeals Centre Europe, in Dublin. The Appeals Centre then, is headed by Thomas Hughes, the former Director of the Oversight Board. Further, isomorphism of structure and vision between some of the ODSs and the Oversight Board appears driven by a shared quest, which is the overarching question of this book: how to control globally active, vastly powerful private power structures. One answer seems to be through private law structures that seek to incorporate public law elements.

However, igniting these actors' creative drive – not least motivated by the opportunity to tap the deep pockets of social media platforms – yields, I argue, two fundamentally important effects which have the potential to significantly alter content moderation, the administration of justice in general and, from a European perspective, the functionality and autonomy of EU law.

We begin by contrasting the defining characteristics of three distinct bodies involved in this landscape. These differences highlight the varying institutional forms that ODSs might take in practice and, crucially, underscore the divergent goals they pursue. For instance, some bodies, like ADROIT – the first-ever certified ODS – may focus primarily on resolving disputes related to economic activity on platforms, with little emphasis on content moderation. Others, such as User Rights, may prioritize advancing EU fundamental rights in the context of platform governance, particularly with respect to rectifying individual content moderation decisions. Still others, such as the Appeals Centre, might aim to drive structural change by facilitating mass dispute resolution and providing feedback on systemic risks, though they may operate somewhat independently of EU law. The one body that was already active at the time of this writing but which this chapter does not explore in greater detail is the Hungarian "Online Platform Vitarendezö Tanács," an ODS focused exclusively on Hungarian content.[252]

These diverse approaches are not mutually exclusive; rather, they are complementary, each presenting its own opportunities and challenges. In the second part of this discussion, we will therefore examine three key issues that could have seismic implications. First, we will explore the use of large language models in ODS decision-making, then turn to the evolving compliance ecosystem, and finally consider the potential erosion of traditional notions of the unity and autonomy of EU law.

3.8.1 *Experiments and Experiences*

All three, ADROIT, User Rights, and the Appeals Centre, show important similarities. They all build on Article 21 DSA, they all are certified by their respective Digital Services Coordinators in Malta, Germany, and Ireland respectively, and they all, in one way or the other, seek to settle disputes between individuals and platforms to hold the latter accountable, and make a profit themselves. All three bodies are profit-oriented, all three are expected to handle a high case load and all seem poised to experiment with some degree of automation.

3.8.1.1 ADROIT

In summer 2024, in scorching Malta, the Maltese Digital Services Coordinator certified the European Union's very first ODS. That ODS is run by a company called RGOAL Ltd., trading as ADROIT – short for alternative dispute resolution of information technologies – with a registered address and physical office located in the building of a five star resort and conference hotel just outside Valletta. ADROIT's website comes in six languages, including English, French, German, and Italian.

252 See further Daniel Holznagel, 'Article 21 DSA Has Come to Life' (*Verfassungsblog*, 5 November 2024) <https://perma.cc/YRK8-3XVH>.

ADROIT can be seen as a paradigmatic example of the traditional ADR-focused vision for ODSs. It mirrors, to an extent, earlier private law inspired models for ODSs that were discussed in the legislative process.[253] Founded by a group of Malta-based German lawyers and a Maltese technical auditor with prior experience in legal tech, ADROIT is part of a broader trend of companies addressing compliance issues for online marketplaces, particularly in the realm of online gambling dispute resolution.

What sets ADROIT apart, however, is its emphasis on one crucial element for the future development of ODSs: entrepreneurship. After all, ODSs are not just legal tools. They are businesses in their own right. Under Article 21 of the DSA, platforms are required to participate in ODS proceedings and cover the associated fees. Given the vast user bases of online platforms in Europe, this creates a potentially lucrative market. ADROIT's model suggests that we are likely to see highly specialized ODSs emerge, focusing on niche areas such as disputes involving demonetized influencers, app store missteps, or the increasingly profitable world of in-app and in-game purchases (with some games themselves functioning as platforms). Furthermore, we might witness the rise of specialized ODSs catering to particular platforms, types of disputes (e.g., defamation, hate speech, cyberbullying), or even political ideologies (conservative, progressive, etc.). The key for legal entrepreneurs is identifying user groups with sufficient grievances to generate a steady stream of complaints – and thereby revenue.

It is important to note that ADROIT, with its roots in traditional consumer ADR, is not focused on complex content moderation issues that involve fundamental rights.[254] Instead, ADROIT's core focus lies in resolving transactional disputes – particularly those related to monetary or contractual issues between individuals and platforms.[255] According to interviews with ADROIT staff, these often involve matters such as disputes over the pricing and functionality of in-app purchases.[256]

Consequentially, ADROIT positions itself as a mechanism between individuals and platforms to "minimize compliance costs" for the latter.[257] To achieve this, ADROIT retains the right to "agree on tailored pricing

[253] See at 3.3.3.
[254] Interview with ADROIT Founder (30 October 2024); Interview with ADROIT Staffer 1 (30 October 2024); Interview with ADROIT Staffer 2 (30 October 2024).
[255] Interview with ADROIT Staffer 1 (n 255).
[256] Interview with ADROIT Founder (30 October 2024); ibid.
[257] ADROIT, 'Fee Model' s A. IV <https://perma.cc/R5L9-T526>.

packages depending on the size, complexity, and (expected) caseload of individual Online Platforms."[258] Moreover, the company intends to enter into "Mutual Administrative Assistance Agreements ... with ... Online Platforms," which also cover "case decision fees."[259] The company notes that when "proceedings become somewhat repetitive due to a high number of similar cases concerning the same respondent, this may result in lower average processing costs per case."[260] The founder of ADROIT, a lawyer, argues that

> it would not be in the users' interest if our proceedings incur incalculable costs on the platforms. This would, eventually, make platforms adversarial and ultimately derail the DSA. We believe we have to work with the platforms together – independent, of course – but at the end of the day, we solve problems for both sides, not only for users.[261]

From multiple angles, this approach is eminently reasonable. Most importantly, ODS decisions lack legal binding force. Thus, persuading and enticing platforms into compliance, rather than coercing them (with what tools, after all?), emerges as a pragmatic strategy. This holds especially true when one adopts a holistic view of what it means to "implement" a decision within sprawling organizational structures. Only when the relevant actors in key positions of power within a platform's hierarchy grasp and are genuinely persuaded by external feedback will they be inclined to recalibrate internal practices in response. Such recalibration is likely to occur only if platforms perceive compliance as aligning with their own interests. In this light, compliance fundamentally depends on corporations seeing ODSs not as external impositions but as effective problem-solvers for the platforms themselves.

However, this perspective also highlights the diverse ways in which different ODSs interpret their mandates. Some ODSs position themselves as protectors of fundamental rights – perhaps even adversarial advocates for users against platforms. Others, shaped by their institutional backgrounds, take a markedly different approach. In this light, one might interpret the "Mutual Administrative Assistance Agreement" as ADROIT reserving the right to make structural noncompliance with applicable norms less costly for platforms. Given the nonbinding nature of ODS decisions, this strategy appears logical. Yet, making noncompliance

[258] Ibid.
[259] ADROIT Fee Model (n 257) s G. II.
[260] Ibid G. I.
[261] Interview with ADROIT Founder (n 255).

cheaper seems, to me, contrary to some of the original intentions of Article 21. This does not necessarily mean such developments would prove detrimental. However, the prospect reveals two critical points. First, it remains an open question whether the carrot is genuinely more effective than the stick when it comes to motivating platforms. Second, if the "stick" was meant to take the form of financial disincentives, further lowering the cost of noncompliance risks extinguishing any lingering hope that ODSs could, through cumulative costs, nudge platforms toward better practices. Remarkably, making procedures cheaper along the way might not even end up being a strategic choice for ODSs but a legal requirement. Article 21(5)(3) demands that the fees charged to the platform "shall in any event not exceed the costs incurred by the body." If, economics of scale indeed drive down the costs of ODSs', one could argue that ODSs are even *obliged* to lower their fees vis-à-vis platforms.

3.8.1.2 User Rights

While the economic realities and motivations discussed are broadly similar among ODSs, they diverge notably in their orientation toward public law. In this regard, User Rights, the first ODS certified in Germany, represents a distinct model. Certified a few months after ADROIT, User Rights stems from a fundamentally different context, cofounded by a former Oversight Board staffer – an intriguing point of intersection between the two case studies. According to its website and internal documents, including initial decisions I reviewed, User Rights conceptualizes its role as almost entirely driven by public law principles. It ambitiously describes its mission as

> Social media platforms are more than just a means of communication – they shape public debate and the exercise of the right to freedom of expression. We offer effective procedures for resolving content moderation disputes with social media platforms. Our decisions help to protect the legal order, democratic values and fundamental rights online.[262]

User Rights further emphasizes that platforms are obliged to "cooperate in good faith" with its decisions. The decisions I reviewed – particularly one in a more "complex" case – read much like court rulings, notably resembling judgments by a German Verwaltungsgericht, or administrative court

[262] In my opinion, it is far from clear which role Article 14(4) DSA foresees for fundamental rights in content moderation in Europe. Eventually, it will be what the Commission and the Court make it to be, which might take years.

(unsurprisingly so as User Right's founders are German-educated lawyers).[263]

Strikingly, User Rights decision-makers have directly applied the CFR to online platforms, adopting what is, at present, a broad interpretation of the ECJ jurisprudence. According to User Rights, Article 14(4) DSA merely formalizes a pre-existing obligation for platforms to enforce fundamental rights.[264] This approach could certainly merit a standalone analysis.[265] However, I limit myself here to the more cautious observation that the direct application of EU fundamental rights to social media platforms appears rooted in a noble intent – though its long-term efficacy remains uncertain, given the nonbinding nature of the decisions mandating such application.

When questioned about the nonbinding status of their decisions, one of the cofounders of User Rights emphasized two points. First, he saw one primary challenge to "introduce public law" to platforms' managerial ecosystem.[266] While not explicitly stated – though discussed in Chapter 2 – it is understood that public law currently only plays a minimal role in platforms' internal content moderation due to their global scale. ODSs, then, may represent the first opportunity to compel platforms to engage with local law on a case-by-case basis.[267] Second, to users, the interviewed cofounder characterizes their role as providing a "right to be heard, akin to a court" and delivering a comprehensive legal analysis.[268] Once established, the cofounder argues, a well-reasoned, rigorous legal assessment would be difficult for platforms to disregard.[269] For instance, given that Article 21 DSA is one of the few provisions offering users substantively new options, the User Rights cofounder reported that at numerous conversations in Brussels, the European Commission reiterated its commitment to "make Article 21 DSA work."[270]

Bringing public law principles into private, managerial settings is no small feat. As discussed in this chapter, ODSs have limited power to

[263] Decision on file with the author.
[264] Decision on file with the author.
[265] The issue has been discussed extensively in both domestic and European contexts. See e.g. Quintais, Appelman and Ó Fathaigh (n 91); Kulick (n 91) 279 et seq; David Gray, 'Is Google a State Agent?' (2024) 27 Stanford Technology Law Review 206, 219 et seq.
[266] Interview with User Rights Co-Founder (n 257).
[267] Ibid.
[268] Ibid.
[269] Ibid.
[270] Ibid.

compel platforms to act against their preferences – a reality underscored by platforms' demonstrated resilience in deflecting external pressures throughout the legislative process.

Yet, there are still grounds for cautious optimism. Well-reasoned decisions and ongoing monitoring by the European Commission could foster an ecosystem in which platforms find it increasingly difficult to ignore the external feedback provided by ODSs like User Rights. This feedback's impact may be amplified by the persuasiveness of legal argumentation, pressure from the Commission, and the legitimizing role of external experts. Just as the Oversight Board leverages the authority of its high-profile members – including a former Head of State, a Nobel Peace Prize laureate, and law professors, which we will examine in the next chapter – User Rights has established an "Advisory Board" on a smaller but similarly strategic scale. Currently, this Advisory Board comprises several renowned young academics from across European jurisdictions (the Netherlands, Croatia, Portugal, and Germany) who are tasked with advising User Rights on complex issues and exploring the future role of ODSs.

3.8.1.3 Appeals Centre Europe

The third player then is the Appeals Centre Europe (the "Appeals Centre"), which set up shop with twenty-five employees in Dublin. It received a whopping fifteen-million-dollar kick off funding by the Oversight Board Trust.[271] That trust is behind what we know as "the Oversight Board" and about which we will learn more in the next chapter.[272] The Appeals Centre is headed by Thomas Hughes, the founding Director of the Oversight Board and former Executive Director of Article 19, a globally active free speech advocacy group named after the respective provision in the International Covenant on Civil and Political Rights.[273]

Unlike ADROIT, which focuses more on commercial disputes, and User Rights, which focuses on EU fundamental rights, the Appeals Centre seeks to advance structural reform. In that it is clearly a brainchild of the experiences at the Oversight Board. According to an early interim webpage, holding the place until the official website is launched and the

[271] Holznagel, 'Article 21 DSA Has Come to Life' (n 253).

[272] See at 4.3.1.2.

[273] A few months before the Board went public with its plans to start its own ODS, Hughes, then the Director of the Board's administration, explored the potential of Article 21 DSA in a blog post, see Thomas Hughes, 'Practical Considerations for Out-of-Court Dispute Settlement (ODS) under Article 21 of the EU Digital Services Act (DSA)' (*DSA Observatory*, 8 February 2024) <https://perma.cc/6BNZ-U2WL>.

Appeals Centre begins accepting cases, the Centre posits that it "sees the potential for out-of-court dispute settlement bodies to contribute to ensuring greater accountability and transparency of social media companies, through helping to identify recurring areas of concern and systemic risk arising from how their platforms function."[274] That is noteworthy for several reasons.

First, compared to the other and at this point smaller ODSs, the Appeals Centre's focus seems to shift a little from settling individual disputes to using those disputes as leverage to remedy larger, more structural governance flaws at platforms. In an interview, the Director of the Appeals Centre explains that the thinking was, from the start, to operationalize individual cases as structural remedies.[275] The Director envisions the Appeals Centre as a "heat map" that can identify particularly pressing issues in content moderation.[276] The Appeals Centre adjudicates very differently to the Oversight Board. The latter decides only a few cases per year and gives structural governance advice. It is, in many respects, not at all about solving disputes. The Appeals Centre, in turn, is about settling as many disputes as possible and, as a side effect, getting a better understanding what the structural problems are. When asked about the relationship between the Appeals Centre and the Oversight Board, Hughes smiled and says "although I'm really not a fan of the Supreme Court analogy when it comes to the Oversight Board, in relation to us it has something to it. The Oversight Board focuses on a few important cases and gives guidance. We, in turn, are a small claims court in this analogy."[277]

Second, it connects Article 21 DSA to "systemic risk assessments" and "independent audits" as foreseen in Articles 33–37 DSA, a section of the DSA that never came up in interviews with EU lawmakers as connected to ODSs.[278] The idea is simple. The DSA requires that very large online platforms – actors like Facebook and X – self-assess the "systemic risks

[274] Appeals Centre Europe, preliminary website, via <https://perma.cc/EM28-EV3D>.
[275] Interview with Appeals Centre Director (1 November 2024).
[276] Ibid.
[277] Ibid.
[278] Of course, this does not rule out the possibility that some EU lawmakers may have considered systemic risk assessments when pondering how to give teeth to Article 21 of the DSA. However, given that the legally binding nature of ODS decisions was only stripped late in the drafting process – and that systemic risk assessments remained conspicuously absent across two years of discussions and numerous interviews – it seems safe to assume that these elements were initially seen as rather separate facets of the DSA.

in the Union stemming from the design or functioning of their service," Article 34(1) DSA. Such systemic risks might include the "dissemination of illegal content" or "any actual or foreseeable negative effects on civic discourse and electoral processes, and public security," Article 37(2)(a) and (c) DSA. In principle, these platforms conduct these reports themselves. Yet, given that they have little incentive to declare their services excessively risky to the societies they operate in, such self-assessments may not be particularly rigorous. External and independent actors could be more reliable stewards of systemic risk assessment. For this reason, the DSA mandates that very large online platforms submit to independent audits once a year.

However, to readers who, like the author, have some – even if only modest – experience working in corporate law, these audits might not seem especially promising on closer inspection. Auditors are tasked with assessing whether Very Large Online Platforms (VLOPs) comply with obligations to assess and mitigate systemic risk, but these are procedural rather than substantive obligations. It would hardly be surprising if VLOPs found it fairly easy to present assessments and mitigation efforts as compliant, while leaving their core practices untouched.

Enter, the Appeals Centre. Given its "small claims court"-like intake of potentially tens of thousands of cases in short periods of time, the Appeals Centre might very well be in a position to "identify, analyse, and assess" systemic risks posed by large online platforms. The Appeals Centre appears, therefore, to already work on ways to manage the "data," as its interviewed Director put it, of all the cases it handles to aggregate and translate them into modes of action eventually fostering structural governance reforms at platforms.[279]

The appeal of this approach is clear. Unlike the systemic risk assessments conducted by platforms or the independent audits by auditors – an industry with well-known issues across sectors – the Appeals Centre's assessments of 'systemic risks' are grounded in real complaints from actual users. Moreover, platforms are required to fund the Appeals Centre while users pick the ODS, which mitigates a structural moral hazard familiar from rating agencies and auditors, where leniency may be motivated by fear of losing lucrative clients.[280] With a nominal five-euro fee charged to users to deter frivolous appeals, we can reasonably

[279] Interview with Appeals Centre Director (n 276).

[280] Roy C Smith and Ingo Walter, 'Rating Agencies: Is There an Agency Issue?' in Richard M Levich, Giovanni Majnoni and Carmen M Reinhart (eds.), *Ratings, Rating Agencies and the Global Financial System* (Springer US 2002); Pepa Kraft, 'Do Rating Agencies Cater?

assume that most of these appeals will highlight genuine grievances, which, as noted in Chapter 2, often reveal underlying structural governance issues.

3.8.2 Opportunities and Challenges

The emerging diversity of ODSs offers opportunities and challenges. The following are, I believe, the most important ones.

3.8.2.1 Automated Justice and Large Language Models

First, we are already witnessing productive experimentation within the field of ODSs. Remarkably, the most groundbreaking initiatives appear driven by a blend of profit motives and efforts to operationalize public law principles vis-à-vis platforms. To achieve profitability, ODSs must operate on a substantial scale, processing large volumes of texts and images. Consequently – and this, arguably, was unforeseeable during the drafting of the DSA prior to the launch of ChatGPT – most, if not all, ODSs will likely rely extensively on "artificial intelligence," especially large language models, to streamline operations.

ODSs aim to establish decisional systems that can manage high case volumes, apply normative frameworks, and – following some degree of human review – issue reasoned decisions or, to be precise and depending on the grade of automation, produce texts that read like reasoned decisions.[281] Some systems are oriented more toward business considerations, others toward fundamental rights, and others still with a direct focus on structural governance. Yet, these are differences of emphasis rather than of fundamental approach. By combining normativity with technological sophistication, ODSs strive to construct what neither content moderation (limited by its profit motive) nor conventional courts (limited by lack of technological expertise) could achieve in the past decade: an efficient, moderately profitable system that processes large quantities of text, applies normative standards, and produces consistent, coherent decisions in individual cases. We are currently in the very early stages of understanding the limitations of integrating automated systems into justice frameworks – and the warnings are plentiful. However, should the bodies established under Article 21 DSA succeed in effectively

Evidence from Rating-Based Contracts' (2015) 59 Journal of Accounting and Economics 264.

281 For the complexities of erecting such systems see (n 94).

embedding AI into their services, the potential insights gained could be transformative.

Therefore, in essence, ODSs represent large-scale experiments on integrating AI into content moderation, administrative justice, and judicial proceedings. As such, ODSs hold significant implications for both private and public administrators and adjudicators, as Chapter 2 theorizes that distinctions between these activities are largely matters of degree. While these domains might (and should) follow somewhat distinct norms and procedures, this book demonstrates that sustaining public values will inevitably depend on private administration and enforcement.

All ODSs seem committed to incorporating some degree of automation into their workflows, from automating case handling systems to elements of case assessment and potentially generating written outputs. However, they uniformly assert that the "decision," as required by Article 21 DSA, will ultimately be made by a human.[282] Whether this commitment is realistic remains an open question, largely hinging on scale: if each individual decision takes approximately two hours, like ADROIT anticipates it in its Fee Model, ODSs would need hundreds, potentially thousands, of decision-makers.[283] This would eventually turn ODSs into operations reminiscent of the content moderation mills of earlier years – a distinctly undesirable prospect. Clearly, automation has a significant role here, and ODSs are poised to advance these solutions. How to keep this process transparent, identify reliable indicators of success and failure, and determine precisely when a human truly makes the final decision are all questions that remain open – and these issues extend beyond ODSs to the broader use of "artificial intelligence" as a whole.

As one cofounder of User Rights noted, they are "experimenting with how to integrate large language models (LLMs) or, eventually, agentic AI into case analysis, initial normative assessments, and text production."[284] Similarly, the Director of the Appeals Centre observed that "LLMs are ideally suited to this type of work" and mentioned potential uses for "triage," facilitating the further processing and escalation of cases.[285] Setting up and maintaining an LLM is costly; in this respect, the fifteen million in initial funding provided by the Oversight Board Trust

[282] Interview with User Rights Co-Founder (n 257); Interview with ADROIT Founder (n 255); Interview with Appeals Centre Director (n 276).

[283] cf. for the estimation of hours ADROIT (n 258) s C. III. 3.

[284] Interview with User Rights Co-Founder (n 257).

[285] Interview with Appeals Centre Director (n 276).

gave the Appeals Centre a considerable advantage. When questioned on whether the Appeals Centre would use Meta's LLMs, the Director clarified that, for the time being, they intended not to use models developed or operated by Meta.[286] Designing LLMs that truly align with public law values, if possible at all, likely calls for building them from the ground up rather than adapting potentially normatively compromised existing models.

Should some ODSs – each organized as private entities – succeed in unraveling the Gordian knot discussed in Chapter 2, namely, the perceived tension between public-minded decision-making and efficiency on one hand, and profitability on the other, they could set a compelling example for scalable justice systems on a larger scale.

3.8.2.2 Compliance Ecosystem

Another intriguing aspect – both an opportunity and a challenge – emerging from the diversity of ODSs is their potential to broaden the range of compliance mechanisms. So far, we have seen how legislative wrangling eroded many initially intended compliance tools for Article 21 DSA, such as binding decisions, punitive costs, and possibly even naming and shaming. Yet as the varied landscape of ODSs develops, we may witness the beginnings of a complex, multilayered compliance ecosystem.

In other words, the normative force of ODS decisions – despite their lack of classic mediation roles and the minimal direct exchange between platforms and individuals, even within ODSs – might gradually crystallize through a mix of approaches. Although these decisions are nonbinding, the European Commission seems prepared – and reportedly has conveyed as much to ODS founders, according to several interviewees – to support the adjudicative outcomes of ODSs.[287] While the Commission cannot strictly enforce individual ODS decisions, it could demand explanations for instances of structural or even individual noncompliance by platforms, creating substantial compliance pressure despite the absence of legal obligation.

Second, ODSs might enlist support from academics and activists to examine and advocate for implementation, thereby applying social and discursive pressure for adherence to ODS decisions. Third, we are likely to see trends of specialization, competition, and convergence among the

[286] Ibid.

[287] Interview with User Rights Co-Founder (n 257); Interview with Appeals Centre Director (n 276).

various ODSs. Some may focus on national contexts, such as the Hungarian "Online Platform Vitarendezö Tanács." Others, like ADROIT, might veer away from content moderation entirely, focusing on other types of issues. Some may prioritize fundamental rights but reflect national predispositions due to language or legal traditions. There could even be ODSs dedicated to specific platforms or issues, like an ODS for art-related disputes or one for LGBTQI issues. Such specializations could enhance expertise and foster identifiable, "manageable" publics that, through intermediaries, may be motivated to demand compliance.[288]

This diversity, however, also presents challenges. We may see vastly different normative interpretations and approaches, along with ODSs potentially influenced by vexatious litigants or politically motivated groups, each pushing content moderation in divergent directions. The influence of coordinated efforts by special interest groups should not be underestimated – as will be discussed in the next chapter.

3.8.2.3 Normative Fragmentation and the Autonomy of EU Law

This diversity poses a fundamental challenge to the prevailing notions of unity and autonomy in EU law. The EU – and particularly the ECJ – may find itself in a "genie out of the bottle" situation. ODSs are now adjudicating fundamental rights, albeit in varied and, over time, inevitably centrifugal ways. This will generate a growing body of (formally nonbinding) decisions, interpretations, and doctrines that apply EU law – especially the CFR – in a patchwork of interpretations.

This isn't necessarily a problem. From the perspectives of legal pluralism, federal diversity, and specialized expertise, it could even be considered beneficial. After all, one aim of localizing DSA enforcement is to align review processes more closely with the social norms of specific communities (how feasible this is remains to be seen, especially given the influence of large language models, which rely on foundation models that are anything but local).

Yet, from a contemporary standpoint on the autonomy of EU law, the situation seems peculiar.[289] The EU, typically committed to eradicating

[288] For a theorization of publics and their relation to infrastructure – and ODSs can be understood as a procedural infrastructure – see Benedict Kingsbury and Nahuel Maisley, 'Infrastructures and Laws: Publics and Publicness' (2021) 17 Annual Review of Law and Social Science 353.

[289] For a reconstruction of the ECJ's jurisprudence on the autonomy of EU law see Charlotte Langenfeld, *Die Autonomie des Unionsrechts in der EuGH-Rechtsprechung* (Mohr Siebeck 2024).

divergent interpretations of core principles, has created quasi-adjudicative bodies tasked with applying EU law – yet without any supervisory mechanism over their decisions. Under current doctrine, none of these bodies can refer questions to the ECJ via the preliminary reference procedure, as none qualifies as a "court or tribunal of a Member State." And why should they? A traditionalist might argue that ODSs are not courts, and their "decisions" are not legally binding; some might not even consider their decisions as law. But this view would be shortsighted. Out-of-court dispute settlements bodies are, by design, normative actors. They are tasked with applying the law and protecting fundamental rights. They are meant to be the first, fastest, and most knowledgeable venue for fundamental rights protection in European content moderation.

ODS decisions will inevitably matter, even if they only contribute to a thick layer of conflicting interpretations, expectations, and degrees of compliance. This accumulation of diverse interpretations will undeniably shape the practical reality of EU law and, particularly, the CFR in the online sphere. The pressing question now is whether the EU – and especially the ECJ – will devise a mechanism to integrate these diverse, imperfect, yet inventive guardians of EU fundamental rights dynamically into the Union's legal system.

3.9 Conclusion

Thus, for now, the conclusion remains ambivalent. On the one hand, on paper, one can only conclude that ODSs represent an innovative idea that fell victim to political horse-trading. In their final design, ODSs lack potent control tools. As outlined above, Emulating Guardians have three types of control tools at their disposal. First, they could be given the authority to issue legally binding decisions. Second, they can issue nonbinding general normative statements that enhance the controlled entity's general governance practices (reminiscing Chayes' public-law litigation approach). Third, other specialized forms of control depend on the specific field and economic incentives. As of now, and arguably never in reality, ODSs cannot "bindingly" adjudicate when it comes to platforms. They are not mandated to issue general normative sentences and advice following the model of "public law litigation."

Lastly, they seem unlikely to be able to economically incentivize platforms to improve governance as the asymmetric cost structure implied in the DSA appears flawed for two reasons. First, the "compulsory and compensated ADR" model, as set out in the DSA's Article 21 provisions, will be dysfunctional as long as platforms maintain unilateral control over most of the pertinent rules (namely, the terms of service) upon which ADR bodies will presumably be basing their decisions. If platforms can change the rules, they can avoid recurring decisions and thereby hobble the "economic incentive" argument. On the other hand, Article 21 of the DSA's cost-incentive model is restricted to fees and reasonable expectations. Therefore, it lacks a big enough carrot to incentivize platforms.

Second, since the summer of 2024, we have witnessed a dynamic and inspiring wave of ODS certifications. While all certified ODSs operate according to the same general framework, each brings its own distinct focus. Some prioritize transactional disputes, others emphasize fundamental rights, and still others concentrate on systemic risks. All, however, can be seen as experiments in integrating large language models into mass decision-making – a process that, if successful, could have far-reaching implications beyond the realm of content moderation. As such, the final judgment on ODSs remains pending. What is clear, however, is that this area promises to be a crucial and fertile field for future research.

Chapter 5 analyzes the three ingredients that would be needed for Emulated Guardians such as ODSs to be able to exert meaningful control or to at least become accountability forums for online platforms: external, legitimate, and concise rules; guardianship and authority; and an accountability culture. But now follows Chapter 4, which analyzes the Oversight Board.

4 The Oversight Board

4.1 Introduction

Announced in 2018 and operational since 2020, the Oversight Board immediately created quite a buzz. Since then, the Board's practices left a lasting impression on debates about how to control social media platforms' immense rulemaking and rule enforcement capacities. Some criticized the Board as a presumptuous Silicon Valley legitimacy-grab.[1] Others highlighted the ambiguous and potentially performative effects of the "Supreme Court" label that Meta had managed to pin on the Board.[2] Others again consider the Board an imperfect but innovative and potentially positive step for more platform accountability.[3] Scholars and practitioners have analogized the Board

[1] See esp. Evelyn Douek, 'Facebook's "Oversight Board:" Move Fast with Stable Infrastructure and Humility' (2019) 21 North Carolina Journal of Law & Technology 1; Julie Cohen, 'From Lex Informatica to the Control Revolution' (2021) 36 Berkeley Technology Law Journal 1017, 1038 et seq; Riku Neuvonen and Esa Sirkkunen, 'Outsourced Justice: The Case of the Facebook Oversight Board' (2022) 12 Journal of Digital Media & Policy; David Wong and Luciano Floridi, 'Meta's Oversight Board: A Review and Critical Assessment' (2023) 33 Minds and Machines 261; Evelyn Douek, 'The Meta Oversight Board and the Empty Promise of Legitimacy' (2024) 37 Harvard Journal of Law & Technology 373.

[2] Josh Cowls, Philipp Darius, Dominiquo Santistevan and Moritz Schramm, 'Constitutional Metaphors: Facebook's "Supreme Court" and the Legitimation of Platform Governance' (2024) 26 New Media & Society 2448. See further from a more normative perspective Thomas Kadri, 'Juridical Discourse for Platforms' (2022) 136 Harvard Law Review (Forum) 163; highlighting the general relevance of performative institutions in internet governance: Matthias C Kettemann, *The Normative Order of the Internet* (Oxford University Press 2020) 242; implicitly also: Rotem Medzini, 'Enhanced Self-Regulation: The Case of Facebook's Content Governance' 24 (2022) New Media & Society 2227.

[3] See especially: Kate Klonick, 'The Facebook Oversight Board: Creating an Independent Institution to Adjudicate Online Free Expression' (2020) 129 Yale Law Journal 2232; Kate Klonick, 'Inside the Making of Facebook's Supreme Court' *New Yorker* (12 February

to the US Supreme Court,[4] US courts,[5] international courts,[6] administrative tribunals,[7] human rights tribunals,[8] "courts" in authoritarian regimes designed only to deflect responsibility,[9] human rights grievance mechanisms,[10] customer- service,[11] "fourth-branch" institutions, or transnational hybrid adjudicators.[12] The Board's founders have described it as a "non-judicial grievance mechanism" as envisaged by the terms of the UN's *Guiding Principles on Business and Human Rights*.[13] Meta also compares the Oversight Board to human rights grievance mechanisms, presenting it as "a new mechanism for independent review of certain content decisions."[14] Meta figures have also mentioned the possibility of future emulation of the Board by other actors as the company "hope[s] [the Board] serves as a useful model for other companies and initiatives."[15]

However, this self-description is merely stating the obvious. Clearly, the Board is not a traditional judicial institution but an organizational unit established and financed by a private entity, in this case a social media company. Arguably, it will manage to remedy a few particular grievances.

2021) <https://perma.cc/44Y7-S8VH>; see further: Laurence R Helfer and Molly K Land, 'The Facebook Oversight Board's Human Rights Future' (2023) 44 Cardozo Law Review 2223; Nele Meier and Angelo Jr Golia, 'The Emerging Normative System of Meta's Oversight Board: An Introduction' MPIL Research Paper Series No. 2022–09; Rishi Gulati, 'Meta's Oversight Board and Transnational Hybrid Adjudication: What Consequences for International Law' KFG Working Paper Series No. 53 March 2022; Paul Gowder, *The Networked Leviathan: For Democratic Platforms* (Cambridge University Press 2023) 140 et seq; Cowls, Darius, Santistevan and Schramm (n 2) 17 et seq.

4 Klonick, 'Inside the Making of Facebook's Supreme Court' (n 3).

5 Klonick, 'The Facebook Oversight Board: Creating an Independent Institution to Adjudicate Online Free Expression' (n 3) 2476–2487. But see n 323 at ibid 2476.

6 Marlene Brosch, 'Alles neu macht das . . . Facebook Oversight Board?' [2021] MultiMedia und Recht (MMR) 26, 26.

7 Klonick, 'The Facebook Oversight Board: Creating an Independent Institution to Adjudicate Online Free Expression' (n 3) 2477. Highlighting the Board's function as "ex post review one would expect from a judicial body," Evelyn Douek, 'Content Moderation as Systems Thinking' (2022) 136 Harvard Law Review 526, 568.

8 Laurence R Helfer and Molly K Land, 'Is the Facebook Oversight Board an International Human Rights Tribunal?' (*Lawfare*, 13 May 2021) <https://perma.cc/AZ4W-PSBR>.

9 Evelyn Douek, 'Facebook's "Oversight Board:" Move Fast with Stable Infrastructure and Humility' (n 1) 15 et seq.

10 Interview with Oversight Board Staffer 2 (13 April 2022).

11 Interview with Oversight Board Staffer 3 (6 May 2022).

12 Gulati (n 3).

13 The full quote reads that the UN Guiding Principles on Business and Human Rights "specify that non-judicial grievance mechanisms (such as the Oversight Board) should deliver outcomes that accord with internationally recognized human rights."

14 Meta, Corporate Human Rights Policy at 03 – accessible via: <https://perma.cc/EK3G-FC7E>.

15 Ibid.

But the need to remedy individual grievances does not fully account for the Board's characteristics, origins, context, and function. Instead, and in contrast to the EU's out-of-court dispute settlement bodies (ODSs) discussed in the previous chapter, the Oversight Board firmly aims to elicit *structural* change at Meta beyond the resolution of (very few) disputes between the company and its users. The disputes and the Board's dispute resolution capacity must be understood mainly as a means to that end. This should come as no surprise, since the Board bends existing categories and draws bits and pieces from various role models that draw from both public- and private-law roots. However, viewing the Board solely from a legal perspective, especially through the lens of human rights, risks neglecting the legitimacy issues pertinent to it from an institutional perspective. In turn, dismissing the Oversight Board as a PR gimmick, a superficial take on content moderation, or even as a solely *private* body with little or no public relevance risks underestimating the possibly novel paradigm the Board (and bodies like it) may represent. In our increasingly globalized and interwoven world, private organizations wield ever more power.[16] This power manifests especially through rulemaking and rule enforcement.[17] Controlling this power requires new mechanisms that warrant at least experimentation beyond traditional, private law-inspired control instruments like liability or competition law. Notwithstanding Meta's self-serving interests, we can approach the Board as a pioneering experiment in bringing into being a new kind of control mechanism – even though, or precisely because, many of its features and underlying ideas replicate

[16] From the vast literature on private domination in the digital constellation see esp. Linnet Taylor, 'Public Actors Without Public Values: Legitimacy, Domination and the Regulation of the Technology Sector' (2021) 34 Philosophy & Technology 897; see in general: Alfred C Aman, 'The Globalizing State: A Future-Oriented Perspective on the Public/Private Distinction, Federalism, and Democracy' (1998) 31 Vanderbilt Journal of Transnational Law 769, 816 et seq; Jody Freeman, 'The Private Role in Public Governance' (2000) 75 New York University Law Review 543; Gunther Teubner, *Verfassungsfragmente: Gesellschaftlicher Konstitutionalismus in der Globalisierung* (Suhrkamp 2012) 18 et seq; illuminating on the reflexive relationship of legal and commercial globalization: Doreen Lustig, *Veiled Power: International Law and the Private Corporation 1886–1981* (Oxford University Press 2020); for free expression in today's mediated society: Jack M Balkin, 'Free Speech Is a Triangle' (2018) 118 Columbia Law Review 2011. See further already Matthias Ruffert, *Die Globalisierung als Herausforderung an das Öffentliche Recht* (Boorberg 2004).

[17] Douek highlighted that content moderation is more than billions of individual decisions based on preset rules. However, thinking of adjudicators' historical role in controlling administrative(-like) structures, rulemaking and rule enforcement are perhaps the practices most receptive to adjudicatory control (in contrast to, e.g., platform design). cf. Douek, 'Content Moderation as Systems Thinking' (n 7) 530 et seq.

preexisting ones. Therefore, reduced to its essentials, the Board can best be characterized as an emulation (albeit imperfect) of *individual rights adjudication*. The Board adjudicates claims about individuals' rights to curtail Meta's power, particularly regarding rule enforcement and, increasingly, with respect to rulemaking. Board members exercise impartial judgment, and the body presents itself as operationally independent in many (if not all)[18] respects, decides disputes between individuals and a dominant power structure, and bases its decisions on norms, especially those enshrined in international human rights law. And yet it is a private body with a circumscribed adjudicatory authority. In other words, the Oversight Board is also an *Emulated Guardian*.

The key takeaway from this case study is as dialectic as it is cautiously optimistic. On the one hand, the Oversight Board, comparable to the Digital Services Act (DSA)'s ODSs, reflects the idea of using individual rights adjudication to control platforms' private bureaucracies, in this case Meta's content moderation machinery. But although Meta promoted the Oversight Board as "a Supreme Court for Facebook," the corporation never designed it to be a *potent* adjudicator. One could therefore dismiss the Board as a merely ceremonial appropriation of symbolism that is meant to publicly legitimate Meta's scolded content-moderation behemoth. However, and this is the dialectic aspect, as the case study shows, the Board's design, staffing, and the public's perception of it as an adjudicator enabled the Board to incrementally expand its guardianship over Meta. In other words, the Oversight Board is enough of an adjudicator to (somewhat successfully) play with the perception of being an adjudicatory guardian and thereby performatively construct its authority. To be clear, the Board is far from being a fully fledged adjudicative controller of Meta's administration-like rulemaking and rule enforcement. Yet the same mechanisms – juridification, judicialization, and individual rights adjudication – that provided the conceptual soil for the Board's creation in 2018, later enabled it to go beyond its in-built restrictions. The Board is a more "activist" adjudicator than initially thought – with all the positive and negative consequences this entails. These issues have become even more pronounced since Meta CEO Mark Zuckerberg announced in early 2025 that the company would scale back certain policies, including its collaboration with external fact-checkers and its rules on hate speech. How this will affect the Oversight Board remains to be seen, but a deep understanding of the Board's operation up to this point is essential for

[18] See at 4.3.

assessing future developments in what appears to be a more conservative and libertarian era of online governance emerging in the mid-2020s.

The case study progresses in six steps. It recapitulates the Board's origins, analyzes the details of its institutional organization, the rules on which it bases its decisions, some of its decisions themselves, and whether Meta in fact implements them.

Before we begin, one last word on terminology. In 2021, Facebook, the parent company of Facebook, Instagram and Threads (social networks), WhatsApp (a chat app), and several other companies renamed itself Meta. Many of the Oversight Board's governing documents were crafted before said rebranding and therefore speak of Facebook instead of Meta. To represent existing textual material as directly as possible, the case study, therefore, uses sometimes also the term Facebook (especially, when directly quoting or referencing governing documents with the old terminology).

4.2 Origins

Others have already told the story of the Oversight Board's genesis at length.[19] This section therefore builds on existing accounts and reconstructs three aspects of the Board's origins which in turn highlight three factors driving its inception. Firstly, the Board was based from the start on the idea of *emulating* individual rights adjudication. Irrespective of the company's presumably self-serving (because profit-driven) motives, the organization its executives created utilizes personnel, institutional designs, normative material, and practices known from the traditional context of adjudicative control over (public) power. Second, this section sheds light on the decisive role played by lawyers and legal academics in the Board's origin (and practice). The Board is the offspring of these juridical arguments – that Meta executives decided to establish an adjudicator and not, say, an ombudsperson is no coincidence. In other words, we will examine the performative effects of juridical concepts presented in internal debates about how to make the platform's content moderation more accountable. Third, the section draws attention to excluded

[19] Extensively: Klonick, 'The Facebook Oversight Board: Creating an Independent Institution to Adjudicate Online Free Expression' (n 3). See further: Douek, 'Facebook's "Oversight Board:" Move Fast with Stable Infrastructure and Humility' (n 1); Klonick, 'Inside the Making of Facebook's Supreme Court' (n 3); Kate Klonick, 'The New Governors: The People, Rules, and Processes Governing Online Speech' (2018) 131 Harvard Law Review 1598.

perspectives and initial reactions from outside actors, some of whom were challenging the presumed 'rationality' of lawyers working for Meta who were defending the company's right to emulate an adjudicatory body. Contrasting these two perspectives highlights one major side effect of the Board's adjudicative design: a usurping of the public legitimacy attached to juridical arguments, personnel, and institutions. Fourth, we take a step back and look at the discursive effects of Meta's use of juridical concepts and constitutional metaphors in general. Discussions surrounding the Board's justification and purpose can be seen as a discursive intervention that shifted debates away from then prevalent discussions about election interference and privacy (remember Cambridge Analytica) and toward content moderation and accountability mechanisms. This external performative effect of the Board yields considerable path dependencies as debates about privacy and content moderation are separated – even though they share the same underlying problem – that is, "business models based on data collection, behavioral advertising, and other aspects of surveillance capitalism."[20]

4.2.1 *Emulation as the Board's Leitmotif*

Since the mid-2010s, social media platforms and especially Facebook, the world's largest social media network, have faced growing criticism. Politicians, journalists, and scholars started questioning platforms' role in a series of (arguably interrelated) political events, like Brexit, and the election of Trump as US President, or, later, the Rohingya's violent persecution in Myanmar.[21] Further, a string of scandals revealed social media companies' troubled relationship with privacy, content moderation, and

[20] Jack M Balkin, 'How to Regulate (and Not Regulate) Social Media' (2021) 1 Journal of Free Speech Law 71, 88.

[21] See esp.: Balkin (n 16); Klonick, 'The New Governors: The People, Rules, and Processes Governing Online Speech' (n 19); Tarleton Gillespie, *Custodians of the Internet: Platforms, Content Moderation, and the Hidden Decisions That Shape Social Media* (Yale University Press 2019); Julie Cohen, 'Law of the Platform Economy' (2017) 51 University of California Davis Law Review 133; Julie Cohen, *Between Truth and Power: The Legal Constructions of Informational Capitalism* (Oxford University Press 2019); for journalistic takes (in chronological order) see e.g.: Ben Mezrich, *The Accidental Billionaires* (Doubleday 2009); David Kirkpatrick, *The Facebook Effect: The Real Inside Story of Mark Zuckerberg and the World's Fastest Growing Company* (Virgin 2010); Steven Levy, *Facebook: The Inside Story* (Blue Rider 2020); Sheera Frenkel and Cecilia Kang, *An Ugly Truth: Inside Facebook's Battle for Domination* (Harper 2021); for more activist takes see e.g.: Jillian York, *Silicon Values: The Future of Free Speech under Surveillance Capitalism* (Verso 2021); Christopher Wylie, *Mindf*ck: Inside Cambridge Analytica's Plot to Break the World* (Profile Books 2019).

potential external effects arguably exacerbated by their products.[22] In particular, the way platforms regulated the communication of their users, a process often euphemistically called content moderation, was characterized as unaccountable, arbitrary, and opaque.[23] These political events and platform-related scandals have led to an (ongoing) public relations crisis for Meta and have increased public pressure on regulators to ramp up their regulatory regimes for tackling possible abuses on (and by) platforms, which eventually resulted in the drafting and passing of the DSA (a complex process discussed in Chapter 3). These events also resulted in numerous hearings where company executives were brought before the US Congress and the European Parliament.

The story of the Oversight Board begins a few days before Mark Zuckerberg, Meta's founder and chief executive, was summoned to Capitol Hill in mid-April 2018. Anticipating angry lawmakers questioning the company's fumbled response to allegations of interference by the Russian regime in the 2016 Presidential election, its monopoly-like market power and, importantly, privacy concerns, Zuckerberg outlined his vision of "building a fair system" granting individual users "a right to appeal [Facebook's] decisions on individual posts."[24] Zuckerberg proposed emulating one of the oldest ideas in public law: individual rights adjudication. In other words, Meta was taking it upon itself to put in place *its own* system of adjudicative control over its content moderation bureaucracies. In the phrasing of this book, Meta vowed to establish its own Emulated Guardian. In an interview just a few days before his hearing on Capitol Hill, Zuckerberg said:

> [My goal is to create some] sort of independent appeal process. Right now, if you post something on Facebook and someone reports it and our community operations and review team looks at it and decides that it needs to get taken down, there's not really a way to appeal that. I think in any kind of good-functioning democratic system, there needs to be a way to appeal. And I think we can build that internally as a first step.

[22] See especially Shoshana Zuboff, *The Age of Surveillance Capitalism: The Fight for a Human Future at the New Frontier of Power* (PublicAffairs 2019).

[23] See e.g. Klonick, 'The New Governors: The People, Rules, and Processes Governing Online Speech' (n 19) 1630 et seq; Gillespie (n 21) 45 et seq; Douek, 'Content Moderation as Systems Thinking' (n 7) 535–564.

[24] Facebook, Social Media Privacy, And the Use and Abuse of Data – Joint Hearing before the Committee on Commerce, Science, and Transportation in the United States Senate and the Committee on the Judiciary in the United States Senate, Serial No. J-115-40 (n 121) 200 at Question 59(c) by Senator Roy Blunt. See also ibid 176, 179, 181, 186, 306, 320.

> But over the long term, what I'd really like to get to is an independent appeal. So maybe folks at Facebook make the first decision based on the community standards that are outlined, and then people can get a second opinion. You can imagine some sort of structure, almost like a Supreme Court, that is made up of independent folks who don't work for Facebook, who ultimately make the final judgment call on what should be acceptable speech in a community that reflects the social norms and values of people all around the world.[25]

These statements are striking for several reasons. First, the company's founder is outlining the idea of his own company devising an adjudicatory entity that is somehow to be "almost like a Supreme Court." This "supreme court" metaphor is what the interview is famous for. However, there are at least two other notable remarks. That is, on the one hand, how Zuckerberg portrays *democratic* government as the role model for his company's governance of user communication. He draws inspiration from "any kind of good-functioning democratic system." Further, not only did he make reference to a "democratic system" as an inspiration and announced a "Supreme Court" as a governance solution, but he also mainly talked about introducing "a way to appeal" content moderation decisions – a thinly veiled reference to *administrative* governance.

Such references to legitimizing concepts like "supreme court" or democracy are by no means random. Speaking about his private company in public-law terms, his co-opting of constitutional vocabulary served to throw a veil of publicly legitimizing imagery over the at the time toothless accountability structures in place. Many media outlets picked up on the "supreme court" metaphor and started talking of the Oversight Board as Facebook's "Supreme Court."[26] However, despite nods to the notion of constitutional governance, the idea behind the Oversight Board's genesis and resulting practices indeed emulates policy choices and organizational designs that have historically been diffused as individual rights adjudication.[27] To be clear, the Board's actual powers are far more limited than initially foreseen, and allusions to a Supreme Court-like body were merely meant to be taken as metaphorical, a fact admitted by Zuckerberg himself.[28] However, even though initial plans were scaled down

[25] Ezra Klein, 'Mark Zuckerberg on Facebook's Hardest Year, and What Comes Next' *Vox.com* (2 April 2018) <https://perma.cc/5W3N-Y37S>.

[26] Cowls, Darius, Santistevan and Schramm (n 2) 5 et seq.

[27] For the theory and historical background on individual rights adjudication see at 2.2.

[28] In an interview conducted by a legal academic Meta's CEO said: "This is certainly a big experiment. It's certainly not as broad as everyone would like it to be, upfront, but I think there's a path for getting there," see Klonick, 'Inside the Making of Facebook's Supreme Court' (n 3).

significantly, the Board is a tentative step to establishing a privately run adjudicatory body whose own goal is to incrementally increase its guardianship over one of the world's largest private governance operations: the way Meta "moderates" content on Facebook, Instagram, and Threads.

This distinction between, on the one hand, the Board's formal mandate and, on the other hand, the Board's practice is important. As we will see, due to performative self-legitimation by savvy lawyers, the Board managed to relatively quickly sewer its own institutional interest – that is, essentially, to do its own thing – from that of the company, whose executives arguably liked the idea of experimenting with the Board without giving it too much power.

The normative and institutional structures required to install such a novel guardian are reminiscent of public-law tenets and, especially, the principles underlying administrative law.[29] To assume this essentially public function, the Oversight Board combines, by way of emulation, public- and private-law elements.

4.2.2 *Lawyers, the Supreme Court Label, and Juridification*

The second context-related aspect of the Board's inception is the dominance of lawyers, legal scholars, and "constitutional metaphors" (in my coauthors' and my phrasing) or "juridical discourse" (in Thomas Kadri's phrase) in its creation.[30] From the start, the Board was conceived as a juridical, rights-focused, public law-inspired adjudicative body.[31] Even though many ambitious initial plans were scrapped, the underlying rationale seemingly always was to build a body that would be (perceived as) independent, norm-based, and with (some) authority to decide on disputes. In other words, creating the Board was always directed toward *emulating* an adjudicator.[32] Meta is a big and multilayered company. Presumably, different people working for it had differing visions for the Board at various times. What is remarkable though is that internal

[29] cf. Douek, 'Facebook's "Oversight Board:" Move Fast with Stable Infrastructure and Humility' (n 1) 28 et seq.

[30] See already Cowls, Darius, Santistevan and Schramm (n 2); Kadri (n 2).

[31] Interview with Academic, Consultant to Facebook in 2018 (1 November 2021). See further, Klonick, 'The Facebook Oversight Board: Creating an Independent Institution to Adjudicate Online Free Expression' (n 3) 2476; Douek, 'Facebook's "Oversight Board:" Move Fast with Stable Infrastructure and Humility' (n 1) 28.

[32] Douek, 'Facebook's "Oversight Board:" Move Fast with Stable Infrastructure and Humility' (n 1) 28.

documents show that the *perception* of whatever entity would emerge from this experiment seems to have been a crucial factor for Meta.[33]

4.2.2.1 From Supreme Court to Amorphous Adjudicator

The first to say that Facebook should subject its content moderation to a private *adjudicative* body was Noah Feldman. Feldman is a Harvard-based law professor specializing "in constitutional studies, with particular emphasis on power and ethics, design of innovative governance solutions, law and religion, and the history of legal ideas," to quote from his profile on the university's website.[34] As he later recalled, it all began on "a long bike ride up in the hills behind Palo Alto."[35] After talking to legal scholars at Stanford University as well as people working for Facebook, Feldman had the idea of reproducing institutional designs from liberal democracies for online platforms.[36] He says that

> platforms could benefit by the introduction of a governance mechanism that has traditionally been used, and intensively, in the last 50 or 60 years in liberal democracies, to manage the social conflict around what speech should be allowed and what should not be allowed, namely the constitutional court or the supreme court model. That is, in its essence, a model where there is an independent body that is not directly answerable to the primary, first-order decision-maker that has a set of principles that are clearly articulated on which it relies to make decisions.[37]

In late-January 2018, roughly two months before Zuckerberg announced his "Supreme Court" plan, Feldman sent a memorandum to his old college friend Sheryl Sandberg, Facebook's number two at the time.[38] Sandberg forwarded the memo to Zuckerberg.[39] The two-page document was titled

[33] An internal memo by Noah Feldman to Mark Zuckerberg from March 2018 states that one of two aims behind the whole operation "is to create a durable institution to deliver principled, reasoned decision-making *that would be widely understood as legitimate*," see Noah Feldman, 'Facebook Supreme Court: A Governance Solution (March 2018), published in: Global Feedback and Input on the Facebook Oversight Board for Content Decisions Appendix, Appendix D' 104 (emphasis added).

[34] See Harvard Law School, Faculty Directory, accessible via <https://perma.cc/95A8-BMXH>.

[35] Noah Feldman, at the GovAI Webinar – Noah Feldman on the Design of Facebook's Oversight Board, University of Oxford, Faculty of Philosophy, 16 September 2020, transcript accessible via: <https://perma.cc/NVH7-QH35>.

[36] Ibid.

[37] Feldman (n 35).

[38] For more details see the preeminent text on the Oversight Board's creation, which is Klonick, 'The Facebook Oversight Board: Creating an Independent Institution to Adjudicate Online Free Expression' (n 3) 2448 et seq.; see further Kadri (n 2) 170 et seq.

[39] Klonick, 'The Facebook Oversight Board: Creating an Independent Institution to Adjudicate Online Free Expression' (n 3) 2448 et seq.

"A Supreme Court for Facebook."[40] In this memo, Feldman framed Facebook's problem with hate speech as a battle between committed advocacy groups who want Facebook to ban certain types of speech and the general, societal interest in free speech.[41] In a binary interpretation, he argues that the "problem is the asymmetry between those who seek censorship and those who favor freedom."[42] Implicitly, Feldman seems to view the company as on the side of societal interests in safeguarding free speech. In Feldman's eyes, Facebook lacked a committed voice and a specific institution to help it defend free speech.[43] Without such an institution, well-organized lobbying groups demanding "censorship" could easily advance their agenda as "nobody is pushing hard on the other side of the door."[44] However, Feldman argues, "there is a solution, one borrowed from the free-speech lessons experienced by governments over the last hundred years."[45] This solution, Feldman says, is for Facebook to adopt free expression as its most fundamental normative basis, as a kind of "constitutional rule," and to establish an adjudicative body to defend it.[46] Courts, he clarifies, unlike majoritarian institutions such as legislators, "can say 'no' . . . [to] demands of advocates seek[ing] to limit speech."[47]

Feldman portrays adjudication as *the* model for Facebook to counter demands for "censorship" and to upgrade how it exercises power over its users.[48] His memo advocated that platforms should set up "their own quasi-legal systems" and that "we need a Supreme Court for Facebook" to mitigate the "dangers social media platforms pose to free speech."[49] In March 2018, Feldman sent the company a second memo, titled "Facebook Supreme Court: A Governance Solution."[50] This outlined how "a Facebook Supreme Court . . . [a]long with lower appeals courts" should adjudicate free speech on

[40] Noah Feldman, 'A Supreme Court for Facebook (January 2018), Published in: Global Feedback and Input on the Facebook Oversight Board for Content Decisions Appendix, Appendix D' (2018) 101 et seq.

[41] Ibid 101.

[42] Ibid.

[43] Ibid 102.

[44] Ibid 101–102.

[45] Ibid 101.

[46] Ibid.

[47] Ibid.

[48] The overly broad use of the word "censorship" should be seen rather critical in this context as it levels the difference between legitimate demands to take down content, e.g., because it is defamatory, and illegitimate censorship of oppositional speech in authoritarian regimes.

[49] Feldman (n 40).

[50] Feldman (n 33).

Facebook and "create a durable institution to deliver principled, reasoned decision-making that would be widely understood as legitimate."[51] One interviewee, who worked at Facebook at the time, said that the "supreme court framework" was there "because of Noah Feldman and because we lawyers tend to think in adjudicative terms."[52] But apart from his attempt to pass off his metaphorically named entity as something "constitutional" and his argument that individual rights adjudication could be emulated, Feldman's influence seems to have gradually waned once more people got involved. One interviewee, who had an advisory role in the Board's creation, pointed out that various ideas were discussed and that

> [t]here are other models of self-regulation. One could be a human rights tribunal, for example, instead of a supreme court. One might be a self-regulatory body. There are many ways to describe tribunals that work along principles other than those of a supreme court.[53]

Nowadays, many interviewed staffers reject the portrait of the Oversight Board as a "supreme court."[54] Further, internal memos from Facebook from late 2018 and early 2019 indicate a wider search for the ideal type of organization. As one interviewee involved in the Board's creation at Facebook remembers, they looked at "the universe of possible solutions."[55] Correspondingly, an internal memo identified different "families" of control regimes for large, administrative power structures, namely "investigative institutions; supervisory institutions; arbitral adjudication processes, administrative adjudication bodies, national judicial systems, including both European continental-style appellate courts and American appeals courts, and international judicial systems."[56] This same memo listed the benefits and downsides of "judicial and quasi-judicial" control of power.[57] Examples range from the European Court of Justice, to Human Rights Courts, French appeals courts, the US Supreme Court, and, notably, to "the [US] system of administrative appeals in federal executive agencies."[58]

51 Ibid 104.

52 Interview with Oversight Board Staffer 4 (27 May 2022).

53 Interview with Oversight Board Trustee (21 September 2021).

54 Interview with Oversight Board Staffer 2 (n 10); Interview with Oversight Board Staffer 1 (25 March 2022); Interview with Oversight Board Staffer 4 (n 52); Interview with Oversight Board Staffer 5 (2 June 2022).

55 Interview with Academic, Consultant to Facebook in 2018 (n 31).

56 Facebook, 'Global Feedback and Input on the Facebook Oversight Board for Content Decisions Appendix' 138 <https://perma.cc/SP5M-Q7G7>.

57 Ibid 140.

58 Ibid 157. Later, the memo presumes that such judges in US administrative appeals are "unlikely to be independent" (ibid). Yet, generally dismissing the independence of

This reference to "administrative appeals" in US administrative law is worth commenting on as it plays into the point about the increasing "administrification" of platform governance in Chapter 2.[59] To recapitulate, Meta's rulemaking and rule enforcement, just like administrative law, concerns a powerful institution (Meta), a group of individuals (users), and rights that are traditionally understood as coming under the purview of public law (freedom of speech). Further, the main function of all normative material governing Meta's governance of communication is supposed to ultimately delineate how Meta exercises its power vis-à-vis a growing and anonymous (indeed, anonymized) group of users. This picture structurally resembles the function of administrative law.[60] Controlling such a complex "system of administration" (following Douek's description) would seem to require a panoply of guardians.[61] As outlined in Chapter 2, various guardians of administrative or administration-like power exist, ranging from traditional, generalist courts to other adjudicatory institutions to various notionally independent operators like ombudspersons or auditors.

4.2.2.2 Juridification and the "Appropriate" Policy Choice

However, since Meta tasked mainly lawyers with building the edifice that would eventually become the Oversight Board, the "appropriate" policy choice to emulate, in the legal team's eyes, was *individual rights adjudication*. As one interviewed legal scholar, who advised Meta on creating the Board, put it:

> Personnel matters in these kinds of things too. When you have a bunch of lawyers . . . work[ing] on this thing, inevitably, what's going to come out is going to be something familiar to lawyers, and just the way in the world that lawyers work.[62]

This is a telling explanation. Because lawyers dominated the Board's creation process (and, so far, its later practice), the project to design

adjudicatory bodies attached to US agencies could be considered simplistic. Many authors consider judges beyond Article III courts in the US in general sufficiently independent to fairly adjudicate in their jurisdiction. cf. James E Pfander, 'Article I Tribunals, Article III Courts, and the Judicial Power of the United States' (2004) 118 Harvard Law Review 643.

59 See also Moritz Schramm, 'Platform Administrative Law: A Research Agenda' (SSRN, 24 July 2024) <https://perma.cc/JH2A-8ZW2>.

60 cf. at 2.3.

61 Douek, 'Content Moderation as Systems Thinking' (n 7).

62 Interview with Academic, Consultant to Facebook in 2018 (n 31).

a guardian to oversee Meta's massive power quickly became funneled into emulating bits and pieces from different models of adjudicatory oversight over public power. This is why the Oversight Board, despite its generic and inoffensive-sounding name, is more than a mere panel of experts, an ombudsperson, or some other type of "guardian." From the start, its creators were perhaps subconsciously united by their respective preconceptions of what adjudicative control over power might look like. In turn, the structure that eventually emerged reflects the Board's limitations as a private law-inspired entity.[63]

From the perspective of organizational sociology, one cannot overstate the preeminence of this mélange of lawyer-dominated staff, uncertainty, and the woolly aim to "create an independent appeals mechanism." Uncertainty is the seed of emulation.[64] As DiMaggio and Powell said, "[w]hen goals are ambiguous, or when the environment creates symbolic uncertainty, organizations may model themselves on other organizations."[65] Emulating preexisting institutions, like individual rights adjudication, to increase an organization's public legitimacy is a common driver of new formal structures. As explained in Chapter 2, emulating institutions and formal structures is relatively straightforward and an "easy sell" to the public. In contrast, it is much harder to implement more deeply rooted changes in policy, strategy, or practice. These are often harder to comprehend for laypeople and thus cannot be legitimized in people's perceptions in the same way as the idea of emulating existing institutions by putting in place formal structures.[66] As Evelyn Douek noted, the "fundamental purpose [of the Oversight Board] is to bring greater legitimacy to Facebook's content moderation ecosystem."[67] According to Douek and many other critics, the Board is only a means to an end for Meta to increase its own public legitimacy in societal discourse.[68] Thomas Kadri points out that platforms "exploit" juridical arguments and structures like the Oversight Board to buttress their public legitimacy.[69] Similarly, DiMaggio and Powell argued already in the 1980s that private, for-profit enterprises "tend to model themselves after

[63] See in detail at 4.3.

[64] Speaking of "imitation" and "mimetic" acts Paul J DiMaggio and Walter W Powell, 'The Iron Cage Revisited: Institutional Isomorphism and Collective Rationality in Organizational Fields' (1983) 48 American Sociological Review 147, 151.

[65] Ibid.

[66] Ibid 52.

[67] Douek, 'Facebook's "Oversight Board:" Move Fast with Stable Infrastructure and Humility' (n 1) 46.

[68] Ibid.

[69] Kadri (n 2) 167.

similar organizations in their field that they perceive to be more legitimate or successful."[70] As discussed in Chapter 2, individual rights adjudication is one of the most legitimate and successful institutions controlling wide-reaching rulemaking and rule enforcement enterprises.[71] Hence, corroborating the theorization about emulation outlined in Chapter 2, Meta's "Governance and Strategic Initiatives" team followed a common pattern in modeling the company's Board after existing institutions. This team was the main driver behind the Board's development.[72] It was run by Brent Harris, a lawyer who joined Facebook that year.[73] Apart from Harris, it consisted of ten people.[74] Further, "dozens" of "cross-functional" people would contribute to the governance team's work.[75] The number of people involved in creating the Board, either as employees or outside consultants, was described by interviewees as in the low double-digits.[76] All of the lawyers involved with Facebook were highly educated and most had received law degrees in the US.[77] One interviewee, who was an in-house adviser to the company, recollected the internal debates at Facebook as follows:

> I think that understandings of the way that courts relate to the people over whom they exercise authority definitely were in the room. Whether they were in the room because anybody wanted to consciously think about them, or whether they were in the room just because of the personnel and communicative context of the thing is not as clear.[78]

How far this emulation went – and whether it can reproduce at least some of the success of adjudicatory control over power in the context of national states or nation-spanning conglomerations like the EU – follows later in this chapter.

70 DiMaggio and Powell (n 64) 152. Their argument, however, did not directly concern the emulation of state structures in private corporations but rather isomorphism among private actors. The here described trend, therefore, seems to be an evolutionary step beyond those observed in the past by DiMaggio, Powell, and many other sociologists.

71 See esp. at 2.2.

72 Klonick, 'The Facebook Oversight Board: Creating an Independent Institution to Adjudicate Online Free Expression' (n 3) 2452–2453.

73 Ibid 2452.

74 See Klonick, based on an email by Caroline Glanville, Policy Communications (Governance Board), Facebook, to Klonick on (May 25, 2020), see in Klonick's text at note 154 – ibid 2453.

75 Ibid.

76 Interview with Academic, Consultant to Facebook in 2018 (n 31).

77 Ibid.

78 Ibid.

4.2.3 *Excluded Perspectives*

Building an edifice with the help of (mostly) US-educated lawyers will necessarily exclude a range of options. To include more diverse perspectives but also to buy time, in 2019 Meta organized a series of workshops focusing on ideas for the Board's design. This global consultation included a series of consultations with stakeholders such as nongovernmental organizations (NGOs) and civil-society advocacy groups.[79] The company also held several "workshops and roundtables" in, to name just a few places, Singapore, Berlin, Oklahoma City, New York, Paris, Nairobi, Mexico City, and Taipei.[80] Presumably these roundtables were the first occasions when the ideas advanced by Meta's lawyers (presumably with Zuckerberg's sanction) were presented to activists, stakeholders, and practitioners from outside the company.[81] The first roundtable, held in Singapore, featured a moot court-like debate about specific cases.[82] Participants were split into groups and received a hypothetical case upon which they had to decide on the basis of predefined norms.[83] As one interviewed activist, who participated in the Berlin workshop in the summer of 2019, recalls:

> [T]hey gave us test case studies ... These were blunt cases, and the people invited to this thing were, again, Westerners. There was one done in Latin America and there was maybe one in Africa, but I know people who were at both of them, and they said that there were still a lot of white people at both.... I would say it was more like a college debate team than a court. It felt nothing like a court to me. It was me sitting around a table with a bunch of other overprivileged white people, discussing a case where actual harm hadn't been done. ... I don't think it set them up well for understanding the cases that would come to them or what they would mean for people on the ground. I think it already came out, so to be clear, they focused solely on European, American right-wing propaganda kind of cases.[84]

Although it is impossible to identify who participated in these workshops, we can reasonably assume that Facebook wanted participants to discuss

[79] Facebook (n 56) 11 et seq.

[80] Ibid 39 at endnotes 40, 41.

[81] Apparently, Zuckerberg remained deeply involved in the whole creation process, e.g. editing various materials. See Klonick, 'Inside the Making of Facebook's Supreme Court' (n 3).

[82] Klonick, 'The Facebook Oversight Board: Creating an Independent Institution to Adjudicate Online Free Expression' (n 3) 2451–2457.

[83] Ibid 2451–2452.

[84] Interview with Activist (1 December 2021).

how they would like an adjudicative institution to look like. In contrast, *if* an adjudicative institution was even the right idea in the first place was not under discussion.

Further, the critical remarks by the participant indicate that Meta's governance team's preconceptions diverged from the needs of affected users. Especially in non-"Western" parts of the world, the same interviewee recalls that

> [T]here's just a lot of eye-rolling at the Oversight Board, to be honest . . . I think that there's a lot of "What's the purpose of putting all of this money behind the Oversight Board when we've been saying these things all along?" which is a fair critique. . . . I think the Oversight Board's most useful function . . . is, in fact, that it formalizes and makes explicit a lot of those recommendations, synthesizes them, really. To be honest, from my colleagues in the Middle East I haven't heard that many positive things about the Oversight Board. It's not so much negative as just "What's the point?"[85]

What the activist is alluding to here is important. The Oversight Board was constructed by those with a specific mindset governed by ideas about individual rights, adjudicative control over power, and shot through with the largely metaphorical language of "supreme" courts and "constitutions." As we will see, the Board somewhat falls short of these expectations. Most importantly, its authority is severely restricted, and it decides too few cases to offer any meaningful judicial protection to the users of its services. This reasonably brings us to question the institution's overall validity. As the activist put it: "What's the point?"

4.2.4 *Foreclosed Debates*

The dominance of lawyers in the discourse, as well as the predominance of constitutional metaphors and juridical framings, construed the Board as an adjudicative solution to Meta's unaccountable methods of content moderation, which was itself portrayed as an issue of how to police billions of free-speech acts. In other words, the question the Oversight Board was designed to handle was that of free speech.[86]

85 Ibid.

86 See e.g. Klonick, 'The New Governors: The People, Rules, and Processes Governing Online Speech' (n 19) 1667–1678. For a critique of Facebook's "exploit[ation]" of juridical discourse see Kadri (n 2) 167 et seq. For the relevance of constitutional metaphors in debates on platform governance see already Cowls, Darius, Santistevan and Schramm (n 2). For a critique of the rights-focused "standard picture" of content moderation see Douek, 'Content Moderation as Systems Thinking' (n 7).

However, when we jump back to the beginning of the Oversight Board's story in early 2018, we see an unusual discursive shift. Back then, content moderation was arguably not Meta's biggest, let alone its only, problem. Instead, Meta was drawing strong criticism from scholars, journalists, and politicians for its handling of personal data and its interface design.[87] To begin with, Meta was using algorithms to "personalize" user experiences, leading to the potential creation of "echo chambers" and an entrenching of attitudes and opinions.[88] Then, Meta's flawed privacy governance schemes were allowing outside parties to access and retrieve huge amounts of personal data. The most infamous of these data breaches was orchestrated by a company called Cambridge Analytica.[89] Cambridge Analytica managed to gain access to the personal data of eighty-seven million US citizens and later allegedly used at least some of that data to tamper with the 2016 Presidential election.[90]

Zuckerberg announced the setting up of the Board a few days before his hearing on Capitol Hill, and around the time those data breaches became public, in April 2018. Although the hearing was also about content moderation, fundamental rights, and accountability, its main concerns were election interference and privacy in the context

[87] Insightful: Asunción Esteve, 'The Business of Personal Data: Google, Facebook, and Privacy Issues in the EU and the USA' (2017) 7 International Data Privacy Law 36; see further Zuboff (n 22) defining Google's "discovery of behavioral surplus" 74–87, for Facebook e.g. at 483–485, 497 et seq.

[88] Seth Flaxman, Sharad Goel and Justin M Rao, 'Filter Bubbles, Echo Chambers, and Online News Consumption' (2016) 80 Public Opinion Quarterly 298; Rune Karlsen and others, 'Echo Chamber and Trench Warfare Dynamics in Online Debates' (2017) 32 European Journal of Communication 257; regarding Facebook's "like button" Zuboff (n 22) 455–461; in general regarding the psychological underpinning of designing online interfaces Chris Nodder, *Evil by Design: Interaction Design to Lead Us Into Temptation* (Wiley 2013). See further Niklas Eder, 'Beyond Automation: Machine Learning-Based Systems and Human Behavior in the Personalization Economy' (2021) 25 Stanford Technology Law Review 1, 19 et seq.

[89] The scandal broke after a data analyst at Cambridge Analytica leaked several documents to the Guardian. The whistleblower later published a memoir describing how Cambridge Analytica, apparently with the help of far-right political strategist Steve Bannon and Russian state affiliates retrieved and utilized data about millions of American voters, see Wylie (n 21) 95–155.

[90] Issie Lapowsky, 'Facebook Exposed 87 Million Users to Cambridge Analytica' (*Wired*, 4 April 2018) <https://perma.cc/D3UV-KH3T>; Remarkably, social media users seem to meet privacy and data breaches with stoic neglect: Hagar Afriat and others, '"This Is Capitalism. It Is Not Illegal": Users' Attitudes toward Institutional Privacy Following the Cambridge Analytica Scandal' (2021) 37 The Information Society 115.

of the Cambridge Analytica scandal.[91] The Congress hearing took place under the title "Facebook, Social Media Privacy, and the Use and Abuse of Data."[92] Senators pressed Zuckerberg mostly on his company's "disturbing" privacy-governance systems that had ended up leaving the door open for Cambridge Analytica to steal personal data.[93]

As Ari Ezra Waldman noted, there are "numerous discourses at play in informational capitalism," some focusing on innovation and possible technological solutions to real-world problems, others highlighting social networks' effects on free speech.[94] Therefore, one can view Meta's project of the Oversight Board – and its metaphorical narration in constitutional-law terminology – as a performative shift in the discourse surrounding the wider role of social media companies in society.[95] Discussing how the Oversight Board might bring accountability to Meta's moderation of speech shifted debates away from Meta's still flawed handling of personal data and the morality of its business model. As revelations by whistleblower Frances Haugen in late 2021 indicated, Meta did not substantively improve its products, its handling of private data, and its overall business model.[96] Instead, the intensifying debates about content moderation approach platforms through the prism of individual rights adjudication but are increasingly detached from discussions regarding social media platforms' business models, ways of handling data, and privacy.[97] Debates

[91] Chairman Chuck Grassley, Senator from Iowa, stated that "the issues [the hearing] will consider range from data privacy and security to consumer protection and the Federal Trade Commission enforcement," 'Facebook, Social Media Privacy, And the Use and Abuse of Data – Joint Hearing before the Committee on Commerce, Science, and Transportation in the United States Senate and the Committee on the Judiciary in the United States Senate, Serial No. J-115-40' (n 24) 2.

[92] 'Facebook, Social Media Privacy, And the Use and Abuse of Data – Joint Hearing before the Committee on Commerce, Science, and Transportation in the United States Senate and the Committee on the Judiciary in the United States Senate, Serial No. J-115-40' (n 24).

[93] Statement of Senator John Thune, US Senator South Dakota, ibid 2. See further the statements by Senators Dianne Feinstein, Bill Nelson, Orin Hatch at ibid 3–8, 21–22, as well as Mark Zuckerberg's statement at 8–13.

[94] *Ari Ezra Waldman, Industry Unbound: The Inside Story of Privacy, Data, and Corporate Power* (Cambridge University Press 2021) 46.

[95] See Cowls, Darius, Santistevan, and Schramm (n 2); criticizing that platforms swayed discourse on content moderation toward "juridical discourses": Kadri (n 2); regarding companies' performative impact on our conception of privacy see Waldman (n 94) 224 et seq.

[96] 'Statement of Frances Haugen' 2–3 <https://perma.cc/3QN6-JMY4>.

[97] Remarkably, Evelyn Douek's comprehensive critique of narrow understandings of content moderation largely skips the aspect of privacy, which Douek considers to be a "related" context, cf. Douek, 'Content Moderation as Systems Thinking' (n 7) 530–533, 571.

surrounding intrusive regulatory intervention when it comes to platforms' business models – or even arguments for breaking up social media companies altogether – are still rife today, although the academic and political winds seem to have shifted toward more reform-oriented approaches.[98] In other words, platforms' wide-ranging regulatory powers seem to be so entrenched that minimizing them, let alone eliminating them, appears increasingly impracticable. This tacit discursive premise in turn paved the way for various reformist ideas to come to the fore, the Oversight Board being just one of the most prominent.

To conclude, we shall recapitulate the two – slightly stylized of course – centripetal forces shaping the Board's creation and its later practice. These are, on the one hand, Meta's striving for public legitimacy and, on the other hand, as a consequence thereof, the nascent adjudicators' unique position and ability to incrementally build on the public's perceptions of what adjudicative authority entails. In other words, the fact that Meta decided to create the Board as an adjudicator and not as, say, an ombudsperson, potentially enables the Board to performatively play with the perception of being an adjudicator and thereby provide some accountability for Meta. Even though the next sections show the serious limitations built into the Board's institutional framework, the story of the Board's genesis and practice are thus evidence of the shortcomings, and dangers, but also of the potentially paradigmatic potential of Emulated Guardians.

[98] For example, the US Federal Trade Commission's (FTC) sued Meta for its acquisition of Instagram and WhatsApp in 2020. If successful, the FTC would require Meta to break up parts of its business. See Federal Trade Commission, 'FTC Sues Facebook for Illegal Monopolization (Press Release)' (9 December 2020) <https://perma.cc/N6RX-AX8Q>. Lina Khan, the FTC's chairwoman under the Biden administration, previously wrote a widely influential article in the Yale Law Review arguing for ramping up antitrust toward the platform economy. However, preparations for the case against Meta because of its acquisition of Instagram and WhatsApp began already under the first Trump administration. For the scholarly groundwork of Ms. Khan see Lina M Khan, 'Amazon's Antitrust Paradox' (2017) 126 The Yale Law Journal 710. Khan's title references (and problematizes) the foundational text of the dominant "consumer welfare" paradigm in US antitrust: Robert H Bork, *The Antitrust Paradox* (Basic Books 1978).

See further already the influential Stigler Report, which demanded, among other things, more "aggressive antitrust": Stigler Center for the Study of the Economy and the State (University of Chicago), 'Stigler Committee on Digital Platforms Final Report' (2019) 7–9, 16–17, 92–121.

4.3 Institution

This section investigates the Board's institutional characteristics. To emulate individual rights adjudication, Meta needed to construct the Oversight Board as a private adjudicator that would adjudicate the public rights of users or, in other words, provide accountability for Meta's private governance by using public-law mechanisms. Now we look at the Board's organizational structure and personnel, as well as its jurisdiction, before reflecting on its impartiality and independence.

4.3.1 *Organization and Personnel*

Owing to its entirely private nature, the Board's institutional structure differs significantly from many other adjudicative bodies controlling traditional administrative power.

The Oversight Board does not exist as a uniform entity.[99] Instead, it consists of four actors working together, governed by a set of founding documents. These are the "Oversight Board Trust," an irrevocable Delaware noncharitable trust with several trustees ("the trust").[100] The trust funds the Board's operations and makes management decisions concerning its operation. The trust created a limited liability corporation (LLC) under Delaware law that rents office space and hires staffers.[101] Further, the trust filed the individual contracts of the Board members who bear ultimate responsibility for the Board's adjudication. At the time of writing, the Board had between seventy and ninety staffers, who are employed by the LLC and who run the Board's operations.

4.3.1.1 The Founding Documents

Four documents govern the Oversight Board. These are the *charter*, a vague and lofty text setting out the Board's purpose and function; the *trust agreement*, a detailed contract establishing a Delaware noncharitable trust; the *LLC agreement*, a contract establishing a limited liability

[99] Even formally uniform adjudicatory entities like "the" Bundesverfassungsgericht collapse into various complementary sub-units if one looks closely enough. See Matthias Jestaedt, 'Autorität und Zitat – Anmerkungen zur Zitierpraxis des Bundesverfassungsgerichts' in Mathias Mayer and Joachim Jacob (eds.), *Im Namen des Anderen – Die Ethik des Zitierens* (Wilhelm Fink Verlag 2010) 147–148.

[100] Trust Agreement Section 1. For the provisions concerning trustees see Section 6.

[101] Trust Agreement Section 2.1.

corporation; and a set of detailed *bylaws*.[102] The charter, bylaws, and trust agreement were drawn up exclusively by Meta's lawyers. Meta then drafted the bylaws; the Board approved them and may amend parts of them subject to approval by Meta executives.[103] Further, several later crafted documents emerged as important throughout the case study and will be discussed in greater detail below. These are the code of conduct for Board members and staff as well as the Board's self-given *Rulebook for Case Review and Policy Guidance* of November 2020.[104]

In organizational terms, the trust agreement in particular has been described as perhaps the most consequential because the trust agreement is a formal contract, whereas the charter was just "declared" by the company.[105] The trust agreement, LLC agreement, and bylaws are much more detailed – and restrictive – than the charter. Yet, the exact relationship and order of precedence between those documents is complex. Especially in terms of organizational or operational hierarchy, it is not intuitively clear how some of the documents relate to one another. For example, the bylaws restrict the Board's jurisdiction over subject matter to removal of particular types of content, whereas the charter uses general language, allowing "people who disagree with the outcome of Facebook's decisions … a request for review."[106] Intuitively, the use of terms like 'charter' and 'bylaws' would imply that rules established by the charter rank more highly than those set out in the bylaws. Similarly, the bylaws describe the charter as "the Board's primary governing document" whereas the bylaws only "detail the operational procedures."[107] Further, the bylaws explicate that "where there is a potential conflict between

[102] For a coeval overview, albeit omitting commentary on the crucial trust agreement, see the series of blogposts on different versions of the charter, Facebook's 'values,' and the Board's bylaws: Evelyn Douek, 'How Much Power Did Facebook Give Its Oversight Board?' (*Lawfare*, 25 September 2019) <https://perma.cc/54D7-X7YW>; Evelyn Douek, 'Why Facebook's "Values" Update Matters' (*Lawfare*, 16 September 2019) <https://perma.cc/527F-7GBZ>; Evelyn Douek, 'Facebook's Oversight Board Bylaws: For Once, Moving Slowly' (*Lawfare*, 28 January 2020) <https://perma.cc/YM8P-T5S2>; ibid; Evelyn Douek, 'What Kind of Oversight Board Have You Given Us?' (*The University of Chicago Law Review Online*, 11 May 2020) <https://perma.cc/6VPV-EZLR>.

[103] Article 5 Section 1 Bylaws.

[104] As the rulebook's introduction states: "The procedures outlined in the Rulebook were established by the Oversight Board Co-Chairs and Members," 'Rulebook for Case Review and Policy Guidance' of November 2020, which can be downloaded here: <https://perma.cc/4BV3-ZA9C>; The Code of Conduct is an appendix to the bylaws and can be downloaded on the Oversight Board website, accessible via <https://perma.cc/CPL4-VPRZ>.

[105] Interview with Oversight Board Trustee (n 53).

[106] Charter Article 2(1).

[107] Bylaws Introduction (p 5).

interpretations of the charter and bylaws, the charter shall prevail."[108] The trust agreement reaffirms that the charter sets forth the "framework for creating the Oversight Board" and that only the charter "specifies the Oversight Board's authority and jurisdiction."[109] But at the same time, the charter states, in Article 6(2), that "the Board's operational procedures will be outlined in its bylaws. The charter and the bylaws will act as companion documents." Whether the charter's vague allusion to the bylaws as a 'companion document' indicates normative equality between charter and bylaws, primacy of the bylaws as *lex specialis* and/or *lex posterior*, or primacy of the charter as *lex superior*, remain an entirely unsettled matter.

The best way to understand the relationship between the founding documents is to keep in mind the documents' different drafting histories.[110] The charter was pinned down first and reflects the initial, high-flying goals from the early "Supreme Court" times.[111] It speaks of "people" instead of users, delineates the Board's "authority to review" and establishes that the "Board's resolution of each case will be binding."[112] The trust document and the LLC agreement, in turn, were crafted as waterproof legal documents by a probably larger und more specialized group of lawyers scrambling to find a private-law form operationalizing the lofty public announcements of Zuckerberg and the terms of the charter.

4.3.1.2 The Trust

The trust was set up in October 2019.[113] According to Section 2.1 of the trust agreement, the "purpose of the Trust . . . is to facilitate the creation, funding, management, and oversight structure that will permit and protect the operation of an Oversight Board." To achieve this, "the

108 Bylaws Introduction (p 5) (at the very end).

109 Trust Agreement Section 2.1.

110 See also Evelyn Douek, 'Facebook's "Draft Charter" for Content Moderation: Vague, But Promising' (*Lawfare*, 31 January 2019) <https://perma.cc/52RW-7E7A>; Douek, 'Facebook's Oversight Board Bylaws: For Once, Moving Slowly' (n 102).

111 See below at 4.3.2.

112 cf. Charter Introduction, Article 2, Article 4. Apparently, said change was initiated by Meta CEO Mark Zuckerberg himself or his personal team. In an interview with Kate Klonick, who was embedded as an observer at Facebook, the head of the company's governance team said that "Feedback is coming from very high up in the company." Further, the CEO edited the charter to make it "more approachable." See Klonick, 'Inside the Making of Facebook's Supreme Court' (n 3).

113 cf. Trust Agreement Section 1.1.

Trustees," of which there are six, "shall form and fund a limited liability company ('the LLC') of which the Trust will be the sole member through its Trustees," according to Section 2.1 paragraph 2 of the trust Agreement. The purpose of the LLC is to "establish, administer, and attend to the ongoing operation of the group of individuals who make up the Board Members," the paragraph continues. In 2019, Meta announced a contribution of 130 million dollars to the trust.[114] In 2022, Meta allocated another 150 million dollars to the trust, bringing the total amount to 280 million dollars.[115]

4.3.1.3 The Board Members

The most public and perhaps the most important component of the Board are its members. Members are individual contractees of the trust, meaning they are not employed by the LLC, to maintain their independence. Their compensation, described as "six-figure salaries," is not disclosed and might differ from member to member as "each Board member contract shall be based upon provisions suggested by ... [the trustees] and the Oversight Board."[116] Members do not work full-time for the Oversight Board but are contractually expected to work fifteen hours a week for it.[117] However, several interviewees indicated that members often spend considerably more time preparing and deliberating.[118] Members need not be physically present at the Board's offices around the world. Many of their deliberations happen online, spanning several time zones and continents. The members bear ultimate responsibility for the Board's decisions, recommendations, and policy advice.[119] In November 2024, the Board had twenty-one members, though it can have up to forty.[120] According to the charter, Board members are appointed for a fixed term of three years, renewable twice.[121]

114 Oversight Board, 'Securing Ongoing Funding for the Oversight Board (Press Release)' (22 June 2022) <https://perma.cc/Y859-KUEF>.

115 Ibid.

116 For the quote on the salaries see Klonick, 'Inside the Making of Facebook's Supreme Court' (n 3) 10. For the latter quote see LLC Agreement Section 5.3(a)(i).

117 Ibid.

118 Interview with Oversight Board Staffer 1 (n 54); Interview with Oversight Board Staffer 5 (n 54).

119 For the details of the different types of decisions see below at 4.5.

120 Charter Article 1 Section 1.

121 Charter Article 1 Section 3.

Powers

The members are vested with several "collective powers," according to Article 1(4) of the charter. They can request Meta to provide information, instruct Meta to allow or remove content and to explain its own decisions. According to Article 1(4)(2) of the charter, members may collectively "interpret Facebook's community Standards and other relevant policies ... in light of Facebook's articulated values." The Board can issue "policy guidance" but "will have no authority or powers beyond those expressly defined by this charter," according to Article 1(4) of the charter. Later sections – in Article 2 of the charter – refer to the Board's "authority to review."

Qualifications and Selection of Members

Qualifications to become a member are vaguely expressed. According to the charter, members shall "possess and exhibit a broad range of knowledge, competencies, diversity and expertise."[122] They should be able to work in a team and have "familiarity with matters relating to digital content and governance."[123] The Board appears to be relatively diverse when compared to traditional adjudicative bodies but not necessarily when compared to international adjudicators, which often have strict rules safeguarding proportional representation on their bench. According to its bylaws the Board must always include a "globally diverse set of members" representing all world regions.[124] Naturally, these regions are broadly defined – mainly by continent – and members might tend not to be familiar with the particular local contexts of appeals or the jurisdictional realities applying in the regions from where the appeals emanate. Nevertheless, the panels tasked with drafting decisions must include at least one member from the specific region.[125]

More than half of the Board's twenty-one members as of November 2024 have a law background.[126] Among the Board's members are several journalists, a former politician, a Nobel Peace Prize laureate, and a media and communications scholar.[127] As of November 2024, the membership's composition appears almost gender-balanced (eleven male, ten female) and features members from all world regions, however with a US

[122] Charter Article 1 Section 2.

[123] Ibid.

[124] Bylaws 1.4.1.

[125] Bylaws 3.1.3.

[126] Meet the Board section at the Board's website, accessible via <https://perma.cc/PYP5-L9M9>.

[127] Ibid.

dominance (six members), followed by Asia (five members), Europe (four members), South and Central America, the Middle East (two members each), and Africa and Oceania (one member each).[128] The initial four members of the Board were selected by Meta.[129] The later members were selected by the Board's cochairs, who are also members, and Meta.[130] Since the Board became operational, its members autonomously decide who joins their ranks (but seemingly only based on a shortlist reviewed by Meta).[131] From a comparative perspective, this is a rather unusual structure, as appointment and nomination procedures tend to tie adjudicators to the entities they are tasked with controlling. Given the spotlight on the Board's independence and Meta's seeming inability to offer a more legitimate appointment or nomination process, this model appears to be a sensible one. We should not forget that many such arrangements owe their existence to the fact that Meta remains a private company – with all the structural reluctance toward external oversight that comes with it. If ever, external, meaningful guardianship over the world's largest content moderation machinery will build incrementally, not overnight.

Juridified Practice

Although the Board needs to function as an adjudicative body, its members do not have to be lawyers. Yet, as mentioned above, more than half of its twenty-one members active in November 2024 either studied law and/or work in law-related fields like human rights activism or are legal scholars. The dominance of lawyers among the Board members has several consequences.[132] For instance, the company's executives presumably viewed lawyers as particularly capable of building the internal procedures, substantive reasoning, and external legitimacy of a body that was supposed to *function* and *be perceived as* adjudicative. Intuitively, this makes sense. Who else but lawyers could (or would) build an adjudicative institution? It also mirrors the dominance of lawyers in the Board's creation at Facebook.[133] US lawyers dominated the internal debates at Facebook's "Governance Team" that rolled out the Board's institutional design between 2018 and 2020. Arguably, this lawyer-dominated group

[128] Ibid.

[129] LLC Agreement Section 5.3(a)(i).

[130] Charter Article 1 Section 8.

[131] Bylaws 5.3 (a) (i); cf. Steven Levy, 'Inside Meta's Oversight Board: 2 Years of Pushing Limits' (*Wired*, 8 November 2022) <https://perma.cc/SUP5-RQCV>.

[132] For an illuminating analysis of the impact of 'juridical discourse' on the Board see Kadri (n 2) 171–176.

[133] See above at 4.2.2.

contributed to the Oversight Board being "an adjudicative body" (and not, say, one with a more parliamentary flavor). As one interviewee, who advised Meta's governance team when creating the Board, recalls:

> The fact of the matter is that the Oversight Board clearly started down one path. They could have started totally different paths. They could've issued three-page decisions, like the court of cassation does. It could've done that. It didn't. There's nothing in the charter or whatever that will tell you that it didn't do. It didn't do because of sociological factors, because they put a bunch of US lawyers in charge. What the fuck happens when you put a bunch of US lawyers in charge? Well, they started doing things that they're familiar with.[134]

Similarly, most people staffing the institution are lawyers as well. Whereas no member can have held a prior position at Meta, some high-level staffers at the Oversight Board were part of Facebook's effort in creating the Board in the first place.[135]

The dominance of lawyers among members pushed two normative aspects higher up the Board's agenda than initially foreseen. These are, first, human rights and, second, public- and administrative-law principles. The expertise in public law and human rights law of many Board members explains why the Board took a different turn than the company, or at least some people in the company, had presumably intended at its inception. The charter posits that the "Board will review content enforcement decisions and determine whether they were consistent with Facebook's content policies and values."[136] In contrast, the Board should only "pay particular attention to the *impact* of removing content in light of human rights norms protecting free expression."[137] Therefore, based on a strict reading of the charter, it seems as though Meta initially envisaged normative material unilaterally produced by Meta itself (its policies and values) and not human rights law as the key normative yardstick for the Board's decision-making.[138] Of course, many people were involved in creating the Board, and competing visions may have circulated at Meta and within the governance team.

[134] Interview with Academic, Consultant to Facebook in 2018 (n 31).

[135] See above at 4.2.2.

[136] Charter Article 2(2).

[137] Ibid (emphasis added).

[138] In that sense also Klonick, 'The Facebook Oversight Board: Creating an Independent Institution to Adjudicate Online Free Expression' (n 3) 2477–2479 (not even mentioning international human rights law and pointing to other cautious, and rather limiting formulations in the charter).

That said, the Board seems to focus particularly on international human rights law and to a much lesser extent on Meta's own devised rules. As we will explore in detail in Section 4.5 below, much of the Board's normative reasoning revolves around, and is framed in, the language of international human rights law, most notably Article 19 of the International Covenant on Civil and Political Rights (ICCPR).[139] For example, the Board allows for restrictions of freedom of expression only if "provided by law" and "necessary" to protect the rights of others, national security, public order, public health or morals, in the sense of Article 19(3) of the ICCPR. This external and arguably stricter normative framework can be understood as going beyond the initial design in the charter. The human rights background of many Board members (and staffers, as we will see in the following section) likely contributed to the Board's tendency to focus on international human rights law instead of Meta's vague and self-given "values," "charter," or "community standards." The policies and values that Meta executives had devised are still referenced in all decisions, but most of the Board's ink is dedicated to human rights-related reasoning.[140] This focus on human rights also constitutes, as we will soon see, one of the key differences from the DSA's ODSs, the other Emulated Guardian examined in this work.

Further, the Board used this human rights framework to infuse administrative-law principles into their recommendations based on legality and proportionality assessments, as specified in Article 19 of the ICCPR. It often deliberates on the basis of arguments like normative clarity and accessibility, users' right to remediation, the duty of the company to give reasons, and to translate its decisions and rules, for example. In this way, the Oversight Board aims to incentivize Meta to improve the normative framework for its content moderation. As one interviewee put it:

> The Board is attempting to infuse content moderation with juridical norms and procedures. We might call this a process of juridification ... In partnership with Meta, and in light of existing human rights norms, the Board articulates norms by which Meta's content moderation decisions should be settled. It seeks to ensure that these norms will be enforced according to public law procedures. The upshot is to take a private for-profit corporation like Meta and to juridify its content-moderation operations.[141]

The rules that are supposed to "juridify" Meta's content moderation are public-law rules. Legality, proportionality, right to a remedy, and the duty

[139] See below at 4.4 and 4.5.
[140] See below at 4.5.2 et seq.
[141] Interview with Oversight Board Trustee (n 53).

to give reasons for a decision, for example, are basic, almost universal administrative-law principles. The interviewee continues:

> To me, the issue is the infusion into management of public law principles. Now, I don't know whether that's the precise idea of juridification, but that seems to me the precise challenge of the Oversight Board.[142]

Similarly, in its decision regarding whether Facebook was justified in banning former US President Trump from its platform after his role in the attack on the Capitol on January 6, 2021, the Board assessed whether Facebook's rules were "clear and accessible."[143] In classic administrative-law fashion, the Board "reiterates that the patchwork of applicable rules makes it difficult for users to understand why and when Facebooks restricts accounts, ... [this] raises legality concerns."[144] In the same vein, the Board argued that "[a]ppropriate limits on discretionary powers are crucial to distinguish the legitimate use of discretion from possible scenarios around the world in which Facebook may unduly silence speech not linked to harm or delay action critical to protecting people."[145] The discursive might of such public law arguments is remarkable. While the Board had used general public law arguments to contain (and justify) Meta's power in its 2021 *Former President Trump's suspension* decision, the Board further expanded this approach in 2023. Then, when faced with incendiary posts by another head of state, the Board used more substantive human rights arguments and weighed, in quite some detail, the conflicting arguments for and against shutting down the profile of the Cambodian Prime Minister, who had used his Facebook account to incite violence in the run up to an election. Both cases dealt with Facebook's infamous "newsworthiness allowance," a rule that essentially excludes important people from otherwise enforced rules against hate speech and the incitement of violence. In 2023, the Board demanded that the company would not only delete content posted by the Cambodian Prime Minister but recommended to Meta to temporarily suspend his profile altogether.[146] That head of state, Hun Sen, had disseminated incendiary rhetoric through his Meta accounts, which arguably led to physical violence.[147]

142 Ibid.
143 Former President Trump's suspension [2021] Oversight Board 2021–001-FB-FBR.
144 Ibid at 25, 26.
145 Ibid at 26.
146 Cambodian Prime Minister [2023] Oversight Board 2023–003-FB-MR.
147 Ibid.

Such clear borrowings from public law would be impossible if not for the preponderance of lawyers among the Board's members (and staff). Hence, the dominance of lawyers among the Board's creators, members, and staffers aligned its design and practice closely with what lawyers are familiar with – that is, adjudicatory institutions. This again led to direct borrowings from public- and especially administrative-law principles to "juridify" Meta's content management operations.

4.3.1.4 The Staff

Apart from its members, the Board relies on the efforts of a considerable number of staff. Between seventy and ninety people work in offices around the world. In 2024, the London office was the largest, with roughly forty staffers working there.[148] As Board members only work part-time for the Oversight Board and are scattered around the globe, the staff have assumed a key – and largely overlooked – role in shaping the Board's strategic vision and practice. Staffers fulfill a dual function. On one hand, staffers are sherpas, helping the Board members navigate intricate legal and technical terrain. On the other, staffers are strategists themselves. By dint of their full-time and long-term positions working for the Board and their expertise in the field, they know many cases by heart and infuse their own normative and strategic considerations into the Board's deliberative remit. Staff members have thereby played a crucial part in fashioning the Board as a formal structure independent of Meta.

Permanent Position and Expertise

In light of many social theorists' focus on practice and cultural perspectives,[149] recent sociological and legal scholarship has highlighted the often overlooked but prime importance of staffers, secretariats, and "back-room personnel" in the business of international adjudication.[150]

148 Interview with Oversight Board Staffer 1 (n 54) 1.

149 The foundational work is arguably: Pierre Bourdieu, *Outline of a Theory of Practice* (Cambridge University Press 1977); for an overview see: Andreas Reckwitz, 'Toward a Theory of Social Practices: A Development in Culturalist Theorizing' (2002) 5 European Journal of Social Theory 243; for a theory of social norms through a praxeological lens see: Christoph Möllers, *The Possibility of Norms: Social Practice beyond Morals and Causes* (Oxford University Press 2020).

150 For EU law Tommaso Pavone, *The Ghostwriters: Lawyers and the Politics behind the Judicial Construction of Europe* (Cambridge University Press 2022) 129; already Antoine Vauchez, *Brokering Europe: Euro-Lawyers and the Making of a Transnational Polity* (Cambridge University Press 2015) 24–35. Antonin Cohen and Antoine Vauchez, 'The Social Construction of Law: The European Court of Justice and Its Legal Revolution Revisited' (2011) 7 Annual Review of Law and Social Science 417. For a similar perspective on

Especially in diversely staffed international adjudicative institutions, advisers, lawyers, and staffers are an indispensable pillar for organizational efficacy. Typically, their role is particularly prominent wherever adjudicating personnel work in globally dispersed, ad hoc, or part-time conditions. Yet most courts, tribunals, and other adjudicators remain coy about the precise roles their staff play. Instead, adjudicators often seek to "maintain the 'fiction' of rulings being delivered from on high …, whereas in fact, a large team of permanent staff is devoted to handling increasingly complex disputes."[151] Other scholars have suggested that this applies for other international and transnational adjudicators like the European Court of Justice and the World Trade Organization (WTO)'s appellate bodies, and this is equally true for the Oversight Board.[152]

The main reason for the staff's prominent role in the Board's practices is that, in contrast to Board members, staff are full-time employees. Plus, there are a lot more staffers than Board members. To repeat the figures, while the staff totals between seventy and ninety people, the Board has only roughly twenty members. Around thirty-five staffers, deployed to the so-called "content team," work directly on all cases. The content team has several subteams. These are: a case selection team; a project management team; a case and policy team; and the data and implementation team. All staffers work under the supervision and at the direction of Board members. Yet, the content team's permanent positions, expertise, and involvement with all aspects of each case seem to allow staffers to dig deep into issues they consider relevant and bring questions to Board members' attention.[153] Staffers contribute – and thereby shape – the Board's practices and strategies in various ways. They create longlists for consideration by a subteam

international adjudication see Tommaso Soave, *The Everyday Makers of International Law: From Great Halls to Back Rooms* (Cambridge University Press 2022); Jeffrey L Dunoff and Mark A Pollack, 'International Judicial Practices: Opening the "Black Box" of International Courts' (2018) 40 Michigan Journal of International Law 47. For a sociological perspective on the influence of specialized staffers see RR Ritti and Fred H Goldner, 'Professional Pluralism in an Industrial Organization' (1969) 16 Management Science 233, 233–246; DiMaggio and Powell (n 64) 150, 155. See further for so-called "fourth branch" institutions: Mark V Tushnet, *The New Fourth Branch: Institutions for Protecting Constitutional Democracy* (Cambridge University Press 2021) 45–46.

[151] Pauwelyn and Pelc (n 15) 538 (referencing a quote by Thomas Cottier who himself was a WTO Appellate Body member).

[152] See for an empirical account of the WTOs' Appellate Body's secretariat: ibid. See for reminiscent phenomena in national judiciaries already Owen M Fiss, 'The Bureaucratization of the Judiciary' (1983) 92 Yale Law Journal 1442.

[153] Interview with Oversight Board Staffer 1 (n 54); Interview with Oversight Board Staffer 2 (n 10); Interview with Oversight Board Staffer 3 (n 11); Interview with Oversight Board Staffer 4 (n 52).

of members, the Case Selection Committee, which then draws up a shortlist of, in their view, the most serious cases.[154] Staff also provide evidentiary material to inform deliberations at the direction of the Board members and help with fact-finding in relation to complex technical and normative questions. During the deliberations of Board members, staffers are also allowed to respond to questions about the briefing materials when asked.[155]

Further, Oversight Board staffers are highly qualified. Many staffers are lawyers, and many have a human rights background.[156] This enables staffers to contribute to the Board's adjudicative practice while reflexively reinforcing the Board's adjudicative nature and perceptions thereof. Appropriately enough, staffers and members are subject to the same code of conduct.[157] Requirements to disclose conflicts of interest or the obligation to be independent, for example, amount to virtually the same thing as the organization's code of conduct always refers to "members and staff."[158] This indicates the staff's importance for the decision-making process and the Board's overall strategy. Another factor reinforcing the staff's position within the institution is staff members' identification with the Oversight Board's mission. A strong sense of commitment and the perceived societal relevance of their work was quite prevalent in every interview and supplementary discussion. Many of the interviewed staffers working in content teams perceive their work as helping to resolve problems for society.[159] Many have a background in NGO work, courts, or other judiciary-related jobs.[160] One staffer describes the staff as having a "very strong sense of identification" with the Board and its mission,[161] while another mentioned their work's main objectives to "protect individual rights" and to "mitigate the negative systemic effects on the basis of individual cases."[162] Even though these qualitative insights are

[154] cf. Rulebook (November 2021) (n 104) 8; Email Oversight Board Staffer 7 (on file with the author) (3 February 2023).

[155] Interview with Oversight Board Staffer 1 (n 54).

[156] Interview with Oversight Board Staffer 1 (n 54); Interview with Oversight Board Staffer 2 (n 10); Interview with Oversight Board Staffer 3 (n 11); Interview with Oversight Board Staffer 4 (n 52).

[157] See Code of Conduct attached to the Bylaws.

[158] See e.g., Code of Conduct Sections "Introduction," "Independence and Impartiality."

[159] Interview with Oversight Board Staffer 1 (n 54); Interview with Oversight Board Staffer 2 (n 10).

[160] Interview with Oversight Board Staffer 1 (n 54); Interview with Oversight Board Staffer 2 (n 10).

[161] Interview with Oversight Board Staffer 1 (n 54).

[162] Ibid.

inherently subjective and reflect, at best, the perspective of the interviewed staffers and not the entire group of employees, we should consider them tentative indicators of many staffers' attitudes to their work.

However, staff expertise also raises one problematic issue. Several staffers are former Facebook employees, some even from the Governance and Strategic Initiatives team that created the Oversight Board.[163] On the one hand, intimate knowledge of how Meta works is crucial for the Board's success. On the other, staffing a guardian institution with former employees of that same "guarded" organization brings with it connotations of personal connections between controller and controlled. In that sense, the questions surrounding the Oversight Board's institutional design are not at all new or unprecedented. In fact, they remind us of Iuvenal's classic "*quis custodiet ipsos custodes?*" (who guards the guardians?) question.[164] Correspondingly, the Oversight Board's code of conduct considers "being a former ... employee of Facebook, Inc." a conflict of interest for "members *and* staffers."[165] Further, Board members and staffers must disclose several potentially disqualifying facts, one of them being previous employment at Facebook.[166] However, former employment does "not necessarily automatically disqualify" someone from working for the Board, as these cases would "be reviewed by the trustees to determine the appropriate course of action."[167] A reading of the applicable governance documents indicates that such conditions (and the accompanying potential conflicts of interest) were reviewed and validated by the trustees in several cases. From a pragmatic perspective this makes sense, because outside hires would presumably be less familiar with the inner workings of Facebook's content-moderation activities. However, this episode adds to the impression that the normative material applicable to the Board is met by considerable centripetal

[163] Interview with Oversight Board Staffer 4 (n 52).

[164] Iuvenal, *Satires* VII 347–348.

[165] Code of Conduct, Article 1 bullet point 1 No 1 (emphasis added). Verbatim that paragraph reads: "[M]embers, staff, and their immediate family will not create or maintain conflicts of interest, which include but are not limited to the following: ... Personal or professional conflicts of interest that may impact (or appear to impact) the ability of Board members or staff to perform their duties, such as: (1) being a former or current employee of Facebook, Inc. or having an immediate family member employed by Facebook, Inc," Code of Conduct Article 1 bullet point 2.

[166] Article 3 Code of Conduct in conjunction with Appendix A (to the code of conduct) 'Disqualifications and Required Disclosures' (Bylaws January 2021, p 45).

[167] Appendix A (to the code of conduct) 'Disqualifications and Required Disclosures' (Bylaws January 2021, p 45).

forces of seeking legitimacy (by the use of constitutional metaphors and strict codes of conduct, for example) while maintaining practical operability (in other words, needing people who actually know what Meta is doing).[168]

"Fishing Mode"

Driven by what appeared like a high degree of personal motivation, the staffers working on the Board's adjudicative processes operate and help fine-tuning the Board's focus, "jurisprudence," and procedures. Each of the content subteams consists of several staffers, and there are usually fewer than ten on each subteam.[169] These content subteams fulfill specific tasks concerning the Board's adjudication and are present at every step while a case makes its way through the Oversight Board.[170] Staffers in the Case Selection Team, which is made up of several lawyers and political scientists, aid in selecting cases at the direction and supervision of the Case Selection Committee, which comprises a rotating membership of Board members.[171] Staffers also prep Board members in substantive, procedural, and factual matters.[172] Even though staffers do not write formal drafts of the Oversight Board's decisions or advisory opinions, it is plausible that the extensive reports written by the Case and Policy Team lay the groundwork for the later draft produced by Board members.[173] At least some of the "content team" staffers are present when Board members deliberate but do not contribute to deliberations and are not encouraged to share their opinions.[174]

And so, even though they are not vested with formal decision-making authority, staffers are an indispensable part of the decision-making process in a broader sense. One striking example of the staff's value and strategic vision was what one interviewed staffer called "fishing mode."[175] This describes how a group of fewer than ten staffers draws up a longlist of a few dozen cases from the many thousands submitted to the Board by

[168] Whereas it might be even questionable whether former members of the Governance and Strategic Initiatives team would be experts in content moderation as the team's job was precisely not to look at what Facebook is doing but to invent an institution that would control Facebook.

[169] Interview with Oversight Board Staffer 1 (n 54).

[170] Ibid.

[171] Ibid.

[172] Ibid.

[173] Ibid.

[174] Email Oversight Board Staffer 7 (on file with the author) (n 154).

[175] Interview with Oversight Board Staffer 3 (n 11).

users of Meta's services. Board members provide staffers with criteria, which staffers then apply when filtering appeals.[176] A high-ranking staffer described these case-selection criteria as a blend of specific content, like "breasts of transitioning people that are deleted as female nudity," with general aspects like "posts from conflict regions."[177] Hence, filtering appeals works in an aim-oriented fashion. "Fishing mode" depicts the case selection team's angling for "good cases" after first filtering the cases based on criteria like metadata, region, language, views, and violated community standard.[178] Like Captain Ahab and the crew of the Pequod, the case selection team stands in the crow's nest looking for tell-tale ripples in the water, hinting at a whale under the surface. But how to spot a metaphorical whale in this ocean of cases? The same interviewee mentioned that a key consideration in longlisting is the user statement.[179] It increases the chances of selection where the user shows serious engagement with the matter and an understanding of what "the problem" is.[180] This has a practical background. It makes it more likely that the user will keep their post up and does not delete it once informed that the Oversight Board is investigating it.[181] The staffer described finding good cases as follows:

> It's not like finding the needle in the haystack. It's more like finding a particularly nice-looking piece of hay in the haystack.[182]

Clearly, one key question is what makes a "good" case. It is not only the criteria but also the structural issues underlying Meta's decision-making processes that the case is potentially addressing.[183] Yet the staffer points out that it is hard to interpret these structural aspects from the limited amount of information they are able to glean from the submissions.[184] Often, the Board recommends Meta to change its rules to be more concise and transparent and align its procedures more with principles of public law, administrative law, and good governance. To buttress its argument, the Board refers to public-law standards as they appear in the wording of legislation like Article 19 of the ICCPR, for example – standards like

176 Bylaws Article 1 Section 3.1.2.
177 Interview with Oversight Board Staffer 3 (n 11).
178 Ibid.
179 Ibid.
180 Ibid.
181 Ibid.
182 Ibid.
183 Ibid.
184 Ibid.

legality and proportionality.[185] Further, the Board repeatedly recommended that Meta should notify users about content-moderation decisions, that it should state reasons and, where necessary, provide timely translations of its rules and decisions.[186]

4.3.1.5 The LLC

Lastly, there is the limited liability company, which is the legal person at the center of much of the Oversight Board's contracting. The purpose of the LLC is solely organization related. The sole member of the LLC is the Oversight Board Trust, according to Article 2.2 of the LLC agreement. The trustees serve as the LLC's managers. The corporation is obliged to rent office space, draw up contracts with staffers (as employees), and draw up individual contracts with Board members.[187]

4.3.2 *Jurisdiction*

Because Emulated Guardians are adjudicators, they must have jurisdiction. To be effective controllers of organizational power, said adjudication must also be compulsorily applied to the organization these guardians are tasked with controlling.

4.3.2.1 Subject Matter Jurisdiction

The Board's purpose is to control Meta's content-moderation activities. To achieve this aim, the Board's founding documents outline the Board's "jurisdiction." The charter states that Meta users "may bring forward content for Board review" whenever they "disagree with the outcome of Facebook's decision and have exhausted appeals."[188] In contrast, the bylaws are formulated more narrowly. They had initially restricted the Board's jurisdiction to review only "individual pieces of content, such as specific posts, photos, videos, and comments" that had been "removed for violations of . . . 'Community Standards' or 'Community Guidelines.'"[189] Because of this, the Board appeared to be barred from reviewing a multitude of other actions and design choices impacting how Meta

[185] See e.g. Pro-Navalny Protests in Russia [2021] Oversight Board 2021–004-FB-UA at p 13 to 16 (of the PDF version) for the "legality" and proportionality assessment as well as recommendation No 6 (notification).

[186] See e.g. COVID lockdowns in Brazil [2021] Oversight Board 2021–008-FB-FBR at 10.1.

[187] LLC Agreement Section 5.3.(a)(i) and (vii).

[188] Charter Article 2 and 2(1).

[189] Bylaws Article 3 Section 1.1.1.

exercises power over its users. Scholars have repeatedly criticized these reduced terms of reference as the "biggest disappointment" of the Board.[190] Allowing users *other than* the original uploader to appeal moderation decisions is essential, as it will typically be the former whose rights may be infringed. For example, to protect the rights of victims in cases of defamation, libel, or revenge porn, victims must be able to challenge moderation decisions. Correspondingly, respective provisions were included in the list of possible appellants to ODSs in the EU's DSA.[191] Since April 2021, and pursuant to a clause in the bylaws,[192] which opened the door for future expansions of jurisdiction, the Board now accepts appeals *for* the removal of content from Facebook and Instagram (that is, appeals *against* Meta's decision to leave content up).[193] In 2024, the Board expanded its jurisdiction to Meta's Threads, a social network the company set up in 2023 to compete with X after Elon Musk's takeover.

Interestingly, the bylaws already indicate that the Board might move toward a more comprehensive interpretation of its powers in the future.[194] Apparently, this issue emerged during the global consultation period, prompting the company to concede, in an attachment to the global consultation report, that "[o]ver time, the Board may look to decide upon other actions (e.g. downranking or applying interstitial warnings)."[195] Correspondingly, Article 3 Section 1.1.2 of the bylaws states that "in the future, people will have the opportunity to request the Board's review of other enforcement actions." As mentioned previously, the Oversight Board has already made use of that provision and expanded its jurisdiction. Further, in October 2022, the Board ventured further down the path of these more graded forms of moderation as it demanded Meta to put up warning screens like "sensitive or disturbing content."[196] In several interviews, staffers and Board members indicated their willingness to focus on

190 Douek, 'What Kind of Oversight Board Have You Given Us?' (n 102). See further Helfer and Land (n 3) 12–15.

191 See at 3.3.4.1.

192 Bylaws Article 3 Section 1.1.2.

193 Oversight Board, 'The Oversight Board Is Accepting User Appeals to Remove Content from Facebook and Instagram (Press Release)' (April 2021) <https://perma.cc/FTD9-8SE2>.

194 Bylaws Article 3 Section 1.1.2.

195 See at tenth question, topic: resolution under "implementing feedback" in Facebook, Capturing Feedback: Charter for the Oversight Board, accessible via: <https://perma.cc/XZ37-MBQG>. See also Douek, 'How Much Power Did Facebook Give Its Oversight Board?' (n 102).

196 Oversight Board, 'Oversight Board Publishes Transparency Report for Second Quarter of 2022 and Gains Ability to Apply Warning Screens (Press Release)' (October 2022) <https://perma.cc/6C3F-WHPT>.

"other enforcement actions" like the amplifying or demoting of content, which may highlight or restrict the visibility (and therefore harmfulness) of content without deleting it.[197]

Therefore, prominent criticism that the Oversight Board would exemplify a simplistic, "stylized" understanding of content moderation as an endless string of customized decisions seems not entirely fair.[198] Although such a viewpoint may have colored the earliest visions for the Board, its practice indicates a nuanced and comprehensive understanding of the structural challenges of content moderation.[199] As we will shortly see, the Board's key normative output is *not* made up of individual decisions but general, structure-focused recommendations, which aim at improving Meta's governance procedures and structures instead of deciding only on a few paradigmatic cases.[200] Thus, the Oversight Board is not a solely binary adjudicator allowing "individual appeal to a human in every case."[201] Quite the opposite, because the Board decides only very few individual appeals. Instead, the Board uses the few cases it adjudicates to formulate general normative sentences that its members believe should apply to Meta. Based on these general normative sentences, the company might then improve its governance and decision-making practices.

In conclusion, the Board's jurisdictional focus rests on one important, and publicly visible, aspect of Meta's content moderation: the removal or retention of individual pieces of content for violation of community standards. However, the company exercises power over its users in a more wide-ranging way than this. Meta retains content even though other users may want it removed. The company shows content according to algorithmic metrics and has, after all, designed the technical infrastructure that allows users to communicate in the first place. All these decisions, one way or another, "moderate" the communication of users on the platform. For the time being, the Board's "jurisdiction" seems not to have plunged further into those deeper layers of moderation. Ultimately, those deeper and darker waters is where the

[197] See for an informative introduction to this governance practice on the network TikTok by Jing Zeng and Bondy Valdovinos Kaye, 'From Content Moderation to Visibility Moderation: A Case Study of Platform Governance on TikTok' (2022) 14 Policy & Internet 79.

[198] For the criticism see Douek, 'Content Moderation as Systems Thinking' (n 7) 528, 567 et seq.

[199] For the Board's origins see above at 4.2.

[200] See at 4.5 and 4.6.

[201] Douek, 'Content Moderation as Systems Thinking' (n 7) 568.

whale is. Yet, on the evidence of decisions made up until now and the tentative expansion of the Board's jurisdiction following the remit allowed by the bylaws' provisions, it appears that the Board might incrementally venture toward a more comprehensive jurisdiction over the various aspects of content moderation which go beyond individual decisions that enforce rules relating to individual pieces of content.

4.3.2.2 Compulsory Jurisdiction

In principle, the Board's jurisdiction is *compulsory* for Meta for the appealable content outlined above. According to Article 2(1) of its charter, the company "will commit to the Board's independent oversight." However, appeals may be ineligible for Board review if they concern content that is "criminally unlawful" or if a Board decision was likely to trigger "criminal liability" allegations or "adverse government reactions" for Facebook, its employees, or the Board.[202] For such pieces of content, Meta can contest the Board's "jurisdiction." The Board and the company found a somewhat peculiar way to ensure that the Board stays within the bylaws' and charter's limits. The Board typically shows the company the shortlisted cases prior to selecting the appeals for review. At this prior stage, the company might then object to the Board choosing, or technically: shortlisting, a specific case for the above-mentioned reasons.[203] Neither the charter nor the bylaws had stipulated any requirement for this prior "legal review" by the company.[204] But it appears to be now standard practice that the Board shares shortlisted cases for prior "legal review" with Meta. The company's legal department then may "exclude" certain appeals from the list due to legal problems in the cases' respective jurisdictions. As stated in the Board's *Rulebook for Case Review and Policy Guidance*, which Board members adopted in November 2020: "shortlisted cases will be sent to Facebook for legal review. Facebook may exclude from the shortlist cases that are not eligible for review by the Oversight Board, in accordance with the Bylaws, such as cases that could result in criminal liability or adverse government action if reviewed."[205]

This is remarkable. In principle, Meta's interest in avoiding negative legal consequences by subjecting itself to the Board appears legitimate.

202 Bylaws Article 2 Section 1.2.2.
203 Interview with Oversight Board Staffer 1 (n 54) 1.
204 See Charter Article 3 and Bylaws Section 3.
205 Rulebook (n 104) Step 2 No 1 (p 8)

Despite all the metaphorical bravado, the Board remains an Emulated Guardian that resides, in contrast to the DSA's ODSs, outside the realms of democratically set law, and only time will tell whether the Board will incrementally build adjudicatory authority.[206] However, the fact that the company has retained at least the possibility of weighing in on the Board's case selection is a blot on the latter's authority. From the perspective of individual rights adjudication, Meta should be able to *contest* the eligibility of cases but not *decide* whether they are ineligible. Thus, at the end of the day, we see how Meta's interest in sustaining autonomy collides with the Board's public image and function as (adjudicatory) guardian. Yet, historically, adjudicatory control over bureaucratic power structures grows gradually and incrementally.[207] Thus, possibly existing communicatory channels leading from the company to the Board should warn us not to enthusiastically drape the Board with the ceremonial garb of "supreme court," as the Board is still in the process of building up its organizational muscles.

4.3.2.3 Appeals, Referrals, and Policy Advice

Users whose content has been deleted by Meta or who filed an unsuccessful notice for other users' content to be deleted have "standing" to file an appeal to the Board.[208]

Further, Meta may "directly refer cases to the Board that are significant and difficult."[209] For example, in January 2021, the company referred the decision to the Board as to whether it was justified in permanently deleting the Facebook and Instagram accounts of then US President Trump after his role in the January 6, 2021 storming of the Capitol. Using Article 19 of the ICCPR's criteria for legality, the Board harshly criticized the company's incomplete and imprecise sanctioning policies. Ultimately, the Board argued that the company had no right to permanently ban Trump's accounts because such a sanction was not stipulated in its terms of service at the time. However, the Board allowed that a temporary ban on Trump's accounts would have been a proportionate response given the threat of real-world harm emanating from many of the posts on his accounts.

[206] See at 3.7, 4.5, 4.6, and 5.3.
[207] See at 2.2.
[208] Bylaws Article 3 Section 1.1.1 and see above at 3.2.1.
[209] Bylaws Article 2 Section 2.1.1.

Lastly, separate from individual case review, the company may request "policy guidance" and a "policy advisory statement from the Board."[210] These are general normative sentences on structural issues. Even though the various documents and the Board's decisions themselves do not use consistent vocabulary, we can distinguish between policy advisory statements and specific recommendations following *general* requests by the company, and policy advisory statements and "recommendations" concerning the underlying governance issues at the company, but which are retrospectively issued as a byproduct of individual decisions.[211]

4.3.3 *Impartiality and Independence*

To emulate adjudicative control over administrative power, the Oversight Board must be *impartial* and *independent*. As outlined in Chapter 2, independence refers to the adjudicating institution's structural design, whereas impartiality signifies the fair-mindedness and objectivity of the person adjudicating.[212] Adjudicators must be externally autonomous – that is, not bound by hierarchical command or factual constraint – and internally objective and fair-minded in terms of the procedure's outcome and the rules applied.[213] When applying these standards, we should remind ourselves of the words of Martin Shapiro who, based on extensive historical work, cautioned: "persons and institutions to which we normally award the titles judges and courts, . . . in reality . . . are simply at one end of a spectrum rather than constituting an absolute distinct entity."[214] For example, specialized adjudicators that control administrative power often have a legal, organizational, and practical nexus to the organization they control. Often, sub-court administrators like UK administrative tribunals, American Article-I courts, or EU Boards of Appeal may even operate attached to specific administrative agencies. Yet they all have structural safeguards in place to shield their adjudicative decision-making processes and people from undue influence by the controlled entity. Therefore, certain organizational overlaps are often necessary in

210 Bylaws Article 1 Section 2.1.3.

211 See at 4.5.

212 For a US perspective see James E Moliterno, 'The Administrative Judiciary's Independence Myth' (2006) 41 Wake Forest Law Review 1191, 1199–1208.

213 cf. the recent case-law by the ECJ on Poland's judiciary, see Independence of the Polish Supreme Court [2019] European Court of Justice (Grand Chamber) C-619/18, ECLI:EU:C:2019:531 paras 71–77.

214 Martin M Shapiro, *Courts: A Comparative and Political Analysis* (University of Chicago Press 1981) 8.

practice or, for the purposes of gaining greater expertise, even desirable. Adjudicatory impartiality and independence hence call for an appropriate institutional, personal, and procedural setup that helps to safeguard externally autonomous decision-makers and internally objective decision-making while maintaining operability.

Viewed against this yardstick, I argue that the Board is – albeit organizationally and financially intertwined with Meta – in practice sufficiently autonomous and its members fair-minded to be considered impartial. However, when it comes to the Board's independence we see a more blurred picture. On the one hand, the (irrevocable) trust installed a seemingly effective organizational buffer between Board and company. On the other, Meta retained avenues of influence over who gets nominated[215] and may "exclude" cases from review if "they are not eligible for review by the Oversight Board."[216] To what extent Meta treads these paths of influence is unclear and it should be noted that during interviews nobody indicated any undue influence being applied.[217] However, these two organizational and procedural aspects are clear "no-go's" from a classic perspective on adjudicatory independence. The crux is: the Board is only of value to Meta if it is publicly perceived as sufficiently independent. This is arguably why, for example, Meta's preliminary "legal review" of the cases entering the Board's docket is not explicitly stipulated in the provisions of the charter or in the bylaws but only in a rather ominous sounding "rulebook," which "nonbindingly" specifies the bylaws.[218]

The following section analyzes the decisive aspects of independence and impartiality for adjudicators controlling administration-like operations. The Board is not entrenched in Meta's hierarchy, though the company nevertheless retains some influence over its docket. Further, we reflect on the trust's role as mediator between the Board and Meta, and on how "dangerous" the Board effectively is for Meta. We then look more deeply into the Board's nomination and removal procedures and investigate its operational and financial autonomy.

[215] See also especially at 4.3.3.1.

[216] For the Stephen Levy article see Levy (n 131) 14–16; for the quote see Rulebook (n 104) Step 2 No 1 (November 2020).

[217] The journalist Stephen Levy reported in a leading outlet for tech journalism that "Meta employees remain deeply involved in hiring and are a factor in why the Board is still far short of the total number set out in its charter." Levy also reported that Meta directly prevented one critical researcher from becoming a Board member, cf. ibid 14.

[218] See Rulebook (n 104) Step 2 called "Facebook Legal Review" at 8; in contrast Bylaws Section 3.1.

4.3.3.1 No Hierarchy, but Docket Influence?

For the Board to be independent, its members must not be subject to hierarchical command governing their decision-making. The Board's independence was a key concern during its creation.[219] Article 1 Section 1 of the bylaws, as well as Article 1 of the charter, stipulate that members "will exercise neutral, independent judgment and render decisions impartially." Even though the founding documents retain some veto powers with the company when it comes to certain management decisions by the trust (for example, changing one or more bylaws), Meta cannot issue any "commands" to Board members.[220] Correspondingly, no interviewee voiced concerns about company overreach. Even though their responses do not guarantee that there was no overreach by the company,[221] the way the Board's decisions developed suggests that it indeed operates largely autonomously from the company's influence. In many decisions, the Board has thrown light on and condemned Meta's governance practices. For example, in the Trump decision, the Board criticized the company's request to *formulate* rules. It stated:

> [t]he Board rejects Facebook's request for it to endorse indefinite restrictions, imposed and lifted without clear criteria. Appropriate limits on discretionary powers are crucial to distinguish the legitimate use of discretion from possible scenarios around the world in which Facebook may unduly silence speech not linked to harm or delay action critical to protecting people.[222]

The Board's forceful repudiation of the company's formally referred request, the founding documents' focus on the Board's independence, as well as the Board members' status as independent contractees, makes hierarchy-based subordination of the Board to the company unlikely. Similarly, several interviewees said that they had seen a drop in public criticism of the Board's purported independence after the Trump decision.[223]

219 See for the role of the trust in safeguarding independence at 4.3.3.2; see for the Board's genesis in general at 4.2.

220 cf. Bylaws Article 5. See further Klonick, 'The Facebook Oversight Board: Creating an Independent Institution to Adjudicate Online Free Expression' (n 3) 2481 et seq.

221 We should not forget that, after all, the interviewees working for the Board have a self-interest to be perceived as independent as possible.

222 When Facebook referred the case to the Board, it specifically requested "observations or recommendations from the Board about suspensions when the user is a political leader." cf. Former President Trump's suspension (n 143) 5.

223 Interview with Oversight Board Staffer 1 (n 54); Interview with Oversight Board Staffer 2 (n 10); Interview with Oversight Board Staffer 4 (n 52).

Yet even though the company does not appear to be exercising undue influence on the Board's decision-making and especially its deliberations, Meta retains at least the possibility of exerting influence over the Board's docket. Board members who are part of the Case Selection Committee are in theory free to compile a shortlist of possible cases to take forward. However, before the Case Selection Committee decides which cases to adopt for decision, that shortlist, according to the Board's internal "rulebook" *must* be sent to Meta. It is unclear what would happen if longlisted cases were not sent to legal review by Meta. As mentioned previously, the company "may exclude from the shortlist cases that are not eligible for review by the Oversight Board, in accordance with the Bylaws, such as cases that could result in criminal liability or adverse government action if reviewed."[224]

Naturally, if Meta ends up removing cases from the shortlist, the Case Selection Committee cannot select them, and the Board cannot decide whether to take them forward. Neither the bylaws nor the charter regulate this "Facebook Legal Review," although the company's intervention is supposed to be just part of the "non-binding … practical guidance … detailing case review and policy guidance procedures."[225] Judging from transparency reports, Meta indeed conducts such legal reviews for each case and, in early 2021, Meta did exclude at least one case, and possibly more, from the shortlist through its use of this "legal review."[226]

An adjudicator whose docket is subject to any caveats emanating from the entity it is supposed to be controlling does not match up to the traditional standards of independence familiar in other adjudicative bodies. Even nonadjudicative guardians like ombudspersons or other "fourth branch" actors often enjoy more autonomy in selecting and rejecting cases. As Klonick observed, Meta's "delegation of authority to the Trust [and the Board in general] is far from absolute."[227] In sum, Meta granted the Board independence in the most literal sense, as the Board is

224 Rulebook (n 104) step 2 No 1.

225 Rulebook (n 104) Introduction.

226 The transparency report only states "Of the 39 cases shortlisted in this period. 34 were confirmed as eligible by Facebook's legal team and five cases were removed from the Board's review either by the person who appealed the content or through Facebook's legal review." Whether it was just one of those five, two, three, or four, which Meta excluded we do not know. If it would have been four (it cannot be five as that would not leave one for the user removal), Meta would have excluded more than 10 percent of the longlisted cases in that quarter. See Oversight Board Transparency Report Q 4 2020, Q1 & Q2 2021, 30 – accessible via: <https://perma.cc/JTJ8-DTHD>.

227 Klonick, 'The Facebook Oversight Board: Creating an Independent Institution to Adjudicate Online Free Expression' (n 3) 2481. See also again Levy (n 216) 14–17.

not formally entrenched into Meta's hierarchical structure. However, depicting the Board as independent in the traditional, adjudicatory sense of the word would, at the moment, be inaccurate for the simple reason that Meta retains some influence over the Board's docket.

4.3.3.2 The Role of the Trust

Even though the Board does not receive directives from the company, organizationally speaking, the two bodies are intertwined. Central to these ties – but also, simultaneously, to the Board's far-reaching practical autonomy vis-à-vis the company – is the trust. The irrevocable, noncharitable "Oversight Board Trust" (established in Wilmington, Delaware) serves as a buffer between Meta (as a private company) and the Board, which, although privately organized, performs the public law-like function of controlling Meta's administration-like content moderation. Six trustees are obliged to isolate the Board's adjudicatory decision-making from the company as much as possible. Board members and trustees communicate mostly in regular (though none too frequent) meetings, where they discuss organizational requirements and administrative issues, for instance.[228]

According to Article 2.2 of the trust agreement, the trust and the individual trustees have to "protect the independent judgment of the Board Members and their ability to fulfil their stated purpose." To do so, many organizational aspects are delegated to the Board itself. For example, the Board can propose new members, establish new procedural rules (within the limits of the bylaws), or engage in new practices like issuing quarterly reports to measure the impact of its decisions and policies. In turn, the trustees are obliged to allocate resources to the LLC for office space, travel, accommodation, workshops, and work retreats for teams scattered around the globe. The trust also handles contracts for Board members and employees. Trustees do not participate in case selection, neither do they take part in deliberations, voice opinions, or anything else that could directly influence the Board's adjudicatory work. One trustee describes their involvement with the Board's day-to-day work as follows:

> We [the trustees] stay completely independent of the Board when it comes to selecting and deciding cases. But with respect to the actual administration of the OSB entity, there are channels of communication. There must be, because we need to set up an organization that works for the Board members, but we must do so in ways that are consistent with our own fiduciary responsibilities.[229]

[228] Interview with Oversight Board Trustee (n 53).
[229] Ibid.

Hence, beyond formal channels of communication, informal avenues between trustees and Board members arguably exist. After all, the group of Meta executives and employees creating the Board, its members, and staffers is fairly tight knit. Most of them went to (and sometimes teach at) elite US law schools. The effects of these personal and habitual connections among practitioners, lawyers, and legal scholars have been identified as a common factor for fostering the emergence of normative orders.[230] Such "field effects" (borrowing from Pierre Bourdieu) should not be underestimated when it comes to the makeup and operations of the Oversight Board.

Correspondingly, even though most people working for the Board, or the trust seem to have, at some time or other, shared their strategic ideas for how the Board should operate, the Board's practice isolates its decision-making from the company and even the trustees. Trustees seem largely isolated from personal or strategic considerations relating to the people working for the Board. One trustee said:

> Of course, I stay completely away from the decision-making processes. That has nothing to do with me. But the larger strategic positioning and functioning of the Board is an entirely different question. We need to establish a model that will provide criteria of success with respect to these larger strategic issues. I myself have many ideas, but in the end the Trustees and Board members will need to reach a common agreement.[231]

This trustee alludes to a thread emerging during the conversations and interviews conducted for this present work: the Oversight Board's ongoing soul-searching. The Board's complicated institutional and internal structure, the public demands on it (some of which Meta and the Board itself drummed up), and the challenge of using private-law mechanisms to accommodate its own emulation of individual rights adjudication – at heart an intrinsically public function – complicates the Board's soul-searching. In short, controlling one of the largest experiments in (private) global governance while being an entirely private and relatively small institution is a conflicting, ambiguous, and perhaps impossible task. Again, the same trustee explained that:

> We're using the structures of private law to create an entity that's essentially responsible for establishing public law norms. We have to work out exactly how

230 See for early community law Pavone (n 127). For EU law in general: Cohen and Vauchez (n 127); Vauchez (n 127). See further Yves Dezalay and Bryant G Garth, *Dealing with Virtue: International Commercial Arbitration and the Construction of a Transnational Legal Order* (University of Chicago Press 1998); Pauwelyn and Pelc (n 151).

231 Interview with Oversight Board Trustee (n 53).

these two distinct legal paradigms intersect. The role of the trustees is to guarantee the independence of the Board. That obligation is clear enough when it comes to actually selecting and deciding cases. But what about if the Board decides that to be independent it requires certain staffing levels or administrative assistance? How do we reconcile *that* kind of independence with our own fiduciary responsibility to the *res* of the trust? These kinds of issues raise complicated and unresolved questions. We're trying to feel our way towards solutions.[232]

Reflecting on the trust's role in setting down a procedural framework for the Board's external autonomy and internal fair-mindedness, we arrive at some (partly conflicting) conclusions. For a start, the trust constitutes a formal as well as informal link between the Oversight Board as an organization, its members as individuals, and Meta as a company. Communication exists and, all symbolic distance aside, it would be naïve to assume that the Board operates in isolation from the company. The issue is then whether such communication impairs the Board's external autonomy and internal fair-mindedness. Reasonably assessing the fair-mindedness of Board members (and staffers), if it were possible at all, would require an array of psychological surveys that is far beyond the scope of this book. However, if this author's subjective impressions based on the conducted interviews are of any value, a "pro-Meta bias" was not detected among the interviewed staffers or Board members. Some interviewees even described the Board's internal culture as expressly "adversarial" toward Meta,[233] while others compared it to a "human rights NGO."[234] At the same time, interviewees characterized the Board's impact as relatively limited and rejected the idea that it had any "supreme court"-like influence over Meta.[235] But they seemed confident that their adjudicatory practice, based largely on human rights and administrative law, could be valuable for the interests of users – and that they were not in their jobs just to do Meta a favor.[236]

This leaves us with the question of the Board's external autonomy. This autonomy would be impaired if the trust or the company could somehow pressure the Board to decide in a certain way. The trustees' fiduciary duty is to enable the Board to exercise "independent judgment."[237] Trustees

232 Ibid.

233 Interview with Oversight Board Staffer 5 (n 54).

234 Interview with Oversight Board Staffer 6 (23 November 2022).

235 Interview with Oversight Board Staffer 1 (n 54); Interview with Oversight Board Staffer 2 (n 10); Interview with Oversight Board Staffer 3 (n 11).

236 Interview with Oversight Board Staffer 1 (n 54); Interview with Oversight Board Staffer 2 (n 10); Interview with Oversight Board Staffer 3 (n 11); Interview with Oversight Board Staffer 6 (n 234).

237 Trust Agreement, Section 2.2.

have no obligations vis-à-vis the company, and none of the interviewees suggested that the company exerts influence via the trustees. Further, baseline communication between adjudicator and controlled entities seems normal and does not necessarily impair external autonomy or internal fair-mindedness. Based on the limited impressions from the conducted interviews, therefore, the trust seems to work reasonably well as a buffer between company and Board.

In that context, it is important to keep a realistic perspective when it comes to how big a "threat" the Board really is for the company.[238] Apart from individual decisions on specific pieces of content, Board decisions are not binding. Arguably, and given the hundreds of millions of dollars Meta already invested, it would not make sense for Meta to weigh in the Board's decision-making process because the Board's main normative feedback to Meta, the nonbinding recommendations (see at Section 4.6.2), require Meta's involvement for them to be implemented anyway. If Meta policymakers want to circumvent the Board, it would be much easier to delay and tacitly thwart the implementation of the Board's decisions, recommendations, and policy advisory statements.[239] Direct meddling with the Board tends to result in disastrous publicity and thwarts the (assumed) aim of Meta to (also) use the Board as a publicly legitimizing formal structure.

Take as example an episode about Meta's withdrawal of a policy advisory opinion on the company's handling of hate speech in the context of Russia's war in Ukraine.[240] The company requested a policy advisory opinion from the Board, whose importance several interviewees described as equal to that of the Trump case. Yet, very late in the process, Meta reversed and withdrew its request. In an unusual press release, the Board subsequently criticized the company stating that it "believe[s] that the request raises important issues and … [the Board is] disappointed by the company's decision to withdraw it." Press reactions to Meta's withdrawal were equally negative, some depicting the move as "undercutting" the Board's authority whose "only role is to handle the easy questions," prompting the question "why bother with it at all?" Neither charter nor bylaws explicate that Meta had the right to withdraw an already referred request for a policy advisory opinion. Article 2

[238] See below at 4.6 and Chapter 5.

[239] See at 4.6.

[240] cf. for the whole paragraph: Oversight Board, 'Protecting Freedom of Expression and Human Rights in Ukraine and Russia (Press Release)' (May 2022) <https://perma.cc/59Z2-WLKY>; Interviewees: Interview with Oversight Board Staffer 2 (n 10) 2; Interview with Oversight Board Staffer 3 (n 11); Interview with Oversight Board Staffer 4 (n 52) 4.

For the press coverage see: Casey Newton, 'How Facebook Undercut the Oversight Board' (*The Verge*, 5 December 2022) <https://perma.cc/H6RE-S57F>.

Section 2.1.3 of the bylaws states that the company "may request" such statements and that the Board "may accept or reject" such requests.

4.3.3.3 Nominations and Removal of Members

Another factor relevant for independence are the nomination and removal procedures for Board members. A body consisting only of people hand-picked or waved through by the controlled entity raises concerns about independence. Moreover, adjudicators' personal sense of fair-mindedness requires that they should not worry about being sacked for any decisions they might make. The removal aspect does not appear particularly problematic. According to the charter and the bylaws, Board members can be prematurely removed from the Board only for just cause but not "due to the content decisions they have made."[241] Instead, removing Board members requires a "two-thirds vote of the Board (not counting the member(s) in question), subject to approval of the trustees . . .; and may be considered only for a violation of the code of conduct."[242]

The code of conduct regulates in detail how members and staff "must conduct themselves, both in their professional and personal capacities" which means "avoiding even the appearance of impropriety and flagging all potential conflicts through proper channels."[243] Therefore, members, staff, and their immediate family should not, for example, receive gifts, loans, or financial assistance on the basis of their position on or relationship with the Board.[244] Further, the idea of removal just because Meta wants a Board member to be removed appears unlikely. The trustees' fiduciary duty is to protect the Board's independence, not Meta's interests, and Board members themselves would hardly vote against their own institutional interests. Hence, the Board's removal regime protects Board members from removal by the company.

However, nomination procedures for members are not fully beyond Meta's grasp. Neither the charter nor the bylaws detail the process of nominating new Board members. Article 4 Section 2 of the bylaws stipulates that "trustees will formally appoint" Board members. None of the governing documents further specifies the nomination procedure except for allusions to the preferred professional qualities of potential nominees. According to an article by Steven Levy, Meta has wielded its influence over

[241] Charter Article 1 Section 8.
[242] Bylaws Article 1 Section 1.2.2.
[243] Code of Conduct, Introduction.
[244] Code of Conduct, Articles 1, 4.

the Trust to prevent people its executives perceived as too critical from becoming Board members.[245] According to Levy, a candidate's previous and repeated criticisms of Meta resulted in some of its management (internally of course) voicing "reservations," which ultimately "put the kibosh on the nomination."[246] Such reporting is perhaps even more damaging for Meta than it is for the Board, as it emphasizes how reluctant the company is to cede authority to the Board and subject itself to truly independent external feedback. That is, however, neither surprising nor particularly worrying – authority of external guardians emerges incrementally, through continuous wrestling and discourse, rather than immediate submission by the controlled power structure.

4.3.3.4 Operational Autonomy and Budget

When focusing on its day-to-day work, the Board is simultaneously autonomous – as the company does not meddle with the Board's decision-making – and dependent on operational support by the company. In particular the Board's IT relies heavily on Meta's support. From a pragmatic perspective, such organizational semi-dependence is inevitable. Yet at times, it may be delicate as highlighted by severe disruptions of the Board's web infrastructure in 2021. For example, the bylaws state that "Facebook will maintain responsibility for the development and maintenance of tools that the Board uses to review and decide upon cases, including the Board's website and case management tool."[247] This web infrastructure is crucial for the Board to be able to receive user requests and handle its massive caseload. This "case management tool" refers to "the platform used by the Oversight Board to receive and review case submissions and collect and store case files."[248] What at first sounds mundane in fact generally shapes case selection. One staffer remembered that the case management tool malfunctioned when the Board started to accept the first appeals in early 2020.[249] Another staffer, in May 2022, mentioned that the case management tool, albeit working well overall, was still having occasional technical issues.[250] Therefore, organizationally, the Oversight Board, with its workforce of only seventy to ninety people,

245 Levy (n 216) 14 et seq.
246 Ibid 14.
247 Bylaws Article 2 Section 1.3.2 (at the very end).
248 Bylaws, Definitions "case management tool," at 34.
249 Interview with Oversight Board Staffer 2 (n 10).
250 Interview with Oversight Board Staffer 5 (n 54).

remains a relatively small entity for controlling the rulemaking and rule enforcement of the world's largest social network, an organization with tens of thousands of employees. This necessarily leads to a considerable degree of dependence when it comes to day-to-day operations because the Board often requires Meta's engineers to provide, for example, IT support.

Lastly, the Board depends on Meta's contribution to the irrevocable trust.[251] The Board itself cannot raise any money.[252] As mentioned before, in 2019 Meta contributed 130 million dollars to the trust. Meta initially estimated that the first tranche would last six years, but in July 2022 the company announced putting another 150 million dollars into it.[253] Presumably, the Board spent more money than anticipated but this supposition could not be confirmed by any of the interviewees.

The trustees retain prerogative over all major spending decisions.[254] The trustees are independent of Meta and have a fiduciary duty to "facilitate the creation, funding, management, and oversight" of the Board.[255] Therefore, trustees have the power to invest in and sell property, establish the LLC, open accounts and exercise transactions, enter into contracts, and anything else necessary to keep the Board running.[256] To date, the biggest investment seem to have been the fifteen million seed funding for the newly founded Appeals Centre Europe – an Oversight Board spin off that was certified as an ODS under Article 21 DSA in late summer 2024 and might become an independent funding stream for the Board.[257] However, forming additional "companies for the purpose of effectuating the purpose" of the trust requires Meta's consent.[258] Even though Meta initially conceived of and initiated the Board as a six-year experiment, the early recapitalization of the trust in July 2022 is a sign of the Board's financial independence for the foreseeable future. However, in line with 2023 cost-cutting measures at Meta, the company appeared poised to gradually limit the Board's financial basis, prompting the Board to moderately consolidate in 2024.[259]

251 Trust Agreement Section 1.4.
252 Although the Trust an LLC agreement allows the LLC to be commercially active.
253 Oversight Board, 'Securing Ongoing Funding for the Oversight Board (Press Release)' (n 114).
254 Trust Agreement Sections 2.1, 2.3, and 4.
255 Trust agreement Sections 2.1 and 6.8.4.
256 Trust Agreement Section 4.
257 See at 3.8.1.3.
258 Trust Agreement Section 4.7.
259 Naomi Nix, 'Meta's Oversight Body Prepares to Lay off Workers' *Washington Post* (29 April 2024) <https://perma.cc/Z8SS-MKSW>.

4.4 Rules

This section introduces the different normative layers governing content moderation and the Board's adjudication. We can differentiate between internal rules devised by Meta and external international human rights law. By way of context, the Board has so far not substantively interacted with EU law. The key takeaway of this section has two parts. We find out that the practically relevant internal rules of content moderation are, in contrast to what is often argued, not the terms of service but a variety of subsidiary rules that detail the normative regime. Then, we also discuss Article 19 of the ICCPR, which provides the Board with a normative scaffolding to evaluate what Meta is doing.

4.4.1 *Internal Rules: Values and Content Policies*

The initially intended normative focus of the Board were the rules that Meta (or Facebook) had unilaterally and internally devised. These were a set of "values," and Meta's "content policies" which are terms of service and, crucially, the huge list of rules governing user communication known as "community standards."

4.4.1.1 Meta's "Values"

In early 2018, when the specific shape of the Oversight Board was still unclear, Meta executives considered setting up the company's "own quasi-legal system where clearly stated policy rules can be applied to the plethora of real-world expression challenges."[260] The normative core (a privatized Kelsenian *Grundnorm* so to speak), should have been an "iconic, one-sentence values commitment Facebook would adopt."[261] To a degree, the Board's foundational documents still reflect this idea, stating that the Board "will review content enforcement decisions and determine whether they were consistent with Facebook's . . . values."[262] However, identifying these values is not that simple. Neither the charter nor the bylaws explain what these values are. Instead, both charter and bylaws premise that Meta "articulate" them.[263] There is no public process or document of perceptible legal quality establishing what these values ought to be. The only source naming and detailing the values is a blog post by Meta's then Vice President for Global Policy Management

[260] Feldman (n 40) 101.
[261] Feldman (n 33) 104.
[262] Charter Article 2 Section 2.
[263] Charter Article 1 Section 4 No 3.

on the company's own public relations blog.[264] The executive writes that the company was "expanding the values that serve as the basis for [its] decision-making."[265] According to this post, the "paramount" value is "voice," whereas other values – "authenticity," "safety," "privacy," and "dignity" – might limit the free expression of that "voice."[266] The text goes on to briefly explain what these values mean. "Voice" relates to a far-reaching, US-informed interpretation of free expression.[267] Of course, voice and expression on Meta are exercised by way of users posting content, which is the basis of Meta's business. "Authenticity" means ensuring that users do not "misrepresent who they are or what they're doing."[268] "Safety" prohibits intimidating other users, as well as the dangers of excluding, or silencing content.[269] "Privacy" aims to "give people the freedom to be themselves," while "dignity" refers to the executive's assertion that Meta "believe[s] that all people are equal in dignity and rights."[270]

In short, various Meta employees' own (unexamined) definitions of "values" should serve as the primary normative framework for the Board's assessment of Meta's rule enforcement and arguably also its rulemaking.[271] Given the vagueness of their definitions, as well as the limited public visibility and legitimacy of those expounding the ideals upon which these "values" are purportedly based, "values" cited in a blog hardly provide appropriate normative material to control what Meta is doing.

4.4.1.2 Content Policies

As argued above, the Board is supposed to assess whether Meta's enforcement actions comply with its "content policies." The charter mentions that "Facebook's Community Standards and other relevant policies" are "collectively referred to as content 'policies.'"[272] These are unilaterally devised rules that manifest in at least three layers.

[264] Monika Bickert, 'Updating the Values That Inform Our Community Standards' (*Meta Newsroom*, 12 September 2019) <https://perma.cc/6TPQ-MW35>.
[265] Ibid.
[266] Ibid.
[267] Ibid.
[268] Ibid.
[269] Ibid.
[270] Ibid.
[271] Douek, 'Why Facebook's "Values" Update Matters' (n 102).
[272] Charter Article 1 Section 4 No 2.

Terms of Service

The top layer of social media companies' rules are their terms of service. These represent nothing less than the contractual basis governing the relationship between Meta and the users of its services. The terms of service are relatively brief and do not regulate user communication substantively. When it comes to content moderation, the terms of service only establish that users must not violate the "community standards" and "other terms and policies." These community standards and other terms and policies make up a second layer of rules. These are a variety of normative texts, appear under different titles, and are not immediately obvious as a part of the terms of service. Instead, the terms of service only reference the community standards and other rules. Therefore, in general, the actual terms of service are only germane because they signpost the much more decisive second normative layer, which are the community standards (and the other, unspecified, rules).

Community Standards and Other Policies

The decisive normative layer governing online communication in Europe and beyond consists of unilateral rules devised by platforms detailing what communication is allowed on a given platform. These community standards are binding with respect to users because the platforms' terms of service (which the user has to agree to) reference them. In the case of Meta, community standards claim to "apply to everyone, around the world, and to all types of content."[273] They are split by topic into more than twenty different "standards," dealing with issues such as "hate speech" to "bullying and harassment" to "cybersecurity."[274] Each standard has a "policy rationale" which outlines the aim of the specific community standard. The community standards – with varying concision and specificity – then provide definitions and examples of prohibited communication acts. To illustrate this, we can look at Facebook's community standard covering hate speech. As of November 2024, almost thirty updated versions of the standard were published on Meta's website. The first hate-speech community standard published by Facebook dates to May 25, 2018.[275] Since then, Meta has amended the hate-speech standard roughly every few months.[276] The hate-speech standard's "policy rationale" states that people should be able to "use their voice and connect more freely when they don't

[273] See Meta, Community Standards accessible via <https://perma.cc/6PBT-KJSD>.
[274] Ibid.
[275] Ibid.
[276] See how this might complicate the EU's rationale behind Article 21 DSA at 3.5 and 3.7.4.

feel attacked on the basis of who they are." There then follows a "definition" of hate speech. Facebook defines this as

> a direct attack against people – rather than concepts or institutions—on the basis of what we call protected characteristics: race, ethnicity, national origin, disability, religious affiliation, caste, sexual orientation, sex, gender identity and serious disease. We define attacks as violent or dehumanizing speech, harmful stereotypes, statements of inferiority, expressions of contempt, disgust or dismissal, cursing and calls for exclusion or segregation.[277]

The practical complexity of such a definition is obvious. How to draw a line between "direct" and "indirect" attacks against people? How to handle necessarily subjective, value-laden, and context-dependent adjectives like "violent," "harmful," or "dehumanizing"? Which diseases are "serious"? Does only the content of a communication act make it "hate speech" or also the attitudinal stance(s) of the person who expresses it? What about the temporal and territorial space in which an utterance was made?[278] Are we even capable of identifying the past, current, and future social, political, and cultural contexts of an utterance with sufficient certainty? What about contexts that are culturally foreign to Meta's predominantly North American rule makers? Interviewed practitioners described content moderation as "phenomenally difficult,"[279] and scholars[280] and tech journalists[281]

[277] See Community Standard Hate Speech, accessible via <https://perma.cc/GGB3-XST8>. Loosening this standard was one of Zuckerberg's most significant public gestures of acquiescence to the incoming Trump administration in January 2025. However, the first sentence's original wording remained in place until the time of this manuscript's revisions in late February 2025, with the arguably largely symbolic change of renaming "hate speech" to "hateful content." In practice, the specifics of the standard were scaled back, and the already somewhat convoluted definition of what constitutes an attack appears to have been pared down. Ultimately, the key issue is not the exact wording of these standards but how Facebook enforces and implements them. Changing the wording, in turn, is a process that, like many other aspects examined in this book, may remain largely ceremonial.

[278] In essence, these questions point to one of the central aporias of the philosophy of language. See Judith Butler's critique of J. L. Austin's "total situation" approach. In his foundational work 'How to do things with words' Austin argued that context – meaning mostly spatial and temporal aspects – would, if "totally comprehended" arguably allow for an absolute interpretation of certain speech acts. Butler disagrees. cf. Judith Butler, *Excitable Speech: A Politics of the Performative* (Routledge 1997) 2–13. See further John L Austin, *How to Do Things with Words* (Oxford University Press 1962); John R Searle, *Speech Acts: An Essay in the Philosophy of Language* (Cambridge University Press 1969). For a US law perspective see especially Robert Post, 'Participatory Democracy and Free Speech' (2011) 97 Virginia Law Review 477.

[279] Interview with Oversight Board Staffer 3 (n 11).

[280] Douek, 'Content Moderation as Systems Thinking' (n 7) 533, 568.

[281] Mike Masnick, 'Masnick's Impossibility Theorem: Content Moderation At Scale Is Impossible To Do Well' (*TechDirt*, 20 November 2019) <https://perma.cc/Q97F-CFHB>.

have even pronounced content moderation an impossible endeavor. Platforms' increasing reliance on automated moderation (despite the well-known shortcomings of natural-language processing)[282] only exacerbates these difficulties.

To drain the seemingly endless swamp of possible contextual layers, each community standard therefore provides further, generalized explanations. These general "explanations" often consist of normative statements relating to those whom the company wishes to protect. For example:

> We also prohibit the use of harmful stereotypes, which we define as dehumanizing comparisons that have historically been used to attack, intimidate, or exclude specific groups, and that are often linked with offline violence.[283]

The sections then elaborate – in a section entitled "do not post" – on specific examples of the types of content that meet the above-mentioned definitions. The "do-not-post" content subdivides into several "tiers." A "tier 1" attack includes, for example,

> (d)ehumanizing speech or imagery in the form of comparisons, generalizations, or unqualified behavioral statements . . . to or about . . . insects, animals that are culturally perceived as intellectually or physically inferior, . . . sub-humanity.

In sum, Meta's community standards reflect the reactive and incremental nature of their creation. They are lengthy, convoluted, sometimes contradictory, and highly subjective. As one interviewee recalls, "[t]he process for making content rules is basically a room full of US lawyers sits down and makes the rules after the latest crisis."[284] Accordingly, "ad-hockery," imprecise terminology, and structural deviations between (and within) standards characterize the resulting "community standards." Simply put, if you want to take down a communication act (usually a post), you are likely to find a community standard that prohibits this post. Yet most standards and their cascading "explanations" are crammed with adjectives and imprecise terminology that can be interpreted in many ways. To an extent, such normative uncertainty is inevitable – especially if you are aiming to regulate the communications of two or more billion people. However, like any

[282] Robert Gorwa, Reuben Binns and Christian Katzenbach, 'Algorithmic Content Moderation: Technical and Political Challenges in the Automation of Platform Governance' (2020) 7 Big Data & Society 1. See also Paul Friedl, 'Dis/Similarities in the Design and Development of Legal and Algorithmic Normative Systems: The Case of Perspective API' (2023) 15 Law, Innovation and Technology 25.

[283] See <https://perma.cc/2YRS-K46C>.

[284] Interview with Academic, Consultant to Facebook in 2018 (n 31); see further Klonick, 'The New Governors: The People, Rules, and Processes Governing Online Speech' (n 19).

sanctioning approach, restricting "speech" on social media requires a minimum level of normative foreseeability and consistency if it is not to be totally arbitrary. We will re-encounter these deeper levels of platform rulemaking in Chapter 6 because they point to one practical shortcoming of many scholarly or regulatory takes on reforming content moderation.[285] Just infusing fundamental rights, which are broad normative categories, without specifying how this affects these sublayers of specific rules, will not solve content moderations' normative shortcomings.

4.4.2 *External Rules: International Human Rights Law*

The third set of norms the Board uses to control Meta is international human rights law. Meta is a private company and therefore cannot, of course, be a signatory of international human rights treaties like the ICCPR. Furthermore, despite scholarly criticism, international law does not provide for the immediate application of human rights law to private actors even if they are powerful transnational companies.[286] This section briefly outlines how the charter largely omits human rights, introduces the UN Guiding Principles as the tool that makes international human rights law relevant for corporations like Meta, and introduces the ICCPR, and especially Article 19, as the normative fulcrum that underpins the Board's reasoning.

4.4.2.1 The Charter's (Superficial) Reference to Human Rights

The charter only superficially references human rights. In Article 2 Section 2 – entitled "basis for decision-making" – the charter explains that "the Board will review content enforcement decisions and determine whether they were consistent with Facebook's content policies and values." In other words, the charter implicitly excludes human rights as a normative standard for the Board to "review" actions by the company.[287] Instead, it merely stipulates that "[w]hen reviewing decisions, the Board will pay

[285] See at 6.1.2.

[286] For recent criticism see from a general perspective the late Antonio Cassese (ed.), 'Introduction' in *Realizing Utopia* (Oxford University Press 2012) xix. See specifically Andrew Clapham, *Human Rights Obligations of Non-State Actors* (Oxford University Press 2006) 195; Marco Fasciglione, 'A Binding Instrument on Business and Human Rights as a Source of International Obligations for Private Companies: Utopia or Reality?' in Martina Buscemi and others (eds.), *Legal Sources in Business and Human Rights* (Brill Nijhoff 2020). For the term "transnational corporation" see Clapham 199–201.

[287] In that sense also Klonick, who considers this "far from a broad or robust adoption of human rights," Klonick, 'The Facebook Oversight Board: Creating an Independent Institution to Adjudicate Online Free Expression' (n 3) 2478.

particular attention to the *impact* of removing content in light of human rights norms protecting free expression."[288] The other relevant documents, especially the bylaws, only partially reproduce the charter's wording regarding the community standards while entirely omitting human rights law in the context of case review.[289] Therefore, Meta's initial vision for the Board did not include a prominent role for anything but rules made by Meta executives themselves, especially not for international human rights law.[290] Instead, at least one strong idea in the creation process was to base the Oversight Board's control entirely, or at least predominantly, on rules and "values" devised by the company itself. Hence, just as with Article 21 of the DSA's review of the criteria governing "incompatibility," Meta's idea for the Oversight Board was to create an adjudicator that would, however, only apply Meta's internally devised rules to control the company.[291]

4.4.2.2 UN Guiding Principles on Business and Human Rights

Although international human rights law is not binding for private companies and even though the Board's foundational documents do not grant it a prominent place, normative bridges between international human rights law and bodies like the Oversight Board do exist. The main bridge connecting corporations and international human rights are the *United Nations Guiding Principles for Business and Human Rights* (UNGP).[292] According to its author, UN Special Representative John Ruggie, this UN normative framework rests, apart from states' (and the EU's) duty to protect individuals from human rights abuses by corporations, largely on a voluntary "responsibility" of corporations "to respect human rights" as well as on "remediation through legitimate processes."[293] Also, the UNGP demand "judicial and non-judicial remedies" by states.[294] Further, they stipulate that "[i]ndustry . . . should ensure

[288] Charter Article 2 (2) (emphasis added).

[289] cf. Bylaws Article 1 Section 3.

[290] See at 4.2 and especially the Feldman memo referenced in n 33.

[291] ODSs review content moderation on grounds of "illegality," which is a normative framework external to platforms, and "incompatibility" with platforms' terms of service, which remain an internal normative framework. See in detail at 3.5.

[292] For an introduction see Radu Mares, 'Business and Human Rights After Ruggie: Foundations, the Art of Simplification and the Imperative of Cumulative Progress' in Radu Mares (ed.), *The UN Guiding Principles on Business and Human Rights* (Brill Nijhoff 2012) 1–49.

[293] UN Guiding Principles para 6 and Principle 22.

[294] UN Guiding Principles para 6.

that effective grievance mechanisms are available."[295] However, as betrayed by its title, the UN's "principles" in this context are "guiding," not legally binding. They also tend often to be vaguely formulated, asserting for example that "[b]usiness enterprises should respect human rights. . . . [which] refers to internationally recognized human rights."[296] How stringently corporations are expected to honor their "responsibility to respect" in this UN framework is not a question of legal accountability but of managerial competence and operational feasibility against the backdrop of the profit motive.

4.4.2.3 The ICCPR, Especially Article 19

Among these internationally recognized human rights mentioned in the UNGP is the ICCPR. The ICCPR contains several human right provisions. Crucial for our context is Article 19, which establishes an individual right to freedom of expression. A close reading paired with a word-count analysis of the Board's decisions taken up to November 2024 shows that Article 19 of the ICCPR – and not Meta's values or content policies – is the prime norm-oriented focus of the Board. The justification requirements of Article 19 of the ICCPR inform the Board's core normative considerations. The decisive parts of Article 19 of the ICCPR read:

> 2. Everyone shall have the right to freedom of expression; . . .
> 3. The exercise of the rights provided for in paragraph 2 of this article carries with it special duties and responsibilities. It may therefore be subject to certain restrictions, but these shall only be such as are provided by law and are necessary:
>
> (a) For respect of the rights or reputations of others;
> (b) For the protection of national security or of public order (ordre public), or of public health or morals.

Based on these paragraphs, the Oversight Board came up with a three-pronged test for Meta's compliance with its "human rights responsibilities," as the Board refers to them. The subject of this test can be either Meta's rule enforcement (for example, because it deleted a post), or Meta's rulemaking (because it prohibited a post). Often, both aspects are tested together, lacking a formal distinction.[297] The three prongs are: legality; legitimate aim; and necessity and proportionality. While the "legality"

[295] UN Guiding Principles 30.
[296] UN Guiding Principles 11 and 12.
[297] At least a formal distinction that would show in a specific title, header, or marking.

section mainly tests the quality of Meta's rulemaking, the "necessity and proportionality" section often mixes rulemaking and rule enforcement.

4.4.3 *Detached from EU Law*

Despite its engagement with international human rights law, the Board does not engage with regional human or fundamental rights regimes. Notably, neither does it reference or apply the EU's Charter of Fundamental Rights (CFR) to cases dealing with content posted within the bloc or by users residing in the EU.

In principle, the CFR binds the EU and Member States when applying EU laws.[298] In principle, it does not bind corporations. However, the European Court of Justice (ECJ) applies several CFR provisions and other guarantees that could be understood as fundamental rights – such as nondiscrimination and equal pay – to private actors.[299] Further, various member-state domestic courts have regularly infused the principle of fundamental rights into their assessment of relevant contractual relations, subjecting the corporation then known as Facebook to due-process requirements.[300] As we saw in the previous chapter, at least one newly certified ODS in the EU outrightly applies the charter between social media platforms and individuals.[301] This descriptive part is not the place to discuss whether the Board might be under a legal obligation to apply EU law, and particularly the CFR, in cases legally located in the EU. For the purposes of this section, it is sufficient to note that the Oversight Board operates entirely detached from the normative layers of supranational or domestic law. For example, cases "where the underlying content has already been blocked, following the receipt of a valid report of illegality, and not removed for Community Standards violation" are inadmissible. In other words, the Board does not aim to interfere with regimes like Germany's now defunct Network Enforcement Act (*NetzDG*) or the DSA. Rather it aims to operate free from such legal constraints, using only Meta's own standards as well as

298 Article 51 CFR.

299 See e.g. Defrenne v Belgian State [1971] European Court of Justice C-80/70; Defrenne v SABENA [1976] European Court of Justice C-43/75; Egenberger [2018] European Court of Justice C-414/16; Stadionverbot [2018] Federal Constitutional Court (Bundeserfassungsgericht) 1 BvR 3080/09, BVerfGE 148, 267–290.

300 See e.g. Hassrede [2021] Federal Court of Justice (Bundesgerichtshof) III ZR 179/20 and III ZR 192/20.

301 See at 3.8.1.2.

international law. From the global perspective in which Meta operates, such an approach makes sense, especially for a private company. From an economic standpoint, diversifying standards for different regions across the world would make Meta's governance structure more costly.[302] But it also means that the Board's norm-based reasoning does not reflect regional (specifically EU) legal frameworks.

4.5 Decisions

After the previous section introduced the normative layers guiding the Board's decision-making – Meta's values and content policies as well as international human rights law – this section investigates how the Oversight Board applies these rules in its decisions. To do so, the section presents qualitative insights as well as a quantitative analysis of the word count in different parts of Board decisions. To anticipate: almost all Board decisions follow the same overall structure for their different normative layers as well as, where applicable, within the human rights assessment it produces. This allows us to compare how much the Board writes and argues on certain aspects by counting and comparing the word distribution among these sections. Word count does not necessarily equate to the quality or "importance" of a text's normative reasoning. However, insights from interviews and a close reading of Board decisions indicate that international human rights law, and especially Article 19 of the ICCPR, is *the* normative focus of the Board. Thus, a thorough understanding of how many words the Board allots to analyzing Article 19 of the ICCPR, in comparison to other normative phenomena like values or community standards, might hint at the relevance of human rights law for the Board's practice.

After a brief introduction to the general layout of Board decisions, this section then engages with some of the Board's reasoning to gain an impression of how the Board uses human rights thinking in its deliberations. After outlining how using word count as the basis for a quantitative analysis may corroborate these qualitative insights and statements made by interviewees, the section proceeds to examine how

[302] Such "nondivisibility" of business operations is one of the key enabling factors for the so-called Brussels Effect, see Anu Bradford, *The Brussels Effect: How the European Union Rules the World* (Oxford University Press 2020) 25 et seq. For a critical review whether the DSA may really unfold such a global effect see Moritz Schramm, 'Curb Your Enthusiasm: Why the Digital Services Act Might Not Have a "Brussels Effect"' (2025) 16 European Journal of Legal Studies (Special Issue) 61.

much the Board writes in terms of the three normative layers – content policies, values, and human rights – as well as in the three subsections within the human rights assessment. This provides us with a quantitative basis upon which to draw several conclusions.

4.5.1 *What Board Decisions Look Like*

The Board published its first decisions on January 28, 2021. Since then, it has issued more than 100 decisions (as of November 2024). Initially, all decisions followed the same procedure and textual structure. However, after some criticism that the Board was too hesitant and slow, the Board began issuing three different types of decisions. These three types are "standard," "summary," and "expedited." Standard decisions are in-depth reviews of specific and often systemic issues, whereas the function of summary decisions largely seems to be to check on the implementation of prior standard decisions. Expedited decisions are relatively rare and offer fast-tracked procedures in situations of imminent real-world harm, for example regarding videos of abducted Israelis in the context of the October 7 attacks or the aftermath of an Israeli strike on Al-Shifa hospital in Gaza. Whereas summary decisions offer only cursory analysis and reasoning, expedited decisions go into considerable detail. Both do not include a public comment section. The following largely focuses on standard decisions. Until the time of writing in November 2024, the Board issued sixty-eight standard decisions (one of which was essentially empty as the user withdrew their appeal, so it is effectively sixty-seven decisions).

All decisions are published on the Board's website.[303] They are published in English and, at least in standard and expedited decisions, the language(s) of the original dispute. The texts have a serial number and a title.[304] Titles are crisp and reference the subject matter of the case, for example "Former President Trump's suspension" when the Board decided whether Meta was right to indefinitely suspend Trump's accounts from its platforms after his role in the 6 January 2021 riots.[305] Other titles point to the wide range of topics and contexts the Board deals with, for instance "Alleged crimes in Raya Kobo" (about communication related to ethnic tensions in Ethiopia), "Colombian protests" (about criticisms of the Colombian President),

303 Accessible via: <https://perma.cc/BK4R-ZYUD>.

304 All cases following the year-number-platform-type of referral pattern, e.g., 2021-001-FB-FBR, which stands for first case of 2021 on Facebook (FB) which was referred by Facebook (FBR). Further, all decisions receive a name, e.g. Öcalan's Isolation [2021] Oversight Board 2021-006-IG-UA.

305 Former President Trump's suspension (n 143).

"Mention of the Taliban in news reporting" (covering reporting on terrorist regimes), "Claimed COVID cure" (relating to misinformation about the Covid-19 pandemic in France), or "Cambodian Prime Minister" (when the Board recommended to Meta to suspend the account of Hun Sen).

All standard decisions contain roughly the same sections, typically in the same sequence, with slight variations over time. Usually, decisions begin with a case summary and a summary of the Board's key findings. The decision's text is separated into several parts, typically nine or ten. These are, a decision summary, a description of the case, a few remarks on the authority and scope of the Board's review, and a description of the relevant normative standards. In this part, the Board typically cites the relevant paragraphs of the community standard and sets out the human rights-related norms it sees as pertinent to the case. Here, the Board does not engage in substantive reasoning. Further, the decisions summarize the statements made by the user in their appeal, as well as Meta's explanation for its decision, and submissions by third parties. Then, the Board engages in a normative assessment called "Oversight Board Analysis." In earlier decisions this was always part eight and since mid-2024 part five. This is the only part of the decision where the Board assesses facts, weighs different interpretations, and engages in normative reasoning. Standard decisions usually conclude with one or two brief parts consisting of the Board's nonbinding recommendations and its binding decision. These last two parts are sometimes combined.

Two things are noteworthy about this structure. To begin with, it is quite striking that the Board rather strictly adheres to it. All sixty-seven standard decisions published at the time of this writing follow that structure, with only minor deviations along the way. That a transnational body – one that deliberates via video call and whose decision-makers are spread across five continents – can commit to such a uniform working method already tells us something about the Board's strategic vision and discipline. Further, the sequencing of the parts appears to be deliberate. Outlining facts and normative standards before engaging in normative reasoning to arrive at a conclusion consisting of a decision and several recommendations implies that the Board members see themselves – or at least want to present themselves – as appliers rather than creators of the law. This viewpoint is reminiscent of Montesquieu's famous observation that "*Le juge est le bouche de la loi,*" and mirrors the practice of many international adjudicators.[306] Setting out a decision only at the very end of a twenty- to thirty-page

[306] Nußberger implicitly made a similar argument about the European Court of Human Rights (ECtHR)'s "pedantic" practice to spell out the entire text of each disputed charter

document resembles the style of decision-framing known from practitioners at the European Court of Justice, the International Court of Justice, and the European Court of Human Rights but also EU Boards of Appeals. In contrast, domestic courts like those in Germany or the United States begin their judgments by presenting the decision; they only explain it later.

In its decisions, mostly within the "Oversight Board Analysis" part, the Board engages with various normative materials. These are, international covenants and authoritative commentary, most notably the ICCPR and the UN Human Rights Committee's General Comments.[307] Further, the Board quotes decisions of international courts (especially the European Court of Human Rights),[308] the US Supreme Court,[309] and legal scholars.[310] It engages with decisions and other normative material produced by a wide range of adjudicators, including the UN Human Rights Committee[311] and the Committee on the Elimination of Racial Discrimination (CERD) Committee.[312] In particular, the Board's legality and proportionality assessments engage in some detail with the acquis of international human rights law, most notably Article 19 of the ICCPR.[313] In several decisions the Board reiterated criticism of the company's rule-making and rule enforcement.

provision, see Angelika Nußberger, 'Wer Zitiert Wen? Zur Funktion von Zitaten Bei Der Herausbildung Gemeineuropäischen Verfassungsrechts' (2006) 61 JuristenZeitung 763, 763.

[307] See Former President Trump's suspension (n 89) at 8.3, Depiction of Zwarte Piet [2021] Oversight Board 2021-002-FB-UA at 8.3, Pro-Navalny Protests in Russia (n 81) at 8.3 to general comment, Two Buttons Meme [2021] Oversight Board 2021-005-FB-UA at 8.3 to general comment, Öcalan's Isolation [2021] Oversight Board 2021-006-IG-UA at 8.3, COVID lockdowns in Brazil [2021] Oversight Board 2021-008-FB-FBR at 8.3, Colombia Protests [2021] Oversight Board 2021-010-FB-UA at 8.3, South Africa slurs [2021] Oversight Board 2021-011-FB-UA at 8.3, Wampum Belt [2021] Oversight Board 2021-012-FB-UA at 8.3, Ayahuasca brew [2021] Oversight Board 2021-013-IG-UA, Knin Cartoon [2022] Oversight Board 2022-001-FB-UA at 8.3, Colombian police cartoon [2022] Oversight Board 2022-004-FB-UA at 8.3.

[308] See e.g. Depiction of Zwarte Piet (n 95) at 8.3, Two Buttons Meme (n 95), Ayahuasca brew (n 95) at 8.2. In Alleged Crimes in Raya Kobo [2021] Oversight Board 2021-014-FB-UA at 8.3 III the Board quoted the International Criminal Tribunal for Rwanda.

[309] See Ayahuasca brew (n 95) at 8.1 and 8.2.

[310] See Pro-Navalny Protests in Russia (n 81) at 8.1.

[311] See in Claimed COVID cure [2021] Oversight Board 2020-006-FB-FBR at 8.3, Colombia Protests (n 95) at 8.3. II, Knin Cartoon (n 95) at 8.3. II.

[312] Depiction of Zwarte Piet (n 307).at 8.3 (to decisions), South Africa slurs (n 95) at 8.3 to recommendation and reports, Wampum Belt (n 95) at 8.3 to general recommendations.

[313] See in detail below at 4.5.5.

4.5.2 *Tracing the Board's Turn to Human Rights*

Several interviewees pointed to human rights as determinative normative category in their day-to-day work.[314] Many staffers and several Board members have a background in human rights, and the Board's first Director, Thomas Hughes, previously worked for an NGO literally called "Article 19."[315] Hughes would later run the Oversight Board spin off, the Appeals Centre, in Dublin.[316] Because Meta's community standards and values are so convoluted and vaguely worded, they are of little help in deciding cases. Therefore, what began as a mission to control the enforcement of rules quickly faced the reality that, not only was enforcement problematic, its underlying rules were not fit for purpose as well. To enhance the quality of Meta's rules, especially its community standards, the Board would have to resort to *external* standards. Especially from a legitimation perspective, citing and thereby tying oneself to international law autonomizes and legitimizes the Board vis-à-vis the company as well as in relation to national regulators. From the Board's perspective, this hits two birds with one stone. One interviewed Board member described the system in this way:

> [A] purely formalist review system is meaningless. Yes, there are important things to do in making sure that Facebook is applying its own rules correctly and consistently, but the big issues are substantive. . . . We need some sort of external standards here. . . . Assuming we're not dealing with the legal and we don't have any democratic footing, it seems that human rights is the best bet . . . for . . . a scope of externally justifiable values that have received a lot of consensus-based legitimacy and been drawn out over 50 years.[317]

A close reading of the Board's decisions corroborates important aspects of this member's claim. The Board confines most of its argumentation, reasoning, and citing of other adjudicatory material – for example, by referring to material from the UN Human Rights Committee or the European Court of Human Rights, other texts, such as reports by UN Special Rapporteurs, or the "Rabat Plan of Action," and the arguments of legal scholars – to the "Oversight Board Analysis." In one subsection of that "Analysis" section, the Board analyzes whether Meta is complying

314 Interview with Oversight Board Member (15 November 2022); Interview with Oversight Board Staffer 1 (n 54); Interview with Oversight Board Staffer 2 (n 10); Interview with Oversight Board Staffer 4 (n 52).

315 Interview with Oversight Board Staffer 2 (n 10).

316 See at 3.8, esp. 3.8.1.3.

317 Interview with Oversight Board Member (n 314).

with its human rights responsibilities in the case at hand.[318] Virtually every standard decision features this human rights-focused subsection. Citing other adjudicative decisions, primary and secondary legal material as well as scholarship are key ingredients of adjudicative reasoning.[319] This material situates and thereby legitimizes normative utterances by an adjudicator in the more general system comprising the norms, applications, institutions, and practices of legality.[320] The Board also sometimes discloses internal disagreement in this human rights section. Several decisions feature passages contrasting majority and minority positions among Board members in the Board's human rights assessment.[321] For example, in a decision concerning communication in the context of the Azerbaijani-Armenian conflict, the Board stated:

> The *majority* noted that the post, when read as a whole, made clear the user's choice of slur was not incidental but central to the user's argument that the target group was inferior. Moreover, the post in question was widely disseminated at the height of an armed conflict between the user's State and the State whose nationals the post attacked. . . . A *minority* found Facebook's deletion of the post was not proportionate, on the basis that the risks cited by the majority were too remote, and were not foreseeable.[322]

318 For quotes on ECtHR see Two Buttons Meme (n 307); Öcalan's Isolation (n 304); Ayahuasca brew (n 307). For quotes on scholars see Pro-Navalny Protests in Russia (n 185).
However, this trend is not absolute. For example, in one decision the Board distinguished the case at hand from court cases cited by Meta, including from the US Supreme Court in the section pertaining to Meta's values. Yet, this deviation may even corroborate the argument that the Board focuses more on human rights, whereas the company looks primarily to its own rules. Arguably, the Board only engages with the US Supreme Court in that particular section because Meta referred to it. In contrast, when the Board argues on its own terms, argumentation and court-citation takes place in the human rights section.

319 David J Walsh, 'On the Meaning and Pattern of Legal Citations: Evidence from State Wrongful Discharge Precedent Cases' (1997) 31 Law & Society Review 337, 398. See for a transnational, qualitative perspective differentiating between "domestic," "transnational European," and entirely "foreign" citations: Nußberger (n 306).

320 For reflections on the normativity of applying norms see Möllers (n 149) 107–114.

321 See vividly COVID lockdowns in Brazil (n 178) 8.3.III presenting alternating arguments by the majority and minority, ultimately asserting that "[t]he majority understands the minority's view but respectfully disagrees with it." See further Colombia Protests [2021] Oversight Board 2021-010-FB-UA, were, in a case concerning protests in Colombia, the minority argued that apart from Article 19 ICCPR the right to freedom of assembly, Article 21 ICCPR, should have been assessed in detail. See further Protest in India against France [2021] Oversight Board 2020-007-FB-FBR; Former President Trump's suspension (n 143); Depiction of Zwarte Piet (n 307); Two Buttons Meme (n 307); Alleged Crimes in Raya Kobo (n 308).

322 Armenians in Azerbaijan [2021] Oversight Board 2020-003-FB-UA at section 8.3(c) (emphasis added).

Contrasting minority and majority positions within a multiperson adjudicator has several effects.[323] It might delegitimize the adjudicator as its decisions could then be perceived as the outcome of bargaining or as a subjective interpretation and not as a clear evidence-based consequence of the interpretation of a particular legal text. On the upside, it could be argued that admitting to norm-related disagreements among adjudicators paints a more realistic picture of their actual deliberations and offers a broader variety of perspectives on the decision. This might bolster an adjudicator's legitimacy as it increases transparency and presents adjudication as what it is: a process of reasoning that will usually allow for more than one conclusion.

In contrast, the Board only occasionally engages with Meta's values. For example, in its first closely reasoned decision, the Board wrote 320 words on Meta's compliance with its own community standards, 691 words on compliance with international human rights law, and a meager forty-six words regarding compliance with Facebook values.[324]

4.5.3 *Introducing Word Count as a Quantifiable Unit*

But how does the Board reason, and on what issues? And how can this be studied objectively? This section draws on several quantitative analyses of Board decisions to show that the Board increasingly grounds its reasoning in international human rights law—rather than Meta's self-made rules—and subjects Meta's rulemaking itself to growing scrutiny.

Based on the interviews, a close reading of the decisions, and academic works looking at the value of argumentation and citation in adjudicative texts, we can assume that the Board writes most about what it considers normatively important or otherwise relevant.[325] Writing more will increase word count. Hence, within the Board's normative reasoning (which is always confined to the "Oversight Board Analysis" part), each section's word count, that is, that of the section on Meta's community standards, the company's "values," or crucially, international human rights law, may serve as a proxy indicator for that section's importance.[326] Hence, analyzing the word count

[323] Disclosing minority opinions in judgments is not the same than dissenting opinions, which are much more detailed. See further Ruth Bader Ginsburg, 'The Role of Dissenting Opinions' (2010) 95 Minnesota Law Review 1; Steven Peterson, 'Dissent in American Courts' (1981) 43 Journal of Politics 312.

[324] Myanmar post about Muslims [2021] Oversight Board 2020-002-FB-UA. The very first decision, 2020-001-FB-UA, was moot as the user deleted the post before the Board decided the case.

[325] For more details underlying the methodology of the word-count analysis, see at 1.4.3.

[326] Note: A similar claim could not be made regarding the comparison of the argumentative part ("Oversight Board Analysis") and the more descriptive parts (rest). In these other

aims to answer two questions. First, how much does the Board write about Meta's self-given community standards, "values," and international human rights law respectively? Second, how much does the Board write that relates to the different subsections (i.e., legality, aim, necessity, and proportionality) within its human rights assessment? This again may tell us something about which issues and norms the Board considers particularly important – and which arguments it uses to lend weight to its largely nonbinding normative input vis-à-vis the company.

4.5.4 *Quantifying the Board's Focus on Human Rights*

Let us begin with the first question: How much does the Board write when it comes to each of the three sets of normative material? That is, how many words does the Board allot to community standards, values, and human rights in its decisions? To repeat, all standard decisions follow the same structure. In every decision, the Board's normative reasoning is contained to one specific part labeled "Oversight Board Analysis." Initially, this Oversight Board Analysis part cascaded into three sections, one for each normative level, that is, Meta's community standards, Meta's values, and international human rights law. These "values" are presented by way of five vaguely worded normative statements unilaterally made by the company,[327] whose purpose is to "guide" Meta's enforcement and rulemaking.

However, before digging further, we may have a look at the overall development of the word count of the "Oversight Board Analysis" section. They key takeaway is: on average, it grew considerably. Figure 4.1 shows the total word count of each decision in columns and the trend (exponential regression) as a dotted line. Thus, the Board wrote more and more over time in its normative analysis.

Now, we unpack the different subsections of the "Oversight Board Analysis." As previously noted, the Oversight Board Analysis contains the Board's normative reasoning and initially divided into three, since late 2022 into two parts. That missing third element are Meta's values, which were the shortest section from the very beginning. In all but one of its decisions, fewer than 500 words of text were devoted to discussing Meta's values. Often it was considerably lower, averaging out at 181 words. Later, as those values were

parts, the Board merely describes existing material. That it does so at great length indicates, on the one hand, the complexity of the issues at stake, and on the other hand, the presumed aim of the Board to present its reasoning as flowing from the normative material and the facts of a case.

327 See at 4.4.1.1.

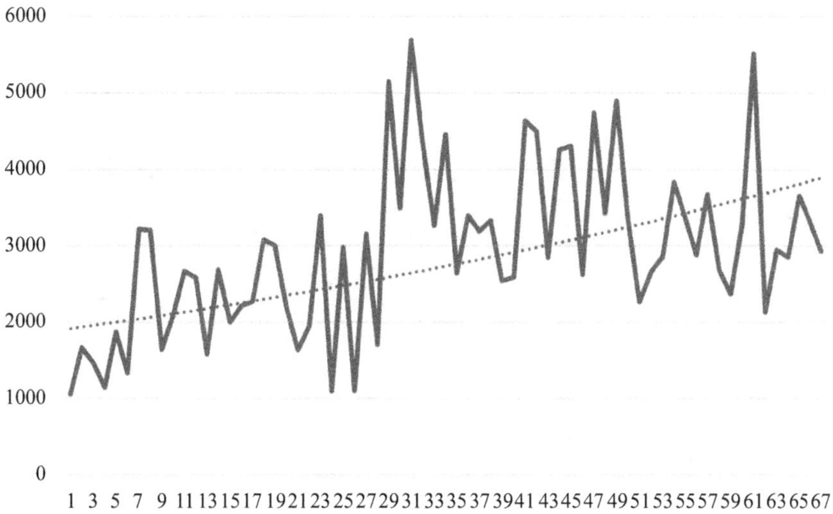

Figure 4.1 Word count Oversight Board Analysis total (2021–11/2024)

ostensibly useless to properly review Meta's exercise of power, the Board largely ceased referencing them. Since late 2022, decisions do not contain a specific section dealing with Meta's "values" anymore.

In turn, the Board's engagement with Meta's community standards and international human rights law seems to have grown consistently over the years. In the first two years, the Board usually allotted between 500 and 1,000 words to its engagement with Meta's community standards. Since 2023, that number climbed considerably to often more than 1,500 words. The overall average as of November 2024 being 855 words. While the growth in words allotted to the community standards appears, on average, steady but not exponential, the human rights section ballooned over the years. Here, the average word count was much higher from the beginning, being roughly 1,500 words in the first two years, reaching almost 2,000 words overall in November 2024 and 2,350 if one looks at only the decisions since 2023. In many decisions, the section on human rights comprised more than 2,000, 3,000 and in one case even more than 5,000 words. In all decisions, human rights standards "received" more words than the sections regarding Meta's values; and almost always more than in the section relating to Meta's community standards.

Figure 4.2 shows the different word counts distinguished by applied normative standard, namely Meta's values and policies, as well as

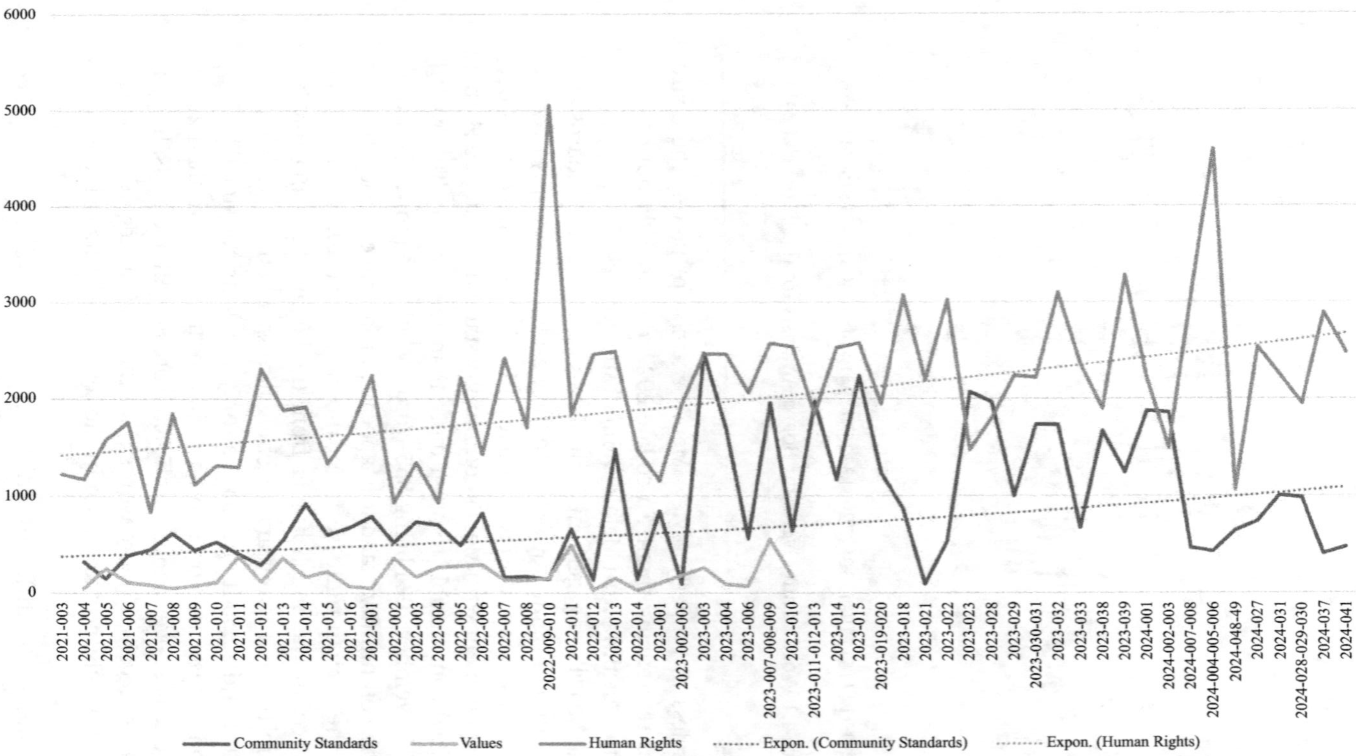

Figure 4.2 Word count of Meta values, Meta policies, and human rights law in the normative reasoning part of Oversight Board decisions (2021–11/2024)

international human rights law. Further, comparing the trends of Figures 4.1 and 4.2 we see that the Oversight Board Analysis and especially its section on human rights became longer over time. In contrast, the section on Meta's values was largely stable and then disappeared while the section where the Board analyzes only Meta's community standards, grew but by far not as strongly as the human rights section. Thus, the expanded word count in the human rights section appears to be the main driver for the (over time) greater amount of text devoted to normative reasoning in the Board's decisions.

In total, the values received roughly 6,000 words, the content policies roughly 60,000 words, and human rights a bit more than 130,000 words. Even though such total values mix together lengthy and more briefly worded decisions, the disparity indicates that the Board's normative reasoning mainly takes place in that part of the decision that focuses on human rights law.

What can we conclude from Figure 4.3? The increase in words may not necessarily indicate that the Board considers human rights more "important" and that therefore the decision's authors take it upon themselves to write more. The text may simply be more imprecise, lengthy, or repetitive.

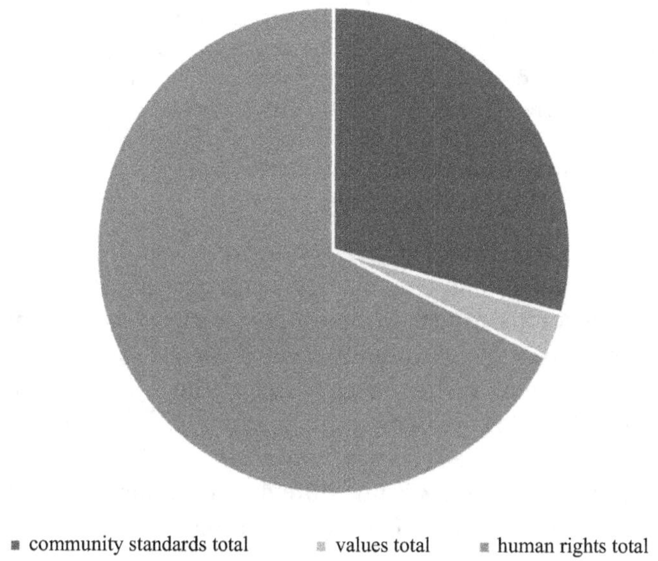

Figure 4.3 Total word count "Oversight Board Analysis" per normative category (2021–11/2024)

However, as a close reading of the decision shows, most of the text allotted to the human rights subsection does indeed read like legal argumentation. For example, in its human rights analysis in the decision relating to the banning of former US President Trump, the Board cautiously constructed a normative standard against which Meta's actions could be measured:

> In international law on freedom of expression, the principle of legality requires that any rule used to limit expression is clear and accessible. People must be able to understand what is allowed and what is not allowed. Equally important, rules must be sufficiently clear to provide guidance to those who make decisions on limiting expression, so that these rules do not confer unfettered discretion, which can result in selective application of the rules. In this case, these rules are Facebook's Community Standards.[328]

After outlining this normative standard by recourse to Article 19 of the ICCPR, the Board applies the facts, cites experts (like a UN Special Rapporteur, for instance), and refers to previous decisions. The same decision argues:

> The clarity [of Meta's community standard] leaves much to be desired, as the Board noted in a prior decision (case 2020–005-FB-UA). The UN Special Rapporteur on Freedom of Expression has also raised concerns about the vagueness of the Dangerous Individuals and Organizations Standard (A/HRC/38/35, para 26, footnote 67). As the Board has noted previously in case 2020–003-FB-UA, there may be times in which certain wording may raise legality concerns, but as applied to a particular case those concerns are not warranted. Any vagueness under the terms of the Standard does not render its application to the circumstances of this case doubtful. The January 6 riot at the Capitol fell squarely within the types of harmful events set out in Facebook's policy, and Mr. Trump's posts praised and supported those involved at the very time the violence was going on, and while Members of Congress were calling on him for help.[329]

In no decision does the Board employ comparable argumentative resources to assess Meta's values and only in a few decisions (and to a lesser extent within those decisions) to Meta's community policies. Although the Board's engagement with Meta's community standards grew over time, the main forum seems to remain human rights law. Therefore, the qualitative insights from the close reading of paragraphs like the above and the insights from the interviews substantiate the claim that we can plausibly assume that the Board has over time shifted its attention away from Meta's own rules and toward human rights. Whether this is because human rights

[328] Former President Trump's suspension (n 143) at 8.3.I.
[329] Ibid.

are perceived as more legitimate, more pertinent, or simply because many employees of the Oversight Board previously worked in a human rights context, is uncertain.

So, to answer the first question, we can conclude that the Board allots by far the most words to the human rights section of its decisions. It writes considerably less in both sections dealing with either Meta's community standards of the later defunct section on Meta's values.

4.5.5 *The Two Forums: Legality and Proportionality*

Now let us move to the second question: how many words does the Oversight Board allot to the three subsections *within* its assessment of Meta's human rights responsibilities? Does the Board write more in the sub-section dealing with the normative basis of a measure, which the Board calls based on the framing of Article 19 ICCPR "legality?" Or does it focus more on a measure's "legitimate aim," or the "necessity and proportionality" of a measure? And what can this tell us about the Board's normative focus?

In Figure 4.4 we see that the Board writes the least in the subsection dealing with the "legitimate aim" of a measure. Here, it typically allocates less than 200 words, averaging out at only roughly 140 words. More usually, but not as a consistent trend across all the decisions, the subsection on "legality" has a greater amount of text. This averages at roughly 440 words but peaks at 1,457 words and dips as low as thirty-five words. In several cases the legality subsection had the highest number of words devoted to it and, when this occurred, this was, at least in the first two years of practice, often in inverse proportion to the word count of the subsection covering a measure's "necessity and proportionality." In other words, when the part of a decision dealing with legality is longer, then the part focusing on issues of necessity and proportionality tends to be shorter, and vice versa. However, this correlation seems to have largely ceased. Decisions of 2023 and 2024 appear to have a more equidistant relationship of the sections on legality and necessity and proportionality. This might be plausibly explained through incrementally manifesting practices within the Board as to its approach and style of reasoning.

Furthermore, we see a trend occurring over time in changes to the word count in the subsections covering legality, aim, and necessity and proportionality.[330] Whereas the (legitimate) aim's word count remains largely stable, the word count increases much stronger over time for the legality and, particularly, the necessity and proportionality sections.

[330] Identified using the exponential regression trend function in Excel.

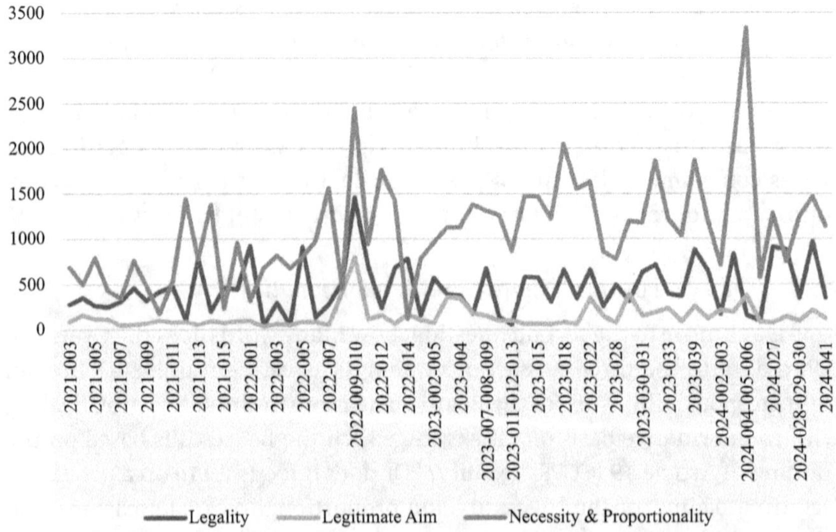

Figure 4.4 Word count of legality, legitimate aim, necessity, and proportionality subsections in the "Oversight Board Analysis" part (2020–11/2024)

Simply put, the Board writes increasingly more about legality and necessity and proportionality than about the legitimate aim.

This could mean that the legality *and* the necessity/proportionality parts are the two main forums for normative argumentation *within* the "Oversight Board Analysis". If that were the case, this would be remarkable. Whereas the necessity and proportionality section typically concentrates on an actor's *enforcement action*, the legality section focuses solely on this enforcement action's legal basis. Traditionally, Art 19 ICCPR requires any restrictions speech to be based on a *legal rule* such as an anti-libel or anti-hate speech law passed by parliament. The Board, however, resorts to Meta's self-made rules as "legal" basis for speech restrictions. In other words, when the Board devotes a lot of words to the legality of Meta's actions and not only their proportionality, this might suggest it is engaging in greater scrutiny of Meta's rulemaking. Simultaneously, the increasing word count in the necessity and proportionality section might also indicate the Board's increased scrutiny of Meta's enforcement procedures.

We now proceed with a close reading of the Board's conclusions about the "legality" of Meta's moderation efforts and their necessity and proportionality.

4.5.5.1 The Board's "Legality" Test

Let us now have a look at the legality section. Legality, a concept rooted in Article 19 of the ICCPR, feels somewhat out of place in the entirely private context we find ourselves navigating here. As envisaged by the United Nations' Guiding Principles, the Board requires Meta's restrictions of free expression to be "provided by law."[331] But what is Meta's "law" in the context of Article 19(3) of the ICCPR? Meta has huge problems producing normative material that works on the worldwide scale on which the company operates. Normative material regulating human behavior must be concise and clear. As we have seen above, most of the rules established by Meta are neither concise nor clear. Further, the notion of "law" in Article 19(3) of the ICCPR is traditionally understood in a rather narrow sense. Based on the Human Rights Committee's "General Comments," this "may include laws of parliamentary privilege … [but not] traditional, religious or other such customary law."[332] The Board, however, never discussed whether notions like "law" or "legality" are applicable for entities like Meta. It just applied them. Meta does not feature a rule-based let alone participatory process of rulemaking.[333] How can its privately devised and ad hoc rules be "law" within the meaning of Article 19 of the ICCPR?

Frictions will always occur when transplanting intrinsically state-centered rules into a private-law context, but this awkward grafting is still striking. On the one hand, the Oversight Board, for good reasons, generally avoids discussions of "sovereignty" or whether an entity like a transnational company or a social media firm is "state-like."[334] On the

[331] Article 19(3) ICCPR.

[332] Human Rights Committee (United Nations), 'General Comment No. 34, Article 19 Freedoms of Opinion and Expression, CCPR/C/GC/34' para 24.

[333] In 2009, Facebook experimented with democratic elements but failed to mobilize enough users to participate in voting. See Nicolas P Suzor, *Lawless: The Secret Rules That Govern Our Digital Lives* (Cambridge University Press 2019) 10 et seq.

[334] A minor digression, but I remain skeptical of analogizing corporations to sovereigns. Sovereignty is an elusive, normatively charged concept with a troubled history, making it ill-suited to scrutinize or describe private power. In fact, sovereignty might not even be particularly helpful for capturing the reality of statehood itself, given the vast disparities in states' power and their ability to exercise the rights tied to idealized notions of sovereignty. Sovereignty, rather, should be understood primarily as a normative, self-legitimizing construct, rooted in Enlightenment-era European conceptions of statehood. Platforms, by contrast, are capitalist corporations. Their internal structures are shaped by the demands of corporate and securities law, not by political projects. They lack participatory – let alone democratic – elements, a shared political community, or the historical continuity that defines states. While platforms wield undeniable power – arguably surpassing that of states in some respects – this does not render them state-like

other side, Article 19 of the ICCPR's legality requirement offers the Board an opening to review not only Meta's "enforcement decisions" but also its rulemaking. In several decisions, the Board's evaluation in the legality section assessed the content and quality of Meta's community standards. Often such assessments result in comprehensive recommendations to Meta outlining what aspects of the community standards the company should change. For example, in a 2021 decision regarding support for the – later deceased – Russian opposition politician Alexei Navalny, the Board demanded a complete overhaul of one of the then twenty-four community standards.[335] Its criticism was that the different subsections and rules of the standard were unclear, that it included many words with unclear definitions (what is the difference between bullying and harassment?) and obscured rather than elucidated the true meaning of the standard. Part of its decision read:

> Facebook should amend and redraft its Bullying and Harassment Community standard to ... explain the relationship between policy rationale and the "Do Nots" as well as the other rules restricting content that follow it. ... Distinguish between bullying and harassment and provide definitions that distinguish the two acts. ... Clearly define its approach to [different groups of users] ... Include illustrative examples of violating and non-violating content.[336]

Such criticism is often renewed in different, subsequent cases, especially in following "summary" decisions. The Board regularly criticizes the company for offering too few examples, for its slow progress in translating standards and decisions, and its unclear and incoherent definitions. For example, in a 2022 decision regarding communication about the Taliban, the Board reiterated that it considers the relationship between two definitions in one particular standard to "remain unclear to users."[337]

In sum, the Board extensively uses its decisions' legality subsection to control – or at least comment on – Meta's rulemaking. The increase in word count for this part of its decisions, coupled with statements by

or sovereign. Their power is of a fundamentally different nature, grounded in markets and profit motives rather than in the intricate, historically contingent construct of sovereignty.

335 Pro-Navalny Protests in Russia (n 187) Recommendation N 10.

336 Ibid at 10.1–4. However, Meta declined implementation of that recommendation, cf. Oversight Board Recommendation Tracker, accessible via <https://perma.cc/76MD-NN32>.

337 Colombian police cartoon [2022] Oversight Board 2022-004-FB-UA at 8.3.1 speaking about the "reporting" allowance in the context of the dangerous individuals and organizations standard.

interviewees, therefore indicates that a prime focus of the Board's deliberation is Meta's *rulemaking*.

4.5.5.2 Necessity and Proportionality

Whereas the legality section focuses on the mostly formal requirements (clarity and consistency) of Meta's rulemaking, the necessity and proportionality section are where the Board scrutinizes Meta's policies of rule enforcement. Typically, the Board's necessity and proportionality assessment has a double focus. On the one hand, it concentrates on the specific enforcement action as it was conducted for the case it is reviewing. For example, in a case dealing with the wrongful deletion of a post promoting breast cancer awareness, the Board established that: "The Board is concerned that the content was wrongfully removed by an automated enforcement system and potentially without human review or appeal. ... In this case, these technologies failed to recognize the words 'Breast Cancer' that appear at the top left of the image in Portuguese."[338]

However, the Board normally embeds assessments of a specific enforcement act in more general statements pertaining to the issue at stake. Therefore, assessing an action's necessity and proportionality allows the Board to say something about the company's procedures in general. For example, in the breast cancer awareness case, the Board inductively drew several general conclusions from its individual assessment of the particular case. Drawing attention to a specific failure of Meta's automated moderation system, the Board criticized Meta's over-reliance on automated tools and pointed out the "limitations" of the technology, especially its "limited ability to understand context." This part of the decision reads:

> This reflects the limitations of automated technologies to understand context and grasp the complexity of human communication for content moderation. ... The Board accepts automated technologies are essential to the detection of potentially violating content. However, enforcement which relies solely on automation, in particular when using technologies that have a limited ability to understand context, leads to over-enforcement that disproportionately interferes with user expression.... Regardless, automated removals should be subject to both an internal audit procedure explained under section 9.2 (I) and appeal to human review should be offered, allowing enforcement mistakes to be repaired. Automated content moderation without necessary safeguards is not a proportionate way for Facebook to address violating forms of adult nudity.[339]

[338] Breast Cancer symptoms and nudity [2021] Oversight Board 2020-004-IG-UA at 8.3.I. c.
[339] Ibid at 8.3.3 (in-text references redacted).

What is striking is how the Board references its own recommendations in a later section of the same decision. It states that "automated removals should be subject to . . . an internal audit procedure explained [below]."[340] In the referenced section, the Board issued a series of recommendations regarding how Meta should improve its overall procedures. Among these recommendations we see again an increasing degree of generalization. The Board issued some recommendations with a specific connection to the case. For example, the company should "[i]mprove the automated detection of images with text-overlay to ensure that posts raising awareness of breast cancer symptoms are not wrongly flagged for review."[341] However, other recommendations are more general. The company should, for example, notify users about the specific rule of the community standard Meta considers to be violated, and it should put in place an "internal audit procedure to continuously analyze a statistically representative sample of automated content removal decisions to reverse and learn from enforcement mistakes."[342] Similar arguments and connections are made in other cases. As will be argued in Section 3.6.2 below, the Board's recommendations constitute a crucial part of its normative output.[343] Therefore, tying them to arguments made in the necessity and proportionality section highlights that section's importance.

In sum, a close reading of the decisions shows that the Board invests considerable argumentative resources on the necessity and proportionality section. Even though it is typically longer than the legality section, this is not always the case, which might indicate the beginnings of a trend toward stricter scrutiny of Meta's rulemaking by the Board. However, the heart of the Board's human rights assessment is making recommendations for Meta to tighten up its content moderation. In other words, the Board "uses" the individual case to inductively generate procedural advice for the company. This advice might be restricted to a particular subject or community standard in question. However, it can often be of a more general nature and based on principles of good governance and administration.

4.5.6 *Interim Conclusion*

This section detailed how the Board uses various normative categories – Meta's community standards, Meta's values, and international human

340 Ibid (emphasis added).
341 Ibid at 9.2.1 first bullet point.
342 Ibid at 9.2.1 fifth bullet point.
343 See this at 4.6.

rights law – in its decisions and arrives at several conclusions. First, the Board does not engage substantively with Meta's "values." Second, the Board does however engage in some detail with the company's community standards as a way to control Meta's enforcement actions. Third, the Board's main normative focus – in every single decision and increasing over time – is *international human rights law*, especially Article 19 of the ICCPR. This is remarkable since the charter only mentions human rights law in passing and the bylaws do not mention it as a basis for review at all. Fourth, as part of its human rights assessment, the Board engages in an increasingly detailed analysis modeled on elements of Article 19(3) of the ICCPR. Typically, this includes a "legality" subsection in the Board's written decisions that tests the normative "clarity" and "accessibility" of Meta's rulemaking, as well as an extensive "proportionality" assessment split into "(legitimate) aim" and "necessity and proportionality" subsections. Sixth, whereas in its earliest decisions the Board tended to focus on the "necessity and proportionality" subsection, we have seen a relative increase over time in words allotted to the "legality" subsection. In the latter, the Board assesses whether Meta's own rules, especially the "community standards", comply with international human rights law. Even though it is too early to speak of a stable trend, we can tentatively conclude that the Board's attention focuses both on controlling Meta's *enforcement* (by questioning the proportionality of Meta's enforcement) and controlling Meta's *rulemaking* (by questioning the clarity and consistency of the rules Meta enforces). So far, the focus on controlling rulemaking has remained at the mainly formal level (relating to the clarity and consistency with which standards are formulated, for instance).

The Board's turn to human rights aligns with remarks by staff members in the interviews who said they were limited in their ability to control individual decisions but wanted to "change how Meta makes these decisions."[344] This turn to human rights might also be explained by the prevalence of people with a background in human rights among staffers (who draft a first legal analysis of each case) and among Board members.

4.6 Implementation

We now explores how (and whether) Board decisions are implemented. The empirical basis for assessing the degree to which Meta implements Board decisions is thin because the company remains coy about how exactly (and

[344] Interview with Oversight Board Staffer 2 (n 10).

if at all) it implements the Board's normative output. However, based on transparency reports by Meta and the Board, several interviews, and a close reading of Board decisions, we might be able to pin down the contours of how Meta implements, or chooses not to implement, Board decisions.

The Board generates several distinct kinds of normative output. Formally, it "decides" individual cases and offers "policy advisory opinions" based on general questions referred to it by Meta.[345] Its decisions feature an operational part that is binding for Meta for that specific case. But the document – known as the "decision" – also includes "policy advisory statements" and/or "recommendations." These are nonbinding, generalized normative recommendations relating to how Meta should improve its rulemaking and rule enforcement. A close reading as well as remarks from several interviewees indicate that these policy advisory statements are the Board's primary normative contribution to Meta. Further, even though policy advisory statements are not binding, many interviewees felt them to be more effective than the (necessarily individual) decision due to the general terms in which these statements were formulated and because of their focus on the company's operations. The Board has begun to build up recurring normative patterns that could be interpreted as doctrines and call for "naming and shaming"-inspired measures to influence the company's behavior.

Due to Meta's largely untransparent implementation of Board decisions, the latter's efficacy cannot be assessed comprehensively. For an adjudicator, this lack of transparency is hard to accept. Even though the Board has quickly adapted – bringing out increasingly sophisticated quarterly transparency reports and, later, a "recommendation tracker" – questions remain regarding Meta's transparency and accountability when it comes to how, or even whether, it implements nonbinding policy recommendations and advice from the Board.

4.6.1 *Set Board Decisions Binding Precedent?*

Each Board decision features a brief "operational part" that assesses whether a specific piece of content should stay on Meta's services or not. This decision is "binding" for Meta, but only for that specific enforcement action relating to the case under review.[346] Decisions do not have precedential status beyond the individual case. Meta should only evaluate whether it is "technically and operationally feasible to apply the Board's

345 The latter is not to be confused with individual referrals of cases by Meta according to Bylaws Article 2 Section 2.

346 Charter Article 4; Bylaws Article 2(2).

decision" in cases with "identical content and parallel context," according to Article 4 of the charter. What "parallel context" means is obscure, but "identical content" can perhaps be pinned down more successfully. Further, even if these criteria are met, the resulting obligation is nothing more than the requirement on Meta's part to exercise due diligence.[347] Thus, Meta is not bound by the Board's decision in cases other than the one decided – their executives need only "take action by analyzing" whether parallel implementation would be feasible. Hence, the "binding" power of the Board's decisions is negligible for the Board's practice. Especially so given the Board's leeway in case selection (subject to Meta's approval) and its relatively small caseload.

4.6.2 *Infusing Public Law Principles Into Private Governance?*

Almost all the Oversight Board's decisions feature nonbinding, more general normative statements called either "recommendations" or "policy advisory statements." These statements inductively generate principles for Meta's rulemaking and rule enforcement. Interviewees described these statements as the normative core of the Board's decisions.[348] One interviewee emphasized that "albeit the Board makes its decisions in a way that can be understood as adjudicative, our main way of exercising our power are the policy recommendations."[349] These are attached to each decision in their own section, typically the tenth. In these recommendations, the Board formulates general guidelines and principles recommending what the Board "should" do to improve its rulemaking and rule enforcement. As one trustee interviewed for this book put it:

> The Oversight Board is going to decide maybe 40 or 50 cases in a year, out of billions of posts. It follows that the Board itself is not the manager of disputes. The Board is not like a police force. Instead, it's infusing the content moderation operations of Meta with public law principles and procedures. It's articulating substantive norms that interpret Meta's community standards in light of human rights principles.[350]

What the interviewee describes as an infusion of "public-law principles" into Meta's managerial way of governing its users are the nonbinding recommendations and advisory statements that the Board attaches as

[347] cf. UK drill music [2022] Oversight Board 2022-007-IG-MR [8.4].

[348] Interview with Oversight Board Staffer 1 (n 54); Interview with Oversight Board Staffer 2 (n 10); Interview with Oversight Board Staffer 3 (n 11).

[349] Interview with Oversight Board Staffer 2 (n 10).

[350] Interview with Oversight Board Trustee (n 53).

supplements to most of its decisions. In its third decision, the Board explicitly formulated such recommendations for the first time.[351] Since then, each decision has featured at least one such "policy advisory statement." These statements draw upon normative or factual assessments made by the Board in its analysis, often with a special focus on human rights-related implications.

For example, in a case concerning posts referring to the – then still alive – Russian opposition figure Alexei Navalny, the Board used the legality assessment of Meta's bullying and harassment community standard to assess this standard's normative coherence. It found that the whole standard was constructed in an overly complex way, making it hard for users to know "what is and what is not allowed."[352] The Board criticized several categories Meta introduced in the standard as it were not clear if they "serve[d] simply as a guidance for the specific rules that follow, or if they must be interpreted conjunctively with the rules."[353] To back up this criticism, the Board then formulated a 'policy advisory statement' outlining what Meta should do. The Board recommended that "[t]o comply with international human right standards, Facebook should amend and redraft its Bullying and Harassment Community Standard."[354] It then formulated six tangible reforms. For example, the Board should "explain the relationship between the policy rationale and the 'Do nots' as well as the other rules restricting content that follow it."[355] Further, the standard should differentiate between bullying and harassment and "should clearly explain to users how bullying and harassment differ from speech that only causes offense and may be protected under international human rights law."[356] Meta should "[c]learly define its approach to different target user categories and provide illustrative examples for each category (i.e. who qualifies as a public figure)."[357]

Most of the Board's recommendations in fact reflect rationales, principles, and notions familiar from public-law contexts. Regarding Meta's rule enforcement, the Board recommended, for example, that the company should provide reasons for its decisions.[358] It should ensure that users are

351 Armenians in Azerbaijan (n 322).
352 Breast Cancer symptoms and nudity (n 318) at section 8.3.I.
353 Ibid at section 8.3.I.
354 Ibid at section 10.
355 Ibid.
356 Ibid.
357 Ibid.
358 See e.g. in Armenians in Azerbaijan (n 299) at section 9.2; Breast Cancer symptoms and nudity (n 318) at section 9.2.I second bullet point; Nazi Quote [2021] Oversight Board 2020-005-FB-UA at section 9.2 first bulletpoint; Depiction of Zwarte Piet (n 298) at section 10 No 2.

notified that their content has been removed and which particular violation had led to its removal.[359] It should also provide timely translations so that its rules are intelligible to users.[360] Users must have the right to appeal, sometimes directly linked to the ICCPR's right to an effective remedy. Several recommendations explicitly referred to the principle of proportionality.[361] Further, the Board recommended specific procedures to Meta for investigating whether its enforcement algorithms might be biased.[362]

In terms of Meta's rulemaking, the Board regularly recommends that the company includes more examples,[363] as well as rules that are worded in a clearer and more concise way.[364]

In sum, the Board's policy advisory statements synthesize principles from external normative material – human rights law and secondary sources (like General Comments from the UN Human Rights Committee), non-governmental or international organizations i documents (the Rabat Plan of Action), and scholarship – and the statements offer recommendations for Meta to implement in order to improve its rulemaking and rule-enforcement efforts.

4.6.3 *Developing Doctrine*

The Board also began to develop normative sentences that could be described as *doctrines*. Although conceptions of what counts as doctrine differ greatly among legal cultures, several characteristics seem identifiable.[365] The function of doctrine is to *stabilize* a normative order

[359] Öcalan's Isolation (n 288) at section 10 No 9; Colombia Protests (n 298) at section 10 No 4; South Africa slurs [2021] Oversight Board 2021-011-FB-UA at section 10 No 1; Wampum Belt [2021] Oversight Board 2021-012-FB-UA at section 10 no 1; Pro-Navalny Protests in Russia (n 177) at section 10 No 6.

[360] Myanmar post about Muslims (n 301) at section 10 No 1; Punjabi Concern over the RSS in India [2021] Oversight Board 2021-003-FB-UA at 10 No 1; Shared Al Jazeera Post [2021] Oversight Board 2021-009-FB-UA at section 10 No 2.

[361] COVID lockdowns in Brazil (n 186); Former President Trump's suspension (n 143).

[362] Shared Al Jazeera Post (n 341) at section 10 No 2.

[363] Nazi Quote (n 358) at 10 No 2, 3; Pro-Navalny Protests in Russia (n 185) at 10 No 3, 4; Öcalan's Isolation (n 304) at 10 No 6; Shared Al Jazeera Post (n 360) at 10 No 1; Colombia Protests (n 307) at 10 No 1, 2.

[364] Former President Trump's suspension (n 143) section 10.; Öcalan's Isolation (n 304) at section 10 No 5; Colombia Protests (n 307) at section 10 No 3; Asking for Adderall® [2022] Oversight Board 2921-015-FB-UA at section 10 No 1.

[365] For an overview see e.g. René Smits, 'What Is Legal Doctrine? On the Aims and Methods of Legal-Dogmatic Research' in Rob van Gestel, Hans-Wolfgang Micklitz and Edward L Rubin (eds.), *Rethinking Legal Scholarship: A Transatlantic Dialogue* (Cambridge University Press 2017) 207; Rob van Gestel, Hans-W Micklitz and Miguel Poiares Maduro, 'Methodology in the New Legal World, EUI Working Papers, Law 2012/13' 3 et seq.

by establishing hierarchy, clarity, and foreseeability. Doctrine creates general normative sentences guiding future behavior.[366] The Board uses citations and references to incrementally construct "doctrines."

On the one hand, the Oversight Board increasingly returns to issues it brought up in earlier decisions but considers insufficiently remedied. The Board clarifies or reiterates prior normative statements and criticizes Meta for insufficient implementation. Such repetitions often include citations of earlier Board decisions. For traditional courts, citing decisions' titles or excerpts is widely considered as a useful tool for maintaining normative stability and developing precedential law and bodies of legal doctrine.[367] Further, the Board references international courts and tribunals. For example, in a case concerning hate speech in the context of ethnic conflicts in Ethiopia, the Board referred to prior decisions as well as to judgments by the International Criminal Tribunal on Rwanda (ICTR). The Board said that it "came to a similar conclusion in decision 2020–003-FB-UA. [And that] . . . cumulative [hate speech] can amount to causation through a 'gradual build-up of effect,' as happened in Rwanda where calls to genocide were repeated [then quoting an ICTR case]."[368]

Citing older cases may not automatically mean that an adjudicator is accurately recreating earlier normative assessments.[369] Citations are also sometimes used "ritualistically."[370] However, for a young but ambitious organization like the Oversight Board, such "ritualistic" practices are important for gaining public legitimacy.

Some of these "doctrines" directly challenge traditional conceptions of international law. The Board increasingly formulates abstract

366 Doctrine's stabilizing function only lasts as long as its proponents in judiciary, practice, and legal academia reaffirm it. See for a daunting example from German history: Bernd Rüthers, *Die unbegrenzte Auslegung: zum Wandel der Privatrechtsordnung im Nationalsozialismus* (9th ed., Mohr Siebeck 2022).

367 The exact difference between the term precedent and doctrine is elusive. Precedents are necessarily court decisions. In principle, doctrines may also result from scholarly writing. However, in practice most doctrines seem to equally originate from judgments. The concepts hence differ mostly regarding their context.

368 Alleged Crimes in Raya Kobo [2021] Oversight Board 2021-014-FB-UA at 8.3.III.

369 Joost Pauwelyn and Manfred Elsig, 'The Politics of Treaty Interpretation: Variations and Explanations across International Tribunals' in Jeffrey L Dunoff and Mark A Pollack (eds.), *Interdisciplinary Perspectives on International Law and International Relations: The State of the Art* (Cambridge University Press 2012) 456.

370 Wolfgang Alschner and Damien Charlotin, 'The Growing Complexity of the International Court of Justice's Self-Citation Network' (2018) 29 European Journal of International Law 83, 86.

interpretations of Meta's normative material and human rights law. Perhaps the most striking example of such an abstract "doctrine" fashioned by the Board is its reference to a state of "public emergency" and Meta's resulting recourse to "emergency powers" to suspend its fundamental rights obligations. We will discuss said "doctrine's" ripple effects in greater detail in the next chapter.[371] For descriptive purposes, we will just briefly look at that decision's decisive paragraph. In a case dealing with potentially incendiary speech about Tigrayans in Ethiopia. The content in question was posted by an individual user, but the Ethiopian government was reported to post similar content. The Board asserted:

> The Board finds that in a country where there is an ongoing armed conflict and an assessed inability of governmental institutions to meet their human rights obligations under international law, Meta may restrict freedom of expression that it otherwise would not (see ICCPR Article 4 on derogations in times of public emergencies).[372]

In other words, the Board emboldens a private, for-profit company to step in whenever it considers governmental institutions to be failing in their human rights obligations in situations of armed conflict. But not only that. The Board essentially emboldens Meta, again, a private company, to declare a state of emergency vis-à-vis a government to justify policing that government tighter than before. We will discuss this in more detail in the following chapter. Yet, I take the liberty of highlighting the audaciousness of such doctrines already here. Arguments like these directly challenge core tenets of international law. They are reminiscent of the earliest plans for the Board, outlined in an internal memo which argued that "by acting to a degree like a sovereign in establishing courts, Facebook presents itself as a responsible decision-maker, prepared to use a method of decision-making deemed valid and legitimate (at least in principle) by most governments on earth."[373] The Board follows this path – even though its actual authority falls far short of earlier ambitions expressed by some within the company.[374] Asked about the audacity of such state-of-emergency arguments, one Board member interviewed, who was not party to the deliberations relating to that specific decision, affirmed that "the Board members

[371] See at 5.2.
[372] Alleged Crimes in Raya Kobo (n 308) at section 8.3.III.
[373] Feldman (n 33) 112.
[374] See e.g., Feldman's memo of March 2018, which envisaged a multitier court system for Facebook and envisaged the company as a "quasi-sovereign," ibid 107, 112 et seq.

are acutely aware of the potential effects of statements like that."[375] Time will tell what the effects will ultimately be, but the significance of the potential downstream effects is hard to overstate.

4.6.4 *The Implementation Conundrum*

Yet, despite intermittently emerging doctrines, the Board's recurring focus on Meta's governance, and the Board's lists of recommendations, the question remains: does it work? Does Meta actually implement the Board's nonbinding recommendations?

As argued in Chapter 2, nonbinding recommendations and doctrines can also have lasting effects. When an adjudicator manages to *convince* the controlled actor, this may lead to more deeply rooted policy changes than the exercise of adjudicatory force through issuing binding decisions.[376] Because adjudicators seek to "adjust future behavior, not compensate for past wrong," their involvement is prolonged as they construct an "ongoing regime of performance."[377] Accordingly, the Board regularly returns to issues it raised in earlier decisions to "guide" the company. Dialogue-based and nonbinding adjudicatory techniques have been extensively explored by legal scholars and, to a degree, might also work for the benefit of the Oversight Board.[378] However, many dialogue-based forms of adjudicatory control are exercised by actual courts, which still have the ultimate tool of comprehensive and binding decisions at their disposal. In contrast, as shown above, the Board's authority to issue binding decisions exists mainly on paper, so the Board – although seen by some as a potent adjudicator – cannot bindingly adjudicate at scale. To make its normative output more effective, the Board could draw on the perceived legitimacy attached to its partly adjudicative status but ultimately it must convince Meta executives to implement its recommendations. Such "good faith"-based implementation reflects the private nature of the Board and of Meta. After all the Board can revert to neither the institutions nor the norms of the rule of law.

375 Interview with Oversight Board Member (n 314).

376 See at 2.2.6.

377 cf. Chayes' characterization of the judge in what he calls "public law litigation," Abram Chayes, 'The Role of the Judge in Public Law Litigation' (1976) 89 Harvard Law Review 1281, 1298.

378 Chayes (n 377); Judith Resnik, 'Managerial Judges' (1982) 96 Harvard Law Review 374; Abram Chayes and Antonia Handler Chayes, 'On Compliance' (1993) 47 International Organization 175; critical in the context of transnational human rights adjudication Veronika Fikfak, 'Against Settlement before the European Court of Human Rights' (2022) 20 International Journal of Constitutional Law 942.

As a consequence, Meta executives regularly choose not to put in place the Board's recommendations in a verifiable way. The story is of fumbled implementing efforts, and the operational complexity of the recommendations. Meta staffers argue that the

> size and scope of the Board's recommendations go beyond the policy guidance that we first anticipated when we set up the Board, and several require multi-month or multiyear investments.[379]

This aligns with statements from interviewed Board staffers who said their counterparts at the company were surprised and even unhappy with the depth and intrusiveness of Board recommendations – which arguably would be a good thing.[380]

To track implementation of its recommendations, the Board first began publishing quarterly transparency reports that assess Meta's implementation efforts. Especially since 2022, the Board scrutinizes how Meta implements its recommendations and uses its quarterly published transparency reports as a "mechanism to force better behavior from Meta."[381] In the first quarterly report of 2022, the Board published a comprehensive assessment of Meta's implementation of all recommendations until then. The report distinguishes six categories of implementation, ranging from "implementation demonstrated through published information" to "recommendation omitted, declined, or reframed."[382] This was later expanded into a section called "recommendation tracker" on the Board's website. The recommendation tracker contains two tables, one listing all published recommendations and one adding two more categories to the six categories just mentioned.

Neither the 2022 quarterly report, which introduced those six implementation categories, nor the later introduced recommendation tracker on the Oversight Board website publish their underlying methodology or the used data. So, the Board's assessment that implementation in these two categories has indeed been "demonstrated" remains at times rather untransparent to outside observers.

Of the 288 recommendations issued by the Board up until November 2024, only fifty-seven recommendations were demonstrably and completely implemented according to the Board. Another forty-one

[379] Jennifer Broxmeyer, 'Facebook's First Quarterly Update on the Oversight Board' (*Meta Newsroom*, 16 July 2021) <https://perma.cc/2YDU-E62C>.

[380] Interview with Oversight Board Staffer 2 (n 10).

[381] Ibid.

[382] Oversight Board Q1 2022 Transparency Report, p 21.

recommendations assessed the Board to be verifiably partially implemented. For many recommendations, Meta reported progress (sixty-seven) or reported implementation without providing corroborating information (forty-six). Meta declined to put in place several recommendations after a feasibility assessment (fourteen), omitted or reframed recommendations (twenty), or declined to implement the recommendation out of principle (thirty-one).

According to Figure 4.5 all but the two top-right categories (implementation demonstrated; partial implementation demonstrated) show recommendations whose normative content was not verifiably adopted. According to the Board, Meta verifiably implemented 21 percent of its recommendations as of November 2024. Further, the Board considers another 15 percent of its implementations to be verifiably "partially" implemented. However, the exact efficacy and relevance of "partial" implementation remains unclear. Also, the Board does not disclose its verification of Meta's implementation. Rather, until this day, the Board and Meta remain in a constant struggle toward, hopefully, incremental improvements in transparency. For example, in a 2023 decision the Board still deemed it necessary to explicate that it "expects Meta to share more data to enable the Board to assess improvements in performance over time."[383] Therefore, this category may be treated with some skepticism. Nonetheless, when comparing the data available in November 2024 with that of the first comprehensive transparency report in 2022, we see that the full implementation indeed increased over time, climbing from 14 percent in 2022 to 21 percent in November 2024; "verifiable partial implementation" more than doubled from 7 percent in 2022 to 15 percent in November 2024.[384]

Between the Board's inception in 2021 and November 2024, Meta reported – without corroborating their self-reporting – either "progress" or even "implementation" on another 113 Board recommendations. However, "progress" only means that "Meta has made a commitment to implementing this recommendation but has not yet completed all necessary actions."[385] Whereas modifications to its publicly accessible normative material can be assessed by the Board, Meta's post-recommendation handling of automated enforcement procedures remains obscure. In particular, it is still unclear how significant an implementation must be

[383] United States posts discussing abortion [2023] Oversight Board 2023-01-IG-UA, 2023-012-FB-UA, 2023-013-FB-UA at 8.2.IV.

[384] Oversight Board, 'Annual Report 2022' 29 <https://perma.cc/MZ3J-86PE>.

[385] Oversight Board Q4 2021 Transparency Report, p 16.

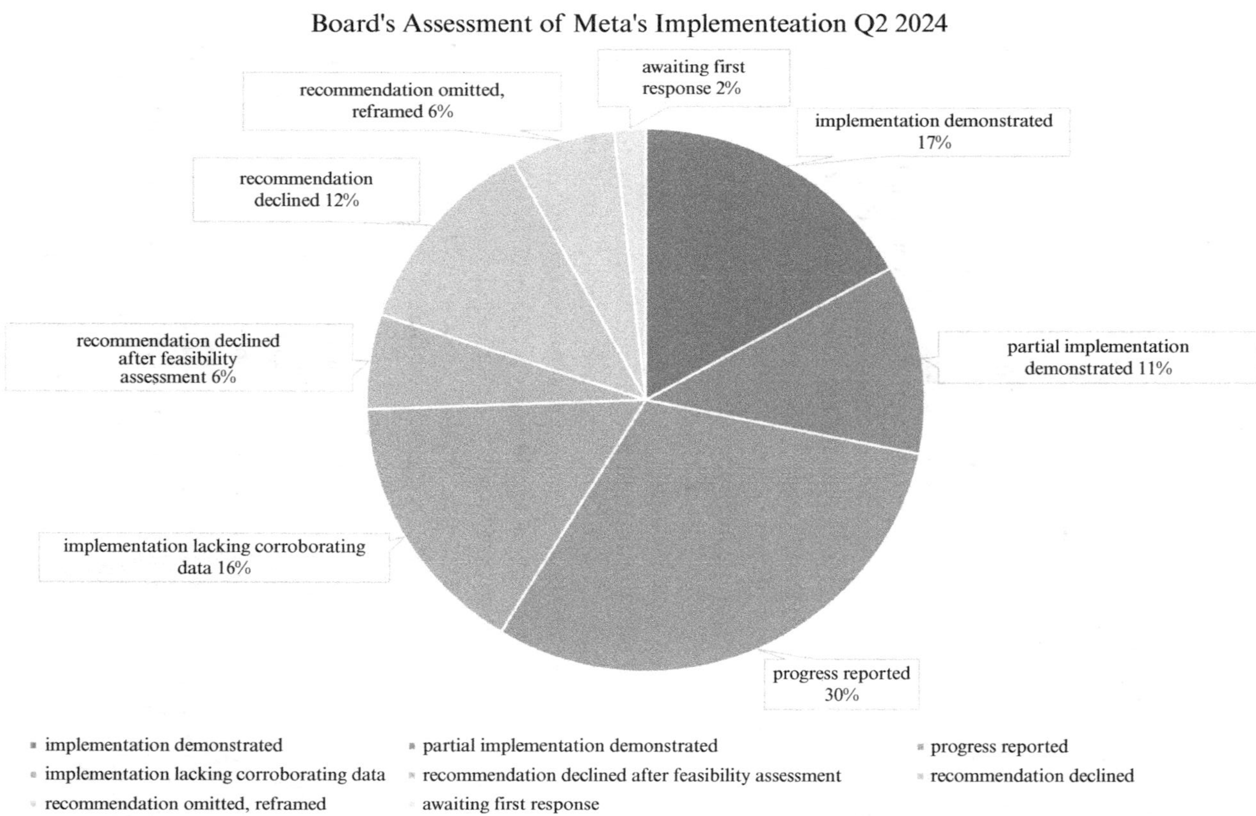

Figure 4.5 The Board's assessment of Meta's implementation of Board recommendations (as of 11/2024)

to count as "progress" and whether "implementation" always pertains to a comprehensive, "word-for-word" implementing of a recommendation.

The success or otherwise of transparency reports as enforcement mechanisms is beyond the scope of this study. However, judging from the anecdotal insights from the interviews as well as a close reading of Meta's updates to its community standards, the tentative answer must be that the Board's recommendations have had mixed success. To some extent, they have been verifiably implemented. Yet 178 out of 276 recommendations until November 2024 were either not fully implemented, their implementation has not been corroborated by any (publicly accessible) data or otherwise failed to materialize. Only roughly a fifth (21 percent) of the total are verifiably implemented recommendations. Conversely, for almost four-fifths (79 percent) of the recommendations made in that period Meta did not corroborate full implementation. Even if one deducts here the 15 percent verifiable partial implementations, one is left with roughly two-thirds of Oversight Board recommendations whose implementation cannot be seriously assessed or is even flat-out rejected by the company.

These figures present a paradox. On one hand, if only one out of five recommendations is fully implemented, it would be premature to declare success. In short, Meta remains obstinate and opaque, a fact the Board itself repeatedly criticized in its decisions. It is also important to look at *which* recommendations Meta implemented and which it rejected. It seems that at least some very salient recommendations were flat-out rejected. Remember the 2023 case on the Cambodian Prime Minister we discussed above?[386] The Board recommended that

> Meta should immediately suspend the official Facebook page and Instagram account of Cambodian Prime Minister Hun Sen for a period of at least six months under Meta's policy on restricting accounts of public figures during civil unrest. The Board will consider this recommendation implemented when Meta suspends the accounts and publicly announces that it has done so.[387]

And indeed Mr. Sen's Facebook page went dark shortly after the Board issued its recommendation to Meta. However, that was not because the company disabled the account. Quite the opposite. The Cambodian Prime Minister appears to have shut down his Facebook account himself, arguably in response to the Oversight Board's decision.[388] The company, in contrast,

[386] See at 3.3.

[387] Cambodian Prime Minister (n 146).

[388] Mike Ives and Sun Narin, 'Cambodian Ruler's Facebook Account Goes Dark after Spat With Meta' *New York Times* (30 June 2023) <https://perma.cc/PPJ9-SCKF>.

expressly "declined" the Oversight Board's recommendation to suspend Mr. Sen's account.[389] Presumably, that is because the company does not wish to cede decision-making capacity in such a vital question to the Board – a remarkable rollback from the stance the company took in its 2021 Trump referral. Back then, the Meta asked the Board to come up with guidelines how the company should handle malevolent heads of state – and the Board tarnished the company for its lack of clear rules on that matter.[390] That Meta now expressly rejects a Board recommendation – based on rules Meta had devised in the meantime – to suspend an account of a government figure who was arguably inciting real-world violence seems deeply troubling. Especially so as all executives at the company must be aware that Facebook infrastructures played – according to the United Nations – a significant role in the displacement and murder of many Rohingya people in Myanmar in 2018. At the same time, the fact that the Cambodian Prime Minister self-suspended his account could be understood as testament to the normativity of Board decisions. Yet, alas, it did not last. Only a month after his exit, shortly before Cambodians went to the polls for a general election, Mr. Sen reactivated his account.[391] In the following election Mr Sen's party won almost all seats – 120 out of 125 – in the Cambodian Parliament.

On the other hand, there is some positive movement. The rate of verifiable implementation in 2024 has significantly improved compared to 2022, which is a crucial indicator of progress. Perhaps, the Board's focused and detailed efforts – such as the implementation tracker, or even external factors such as this very book – are exerting pressure on the company to improve its adherence to recommendations and overall improvement of its content moderation regime.

Looking ahead, two key points warrant attention. First, the Oversight Board was astute in transforming a vice into a virtue by publishing Meta's initially dismal implementation rates. Highlighting how uncooperative the company was during the Board's early years, and likely still is in some respects, appears to have prodded Meta into demonstrably adopting more recommendations. At present, the Board openly calls out Meta's shortcomings in fully implementing its guidance, a strategy that paradoxically risks undermining the Board's own credibility. However, Meta has a clear interest in sustaining the perception of

389 As per the Oversight Board's Recommendation Tracker, accessible via <https://perma.cc/7RY8-CSLH>.

390 Former President Trump's suspension (n 143).

391 Martin Petty, 'Cambodia PM's Facebook Page Reactivated Days before Election' *Reuters* (20 July 2023) <https://perma.cc/KSD7-3NHV>.

the Board as a (somewhat) effective oversight mechanism. As long as the company seeks to benefit from the legitimacy bestowed by external, adjudicative oversight, it remains incentivized to comply – at least enough to avoid entirely eroding the Board's authority. Therefore, it seems entirely plausible that we will see a further uptick in implementation. This would then warrant further, more qualitative research as the mere number of implemented recommendations tells us little about the actual quality of the reforms.

Second, some patience is warranted. The Oversight Board is still a young organization, and many well-established human rights bodies within the UN system arguably have similarly low implementation rates, despite decades of experience. The core challenge, as consistently highlighted in interviews with Board members, staff, and trustees, lies in the social norms and internal culture at Meta – factors that do not change overnight. Consequently, the gradual but steady implementation of Oversight Board decisions is a hopeful sign.

Looking to the future, however, it will be critical for the Board to be transparent about how it assesses "verifiable" implementation, so that independent third parties – particularly researchers – can effectively scrutinize the compliance process.

To summarize, having limited jurisdiction or relying on the good faith of digital corporations may not be immediately fatal for Emulated Guardians. Especially so in post-state governance where many power relations are regulated in vague, nonbinding arrangements. However, a "verifiable" success rate of only 21 percent cannot be seen as representing effective implementation.[392] Maybe Meta implements more than that – but the company's unwillingness to be transparent about measures it puts into practice constitutes a legitimacy problem for the Board, although the latter's transparency reports are bold and innovative in their approach. Eventually, these transparency reports may either gradually push Meta into compliance or, as a result of that transparency itself, their contents might end up chipping away at the Board's image as a credible guardian of power, and thereby undermine its authority.

[392] I am not sure whether many adjudicatory guardians of post-state and international governance could expound higher implementation quotas. See regarding the methodological difficulties assessing implementation, Erik Voeten, 'Domestic Implementation of European Court of Human Rights Judgments: Legal Infrastructure and Government Effectiveness Matter: A Reply to Dia Anagnostou and Alina Mungiu-Pippidi' (2014) 25 European Journal of International Law 229.

4.6.5 *Prospects*

Assessing possible improvements in the Board's efficacy and Meta's implementation will be the work of further studies. To a large degree, this change will depend on a change of culture at Meta. We know how hard and unlikely such a cultural change may be.[393] Also, the whole tech sector shifted or appears poised to shift to the political right, a trend epitomized by but not restricted to Elon Musk's role in the 2024 US presidential election.[394] How lasting and impactful such shifts are remains to be seen. Nonetheless – or perhaps particularly since that election – the Oversight Board, despite its ceremonies, can be seen as a first step toward important yet contested cultural change. In addition, the fact that Meta increased its funding of the trust earlier than it needed to indicates a long-term and perhaps enhanced commitment to adjudicatory oversight. In contrast, other developments foreshadow the long journey still ahead for Emulated Guardians. Evolving such a culture, reflexively, requires institutions and rules to pave the way. The Board and the references to human rights in its decisions may be encouraging such cultural change from the outside. But they will not and cannot *compel* this change.

If, ten years from now, we consider the Oversight Board a failure (or do not recall it at all), it will likely not have been the Board's fault but the company's unwillingness to subject itself to adjudicative oversight. However, for the time being, impatience seems misguided. If the Board turns out to be the next chapter in the saga of adjudicative control over organizational power, assuming authoritative guardianship will take time. Nonetheless, it seems equally possible that the Board – even if it persists in its current form – will become yet one more quaint guardian-like experiment sidelined by more dynamic and powerful organizations.

In any event, I argue the Oversight Board should not be entirely forgotten, as emulation inevitably casts ripples. As we saw in the other case study, we already witness policy diffusion of aspects of the Oversight Board in Europe, most notably through the Appeals Centre Europe but arguably also in User Rights.[395] I suspect this trend will extend beyond content moderation, likely reappearing, *mutatis mutandis*, in future

393 See esp. 'Statement of Frances Haugen' (n 96). See further for anecdotal examples of unsuccessful governance reforms at FIFA, Miguel Maduro and Joseph H H Weiler, '"Integrity," "Independence" and the Internal Reform of FIFA' in Arnout Geeraert and Frank van Eekeren, *Good Governance in Sport* (Routledge 2021).

394 cf. Anja Bossow, Marie Müller-Elmau and Moritz Schramm, 'The Messiah and His Oligarchs' (*Verfassungsblog*, 1 November 2024) <https://perma.cc/55QN-HM2S>.

395 See at 3.8.

governance frameworks. Anthropic, a leading artificial intelligence company, has established a so-called Long-Term Benefit Trust, which is supposed to infuse (some) public-interest considerations into both the company's management and the composition of its board. For future corporations and post-state power structures, someone might once again come up with the same, apparently simple, idea to emulate individual rights adjudication or other canonical ideas of public law.

4.7 Conclusion

This chapter examined the genesis and practice of the Oversight Board, a privately established Emulated Guardian that was set up ostensibly to control the world's largest social network's rulemaking and rule-enforcement efforts. It looked at the ways in which lawyers and juridical concepts shaped the Board's creation as an adjudicatory institution, and examined its institutional structure and personnel. We have seen that the dominance of lawyers among Board members and staffers enabled the Board to attempt to incrementally overcome some of its in-built handicaps. Among these are a complex relationship between, on the one side, an able, impartial group of members and staffers and, on the other, several backdoor channels used by Meta to influence the Board's adjudicative practices, which eventually undermined the Board's hoped-for independence. Crucially, the Board turned to international human rights law as an external normative yardstick against which to measure at least some of Meta's internally devised rules. Although the Board's attempts to infuse public-law principles into a private-law context represent sometimes bold challenges to the status quo, for example when developing a doctrine of "public emergency," its recommendations on the basis of these "infusions" often end up not being verifiably implemented by Meta. Nevertheless, the Board's skillful adaptation of juridical personnel, argumentation, practices, and reasoning might indicate that its incremental build-up of authority has, perhaps, only just begun.

5 Do Emulated Guardians Work?

5.1 Introduction

As the previous two chapters explained how the two Emulated Guardians – the EU's out-of-court dispute settlement bodies (ODSs) and Meta's Oversight Board – came about, this chapter now vets them against the efficacy criteria of any functional adjudicatory guardian of organizational power. These criteria build on the work of Peter Cane, one of common law's most eminent theorists of administrative law. Namely, the three criteria are, first, a set of stable, external, and legitimate rules; second, an authoritative guardian; and third an organizational culture that holistically effectuates rather than undermines the guardian's external feedback.[1]

The key message of this chapter is twofold. On the one hand, neither of the studied Emulated Guardians works or is indeed designed to work as a truly effective adjudicatory overseer of corporate power. The mandates of both bodies are weak and many normative and factual arrangements severely hamstring their ability to effectively hold social media companies accountable. This is, arguably, a common feature of emulative institutions, which quickly reproduce formal structures and institutions, without holistically reproducing the enabling factors – here: democratic

[1] It is worth noting that the elements of "authority" and "culture" represent a slight modification of what Cane originally described as "institution" and "practice." The sociolegal approach of this book required a subtle shift in emphasis, as Cane's original categories – rules, institutions, and practice – seem, to me, deeply interconnected (after all, what are rules and institutions without their practice?). Thus, I took the liberty of focusing on an institution's "authority" and the cultures of implementation and accountability. Peter Cane, *Controlling Administrative Power: An Historical Comparison* (Cambridge University Press 2016).

rulemaking, the rule of law, judicial authority – enveloping the role model in its original context.

However, on the other hand, as flagged in the introduction, theorized in the second chapter and empirically traced in the case studies, both bodies (or their creators) *performatively* play with the symbolism and language of all these contextual factors. Albeit mostly discursive rather than substantively legal, those appropriations of adjudicative symbolism may incrementally position bodies like ODSs or the Oversight Board (or any other Emulated Guardian for that matter) in the public mindset as, somewhat, serious guardians of power. We already observe that the authority and global standing of the Oversight Board seems to stabilize. Likewise, as the very recent practical developments in the context of the first ODSs showed, ODSs might creatively overcome at least some of their serious shortcomings the case study uncovered. They might, as discussed in greater detail, be important experiments for incorporating large language models into decision-making architectures, offering valuable lessons for future automated justice systems. To repeat a catch phrase from the introduction: Emulated Guardians are not powerful because they are courts. Emulated Guardians are powerful because they *appear and act like* courts. Formal labels do not matter here – it is the idea, the insinuation, the performance that counts. This potentially enables Emulated Guardians to incrementally expand their normative bind vis-à-vis the organizations they shall control. Notably, such incremental construction of authority is not at all dubious. Rather, gradual gains in authority and strategic expansions of initially tight mandates are a common adjudicative strategy well studied for domestic courts – think about Marbury v Madison – as well as international courts and the European Court of Justice.[2] The source of that normativity, however, would not primarily be formal mandate but discursive pressure.

In other words, effectuating public law guarantees vis-à-vis private power through emulative arrangements works, ironically, largely *besides* formal public law. As already hinted at in the introduction, this book argues that as long as classic public law ideas like individual rights and adjudicative accountability over powerful organizations remain socioculturally appealing they may be powerful drivers of socially demanded rather than merely regulated change. Making those public law ideas

[2] cf. Chester Neal Tate, 'The Global Expansion of Judicial Power: The Judicialization of Politics' in Chester Neal Tate and Torbjörn Vallinder (eds.), *The Global Expansion of Judicial Power* (New York University Press 1995).

work though requires a different – in many ways more rudimentary and rawer – approach than conventional command and control regulations offer. The ethereal but humongous and deeply institutionalized spheres of globalized, private, and profit-oriented power structures, seem to adopt public law ideas mainly out of self-interest and in contorted form, instead of bona fide implementation of classic public regulation. We will look deeper into this aspect in the final chapter.

Therefore, to come back to the concrete program of this chapter, we now dissect the ODSs and the Oversight Board's ability to exercise effective guardianship vis-à-vis the private, for-profit power structures they are tasked to control. Conducting such an analysis is necessarily a gradual, context-dependent rather than binary endeavor. I therefore refrain from clearly labeling either of the two Emulated Guardians studied here as wholly effective, entirely ineffective, legal, illegal, problematic, or promising. Such labels are simplifying and, I believe, beyond the point.

Absolute assessments are only snapshots anyways. ODSs are just becoming operational in the months the final words of this book were written. There will be a rich variety of different ODSs, national variations and, arguably, social media site-dependent practices. Likewise, the Oversight Board, social media platforms and the whole informational economy develop so fast that "definite" evaluations are not only quickly outdated but at odds with my whole observation that these phenomena are deeply performative and, thus, subject to constant change. Therefore, instead, this chapter offers three criteria – *rules, authority, culture* – to evaluate the efficacy of emulative guardianship over private, for-profit organizations in globalized commerce. The example we look at here is content moderation by social media companies. But, as argued in the introduction, I believe the core idea to emulate individual rights adjudication (or other public law classics) to control powerful organizations beyond the state is all but assured to reappear once we face the next "new" challenge, be it the governance of "artificial intelligence," bio-, geoengineering, space exploration, or something else.

Before we begin, a few words on the elements of an effective control regime. In essence, there are three criteria: rules, authority, and culture. The criterion of "rules" in this context refers to the normative material used by an Emulated Guardian to contain private power structures. "Authority" then denotes the power and efficacy of an Emulated Guardian as an institution and its normative output. Lastly, "culture" points to the various elusive but crucial contextual enabling factors, especially in an organization's sociology and culture. These are especially

a culture to implement, in good faith, external feedback and honestly commit to public law principles like rights and accountability.

One concept I will frequently use as somewhat negative contrast to these three criteria is "ceremony." As a concept, ceremony originates from organization theory and denotes formal, external structures and organizational practices that accommodate public expectations but have little relation or effect on the internal actual practice of an organization.[3] In our example, a "ceremony" would be to establish a wholly ineffective but flashy and PR-savvy accountability forum. That would play well in overall discourse but change little in how platforms moderate down the road. Evelyn Douek called this "accountability theater."[4] In this sense, "ceremonies" and "accountability theater" is clearly negative. As shown in the second chapter, merely ceremonial emulations can be outrightly dangerous if they incrementally erode our shared sense of what kind of actor, what type of action, and what degree of rights protection and enforceability is even *possible* in globalized, transnational spheres. Remember that studies show, on the one hand, that privacy remains to be a cherished societal value, albeit, on the other hand, many grew to accept that privacy may be nice to have but is simply not enforceable. As one participant put it "this is capitalism."[5] If Emulated Guardians were only adjudicative ceremonies without practical benefit, they would, in the long run, erode our shared understanding of how far we *can* protect individual rights online.

Yet, at the same time, ceremonies, understood broadly as flashy but somewhat pointless habits are prevalent and arguably necessary elements of any organization and, arguably, society at large. Every formal organization, especially an adjudicator, features ceremonial structures and practices that are, at least partly, decoupled from their internal practices.[6] Judges wear robes and wigs, and rhetorically reaffirm their

[3] Seminal: John W Meyer and Brian Rowan, 'Institutionalized Organizations: Formal Structure as Myth and Ceremony' (1977) 83 American Journal of Sociology 340.

[4] Evelyn Douek, 'Content Moderation as Systems Thinking' (2022) 136 Harvard Law Review 526, 528, 533.

[5] Hagar Afriat and others, '"This Is Capitalism. It Is Not Illegal": Users' Attitudes toward Institutional Privacy Following the Cambridge Analytica Scandal' (2021) 37 The Information Society 115.

[6] Of course, ceremonial structures and practices in the sense of Meyer and Rowan are also practices in the sense adopted here. For Meyer and Rowan, the key distinction was not between formal structure and practice (although that also is a relevant distinction, as formal structures are especially "ripe" for emulation because they do not have to be necessarily backed by practice) but between internal practice and external structure, cf. Meyer and Rowan (n 3) 349 et seq.

authority in phrases like "in the name of the people" and "all rise." These ceremonial aspects do not undermine the control of adjudicators or judges. Some of these aspects even reaffirm the adjudicator's controlling authority, performatively *making* the judge in the public's eyes. Thus, we see again, the deep ambivalence and transience of Emulated Guardians, which, in my eye, largely prohibit simplistic dismissals (especially as there does not really seem to be a politically feasible alternative to them).

5.2 Rules

We now proceed to the first element of a functional control regime of administrative(-like) power. That element is a set of stable, external, and democratic rules.[7] I argue that the two studied Emulated Guardians face three challenges in this regard. First, most of the rules they apply are embarrassingly undemocratic. Second, the Digital Services Act (DSA) seems to vindicate rather than restrict platform power as it implicitly declares platforms' unilateral, convoluted rules the main standard for free speech in Europe. This severely undermines the potential of ODSs to exercise meaningful guardianship vis-à-vis social media platforms in Europe. Third, as these phenomena are deeply ambivalent, I show how external, arguably legitimate rules like international human rights law, equally carry the potential to severely challenge core tenets of international law and governance. The example I present here is how the Oversight Board, a private body that shall control a private company, tweaks and twists human rights logics to argue that in "states of emergency" the *company* is under different policing duties vis-à-vis individuals *and sovereign states* (or to be precise, their social media accounts). One does not have to invoke an infamous German scholar of the first half of the twentieth century to detect the thinly veiled allusions to sovereignty and potentially paradigm shifting effects of such arguments for international law and governance.

5.2.1 *Platform-Made Rules Are Undemocratic*

Adjudication is third-party review. It only works if the allegedly controlled party cannot unilaterally amend the rules upon which its control is based. In other words, the whole point of individual rights adjudication is that it controls whether a powerful organization, that is, historically

[7] Cane (n 1) 2.

the state, now, perhaps, social media platforms, abides by normative guarantees that are designed to limit their power. It is questionable to which extent Terms of Service and Community Guidelines, which are the most important sets of normative material here, are indeed designed to limit the power of platforms. As Gillespie put it, those community guidelines are "inevitably, provisional lines drawn in shifting sands, the residue of past tensions, and best efforts at workable compromises."[8]

In contrast, classic normative guarantees that are, at least in principle, designed to limit power are fundamental rights, international human rights law, or transnational or national regulation. To an extent, also normative material generated, in one form or the other, by the organization itself may self-restrict organizational power. After all, when courts review the legality of administrative action in national or EU contexts, they also look at statutory (and constitutional) law, which originates just as much from public power as the administrative agency does. However, the key factor waterproofing a rule as a functional basis for adjudicative control over power is the process of its genesis. In other words, while formal labels like public or private seem not decisive, what is decisive is the democratic viability of the rulemaking process. This is particularly important when the substantive matter is speech – a deeply sociocultural phenomenon. If an organization makes rules about online but nonetheless public discourse, those rules should tie back to the people they govern. In a public context, therefore, the rules that constrain power originate, in principle, from a democratic, transparent, and formalized process. Even though administrative agencies are as public as the legislator, the rules governing administrative agencies are not mostly made unilaterally by those agencies. And even those rules which are made unilaterally by administrative agencies only come about in somewhat democratized procedures. These procedures enable affected individuals to participate in the process of rulemaking.

None of this happens for platform rulemaking. Platform rules (meaning terms of service, community guidelines, and all the sublayer rules undergirding them) are unilaterally made and amended by the platforms at whim. One interviewee who advised Meta describes the process of making these rules as "basically a room full of US lawyers sits down and makes the rules after the latest crisis."[9] It is jarring that

[8] Tarleton Gillespie, *Custodians of the Internet: Platforms, Content Moderation, and the Hidden Decisions That Shape Social Media* (Yale University Press 2019) 71.

[9] Interview with Academic, Consultant to Facebook in 2018 (1 November 2021).

many – including the European Union as Chapters 2 and 3 show – came to unquestioningly accept this rather brazen and unintuitive privatization of rulemaking power over absolute core issues of social, cultural, and political speech.

The ubiquitous counter argument is freedom of contract and property. The property argument is that social media companies may use their property – infrastructure, code, and so on – as they please. After all, platforms do own these infrastructures. The contract argument, pretty much up the same ally, holds that parties are free to agree to whatever they want and as users sign, or rather click, those agreements, who are we to weigh in? Both arguments are, frankly, ridiculous. Oil giants cannot dump crude oil in open waters, even though they own the crude oil. Even if they would indeed also own the waters, they would not be allowed to do so. Big Tabaco cannot legally tell us that cigarettes are healthy, and even if I were to legally buy the raw chemicals to produce LSD, I would not be allowed to do with them whatever I want. Property and contract are free only if their usage does not harm others. That is the whole point of living in a society and having laws. However, collective goods – such as each individual's personal construction of the self and society's foundational ability to communicate and address problems – must be governed by principles that extend beyond the pursuit of maximum profit by whoever was fastest to exploit a novel business model. Thus, clearly, reforming platform rulemaking is a question of political will.

5.2.2 The DSA Empowers Rather Than Controls Platforms

The DSA does not remedy the democratic deficit of platform rulemaking. But that is not it. The DSA also stabilizes platforms' preference for internal, rather than external rules to "control" their behavior. The control of content moderation offered by ODSs in this model is, in practice, largely restricted to assessing whether platforms abide by their own rules, that is, the community standards.

Let me explain this. The DSA envisages platforms to base their moderation decisions on two sets of rules. These are, first, the rules made by the platform itself, and second, Member State and Union law. The first category is called "incompatibility" with terms of service; the second category is called "illegality." Illegal refers to any content that "is not in compliance with Union law or the law of any Member State which is in compliance with Union law, irrespective of the precise subject matter or nature of that law," according to Article 2(h) of the DSA. These rules are external to platforms and should therefore provide a functional normative basis for adjudicatory control over platform enforcement. However, due to foreseeable practical impediments, this might not in fact be the case.

The DSA's definition of illegality is so broad that platforms might not be able to identify the relevant rules that should apply to them.[10] Similarly, some EU lawmakers interviewed for this present work assumed that only a minority of the moderation decisions will focus on "illegality," whereas possibly the majority of moderation decisions and ensuing disputes will relate to the platforms' terms of service.[11] That seems plausible. Platforms' enforcement of their own terms of service is a lot more seasoned, centralized, and established than the enforcement regimes required to take down any content that the DSA deems "illegal," especially in a pluralist and federated bloc like the EU.[12] Large social networks like Facebook or Instagram or other content platforms like YouTube moderate billions of pieces of content per month. I am skeptical that it is truly realistic for platforms to entirely overhaul their content moderation regimes to accommodate the specific interests of any given Member State, irrespective of its subject matter or nature."[13] The organizational effort to reflect the specifics of twenty-seven domestic legal systems in platforms' enforcement regimes far outweighs the benefits for platforms. Remember, some Member State legal frameworks arguably cover fewer platform users than the number of people living in a large city. In some cases, it might not even be a particularly big city – Malta, Luxembourg, and Cyprus together do not quite equal the number of inhabitants of Brooklyn. Therefore, from a legal realist perspective, it seems unlikely that platforms will substantively adapt their organizational structures to accommodate the normative specifics of "smaller" Member States.[14] As previous empirical work has uncovered evidence for, platforms favor a centralized system of

[10] Article 2(h) DSA.

[11] Interview with European Commission Staffer 1 (8 July 2022); Interview with European Commission Staffer 1 (29 October 2021); Interview with European Parliament, Staffer 2 (25 November 2022).

[12] Regarding the EU's categorization as federal system see Robert Schütze, *From Dual to Cooperative Federalism: The Changing Structure of European Law* (Oxford University Press 2009).

[13] For the quote see Article 2(h) DSA.

[14] cf. Lauren B Edelman, 'Legal Ambiguity and Symbolic Structures: Organizational Mediation of Civil Rights Law' (1992) 97 American Journal of Sociology 1531.

rules they can apply as uniformly as possible.[15] Scale is a key component of platforms' business models.[16]

From an EU law perspective, that hints to an important finding. On the one hand, many of the DSA's key provisions read so vaguely that platform discretion and ceremonial adaptation may undercut any "Brussels Effect."[17] On the other hand and running counter to the logic of the "Brussels Effect" as described by Bradford, the DSA does indeed *not* establish a uniform, EU-wide substantive standard. Quite the contrary. When it comes to law enforcement, and intuitively so, if one thinks of the EU's federal structure, the DSA tries to enable Member States to muscle through their own standards but does not establish a common European one. Given European pluralism, that makes sense.

However, whether the DSA's uniform procedural framework suffices to motivate platforms to enforce, say, Maltese, Luxembourgian, or Cypriot law (and that of many other Member States) remains to be seen. They might enforce such laws when asked to in notice-and-takedown procedures; but proactively rather not. Eventually, "illegal" content, especially if illegal only as defined by nationally applicable legislation in some Member States, might not play a central role in platforms' moderation efforts. If such content is not deleted for its illegality but for its incompatibility with terms of service, however, ODSs will not adjudicate on the "illegality" of content.[18]

The other of these two categories, "incompatibility" with a platform's terms of service, imperfectly builds a control system on adjudicating

[15] Gillespie (n 8) 45 et seq. See also Kate Klonick, 'The New Governors: The People, Rules, and Processes Governing Online Speech' (2018) 131 Harvard Law Review 1598, 1631.

[16] cf. Stigler Center for the Study of the Economy and the State (University of Chicago), 'Stigler Committee on Digital Platforms Final Report' (2019) 34 et seq.

These are, incidentally, pertinent observations for debates about the EU's democratic deficit. In principle, one of the EU's major democratizing effects—despite other institutional flaws—has been to level the playing field between smaller and larger European states. However, federalizing enforcement and normative input vis-à-vis globally active, infrastructure-controlling, and vertically integrated digital corporations may undermine this empowering effect. Against that backdrop, the EU faces a difficult choice: while internal differentiation holds appeal from a legal pluralism perspective, the Union's strength in the global arena – whether in trade or digital regulation – derives precisely from acting as a cohesive bloc.

[17] Martin Husovec and Jennifer Urban, 'Will the DSA Have the Brussels Effect?' (*Verfassungsblog*, 21 February 2024) <https://perma.cc/DCX4-6FYK>; Moritz Schramm, 'Curb Your Enthusiasm: Why the Digital Services Act Might Not Have a "Brussels Effect"' (2025) European Journal of Legal Studies (Special Issue) 61.

[18] If at all, ODSs will adjudicate the "illegality" mainly based on appeals launched by so-called "trusted flaggers" (people who report other users, see esp. Article 22 DSA) but those will arguably be way fewer cases than by people whose content was deleted for violating a platform's community standards.

internal rules. These platform-made rules, however, cannot be an appropriate normative yardstick for controlling platforms because platforms have so much leeway in devising and amending them. The best outcome that such control could bring is what one adviser to the Commission called an "arbitrariness check" – that is, monitoring whether platforms follow their own dysfunctional rules.[19]

Intuitively, one might say that for controlling private power such scanty control could suffice. Moreover, indeed, stringent enforcement of platform-made rules would signify progress compared to the situation we have now. However, the root of the problem is not only platforms' enforcement of their rules but how these rules have come about. Terms of service (and the cascading community guidelines) are neither procedurally nor normatively linked to the individuals they govern. As argued above, terms of service are deeply undemocratic. They mirror what a group of corporate lawyers and product managers at social media companies deem good policy (for the company, not necessarily the public writ large). Yet, those rules code and normalize a very particular and presumably rather corporate understanding of global speech norms.[20] This undermines the EU's own goal to reign in on digital corporations. Therefore, the rules determining free speech in Europe are unlikely to be any more "European" than those determining online speech in Indonesia, Argentina, or South Africa. Overall, we will have (or already have) a global standard. That standard is not set by the EU but by private companies. And with the DSA, the EU valorizes rather than democratizes this corporate standard.

5.2.3 *From Flawed Design to Better Practice*

That being said, not every design flaw ends up staining later practice. It seems very well plausible that at least some ODSs overcome those in-built design flaws and develop ODSs into more than they are designed to be. The developments around ADROIT, User Rights, and the Appeals Centre – three ODSs fresh off the shelf – offer a shimmer of entrepreneurship and institutional innovation. As some of these new ODSs are run by people coming from content moderation, rather than from a consumer protection side, we may observe strategic sensitivity that external and concise rules are important, and that solid adjudicative argumentation and cautious institution-building

[19] Interview with Academic, Consultant to the European Commission (29 June 2022).

[20] This reminds of the "coding" of corporate law through global elites of corporate lawyers described in Katharina Pistor, *The Code of Capital: How the Law Creates Wealth and Inequality* (Princeton University Press 2019).

are arguably necessary to make an ODS work. At the same time, as ADROIT indicated, also the consumer protection ADR has its place in this new ecosystem.

Similarly, the Oversight Board quickly overcame some of its in-built design flaws. For example, the Oversight Board's charter establishes that the Board's main review function is to "determine" whether content enforcement decisions are "consistent with Facebook's content policies and values."[21] In contrast, the role for human rights law, which would have been an external and legitimate basis for review, could be read as merely decorative. The Board should only "pay particular attention to the *impact* of removing content in light of human rights norms protecting free expression" but, at least according to the wording of the charter, the Board should not use international human rights law as a basis for its review of Meta's enforcement decisions.[22] Judging from its normative fundamentals, the Board was thus largely restricted to applying Meta's own, internally devised rules. However, for meaningful adjudicatory review, Facebook's content policies and values are woefully inadequate. In the Board's own words, they are often "inconsistent" and "lack clarity" while the way they are handled by the company remains "vague" and "uncertain."[23] Further, Meta may (and does) unilaterally amend these policies and values, thereby rendering any adjudicatory control based on them largely ceremonial.[24] Therefore, if we look at the Oversight Board's institutional design, we must conclude that this design could be viewed as largely ceremonial.

However, in practice, the Oversight Board overcame this in-built limitation of only being able to work with Meta's internal rules. As argued in Chapter 4, the Board does in fact draw upon international human rights law to derive normative standards for Meta's actions.[25] The Board regularly assesses Meta's internal decision-making, communication with individuals, and the quality of the rules Meta applies in terms of whether these adhere to international human rights law. Admittedly, the Board's normative assessments often focus on establishing standards and not on the kind of extensive reasoning that occurs in domestic courts.[26] In other words, the

[21] Charter Article 2 Section 2.

[22] Charter Article 2 Section 2 (emphasis added); see also in detail at 4.4.2.1.

[23] For the former see Breast Cancer symptoms and nudity [2021] Oversight Board 2020-004-IG-UA. For the latter see Former President Trump's suspension [2021] Oversight Board 2021-001-FB-FBR. at section 8.3.I.

[24] See at 4.1.2.2 and 4.5.4.

[25] See at 4.5.

[26] Ibid.

Board itself expounded an external normative framework beyond Meta's control. It arguably did so out of self-interest. Adjudicating based on, and in the language of, human rights is a legitimacy-affording asset for the Board vis-à-vis the company (and other organized powers like states or the EU). And it seems to be working. Some commentators are already comparing the Board to a UN human rights treaty body and even point to a "human rights future."[27] For the Board, recourse to human rights is a means to build legitimacy incrementally. Hence, despite the normative straitjacket imposed on it by the charter, the Board seems to be emulating what adjudicators have arguably done for centuries: reinterpreting its role more broadly than initially foreseen.

Does all this mean that the Board or experiments like it will single-handedly save us? Surely not. But it shows that dynamics of contestation, voice, and accountability, of reform and critique follow power structures we too often view only through the limiting lens of private law and economics.

5.2.4 *Why Human Rights Law Is Ambivalent Too*

Broadly and boldly interpreting its role as human rights guardian also comes with ambivalence. For example, its turn to international human rights law might legitimize the Board vis-à-vis the company but simultaneously somewhat shields it from national regulation. This is, from Meta's perspective, of course a good thing. However, from a democratic perspective one may rightly question the legitimacy of claims of a private actor which basically ties itself to public international law – on very convenient terms, as none of this public international law is formally binding for it – instead of the usually more strict and (perhaps) concise regulatory demands of, say, the European Union.

The ambivalent role of public international law as grounds for private adjudicative review for private power becomes particularly vivid whenever actual international actors are involved. By now, there are several Oversight Board cases concerning, in one way or the other, government speech. There is, of course, the famous Trump decision. But there are more. For example, in the context of ethnic unrest in the Tigray region in Ethiopia, the Ethiopian government ushered several statements through

[27] Laurence R Helfer and Molly K Land, 'The Facebook Oversight Board's Human Rights Future' (2023) 44 Cardozo Law Review 2223; see also Nele Meier and Angelo Jr Golia, 'The Emerging Normative System of Meta's Oversight Board: An Introduction' MPIL Research Paper Series No. 2022-09 41.

its social media accounts that could easily be described as inflammatory. In fact, inflammatory statements occur regularly on social media profiles of government officials, as we saw, for example, also in Cambodia, Myanmar, and the United States. So, the Board faced the somewhat fundamental question how it and the company should deal with government communication that could be seen as at least mediately entailing the risk of further violence and real-world harm.

Some of the "doctrines" developed in this context read like a direct challenge to core tenets of international law. Let us, for example, have a look at the Alleged Crimes in Raya Kobo case. In Alleged Crimes in Raya Kobo the Board had to assess whether Meta was right to delete content posted by a private individual in the context of the Ethiopian conflict with Tigrayans. One critical factor in this case was that, although that specific piece of content had not been posted by the Ethiopian government, that same government been posting similar or even more concerning things. Thus, discussing Meta's right to remove this specific piece of content implicitly discussed whether Meta was allowed to moderate similar content posted by the Ethiopian government. For example, only several weeks before the decision was published, Meta removed a post by the Ethiopian prime minister urging civilians to take up arms and "bury" Tigrayan rebels.[28] It should be noted that UN experts sent to Ethiopia have repeatedly highlighted the prevalence of hate speech and its contributory role in atrocities.[29]

The question the Board then faced was how to legitimize Meta's role as a "speech" moderator in potentially life-threatening circumstances.[30] The

[28] 'Facebook Deletes Ethiopia PM's Post That Urged Citizens to "Bury" Rebels' (*BBC*, 3 November 2021) <https://perma.cc/7VAB-XABF>.

[29] See e.g. Human Rights Council, 'Report of the International Commission of Human Rights Experts on Ethiopia, A/HRC/51/46' (2022) para 23, and explicitly referencing the 2014 UN Framework for Analysis of Atrocity Crimes 127.

[30] Regarding the situation on the ground, the Board assessed: "the content could contribute to ethnic hatred. Ethnic conflict situations call for heightened scrutiny over how people should report on and discuss human rights violations committed by parties to the conflict. These considerations apply to Facebook posts, which can be used to spread unverifiable rumors at great speed. The Board notes that some Ethiopian government officials have instigated or spread hate speech targeting Tigrayans ... On its own, an unverifiable rumor may not directly and immediately cause harm. However, when such content appears on an important, influential and popular social media platform during an ongoing conflict, the risk and likelihood of harm become more pronounced. ... Furthermore, cumulative impact can amount to causation through a 'gradual build-up of effect,' as happened in Rwanda where calls to genocide were repeated (see the Nahimana case, Case No. ICTR-99-52-T, paras 436, 478, and 484-485)." Alleged Crimes in Raya Kobo [2021] Oversight Board 2021-014-FB-UA 8.3 III.

Ethiopian government's involvement in communicating hate speech further complicates the matter. Some of the communication the company would have to suppress, and already had suppressed,[31] directly or indirectly stemmed from the (democratically elected) Ethiopian government. And yet serious allegations of human rights violations were being directed at that self-same government.[32]

Therefore, one of the main questions was how to balance, on the one hand, Ethiopian sovereignty and, on the other, the potentially lethal effects of (government-propagated) hate speech in that context.[33]

The human rights rules the Board applied to this situation go to the heart of public law and the notion of sovereignty. The Board framed this whole predicament as a balancing question between, on the one hand, freedom of expression, which in this case would protect the communication of the government on Meta's infrastructures, and on the other hand, Ethiopian sovereignty. Remarkably though, the Board held the company's commitments to free expression would and should be "derogate[ed] in times of *public emergency*."[34] It would be, unsurprisingly, the company which ultimately decides then what counts as state of emergency. In its decision, the Board reasoned:

[31] See above n 28.

[32] UN Office of Genocide Prevention and the Responsibility to Protect, 'Statement by Alice Wairimu Nderitu, United Nations Special Adviser on the Prevention of Genocide, on the Continued Deterioration of the Situation in Ethiopia' (2021) <https://perma.cc/ZX3W-V4V4>; Office of the High Commissioner for Human Rights, 'Ethiopia: Bachelet Urges End to "Reckless" War as Tigray Conflict Escalates (Press Release)' (2021) <https://perma.cc/L2BY-GWPX>.

[33] Reminiscent questions surfaced when the Board had to decide whether Meta could permanently ban then US President Donald Trump from its platforms. Prior to his ban, the former President used Meta's services in ways plausibly contributing to the violent attack on the US Capitol on 6 January 2021. The Board noted that "[Trump's] posts were made during a dynamic and fluid period of ongoing violence. There was a clear immediate risk of harm to life, electoral integrity, and political participation. The violence at the Capitol started within an hour of the rally organized through the use of Facebook and other social media. . . . Analyzing these factors, the Board concludes that . . . Facebook's imposition of account-level restrictions on January 6 and the extension of those restrictions on January 7 was necessary and proportionate," Former President Trump's suspension (n 23).

Even though the Board did not directly invoke the "public emergency" argument in its Trump decision, functionally, its reasoning is similar. Because of the real-world harm that followed the President's remarks (several people died at the Capitol riot, not to speak of the lasting damage to American democracy), the company restricted official communication on political issues – even if uttered by a democratically elected head of state.

[34] Alleged Crimes in Raya Kobo (n 30) 8.3 (emphasis added).

The Board finds that in a country where there is an ongoing armed conflict and an assessed inability of governmental institutions to meet their human rights obligations under international law, Meta may restrict freedom of expression that it otherwise would not (see ICCPR Article 4 on derogations in times of *public emergencies*).[35]

In simple terms this means that Meta, a private, for-profit company declares a state of emergency vis-à-vis a government and may then restrict the communication of said government. And the core argument for this is the ICCPR. This is, from a conventional perspective a pretty remarkable argument. The traditional "who does what" in international law is that states ought to protect human rights and may, under very narrow circumstances, declare emergencies. In contrast, private corporations typically have little to do with neither, especially the latter.

From a human rights perspective, some might find the Board's expansive reasoning logical. For decades, scholars and activists have demanded stricter human rights responsibilities from nonstate actors, and especially private companies.[36] Indeed, as this book seeks to emphasize, thinking about the power of some corporations discursively triggers and theoretically warrants conceptualization in public law terms. It does so, incidentally, not because these companies should be likened to states, but because public law is fundamentally about anchoring organized power to the public will and interest – regardless of the historically contingent nature of that power.[37] Using international human rights law instead of Meta's own rules makes the Board appear less ceremonial and underscores the fact that the Board takes its control function seriously. This is, from a purely functional viewpoint, a positive sign. Who would not agree that powerful organizations should strive to mitigate the social and political perils that may arise from "improper" use of their products and services, especially in scenarios of possible ethnic cleansing or even genocide. It would be absurd to assert that private governance actors

35 Ibid 8.3 III (emphasis added).

36 For an overview over the debate see Andrew Clapham, *Human Rights Obligations of Non-State Actors* (Oxford University Press 2006); from the UN context see esp. John Ruggie, 'Report of the Special Representative of the Secretary-General on the Issue of Human Rights and Transnational Corporations and Other Business Enterprises, John Ruggie' (United Nations, Human Rights Council, 17th session 2011) A/HRC/17/31; and Astrid Sanders, 'The Impact of the "Ruggie Framework" and the "United Nations Guiding Principles on Business and Human Rights" on Transnational Human Rights Litigation' in Jena Martin and Karen E Bravo (eds.), *The Business and Human Rights Landscape* (Cambridge University Press 2015).

37 See in this context also n 334 on sovereignty in the previous chapter at 4.5.5.1.

like Meta should stay on the sidelines and thereby become complicit in government actions like inciting racial hatred or thwarting an election.

5.2.5 *Private Checks on Public Power?*

However, a bitter aftertaste remains. In front of these scenarios, we develop a better sense of how fundamentally Emulated Guardians may transform global governance. One does not need to invoke a certain German scholar to stress the implications of granting a private corporation the authority to decide what constitutes a "public emergency." Allowing Meta to declare a "public emergency," would allow the company to suspend its own commitment to respecting free expression in a specific context. It alleviates the company to what could be described as ultimately "sovereign" position, whereas individuals as much as states are subjects to the platform's unilateral emergency powers. In short, the Oversight Board's invoking of a "state of public emergency" shows how platforms incrementally become private *checks* on public power.

In principle, it is not so remarkable that private companies seek to sway and "discipline" public actors in situations of atrocities or other human rights violations. There were, for example, company boycotts of Apartheid-era South Africa or the Russian Federation after its full-scale invasion of Ukraine in 2022. Also, some American companies pledged to fulfill emission-reduction goals even though the Trump government pulled out of the Paris Accord. Yet, the situation described here appears different as it directly emulates a legal and quite direct, formalized method of disciplining public power. When online platforms restrict government communication, governments lose an important channel for communicating and conducting their policies. This can be viewed as a de facto, corporate, private check on public power, which is a remarkable development. In fact, one interviewed Board member mentioned – as already briefly discussed in the previous chapter – that they were "acutely aware of the implications of statements like that of a public emergency."[38]

So far, the Board has exercised this check in line with "liberal" expectations. It asserted that governments should not encourage ethnic hatred and/or impede the peaceful transfer of power. From a normative perspective, the Board arguably could hardly have decided otherwise. The Board's normative reasoning has perhaps even helped prevent future harm.

[38] Interview with Oversight Board Member (15 November 2022). For the discussion in the previous chapter see at 4.6.3.

However, this specific Emulated Guardian, the Oversight Board, is still a private body without a democratic mandate; Meta even more so. Both lack meaningful procedural or participatory connections to the people they are claiming to protect. Hence, Emulated Guardians risk delegating decisions to actors lacking the (legitimate) procedures, norms, and institutions originally tasked with making such decisions – that is, international law and governments.

However, would private complicity in alleged government terror be the better solution? Hardly so. Are despotic governments more legitimate decision-makers than private organizations, especially when the latter are nominally accountable to an Emulated Guardian? Hard to say. Do we have any guarantee that private power structures align themselves meaningfully with public law ideals or are they themselves – arguably hinging on the political preferences of their owner – prone to authoritarian tendencies? Properly answering those questions requires thoroughly deconstructing notions of public and private as well as the presumed higher normative legitimacy of ideals of public power which, this self-awareness seems warranted, is a presumption much more common in Europe than the United States. Would it be even desirable if state-oriented notions of international law block novel, adjudicative actors operating outside the conventional scope and mechanisms of international law?

The empowerment the Board derives from international human rights law vis-à-vis the company also, paradoxically, encapsulates the Board and, by extension, the company from regulatory intervention. Visualized in the classic pyramid of legal hierarchy, the Board tries to elevate the problems Meta faces to the international-law level, thereby decoupling Meta's governance from domestic or supranational regulation. This feeds into the narrative of successful self-regulation, pushing the company's administration-like practices (discursively) out of the reach of regulators. The Board's coy labeling of itself as a "non-judicial grievance mechanism" thus belies the reality that Meta retains decision-making power over what constitutes a "public emergency."[39] Such decision-making powers are not trivial or necessarily business-related but historically linked to the very heart of sovereignty.

There are no easy, and hardly definitive answers to these questions. All point to a rather fundamental reshuffle of power, form, and expectation. What seems for certain though is, to reiterate, that public law ideas – like

[39] Claimed COVID cure [2021] Oversight Board 2020-006-FB-FBR at 8.3; see also Meta, Corporate Human Rights Policy at 03, accessible via <https://perma.cc/EK3G-FC7E>.

individual rights adjudication, judicial review of administrative power, fundamental rights, and so on – increasingly escape the classic forms and mechanisms of public law. Yet, public law ideas, for their sheer sociocultural entrenchment, appear to remain a *leitmotif* of future discourse and practice shaping future governance institutions. Those future governance institutions, however, may build on past experiences with public law without being public legal actors themselves. This is a challenging, and at least from a scholarly perspective, vastly exciting prospect. We will discuss this outlook in more detail in the remaining pages of this book.

5.3 Authority

The second criterion determining the might of the two Emulated Guardians studied here is their adjudicative authority. Are the EU's out-of-court dispute settlement bodies and the Oversight Board authoritative enough to steer private governance operations into a more normatively desirable direction? In other words, can they exercise meaningful control vis-à-vis the corporate behemoths of our time? Can they – and, by extensions, Emulated Guardians as a class of actors – remedy rights violations and thereby advance justice for individuals? Do nonbinding decisions and recommendations foster accountability or merely sugar-coat unchanged practices?

As seen in the case studies, both Emulated Guardians have several means at their disposal to exert control and advance accountability. However, in comparison to traditional public law adjudication, these mechanisms are embryonic. ODSs' decisions are expressly nonbinding.[40] The Board's decisions "bind" Meta, but the Board makes so few decisions that any normative influence it has resides mainly in its nonbinding recommendations.[41] To put it bluntly, the authority of Emulated Guardians to formally adjudicate is minuscule. Yet, neither is formal mandate the only source of authority, nor are formal legal rules and decisions the only well of normativity. Broadly understood, the authority of accountability forums like Emulated Guardians depends on their efficacy – in which way whatsoever – to curb corporate misconduct and advance individual freedom vis-à-vis the dominant power structures of the digital sphere. The fact that Emulated Guardians, to an extent, mirror the judicial process does not necessarily mean that they are limited to the

[40] See at 3.6 and 3.7.
[41] See at 4.6.

same tools an, anyways idealized, understanding of courts would imagine, that is, communicate exclusively through binding decisions. Rather, Emulated Guardians offer various forms of external feedback and, inevitably, turn to society as main driver to force digital corporations to implement that feedback. If your feedback is not *legally* binding, you may still orchestrate enough public pressure to nonetheless lend it the weight of thousands or perhaps even millions of disgruntled individuals.

Both types of Emulated Guardians, the emerging rich variety of ODSs as well the Oversight Board, feature mechanisms that seem to buttress their nonbinding normative pronouncements vis-à-vis the private governance structures they control.[42] These could be costs, public pressure, and dialogue-based engagement.

We will focus here on the latter two elements. At the time of writing, we simply lack empirical data to assess the efficacy of the DSA's litigation fees in the context of Article 21; even more so the disciplinary efficacy of Commission fines under the DSA.

In contrast, we have plenty of real-world examples of attempts to rein in on Meta through dialogue and public pressure. Most examples are not necessarily promising. For example, whistleblower Frances Haugen, a former high-ranking Facebook executive, testified to Congress that

> The company's leadership knows ways to make Facebook and Instagram safer and won't make the necessary changes because they have put their immense profits before people. . . . [I]f there is one thing that I hope everyone takes away from these disclosures it is that Facebook chooses profit over safety every day.[43]

So, given such dire in-house perspectives, how persuasive and effective is Emulated Guardians' feedback to corporate actors really? As discussed in the third and fourth chapter, the Oversight Board and ODSs differ in many respects. The Oversight Board is a relatively small, unitary, and tightly run organization. It has a clear focus on structural deficits within Meta. It decides relatively few cases per year and its main normative output are not its decisions but its nonbinding recommendations, which it seeks to buttress by naming and shaming efforts and strategic communication. In contrast, ODSs will be very diverse. The four ODSs certified at the point of this writing all are vastly different.[44] They will reflect the diverse jurisdictional cultures from which they originate. Being a business themselves, ODSs must decide as many cases as possible.

[42] See at 3.7 and 4.6.

[43] 'Statement of Frances Haugen' <https://perma.cc/3QN6-JMY4>.

[44] See in detail at 3.8.

They are not designed to orchestrate extensive naming and shaming campaigns or engage in other forms of strategic communication. Rather, the key factor behind Article 21 DSA is mass. The EU envisages simply so many cases that platforms, at some point, simply "have to" comply. The crux is, however, whether enough users will indeed play along as it is unclear whether the prospect of nonbinding procedures with unclear effects indeed motivates enough people to ramp up pressure vis-à-vis platforms.

Therefore, this section investigates two things. First, we assess whether Meta indeed changes its practice based on the Oversight Board's feedback. Second, we question, from a more theoretical angle, whether the European social media users are likely to be altruistic enough to effectuate ODSs, which, lacking binding decision-making powers, might not be able to remedy all those individual grievances.

5.3.1 *Does Meta Care for the Oversight Board?*

So, does Meta take the Board seriously enough to adopt its recommendations, accept its normative guidance, and ultimately subject itself to the Board's emulation of public law adjudication?

Referring to "key audiences," the Oversight Board's decisions have been examined by stakeholders and legal academics and, as we have seen, Meta has verifiably followed some of its recommendations. Clearly, Meta's lack of transparency as to how far it really applies with the Board's recommendations is still a problem. One interviewee at the Board, for example, said they thought many people at Meta "do not care about the Board."[45] The shifts in corporate policy and personnel in early 2025, aimed at aligning Meta with the second Trump administration – including the outright denunciation of previous content moderation as "censorship" – do not inspire much confidence that Meta's rank and file will show greater regard for the Board in the near future. A particularly dispiriting aspect of this policy shift was, arguably, the manner in which it unfolded. When Zuckerberg decided to ban then-US President Trump from Meta following his use of the platform during the storming of the Capitol on January 6, 2021, he quickly engaged with the Oversight Board to outline the rules for removing high-profile figures. Yet now, as Meta scales back enforcement and revises its policies, he appears to have bypassed the Board entirely. Moreover, given the Board's own assessment that the company had only verifiably fully put in place fifty-seven out of 288 of

[45] Interview with Oversight Board Staffer 6 (23 November 2022).

its recommendations by November 2024, we cannot talk of meaningful accountability yet.[46] However, the fifty-seven recommendations the Board deemed *had* been verifiably fully implemented are a significant improvement compared to the sixteen recommendations in that category in the first quarter of 2022.[47]

Figure 5.1 shows another trend worth monitoring. That is the decline in appeal numbers, which have steadily decreased since early 2022. The implications of this decline are unclear. On the one hand, it could either indicate user disillusionment with the Oversight Board – perhaps due to the near-zero chances of their cases being adjudicated or Meta's inconsistent implementation of the Board's recommendations. Assuming the average user is less aware of the developments surrounding the Board than the somewhat niche group of people studying it, the former explanation seems more plausible.

On the other hand, the decline might reflect a normalization of user interest, as users gain a clearer understanding of the Board's purpose and the initial hype – especially following the Trump decision, which likely drove the mid-2021 to early-2022 spike – gradually subsides. If so, this is not necessarily a bad thing. Fewer appeals could, in fact, simplify the

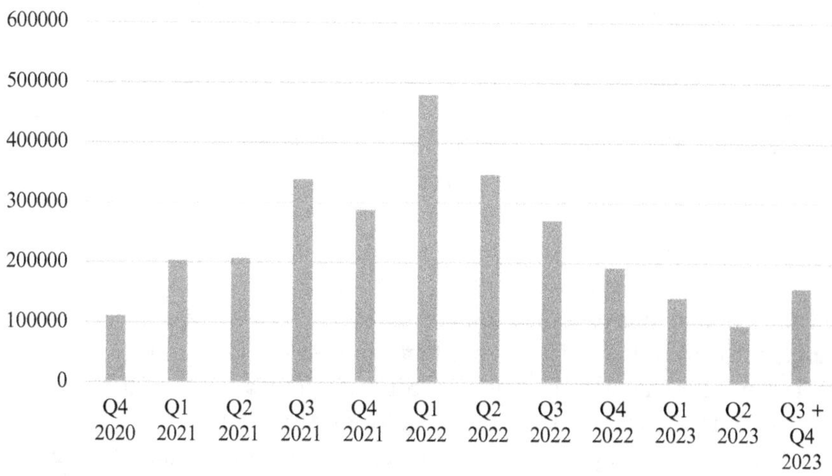

Figure 5.1 User appeals to the Oversight Board (2020–2023)

[46] Oversight Board 'Recommendation Tracker' as of November 2024, accessible via <https://perma.cc/4M6Y-WX7Q>.

[47] Transparency Report Q 1 2022, p 21, accessible via <https://perma.cc/G4YL-S68T>.

process of selecting cases, a task Oversight Board staffers jokingly refer to as "fishing mode."

Nonetheless, the Oversight Board's unique strength has always been its ability to generate highly targeted discourses. As it stands, it remains the only Emulated Guardian with the research capabilities, public relations influence, and academic and policy networks necessary to rally global public support for specific policy reforms at Meta. To sustain this role, a dramatic drop in appeal numbers would be problematic. That said, even if the Board received a low six-figure number of cases annually, its members would still have plenty of material to work with.

To me, the key impression is that the Board quickly identified and began establishing the mechanisms that would be necessary to assume a (partially) controlling role over Meta – it refers to external legitimate rules, dialogically engages with the company and drums up and takes on public discourse around specific issues that it then channels into recommendations. Thanks to the Board's legal experts and its overall adjudicative perception, the Board has been able to do what many other adjudicators had done before it: engage in the slow, incremental construction of authority vis-à-vis the power structure it controls. The "strength" of adjudicatory authority escapes simple scales or indicators but must be assessed on a context-sensitive, case-by-case basis. For the Oversight Board, that context could be better – especially regarding Meta's presumably underdeveloped "accountability culture" (see below at Section 5.4).

However, so far, it could also be a whole lot worse. Entirely ceremonial corporate legitimacy stunts usually do not cost several hundred million dollars and hire substantial amounts of serious people, many of whom elite-educated lawyers. Of course, a big check and a few Ivy League lawyers do not make a potent guardian. But roughly 100 highly qualified, motivated people, who operate largely independently in their day-to-day, and who are backed by more than a quarter billion dollars for several years while under intense global scrutiny to hold Meta accountable, indeed sound like the ingredients to potentially shake things up. To compare, the annual budget of the International Court of Justice amounts to roughly 30 million dollars these days, that of the European Court of Justice, which employs more than 2,300 people to almost 500 million euros, and the European Court of Human Rights has roughly 75 million euros to spend annually.[48]

[48] International Court of Justice, 'Report of the International Court of Justice, 1 August 2023- 31 July 2024, A/79/4' para 300 <https://perma.cc/PX8M-5HJK>; European Court of Justice, 'Annual Report 2023' 16 <https://perma.cc/H7R9-ZKUD>; European Court of Human Rights, 'ECHR Budget 2024 (Press Release)' <https://perma.cc/6685-KQNP>.

Clearly, from Meta's perspective, there is a ceremonial element to the Board. But from the Board itself, whose day-to-day operations seem to function (with some exceptions) largely independent from Meta,[49] neither this research nor other reporting indicated any serious penchant for timidity when it comes to Meta. How this would unfold if Meta were indeed to scale back large parts of its content moderation remains uncertain. Either way, for various reasons outlined in this and the next chapter Emulated Guardians like the Oversight Board must be seen as a first step on a long journey toward comprehensive protection of individual freedoms and the public interest in a world of global governance that seems increasingly dominated by vastly powerful corporations controlled by a handful of men. Whether the Oversight Board and Meta will ultimately be the key players in the broader effort to reclaim public accountability for private, unilateral power structures like digital corporations remains to be seen.

The fact that the Board is – and will remain – bereft of any public and democratic mandate makes it unusual in the otherwise crowded arena of globally active, individual rights-focused adjudicators. International adjudicators in the traditional sense of the word originate from treaties or other expressions of sovereign will.[50] Private international adjudicators can also come into being by the consent of two disputing parties, for the purpose of dealing with contractual disputes – not the administrification of private governance. Other specialized adjudicators like the Court of Arbitration for Sport (CAS) or the dispute settlement system at the International Corporation for Assigned Names and Numbers (ICANN) also are only a semi-good fit as neither of them customarily deal with controlling the rulemaking and rule enforcement of massive, administration-like operations like Meta's private governance.[51]

Whether the Board succeeds in combining public pressure with dialogue-based oversight remains to be seen – and will largely depend on Meta executives' internal approach to the Board. The Board's most realistic path forward may be to take up activists' ideas and demands for reform. In this way, Board members' reasoning, decisions, and recommendations may become a valuable normative point of reference and

[49] See at 4.3.3.

[50] For a theoretical overview highlighting also other sources of normative legitimacy than state consent see Armin von Bogdandy and Ingo Venzke, *In wessen Namen? Internationale Gerichte in Zeiten globalen Regierens* (Suhrkamp 2014).

[51] For an overview see John G White, 'ICANN's Uniform Domain Name Dispute Resolution Policy in Action' (2001) 16 Berkeley Technology Law Journal 229.

"legitimacy asset" for factions within the company.[52] These factions could use Board recommendations to force through governance changes that they would otherwise not be able to.[53] Referring to Eleanor Westney's study of Japan's emulations in the Meiji era, we recall that a "foreign organizational model may be used to legitimate changes that are desired by the innovators, but which require justification by the appeal to an outside model."[54] Using the Oversight Board and its decisions as an external point of reference may hence be a legitimizing factor for power struggles within the company. Whether this transpires remains to be seen – and will be verifiable only after some time and only with the help of sufficient data and transparency from the company. As yet, we only have anecdotal evidence pointing to this possibility, like the story about a powerful Meta executive (who helped design the Board), who now heads the company's content policy unit, increasingly considering the Board's (potential) view of the company's decisions.[55]

Yet we do not know how representative these indications for Meta's responsiveness to Board recommendations are. Judging from publicly disclosed material and accounts of the company's internal decision-making by Frances Haugen, we might put a (big) question mark on whether all Meta's departments are indeed that welcoming of the Board.[56] These observations are not mutually exclusive since the above-mentioned Meta executive is arguably one of the people at Meta "supporting" the Board; these are perhaps not representative but could, for example, be presented as such to a journalist writing a piece about the Board for a news story.[57] Admittedly, this scenario seems humbler than

[52] See the statement by an interviewed activist at 4.2.3.

[53] The concept of "legitimacy assets" refers to communicative strategies and performative constructions of expertise, tradition, etc. employed by actors in complex, multi-stakeholder governance process to ascertain what Venzke and Mendes call "relative authority." See Ingo Venzke and Joana Mendes, 'The Idea of Relative Authority in European and International Law' (2018) 16 International Journal of Constitutional Law 75.

[54] Eleanor Westney, *Imitation and Innovation The Transfer of Western Organizational Patterns to Meiji Japan* (Harvard University Press 1987) 27.

[55] Steven Levy, 'Inside Meta's Oversight Board: 2 Years of Pushing Limits' (*Wired*, 8 November 2022) <https://perma.cc/SUP5-RQCV>.

[56] In her written testimony to congress, former Meta executive Frances Haugen argued that the company would choose "profit over safety" every single time, cf. 'Statement of Frances Haugen' (n 43).

[57] That executive is Monika Bickert, a Harvard-educated lawyer who served in various leading policy-related positions at Meta and Facebook. Bickert also appears recurrently in Klonick's earlier accounts on the development of content moderation at Meta and the Oversight Board.

commonly held perceptions of Herculean judicial guardians striving to control power cleaning out the Augean stables of corporate over-reach.[58] But from a sociolegal perspective, the mechanisms that put transnational adjudication to work are often multifaceted, ranging from formal and idealistic aspects to self-interested horse-trading.[59] Hence, such slow, incremental expansion of authority is normal for novel adjudicators.

5.3.2 *Performative Authority*

Authority does not necessarily derive from mandate. It may derive from perception. This leads us to perhaps the ultimate question regarding the Board's authority: does the Board manage to performatively build its authority vis-à-vis the company (and public regulators) through appropriating public law symbolism, its legalese, its references to rights, international law and courts, and overall appearance?

If the Board fails to further build its authority through such discursive, rather than formal legal means it will likely remain largely ceremonial. Skeptics as well as optimists could both point to developments to back up their views.

Crucially, some of Meta's highest echelons (claim to) support the Board. In a company whose controlling shareholder and CEO is a single individual, that person's support is key. However, it is unclear how widespread the support for the Oversight Board is at Meta. Here, we reach a clear methodological limitation of my empirical work, as I did not have the opportunity to investigate empirically these matters within Meta.[60] However, one Oversight Board staffer confided that, in their personal opinion, some people at Meta might "not care for the Board."[61] How representative such skepticism toward the Board was for Meta executives remains unclear. Yet Meta seems to operate in an untransparent way in its relationship with the

[58] For the latter see famously Ronald Dworkin, 'Hard Cases' in *Taking Rights Seriously* (Harvard University Press 1977) 105.

[59] For example, one key factor widely considered contributing to the success of EU law's preliminary reference procedure was lower courts' valorization through direct dealings with the ECJ – bypassing their superior domestic courts, Joseph HH Weiler, 'A Quiet Revolution: The European Court of Justice and Its Interlocutors' (1994) 26 Comparative Political Studies 397, 523.

[60] In 2021, I reached out to several current and former Meta employees who deal or dealt with the Oversight Board but to no avail. In 2022, I decided not to broaden the scope of potential interviewees to Meta as this would have been beyond time and resource capacities. Empirical research into how Meta implements those decisions would be a fruitful avenue for further research.

[61] Interview with Oversight Board Staffer 6 (n 45).

Board. In one instance, and to the "disappoint[ment]" of the Board, Meta withdrew a request for the Board to draw up a policy advisory statement regarding the company's handling of content in the context of Russia's invasion of Ukraine.[62] Meta executives seem not to grant the Board access to internal data to verify whether it implements the Board's recommendations, as the company claims to do. Further, Meta only grudgingly offers the Board relevant technical assistance to assess the technical context of specific cases.[63] At least in one instance, the company flagrantly lied to the Board – its denial that it had done so was later debunked by a series of leaks to an American newspaper.[64] Therefore, it can be validly claimed that the Board remains largely ceremonial – despite its sophisticated naming and shaming efforts, its well-equipped and capable team, and its crucial turn to human rights law. If the controlled organization simply does not acknowledge a guardian's oversight, the guardian cannot be a meaningful control mechanism. Lacking a rule of law-style enforcement system, then normative output controls the company as much as the company voluntarily subjects to this control. This situation epitomizes what Meyer and Rowan described as a decoupling of ceremonial façades conforming to popularized "myths" from an organization's actual work requirements.[65]

Yet, despite well-warranted caution, not all seems lost. I believe entirely dismissing phenomena like the Oversight Board on the ground that they are not yet as effective as we would like them to be underestimates two aspects, which, in the long run might give reason to hope. On the one hand, one can hardly overestimate the challenge of the task Emulated Guardians face. Their work is not about improving content moderation (this alone would be phenomenally difficult), but the challenge is to fundamentally reform the organizational structure, culture, and, by

[62] Ibid; Interview with Oversight Board Staffer 4 (27 May 2022). See further Oversight Board, 'Protecting Freedom of Expression and Human Rights in Ukraine and Russia (Press Release)' (May 2022) <https://perma.cc/59Z2-WLKY>.

[63] An example for the latter is the company's reluctance to grant the Board access to a tool called "CrowdTangle" which would have allowed the Board to analyze how many people see and interact with Facebook and Instagram posts. Yet, as one interviewee claimed, the Board had to go wrestle the company at painstaking lengths to eventually get access to the tool. Interview with Oversight Board Staffer 6 (n 107); see also Levy (n 55).

[64] This concerned the prevalence of the so-called "Cross Check" system, which allowed the accounts of famous people, such as then US President Donald Trump, to communicate in ways otherwise prohibited. A prominent example was his statement "when the looting starts, the shooting starts," which was widely considered dangerous in a situation of civil unrest and could be read as thinly veiled encouragement to vigilantism, and given the specific context, even racialized lynching. See further Levy (n 55).

[65] See Meyer Rowan (n 3) 356 et seq.

extension, economic rationale of humongous digital corporations. This is incredibly complex. Unsurprisingly, no single actor could do that. Fundamentally reforming the power dynamics in the digital economy requires a multipronged approach.

Second and this reflects the bit of public law idealism left in me, one should not underestimate the performative power that societal imaginaries still bestow on adjudicatory bodies and public law symbolism. Remember, public law is relevant here not because these companies are "like states." Public law is relevant because it is a well-tested and widely supported set of tools to tie organized power structures to majoritarian will, egalitarian principles, and the public good. Public law, that is constitutional, administrative, and civil rights law, is not about the state per se – it is about controlling organized power. If that organized power manifests beyond the state, we might as well think about how to make the ideas of public law work in these private, profit-oriented contexts.

The more the Board is seen as a credible, serious, and (at least partly) legitimate adjudicator, the more likely it would be to become one eventually. A neo-institutionalist approach would suggest that Meta set up the Board because it wanted to conform to certain societal institutions, namely that of individual rights adjudication.[66] Yet public expectations do not necessarily cease once a new organization has been set up to somehow remedy these rights – institutionalized expectations toward Meta might eventually demand results. If the Board manages to capitalize on these institutionalized images and expectations and become ever more like an adjudicator, effectuating the Board's decisions and recommendations will become a source of legitimation for the company. The Board can, through performance, "de-ceremonize," or, in Evelyn Douek's framing, "de-theater" itself. Eventually, accepting the Board's authority might, eventually, be in the company's own interests and this development would thereby, reflexively, performatively construct and reaffirm the Board's authority. This would indeed be a revolutionary – and perhaps unlikely – development. But who could have foreseen many of the developments we consider natural today?

Similarly, the general perception of the Board appears to be shifting from an early lack of appreciation and toward a grudging respect by human rights organizations, academics, and public bodies like the UN

[66] See in general at 2.4 and 4.2.

High Commissioner for Human Rights.[67] Evelyn Douek, a vocal critic who (arguably accurately) declared the company's announcement of a "supreme court" an authoritarian legitimacy-grab, later said that "[p]eople thought it would be a total fiasco. But in some real ways, it has brought some accountability to Facebook."[68] The reasons for these minor successes, lie in many of the discourses of our era – namely juridification, judicialization, and the sociopolitical importance of courts, rights, and adjudication, as well as narratives about individual agency. The following section will look at the practical problems arising from some of these aspects, most notably the DSA's novel adjudicators that promise only circumscribed enforcement prospects, as well as EU policymakers' apparently continuing belief that individuals are easy to mobilize for the greater good, even bereft of immediate rewards. The Board's dwindling appeals docket may be a warning sign in this regard. It also remains to be seen how the second presidency of Donald Trump, along with the internal policy shifts at Meta announced in January 2025, will affect the Board. However, these developments should be assessed with nuance, rather than through quick or fatalistic conclusions.

5.3.3 *Are Europeans Altruist Enough to Make Article 21 DSA Work?*

The previous section suggested that the Oversight Board has the potential to gradually develop into a more-than-ceremonial adjudicator. This section now examines whether ODSs also have access to paths that could lead to meaningful accountability. We learned about plans of some people to equally performatively expand the authority of ODSs through qualitative reasoning and close cooperation with legal academia, a strategy also not foreign to the Oversight Board. However, lawyers in general and legal academics in particular perhaps overestimate the real-world efficacy of their profession. As argued above, even if some ODSs become widely

[67] For example, in February 2022, the Oversight Board submitted a report to the OHCHR outlining its practice, Oversight Board, 'The Oversight Board: Operationalizing the UN Guiding Principles on Business and Human Rights: Submission to the Office of the High Commissioner for Human Rights, United Nations on the Practical Application of the UNGPs to the Activities in Technology Companies' (2022) <https://perma.cc/PS65-ENNM>.
For positive, human-rights focused evaluations of the Board in the literature see e.g. Meier and Golia (n 27) 40–41; Helfer and Land (n 27) 51–63; Levy (n 55); Kate Klonick, 'Inside the Making of Facebook's Supreme Court' *New Yorker* (12 February 2021) <https://perma.cc/44Y7-S8VH>; Rishi Gulati, 'Meta's Oversight Board and Transnational Hybrid Adjudication: What Consequences for International Law' KFG Working Paper Series No. 53 March 2022 19 et seq.

[68] Levy (n 55).

accepted, they remain persuasive rather than binding accountability forums. Their normative force will hinge on the depth of their public support. Therefore, the decisive stakeholders for accountability in this scenario are EU citizens. Only if people across Europe become "active" – perhaps altruistic would be a better word – might the DSA's enforcement mechanisms work.[69] In short, one contextual factor may build ODSs' authority, while two contextual aspects may quickly undermine it.

First to the more optimistic aspect. Compared to Meta's Oversight Board, ODSs have one great authority-conferring and legitimizing advantage. That is that ODSs are the product of a democratic process. Out-of-court dispute settlement bodies are based on an EU regulation and are certified by the relevant authorities at the Member State level.[70] The European Commission arguably cares a great deal about making the DSA a success as its own output legitimacy depends on it. In interviews, representatives of three already certified ODSs – ADROIT, User Rights, and the Appeals Centre Europe – highlighted that they had the impression that the Commission will throw its weight behind them, even though their decisions are formally nonbinding.[71] The fact that ODSs spring from democratic, supranational lawmaking instead of from untransparent management efforts situates ODSs in a different sphere than the Oversight Board.[72] They face fewer legitimacy challenges as they are based on a public mandate as well as being certified by states and closely monitored by regulators. Moreover, EU lawmakers never intended to formally replace traditional judicial redress with ODSs, which are intended to be complementary to judicial redress in the Member States outside the DSA.[73] Ideally, these bodies will take some of the burden off Member State courts and provide a newer and more easily accessible path to justice. Hence, from a norm-oriented public law perspective, ODSs that base their decisions on EU and Member State law and whose decisions are (voluntarily) implemented would come close to the ideal of an Emulated Guardian. They could, for example, seek to apply a legitimated (though only in the EU), external normative framework to digital corporations' content moderation, remedy millions of individual rights violations and push companies toward improving their governance practices. If this

[69] cf. Martin Husovec, 'Will the DSA Work?' (*Verfassungsblog*, 9 November 2022) <https://perma.cc/FV8G-UPHZ>.

[70] See at Chapter 3, regarding certification especially at 3.4.2.

[71] Interview with ADROIT Founder (30 October 2024); Interview with User Rights Co-Founder (25 October 2024); Interview with Appeals Centre Director (1 November 2024).

[72] Regarding the importance of a democratic footing of international adjudicators see Bogdandy and Venzke (n 50) 215 et seq.

[73] See at 3.2 and 3.3.

were indeed to transpire, it would provide meaningful accountability for digital corporations in Europe. And yet, because of the expected limitations of this model, especially the fact that EU and Member State law will only play a minuscule role when compared to the platforms' own terms of service, this idealized version of out-of-court dispute settlement bodies might not transpire.

However, despite these presumed setbacks, ODSs could offer what, from an individual's perspective, would be a key benefit compared either to the Oversight Board or to traditional courts. Out-of-court dispute settlement bodies will be much more accessible than traditional courts. They will also, unlike the Oversight Board, decide on (almost) every appeal brought to them.[74] Therefore, ODSs might in theory broaden access to justice in online-speech related disputes in the EU.[75] Given the sheer size of content moderation machineries and the structural, rather than individual root causes of recurring fundamental rights violations, the EU's focus on individual justice rather than structural reform seems overall questionable.

The question then is whether platforms will implement (hundreds, thousands, millions of) ODS decisions even though these will not be binding. As explained in Chapter 3, I am deeply skeptical as to whether Article 21 of the DSA will inflict heavy enough costs on platforms to incentivize the latter to make substantive and positive changes to their operations.[76] In addition and given the expected diversity of ODSs across Member States, we should not assume that orchestrated naming and shaming campaigns will exert pressure on platforms to enforce ODS decisions. Whether dismissing individual decisions may generate enough public outcry to nudge social media platforms into obeying ODS decisions is also doubtful. In a similar vein, interviewed staffers from the European Parliament, who were involved in legislating the ODSs into existence, voiced skepticism as to whether these economic incentives would work – especially for very large online platforms.[77] Even the academic who helped the Commission draft its proposal for ODSs has recently called the version that survived the legislative process mere "expert panels."[78]

[74] They can, for example, dismiss cases that were already decided, cf. Article 21(2) subpara 2 DSA.

[75] For an introduction, coming, however, more from a contractual, consumer protection perspective see Richard E Susskind, *Online Courts and the Future of Justice* (Oxford University Press 2019) 95 et seq.

[76] See at 3.7.4.

[77] Interview with European Parliament, Staffer 2 (n 11); European Parliament, Staffer 1, Email to the Author (on file with the author) (17 November 2021).

[78] For the latter see Husovec (n 69).

Further, ODSs focus on individual justice paired with the absence of authority to bindingly remedy rights violations risks *demotivating* appellants. It is unclear whether there will be a steady stream of people applying for dispute resolution to fuel the DSA's cost-inflicting machinery. As Husovec argued, the DSA depends on "active individuals" as well as societal structures that would help push platforms toward improved governance.[79] Yet such structures "need to be built bottom-up and sometimes locally in each Member State. If their creation fails, the regulatory promises might turn out to be a glorious aspiration."[80] As of now we cannot reasonably assess whether such structures will emerge and whether people will indeed become active in demanding their rights are enforced. What we do know, however, is that given ODSs' current authority, rights enforcement remains a euphemism. The DSA's ODSs cannot *enforce* users' rights in any immediate way. Interviewed Parliament staffers openly questioned whether individuals would be motivated in sufficient numbers – especially once they learn that ODSs cannot guarantee *binding* remedies to successful appellants.[81]

Alternative strategies for how to enable ODSs bodies to help generate naming and shaming campaigns were not discussed while they were being legislated for.[82] After all, until pretty much the end of the legislative procedure ODS decisions should have been binding. Yet, as analyzed in Chapter 3, a concerted effort of some Member States, activist groups, and industry actors advocated gutting the authority of ODSs. This is, by the way, not necessarily a bad thing. Vesting those bodies with the authority to bindingly adjudicate the online free expression of hundreds of millions of Europeans without having devised any procedural law or a mechanism to maintain jurisprudential coherence between those bodies would have likely ended in chaos.

Now, it seems that the DSA may itself risk partially succumbing to ceremony. Simply put, the DSA – or especially the political discourse surrounding it – might have overpromised compared to what it actually delivers. At first sight, some DSA provisions apparently promise to protect fundamental rights online. However, if one takes a closer look,

[79] Ibid.

[80] Ibid.

[81] Interview with European Parliament, Staffer 2 (n 11); European Parliament, Staffer 1 (n 77).

[82] A possible alternative route might be using the Digital Services Coordinators' reports, see in detail 3.7.3. Source of the descriptive statement: Interview with European Parliament, Staffer 2 (n 70).

they fail to set forth an effective remedy for violations of those rights. Once people begin to understand this, the whole idea of a mass of appeals to ODSs in the hope that they will inflict costs that would motivate platforms to change their rules might burst like a bubble. Here, the continuously declining appeal numbers to the Oversight Board are a warning sign. If even the well-staffed and loaded Oversight Board attracts less than a quarter of the cases it did just two years ago, how are we expecting a diverse and arguably quite chaotic ecosystem of ODSs fare better? Especially so as the practical relevance of these ODSs will arguably hinge on how easy it is to access them. The easiest way to do so will be buttons and automatic redirections on social media websites themselves. How this potentially concentrates markets around several particular ODSs – especially the Appeals Centre – and if this constitutes a problem from an independence perspective remains to be seen.

To be fair, at the time of this writing, the DSA just became applicable. As with the Oversight Board, many things might change once more ODSs become operational and the few that already are have a few years of practice under their belt. Depending on the staff they employ, the publicity they seek, and the quality of the decisions they issue, ODSs may fare better than their current institutional design would suggest. As we saw in the third chapter, the creativity unleashed by the business opportunity to start an ODS and make it profitable by designing a large language model might yield positive results – if not for European internet users at least as general experiments of algorithmic justice systems.[83] We will likely see great variety among ODSs, with some managing to eke out incremental progress toward functional accountability while others remain largely on the ceremonial side.

5.4 Culture

We have seen that both Emulated Guardians show mixed results regarding their normative framework, putting them on the more ceremonial side of the scale, although the Oversight Board, since its turn to human rights, is slightly nearer to the scale's "control" endpoint. As the previous two sections showed, Emulated Guardians' success largely depends on factors beyond their immediate control. Another key factor, and the third

[83] See in detail at 3.8.

constitutive element of any functional accountability regime, is a *culture* of accountability. As Jack Balkin argued, "[s]ocial media companies have to become key institutions for fostering a healthy public sphere. They can't just serve economic incentives. They have to adopt public-regarding professional norms related to the important public function that they serve in the digital public sphere."[84]

Balkin is right. But infusing such "public" norms into private corporate cultures will prove fiendishly difficult. Establishing an accountability culture would require habitualized bona fide application of the normative framework by the guardian, public demand for said control, and internal adaptation on the part of companies. Given Emulated Guardians' recent emergence, evaluating such an emerging accountability culture necessarily remains cursory. Pointing out, however, that accountability culture is decisive for the success of any Emulated Guardian – any guardian institution frankly – appears mandatory. I conclude this chapter by briefly reflecting on the internal and external elements of a culture of accountability and examining the first signs of accountability that have emerged from the case studies.

5.4.1 *Emerging Accountability Cultures*

The notion of accountability cultures refers to a minimum of public support for, and the institutional pattern of, bona fide practices, expectations, customs, and traditions regarding the accountability of administration-like power.[85] Accountability cultures develop over time,

[84] Jack M Balkin, 'How to Regulate (and Not Regulate) Social Media' (2021) 1 Journal of Free Speech Law 71, 82.

[85] See for example the work of Tarunabh Khaitan who highlights the role of "political cultures" in enabling and restricting fourth branch institutions (which could be understood as closely related to Emulated Guardians as they also shall be independent and, in one way or the other, safeguard the public interest). Khaitan highlights the performative effects of accountability cultures: "Political cultures matter a great deal. Providing institutional guarantees in a relatively stable, peaceful, egalitarian, affluent society with a high degree of political trust and low levels of corruption is likely to be a lot easier than in a post-conflict transitional context marred by poverty, inequality, and mistrust. If anything, effective design matters more rather than less in the latter context. In either case, it is not enough that the initial design of the institution is credible – it must remain credible over time. A guarantor institution can, therefore, become an ordinary regulatory agency by losing credibility, and a formerly ruling-party-controlled regulator could, over time, acquire enough effectiveness and credibility to qualify as a guarantor institution," Tarunabh Khaitan, 'Guarantor Institutions' (2021) 16 Asian Journal of Comparative Law 40, 45, see also at 53.

closely link to societal institutions, and transcend legal obligations.[86] They require structured and habitualized practices paired with the expectations these practices produce.[87] Culture, in this broader sense, does not refer to traditional "cultural" phenomena like literature or music, but rather to the comprehensive institutionalization and symbolism of a guardian's accountability practice.[88] It includes an organization's practice of rules as much as the relevant public's expectations regarding this practice. In this conception, culture includes *internal* and *external* perspectives on adjudication. Adjudication as an accountability mechanism is therefore both individual – because it deals with individual rights – as well as public-facing in that it lets people assess whether a given power structure is acts accountable.[89]

This internal–external aspect should not, however, make majority opinion an absolute. It just points out the salience of public opinion

[86] In some contexts, the term culture comes with baggage. It can be used exclusionary. As Adorno noted, culture may still convey "brutal claims to societal power." I do not refer to such an exclusionary meaning here but use the term "culture" to highlight a holistic, sociocultural perspective on accountability in practice. For the quote see Theodor W Adorno, *Gesammelte Schriften 9.2 Soziologische Schriften II (Zweite Hälfte)* (Suhrkamp 1975) 276 (translation by the author).

[87] I use the term "(accountability) culture" instead of "practice" as the latter already closely relates to my understanding of rules and authority. To understand a rule, one must look at the practice of it, not only its letter. To build authority, adjudicatory practice is crucial. Peter Cane, on whose three-pronged distinction of control systems I structured this chapter, instead speaks of "practices" and not of culture. Cane argues that said control practices refer to "non-normative patterns of behaviour or, in other words, the way control institutions in fact perform their controlling functions, and the ways they interact with each other and with the . . . agencies they can control." Culture also puts a bigger emphasis on societal expectations and, to speak with Bourdieu, its structure-making, eventually habitualizing effect.

For Cane's account see (n 1) 2 et seq. For a reconstruction of what could be described as transnational law's specific culture see e.g. Martti Koskenniemi, 'Performing Legal Expertise: Reflections on the Construction of Transnational Authority' in Emilia Korkea-aho and Päivi Leino-Sandberg (eds.), *Law, Legal Expertise and EU Policy-Making* (Cambridge University Press 2022). For the importance of 'culture' in guiding actors' behavior see e.g. R Jepperson and J Meyer, 'Reflections on Part II: Institutional Theory' in John W Meyer and Ronald L Jepperson (eds.), *Institutional Theory: The Cultural Construction of Organizations, States, and Identities* (Cambridge University Press 2021) 130 et seq.

[88] Albeit I borrow from Bourdieu, e.g., the concepts of practice, structure, and habitualization (not habitus in a strict sense as I do not study the personal behavior of people), my understanding of "a culture of accountability" is not synonymous with culture as used in most of Bourdieu's work dealing with societal distinction based on "cultural capital." For the latter see e.g. Pierre Bourdieu, *Distinction* (Harvard University Press 1984) 260 et seq.

[89] cf. for actors' embeddedness to individual and collective cultural frames: Jepperson and Meyer (n 87) 129 et seq.

when it comes to motivating organizations to act in certain ways. Hence, no particular type of culture (like a rule of law-inspired culture of judicial review) can be a one-size-fits-all solution.[90] Varying sets of rules and guardians work differently depending on the context. Ombudspersons, for example, are often found in centralized systems of government as in the UK or Australia and are embedded in cultures of transparency and public accountability common in Scandinavian countries. The establishment of a European Ombudsman for a highly diffused European governance system lacking such an "ombudspersons culture" has hence been seen by some commentators as puzzling.[91] And indeed, as we had to painfully learn from, not all EU institutions indeed "care" all too much about the European Ombudsman. Comparable experiments transplanting the Ombudsperson model into the US administrative state have likewise produced mixed results.

In other words, institutions, rules, and cultures necessarily reflect context. Cultural studies-inspired perspectives on law have argued that looking at the cultural underpinning reproduced by legal institutions helps us gain insights into these institutions.[92] To turn this around, this means that guardians will not be able to function "properly" if they operate in, and with, a culture opposed to their mission. Rules and institutions require bona fide practices that truly aim to control administration-like power.[93]

The effectiveness of an accountability system, correspondingly, hinges not just on formal mechanisms but also on cultural, informal, and societal dynamics. A guardian's cultural alignment with, and influence on, a governance constellation's institutional framework often outweighs doctrinal analyses of formal structures or the predictive allure of principal-agent and rational-actor theories. As Martin Shapiro demonstrated in his comparative study of courts – from US courts to Islamic tribunals to arbitral systems in imperial China – functional guardians adapt reflexively to their cultural environments. Imposing guardians that

90 See for a reflection on positionality at 1.5.

91 Peter Cane, 'A Framework for Historical Comparison of Control of National, Supranational and Transnational Public Power' in Susan Rose-Ackerman, Blake Emerson and Peter L Lindseth (eds.), *Comparative Administrative Law* (2nd ed., Edward Elgar Publishing 2017) 611.

92 Paul W Kahn, *The Cultural Study of Law: Reconstructing Legal Scholarship* (University of Chicago Press 1999).

93 Similar arguments have been recently made about the robustness of constitutional regimes for preventing democratic backsliding, see Steven Levitsky and Daniel Ziblatt, *How Democracies Die* (Penguin Books 2019). For a historical perspective see Benjamin Carter Hett, *The Death of Democracy: Hitler's Rise to Power and the Downfall of the Weimar Republic* (Windmill Books 2019).

lack this cultural resonance onto governance systems, however well intentioned, tends to end in failure.[94] In much, the same vein, Karen Alter, Laurence Helfer, and Mikael Madsen explained international adjudicators' sometimes-sluggish path toward authority in terms of struggles to adapt to contexts and cultures. International adjudicators "are for the most part new institutions. As such, their rulings may conflict with, and seek to displace, well-established or assumed interpretations of legal rules or social norms. Displacing entrenched ideas and practices is always difficult."[95] Indeed, despite the internet's breakneck speed, governance reforms often move slowly, grinding through overlapping spheres of authority, endless contestations, and persistent uncertainties.

5.4.2 *Globalizing Accountability Culture*

The previous section pointed to the relevance of cultural factors for Emulated Guardians to function as meaningful controllers of power structures. Given Emulated Guardians' relatively recent origins, expecting them to have already developed "cultural" aspects in their practices may be premature. But Emulated Guardians' very existence points to an underlying cultural shift in societal expectations that private governance should be held to account. Indeed, the speed of events is striking. In 2018, Kate Klonick criticized platforms' lack of accountability in the Harvard Law Review.[96] That same year, Meta announced its plans for the Oversight Board and, while many countries were entering a second Covid lockdown in late 2020, the European Commission published its proposal for a comprehensive regulation advancing accountability for these platforms. Related regulatory plans have also been presented in the US and the UK.[97] India, the largest democracy on the planet and with a history of ethnically and religiously driven hate speech set up three so-called "Grievance Appellate Committees" to adjudicate on disputes over content

[94] cf. Martin M Shapiro, *Courts: A Comparative and Political Analysis* (University of Chicago Press 1981).

[95] Karen J Alter, Laurence R Helfer and Mikael Rask Madsen, 'How Context Shapes the Authority of International Courts' in Karen J Alter, Laurence R Helfer and Mikael Rask Madsen (eds.), *International Court Authority* (Oxford University Press 2018) 26–27.

[96] Kate Klonick, 'The New Governors: The People, Rules, and Processes Governing Online Speech' (n 15) 1668.

[97] In the US and in the UK, legislative proposals were tabled that partly mirror the DSA (yet none has a direct emulation of Article 21 DSA). See for the US, Lori Trahan, Adam Schiff and Sean Casten, Digital Services Oversight and Safety Bill [introduced], H.R. 6796 – 117th Congress (2021–2022) 2022; UK Online Safety Bill [HL Bill 87-EN].

moderation.[98] These government-run committees decide appeals by Indian users against content moderation measures within thirty days.[99] Establishing these appeal bodies was necessary, as the relevant Indian ministry has said: "due to large numbers of grievances being left unaddressed or unsatisfactorily addressed by internet Intermediaries. GAC is expected to create a *culture* of responsiveness amongst all internet Platforms and Intermediaries toward their consumers."[100]

For the DSA, these developments in India might indicate that administrifying platforms and fostering, as the Indian bill put it, a "culture of responsiveness" is a pressing though difficult task.

However, whenever the DSA's attempts to make platforms better administrators lack clear definitions and are at odds with social media platforms' business interests, the platforms' further administrification risks remaining ceremonial rather than substantive – even within the DSA framework. Many of the DSA's procedural impositions are vague, qualified, and adjective-heavy. For example, platforms are expected to "handle complaints submitted through their internal complaint-handling system in a timely, diligent and objective manner," according to Article 15(3) of the DSA. The DSA does not detail precisely what "diligent" and "objective" procedures would look like. This might improve through later practice and litigation. However, although the administrification of platform governance, in part, has already been evidenced in empirical studies, we know relatively little about platforms' actual internal operations, the habitualized practices of their employees, and the norms and values underpinning their choices. Most of what we do know – often from leaks – points to a corporate culture favoring growth, user engagement (the euphemism for the time users spend on a program), and profit, over sound, balanced practices regarding rulemaking and rule enforcement (not to mention firms' datamining activities).[101] So, even

98 Ministry of Electronics and Information Technology (India), 'Three Grievance Appellate Committees (GACs) Notified on the Recently Amended "IT Rules 2021" (Press Release)' (28 January 2023) <https://perma.cc/98M3-5DQG>.

99 Ibid.

100 Ibid (emphasis added).

101 cf. Jillian York, *Silicon Values: The Future of Free Speech under Surveillance Capitalism* (Verso 2021); Shoshana Zuboff, *The Age of Surveillance Capitalism: The Fight for a Human Future at the New Frontier of Power* (PublicAffairs 2019); and especially for Facebook (although similar things presumably apply to all tech giants): Jeremy B Merril and Will Oremus, 'Five Points for Anger, One for a "Like": How Facebook's Formula Fostered Rage and Misinformation' *Washington Post* (26 October 2021) <https://perma.cc/7E55-RPZL>; Sheera Frenkel and Cecilia Kang, *An Ugly Truth: Inside Facebook's Battle for Domination* (Harper 2021).

though the sheer size and functional logic of platforms partially mirrors (or even supersedes) traditional administrative institutions, we should assume that their normative underpinning and cultural embedding continues to reflect their private and profit-oriented nature.

Implementing individualized, in-depth assessments of individual cases in the context of Articles 14, (moderation), 17 (reason giving), or 20 (internal complaints) of the DSA could give rise to potentially huge costs for platforms. It seems therefore likely that platforms will instead adopt "ceremonial" procedures that invoke the perception of legitimacy without the need for extensive modifications to governance. In turn, in sociological parlance: platforms might design "a formal structure that adheres to the prescriptions of myths in the institutional environment" and thereby demonstrate that they "act ... on collectively valued purposes in a proper and adequate manner."[102] Yet these formal structures often remain ceremonial and decoupled from organizations' actual work activities.[103] Hence, the DSA's goal of holding platforms accountable and protect fundamental rights may advance administrative ceremonies but not necessarily trigger a fundamental shift toward more "responsible and diligent behavior" by platforms, which the EU rightly considers "[e]ssential for a safe, predictable and trusted online environment and for allowing Union citizens and other persons to exercise their fundamental rights."[104] In short, installing a meaningful accountability culture within digital corporations might be indeed the thorniest of all three elements required to establish an accountability regime. The struggle over these cultural and regulatory frameworks has only just begun, with allegiances becoming ever more complex. Key corporations in the tech sector began aligning themselves with the second Trump administration, while the European Union and United States governments finds themselves in a challenging geopolitical position as matters of digital, trade, and security policy appear increasingly intertwined.

5.5 Conclusion

Our evaluation of the DSA's ODSs and the Oversight Board offers an ambiguous picture. The case studies showed that some pioneering thinkers – whether academics, politicians, executives, or public servants – from both

102 Meyer and Rowan (n 3) 349.
103 Ibid 357 et seq.
104 DSA Recital 3.

sides of the Atlantic had a similar idea at the same time: subjecting private power to individual rights adjudication. Yet, the formal mandates of both Emulated Guardians are limited. The Oversight Board gives nonbinding feedback on structural governance problems within Meta. The EU created a class of actors, the ODSs, which shall remedy millions of individual grievances, however, without being able to issue binding decisions. Simultaneously, neither the Oversight Board nor the European Union seem to dare, yet, to take on the truly crucial issues with content moderation, such as platforms' business model or, at least, the undemocratic nature of platform rules.

Nonetheless, dismissing Emulated Guardians as useless ceremonies would be premature. Especially the first years of the Oversight Board also offer indications for some cautious optimism: with the people who work for the Board, the financial resources they have, and the comprehensive, structure-focused interpretation of their mission, one would be justified in viewing the Oversight Board a worthwhile experiment, shining a spotlight on the important normative and organizational issues of content moderation and the private governance structures of global companies. As the Oversight Board shows, they may performatively play with judicial symbolism and discursively construct rather than legally exercise their authority vis-à-vis the companies they shall control. Public law ideas still seem to carry significant discursive might – even if public law's enforcement through "classic" institutions and mechanisms appears ever more challenging.

Remarkably, the external elements of an accountability culture are emerging. This is a good sign. That platforms constitute problematic power structures today seems widely – even if not unequivocally – accepted.[105] This alone is a significant achievement compared to many governance discourses between the 1980s and the recent "techlash" that has been around since roughly 2016. This shift in overall narrative and political climate may very well be the soil in which Emulated Guardians

[105] The Supreme Court's jurisprudence on this issue – and the broader American political discourse underpinning it – could easily fill an entire comparative study. In Europe, government regulation of content moderation tends to be a rallying cry for the left, while in the United States, it became predominantly a cause championed by the right. Many US conservatives essentially view the entire content moderation apparatus as a liberal enterprise designed to marginalize conservative viewpoints. As a result, although the current majority on the US Supreme Court largely maintains a libertarian stance on the issue, the most pointed critiques of platform power have come from Justices Thomas and Alito, both on the right end of the Court's composition. In contrast, liberal justices like Elena Kagan and Sonia Sotomayor appear untroubled by this particular concentration of corporate influence, cf. Moody v Netchoice 603 US ____ (2024) (United States Supreme Court).

grow to become "masters of their own destinies" and incrementally build their authority vis-à-vis social media platforms.[106] Further, we are already seeing other jurisdictions debating whether to pass regulations (loosely) modeled on the DSA. India has recently established adjudicatory mechanisms to control content moderation that could perhaps be described as Emulated Guardians (although we do not know whether India purposely emulated the Commission proposal in that regard).

However, the emergence of an accountability culture and successful narratives of "self"-regulation may bolster platforms' all too natural "instinct" to erect ceremonial façades instead of embarking on structural reform. Fostering an institutionalization of meaningful control above and beyond the mere appearance of accountability will be a pressing task for the coming years. Although both Emulated Guardians show promising features, they can only be the first arenas for a new set of actors entering the power struggle between public, value-based, and ideally democratic governance of digital communication and its current domination by private and profit-driven interests.

Because we are just setting out on this somewhat ethereal journey for more accountability in the digital economy (and beyond), the idea behind Emulated Guardian remains malleable. As they rest on social and discursive rather than formal legal authority anyway, they are potentially quick in adapting and improving. We may hence remedy the shortcomings of the two studied specimens in the future.

The following final chapter therefore makes some tentative generalizations as a result of insights from the two case studies and this analysis chapter. The key ideas I will discuss in this last chapter are the following. First, I believe that focusing on individual rights – as much of current political and scholarly debates do – is insufficient. We should focus less on individual rights and more on structural deficits in the governance architectures and infrastructures of the digital economy. Second, we should learn more from administrative law to improve private governance. Third, perhaps the most important intake from administrative law for private governance is that private rulemaking in content moderation should be much more participatory. Fourth, looking back at the whole research and writing process of this book, I argue that we observe the

[106] This, of course, references an optimistic perspective on international courts that remains prominent in much legal and political science scholarship. However, even the initial optimists of "classic" international courts employ many more caveats than in the early 2000s, see Karen J Alter, Laurence R Helfer and Mikael Rask Madsen (eds.), *International Court Authority* (Cambridge University Press 2018) 435 et seq.

emergence of a new type of public law-inspired yet privately enforced *accountability law* in globalized, private, and often profit-driven contexts. These *New Accountability Norms* transgress classic public-private distinctions. They respond to public demands for accountability of private, profit-driven actors. I studied those norms here for social media companies. But I would not be surprised to find similar phenomena in other digital or otherwise globalized contexts. The next chapter will sketch out the contours of these New Accountability Norms.

6 New Accountability Norms

6.1 Where We Stand

This final chapter offers a brief recap of where our inquiry has led us thus far and provides an outlook for what may lie ahead. I propose that we are witnessing the emergence of an entirely new class of norms, mechanisms, and institutions aimed at constraining the immense power wielded by privately incorporated governance structures. Content moderation, and particularly experiments such as the Oversight Board or the EU's out-of-court dispute settlement bodies (ODSs), provide a vivid – if ambivalent – example of the fascinating and innovative efforts to address the core question posed at the outset of this book: how do we control corporate power structures when the traditional locus of authority, the state, is gradually fading? Or, to put it more starkly, how can we constrain powerful corporations that govern critical sectors of the future – platforms, artificial intelligence, space travel, satellites, biotech, quantum computing, and beyond – when they outpace and outscale the regulatory capacity of public institutions?

Over the last 300 or so pages we analyzed these and other questions in the realm of content moderation, particularly how private and regulatory actors alike flocked to emulating a canonized classic of public law – individual rights adjudication – to provide accountability to the fledgling, privately incorporated power structures of social media companies. Such emulative moves are a common pattern in politics as well as managerial practice. Therefore, it seems likely that regulators, academics, and publics will, again and again, draw on historical approaches that have proven effective in the past to solve future problems of organizational and especially corporate power. A crucial role model for controlling private organizational power will remain, for the time being, public law. By public law, I refer mostly to constitutional, civil rights, and administrative law. In contrast, by private law, I refer to the body of law governing relationships between private parties, such as contracts and company law. The ideas of public law – self-governance, participation, due process, reason-giving, third-party review – hold a lot of social sway. But like for content moderation, we will, inevitably, face the necessity of adapting those role model solutions to the private law context in which these new power structures operate. These emerging frameworks could well be described as the beginning of a set of new accountability norms – an attempt to rein in corporate power in ways that acknowledge its vast reach and innovative force while seeking to instill checks, balances, and accountability within these unprecedented governance systems.

But before we get to these future developments, we must briefly recapitulate and critically complement the core arguments this book puts forward. The introductory chapter already anticipated these arguments. However, to refresh our memory and frame the preceding chapters, I take the liberty to briefly recapitulate them here once again. First of all, I argue that it makes sense to think about new institutional and normative arrangements in digital governance, and, for the fact of the matter, arguably the governance of many future sectors. In other words, we witness *governance by emulation*. Emulation means the reproduction of commonly known role models from prior contexts in new contexts.[1] Here it means the emulation of individual rights adjudication vis-à-vis a dominant power structure, in this case social media companies' content moderation machineries. Remarkably, emulating public law ideas is by no means a liberal shtick. Various kinds of conservative or libertarian critiques of regulatory programs or platform (self-)governance invoke arguments about viewpoint discrimination, majoritarianism, free speech, and accountability – all public law concepts in their own right. But that more recent episode, arguably the backlash against the phenomena analyzed in the empirical chapters, has to be studied in future work. This book focused on the "liberal" era of platform governance. The case studies analyzed how users might seek to enforce their individual rights vis-à-vis platforms through new adjudicators like the Oversight Board or ODSs. I called these novel adjudicators Emulated Guardians, the latter term referencing the classic question of public law: Who guards the guardians? Emulated Guardians' reproduction of individual rights adjudication for this context is pretty intuitive. After all, who would be against

[1] See Chapters 1 and 2.

trying to empower users to adjudicate their rights and hold platforms accountable. However, one must pay attention to the contextual factors that enabled the role model in its original context. The two Emulated Guardians that I studied here – the ODSs certified according to Article 21 Digital Services Act (DSA) and Meta's Oversight Board – struggle with lacking the formal powers and institutional postures of their role model.[2] Also, crucially, emulations regularly operate in a context that is markedly different than the original one, here, for example, the new context are profit-driven private governance regimes whereas the role model's context were continually grown rule of law systems. However, second, contexts may change. The characteristic strength of emulative arrangements is their *performative* potential.[3] Emulated Guardians can be powerful not because they are courts but because they *remind* us of courts. Especially the Oversight Board performatively plays with the perception of adjudicative power and reasoning, international human rights law and thereby taps into the still much venerated imaginary of public law-based accountability of organized power. Yet third, every phenomenon carries its own dialectics. The lack of formal powers and inevitable proclivity to public perception may give rise to merely superficial, or as I call it borrowing from organization theory, *ceremonial* compliance.[4] Such ceremonial arrangements may occur whenever an allegedly controlled power structure adopts external feedback but effectuates only outside-facing changes while keeping internal, potentially harmful practices intact. These three elements – emulation, performativity, and ceremony – are inseparably intertwined. Therefore, one should not hope or even wish for governance arrangements that entirely overcome one of them. Emulation, performativity and, to a degree, ceremony can be very fruitful means of organizational growth and the construction of authority. Therefore, we should invest time and attention into continually monitoring and improving the governance arrangements we encounter. Fourth, concretely, regarding the two studied Emulated Guardians – the ODSs and Meta's Oversight Board – I argue that both are innovative fusions of public and private law models.[5] They have, upon closer inspection, vastly different functional logics, and will end up focusing on different things. The authority of both types of bodies may be ambivalent

[2] See Chapters 3 and 4.

[3] See Chapter 2 section on performativity; for a practical example see Chapter 4 on reasoning.

[4] See Chapters 2 and 5.

[5] See at 3.2 and 4.2.

and even formally weak. For the performativity-argument made above, they might yet expand their authority, nonetheless. Also, for the EU's ODSs, one might even say that at least some of them may develop into mere mediating bodies, which can be a good way to filter out many disputes before they reach the lengthy and costly stage of formal litigation. As the first ODSs became operational through 2024, we also observed another innovative aspect that was not foreseen by the EU. That is ODSs' experimentation with large language models as tools to handle large amounts of cases and construe automated justice architectures; a development that, if successful, might hold fundamental lessons for any form of individualized decision-making in normative contexts ranging from classic bureaucratic tasks to the judiciary. At the time of writing, it is too early to tell how such experiments will turn out. Then, fifth, the book seeks to caution against some claims by regulators, especially the European Union, that platforms are indeed applying the regulators' rules instead of their own. As Chapters 2 and 3 showed, we observe rather the opposite. The European Union largely ceded rulemaking and rule-enforcement capacity to digital corporations, which it then adorns with the public legitimizing label of being tightly regulated by Brussels.[6] How this plays out once the Commission ramped up implementation remains to be seen. Sixth, I believe, and have outlined elsewhere, that for concrete improvements of content moderation regimes and the implementation (and drafting) or regulation thereof, administrative law holds much to offer.[7] Questions of normative hierarchy and deference, scale and unity in complex systems are well studied and, I would argue, reasonably well answered in administrative law. Content moderation is a bureaucratic endeavor, even if it is highly technicized (as most bureaucracies are). Bureaucratic in this sense refers to large, partially hierarchical, partially project-based organizations that deal with high volumes of recurring tasks. Administrative law offers mechanisms and norms to make sense of this and, eventually, improve such bureaucracies whenever they act on the public. And then, lastly, seventh, I believe that all prior points lead to a simple but very exciting prospect: we are witnessing the emergence of new norms of accountability and control for private power structures that exercise global governance.

[6] See Chapters 2 and 3. See also Moritz Schramm, 'Curb Your Enthusiasm: Why the Digital Services Act Might Not Have a "Brussels Effect"' (2025) European Journal of Legal Studies (Special Issue) 61.

[7] See at 2.3 and Moritz Schramm, 'Platform Administrative Law: A Research Agenda' (SSRN, 24 July 2024) <https://perma.cc/JH2A-8ZW2>.

This book studied said accountability structures for content moderation. But these are, in my opinion, only one of many examples where similar centralized but private, for-profit, corporate-driven global governance arrangements emerge. Think of, for example, artificial intelligence, autonomous vehicles, quantum computing, commercial space travel, satellite infrastructure, health governance, biotechnology, human "enhancement," carbon capture, private surveillance technologies, and so much more. Not all these sectors necessarily will flourish. But some most likely will. And in all these sectors it will to a large extent be private actors making and enforcing the decisive governance decisions. They simply outpace and outscale public power structures. This, however, evinces the necessity to erect new perspectives on and structures of the legitimate exercise of power. Emulated Guardians are a paradigmatic example for this new sphere of norms one could call new accountability norms. These new accountability norms will be the main topic of the remaining pages of this book.

However, before we go there, let me briefly address some of the complementary, more critical takeaways complementing six of the seven core arguments of this book. I make two more critical points. First, that we should not put too much hope in individual rights and adjudicators, second that rulemaking in content moderation requires more ex ante input from the publics bound by the rules. These observations then also pave the way to our outlook at the new accountability norms, which I discuss in the second part of this chapter.

6.1.1 *The Limits of Rights and Courts*

First, one might question whether the European Union and Meta selected the appropriate model by emulating individual rights adjudication.[8] For lawyers, using an adjudicator to operationalize individual rights and hold digital corporations accountable seems self-evident. However, as many scholars – both empiricists and theorists – have argued, the real-world effectiveness of this rights-focused, court-centered approach is far from certain.[9] Only idealistic, and perhaps somewhat self-absorbed, lawyers

[8] Critical of individual rights in this context in general: Rachel Griffin, 'Rethinking Rights in Social Media Governance: Human Rights, Ideology and Inequality' (2023) 2 European Law Open 30.

[9] Gerald N Rosenberg, *The Hollow Hope Can Courts Bring About Social Change?* (University of Chicago Press 1991); Michael Blauberger and others, 'ECJ Judges Read the Morning Papers. Explaining the Turnaround of European Citizenship Jurisprudence' (2018) 25 Journal of European Public Policy 1422.

would believe that all it requires to domesticize a recalcitrant bureaucratic behemoth is a courageous, Herculean court. This was arguably never true of traditional legal systems, and it is certainly not the case today. There is little reason to believe that Emulated Guardians like ODSs or the Oversight Board, inherently imperfect adjudicators with limited authority, could succeed where their predecessors failed. Dismantling entrenched organizational structures that follow potentially harmful incentives is very, very complicated and takes a lot of external and internal pressure.

Consider, for the sake of argument, one of the biggest presumed victories of rights-based-approaches and courts: the desegregation of public schools in the United States. Many lawyers might intuitively believe that the Supreme Court resolved this issue with Brown v Board of Education in 1954. That decision operationalized the individual rights of several Black students to equal treatment, making a normative statement about the governance of public schools across the United States, where many institutions denied equal access to Black students. However, school desegregation did not occur immediately following the decision.[10] The widely recognized images of the National Guard escorting Black students into a school only represent a specific moment in time, and beyond that event, segregationist practices remain(ed) deeply entrenched. As Lani Guinier observed:

> On its fiftieth anniversary, *Brown v. Board of Education* no longer enjoys the unbridled admiration it once earned from academic commentators. . . . The fact is that fifty years later, many of the social, political, and economic problems that the legally trained social engineers thought the Court had addressed through *Brown* are still deeply embedded in our society.[11]

Evidently, this is not to say that governance practices in content moderation are comparable to past and prevalent racial injustices in US bureaucracy. But the point is that structural change seldom transpires only because of courts, even if it is one of the most prominent decisions of what was at the time perceived the world's most powerful court dealing with an injustice so obvious, few would openly dare to defend it.[12]

10 See e.g. Alexander M Bickel, 'The Decade of School Desegregation: Progress and Prospects' (1964) 64 Columbia Law Review 193.

11 Lani Guinier, 'From Racial Liberalism to Racial Literacy: Brown v. Board of Education and the Interest-Divergence Dilemma' (2004) 91 Journal of American History 92, 92.

12 To be fair, rights-based approaches rely never on courts alone but typically build on a rich variety of different stakeholders. This is a point underscored by social mobilization

Therefore, if even in such a constellation – powerful court, obvious injustice – individual rights adjudication reaches its limits, why are many putting so much hope into an emulated, feeble version of individual rights adjudication to solve problems that appear normatively much more nuanced and whose remedy is much less straightforward?

Arguably, the reason Meta and the EU chose to emulate adjudicators rather than, say, parliaments lies in the deep-seated sociocultural veneration of the former. There is something inherently appealing about the idea of empowering individuals through rights-based adjudication – even if it does not always deliver the structural transformation one might hope for. Much ink has already been spilled on the complexities of courts, individualism, and rights-based approaches, often with far greater theoretical and historical nuance than I can provide here.[13] Therefore, I restrict myself to flagging this issue. These kinds of structural criticism of the Oversight Board, the DSA, and content moderation are important. However, many of these critiques merely reflect well-known general critiques of over-relying on rights and court-based approaches.

There is, however, a more cynical way to look at things. Perhaps individual rights adjudication was not chosen despite its shortcomings in driving real change, but precisely because of them.[14] After all, the effectiveness of such adjudication depends heavily on the rule of law, which in turn relies on the social norms that sustain it. Courts may boast neither purse nor sword, but individual rights and independent review are so deeply embedded in our

theory. However, even when embedded into a broader movement, it remains unclear how important courts actually are compared to public pressure, changing politics, and culturalized habits, cf. for a more optimistic perspective Charles R Epp, *The Rights Revolution: Lawyers, Activists, and Supreme Courts in Comparative Perspective* (University of Chicago Press 1998); Gráinne de Búrca, 'Human Rights Experimentalism' (2017) 111 American Journal of International Law 277.

[13] See, somewhat eclectically, esp. Karl Marx, 'Zur Judenfrage' [1844] Deutsch-Französische Jahrbücher 182; on the *right to have rights*: Hannah Arendt, *The Origins of Totalitarianism* (Harcourt, Brace and Company 1951); Frantz Fanon, *The Wretched of the Earth (1963)* (Grove Press 2004); Michael J Sandel, *Liberalism and the Limits of Justice* (2nd ed., Cambridge University Press 1998); Gayatri Chakravorty Spivak, 'Can the Subaltern Speak?' in C Nelson and L Grossberg (eds.), *Marxism and the Interpretation of Culture* (Macmillan 1988); Catharine A MacKinnon, *Toward a Feminist Theory of the State* (Harvard University Press 1991); Duncan Kennedy, *A Critique of Adjudication: Fin de Siècle* (Harvard University Press 1998); Samuel Moyn, *Not Enough: Human Rights in an Unequal World* (Belknap 2019); Jamal Greene, *How Rights Went Wrong: Why Our Obsession With Rights is Tearing America Apart* (Houghton Mifflin Harcourt 2021).

[14] This point was made also early on regarding the Oversight Board, see esp. Evelyn Douek, 'Facebook's "Oversight Board:" Move Fast with Stable Infrastructure and Humility' (2019) 21 North Carolina Journal of Law & Technology 1.

cultural fabric that setting up these systems offers a win-win opportunity for both the European Union and Meta – even if the structural shifts ushered in by these Emulated Guardians unfold at a glacial pace.

The real beauty, from a strategic standpoint, lies in the shift of responsibility. Once these bodies are in place – and the Oversight Board's immense caseload suggests it already is well on its way – the question of who bears the burden of protecting online rights begins to drift. No longer will Meta or the European Union be the primary targets of scrutiny. Instead, public attention and potential criticism might now zero in on the guardians themselves. And that, in the end, suits both Meta and the EU quite nicely.

6.1.2 *Participation*

Building on the previous observation, the current discourse surrounding the legitimacy of content moderation remains overly focused on ex post review – hence the fixation on emulating individual rights adjudication – while largely neglecting ex ante improvements. The quality of the rules applied by platforms remains deeply problematic: they are unsystematic, incoherent, and one can only speculate about the quality of algorithmic enforcement of rules that, even for human readers, allow for a wide range of interpretations. As one interviewed former consultant to Facebook put it, "[t]he process for making content rules is basically a room full of US lawyers sits down and makes the rules after the latest crisis."[15] And, as the interviewee continued, "[w]hat the fuck happens when you put a bunch of US lawyers in charge? Well, they started doing things that they're familiar with," which was in this case to come up with more rules and, eventually, an external adjudicator.[16] Admittedly, creating globally scalable speech rules is a Sisyphean task. However, from the perspective of the affected publics and a liberal instinct for self-governance, it is striking how little influence users have in shaping the very rules they are expected to follow.

Calls for more participatory elements in the rulemaking processes of social media companies are not new, and neither are the widely held objections to increased user participation in platform rulemaking.[17] There are three primary objections.

[15] Interview with Academic, Consultant to Facebook in 2018 (1 November 2021); see further Kate Klonick, 'The New Governors: The People, Rules, and Processes Governing Online Speech' (2018) 131 Harvard Law Review 1598.

[16] Interview with Academic, Consultant to Facebook in 2018 (n 15).

[17] See (in chronological order) in a sense already Yochai Benkler (ed.), *The Wealth of Networks: How Social Production Transforms Markets and Freedom* (Yale University Press

First, it is argued that users do not constitute a *demos* – they would lack the shared identity or cohesion that forms an actual polity. This argument is, in my mind, a tat esoteric. Claims to self-governance arise from shared affectedness and agency, not from an otherwise constructed ideological, ethnic, or historical bond. As the eminent US constitutional theorist – and Oversight Board trustee – Robert Post put it: "Democratic forms of social ordering have a particular and bounded sphere of appropriate application, which is defined by ... those aspects of society deemed necessary for the success of collective processes of self-determination."[18]

Evidently, a claim to self-governance arises vis-à-vis a state in a different form and quality than vis-à-vis a social media platform. The disciplinary powers of the former are (as of now) significantly more intimidating than deplatforming or downranking of social media posts.[19] However, if digital corporations in general, and social media platforms in particular, were not in some way exceptional – and

2006); Rebecca MacKinnon, *Consent of the Networked: The Worldwide Struggle for Internet Freedom* (Basic Books 2012); Aaron Wachhaus, 'Platform Governance: Developing Collaborative Democracy' (2017) 39 Administrative Theory & Praxis 206; Hannah Bloch-Wehba, 'Global Platform Governance: Private Power in the Shadow of the State' (2019) 72 SMU Law Review 27, esp. 75–76; Bart Cammaerts and Robert Mansell, 'Digital Platform Policy and Regulation: Toward a Radical Democratic Turn' (2020) 14 International Journal of Communication 135; Moritz Schramm, 'Where Is Olive? Or: Lessons from Democratic Theory for Legitimate Platform Governance' (*The Digital Constitutionalist*, 26 January 2022) <https://perma.cc/RL93-CGSY>; Blayne Haggart and Clara Iglesias Keller, 'Democratic Legitimacy in Global Platform Governance' (2021) 45 Telecommunications Policy 102152; Paul Gowder, *The Networked Leviathan: For Democratic Platforms* (Cambridge University Press 2023). See also for data governance Salomé Viljoen, 'A Relational Theory of Data Governance' (2021) 131 Yale Law Journal 370.

18 Robert C Post, *Constitutional Domains: Democracy, Community, Management* (Harvard University Press 1995) 8. See further Benedict Kingsbury and Nahuel Maisley, 'Infrastructures and Laws: Publics and Publicness' (2021) 17 Annual Review of Law and Social Science 353, 357 et seq; Jeremy Waldron, *Law and Disagreement* (Oxford University Press 1999); Jeremy Waldron, 'The Principle of Proximity, NYU School of Law, Public Law Research Paper No. 11-08' (SSRN, 20 January 2011) <https://perma.cc/2JWS-BU2Q>; classic also: Benedict R O'G Anderson, *Imagined Communities: Reflections on the Origin and Spread of Nationalism* (Verso 1983); Elinor Ostrom, *Governing the Commons: The Evolution of Institutions for Collective Action* (Cambridge University Press 1990).

19 Nonetheless, for example, if we consider also surveillance as "disciplinary" platforms arguably are entirely unprecedented disciplinary regimes, see e.g. Niklas Eder, 'Beyond Automation: Machine Learning-Based Systems and Human Behavior in the Personalization Economy' (2021) 25 Stanford Technology Law Review 1.

this exception lies in their nearly absolute power over crucial aspects of our lives – this entire conversation would not be happening. Digital corporations possess, program, and structure the very means of our collective processes of self-determination, are indispensable mediators of societal decision-making, in the case of communicative services, and broader societal and economic development, in the case of other industries. Whenever an organization regulates human behavior at this scale, the liberal instinct should not be to condone that exercise of power even if it seems unjust merely because the power structure is incorporated as a private company. Instead, we ought to ask why there is so little say in how these actors govern our online activities. None of this means that participation must be equivalent to what one might consider a democratic ideal. Arguably, that would be counterproductive, as these actors remain corporations, not states or other public entities. Yet, the idea that being ruled necessitates some voice in how one is ruled seems intuitive.

Second, there is the claim that users simply do not care. This is indeed a real problem, amusingly enough one familiar from public governance as well.[20] And admittedly, Meta's experiment with direct voting on some of its terms of service attracted participation from less than one percent of users.[21] However, once we accept that content moderation and comparable power relations in private governance may give rise to valid claims for elements of self-governance, the question becomes how, rather than if. As the Meta example shows, general voting might not be a good idea, and for several other reasons, well explored in democratic theory, general voting might fail. However, various other mechanisms and procedures are necessary and exist to help infuse the interests of affected publics into rulemaking processes.[22] There are numerous civil society groups and activists who could professionalize this participation. None of these processes would be perfect, and all would require continuous review and improvement. However, engaging people before imposing rules on their expression, rather than only revising the most problematic rules after sufficient complaints, would overcome the Silicon Valley-inspired "release early, release often" mentality and reflect a more

[20] Critical of participatory elements in administrative rulemaking (yet conceding the inevitability thereof) Richard B Stewart, 'The Reformation of American Administrative Law' (1975) 88 Harvard Law Review 1667.

[21] Kalev Leetaru, 'Facebook Was a Democracy 2009–2012 But We Didn't Vote So it Turned into a Dictatorship' *Forbes* (13 April 2019) <https://perma.cc/Z5PG-3MBD>.

[22] Iris Marion Young, *Inclusion and Democracy* (Oxford University Press 2002).

mature understanding of the governance task these companies have assumed. In that sense, and as I argued in greater detail in Chapters 2 and 3, the DSA disappoints.[23] The claims of the EU that "the rules of the game" were now made by Europeans rather than platforms are, unfortunately, largely empty political rhetoric. In fact, it seems plausible that the DSA stabilizes rather than curtails platform power in Europe.

The third and perhaps most problematic objection is the frequently invoked claim that platforms, being private entities, are inherently insulated from any participatory elements in how they regulate user behavior. This argument, however, is unconvincing for both practical and deeper theoretical reasons. On a practical level, it seems contradictory to deny participation in rulemaking while simultaneously framing terms of service and other implementation rules as contractual in nature.[24] If these rules are truly contractual, they ought to be negotiated, not unilaterally imposed.[25] The very essence of a contract is the negotiation between two parties to reach a mutually agreeable arrangement.[26] Of course, this ideal does not fully apply to mass contracts, but to dismiss entirely the idea of user participation in platform rulemaking on the grounds that it would violate platforms' "freedom of contract," as some Commission agents have argued in interviews conducted for this book, strikes me as unpersuasive.[27]

We see many types of contracts where participatory elements are well-established practices, from labor law to shareholder rights in corporate law. Some forms of participation may be mediated through property – such as shareholder voting rights – but others arise purely from the recognition that private entities possess far more power than the individuals whose contributions are crucial to the entities' economic success.

[23] See at 3.2.4.

[24] Another option is, consequentially, to argue that digital corporations' terms of service are not contracts, see e.g. Przemyslaw Jacek Palka, 'Terms of Service Are Not Contracts: Beyond Contract Law in the Regulation of Online Platforms' in Stefan Grundmann (ed.), *European Contract Law in the Digital Age* (Intersentia 2018).

[25] Criticizing "boilerplate" contracts as a problem for the rule of law: Margarete Jane Radin, 'Boilerplate: A Threat to the Rule of Law?' in Lisa M Austin and Dennis Klimchuk (eds.), *Private Law and the Rule of Law* (Oxford University Press 2015).

[26] Some go even further and argue that only such agreements that align with values such as equality and democracy are legitimate contracts, see esp. Martijn W Hesselink, 'Democratic Contract Law' (2015) 11 European Review of Contract Law 81; others highlight the autonomy of private law Matthias Ruffert, *Vorrang der Verfassung und Eigenständigkeit des Privatrechts: Eine verfassungsrechtliche Untersuchung zur Privatrechtswirkung des Grundgesetzes* (Mohr Siebeck 2001).

[27] Interview with European Commission Staffer 1 (29 October 2021).

This is, after all the foundational principle behind collective bargaining, a practice with a long history that acknowledges the imbalance of power and seeks to redress it through participatory means.

Further, the argument that private incorporation alone grants platforms the right to exclude users from rulemaking doesn't hold up on a deeper theoretical level. To grasp why, we need to briefly revisit the historical purpose of distinguishing between public and private power. This will also set the stage for the discussion in the next section on new accountability norms.

Historically, the public-private divide was designed to safeguard individual freedom from the biggest threat to liberty at the time: the state.[28] Private individuals, privacy, private property, and private law – all these institutions emerged to empower individuals vis-à-vis a power structure that was not only dominant, but utterly all-encompassing. Rulemaking authority gradually shifted away from Church and Crown to guilds, cities, and eventually republics. Conceptualizing those organized power structures, especially the State, as "public" tied it to certain ideals of publicness and, in turn, carved out spheres of individual and collective freedom, the "private."[29] Seen from an abstract vantage point, however, erecting public and private as opposing categories typically sought to defend individual freedoms and confine powers.[30] The purpose of this ideational dichotomy – which in practice is much less pronounced than in theory anyway, for anything private existing in a public context and anything public being constituted by and for private people – was never to blindly distinguish based on form, but eagerly protect individual liberty from emergent power structures.

A bit later, in the late-nineteenth century, the private business corporation emerged as a distinct legal entity.[31] It only gradually disentangled itself from the state, most notably in colonial settings where private incorporation had a "convenient" side effect for its masters: it shielded

[28] From the rich literature on this issue see esp. Morris Cohen, 'Property and Sovereignty' (1927) 13 Cornell Law Quarterly 8; Duncan Kennedy, 'The Stages of the Decline of the Public/Private Distinction' (1982) 130 University of Pennsylvania Law Review 1349; Jody Freeman, 'The Private Role in Public Governance' (2000) 75 New York University Law Review 543; Martin Loughlin, *The Idea of Public Law* (Oxford University Press 2004).

[29] Martin Loughlin, *Foundations of Public Law* (Oxford University Press 2010).

[30] Remarkably, at least the baseline contours of this assessment are canonical to various epistemic traditions, cf. John Locke, *Two Treatises of Government* (1689); Hannah Arendt, *The Human Condition* (2nd ed. [1998], University of Chicago Press 1958); Isaiah Berlin, 'Two Concepts of Liberty (1958)' in *Four Essays on Liberty* (Oxford University Press 1969).

[31] See esp. Doreen Lustig, *Veiled Power: International Law and the Private Corporation 1886–1981* (Oxford University Press 2020).

corporate executives who commanded armies and effectively governed entire continents from demands for transparency and adherence to public ideals. The downstream consequences of the private form, therefore, are profoundly ambivalent: necessary, yet persistently susceptible to abuse.

Today, a significant threat to liberty comes not from what we label "public power" but from privately incorporated entities like social media companies. Today it is not only one power structure – the local sovereign – but a quite dense and confusing web of overlapping power structures, some of which remain public, like States or the European Union, some, however, are private corporations. The power of some of these corporations, at least within their specific sectors, is immense. Arguing that such corporations – armed with more money, resources, data, and infrastructure than many governments – require essentially unrestricted bargaining power turns the traditional understanding of private law on its head. If even a fraction of the claims about the transformative nature of the digital age is true, it is time to reassess how justified the privileges granted to private entities truly are. The idea that such powerful actors should have unrestricted freedom of contract and property simply because they are incorporated in private form appears, at least to me, an utter misunderstanding of what the distinguishing the private from the public is for.

Here, the dialectics presented in the case studies are striking. On the one hand, companies like Meta assert their right – and undoubtedly possess the means – to intervene in the speech of elected officials, including the President of the United States. From a traditional perspective, this is deeply concerning. On the other hand, why should we expect platforms to be complicit in the dissemination of government-sanctioned hate speech? What if a company, rather than a state actor, defends human rights by preventing a government from inciting human rights violations? Do such actions represent legitimate private checks on public power, as discussed in Chapter 5? Conversely, how can we distinguish between "legitimate" requests of state power and the nefarious cooptation of private governance by authoritarian regimes? For instance, the DSA includes provisions designed to "waterproof" its notice-and-takedown mechanism against potentially malicious demands from increasingly authoritarian Member States.[32] What procedures should companies like Meta follow when deciding how to respond to countries

[32] See Chapter 3.

that adopt platform regulations modeled after the DSA but geared toward authoritarian ends? How can we even make sure that the DSA is not misused for authoritarian purposes in some Member States or even regional authorities, for example against migrants, the LGBTQI community, or simply opposition figures? Should digital corporations comply with potentially authoritarian interpretations (or emulations) of the DSA simply because it claims to advance national sovereignty? Unfortunately, there are no easy answers to these complex questions.

Also, elements of self-governance and participation need to be carefully adapted to fit their new environment. Much of the relationship between individuals and platforms remains private, transactional, and shaped by contractual agreements. And rightly so. It is essential to recognize that ideas often seen as belonging to the public sphere – such as participation and self-governance – also appear in private contexts, though under different names.[33] However, this is not an argument for turning digital corporations into state-like entities, as if that would solve all problems. Such a transformation would be neither politically viable, nor practical, nor desirable. The profit motive driving platforms is vital, as it promotes innovation and efficacy. Moreover, states themselves are not without flaws; many struggle with inefficiencies, and some fail to uphold even basic democratic principles.

As discussed in Chapters 4 and 5, serious dilemmas arise when powerful corporations act as private checks on public power. In certain cases – such as when governments fuel hate speech during ethnic unrest – corporate intervention can prevent real harm.[34] Yet, such actions also undermine key principles of international law and further erode the already fragile concept of state sovereignty. This creates a complex tension: preventing harm on the one hand, while weakening legal norms and sovereignty on the other.

6.2 New Accountability Norms

Reflecting on these ideas, we turn now to consider the future. It is reasonable to assume that in the coming years – indeed, even now – corporate-driven, private governance arrangements will continue to wield vast, largely unchecked power over key sectors of human activity, particularly in the economic realm. Public power still plays a role in all of

[33] Seminal: Philip Selznick, *Law, Society, and Industrial Justice* (Russel Sage Foundation 1969).
[34] See at 4.6.3 and 5.2.4.

these future sectors. The US government, for instance, funds a significant portion of the research and helps creating demand for new private, profit-driven space corporations.[35] International organizations hold fact-finding commissions and are scrambling to establish normative frameworks for artificial intelligence, while sectors such as quantum computing, biotechnology, human enhancement, and carbon capture thrive on state-funded foundational research.[36] Yet, despite these efforts, the sheer scale, speed, and infrastructural control of many of these industries mean they are predominantly governed by the techno-normative frameworks devised by the small number of corporations that invent and control the relevant technologies and services.[37]

Take, for example, the ongoing discussions around "global AI governance." These debates often focus on abstract normative goals for how this still poorly understood technology should or should not be used. But merely generating rules, reports, and guidelines is far from effective governance. The real governance power – as this book has shown – rests with internal factions within these companies.[38] These are engineers and product developers on one side, compliance, legal, and public relations teams on the other. These actors truly determine how a given technology or service is employed. And indeed, they may consider external norms or regulations. But given the global reach and scale of their operations it appears naïve to hope for the enforcement of public law through traditional public mechanisms.

[35] cf. Mariana Mazzucato and Douglas KR Robinson, 'Co-Creating and Directing Innovation Ecosystems? NASA's Changing Approach to Public-Private Partnerships in Low-Earth Orbit' (2018) 136 Technological Forecasting and Social Change 166.

[36] For the United Nations and the Council of Europe see United Nations and AI Advisory Body, 'Governing AI For Humanity (Final Report)'; European Council, Framework Convention on Artificial Intelligence and Human Rights, Democracy and the Rule of Law (September 2024); see in general Nathalie Smuha, 'From a "Race to AI" to a "Race to AI Regulation": Regulatory Competition for Artificial Intelligence' (2021) 13 Law, Innovation and Technology 57.

[37] For different perspectives on this infrastructural perspective see Langdon Winner, 'Do Artifacts Have Politics?' (1980) 109 Daedalus 121; Geoffrey C Bowker and Susan Leigh Star, *Sorting Things Out: Classification and Its Consequences* (MIT Press 1999); Paul N Edwards, 'Infrastructure and Modernity: Force, Time, and Social Organization in the History of Sociotechnical Systems' in Thomas J Misa, Philip Brey and Andrew Feenberg (eds.), *Modernity and Technology* (MIT Press 2002); Laura DeNardis and Francesca Musiani, 'Governance by Infrastructure' in Francesca Musiani and others (eds.), *The Turn to Infrastructure in Internet Governance* (Palgrave Macmillan 2016); Kingsbury and Maisley (n 18).

[38] See also Ari Ezra Waldman, *Industry Unbound: The Inside Story of Privacy, Data, and Corporate Power* (Cambridge University Press 2021).

In many sectors, public power seems to have hit a ceiling in terms of shaping and enforcing its normative demands on these economically powerful, globally active corporations. This was laid out in detail in Chapter 3. The European Union, for instance, is often celebrated as a strict regulator. However, even in one of its flagship political projects of recent years, the DSA, the EU appears to have consolidated, rather than diminished, platform power.[39] Put simply, it seems the regulatory process is no longer capable of generating the kind of outcomes that could meaningfully alter the governance practices of these corporations, at least not to the degree publicly promised.

This leads to an inevitable conclusion: governance will, and arguably must, be exercised also by forces other than public power. And this is not about mundane governance; it is about the control, distribution, and creation of fundamental aspects of social, economic, and public life. For staunch defenders of traditional public law, this may sound heretical. It is worth noting that my own perspective on this issue has shifted – albeit gradually – over the course of writing this book. The book seeks to portray a somewhat transient perspective, combining European and American takes to a hopefully interesting whole. However, based on the power dynamics we have explored, insisting solely on the supremacy of the state in governing these technologies and organizations feels, as Martti Koskenniemi put it, "trite."[40] The world is moving on.

If private ordering is set to become even more prevalent, several questions appear increasingly pressing. How should we think about the legitimacy of these power structures? Should we consider their legitimacy at all? Who should have a say in shaping, implementing, and overseeing these structures? How can we reconcile the legally protected (and often essential) profit motive – after all, we need innovation and efficiency – with broader public concerns? How can we formulate and operationalize normative demands if power is indeed exercised not through communication or human action but via computing and infrastructure? How should the burdens be shared, profits allocated, and externalities mitigated? What should be the fundamental principles – the "grammar" – governing the norms that regulate these corporations? This grammar, spanning from self-imposed standards and technical frameworks to

[39] See Chapters 2 and 3.

[40] Referring not exclusively to private power in transnational governance though, Martti Koskenniemi, 'Performing Legal Expertise: Reflections on the Construction of Transnational Authority' in Emilia Korkea-aho and Päivi Leino-Sandberg (eds.), *Law, Legal Expertise and EU Policy-Making* (Cambridge University Press 2022) 40.

traditional laws, becomes all the more critical in a landscape of regulatory fragmentation, revolving doors between public and private sectors, and the codification of assumptions that tend to privilege corporate over public interests. How can such norms even be enforced when private corporations are far more centralized and resilient than many entities claiming to act in the public interest?

Attempting to answer these questions could easily fill another book. However, much of it seems to boil down to incorporating better governance and publicness within the power structures as they are. Here, emulation will be an important tool – for all its virtues and vices. Two things will be essential: First, we must repurpose "private" law in global governance, especially corporate and contract law.[41] At a practical level, current private law frameworks struggle to accommodate the public-oriented demands that arise when certain private actors accumulate significant governance power. Also, on a theoretical level, we ought to focus more on the power relationships at play than legal privileges latched to the private form. Yet, classifying something as private has profound legal consequences, many of which may be unjustified given the current power dynamics. Second, it is unclear what role traditional law or other forms of explicated normative material might play in future governance scenarios. In such scenarios, code and infrastructure will be crucial determinants, effectuating their very own ways of closure, discipline, and steering. Lastly, from a normative perspective, any new governance arrangement must be responsive to the affected publics, not just the corporations involved. The mechanisms for ensuring this responsiveness will vary and evolve incrementally, but the trajectory should be one of public accountability rather than unchecked centralization. I firmly believe that the principles of public law will continue to play a pivotal role in advancing these ideals, even if their influence increasingly extends beyond the realm of traditional public law regulation. Public law's adaptability as both a method and a mindset ensures its relevance in shaping the norms and institutions required to navigate the complexities of modern governance. Its ideals of accountability, fairness, and public interest remain indispensable, even as the mechanisms for achieving them evolve. However, this optimistic note is deliberately reserved for the epilogue. By concluding on this forward-looking note, I aim to leave readers with a sense of the transformative potential of public law ideals –

[41] I am indebted to Benedict Kingsbury for the "repurposing" framing.

an antidote to the fragmentation and uncertainty that so often dominate the landscape.

That is because, on a practical level, it will be extraordinarily challenging to build accountability structures and public-minded governance institutions solely through the private law mechanisms discussed here.[42] This is not to simplistically juxtapose an idealized public and an inherently nefarious private. As said repeatedly throughout the book, private ordering is neither good nor bad. The profit motive is an important driver of innovation and efficiency and, vice versa, the state far off being an always legitimate, let alone effective exercise in organized power. Especially at a global scale, there are few simple answers or absolute truths as to which things should be governed in what way. Likewise, the uncritical idealization of public power that underlies other criticism is itself rather ahistorical. Wherever power becomes comprehensive, it ought to be exercised in alignment with ideals of publicness and self-governance. We simply have more historical experience—and conceptual vocabulary—for thinking about these demands in relation to the state. But they are by no means exclusive to it.

This book showed how private, for-profit actors can be a very effective and indeed important check on state actors. Think of the Oversight Board's attempts to nudge Meta to restrain government hate speech on its services. Consider Meta's ability to do just that, quite literally by pulling the plug. Or think of AI companies' control over foundation models: adjusting such a model even slightly, making it more "aggressive,", more "lenient," or simply less accurate can have immense sociocultural, political, and economic repercussions. The scale of this influence is astonishing, and, I would argue, the way it is governed should be a matter of serious concern. Private law structures characterized by fiduciary duties, trusts, and contracts might very well be an important part of pragmatically repurposing certain private law institutions for publicly minded governance. Such incremental repurposing of contractual vehicles is also neither entirely new nor particularly understudied on an abstract level as numerous conceptual works on transnational law, *lex mercatoria*, private ordering, and entangled legalities indicate.[43]

[42] Drastic: Dorothy Lund and Elizabeth Pollman, 'The Corporate Governance Machine' (2021) 121 Columbia Law Review 2563.

[43] Philip C Jessup, *Transnational Law* (Yale University Press 1956); Avery Katz, 'Taking Private Ordering Seriously' (1996) 144 University of Pennsylvania Law Review 1745; Gunther Teubner (ed.), *Global Law without a State* (Dartmouth 1997); Alfred C Aman, 'The Globalizing State: A Future-Oriented Perspective on the Public/Private Distinction,

In this sense, these emerging governance arrangements hold both promise and peril. As the case studies show, technological advancements can be harnessed for the common good, but they can just as easily be used for harmful purposes. At the global level, it remains unclear who will differentiate between these two paths, according to what rules, and through which processes. As we move toward addressing these questions of normative and institutional design, we are likely to witness more instances of emulation – complete with both its opportunities and challenges. But there is reason for optimism. The liberal State – which today appears to be under pressure in many parts of the world – did also not emerge overnight. It took decades of protests, reforms, bills, and public pressure to entrench the separation of powers, due process, and democracy in public power structures. No categorical reason exists why similar – but not identical – improvements could not be made for future governance constellations.

6.2.1 *Repurposing Private Law in Global Governance*

Let us now dig briefly into each of these points. The first argument is that we – meaning academics, practitioners, and lawmakers – need to rethink and eventually repurpose private law in constellations of global governance.[44] This is, in essence, an obvious thing to do but it reverberates through our whole conception of the legal system and shakes deep-rooted priors of the role of law, the state, and corporate power.

Unlike the 1990s and 2000s, when private ordering was hailed by some as the inevitable next step in globalization under the Pax Americana, contemporary global governance increasingly unfolds through code, technology, and infrastructural control.[45] At the heart of this shift lie corporations – at the time of this writing predominantly American, with

Federalism, and Democracy' (1998) 31 Vanderbilt Journal of Transnational Law 769; Matthias C Kettemann, *The Normative Order of the Internet* (Oxford University Press 2020); Nico Krisch (ed.), *Entangled Legalities Beyond the State* (Cambridge University Press 2021).

[44] On the national level, some of such rethinking and repurposing is already well under way (and contested) in antitrust law, evinced most prominently by the Neo-Brandeisians in the United States. See esp. Lina M Khan, 'Amazon's Antitrust Paradox' (2017) 126 The Yale Law Journal 710; Tim Wu, *The Curse of Bigness: Antitrust in the New Gilded Age* (Columbia Global Reports 2018).

[45] Frank Pasquale, *The Black Box Society: The Secret Algorithms That Control Money and Information* (Harvard University Press 2016); Shoshana Zuboff, *The Age of Surveillance Capitalism: The Fight for a Human Future at the New Frontier of Power* (PublicAffairs 2019); Julie Cohen, *Between Truth and Power: The Legal Constructions of Informational Capitalism* (Oxford University Press 2019); Gerald J Postema, *Law's Rule: The Nature, Value, and Viability of the Rule of Law* (Oxford University Press 2023) 263 et seq; for a critical account of corporate power in globalization

a few Chinese contenders – that have centralized the governance of many industries with planetary significance. Meanwhile, the billionaire owners of these corporations, along with Silicon Valley's venture capital vanguard firms, have not only amassed extraordinary influence but have also embedded themselves within the US government – a trend dramatically accelerated by Donald Trump's re-election in 2024.[46] This concentration of wealth, infrastructural control, technological dominance, and legal immunity benefits a small cadre of men – especially Elon Musk, Jeff Bezos, Marc Andreessen, Mark Zuckerberg Larry Page, Larry Ellison, Sergey Brin, and Jensen Huang. As Julie Cohen aptly described, these figures are modern-day oligarchs, wielding power that resembles feudal hierarchies far more than democratic or even traditional market-based systems.[47] In other words, private power structures are becoming ever more dominant, fueled by the ideologies of "tech-solutionism" and underpinned by the prevailing paradigm of American political economy. To an extent, all these actors benefit profoundly from the globally diffused fundamental grammar of private law that champions property rights and contractual freedom rather than communitarian let alone planetary interests, an observation already well established for the US context.[48] Therefore, if the goal is improved governance of such future industries, this book holds several inductive lessons from the regulatory and self-regulatory practices in content moderation in Europe and the United States as to why and how repurposing of the "private" in global governance and particularly private law could take place.

To begin, we must reconceptualize corporate domination not merely as commerce or capitalism, but as a distinct form of governance. To fully comprehend corporate power as a comprehensive form of governance, a historical lens is instructive. By looking back, we can trace how corporations have transitioned from purely economic entities to actors wielding significant influence over societal norms, political structures, and even

since the late 1980s see Susan Strange, *The Retreat of the State: The Diffusion of Power in the World Economy* (Cambridge University Press 1996).

46 Anja Bossow, Marie Müller-Elmau and Moritz Schramm, 'The Messiah and His Oligarchs' (*Verfassungsblog*, 1 November 2024) <https://perma.cc/55QN-HM2S>.

47 For the oligarchy quote by Cohen see ibid; referencing feudalism Shoshana Zuboff, 'Big Other: Surveillance Capitalism and the Prospects of an Information Civilization' (2015) 30 Journal of Information Technology 75. See further Cohen, 'Oligarchy, State, and Cryptopia' (SSRN 8 March 2025) <https://perma.cc/HU7F-LF94>.

48 Katharina Pistor, *The Code of Capital: How the Law Creates Wealth and Inequality* (Princeton University Press 2019); Marc Galanter, 'Why the "Haves" Come out Ahead' (1974) 9 Law & Society Review 95.

legal systems.[49] It is, for example, a mistake to think that particularly questionable extractive practices are illegal – many are not. From a substantive normative perspective, the legal system accommodates such extractive practices through protections of property and contract rather than elevating structurally weaker parties through substantive guarantees.[50] This historical perspective underscores that the power of these entities is not a natural evolution of capitalism but a deliberate engineering of governance structures that prioritize private interests over public accountability. Historically, however, even more extreme government by corporations is not at all unprecedented. Europeans, for example, subjected hundreds of millions of colonized people in India to the privatized "government" of the East India Company. The period between 1773 and 1858 is commonly referred to as one of "company rule" in India. The East India Company, a privately owned corporation, managed from London its own administration, legislation, judicial system, and military forces on the Indian subcontinent.[51] This story is not exclusive to India. Similar sufferings were brought, for example, upon the people of the West Indies by the Danes, upon Borneo by the Dutch, and upon Mozambique by the Portuguese.[52] In other words, substantial parts of sovereignty's nastiest aberration, colonialism, were *privately* governed.[53] These corporations, through their charters, were deeply entwined with the state while simultaneously cultivating

[49] Max Weber, *Wirtschaft Und Gesellschaft (1922)* (Zweitausendeins 2005); Karl Polanyi, *The Great Transformation: The Political and Economic Origins of Our Time* (Beacon Press 1944); Alfred Dupont Chandler, *The Visible Hand: The Managerial Revolution in American Business* (Harvard University Press 1877); Strange (n 45).

[50] cf. Lisa M Austin, 'Enough About Me: Why Privacy Is About Power, Not Consent (or Harm)' in Austin Sarat (ed.), *A World without Privacy: What Law Can and Should Do?* (Cambridge University Press 2014); Julie Cohen, 'Law of the Platform Economy' (2017) 51 University of California Davis Law Review 133.

[51] The literature on the East India Company is vast. See for a coeval account (with the uncritical perspective that entails): John William Kaye, *The Administration of the East India Company* (2nd ed., Richard Bentley 1853). See further Bankey Bihari Misra, *The Central Administration of the East India Company 1773–1834* (Oxford University Press 1959); HV Bowen, *The Business of Empire: The East India Company and Imperial Britain, 1756–1833* (Cambridge University Press 2005).

[52] Eric Allina-Pisano, *Slavery by Any Other Name: African Life under Company Rule in Colonial Mozambique* (University of Virginia Press 2012); Kennedy G Tregonning, *Under Chartered Company Rule: North Borneo 1881–1946* (University of Malaysia Press 1959); Waldemar C Westergaard, *The Danish West Indies under Company Rule (1671–1754)* (Macmillan 1917).

[53] For a critical reconstruction of international legal thought in the wake of its imperial and colonial context in the nineteenth century see Martti Koskenniemi, *The Gentle Civilizer of Nations: The Rise and Fall of International Law 1870–1960* (Cambridge University Press 2001) 98 et seq.

a distinct autonomy. Remarkably, at one point, members of the East India Company's Board perceived the organization as equal to – or perhaps entirely independent of – the Crown, a view supported by archival evidence suggesting claims to corporate sovereignty.[54] To be clear, this is not to conflate contemporary digital corporations with historical colonial enterprises. However, reflecting on the historicity and discursive construction of our conceptual frameworks enables us to overcome the widespread difficulty of imagining entities like Meta, Google, SpaceX, Starlink, or TikTok beyond the narrow confines of business law. In that sense, such a historically informed perspective also helps complementing existing experimentalist approaches.[55]

From a historical vantage point, the contemporary reluctance in the United States to view centralized and immensely powerful digital corporations as anything more than mere business enterprises is perplexing. In the eighteenth century, Americans openly debated whether Congress should have the authority – mirroring British colonial practices – to charter corporations for both colonial and domestic purposes. At the Constitutional Convention in 1787, James Madison proposed empowering Congress to "grant charters of incorporation where the interest of the US might require & the legislative provisions of individual States may be incompetent."[56] Yet, this motion failed, driven by fears of monopolistic dominance – particularly in banking – and state overreach. In essence, the notion of outsourcing governmental functions to chartered corporations was deliberated and dismissed in the United States over two centuries

[54] Swati Srivastava, 'Corporate Sovereign Awakening and the Making of Modern State Sovereignty: New Archival Evidence from the English East India Company' (2022) 76 International Organization 690.

[55] In governance research, experimentalism became increasingly popular to describe federal and privatized modes of project-oriented governance in the 2010s and is now increasingly applied to platform regulation. For the latter see esp. Evelyn Douek, 'Content Moderation as Systems Thinking' (2022) 136 Harvard Law Review 526, 584 et seq; Elettra Bietti, 'Experimentalism in Digital Platform Markets: Antitrust and Utilities' Convergence' (2024) 2024 University of Illinois Law Review 1277, 147 et seq; more generally Charles F Sabel and Jonathan Zeitlin, *Experimentalist Governance* (Oxford University Press 2012); Gráinne de Búrca, 'Human Rights Experimentalism' (2017) 111 American Journal of International Law 277.

[56] For the Madison quote see Max Farrand, *The Records of the Federal Convention of 1787 Vol 2* (Online Library of Liberty – Ebook 2011) (1911) 491. See further Adolf A Berle, 'Constitutional Limitations on Corporate Activity: Protection of Personal Rights from Invasion Through Economic Power' (1952) 100 University of Pennsylvania Law Review 933, 944 et seq (esp n 19); for a recent reassessment see Elizabeth Pollman, 'Quasi Governments and Inchoate Law: Berle's Vision of Limits on Corporate Power' (2019) 42 Seattle University Law Review 617.

ago, precisely due to concerns about monopolization and concentrated power. Ironically, these very concerns, if raised today regarding digital giants, are often dismissed as radical, interventionist fantasies. In short, the private corporate form has always served – and continues to serve – as a convenient shield against legitimate and pressing demands for better governance. This tactic is not a historical relic but a persistent strategy, cleverly exploited to deflect responsibility and stave off accountability.

Once we accept that these corporations function as global governors, our focus must shift to the ends they pursue and the means through which they exercise governance. What are their objectives, and what tools do they deploy to achieve them? As organizational theory has taught us, these ends are often conflicting, and the means can be overlapping. For instance, as this book demonstrates, reforms that appear ineffective in addressing structural governance flaws may serve effectively as public relations rituals, deflecting responsibility while shielding unchanged practices from external scrutiny.

The theoretical leap, then, is not simply to advocate for more public regulation of private actors – a model with evident limitations – but to reinterpret enduring ideals such as self-governance, accountability, and privacy for the new realities of private, corporate, for-profit power structures. Consider the example of shifting privacy expectations towards Facebook in the aftermath of the Cambridge Analytica scandal. Chapter 2 (Section 2.1.2 to be precise) revealed disheartening findings: while users still valued privacy, they resigned themselves to a lack of enforcement power, tacitly accepting privacy's erosion. Yet, this does not preclude a more optimistic, normative stance in other matters. Public law ideals like privacy, as hard-won achievements, deserve reinterpretation in light of private power structures. Julie Cohen offers a compelling argument here, suggesting that privacy should no longer be viewed merely as the "protection of the liberal self" as framed during the Enlightenment.[57] Instead, she contends, "[p]rivacy shelters dynamic, emergent subjectivity from the efforts of commercial and government actors to render individuals and communities fixed, transparent, and predictable."[58] Much in the same vein, Lisa Austin's genealogy of privacy unveiled that its contemporary linkage to property and trespassing, which is the basis for the idea that extractive practices are basically merely a matter of consent, cuts out a second, but arguable more

[57] Julie Cohen, 'What Privacy Is For' (2013) 126 Harvard Law Review 1904, 1905.
[58] Ibid 1905.

important public law dimension of privacy, namely that of the rule of law and protections against search and seizure. In Austin's telling,

> [a] broad rule-of-law approach [of privacy] would focus on the surveilling party and questions of power, its possibility of abuse, and legal safeguards. It would place questions of transparency and accountability at the center of the debate rather than as add-ons to the reasonable expectation of privacy analysis.[59]

Similar reasoning can be extended to other principles of good governance and constellations of domination. These ideals are not relics of a bygone era but tools to be reactivated and adapted to confront the threats posed by private power. By reimagining and operationalizing these principles, we can reinvigorate them for the challenges of today and tomorrow.

One effective way to reactivate these public law ideals – participation, due process, equality, and self-governance – is, somewhat paradoxically, through the framework of domestic private law.[60] Despite their global reach, corporate global governors remain bound by the laws of their jurisdictions of incorporation. This presents a significant opportunity: instead of (only) ascending into increasingly abstract discussions of governance, we can focus on creatively reimagining and operationalizing existing mechanisms within contract and corporate law to drive meaningful change. Privately formed, profit-driven bureaucracies already embed fragments of traditionally "public" elements within their structures, whether through reason-giving, participatory processes, or accountability mechanisms.[61] These incorporations are not coincidental but rather pragmatic adaptations to maintain legitimacy and manage complex stakeholder relationships. Contract and corporate law, with its capacity to mediate obligations and responsibilities, becomes a practical tool for embedding public law ideals into private governance practices.

For instance, the principles of participation and reason-giving can be integrated into contracts by mandating transparent decision-making processes or requiring explicit justifications for corporate actions that

59 Austin (n 50) 164.

60 And the osmosis between spheres is by no means novel. For example, US "public forum" jurisprudence distinguishes different types of government property, which then entails different legal obligations for that property's "governance" or "management," see Robert Post, 'Between Governance and Management: The History and Theory of the Public Forum' (1986) 34 University of California Los Angeles Law Review 1713. For a reconceptualization of important aspects of EU law through the prism of "data" see Thomas Streinz, 'The Evolution of European Data Law' in Paul Craig and Gráinne de Búrca (eds.), *The Evolution of EU Law* (3rd ed., Oxford University Press 2021).

61 Selznick (n 33).

affect stakeholders. Similarly, contractual frameworks can enforce accountability by setting clear benchmarks for performance and remedies for noncompliance. Equality and self-governance, too, can find footholds in private law by ensuring equitable terms for all parties involved and enabling stakeholders to have a more substantial say in the governance structures they are subjected to. By definition, contract law is highly adaptable to new challenges – much more so than public law. To reiterate, at least in theory, there are few hard limits to establishing governance frameworks through contracts that embody public-interest principles. This, too, is a form of freedom within property and contract law. Therefore, a pragmatic next step toward new accountability norms might be to first theorize what contractual solutions are needed to govern phenomena like those mentioned above in a more public-oriented way, and then to devise practical solutions to implement them.[62]

A particularly instructive – and cautionary – area is the law governing philanthropy, endowments, foundations, and fiduciary contracts. Drafting a contract that binds a corporate executive to serve a specific public interest – whether improving content moderation or ensuring that the data intake of a large language model reflects values like diversity and inclusion – is not particularly difficult. Private law is brimming with fiduciary relationships.[63] Those can be construed between directors and shareholders, trustees and beneficiaries, and others. Typically, these fiduciary duties are anchored to the profit interests of the principal. But that is not a given. It is entirely feasible to create an entity whose fiduciary duty is, for example, to safeguard environmental sustainability or maintain an impeccable human rights record – at all costs.[64] First – cautious and potentially ceremonial – experiments have already begun. In 2023, Anthropic, a leading artificial intelligence company, established a so-called Long-Term Benefit Trust, which is intended gradually to assume influence over the company's board and to steer the firm toward public-interest objectives. Especially in companies controlled by a small group of people, or even a single shareholder, such structures are not only possible but relatively straightforward to implement.

[62] See e.g. Radin (n 25).

[63] Victor Brudney, 'Contract and Fiduciary Duty in Corporate Law' (1997) 38 Boston College Law Review 595; for an economic perspective see Reinier H Kraakman, 'Gatekeepers: The Anatomy of a Third-Party Enforcement Strategy' (1986) 2 Journal of Law, Economics & Organization 53; Jack M Balkin, 'Information Fiduciaries and the First Amendment' (2016) 49 UC Davis Law Review 1183.

[64] The practical viability of such an arrangement may prove nonetheless complicated, see again Lund and Pollman (n 42).

Choosing not to build such frameworks is, in reality, a normative decision, not a reflection of unavailable options.

In this context, the Oversight Board's model of establishing an irrevocable trust, with trustees whose fiduciary duty is to protect the Board's independent judgment, is a genuinely innovative approach.[65] However, making such arrangements work in practice requires genuine commitment from organizations willing to cede power, capital, and influence on entities whose fiduciary duty is tied to a pre-defined public interest. Separating agents for specific functions is an indispensable structural principle of society and any larger organization.[66] This is also well recognized in economics. Problems arise, the economists taught us, when the interests of the principal diverge from that of the agent.[67] Therefore, any separated entity committed to governance in the public interest must have the authority to challenge practices within the company that conflict with this duty. Establishing such differentiated agents within a single company is not only difficult but likely demands a fundamental cultural shift in how we understand the role of organizations in contemporary economic and social life. Lina Khan has called for such "structural separations" from an antitrust perspective.[68] Evelyn Douek built on this, advocating for a "separation of functions" to disentangle content moderation from the business operations of social media platforms.[69] How exactly these principles might be implemented in practice remains an open question. Yet, it will be the responsibility of lawmakers to offer clear incentives, signaling that these structures are genuinely desired, and ensuring that "internal but separated governance entities" do not become mere ceremonial gestures.

6.2.2 *Infrastructure, Code, and Supply Chains*

But repurposing private law will not be enough. To effectuate new accountability norms, we must move beyond the traditional understanding of the normative. Corporations, after all, are human-run organizations and, as such, are inherently subject to legal regulation and external feedback. Yet, their power extends beyond – indeed, often eclipses – the conventional realm

65 cf. Oversight Board Trust Agreement Section 2.1 and 2.2; also 4.3.

66 Famously Emile Durkheim, *De La Division Du Travail Social* (1893).

67 Michael C Jensen and William H Meckling, 'Theory of the Firm: Managerial Behavior, Agency Costs and Ownership Structure' (1976) 3 Journal of Financial Economics 305; Eugene Fama, 'Agency Problems and the Theory of the Firm' (1980) 88 Journal of Political Economy 288.

68 Lina M Khan, 'The Separation of Platforms and Commerce' (2019) 119 Columbia Law Review 973.

69 Douek (n 55) 586 et seq.

of rulemaking and enforcement. Even in content moderation, this book's example of rather unaccountable private power structures, rulemaking, and rule-enforcement covers only one dimension. As discussed in Chapter 2, also here, and even more so in other technologies, corporate influence operates not only through rules but through code, technology, infrastructure, and hardware. Thereby, corporate global governance often bypasses "traditional" mechanisms – normative documents, reports, or public consultations. Instead, it operates through code, technology, and infrastructural control. Consider, for example, the role of Starlink, Elon Musk's satellite-internet company, during the Ukraine war since 2022. Initially, Ukrainian forces depended heavily on Starlink's infrastructure, until, during a critical counteroffensive, intact systems inexplicably went offline or – prior accounts were later disputed – were never activated in crucial areas.[70] Reports suggest this was due to Musk's acquiescence to Russian President Vladimir Putin's threats against Musk's broader business interests and nuclear war if the company continued to aid Ukraine. Whichever concrete version of the story happened, the example epitomizes the level of immediate infrastructural sway such companies and the individuals controlling them hold over world affairs, an effective – yet troubling – form of governance.

Therefore, I echo demands for conceptual expansion in our understandings of regulation and governance: from focusing narrowly on legal forms to examining the organizational and techno-normative structures where power is enacted.[71] These frameworks encode normative decisions into technological systems, shaping societal interactions and individual experiences. Just as digital platforms have disrupted traditional, localized business-to-consumer relationships, new technologies transform and discipline societal and commercial interaction. Regulating these shifts will require more than traditional rulemaking and theorizing constrained by past experience. The focus must move – and already does so in the academy – to include the underlying infrastructures and computational systems themselves. As those systems are largely operated by private, for-

[70] Walter Isaacson, *Elon Musk* (Simon & Schuster 2023) 428–434; Ella Creamer, 'Elon Musk Biographer Admits Suggestion SpaceX Head Blocked Ukraine Drone Attack Was Wrong' *Guardian* (12 September 2023) <https://perma.cc/YR7U-Q68A>.

[71] Edwards (n 37); DeNardis and Musiani (n 37); Benedict Kingsbury, 'Infrastructure and InfraReg: On Rousing the International Law "Wizards of Is"' (2019) 8 Cambridge International Law Journal 171; for data see esp. Angelina Fisher and Thomas Streinz, 'Confronting Data Inequality' (2022) 60 Columbia Journal of Transnational Law 829. For digital infrastructures see famously: Joel R Reidenberg, 'Lex Informatica: The Formulation of Information Policy Rules Through Technology' (1998) 76 Texas Law Review 553; Lawrence Lessig, *Code: And Other Laws of Cyberspace* (Basic Books 1999).

profit actors, future governance arrangements will arguably further entangle spheres of authority of centralized corporate actors that benefit from stylized guarantees of property and innovative modes of contracting while classic government increasingly adapts entrepreneurial and arguably more pragmatic tactics.[72] Accountability mechanisms and structural, substantive rules should therefore be embedded not only in external regulations, but directly in the code and infrastructure. In this way, good governance must permeate every layer of the complex socio-technological practices we call artificial intelligence, social media, or any other emerging technology.

This task is made all the more challenging by the technological modalities unique to each sector. Two aspects stand out. First, while vertically integrated corporations may retain control over much of these technologies, their dissemination may give rise to new, semi-autonomous systems beyond the reach of their creators. That is especially the case for "artificial intelligence." It is crucial not to conceive of "artificial intelligence" as a single, monolithic entity crafted by one actor. These are intricate, multifaceted systems, interacting with a variety of players across entire "supply chains" of technology and governance.[73] As Jennifer Cobbe, Michael Veale, and Jatinder Singh demonstrate, the intricate interplay of interconnectedness and centralization in these sectors complicates the attribution of legal responsibility. Yet, this is not a problem unique to new technologies; it mirrors issues long observed in global commerce.[74] Governance proposals and heaps of local laws – think tort, product safety, intellectual property, and so forth – for such scenarios already exist. Legal tools to address such injustices are already in place. They may be underutilized or lack enforcement power at present, but this reflects the shortcomings of political economy and questionable alure of statements of "newness" on behalf of corporate executives more than the inadequacy of legal possibilities.[75] In fact, some of these issues may not require entirely new governance structures, but rather a more assertive application and modern interpretation of existing liability regimes.

[72] For the latter see e.g. Fleur Johns, 'From Planning to Prototypes: New Ways of Seeing Like a State' (2019) 82 Modern Law Review 833.

[73] Jennifer Cobbe, Michael Veale and Jatinder Singh, 'Understanding Accountability in Algorithmic Supply Chains', *2023 ACM Conference on Fairness, Accountability, and Transparency* (ACM 2023).

[74] See e.g. Clodia Vurro, Angeloantonio Russo and Francesco Perrini, 'Shaping Sustainable Value Chains: Network Determinants of Supply Chain Governance Models' (2009) 90 Journal of Business Ethics 607.

[75] For the latter see Lee Vinsel and Andrew L Russell, *The Innovation Delusion* (Currency 2020).

Second, positively impacting the politics of artifacts requires restructuring the epistemologies and creative processes that produce these artifacts. In other words, a crucial element in effectuating new accountability norms will be to entrench them in the culture and education of engineers, computer scientists, biologists, economists, and, frankly, lawyers. While professional ethics are often considered ineffective and difficult to enforce, we should not underestimate the power of ethical and cultural norms in organizational contexts and, especially, in higher education. If universities do not teach engineers and economists to think about the harms – politely termed "social costs" – that their practices may cause, how can we expect them to recognize these risks?[76] Conversely, when ethical considerations and social awareness become deeply integrated into a sector's culture – often as a result of earlier scandals – these norms can curb questionable but profitable practices. For example, the field of human genetics research is relatively well-regulated through a combination of ex ante regulation, formal accountability procedures, and a cultural commitment to certain ethical standards.[77] In short, eventually, any system of new accountability norms must combine legal rules, technological means, and people.

6.3 Reasons for Optimism

This brings us to the final, and cautiously optimistic, epilogic notes of this book. Any future governance arrangement – whether private or otherwise – exists within a sociopolitical context. Governance, after all, is about shaping human behavior. Therefore, it should respond to the needs and desires of the humans it governs. Crafting concrete frameworks for this will undoubtedly be complex. Even the very definition of "human" might evolve with advances in artificial intelligence, biotechnology, and human "enhancement" (though one cannot help but notice the hype in some of

[76] That is, of course, if the people running those corporations at all finish their higher education, cf. Daub's analysis of the "drop out" culture permeating Silicon Valley entrepreneurship Adrian Daub, *What Tech Calls Thinking: An Inquiry into the Intellectual Bedrock of Silicon Valley* (Farrar, Straus and Giroux 2020).

[77] cf. Eric S Lander and others, 'Adopt a Moratorium on Heritable Genome Editing' (2019) 567 Nature 165; Britta C van Beers, 'Rewriting the Human Genome, Rewriting Human Rights Law? Human Rights, Human Dignity, and Human Germline Modification in the CRISPR Era' (2020) 7 Journal of Law and the Biosciences 1; Henry T Greely, *CRISPR People: The Science and Ethics of Editing Humans* (MIT Press 2021).

these fields).[78] Yet, whenever groups of people are brought together through the imposition of rules or by reliance on technological infrastructures, they inevitably begin to voice demands. These demands will often reflect the classic ideals of public law: individual rights, self-governance, participation, reason-giving, accountability, equal treatment, and due process.

In other words, when publics form – whether entirely transnational or virtual – demands for good governance will inevitably follow. And delivering good governance often hinges on adapting these public law principles. Whether we still call them – or should call them – public law principles is a different question.[79] Maybe, some of the abstract ideas might go down easier in some sectors if they were conceptually repackaged.

However, the striking development of the last centuries is that this adaptation will increasingly occur beyond the realm of the dominant authorities of the time. Consider this: After the unfathomable horrors of two World Wars and the Shoah, the state was the undisputed locus of supreme authority in Europe. States, at the time, had a distinct shape, trajectory, and ideology (the latter especially fueled by the Cold War). In the West, as a matter of principle, states would protect fundamental rights – more so after 1968 and not necessarily in a fair and equal matter (think of Algerians in France and then still prevalent colonialism in general) but bear with me.[80] Nonetheless, the post-War era is also one of transnationalism, especially in Europe. However, it took the European Union – an entity rooted firmly in public law – decades to build a meaningful human rights framework. At the time, the idea that a supranational organization, primarily focused on facilitating trade in Western Europe, should concern itself with human rights seemed baffling. Twice in the late 1950s, the European Court of Justice explicitly dismissed the notion that human rights law had any place within the

[78] cf. Allen Edward Buchanan, *Better than Human: The Promise and Perils of Enhancing Ourselves* (Oxford University Press 2017).

[79] Conceptual scrutiny is paramount here, cf. Megan Donaldson and Benedict Kingsbury, 'Ersatz Normativity or Public Law in Global Governance: The Hard Case of International Prescriptions for National Infrastructure Regulation' (2013) 14 Chicago Journal of International Law 1, 48 et seq.

[80] For postcolonial perspectives on EU law see Signe Rehling Larsen, 'European Public Law after Empires' (2022) 1 European Law Open 6; Lionel Zevounou, 'For a Postcolonial Reading of EU Law' (*Verfassungsblog*, 21 March 2024) <https://perma.cc/A7P2-U5ZA>. In general on the evolution of EU law see Joseph H H Weiler, 'The Community System: The Dual Character of Supranationalism' (1981) 1 Yearbook of European Law 267; Joseph H H Weiler, 'The Transformation of Europe' (1991) 100 Yale Law Journal 2403.

Community's acquis.[81] But this position evolved. Gradually, the Court "discovered" that the supranational project had a voice in human rights matters.[82] Decades later, the European Union, now an institutional giant tackling everything from climate policy to migration, applies a comprehensive human rights charter – a charter that is, amusingly, used mostly to holding its Member States to account rather than the Union itself.

None of this would have seemed plausible in the early 1950s. And yet it happened – driven, in no small part, by public pressure and savvy lawyers. The lesson here is that power adapts in unpredictable ways. Today, much like then, power structures evolve in response to the demands of the public, though increasingly beyond the familiar corridors of nation-states.

Therefore, this book's final message is one of cautious yet genuine optimism. Both case studies illuminate the complexity of holding novel power structures, such as social media companies, accountable. These entities operate in ways that challenge traditional regulatory paradigms: classic state-based regulation often reaches its limits, and corporate self-regulation remains, at best, incremental. Yet, despite these challenges, the case studies reveal how quickly, and fundamentally groundbreaking organizations normative regimes, and accountability forums can emerge. Their current shortcomings, when measured against the ideals they aspire to emulate, are not a reason for disillusionment. On the contrary, these limitations serve as a call to action – to imagine more ambitious improvements, devise innovative governance concepts, and craft positive scenarios for accountability in the digital age.

Achieving these goals demands a careful balancing act. We must avoid the pitfalls of narrow doctrinalism, which clings too rigidly to traditional legal forms while neglecting the rich variety of governance methods beyond the state. At the same time, we must reject the temptation of purely ceremonial law-mimicry, which risks reducing accountability efforts to symbolic gestures devoid of substantive impact. Instead, we should embrace the creativity and ingenuity displayed in emerging accountability experiments, which offer fertile ground for exploring new models of governance. The enduring ideals of public law remain central to these efforts, even as their application evolves in response to new challenges. Projects like rights, review, and democratic self-governance might have to be repackaged, adapted, and other means of governance repurposed in light

[81] Stork [1959] European Court of Justice C 1/58, ECLI:EU:C:1959:4; Nold [1960] European Court of Justice Joined cases 36, 37, 38–59, 40–59, ECLI:EU:C:1960:36.

[82] Stauder [1969] European Court of Justice C 26–69, ECLI:EU:C:1969:57.

of them. In that sense, public law's principles – its emphasis on accountability, fairness, and the protection of public interests – persist as touchstones, even when traditional legal frameworks falter. I allow myself to come back to a quote by Julie Cohen, who, ever a staunch critic of "performances" like the Oversight Board, nonetheless agrees that

> "rule of law" language is intended to supply a framework for talking about power, calling it to account, and constraining systematic abuse. Designing governance institutions for the networked information era requires new thinking about how to translate those broadly framed rule-of-law commitments into mid-level principles capable of being operationalized within networked digital environments.[83]

Emulated Guardians, like the Oversight Board or the EU's ODSs, exemplify this new thinking. Yet, a skeptic might caution, are these institutions not merely flawed facades – empty rituals crafted by corporate executives and starry-eyed Eurocrats?[84] Some of this critique is well-founded. Yet, as this book argues – particularly through its focus on emulation – there is much to be gleaned from these imperfect regulatory and corporate experiments. While undeniably fragile and flawed, they represent a new breed of institution. Born out of necessity and shaped by the ingenuity of legal entrepreneurs, these entities fuse self-serving corporate interests with gestures toward broader public values. Once established, they take on a life of their own, drawing on the residual faith in rule-of-law rhetoric – though, admittedly, such lofty ideals may resonate more strongly in Europe than in the United States.[85] When approached thoughtfully, the rule-of-law language Cohen references offers precisely the mindset, and attracts precisely the individuals, capable of helping to build innovative accountability structures. Can lawyers accomplish this alone? Certainly not. Must we take into account material and distributive aspects beyond norm-creation and institution-building?[86] Absolutely.

[83] Julie Cohen, 'From Lex Informatica to the Control Revolution' (2021) 36 Berkeley Technology Law Journal 1017, 1038, 1047. For prior discussion of this see at 1.1.

[84] Cohen diagnoses depression masqueraded as optimism among tech scholars who, for the lack of feasible alternatives, turn to apologists of those private governance experiments, ibid 1038–1042. See also Cohen's criticism of the creators of the Oversight Board (notably, not of the Board itself) at ibid 1048.

[85] For the latter see Jack M Balkin, 'Constitutional Crisis and Constitutional Rot' (2017) 77 Maryland Law Review 147.

[86] See esp. Griffin, who rightly highlights the material aspects while also mentioning "democracy," a concept whose realization arguably hinges on effective public law (idea[l]s), cf. Rachel Griffin, 'Public and Private Power in Social Media Governance: Multistakeholderism, the Rule of Law and Democratic Accountability' (2023) 14 Transnational Legal Theory 46.

Yet, until proven otherwise, we might as well explore how the performativity and symbolism inherent in public law ideals can be harnessed to incrementally create meaningful guardians of power that work toward a more just world. I would argue that this is even more critical in times of growing public distrust and widespread uncertainty over who truly holds the reins of power – especially in a world where traditional markers of authority fade away. Arguably, this distinguishes broader questions of governance and organizational power like content moderation from the specific issue of privacy, which lacks a clear organizational program when compared to individual rights adjudication and self-governance, and which therefore appears to be indeed a hard case even for the biggest optimist. Likewise, the shifts in regulatory policy and corporate strategy among US digital corporations in early 2025 – closely aligned with the second Trump administration – underscored just how fluid and precarious these governance arrangements are. To assume that the fight for more accountable technology companies is lost simply because the Oversight Board or the DSA fell short of their initially overblown expectations would accomplish only one thing: further entrenching the status quo.

However, becoming authoritative guardians will require time; after all, courts and other traditional public institutions took generations to achieve their peak authority – an authority, ironically, now seemingly in decline. Yet dismissing these emerging spectacles as fruitless would all but guarantee they yield nothing worthwhile. Public law's role in this shifting landscape transcends formal regulation. It provides a framework for thinking, a lens through which governance can be interpreted and molded. Its enduring power lies in its universality, its ability to resonate with our collective imagination, and its intrinsic value as a guide for accountability and justice. As Megan Donaldson and Benedict Kingsbury have put it, public law is both "a method and a mindset."[87] These qualities ensure that its relevance endures, even as governance increasingly transcends the traditional confines of the state.

Ultimately, public law's legacy lives on not merely through formal statutes or court decisions but through the broader structures that shape how we think, communicate, and envision accountability. It offers a foundation for navigating an uncertain future, not because it has all the answers but because it provides a framework for asking the right questions – and for imagining a governance landscape that is both innovative and principled. The book's opening question centered on how to

[87] Donaldson and Kingsbury (n 79) 48.

control private power structures beyond the state, particularly as the state's ability to exert its authority gradually diminishes. In response, we may conclude that perhaps the most surprising, and also the most encouraging, takeaway of this book is that public law remains a dominant framework in global governance, even beyond the confines of traditional public law and public actors. Concepts from administrative and constitutional law are seeping into private law structures – often in ways that are twisted, occasionally self-serving, and slightly askew, yet undeniably significant. Public law, then, endures as a vital force, not only for what it has been, but also for what it continues to inspire: a vision of governance grounded in ideals that are universally understood, deeply resonant, and, ultimately, built upon good ideas.

Bibliography

Abrams N, 'Administrative Law Judge Systems: The California View' (1977) 29 Administrative Law Review 487

Adorno T, *Gesammelte Schriften 9.2 Soziologische Schriften II (Zweite Hälfte)* (Suhrkamp 1975)

Afriat H and others, '"This Is Capitalism. It Is Not Illegal": Users' Attitudes toward Institutional Privacy Following the Cambridge Analytica Scandal' (2021) 37 The Information Society 115

Alberti J, 'The Position of Boards of Appeal: Between Functional Continuity and Independence' in Merijn Chamon, Annalisa Volpato, and Mariolina Eliantonio (eds.), *Boards of Appeal of EU Agencies* (Oxford University Press 2022)

Alchian AA, 'Uncertainty, Evolution, and Economic Theory' (1950) 58 Journal of Political Economy 211

Allina-Pisano E, *Slavery by Any Other Name: African Life under Company Rule in Colonial Mozambique* (University of Virginia Press 2012)

Alschner W and Charlotin D, 'The Growing Complexity of the International Court of Justice's Self-Citation Network' (2018) 29 European Journal of International Law 83

Alter KJ, *The New Terrain of International Law: Courts, Politics, Rights* (Princeton University Press 2014)

Alter KJ, Helfer LR and Madsen MR (eds.), *International Court Authority* (Cambridge University Press 2018)

'How Context Shapes the Authority of International Courts' in Karen J Alter, Laurence R Helfer and Mikael Rask Madsen (eds.), *International Court Authority* (Oxford University Press 2018)

Aman AC, 'The Globalizing State: A Future-Oriented Perspective on the Public/Private Distinction, Federalism, and Democracy' (1998) 31 Vanderbilt Journal of Transnational Law 769

Anderson BRO, *Imagined Communities: Reflections on the Origin and Spread of Nationalism* (Verso 1983)

Andrew J and Bernard F (eds.), *Human Rights Responsibilities in the Digital Age: States, Companies, and Individuals* (Hart 2021)

Arendt H, *The Origins of Totalitarianism* (Harcourt, Brace and Company 1951)

The Human Condition (2nd ed. [1998], University of Chicago Press 1958)

Aristoteles, *Politics*

Arnull A, 'The Principle of Effective Judicial Protection in EU Law: An Unruly Horse?' (2011) 36 European Law Review 51

Asimov M, 'Five Models of Administrative Adjudication' (2015) 63 The American Journal of Comparative Law 3

Austin JL, *How to Do Things with Words* (Oxford University Press 1962)

Austin LM, 'Enough About Me: Why Privacy Is About Power, Not Consent (or Harm)' in Austin Sarat (ed.), *A World without Privacy: What Law Can and Should Do?* (Cambridge University Press 2014)

Bader Ginsburg R, 'The Role of Dissenting Opinions' (2010) 95 Minnesota Law Review 1

Balkin JM, 'What Is Postmodern Constitutionalism?' (1992) 90 Michigan Law Review 1966

'Populism and Progressivism as Constitutional Categories (Book Review)' (1995) 104 Yale Law Journal 1935

'Information Fiduciaries and the First Amendment' (2016) 49 UC Davis Law Review 1183

'Constitutional Crisis and Constitutional Rot' (2017) 77 Maryland Law Review 147

'Free Speech Is a Triangle' (2018) 118 Columbia Law Review 2011

'How to Regulate (and Not Regulate) Social Media' (2021) 1 Journal of Free Speech Law 71

'To Reform Social Media, Reform Informational Capitalism' in Lee C Bollinger and Geoffrey R Stone (eds.), *Social Media, Freedom of Speech, and the Future of Democracy* (Oxford University Press 2022) 233

Banakar R (ed.), *Rights in Context: Law and Justice in Late Modern Society* (Ashgate 2010)

Barton JH, 'Behind the Legal Explosion' (1975) 27 Stanford Law Review 567

Baude W, 'Adjudication Outside Article III' (2020) 133 Harvard Law Review 1511

BBC, 'Facebook Deletes Ethiopia PM's Post That Urged Citizens to "bury" Rebels' (BBC, 3 November 2021) <https://perma.cc/7VAB-XABF>

Beckers A and others, *The Foundations of European Transnational Private Law* (Hart 2024)

Beetham D, *The Legitimation of Power* (Humanities Press International 1991)

Bélanger F and Crossler RE, 'Privacy in the Digital Age: A Review of Information Privacy Research in Information Systems' (2011) 35 MIS Quarterly 1017

Belli L, Francisco PA and Zingales N, 'Law of the Land or Law of the Platform? Beware of the Privatisation of Regulation and Police' in Luca Belli and Nicolo Zingales (eds.), *Platform Regulations – How Platforms are Regulated and How they Regulate Us* [Official Outcome of the UN IGF Dynamic Coalition on Platform Responsibility] (FGV Direito Rio 2017)

Benkler Y (ed.), *The Wealth of Networks: How Social Production Transforms Markets and Freedom* (Yale University Press 2006)

Berle AA, 'Constitutional Limitations on Corporate Activity: Protection of Personal Rights from Invasion Through Economic Power' (1952) 100 University of Pennsylvania Law Review 933

Berlin I, 'Two Concepts of Liberty (1958)' in Isiah Berlin, *Four Essays on Liberty* (Oxford University Press 1969)

Berry FS and Berry W, 'Innovation and Diffusion Models in Policy Research' in Christopher M Weible and Paul A Sabatier (eds.), *Theories of Policy Process* (Routledge 2018)

Bickel AM, 'The Decade of School Desegregation: Progress and Prospects' (1964) 64 Columbia Law Review 193

The Least Dangerous Branch: The Supreme Court at the Bar of Politics (2nd ed., Yale University Press 1986)

Bietti E, 'Genealogy of Digital Platform Regulation' (2023) 7 Georgetown Law & Technology Review 1

'Experimentalism in Digital Platform Markets: Antitrust and Utilities' Convergence' (2024) 2024 University of Illinois Law Review 1277

Birkenkötter H, 'What the Secretariat Makes It: How International Civil Servants Shape Contemporary International Law' (2023) 20 International Organizations Law Review 426

Blauberger M and others, 'ECJ Judges Read the Morning Papers: Explaining the Turnaround of European Citizenship Jurisprudence' (2018) 25 Journal of European Public Policy 1422

Blichner LC and Molander A, 'Mapping Juridification' (2008) 14 European Law Journal 36

Bloch-Wehba H, 'Global Platform Governance: Private Power in the Shadow of the State' (2019) 72 SMU Law Review 27

Bogdandy A von and Venzke I, *In wessen Namen? Internationale Gerichte in Zeiten globalen Regierens* (Suhrkamp 2014)

Boghossian P, *Fear of Knowledge* (Oxford University Press 2006)

Bork RH, *The Antitrust Paradox* (Basic Books 1978)

Bossow A, Müller-Elmau M and Schramm M, 'The Messiah and His Oligarchs' (*Verfassungsblog*, 1 November 2024) <https://perma.cc/55QN-HM2S>

Bourdieu P, *Outline of a Theory of Practice* (Cambridge University Press 1977)

Distinction (Harvard University Press 1984)

'The Practice of Reflexive Sociology (The Paris Workshop)' in Pierre Bourdieu and Loïc JD Wacquant (eds.), *An Invitation to Reflexive Sociology* (Polity Press 1992)

The Logic of Practice (Stanford University Press 1992)

Boushey G, *Policy Diffusion Dynamics in America* (Cambridge University Press 2010)

Bowen HV, *The Business of Empire: The East India Company and Imperial Britain, 1756–1833* (Cambridge University Press 2005)

Bowker GC and Star SL, *Sorting Things Out: Classification and Its Consequences* (MIT Press 1999)

Bradford A, 'The Brussels Effect' (2012) 107 Northwestern University Law Review 1

The Brussels Effect: How the European Union Rules the World (Oxford University Press 2020)
Digital Empires: The Global Battle to Regulate Technology (Oxford University Press 2023)
'Europe's Digital Constitution' (2023) 64 Virginia Journal of International Law 1
Bradley K, 'Tribunals and Adjudication' in Peter Cane and others (eds.), *The Oxford Handbook of Comparative Administrative Law* (Oxford University Press 2020)
Brenninkmeijer A, Lalikova LF and Siry D, 'Public Audit Accountability' in Peter Cane, Herwig CH Hofmann, Eric C Ip and Peter L Lindseth, (eds.), *The Oxford Handbook of Comparative Administrative Law* (Oxford University Press 2021)
Bretherton C and Vogler J, 'A Global Actor Past Its Peak?' (2013) 27 International Relations 375
Brooks P and Gewirtz P (eds.), *Law's Stories: Narrative and Rhetoric in the Law* (Yale University Press 1996)
Brosch M, 'Alles neu macht das . . . Facebook Oversight Board?' (2021) 28 MultiMedia und Recht (MMR) 26
Brown RH, 'Bureaucracy as Practice: Towards a Political Phenomenology of Formal Organizations' (1978) 23 Administrative Science Quarterly 365
Brudney V, 'Contract and Fiduciary Duty in Corporate Law' (1997) 38 Boston College Law Review 595
Buchanan AE, *Better than Human: The Promise and Perils of Enhancing Ourselves* (Oxford University Press 2017)
Buchheim J and Möllers C, '§ 46 Gerichtliche Verwaltungskontrollen als Steuerungsinstrument' in Andreas Voßkuhle, Martin Eifert and Christoph Möllers (eds.), *Grundlagen des Verwaltungsrechts*, vol. II (3rd ed., Beck 2022)
Buiten MC, 'The Digital Services Act: From Intermediary Liability to Platform Regulation' (2021) 12 JIPITEC 361
de Búrca G, 'Human Rights Experimentalism' (2017) 111 American Journal of International Law 277
Butler J, *Excitable Speech: A Politics of the Performative* (Routledge 1997)
Calliess C and Ruffert M (eds.), *EUV/AEUV: Das Verfassungsrecht der Europäischen Union mit Europäischer Grundrechtecharta: Kommentar* (6th ed., Beck 2022)
Cammaerts B and Mansell R, 'Digital Platform Policy and Regulation: Toward a Radical Democratic Turn' (2020) 14 International Journal of Communication 135
Cane P, *Administrative Tribunals and Adjudication* (Hart 2010)
Controlling Administrative Power: An Historical Comparison (Cambridge University Press 2016)
'A Framework for Historical Comparison of Control of National, Supranational and Transnational Public Power' in Susan Rose-Ackerman, Blake Emerson and Peter L Lindseth (eds.), *Comparative Administrative Law* (2nd ed., Edward Elgar 2017)

Cappelletti M, *The Judicial Process in Comparative Perspective* (Clarendon Press 1989)
Cassese A (ed.), 'Introduction' in *Realizing Utopia* (Oxford University Press 2012)
Cassese S, 'Administrative Law without the State? The Challenge of Global Regulation' (2005) 37 International Law and Politics 663
(ed.), *Research Handbook on Global Administrative Law* (Edward Elgar 2016)
Cauffman C and Goanta C, 'A New Order: The Digital Services Act and Consumer Protection' (2021) 12 European Journal of Risk Regulation 758
Celeste E, 'Digital Constitutionalism: A New Systematic Theorisation' (2019) 33 International Review of Law, Computers & Technology 76
Celeste E, Heldt A and Iglesias Keller C (eds.), *Constitutionalising Social Media* (Hart 2022)
Chamon M and Fromage D, 'Between Added Value and Untapped Potential: The Boards of Appeal in the Field of EU Financial Regulation' in Merijn Chamon, Annalisa Volpato and Mariolina Eliantonio (eds.), *Boards of Appeal of EU Agencies: Towards Judicialization of Administrative Review?* (Oxford University Press 2022)
Chamon M, Volpato A and Eliantonio M (eds.), *Boards of Appeal of EU Agencies: Towards Judicialization of Administrative Review?* (Oxford University Press 2022)
Chandler AD, *The Visible Hand: The Managerial Revolution in American Business* (Harvard University Press 1877)
Chayes A, 'The Role of the Judge in Public Law Litigation' (1976) 89 Harvard Law Review 1281
Chayes A and Chayes AH, 'On Compliance' (1993) 47 International Organization 175
Citron DK, 'Technological Due Process' (2008) 85 Washington University Law Review 1249
Citron DK and Norton HL, 'Intermediaries and Hate Speech: Fostering Digital Citizenship for Our Information Age' (2011) 91 Boston University Law Review 1435
Clapham A, *Human Rights Obligations of Non-State Actors* (Oxford University Press 2006)
Cobbe J, Veale M and Singh J, 'Understanding Accountability in Algorithmic Supply Chains' in *2023 ACM Conference on Fairness, Accountability, and Transparency* (ACM 2023)
Cohen A and Vauchez A, 'The Social Construction of Law: The European Court of Justice and Its Legal Revolution Revisited' (2011) 7 Annual Review of Law and Social Science 417
Cohen J and Fung A, 'Democracy and the Digital Public Sphere' in Lucy Bernholz, Hélène Landemore and Rob Reich (eds.), *Digital Technology and Democratic Theory* (University of Chicago Press 2021)
Cohen J, *Configuring the Networked Self* (Yale University Press 2012)
'What Privacy Is For' (2013) 126 Harvard Law Review 1904
'Law of the Platform Economy' (2017) 51 University of California Davis Law Review 133

Between Truth and Power: The Legal Constructions of Informational Capitalism (Oxford University Press 2019)
'From Lex Informatica to the Control Revolution' (2021) 36 Berkeley Technology Law Journal 1017
'Oligarchy, State, and Cryptopia' (SSRN 8 March 2025) <https://perma.cc/HU7F-LF94>
Cohen M, 'Property and Sovereignty' (1927) 13 Cornell Law Quarterly 8
Coleman JL and Leiter B, 'Determinacy, Objectivity, and Authority' (1993) 142 University of Pennsylvania Law Review 549
Common MF, 'Fear the Reaper: How Content Moderation Rules Are Enforced on Social Media' (2020) 34 International Review of Law, Computers & Technology 126
Corporate Europe Observatory, 'How Corporate Lobbying Undermined the EU's Push to Ban Surveillance Ads' (2022) <https://perma.cc/GC3S-6DQJ>
'Big Tech's Last Minute Attempt to Tame EU Tech Rules: Lobbying in Times of Trilogues' (2022) <https://perma.cc/U2G7-4ESJ>
Costello RÁ, 'Faux Ami? Interrogating the Normative Coherence of "Digital Constitutionalism"' (2023) 12 Global Constitutionalism 326
Cowls J, Darius P, Santistevan D and Schramm M, 'Constitutional Metaphors: Facebook's "Supreme Court" and the Legitimation of Platform Governance' (2024) 26 New Media & Society 2448
Craig PP, *EU Administrative Law* (3rd ed., Oxford University Press 2018)
Creamer E, 'Elon Musk Biographer Admits Suggestion SpaceX Head Blocked Ukraine Drone Attack Was Wrong' (Guardian, 12 September 2023) <https://perma.cc/YR7U-Q68A>
Culnan MJ and Armstrong PK, 'Information Privacy Concerns, Procedural Fairness, and Impersonal Trust: An Empirical Investigation' (1999) 10 Organization Science 104
Curtin D and Senden L, 'Public Accountability of Transnational Private Regulation: Chimera or Reality?' (2011) 38 Journal of Law and Society 163
Czarniawska B, 'Gabriel Tarde and Organization Theory' in Paul Adler (ed.), *The Oxford Handbook of Sociology and Organization Studies* (Oxford University Press 2009)
Daub A, *What Tech Calls Thinking: An Inquiry into the Intellectual Bedrock of Silicon Valley* (Farrar, Straus and Giroux 2020)
De Gregorio G, *Digital Constitutionalism in Europe: Reframing Rights and Powers in the Algorithmic Society* (Cambridge University Press 2022)
DeNardis L and Musiani F, 'Governance by Infrastructure' in Francesca Musiani and others (eds.), *The Turn to Infrastructure in Internet Governance* (Palgrave Macmillan 2016)
Dezalay Y and Garth BG, *Dealing with Virtue: International Commercial Arbitration and the Construction of a Transnational Legal Order* (University of Chicago Press 1998)
Dickinson L, 'Organizational Structure and Culture in an Era of Privatization: The Case of United States Military and Security Contractors' in

Susan Rose-Ackerman, Blake Emerson and Peter L Lindseth (eds.), *Comparative Administrative Law* (2nd ed., Edward Elgar 2017)

Dienlin T, Masur PK and Trepte S, 'A Longitudinal Analysis of the Privacy Paradox' (2023) 25 New Media & Society 1043

Diez T, 'Speaking "Europe": The Politics of Integration Discourse' (1999) 6 Journal of European Public Policy 598

DiMaggio P and Powell WW, 'The Iron Cage Revisited: Institutional Isomorphism and Collective Rationality in Organizational Fields' (1983) 48 American Sociological Review 147

(eds.), *The Neo-Institutionalism in Organizational Analysis* (University of Chicago Press 1991)

Donaldson M and Kingsbury B, 'Ersatz Normativity or Public Law in Global Governance: The Hard Case of International Prescriptions for National Infrastructure Regulation' (2013) 14 Chicago Journal of International Law 1

Douek E, 'Facebook's "Oversight Board": Move Fast with Stable Infrastructure and Humility' (2019) 21 North Carolina Journal of Law & Technology 1

'Facebook's "Draft Charter" for Content Moderation: Vague, But Promising' (Lawfare, 31 January 2019) <https://perma.cc/52RW-7E7A>

'Why Facebook's "Values" Update Matters' (Lawfare, 16 September 2019) <https://perma.cc/527F-7GBZ>

'How Much Power Did Facebook Give Its Oversight Board?' (Lawfare, 25 September 2019) <https://perma.cc/54D7-X7YW>

'Facebook's Oversight Board Bylaws: For Once, Moving Slowly' (Lawfare, 28 January 2020) <https://perma.cc/YM8P-T5S2>

'What Kind of Oversight Board Have You Given Us?' (The University of Chicago Law Review Online, 11 May 2020) <https://perma.cc/6VPV-EZLR>

'Content Moderation as Systems Thinking' (2022) 136 Harvard Law Review 526

'The Meta Oversight Board and the Empty Promise of Legitimacy' (2024) 37 Harvard Journal of Law & Technology 373

Dunoff JL and Pollack MA, 'International Judicial Practices: Opening the "Black Box" of International Courts' (2018) 40 Michigan Journal of International Law 47

Durkheim E, *De la Division du Travail Social* (1893)

Dworkin R, *'Hard Cases', Taking Rights Seriously* (Harvard University Press 1977)

Edelman LB, 'Legal Ambiguity and Symbolic Structures: Organizational Mediation of Civil Rights Law' (1992) 97 American Journal of Sociology 1531

Eder N, 'Beyond Automation: Machine Learning-Based Systems and Human Behavior in the Personalization Economy' (2021) 25 Stanford Technology Law Review 1

Edwards PN, 'Infrastructure and Modernity: Force, Time, and Social Organization in the History of Sociotechnical Systems' in Thomas J Misa, Philip Brey and Andrew Feenberg (eds.), *Modernity and Technology* (MIT Press 2002)

Eifert M, 'Das Netzwerkdurchsetzungsgesetz und Plattformregulierung' in Martin Eifert and Tobias Gostomzyk (eds.), *Netzwerkrecht* (Nomos 2018)

Eifert M, v Ladenberg-Roberg M, Theß S and Wienfort N, *Netzwerkdurchsetzungsgesetz in der Bewährung* (Nomos 2020)

Eifert M, Metzger M, Schweitzer H and Wagner G, 'Taming the Giants: The DMA/DSA Package' (2021) 58 Common Market Law Review 987

Eliantonio M, 'Judicial Review in an Integrated Administration: The Case of "Composite Procedures"' (2015) 7 Review of European Administrative Law 65

Epp CR, *The Rights Revolution: Lawyers, Activists, and Supreme Courts in Comparative Perspective* (University of Chicago Press 1998)

Erie MS and Streinz T, 'The Beijing Effect: China's Digital Silk Road as Transnational Data Governance' 54 (2021) New York University Journal of International Law and Policy 1

Ervo L, Letto-Vanamo P and Nylund A (eds.), *Rethinking Nordic Courts* (Springer 2021)

Esteve A, 'The Business of Personal Data: Google, Facebook, and Privacy Issues in the EU and the USA' (2017) 7 International Data Privacy Law 36

Ewald W, 'Comparative Jurisprudence (II): The Logic of Legal Transplants' (1995) 43 The American Journal of Comparative Law 489

Fama E, 'Agency Problems and the Theory of the Firm' (1980) 88 Journal of Political Economy 288

Fanon F, *The Wretched of the Earth* (1963) (Grove Press 2004)

Farrell H, Levi M and O'Reilly, 'Mark Zuckerberg Runs a Nation-State, and He's the King' (Vox.com, 10 April 2018) <https://perma.cc/UVD9-MDNK>

Fasciglione M, 'A Binding Instrument on Business and Human Rights as a Source of International Obligations for Private Companies: Utopia or Reality?' in Martina Buscemi and others (eds.), *Legal Sources in Business and Human Rights* (Brill Nijhoff 2020)

Feldmann T, 'Zum Referentenentwurf eines NetzDG: Eine Kritische Betrachtung' (2017) 20 Kommunikation & Recht 292

Fikfak V, 'Against Settlement before the European Court of Human Rights' (2022) 20 International Journal of Constitutional Law 942

Fischman-Afori O, 'Taking Global Administrative Law One Step Ahead: Online Giants and the Digital Democratic Sphere' (2022) 20 International Journal of Constitutional Law 1006

Fisher A and Streinz T, 'Confronting Data Inequality' (2022) 60 Columbia Journal of Transnational Law 829.

Fiss OM, 'The Bureaucratization of the Judiciary' (1983) 92 Yale Law Journal 1442

Flaxman S, Goel S and Rao JM, 'Filter Bubbles, Echo Chambers, and Online News Consumption' (2016) 80 Public Opinion Quarterly 298

Foucault M, *The Archaeology of Knowledge* (Pantheon Books 1972)

The Order of Things: An Archaeology of the Human Sciences (Vintage Books 1973)

Franco M, Gaggi O and Pallazzi CE, 'Analyzing the Use of Large Language Models for Content Moderation with ChatGPT Examples' 3rd International Workshop on Open Challenges in Online Social Networks (OASIS '23), 04–08 September 2023, Rome, Italy. ACM, New York <https://perma.cc/Z2LP-KHT9>

Freeman J, 'The Private Role in Public Governance' (2000) 75 New York University Law Review 543

Frenkel S and Kang C, *An Ugly Truth: Inside Facebook's Battle for Domination* (Harper 2021)

Friedl P, 'Dis/Similarities in the Design and Development of Legal and Algorithmic Normative Systems: The Case of Perspective API' (2023) 15 Law, Innovation and Technology 25

Friedman B, *The Will of the People: How Public Opinion Has Influenced the Supreme Court and Shaped the Meaning of the Constitution* (Farrar, Straus and Giroux 2009)

Frosio G and Husovec M, 'Accountability and Responsibility of Online Intermediaries' in Giancarlo Frosio, Giancarlo Frosio and Martin Husovec (eds.), *Oxford Handbook of Online Intermediary Liability* (Oxford University Press 2020)

Galanter M, 'Why the "Haves" Come out Ahead' (1974) 9 Law & Society Review 95

Galletta A, *Mastering the Semi-Structured Interview and Beyond: From Research Design to Analysis and Publication* (New York University Press 2013)

Geese A, 'Why the DSA Could Save Us from the Rise of Authoritarian Regimes' (*Verfassungsblog*, 8 November 2022) <https://perma.cc/E44F-CFU4>

Geiger C, Frosio G and Izyumenko E, 'Intermediary Liability and Fundamental Rights' in Giancarlo Frosio, Christophe Geiger, Giancarlo Frosio and Elena Izyumenko (eds.), *Oxford Handbook of Online Intermediary Liability* (Oxford University Press 2020)

Gersdorf H, 'Hate Speech in Sozialen Netzwerken: Verfassungswidrigkeit des NetzDG-Entwurfs und grundrechtliche Einordnung der Anbieter sozialer Netzwerke' (2017) 20 MultiMedia und Recht 439

Ghaffary S, 'Microsoft, Google and Meta Bet on Fake Data to Build AI Models' (Bloomberg, 2 May 2024) <https://perma.cc/MX2F-NSLU>

Gilardi F, Alizadeh M and Kubli M, 2023. ChatGPT out-performs crowd-workers for text-annotation tasks; arXiv:2303.15056.

Gilardi F and Wasserfallen F, 'The Politics of Policy Diffusion' (2019) 58 European Journal of Political Research 1245

Gillespie T, 'The Politics of "Platforms"' (2010) 12 New Media & Society 347

Custodians of the Internet: Platforms, Content Moderation, and the Hidden Decisions That Shape Social Media (Yale University Press 2019)

'Content Moderation, AI, and the Question of Scale' (2020) 7 Big Data & Society

Gkliati M, 'The EU-Turkey Deal and the Safe Third Country Concept before the Greek Asylum Appeals Committees' (2017) 3 movements 213

Goanta C and Ortolani P, 'Unpacking Content Moderation: The Rise of Social Media Platforms as Online Civil Courts' in Xandra Ellen Kramer and others (eds.), *Frontiers in Civil Justice: Privatisation, Monetisation and Digitisation* (Edward Elgar 2022)

Goldman E, 'Why Section 230 Is Better than the First Amendment' (2019) 95 Notre Dame Law Review 33

Golia A Jr, 'Critique of Digital Constitutionalism: Deconstruction and Reconstruction from a Societal Perspective' (2023) 10 Global Constitutionalism 1

Gorwa R, 'What Is Platform Governance?' (2019) 22 Information, Communication & Society 854

The Politics of Platform Governance: How Governments Shape Online Content Moderation (Oxford University Press 2024)

Gorwa R, Binns R and Katzenbach C, 'Algorithmic Content Moderation: Technical and Political Challenges in the Automation of Platform Governance' (2020) 7 Big Data & Society 1

Gowder P, *The Networked Leviathan: For Democratic Platforms* (Cambridge University Press 2023)

Graham ER, Shipan CR and Volden C, 'The Diffusion of Policy Diffusion Research in Political Science' (2013) 43 British Journal of Political Science 673

Graham L and Warren E, 'When It Comes to Big Tech, Enough Is Enough (Guest Essay)' (New York Times, 27 July 2023)

Gray D, 'Is Google a State Agent?' (2024) 27 Stanford Technology Law Review 206

Greely HT, *CRISPR People: The Science and Ethics of Editing Humans* (MIT Press 2021)

Greene J, *How Rights Went Wrong: Why Our Obsession With Rights is Tearing America Apart* (Houghton Mifflin Harcourt 2021)

Griffin R, 'Rethinking Rights in Social Media Governance: Human Rights, Ideology and Inequality' (2023) 2 European Law Open 30

'Public and Private Power in Social Media Governance: Multistakeholderism, the Rule of Law and Democratic Accountability' (2023) 14 Transnational Legal Theory 46

Grimmelmann J, 'The Virtues of Moderation' (2015) 17 Yale Journal of Law & Tech 42

Guinier L, 'From Racial Liberalism to Racial Literacy: Brown v. Board of Education and the Interest-Divergence Dilemma' (2004) 91 Journal of American History 92

Gulati R, 'Meta's Oversight Board and Transnational Hybrid Adjudication: What Consequences for International Law' KFG Working Paper Series No. 53 March 2022

Habermas J, *Strukturwandel Der Öffentlichkeit: Untersuchungen Zu Einer Kategorie Der Bürgerlichen Gesellschaft* (Suhrkamp 1990)

'Überlegungen und Hypothesen zu einem erneuten Strukturwandel der politischen Öffentlichkeit' in Martin Seeliger and Sebastian Sevignani (eds.), *Ein neuer Strukturwandel der Öffentlichkeit?* (Nomos 2021)

Hafner-Burton EM, 'Sticks and Stones: Naming and Shaming the Human Rights Enforcement Problem' (2008) 62 International Organization 289

Haggart B and Keller CI, 'Democratic Legitimacy in Global Platform Governance' (2021) 45 Telecommunications Policy 102152

Hamilton A, 'Federalist No. 78' (28 May 1788)

Hausman D, 'The Failure of Immigration Appeals' (2016) 164 University of Pennsylvania Law Review 1177

Helfer LR and Land MK, 'Is the Facebook Oversight Board an International Human Rights Tribunal?' (Lawfare, 13 May 2021) <https://perma.cc/AZ4W-PSBR>

'The Facebook Oversight Board's Human Rights Future' (2023) 44 Cardozo Law Review 2223

Helfer LR and Slaughter A-M, 'Toward a Theory of Effective Supranational Adjudication' (1997) 107 Yale Law Journal 273

Hesselink MW, 'Democratic Contract Law' (2015) 11 European Review of Contract Law 81

Hett BC, *The Death of Democracy: Hitler's Rise to Power and the Downfall of the Weimar Republic* (Windmill Books 2019)

Hirschman AO, *Exit, Voice, and Loyalty: Responses to Decline in Firms, Organizations, and States* (Harvard University Press 1970)

Hoffmeister F, *Menschenrechts- und Demokratieklauseln in den vertraglichen Außenbeziehungen der Europäischen Gemeinschaft* (Springer 1998)

Hofmann H and Ziller J (eds.), *Accountability in the EU: The Role of the European Ombudsman* (Edward Elgar 2017)

Holznagel D, 'Ireland Cannot Do It Alone' (*Verfassungsblog*, 27 April 2021) <https://perma.cc/36C6-LYJB>

'The Digital Services Act Wants You to "Sue" Facebook over Content Decisions in Private de Facto Courts' (*Verfassungsblog*, 24 June 2021) <https://perma.cc/6W8K-E3GM>

'Article 21' in Ralf Müller-Terpitz and Markus Köhler (eds.), *Digital Services Act Kommentar* (Beck 2024)

'Article 21 DSA Has Come to Life' (*Verfassungsblog*, 5 November 2024) <https://perma.cc/YRK8-3XVH>

Hughes T, 'Practical Considerations for Out-of-Court Dispute Settlement (ODS) under Article 21 of the EU Digital Services Act (DSA)' (DSA Observatory, 8 February 2024) <https://perma.cc/6BNZ-U2WL>

Husovec M, 'Will the DSA Work?' (*Verfassungsblog*, 9 November 2022) <https://perma.cc/FV8G-UPHZ>

Injunctions against Intermediaries in the European Union (Cambridge University Press 2018)

Principles of the Digital Services Act (Oxford University Press 2023)

Husovec M and Fiala L, 'Using Experimental Evidence to Improve Delegated Enforcement' (2022) 74 International Review of Law and Economics 106079

Husovec M and Roche Laguna I, 'Digital Services Act: A Short Primer' (SSRN, 5 July 2022) <https://perma.cc/JE3Q-55XA>

Husovec M and Urban J, 'Will the DSA Have the Brussels Effect?' (*Verfassungsblog*, 21 February 2024) <https://perma.cc/DCX4-6FYK>

Irmscher PF, *Öffentlichkeit als Sanktion* (Mohr Siebeck 2019)

Isaacson W, *Elon Musk* (Simon & Schuster 2023)

Iuvenal, *Satires*

Ives M and Narin S, 'Cambodian Ruler's Facebook Account Goes Dark after Spat with Meta' (New York Times, 30 June 2023) <https://perma.cc/PPJ9-SCKF>

Jensen MC and Meckling WH, 'Theory of the Firm: Managerial Behavior, Agency Costs and Ownership Structure' (1976) 3 Journal of Financial Economics 305

Jepperson R and Meyer J, 'Reflections on Part II: Institutional Theory' in John W Meyer and Ronald L Jepperson (eds.), *Institutional Theory: The Cultural Construction of Organizations, States, and Identities* (Cambridge University Press 2021)

Jepperson R, 'Institutions, Institutional Effects, and Institutionalism' in Walter W Powell and Paul J DiMaggio (eds.), *The New Institutionalism in Organizational Analysis* (University of Chicago Press 1991)

'The Development and Application of Sociological Neoinstitutionalism (2002)' in John W Meyer and Ronald L Jepperson (eds.), *Institutional Theory: The Cultural Construction of Organizations, States, and Identities* (Cambridge University Press 2021)

Jessup PC, *Transnational Law* (Yale University Press 1956)

Jestaedt M, 'Autorität Und Zitat: Anmerkungen zur Zitierpraxis des Bundesverfassungsgerichts' in Mathias Mayer and Joachim Jacob (eds.), *Im Namen des Anderen: Die Ethik des Zitierens* (Wilhelm Fink Verlag 2010)

Johns F, 'From Planning to Prototypes: New Ways of Seeing Like a State' (2019) 82 The Modern Law Review 833

Jørgensen RF (ed.), *Human Rights in the Age of Platforms* (MIT Press 2019)

Kadri T, 'Juridical Discourse for Platforms' (2022) 136 Harvard Law Review (Forum) 163

Kahn PW, *The Cultural Study of Law: Reconstructing Legal Scholarship* (University of Chicago Press 1999)

Kahneman D, *Thinking, Fast and Slow* (Farrar, Straus and Giroux 2011)

Kanevskaia O, 'Governance of ICT Standardization: Due Process in Technocratic Decision-Making' (2020) 45 North Carolina Journal of Law & Technology 549

Karlsen R and others, 'Echo Chamber and Trench Warfare Dynamics in Online Debates' (2017) 32 European Journal of Communication 257

Katz A, 'Taking Private Ordering Seriously' (1996) 144 University of Pennsylvania Law Review 1745

Kaufman E, 'The New Legal Liberalism' (2019) 86 The University of Chicago Law Review 187

Kaufman IR, 'The Essence of Judicial Independence' (1980) 80 Columbia Law Review 671

Kaye JW, *The Administration of the East India Company* (2nd ed., Richard Bentley 1853)

Keles B, McCrae N and Grealish A, 'A Systematic Review: The Influence of Social Media on Depression, Anxiety and Psychological Distress in Adolescents' (2020) 25 International Journal of Adolescence and Youth 79

Keller D, 'Internet Platforms: Observations on Speech, Danger, and Money, Hoover Institution's Aegis Paper Series No. 1807' (2018)

'The Right Tools: Europe's Intermediary Liability Laws and the EU 2016 General Data Protection Regulation' [2018] *Berkeley Technology Law Journal* 297

'The EU's New Digital Services Act and the Rest of the World' (*Verfassungsblog*, 7 November 2022)

Kennedy D, 'The Stages of the Decline of the Public/Private Distinction' (1982) 130 University of Pennsylvania Law Review 1349

A Critique of Adjudication: Fin de Siècle (Harvard University Press 1998)
Kettemann MC, *The Normative Order of the Internet* (Oxford University Press 2020)
Khaitan T, 'Guarantor Institutions' (2021) 16 Asian Journal of Comparative Law 40
Khan LM, 'Amazon's Antitrust Paradox' (2017) 126 Yale Law Journal 710
'The Separation of Platforms and Commerce' (2019) 119 Columbia Law Review 973
Kingsbury B, 'Infrastructure and InfraReg: On Rousing the International Law "Wizards of Is"' (2019) 8 Cambridge International Law Journal 171
'Frontiers of Global Administrative Law in the 2020s' in Jason NE Varuhas and Shona Wilson Stark (eds.), *The Frontiers of Public Law* (Hart Publishing 2020)
Kingsbury B and Maisley N, 'Infrastructures and Laws: Publics and Publicness' (2021) 17 Annual Review of Law and Social Science 353
Kingsbury B, Krisch N and Stewart RB, 'The Emergence of Global Administrative Law' (2005) 68 Law and Contemporary Problems 15
Kirkpatrick D, *The Facebook Effect: The Real Inside Story of Mark Zuckerberg and the World's Fastest Growing Company* (Virgin 2010)
Klein E, 'Mark Zuckerberg on Facebook's Hardest Year, and What Comes Next' (Vox.com, 2 April 2018) <https://perma.cc/5W3N-Y37S>
Klonick K, 'The New Governors: The People, Rules, and Processes Governing Online Speech' (2018) 131 Harvard Law Review 1598
'The Facebook Oversight Board: Creating an Independent Institution to Adjudicate Online Free Expression' (2020) 129 Yale Law Journal 2232
'Inside the Making of Facebook's Supreme Court' (New Yorker, 12 February 2021) <https://perma.cc/44Y7-S8VH>
'Of Systems Thinking and Straw Men' (2023) 136 Harvard Law Review Forum 339
Knebel S, *Die Drittwirkung der Grundrechte und -freiheiten gegenüber Privaten: Regulierungsmöglichkeiten sozialer Netzwerke* (Nomos 2018)
Kokolakis S, 'Privacy Attitudes and Privacy Behaviour: A Review of Current Research on the Privacy Paradox Phenomenon' (2017) 64 Computers & Security 122
Korkea-aho E, 'Legal Lobbying: The Evolving (But Hidden) Role of Lawyers and Law Firms in the EU Public Affairs Market' (2021) 22 German Law Journal 65
'No Longer Marginal? Finding a Place for Lobbyists and Lobbying in EU Law Research' (2022) 18 European Constitutional Law Review 682
Korkea-aho E and Leino-Sandberg P, 'Interviewing Lawyers: A Critical Self-Reflection on Expert Interviews as a Method of EU Legal Research' (2019) European Journal of Legal Studies (Special Issue) 17
Koselleck R, *Begriffsgeschichten* (Suhrkamp 2006)
Koskenniemi M, 'Performing Legal Expertise: Reflections on the Construction of Transnational Authority' in Emilia Korkea-aho and Päivi Leino-Sandberg (eds.), *Law, Legal Expertise and EU Policy-Making* (Cambridge University Press 2022)
The Gentle Civilizer of Nations: The Rise and Fall of International Law 1870–1960 (Cambridge University Press 2001)

Kovács K and Scheppele KL, 'The Fragility of an Independent Judiciary: Lessons from Hungary and Poland – and the European Union' (2018) 51 Journal of Communist and Post-Communist Studies 189

Kraakman RH, 'Gatekeepers: The Anatomy of a Third-Party Enforcement Strategy' (1986) 2 Journal of Law, Economics & Organization 53

Kraft P, 'Do Rating Agencies Cater? Evidence from Rating-Based Contracts' (2015) 59 Journal of Accounting and Economics 264

Krajewski M, *Relative Authority of Judicial and Extra-Judicial Review: EU Courts, Boards of Appeal, Ombudsman* (Hart 2021)

Krämer H, *Rechtsschutz im EG-Eigenverwaltungsrecht zwischen Einheitlichkeit und sektorieller Ausdifferenzierung: eine Untersuchung unter besonderer Berücksichtigung des Gemeinschaftsmarkenrechts* (Duncker & Humblot 2007)

Krisch N (ed.), *Entangled Legalities Beyond the State* (Cambridge University Press 2021)

Kulick A, *Horizontalwirkung im Vergleich* (Mohr Siebeck 2020)

Kumar D, AbuHashem Y, Durumeric Z, 'Watch Your Language: Investigating Content Moderation with Large Language Models' (17 January 2024) arXiv:2309.14517v2.

Lakoff G and Johnson M, *Metaphors We Live By* (University of Chicago Press 1980)

Lamandini M and Muñoz DR, 'Law and Practice of Financial Appeal Bodies (ESAs' Board of Appeal, SRB Appeal Panel): A View from the Inside' [2020] Common Market Law Review 119

Lander ES and others, 'Adopt a Moratorium on Heritable Genome Editing' (2019) 567 Nature 165

Lang A, 'Netzwerkdurchsetzungsgesetz und Meinungsfreiheit' (2018) 143 Archiv des öffentlichen Rechts 220

Langenfeld C, *Die Autonomie des Unionsrechts in der EuGH-Rechtsprechung* (Mohr Siebeck 2024)

Lanier J, *Ten Arguments for Deleting Your Social Media Accounts Right Now* (Macmillan 2018)

Lapowsky I, 'Facebook Exposed 87 Million Users to Cambridge Analytica' (Wired, 4 April 2018) <https://perma.cc/D3UV-KH3T>

Larsen SR, 'European Public Law after Empires' (2022) 1 European Law Open 6

Lecourt R, *L'Europe des juges* (Bruylant 2008)

Lee CK and Strang D, 'The International Diffusion of Public Sector Downsizing: Network Emulation and Theory-Driven Learning' in Beth A Simmons, Frank Dobbin and Geoffrey Garrett (eds.), *The Global Diffusion of Markets and Democracy* (Cambridge University Press 2008)

Leetaru K, 'Facebook Was A Democracy 2009–2012 But We Didn't Vote So It Turned Into A Dictatorship' (Forbes, 13 April 2019) <https://perma.cc/Z5PG-3MBD>

Legrand P, 'The Return of the Repressed: Moving Comparative Legal Studies Beyond Pleasure' (2001) 75 Tulane Law Review 1033

Leino-Sandberg P, *The Politics of Legal Expertise in EU Policy-Making* (Cambridge University Press 2021)

Lemley M, 'The Benefit of the Bargain' [2023] Wisconsin Law Review 237

Leonardi PM, Huysman M and Steinfield C, 'Enterprise Social Media: Definition, History, and Prospects for the Study of Social Technologies in Organizations' (2013) 19 Journal of Computer-Mediated Communication 1

Levinson JD, Bennett MW and Hioki K, 'Judging Implicit Bias: A National Empirical Study of Judicial Stereotypes' (2017) 69 Florida Law Review 63

Levitsky S and Ziblatt D, *How Democracies Die* (Penguin Books 2019)

Levy S, 'Inside Meta's Oversight Board: 2 Years of Pushing Limits' (Wired, 8 November 2022) <https://perma.cc/SUP5-RQCV>

Facebook: The Inside Story (Blue Rider 2020)

Liesching M and Funke C, *Das NetzDG in der praktischen Anwendung: eine Teilevaluation des Netzwerkdurchsetzungsgesetzes* (Carl Grossmann 2021)

Lindh M and Nolin JM, 'GAFA Speaks: Metaphors in the Promotion of Cloud Technology' (2017) 73 Journal of Documentation 160

Linnanmäki K, 'Mediation: A Change in Finnish Court Culture?' in Laura Ervo, Pia Letto-Vanamo and Anna Nylund (eds.), *Rethinking Nordic Courts* (Springer 2021)

Lobby Control, 'DSA/DMA: Wie Big Tech Neue Regeln Für Digitale Plattformen Verhindern Will' (2020) <https://perma.cc/V8TL-Q3B6>

Lobel O, 'The Law of the Platform' (2016) 101 Minnesota Law Review 87

Locke J, *Two Treatises of Government* (1689)

Loughlin M, *The Idea of Public Law* (Oxford University Press 2004)

Foundations of Public Law (Oxford University Press 2010)

Lubbers JS, 'Federal Administrative Law Judges: A Focus on Our Invisible Judiciary' (1981) 33 Administrative Law Review 109

'Administrative Adjudication: The United States Is the Outlier' in Marc Hertogh and others (eds.), *The Oxford Handbook of Administrative Justice* (Oxford University Press 2022)

Luhmann N, *Legitimation durch Verfahren* (Suhrkamp 1983)

Lund D and Pollman E, 'The Corporate Governance Machine' (2021) 121 Columbia Law Review 2563

Lustig D, *Veiled Power: International Law and the Private Corporation 1886–1981* (Oxford University Press 2020)

Lütz S, 'Policy-Transfer Und Policy-Diffusion' in Arthur Benz and others (eds.), *Handbuch Governance: Theoretische Grundlagen und empirische Anwendungsfelder* (VS Verlag für Sozialwissenschaften 2007)

Machona G, 'Das Provenienz-Problem Der Rechtswissenschaften: Zum Umgang mit Antisemitismus, Rassismus und Sexismus im juristischen Wissenskanon' (2022) 55 Kritische Justiz 437

MacKinnon CA, *Toward a Feminist Theory of the State* (Harvard University Press 1991)

MacKinnon R, *Consent of the Networked: The Worldwide Struggle for Internet Freedom* (Basic Books 2012)

Maduro M and Weiler JHH, '"Integrity," "Independence" and the Internal Reform of FIFA' in Arnout Geeraert and Frank van Eekeren (eds.), *Good Governance in Sport* (Routledge 2021)

Mann RJ and Belzley SR, 'The Promise of Internet Intermediary Liability' (2005) 47 William & Mary Law Review 239

Marcus G and Davis E, *Rebooting AI* (Knopf 2019)

Mares R, 'Business and Human Rights After Ruggie: Foundations, the Art of Simplification and the Imperative of Cumulative Progress' in Radu Mares (ed.), *The UN Guiding Principles on Business and Human Rights* (Brill Nijhoff 2012)

Marx K, 'Zur Judenfrage' (1844) 1(2) Deutsch-Französische Jahrbücher 182

Mashaw JL, *Creating the Administrative Constitution: The Lost One Hundred Years of American Administrative Law* (Yale University Press 2012)

Masnick M, 'Masnick's Impossibility Theorem: Content Moderation At Scale Is Impossible To Do Well' (TechDirt, 20 November 2019) <https://perma.cc/Q97F-CFHB>

Masur PK and Trepte S, 'Transformative or Not? How Privacy Violation Experiences Influence Online Privacy Concerns and Online Information Disclosure' (2021) 47 Human Communication Research 49

Mayers L, *The American Legal System: The Administration of Justice in the United States by Judicial, Administrative, Military, and Arbitral Tribunals* (Rothman 1981)

Mazzucato M and Robinson DKR, 'Co-Creating and Directing Innovation Ecosystems? NASA's Changing Approach to Public-Private Partnerships in Low-Earth Orbit' (2018) 136 Technological Forecasting and Social Change 166

Medzini R, 'Enhanced Self-Regulation: The Case of Facebook's Content Governance' 24 (2022) New Media & Society 2227

Meier N and Golia AJr, 'The Emerging Normative System of Meta's Oversight Board: An Introduction' MPIL Research Paper Series No. 2022–09

Merril JB and Oremus W, 'Five Points for Anger, One for a "Like": How Facebook's Formula Fostered Rage and Misinformation' (Washington Post, 26 October 2021) <https://perma.cc/7E55-RPZL>

Metz C and others, 'How Tech Giants Cut Corners to Harvest Data for A.I.' (New York Times, 6 April 2024) <https://perma.cc/WW5D-EXXS>

Meuser M and Nagel U, 'The Expert Interview and Changes in Knowledge Production' in Alexander Bogner, Beate Littig and Wolfgang Menz (eds.), *Interviewing Experts* (Palgrave Macmillan UK 2009)

Meyer JW and Rowan B, 'Institutionalized Organizations: Formal Structure as Myth and Ceremony' (1977) 83 American Journal of Sociology 340

Mezrich B, *The Accidental Billionaires* (Doubleday 2009)

Misra BB, *The Central Administration of the East India Company 1773–1834* (Oxford University Press 1959)

Moliterno JE, 'The Administrative Judiciary's Independence Myth' (2006) 41 Wake Forest Law Review 1191

Möllers C, *Gewaltengliederung: Legitimation und Dogmatik im nationalen und internationalen Rechtsvergleich* (Mohr Siebeck 2005)

'European Governance: Meaning and Value of a Concept' (2006) 43 Common Market Law Review 313

'Legalität, Legitimität Und Legitimation Des Bundesverfassungsgerichts' in Matthias Jestaedt and others (eds.), *Das entgrenzte Gericht* (Suhrkamp 2011)

The Three Branches: A Comparative Model of Separation of Powers (Oxford University Press 2013)

The Possibility of Norms: Social Practice beyond Morals and Causes (Oxford University Press 2020)

Montesquieu, *The Spirit of Laws* (1748)

Moyn S, *Not Enough: Human Rights in an Unequal World* (Belknap 2019)

Narine M, 'From Kansas to the Congo: Why Naming and Shaming through the Dodd-Frank Act's Corporate Governance Disclosure Won't Solve a Human Rights Crisis' (2013) 25 Regent University Law Review 351

Neuvonen R and Sirkkunen E, 'Outsourced Justice: The Case of the Facebook Oversight Board' (2022) 12 Journal of Digital Media & Policy 1

Newman AL and Posner E, 'Putting the EU in Its Place: Policy Strategies and the Global Regulatory Context' (2015) 22 Journal of European Public Policy 1316

Newton C, 'How Facebook Undercut the Oversight Board' (The Verge, 5 December 2022) <https://perma.cc/H6RE-S57F>

Nielsen LB, 'The Need for Multi-Method Approaches in Empirical Legal Research' in Peter Cane and Herbert M Kritzer (eds.), *The Oxford Handbook of Empirical Legal Research* (Oxford University Press 2010)

Nix N, 'Meta's Oversight Body Prepares to Lay off Workers' (Washington Post, 29 April 2024) <https://perma.cc/Z8SS-MKSW>

Nodder C, *Evil by Design: Interaction Design to Lead Us Into Temptation* (Wiley 2013)

Nou J, 'Dismissing Decisional Independence Suits' (2019) 86 University of Chicago Law Review 1187

Nouwen SMH, '"As You Set out for Ithaka": Practical, Epistemological, Ethical, and Existential Questions about Socio-Legal Empirical Research in Conflict' (2014) 27 Leiden Journal of International Law 227

Nußberger A, 'Wer Zitiert Wen? Zur Funktion von Zitaten bei der Herausbildung Gemeineuropäischen Verfassungsrechts' (2006) 61 JuristenZeitung 763

Okayama H, *Judicializing the Administrative State: The Rise of the Independent Regulatory Commissions in the United States, 1883–1937* (Routledge 2021)

Ostrom E, *Governing the Commons: The Evolution of Institutions for Collective Action* (Cambridge University Press 1990)

Palka PJ, 'Terms of Service Are Not Contracts: Beyond Contract Law in the Regulation of Online Platforms' in Stefan Grundmann (ed.), *European Contract Law in the Digital Age* (Intersentia 2018)

Palmer MJE and Roberts S, *Dispute Processes: ADR and Primary Forms of Decision-Making* (2nd ed., Cambridge University Press 2005)

Pasquale F, *The Black Box Society: The Secret Algorithms That Control Money and Information* (Harvard University Press 2016)

Pauwelyn J and Elsig M, 'The Politics of Treaty Interpretation: Variations and Explanations across International Tribunals' in Jeffrey L Dunoff and Mark A Pollack (eds.), *Interdisciplinary Perspectives on International Law and International Relations: The State of the Art* (Cambridge University Press 2012)

Pauwelyn J and Pelc K, 'Who Guards the "Guardians of the System"? The Role of the Secretariat in WTO Dispute Settlement' (2022) 116 American Journal of International Law 534

Pavone T, *The Ghostwriters: Lawyers and the Politics behind the Judicial Construction of Europe* (Cambridge University Press 2022)

Pech L and Scheppele KL, 'Illiberalism Within: Rule of Law Backsliding in the EU' (2017) 19 Cambridge Yearbook of European Legal Studies 3

Peterson S, 'Dissent in American Courts' (1981) 43 Journal of Politics 312

Petty M, 'Cambodia PM's Facebook Page Reactivated Days before Election' (Reuters, 20 July 2023) <https://perma.cc/KSD7-3NHV>

Peuker E, *Bürokratie und Demokratie in Europa: Legitimität im europäischen Verwaltungsverbund* (Mohr Siebeck 2011)

Pfander JE, 'Article I Tribunals, Article III Courts, and the Judicial Power of the United States' (2004) 118 Harvard Law Review 643

Pistor K, *The Code of Capital: How the Law Creates Wealth and Inequality* (Princeton University Press 2019)

Polanyi K, *The Great Transformation: The Political and Economic Origins of Our Time* (Beacon Press 1944)

Pollicino O, *Judicial Protection of Fundamental Rights on the Internet: A Road towards Digital Constitutionalism?* (Hart 2021)

Pollman E, 'Quasi Governments and Inchoate Law: Berle's Vision of Limits on Corporate Power' (2019) 42 Seattle University Law Review 617

Posner E, 'Making Rules for Global Finance: Transatlantic Regulatory Cooperation at the Turn of the Millennium' (2009) 63 International Organization 665

Posner EA, *The Perils of Global Legalism* (University of Chicago Press 2009)

Post RC, 'Between Governance and Management: The History and Theory of the Public Forum' (1986) 34 University of California Los Angeles Law Review 1713

Constitutional Domains: Democracy, Community, Management (Harvard University Press 1995)

'Participatory Democracy and Free Speech' (2011) 97 Virginia Law Review 477

Postema GJ, *Law's Rule: The Nature, Value, and Viability of the Rule of Law* (Oxford University Press 2023)

Psychogiopoulou E and Casarosa F, 'Social Media before Domestic Courts in Europe: An Analysis of Free Speech Cases' (2020) 27 Maastricht Journal of European and Comparative Law 791

Quintais JP, Appelman N and Ó Fathaigh R, 'Using Terms and Conditions to Apply Fundamental Rights to Content Moderation' (2023) 24 German Law Journal 881

Rachlinski JJ and others, 'Does Unconscious Racial Bias Affect Trial Judges?' (2009) 84 Notre Dame Law Review 1195

Radin MJ, 'Boilerplate: A Threat to the Rule of Law?' in Lisa M Austin and Dennis Klimchuk (eds.), *Private Law and the Rule of Law* (Oxford University Press 2015)

Rasmussen H, *On Law and Policy in the European Court of Justice: A Comparative Study in Judicial Policymaking* (Nijhoff 1986)

Rauchegger C and Kuczerawy A, 'Injunctions to Remove Illegal Online Content under the ECommerce Directive: Glawischnig-Piesczek' (2020) 57 Common Market Law Review 1495

Rawls J, *A Theory of Justice* (rev ed., Belknap 1999 [1971])

Reckwitz A, 'Toward a Theory of Social Practices: A Development in Culturalist Theorizing' (2002) 5 European Journal of Social Theory 243

Redeker D, Gill L and Gasser U, 'Towards Digital Constitutionalism? Mapping Attempts to Craft an Internet Bill of Rights' (2018) 80 International Communication Gazette 302

Reidenberg JR, 'Lex Informatica: The Formulation of Information Policy Rules Through Technology' 76 (1998) Texas Law Review 553

Resnik J, 'Managerial Judges' (1982) 96 Harvard Law Review 374

Reus-Smit C, *Individual Rights and the Making of the International System* (Cambridge University Press 2013)

Reuters Staff, 'Fretting about Data Security, China's Government Expands Its Use of "Golden Shares"' (Reuters, 16 December 2021) <https://perma.cc/XT6C-LFHT>

Ritti RR and Goldner FH, 'Professional Pluralism in an Industrial Organization' (1969) 16 Management Science 233

Roberts ST, *Behind the Screen: Content Moderation in the Shadows of Social Media* (Yale University Press 2019)

Roeben V, 'Judicial Protection as the Meta-Norm in the EU Judicial Architecture' (2020) 12 Hague Journal on the Rule of Law 29

Rose N and Miller P, 'Political Power beyond the State: Problematics of Government' (1992) 43 British Journal of Sociology 173

Rosenberg GN, *The Hollow Hope Can Courts Bring About Social Change?* (University of Chicago Press 1991)

Ruffert M, *Vorrang der Verfassung und Eigenständigkeit des Privatrechts: Eine verfassungsrechtliche Untersuchung zur Privatrechtswirkung des Grundgesetzes* (Mohr Siebeck 2001)

Die Globalisierung als Herausforderung an das Öffentliche Recht (Boorberg 2004)

Law of Administrative Organization of the EU: A Comparative Approach (Edward Elgar 2020)

Ruggie J, 'Report of the Special Representative of the Secretary-General on the Issue of Human Rights and Transnational Corporations and Other Business Enterprises, John Ruggie' (United Nations, Human Rights Council, 17th session 2011) A/HRC/17/31

Rüthers B, *Die unbegrenzte Auslegung: zum Wandel der Privatrechtsordnung im Nationalsozialismus* (9th ed., Mohr Siebeck 2022)

Sabel CF and Zeitlin J, *Experimentalist Governance* (Oxford University Press 2012)

Sailer R, *Untertanenprozesse vor dem Reichskammergericht: Rechtsschutz gegen die Obrigkeit in der zweiten Hälfte des 18. Jahrhunderts* (Hochschulschrift Universität Freiburg i. Br. 1999)

Sandel MJ, *Liberalism and the Limits of Justice* (2nd ed., Cambridge University Press 1998)

Sanders A, 'The Impact of the "Ruggie Framework" and the "United Nations Guiding Principles on Business and Human Rights" on Transnational Human Rights Litigation' in Jena Martin and Karen E Bravo (eds.), *The Business and Human Rights Landscape* (Cambridge University Press 2015)

Sandhu S, 'Grundlagen und Kernbegriffe des Neo-Institutionalismus' in Swaran Sandhu, *Public Relations und Legitimität* (Verlag für Sozialwissenschaften 2012)

Sapir A, *Fragmented Power: Europe and the Global Economy* (Bruegel 2007)

Schepel H, *The Constitution of Private Governance: Product Standards in the Regulation of Integrating Markets* (Hart 2005)

Schrad ML, *The Power of Bad Ideas: Networks, Institutions, and the Global Prohibition Wave* (Oxford University Press 2010)

Schramm F, 'Judges as Narrators of the Climate Crisis? An Illustrative Analysis of the Decision of the German Constitutional Court from 24 March 2021' (2022) 7 European Papers 361

Schramm M, 'Where Is Olive? Or: Lessons from Democratic Theory for Legitimate Platform Governance' (The Digital Constitutionalist, 26 January 2022) <https://perma.cc/RL93-CGSY>

'Michał Krajewski, Relative Authority of Judicial and Extra-Judicial Review: EU Courts, Boards of Appeal, Ombudsman (Book Review)' (2023) 16 Review of European Administrative Law 125

'Shrinks, Priests, and Academic Soul-Searching: Epistemic Reflexivity in Socio-Legal Research' (Frontiers of Socio-Legal Studies, 5 July 2023) <https://perma.cc/EV9F-ZZ72>

'Platform Administrative Law: A Research Agenda' (SSRN, 24 July 2024) <https://perma.cc/JH2A-8ZW2>

'Averting Zombie Mode: Learning from (the Critique of) Global Constitutionalism for Digital Constitutionalism' in Giovanni De Gregorio, Oreste Pollicino and Peggy Valcke (eds.), *Oxford Handbook on Digital Constitutionalism* (Oxford University Press 2025)

'EU Review Bodies beyond the Judiciary' in Melanie Fink (ed.), *Access to Justice and the EU's Remedies System* (Cambridge University Press 2025)

'Curb Your Enthusiasm: Why the Digital Services Act Might Not Have a "Brussels Effect"' (2025) European Journal of Legal Studies (Special Issue) 61

'His Time Has Come' (*Verfassungsblog*, 9 November 2024) <https://perma.cc/4ZF5-6BXS>.

Schütze R, *From Dual to Cooperative Federalism: The Changing Structure of European Law* (Oxford University Press 2009)

Scott J, 'Extraterritoriality and Territorial Extension in EU Law' (2014) 63 American Journal of Comparative Law 87

Searle JR, *Speech Acts: An Essay in the Philosophy of Language* (Cambridge University Press 1969)

Seeliger M and Sevignani S (eds.), 'Ein Neuer Strukturwandel der Öffentlichkeit?' [2021] Leviathan Sonderband 37

Selznick P, *Law, Society, and Industrial Justice* (Russel Sage Foundation 1969)

Shapiro M and Stone Sweet A, *On Law, Politics, and Judicialization* (Oxford University Press 2002)

Shapiro M, *Courts: A Comparative and Political Analysis* (University of Chicago Press 1981)

'APA: Past, Present, Future' (1986) 72 Virginia Law Review 447

Who Guards the Guardians? Judicial Control of Administration (University of Georgia Press 1988)

Shipan CR and Volden C, 'The Mechanisms of Policy Diffusion' (2008) 52 American Journal of Political Science 840

Simmons BA, Dobbin F and Garrett G, 'Introduction: The Diffusion of Liberalization' in Beth A Simmons, Frank Dobbin and Geoffrey Garrett (eds.), *The Global Diffusion of Markets and Democracy* (Cambridge University Press 2008)

(eds.), *The Global Diffusion of Markets and Democracy* (Cambridge University Press 2008)

Simoncini A, The Constitutional Dimension of the Internet – Some Research Paths, EUI Working Papers LAW 2016/15 (2016)

Sinders C, 'Toxicity and Tone Are Not the Same Thing: Analyzing the New Google API on Toxicity, PerspectiveAPI' (Medium.com, 24 February 2017) <https://perma.cc/MK66-NS9J>

Slupska J, 'War, Health and Ecosystem: Generative Metaphors in Cybersecurity Governance' (2021) 34 Philosophy & Technology 463

Smith RC and Walter I, 'Rating Agencies: Is There an Agency Issue?' in Richard M Levich, Giovanni Majnoni and Carmen M Reinhart (eds.), *Ratings, Rating Agencies and the Global Financial System* (Springer US 2002)

Smits R, 'What Is Legal Doctrine? On the Aims and Methods of Legal-Dogmatic Research' in Rob van Gestel, Hans-Wolfgang Micklitz and Edward L Rubin (eds.), *Rethinking Legal Scholarship: A Transatlantic Dialogue* (Cambridge University Press 2017)

Smuha N, 'From a "Race to AI" to a "Race to AI Regulation": Regulatory Competition for Artificial Intelligence' (2021) 13 Law, Innovation and Technology 57

Soave T, *The Everyday Makers of International Law: From Great Halls to Back Rooms* (Cambridge University Press 2022)

Spencer L, 'Comparative Legal Geography: Context and Place in "Legal Transplants"' in Tayanah O'Donnell, Daniel F Robinson and Josephine Gillespie (eds.), *Legal Geography: Perspectives and Methods* (Routledge 2020)

Spivak GC, 'Can the Subaltern Speak?' in C Nelson and L Grossberg (eds.), *Marxism and the Interpretation of Culture* (Macmillan 1988)

Srivastava S, 'Corporate Sovereign Awakening and the Making of Modern State Sovereignty: New Archival Evidence from the English East India Company' (2022) 76 International Organization 690

Staab P and Thiel T, 'Social Media and the Digital Structural Transformation of the Public Sphere' (2022) 39 Theory, Culture & Society 129

Stanchi KM, Berger LL and Crawford BJ (eds.), *Feminist Judgments: Rewritten Opinions of the United States Supreme Court* (Cambridge University Press 2016)

Stebbings C, *Legal Foundations of Tribunals in Nineteenth-Century England* (Cambridge University Press 2006)

Stein E, 'Lawyers, Judges, and the Making of a Transnational Constitution' (1981) 75 American Journal of International Law 1

Steinbeiß-Winkelmann C, '§ 4 Formen der Verwaltungsgerichtsbarkeit auf Reichsebene' in Karl-Peter Sommermann and Bert Schaffarzik (eds.), *Handbuch der Geschichte der Verwaltungsgerichtsbarkeit in Deutschland und Europa* (Springer 2019)

Stewart RB, 'The Reformation of American Administrative Law' (1975) 88 Harvard Law Review 1667

Stigler Center for the Study of the Economy and the State (University of Chicago), 'Stigler Committee on Digital Platforms Final Report' (2019)

Stone Sweet A, 'Judicialization and the Construction of Governance' (1999) 42 Comparative Political Studies 147

The Judicial Construction of Europe (Oxford University Press 2004)

Strandburg KJ, 'Rulemaking and Inscrutable Automated Decision Tools' (2019) 119 Columbia Law Review 1851

Strange S, *The Retreat of the State: The Diffusion of Power in the World Economy* (Cambridge University Press 1996)

Streinz T, 'The Evolution of European Data Law' in Paul Craig and Gráinne de Búrca (eds.), *The Evolution of EU Law* (3rd ed., Oxford University Press 2021)

Struth AK, *Hassrede und Freiheit der Meinungsäußerung* (Springer 2019)

Stylianou K, Zingales N and di Stefano S, Is Facebook Keeping up with International Standards on Freedom of Expression? A Time-Series Analysis 2005–2020 (2022)

Susskind RE, *Online Courts and the Future of Justice* (Oxford University Press 2019)

Suzor NP, 'Digital Constitutionalism: Using the Rule of Law to Evaluate the Legitimacy of Governance by Platforms' (2018) 4 Social Media + Society 1

Lawless: The Secret Rules That Govern Our Digital Lives (Cambridge University Press 2019)

Sylvain O, 'Platform Realism, Informational Inequality, and Section 230 Reform' (2021) 131 Yale Law Journal Forum 475

Tarde G, *The Laws of Imitation* (Henry Holt 1903)

Tate CN, 'The Global Expansion of Judicial Power: The Judicialization of Politics' in Chester Neal Tate and Torbjörn Vallinder (eds.), *The Global Expansion of Judicial Power* (New York University Press 1995)

Taylor L, 'Public Actors Without Public Values: Legitimacy, Domination and the Regulation of the Technology Sector' (2021) 34 Philosophy & Technology 897

Terzis P, 'Against Digital Constitutionalism' [2024] European Law Open 1

Teubner G (ed.), *Juridification of Social Spheres: A Comparative Analysis in the Areas of Labor, Corporate, Antitrust and Social Welfare Law* (De Gruyter 1987)

'Juridification Concepts, Aspects, Limits, Solutions' in Gunther Teubner (ed.), *Juridification of Social Spheres* (De Gruyter 1987) (ed.), *Global Law without a State* (Dartmouth 1997)

Verfassungsfragmente: Gesellschaftlicher Konstitutionalismus in der Globalisierung (Suhrkamp 2012)

Tovo C, 'The Boards of Appeal of Networked Services Agencies: Specialized Arbitrators of Transnational Regulatory Conflicts?' in Merijn Chamon, Annalisa Volpato and Mariolina Eliantonio (eds.), *Boards of Appeal of EU Agencies: Towards Judicialization of Administrative Review?* (Oxford University Press 2022)

Tregonning KG, *Under Chartered Company Rule: North Borneo 1881–1946* (University of Malaysia Press 1959)

Tushnet MV, *The New Fourth Branch: Institutions for Protecting Constitutional Democracy* (Cambridge University Press 2021)

Vallejo Garretón R, 'After Governance? The Idea of a Private Administrative Law' in Poul F Kjaer (ed.), *The Law of Political Economy* (Cambridge University Press 2020)

'The Private Administrative Law of Technical Standardization' (2022) 40 Yearbook of European Law 172

van Ballaert B, 'The European Commission's Use of Consultation during Policy Formulation: The Effects of Policy Characteristics' (2017) 18 European Union Politics 406

van Beers BC, 'Rewriting the Human Genome, Rewriting Human Rights Law? Human Rights, Human Dignity, and Human Germline Modification in the CRISPR Era' (2020) 7 Journal of Law and the Biosciences 1

van Gestel R, Micklitz H-W and Maduro MP, 'Methodology in the New Legal World, EUI Working Papers, Law 2012/13'

Vauchez A, 'The Force of a Weak Field: Law and Lawyers in the Government of the European Union (For a Renewed Research Agenda)' (2008) 2 International Political Sociology 128

Brokering Europe: Euro-Lawyers and the Making of a Transnational Polity (Cambridge University Press 2015)

'The Genie of Independence and the European Bottle: How Independence Became Europe's Most Contentious Legal and Political Category' (2022) 20 International Journal of Constitutional Law 1

Vauchez A and Witte B de (eds.), *Lawyering Europe: European Law as a Transnational Social Field* (Hart 2013)

Venzke I, *How Interpretation Makes International Law* (Oxford University Press 2012)

Venzke I and Mendes J, 'The Idea of Relative Authority in European and International Law' (2018) 16 International Journal of Constitutional Law 75

Vergnolle S, 'Putting Collective Intelligence to the Enforcement of the Digital Services Act: Report on Possible Collaborations between the European Commission and Civil Society' Conservatoire National des Articles et Métiers (CNAM) Paper Series, 2023

Viljoen S, 'A Relational Theory of Data Governance' (2021) 131 Yale Law Journal 370

Vinsel L and Russell AL, *The Innovation Delusion: How Our Obsession with the New Has Disrupted the Work That Matters Most* (Crown Currency 2020)

Voeten E, 'Domestic Implementation of European Court of Human Rights Judgments: Legal Infrastructure and Government Effectiveness Matter: A Reply to Dia Anagnostou and Alina Mungiu-Pippidi' (2014) 25 European Journal of International Law 229

Vogel D, 'The New Politics of Risk Regulation in Europe' [2001] Centre for Analysis of Risk and Regulation, London School of Economics and Political Science

The Politics of Precaution: Regulating Health, Safety, and Environmental Risks in Europe and the United States (Princeton University Press 2012)

Vurro C, Russo A and Perrini F, 'Shaping Sustainable Value Chains: Network Determinants of Supply Chain Governance Models' (2009) 90 Journal of Business Ethics 607

Wachhaus A, 'Platform Governance: Developing Collaborative Democracy' (2017) 39 Administrative Theory & Praxis 206

Wacquant LJD, 'Towards a Social Praxeology: The Structure and Logic of Bourdieu's Sociology' in Pierre Bourdieu and Loïc JD Wacquant (eds.), *An Invitation to Reflexive Sociology* (Polity Press 1992)

Wagner G, 'Private Law Enforcement Through ADR: Wonder Drug or Snake Oil?' (2014) 51 Common Market Law Review 165

Waldman AE, 'Privacy Law's False Promise' (2020) 97 Washington University Law Review 773

Industry Unbound: The Inside Story of Privacy, Data, and Corporate Power (Cambridge University Press 2021)

Waldron J, *Law and Disagreement* (Oxford University Press 1999)

'The Principle of Proximity, NYU School of Law, Public Law Research Paper No. 11-08' (SSRN, 20 January 2011) <https://perma.cc/2JWS-BU2Q>

Walsh DJ, 'On the Meaning and Pattern of Legal Citations: Evidence from State Wrongful Discharge Precedent Cases' (1997) 31 Law & Society Review 337

Watson A, *Legal Transplants: An Approach to Comparative Law* (2nd ed., University of Georgia Press 1993)

Weber M, 'Die "Objektivität" sozialwissenschaftlicher und sozialpolitischer Erkenntnis' (1904) 19 Archiv für Sozialwissenschaft und Sozialpolitik 22

Wirtschaft Und Gesellschaft (Zweitausendeins 2005 [1922])

Webley L, 'Qualitative Approaches to Empirical Legal Research' in Peter Cane and Herbert M Kritzer (eds.), *The Oxford Handbook of Empirical Legal Research* (Oxford University Press 2010)

Weiler JHH, 'The Community System: The Dual Character of Supranationalism' (1981) 1 Yearbook of European Law 267

'The Transformation of Europe' (1991) 100 Yale Law Journal 2403

'A Quiet Revolution: The European Court of Justice and its Interlocutors' (1994) 26 Comparative Political Studies 397

Weizenbaum J, *Computer Power and Human Reason: From Judgment to Calculation* (Freeman 1976)

Westergaard WC, *The Danish West Indies under Company Rule (1671–1754)* (Macmillan 1917)

Westney E, *Imitation and Innovation: The Transfer of Western Organizational Patterns to Meiji Japan* (Harvard University Press 1987)

White JG, 'ICANN's Uniform Domain Name Dispute Resolution Policy in Action' (2001) 16 Berkeley Technology Law Journal 229

Wielsch D, 'Die Ordnungen Der Netzwerke: AGB – Code – Community Standards' in Martin Eifert and Tobias Gostomzyk (eds.), *Netzwerkrecht* (Nomos 2018)

Wilman F, 'The EU's System of Knowledge-Based Liability for Hosting Service Providers in Respect of Illegal User Content: Between the e-Commerce Directive and the Digital Services Act' (2021) 12 JIPITEC 317

Wimmers J, 'The Out-of-Court Dispute Settlement Mechanism in the Digital Services Act' (2021) 12 JIPITEC 421

Winner L, 'Do Artifacts Have Politics?' (1980) 109 Daedalus 121

Wittgenstein L, *Philosophical Investigations* (1st ed., Basil Blackwell 1953)

Wong D and Floridi L, 'Meta's Oversight Board: A Review and Critical Assessment' (2023) 33 Minds and Machines 261

Wotipka CM and Ramirez FO, 'World Society and Human Rights: An Event History Analysis of the Convention on the Elimination of All Forms of Discrimination against Women' in Beth A Simmons, Frank Dobbin and Geoffrey Garrett (eds.), *The Global Diffusion of Markets and Democracy* (Cambridge University Press 2008)

Wu T, *The Curse of Bigness: Antitrust in the New Gilded Age* (Columbia Global Reports 2018)

Wylie C, *Mindf*ck: Inside Cambridge Analytica's Plot to Break the World* (Profile Books 2019)

York J, *Silicon Values: The Future of Free Speech under Surveillance Capitalism* (Verso 2021)

Young AR, 'The European Union as a Global Regulator? Context and Comparison' (2015) 22 Journal of European Public Policy 1233

Young IM, *Inclusion and Democracy* (Oxford University Press 2002)

Zarbiyev F, 'On the Judge Centredness of the International Legal Self' (2021) 32 European Journal of International Law 1139

Zeng J and Bondy Valdovinos Kaye D, 'From Content Moderation to Visibility Moderation: A Case Study of Platform Governance on TikTok' (2022) 14 Policy & Internet 79

Zevounou L, 'For a Postcolonial Reading of EU Law' (*Verfassungsblog*, 21 March 2024) <https://perma.cc/A7P2-U5ZA>

Zhang AH, *High Wire: How China Regulates Big Tech and Governs Its Economy* (Oxford University Press 2024)

Zuboff S, 'Big Other: Surveillance Capitalism and the Prospects of an Information Civilization' (2015) 30 Journal of Information Technology 75

The Age of Surveillance Capitalism: The Fight for a Human Future at the New Frontier of Power (PublicAffairs 2019)

Zürn M, *A Theory of Global Governance: Authority, Legitimacy, and Contestation* (Oxford University Press 2018)

Documents

ADROIT, 'Fee Model' <https://perma.cc/R5L9-T526>

Basic Principles on the Independence of the Judiciary, adopted by the Seventh United Nations Congress on the Prevention of Crime and the Treatment of Offenders held at Milan from 26 August to 6 September 1985

Bickert M, 'Updating the Values That Inform Our Community Standards' (Meta Newsroom, 12 September 2019) <https://perma.cc/6TPQ-MW35>

Broxmeyer J, 'Facebook's First Quarterly Update on the Oversight Board' (Meta Newsroom, 16 July 2021) <https://perma.cc/2YDU-E62C>

Code of Conduct on Countering Illegal Hate Speech online 2016 (European Union and numerous digital corporations)

Council of the European Union (ed.), 'General Approach: Proposal for a Regulation of the European Parliament and of the Council on a Single Market for Digital Services (Digital Services Act) and Amending Directive 2000/31/EC'

'DSA: Council Gives Final Approval to the Protection of Users' Rights Online (Press Release)' (2022) <https://perma.cc/F85X-4QKF>

Digital Rights Europe, 'Digital Serves Act Position Paper' <https://perma.cc/FCP8-5HNW>

European Commission for Democracy through Law (Venice Commission), 'Report on the Independence of the Judicial System Part I: The Independence of Judges' (2010) Study No. 494/2008; CDL-AD(2010)004

European Commission, Proposal for a Regulation of the European Parliament and of the Council on a Single Market for Digital Services (Digital Services Act) and amending Directive 2000/32/EC 2020 [COM(2020) 825 final]

'Commission Staff Working Document, Impact Assessment, Accompanying the Commission Proposal for the DSA, Annex, Part 2/2, SWD(2020) 348 Final'

'Commission Staff Working Document, Impact Assessment, Accompanying the Commission Proposal for the DSA, Part 1/2. SWD(2020) 348 Final'

European Court of Human Rights, 'ECHR Budget 2024 (Press Release)' <https://perma.cc/6685-KQNP>

European Court of Justice, 'Annual Report 2023' <https://perma.cc/H7R9-ZKUD>

European Parliament Committee on Legal Affairs and Tiemo Wölken (Rapporteur), 'DRAFT REPORT with Recommendations to the Commission on a Digital Services Act: Adapting Commercial and Civil Law Rules for Commercial Entities Operating Online (2020/2019(INL))' <https://perma.cc/VC3U-7Y97>

Facebook, 'Global Feedback and Input on the Facebook Oversight Board for Content Decisions Appendix' <https://perma.cc/SP5M-Q7G7>

Farrand M, *The Records of the Federal Convention of 1787* Vol. 2 (Online Library of Liberty – Ebook 2011) (1911)

Federal Trade Commission, 'FTC Sues Facebook for Illegal Monopolization (Press Release)' (9 December 2020) <https://perma.cc/N6RX-AX8Q>

Feldman N, 'A Supreme Court for Facebook (January 2018), Published in: Global Feedback and Input on the Facebook Oversight Board for Content Decisions Appendix, Appendix D' (2018)

'Facebook Supreme Court: A Governance Solution (March 2018), Published in: Global Feedback and Input on the Facebook Oversight Board for Content Decisions Appendix, Appendix D' (2018)

Framework Convention on Artificial Intelligence and Human Rights, Democracy and the Rule of Law

Google, 'Google Transparency Report, YouTube-Community-Guidelines and Their Application (Q1 2024)' <https://transparencyreport.google.com/youtube-policy/removals>

Human Rights Committee (United Nations), 'General Comment No. 34, Article 19 Freedoms of Opinion and Expression, CCPR/C/GC/34'

Human Rights Council, 'Report of the Independent International Fact-Finding Mission on Myanmar, A/HRC/39/64' (United Nations General Assembly 2018)

'Report of the International Commission of Human Rights Experts on Ethiopia, A/HRC/51/46' (United Nations General Assembly 2022)

International Court of Justice, 'Report of the International Court of Justice, 1 August 2023–31 July 2024, A/79/4' <https://perma.cc/PX8M-5HJK>

Kaye D, 'Report of the Special Rapporteur on the Promotion and Protection of the Right to Freedom of Opinion and Expression' (United Nations Human Rights Council 2018) A/HRC/38/35

Ministry of Electronics and Information Technology (India), 'Three Grievance Appellate Committees (GACs) Notified on the Recently Amended "IT Rules 2021" (Press Release)' (28 January 2023) <https://perma.cc/98M3-5DQG>

Netzwerk zur Umsetzung der UN-Kinderrechtskonvention, 'Kinderrechte und das Gesetz über digitale Dienste' (23 March 2022) <https://perma.cc/GZP3-WUUP>

Office of the High Commissioner for Human Rights, 'Ethiopia: Bachelet Urges End to "Reckless" War as Tigray Conflict Escalates (Press Release)' (2021) <https://perma.cc/L2BY-GWPX>

Oversight Board, 'Facebook Supreme Court: A Governance Solution (March 2018), Published in: Global Feedback and Input on the Facebook Oversight Board for Content Decisions Appendix, Appendix D'

'The Oversight Board Is Accepting User Appeals to Remove Content from Facebook and Instagram (Press Release)' (April 2021) <https://perma.cc/FTD9-8SE2>

'The Oversight Board: Operationalizing the UN Guiding Principles on Business and Human Rights – Submission to the Office of the High Commissioner for Human Rights, United Nations on the Practical Application of the UNGPs to the Activities in Technology Companies' (2022) <https://perma.cc/PS65-ENNM>

'Annual Report 2022' <https://perma.cc/MZ3J-86PE>

'Protecting Freedom of Expression and Human Rights in Ukraine and Russia (Press Release)' (May 2022) <https://perma.cc/59Z2-WLKY>

'Securing Ongoing Funding for the Oversight Board (Press Release)' (22 June 2022) <https://perma.cc/Y859-KUEF>

'Oversight Board Publishes Transparency Report for Second Quarter of 2022 and Gains Ability to Apply Warning Screens (Press Release)' (October 2022) <https://perma.cc/6C3F-WHPT>

UN Office of Genocide Prevention and the Responsibility to Protect, 'Statement by Alice Wairimu Nderitu, United Nations Special Adviser on the Prevention of Genocide, on the Continued Deterioration of the Situation in Ethiopia' (2021) <https://perma.cc/ZX3W-V4V4>

United Nations and AI Advisory Body, 'Governing AI For Humanity (Final Report)'

United States House of Representatives, Trahan L, Schiff A and Casten S, Digital Services Oversight and Safety Bill [introduced], H.R. 6796 – 117th Congress (2021–2022) 2022

United States Senate, 'Facebook, Social Media Privacy, And the Use and Abuse of Data – Joint Hearing before the Committee on Commerce, Science, and Transportation in the United States Senate and the Committee on the Judiciary in the United States Senate, Serial No. J-115-40' 1 <www.congress.gov/event/115th-congress/senate-event/LC64510/text?s=1&r=59>

'Statement of Frances Haugen' <https://perma.cc/3QN6-JMY4>

von der Leyen U, 'State of the Union Address by President von Der Leyen at the European Parliament Plenary' (Brussel, 15 September 2020) <https://perma.cc/8KWR-K873>

Index

For EU product safety concerns, contact us at Calle de José Abascal, 56–1°, 28003 Madrid, Spain or eugpsr@cambridge.org.

www.ingramcontent.com/pod-product-compliance
Lightning Source LLC
LaVergne TN
LVHW052025200926
848481LV00005B/1587

* 9 7 8 1 0 0 9 6 3 9 7 7 4 *